"Aimed at educated, experienced travellers, the [Berlitz Travellers] Guides capture the flavor of foreign lands."
—*Entrepreneur*

"Filling a needed niche in guidebooks ... designed to eliminate the cumbersome lists of virtually every hotel and restaurant .... Special out-of-the-way places are detailed.... The books capture the personality and excitement of each destination."
—*Los Angeles Times*

"There's a different tone to these books, and certainly a different approach ... information is aimed at independent and clearly sophisticated travellers.... Strong opinions give these books a different personality from most guides, and make them fun to read."
—*Travel & Leisure*

"Aimed at experienced, independent travellers who want information beyond the nuts-and-bolts material available in many familiar sources. Although each volume gives necessary basics, the series sends travellers not just to 'sights,' but to places and events that convey the personality of each locale."
—*The Denver Post*

"Just the right amount of information about where to stay and play."
—*Detroit Free Press*

CONTRIBUTORS

FRANK VICTOR DAWES worked as a reporter on Fleet Street and later for the BBC, where he specialized in travel programs. The author of *Not in Front of the Servants,* he lived in Sussex. He was the editorial consultant for this guidebook.

CHARLOTTE ATKINS is a freelance travel writer and travel editor of *Woman's Own* magazine. Formerly deputy editor of the *U.K. Holiday Guide* and *Family Holidays in Britain* magazines, she is also coauthor of *The French Channel Ports.*

ANTHONY BURTON has written several books on the industrial history of England—and one on the history of beer and pubs—and has written and presented several television series about England's industrial heritage for the BBC.

CATHERINE CONNELLY took up travel writing after a career in nursing. She has travelled extensively around the world but makes her home near London.

BRYN FRANK is the author of *Everyman's England* and *Short Walks in English Towns*. He is a regular contributor to *British Heritage* and *In Britain* magazines, and he writes occasionally about travel in the U.K. for the London *Evening Standard.*

SUSAN GROSSMAN was born in and lives in London. Currently the editor of *The Best of Britain Guide* (American Express) and editor of *Upbeat* magazine, she frequently writes about hotels and restaurants.

ALEX HAMILTON is the author of seven works of fiction and a travel book on the Trans-Siberian railway. He is a winner of the Fitzgerald Award for travel writing and is travel editor of the British national daily *The Guardian.*

KATIE LUCAS, the author of a best-selling book on walking tours of London, has lived in Suffolk for many years and runs a London-based specialized British tours company.

ANGELA MURPHY is a freelance journalist who has contributed to a number of guidebooks, including the *Shell Weekend Guide Book* to England and the *Hachette Guide to Great Britain*.

PAUL MURPHY'S first book, the *Guinness Guide to Superlative London,* won the 1989 London Tourist Board Guide Book of the Year award. During this period Murphy was also guiding tourists around the capital on walking tours. Since then he has become a full-time travel writer and editor and has written and contributed to travel guides covering many countries.

KEN THOMPSON, journalist and broadcaster, has lived in Cornwall for more than 30 years. He edited the famous *Falmouth Packet* newspaper and was, for 12 years until 1987, Cornwall's chief tourism officer.

DAVID WICKERS contributes regularly to several major British publications, and is travel editor of *Marie Claire* magazine and travel correspondent of the London *Sunday Times*. In 1992 he was named U.K. Travel Writer of the Year.

THE BERLITZ
TRAVELLERS GUIDES

THE AMERICAN SOUTHWEST

AUSTRALIA

BERLIN

CANADA

THE CARIBBEAN

COSTA RICA

ENGLAND & WALES

FRANCE

GERMANY

GREECE

HAWAII

IRELAND

LONDON

MEXICO

NEW ENGLAND

NEW YORK CITY

NORTHERN ITALY AND ROME

PORTUGAL

SAN FRANCISCO &
NORTHERN CALIFORNIA

SOUTHERN ITALY AND ROME

SPAIN

TURKEY

THE BERLITZ TRAVELLERS GUIDE TO ENGLAND & WALES

Sixth Edition

ALAN TUCKER
General Editor

BERLITZ PUBLISHING COMPANY, INC.
New York, New York

BERLITZ PUBLISHING COMPANY LTD.
Oxford, England

THE BERLITZ TRAVELLERS GUIDE
TO ENGLAND & WALES
Sixth Edition

Berlitz Trademark Reg U.S. Patent and Trademark Office
and other countries—Marca Registrada

Published by Berlitz Publishing Company, Inc.
257 Park Avenue South, New York, New York 10010, U.S.A.

Distributed in the United States by
the Macmillan Publishing Group

Distributed elsewhere by Berlitz Publishing Company Ltd.
Berlitz House, Peterley Road, Horspath, Oxford OX4 2TX, England

ISBN 2-8315-1707-9
ISSN 1057-4735

Designed by Beth Tondreau Design
Cover design by Dan Miller Design
Cover photograph © The British Tourist Authority
Maps by Mark Stein Studios
Illustrations by Bill Russell
Fact-checked in London by Paul Murphy
Edited by Patricia Fogarty

Printed in the United States of America
1 3 5 7 9 10 8 6 4 2

THIS GUIDEBOOK

The Berlitz Travellers Guides are designed for experienced travellers in search of exceptional information that will enhance the enjoyment of the trips they take.

Where, for example, are the interesting, out-of-the-way, fun, charming, or romantic places to stay? The hotels described by our expert writers are some of the special places, in all price ranges except for the very lowest—not just the run-of-the-mill, heavily marketed places in advertised airline and travel-wholesaler packages.

We are *highly* selective in our choices of accommodations, concentrating on what our insider contributors think are the most interesting or rewarding places, and why. Readers who want to review exhaustive lists of hotel and resort choices as well, and who feel they need detailed descriptions of each property, can supplement the *Berlitz Travellers Guide* with tourism industry publications or one of the many directory-type guidebooks on the market.

We indicate the approximate price level of each accommodation in our description of it (no indication means it is moderate in local, relative terms), and at the end of every chapter we supply more detailed hotel rates as well as contact information so that you can get precise, up-to-the-minute rates and make reservations.

The Berlitz Travellers Guide to England & Wales highlights the more rewarding parts of the country so that you can quickly and efficiently home in on a good itinerary.

Of course, this guidebook does far more than just help you choose a hotel and plan your trip. *The Berlitz Travellers Guide to England & Wales* is designed for use *in* England and Wales. Our writers, each of whom is an experienced travel journalist who either lives in or regularly tours the city or region of England or Wales he or she covers, tell you what you really need to know, what you can't find out so easily on your own. They identify and describe the truly out-of-the-ordinary restaurants, shops, activities, and sights, and tell you the best way to "do" your destination.

Our writers are highly selective. They bring out the significance of the places they *do* cover, capturing the personality and the underlying cultural and historical resonances of a city or region—making clear its special appeal.

The Berlitz Travellers Guide to England & Wales is full of reliable information. We would like to know if you think we've left out some very special place. Although we make every effort to provide the most current information available about every destination described in this book, it is possible too that changes have occurred before you arrive. If you do have an experience that is contrary to what you were led to expect by our description, we would like to hear from you about it.

A guidebook is no substitute for common sense when you are travelling. Always pack the clothing, footwear, and other items appropriate for the destination, and make the necessary accommodation for such variables as altitude, weather, and local rules and customs. Of course, once on the scene you should avoid situations that are in your own judgment potentially hazardous, even if they have to do with something mentioned in a guidebook. Half the fun of travelling is exploring, but explore with care.

ALAN TUCKER
General Editor
Berlitz Travellers Guides

Root Publishing Company
350 West Hubbard Street
Suite 440
Chicago, Illinois 60610

CONTENTS

This Guidebook	vii
Overview	5
Useful Facts	16
Bibliography	22
London	29
Getting Around	121
Accommodations	126
Dining	141
Pubs and Bars	154
Entertainment and Nightlife	162
Shops and Shopping	170
Day Trips from London	186
Oxford	186
Cambridge	197
Windsor	206
Brighton	213
The Literary Southeast	220
The Wessex Shore	252
The Cotswolds to Winchester	275
Devon and Cornwall	325
East Anglia	375
The Shires of Middle England	430
The Heart of England	476
York	534
The North Country	550
Wales	594
The Industrial Heritage	619

Historical Chronology   635
Index   647

MAPS

England and Wales   2
Greater London   30
London   36
  The City   44
  Central London   54
  Westminster   68
  Knightsbridge and Kensington   78
  Notting Hill and Holland Park   92
  Bayswater   94
  Hampstead to Camden Town   98
  Regent's Park   104
  Islington   108
  East End and Docklands   112
London Environs   187
Oxford   190
Cambridge   198
Upper Thames   207
Literary Southeast   222
Surrey and Hampshire   246
The Wessex Shore   253
The Cotswolds   278
Bath   288
The Salisbury Plain Area   304
Devon   328
Cornwall   350
East Anglia   376
Northamptonshire and Leicestershire   433
Nottinghamshire and Lincolnshire   448
The Peak District   467
The Heart of England   478

Stratford-upon-Avon Town Center and Area 481
Vale of Evesham 487
Warwickshire 491
Worcestershire 497
Herefordshire and the Wye Valley 504
Upper Severn Valley 517
York 536
North Country 552
Yorkshire to Durham 558
North Coast 566
Lake District 577
Border Country 586
Wales 596
Industrial Heritage 620

THE
BERLITZ
TRAVELLERS
GUIDE TO
ENGLAND
& WALES

England
and Wales

0   miles   40

0   40
kilometers

Berwick-
upon-Tweed

Newcastle-
upon-Tyne
WALL

Durham

A1

NORTH
YORKSHIRE
MOORS

NORTH SEA

N

KSHIRE
ALES

Leeds

York

Manchester

A46   Lincoln

E N G L A N D

Nottingham

Norwich

Birmingham

A1

EAST
ANGLIA

M5

Stratford-
upon-Avon

Northampton

A11

M1

Cambridge

Cheltenham

THE
OTSWOLDS

Oxford

M40

London

M11

ath

M4

Windsor

SURREY

M3

River Thames

M2

Canterbury

Dover

Salisbury

Winchester

SUSSEX

KENT

A36

Southampton

Portsmouth

Brighton

Calais

A31

Isle of Wight

F R A N C E

ENGLISH CHANNEL

OVERVIEW

By Frank Victor Dawes

Frank Victor Dawes worked as a reporter on Fleet Street and for the BBC, where he specialized in travel programs. The author of Not in Front of the Servants, *he was a member of the British Guild of Travel Writers.*

History, pageantry, and landscape are what bring tourists to Britain by the millions. Many of the English-speaking visitors are coming to the mother country of a mighty empire that no longer exists, to the "Old Country" some of them have never set eyes on before. England is still a constitutional monarchy, Shakespeare's "sceptered isle, this royal throne of kings," with an innate sense of theater that shows itself as much in the daily rituals of changing the guard at Buckingham Palace and Windsor Castle and the Beefeaters' ceremony of the keys at the Tower of London as in the larger pageantry of royal weddings, funerals, and coronations, Trooping the Colour, or the State Opening of Parliament. The love of pomp and pageantry flourishes in the age of video and television, and the British love dressing up for medieval fairs and performing festivals in Dickensian costume.

The British royal family, apparently a never-ending subject of fascination to republicans around the world, are sometimes likened to characters in a soap opera. This does them less than justice. Windsor, the town whose name they bear and which more than any other of their estates they call home, is where Prince Albert set up the first Christmas tree to be seen in England and the place from which the Queen sends out her annual message to the nation and the Commonwealth. Their castle, with nine centuries of monarchic history, is set in a park of

4,800 acres—most of it open to visitors and an easy day trip to the west of London. Sadly, in 1992 fire destroyed a large part of the building, including the Great Hall.

As well as being a home, Windsor Castle is a museum, and museums in Britain are enjoying a renaissance. No longer are they seen as musty, silent places filled with rows of glass cases and stuffed animals. With all the resources of new technology, the stories of York, Canterbury, Oxford, and Dover are being retold graphically as "heritage experiences." At the same time, the history of Britain's steam-age industries is being promoted as the industries themselves wither away and die. The open-air museum at Beamish in Durham, once a great coalfield, and the museum complex at Wigan Pier (to which George Orwell took his road) in Wigan are outstanding examples of these exciting trends.

Great Britain's maritime heritage is being given its due not just in the national museum at Greenwich but also in such seafaring cities as Bristol, where the SS *Great Britain,* the first steam-powered iron ship, has been rescued from the scrapyard, and Plymouth, where the Pilgrims set sail in the *Mayflower.* Chatham Historic Dockyard brings to life centuries of warship-building history, and Portsmouth ("Pompey" to the Royal Navy) has achieved a remarkable hat trick in setting up Henry VIII's warship *Mary Rose,* Nelson's flagship *Victory,* and the Victorian ironclad *Warrior* as walk-through dockside exhibits. (To get an idea of just how many museums there are in Britain that celebrate the nation's industrial and maritime past, see the Industrial Heritage chapter.)

Profound resistance to new ways and new ideas, along with an ability to adapt superficially, is characteristic of an island race, and Great Britain has a longer past than most countries. But it has a present, too, and has been forced by circumstances to change rapidly in the last few years. Britain is not a museum or a large theme park but a small, highly developed country with a population in excess of 60 million. The fact that its people are extremely mobile, in addition to the influx of tourists, has led to an insatiable demand for more and more motorways; Britain's two major airports, Heathrow and Gatwick, have become the busiest in the world, bar none.

As a member of the European Community's single trading market, Shakespeare's "blessed plot, this earth, this realm, this England" is now irrevocably welded to the Continental mainland. The opening of the new Channel Tunnel underneath the Channel between Dover and Calais in late 1993 or early 1994 realizes the dream of two centuries and makes the connection a physical one. The "Chunnel," as the British call it, uses a shuttle of high-speed, vehicle-carrying trains to link the motorway networks of England and France. It is in fact two 30-mile-long tunnels (with a service tunnel between them) capable of shunting more than 4,000 vehicles per hour in each direction.

LONDON

The British capital is gearing up for a faster pace—too fast for some people. Prince Charles has expressed concern about the effect of the accelerating development of characterless new office buildings on the familiar and much-loved skyline of the old City. The dome of Christopher Wren's St. Paul's Cathedral has been obscured by this explosion of high rises, which is spreading eastward from Aldgate Pump into what used to be the docklands of the East End. All in all, London is witnessing its greatest rebuilding since the Great Fire of 1666, although, inevitably, economic recession has slowed the pace.

London's eight square miles of waterfront, for 150 years the world's foremost seagoing port, had become a wasteland with the decline of the docks. Now from the dereliction a new city is arising between the Norman Tower of London and Canary Wharf, at 803 feet the tallest office tower in Europe. Yet on the opposite bank of the River Thames, the stately front of Greenwich still looks as it did when Canaletto painted it in the mid-18th century. A London City Airport for STOL (short takeoff and landing) flights to Paris, Brussels, and Plymouth has been built on the site of the Royal Docks. Computer-driven overhead trains run every few minutes from Tower Bridge along the length of the Isle of Dogs, where King Henry VIII kept his hunting dogs, surrounded by a wide loop of the River Thames.

And in once-marshy Bankside, south of the Thames, redevelopment has uncovered the remains of Tudor theaters: the Rose and the Globe—the "Wooden O"—where many of Shakespeare's plays, including *Hamlet,* were first performed. After two decades of negotiation and planning, Sam Wanamaker's reconstruction of the Globe Theatre—in timber, wattle, and daub under a tiled roof on the far side of the old bear garden adjoining the original theater sites—has been obliged by financial stringency to push back its opening until the mid-1990s.

Yet for all the new building of offices, shopping precincts, and leisure centers, hotels, concert halls, sports arenas, marinas, and museums, London remains a city of villages. It is a mistake to concentrate on the familiar sights of Westminster and the City and to miss out on Hampstead, Richmond, and Chelsea. London, like some other parts of Britain today, is a rich ethnic mix. The customs and cuisine in the East End, Soho, Notting Hill, and Camden Town are worth exploring.

ARCHITECTURE AND HISTORY

Nor is London by any means Britain. Castles and cathedrals, ancient churches and cottages, ruined abbeys and stately homes are scattered the length and breadth of Shakespeare's sceptered isle, its High Streets displaying a millennium of architectural styles—Norman churches, Tudor half-timbered affairs, Georgian terraces, Victorian Gothic buildings—alongside modern supermarkets. The green and pleasant landscape bears the traces of earlier conquerors and civilizations—a Roman road and villa here, a Viking place name there, Celtic barrows and tumuli and mysterious circles of Neolithic stones, such as Stonehenge on Salisbury Plain.

There are literally hundreds of historic houses and properties open to visitors, and only a few of them remain in private hands. The majority are run by two major organizations, each of which publishes its own guide and list of opening times (which vary enormously) and admission charges. Contact the National Trust at 36 Queen Anne's Gate, London SW1H 9AS, or English Heritage at Keysign House, 429 Oxford Street, London W1R 2HD, for details.

The Great British Heritage Pass, which can be bought in advance at travel agents around the world or, on showing a passport, at tourist information offices in England, gives unlimited access to 600 castles, stately homes and gardens, and other places of interest all over the country. The pass comes with a map-folder listing all the properties, opening times, and locations, and some useful discounts and free admission to tourist attractions.

WALKING PATHS

If you want to tread in the footsteps of Chaucer's pilgrims to Canterbury, the North Downs Way will point you there and beyond to Shakespeare Cliff, the highest point of the wall of chalk fronting the English Channel. This is but one of several long-distance walking paths in England and Wales—the South Downs Way, Cotswold Way, Pennine Way, Offa's Dyke Path, and the Pembrokeshire Coast Path are just some of the others. "Walking in Britain," a useful pamphlet on all these paths, listing guidebooks, maps, and other detailed information, is available from the British Tourist Authority, Thames Tower, Black's Road, Hammersmith, London W6 9EL, or its offices throughout London and around the world. These trails, some of them designated as bridleways (open to cyclists and horse-riders as well as walkers), are waymarked by the Countryside Commission, whose symbol is an acorn. They are a welcome escape from traffic-clogged roads.

Villages and small towns whose peace was rudely disturbed by the coming of the railways in the 19th century were returned to rural slumber in the 1960s:

> When Dr Beeching took his axe
> And gave BR [British Rail] those mighty whacks
> A wondrous gift came free of tax
> For all who love to walk the tracks

Thus Hunter Davies opens his book *A Walk Along the Tracks,* in which he explores former railway cuttings and embankments now given back to wildlife, dog roses, and blackberries, including Three Bridges to East Grinstead in Sussex, York to Market Weighton, Cockermouth to Penrith, the Wirral Way, the Wye Valley, and the Somerset and Dorset. There are 8,000 miles of disused railway in Britain. Here and there the bygone age is lovingly preserved by steam enthusiasts on short stretches of track—the Watercress Line in Hampshire, the Bluebell Railway in Sussex, the North Norfolk, and the North Yorkshire Moors, to name but a few.

REBORN RAILWAYS AND CANALS

Indeed, rail travel in England is enjoying a renaissance with the expansion of InterCity's "Land Cruises" in special trains with sleeper cars from London; Tel: (0543) 25-40-76 for information and bookings. British Rail said farewell to steam in 1968 but now runs Nostalgic Steam Days Out to many parts of England and Wales from London, powered by famous locomotives such as the *Flying Scotsman* and the *Duchess of Hamilton.* Roast beef lunches and afternoon teas are served at your seat: Tel: (0543) 41-94-72.

The elegant umber-and-cream carriages of the Venice Simplon Orient-Express re-create the inter-Wars heyday of the Brighton and Bournemouth Belles with trips to historic castles in Kent, Sussex, and Hampshire, to the seaside at Bournemouth, and to Georgian Bath. There are excursions by Orient-Express to the highlights of the social season—Royal Ascot, Glorious Goodwood, and Henley Regatta; Tel: (071) 928-6000.

An even earlier legacy of the Industrial Revolution—the network of canals carved across England two centuries ago to carry freight in narrowboats drawn by horses—is also finding a new lease on life in tourism. Nearly 2,000 miles of navigable inland waterways remain, and they offer a fascinating inside view of countryside, old villages, and market towns, sometimes off the beaten track. Choose between renting a self-skippered narrowboat (probably painted in traditional style with roses and castles but powered by a diesel engine and comfortably heated, furnished, and equipped) and taking a cruise on a hotel boat. There are well over a hundred companies operating some 1,500 hire boats, spread throughout the canal and river system of England and Wales. One of the largest, and longest established companies is Anglo Welsh Waterways Holidays, with bases spread throughout the country and they can be contacted at their headquarters at The Canal Basin, Market Harborough, Leicestershire LE16 7BJ; Tel: (0858) 466910. A complete list of all hire boats is published annually by A.E. Morgan, Stanley House, 9 West Street, Epsom, Surrey KT18 7R1; Tel: (0372) 741411. Self-skippering means more than just steering your boat—it also involves working locks, opening swing bridges and generally keeping busy. Some might prefer to travel canals the easy way, on a hotel boat, where someone else will do all the work—including the washing-up. A list of hotel boats is available from UK Waterway Holidays, 1 Port Hill, Hertford SG14 1PJ; Tel: (0992) 550616. Several U.S. travel agents handle bookings directly.

DRIVING IN BRITAIN

Britain is good motoring country once the visitor has adapted to driving on the left. There is a network of toll-free motorways and trunk roads that has cut travelling time considerably, and the main car-rental companies have hundreds of branches in all the larger towns and at ports and airports. The completion of the M 25, which orbits London at a radius of 12 to 21 miles, with 32 junctions connecting with motorways and major routes to other parts of the country, has added to the ease of road travel. But England *is* a small and overcrowded island, and at peak times traffic can be very heavy indeed.

"A" roads, usually marked in red on maps, are main routes. "B" roads are secondary two-lane routes, usually in reasonable condition. Motorways (expressways) are designated by the letter M. For those with the time, the "B" roads provide an alternative way of getting around the country and are often surprisingly free of traffic. However, unlike the motorways, they wander this way and that, with frequent junctions and crossroads, and road signs are not always all they might be. An Ordnance Survey or Automobile Association road map will pay dividends in any exploration of Britain's byways.

If you use the motorways to travel from center to center and "A" and "B" roads for an in-depth look at a particular area, ten days is an optimum amount of time for a tour of England and Wales. A couple of days is usually enough time to explore any one area. The British Tourist Association's *Motoring Itineraries in Britain* is available free from its overseas offices (see the Useful Facts section following). It details 15 suggested routes, ranging from five to 15 days, and three theme tours covering writers, gardens, and Norman England. There are more than 600 tourist information centers in all regions and at certain service areas on the motorways, and exits to major historical and heritage sites are clearly marked. Tours of ten key heritage centers in England are efficiently organized by Guide Friday, whose home base is the Civic Hall, 14 Rother Street, Stratford-upon-Avon CV37 6LU; Tel: (0789) 29-44-66. Guide Friday operates also in Bath, Bristol, Canterbury, Cambridge, Chester, Oxford, Plymouth, Portsmouth, Salisbury, Windermere, Windsor, and York.

HOTELS AND GUEST HOUSES

Nowhere is the impact of tourism on Britain more apparent than in its hotels and restaurants. Multinational companies have not only built new hotels but also restored many old coaching inns to their former glory, adding all the facilities that travellers now expect.

The standards of the smaller family-run hotels and guest houses have improved beyond recognition. Fresh local meat, fish, and vegetables are featured on most menus, and good wine, properly served, is now the rule rather than the exception. No longer are overcooked cabbage and warm beer inescapable penalties for travelling in Britain, any more than freezing bathrooms or lumpy beds are. No more do the British consider discomfort to be a virtue.

An offshoot of the affluent 1980s was the spread of individually owned and run country-house hotels, so much so that they were in danger of becoming a standardized package of Laura Ashley fabrics and Crabtree & Evelyn toiletries. In the leaner nineties genuine quality and originality in cooking and comfort are called for to ensure the survival of historic and beautiful houses, such as those assembled in the Pride of Britain consortium; Tel: (0264) 764-44. Most of these offer toll-free telephone numbers from the U.S. only, specifically for reservations from travel agents.

An alternative to a country-house hotel is to rent a gracious country or town house of your own—you don't have to have a butler, necessarily. The Landmark Trust (at Shottesbrooke, Maidenhead SL6 3SW) offers an intriguing selection of properties, ranging from the Gothic Tower in Buckinghamshire, Fox Hall in Sussex, and Marshal Wade's elegant house in Bath to a couple of gatehouses, a water tower on the Queen's estate at Sandringham (Norfolk), and the inelegantly named Pigsty at Robin Hood's Bay in Yorkshire; Tel: (0628) 82-59-25. The National Trust has an even larger range of holiday properties to let, from a large mansion in Cornwall to an isolated former gamekeeper's cottage in North Wales, with a castle folly and a former water tower thrown in for good measure. The majority are available year-round. For details, write to P.O. Box 101, Melksham SN12 8EA.

THE PUB

That other great British institution, the pub, is now allowed to remain open from 11:00 A.M. to 11:00 P.M., Monday through Saturday, thanks to an overdue change in a law introduced during World War I that aimed to keep munitions factory workers sober by shutting pubs in the afternoon. Sunday opening hours are now noon to 3:00 P.M. and 7:00 P.M. to 10:30 P.M. Within these permitted open hours, individual pub owners decide whether to stay open or to call "Time, gentlemen, please!" Most of those in London's West End and in tourist resorts have opted for all-day opening and have increased their range of food service (pub lunches are excellent value). Some even offer morning coffee and afternoon tea in addition to alcohol.

England and Wales
for Travellers

Your choices of areas to tour in England and Wales are wide, and our book is intended to help you make your choice. A day trip south from London takes you to Brighton, a town by the sea, built on misbehavior following the bad example of an extravagant and debauched monarch, George IV, and to the northwest and north, respectively, are the ancient university cities of Oxford and Cambridge. They are miles apart geographically but always paired, with Oxford first, even when the names are merged as "Oxbridge." Each strives to outdo the other in style as well as in their annual boat race on the Thames. Along with Windsor, to the west of London, these three cities are covered in our **Day Trips from London** chapter.

Many tourists venture no farther than Oxford or Stratford-upon-Avon, Stonehenge or Bath, which is a pity because beyond these much-visited centers—and within an hour or two of London—are rarely explored tracts of countryside and unspoiled towns. We describe many such places in our chapters **The Cotswolds to Winchester** and **The Heart of England**.

Sussex

It is all very well to follow the crowds to Scotland via Stratford and the Lake District or York, but it is just as rewarding to make the odd detour, perhaps to seek out the rural retreat of Virginia Woolf and the rest of the Bloomsbury set in deepest Sussex (only an hour south of London)—and rediscover Kipling at the same time—as we suggest in the **Literary Southeast** chapter.

Wessex and West

The ancient kingdom of Arthur and the knights of the Round Table, Wessex no longer exists on the map, but its legends live on in the region extending from the Avon to the beautiful south coast of Hampshire and Dorset, where in 1944 the Allied armies were marshaled for D-Day. This is Thomas Hardy country, too, where literary tourists may identify places described under fictional names in his novels, such as Bournemouth, which appears as "Sand-bourne." The New Forest, hunting ground of kings of ages past, lies just outside Southampton on this coast overlooking the Isle of Wight, where the *America*'s Cup was inaugurated at the Cowes Regatta. See our chapter **The Wessex Shore**.

Bristol, that mercantile base of such world adventurers and explorers as the Cabots, father and son, is a hop away from Bath. Farther west yet is Plymouth, where Sir Francis Drake set sail to beat the Spanish Armada—but not before he had finished his game of bowls on the Hoe. It's a handy base for exploring Cornwall and Devon, the former a place apart that has always attracted poets and painters. See the chapter **Devon and Cornwall**.

The Midlands

A swath of the Midlands, once dubbed the Black Country because its factory chimneys had made it so, is now rediscovering a more ancient past, shared with its outlying bastions, the Roman walled city of Chester, on the River Dee, and Lincoln, with its cathedral of legend; we call this section **The Shires of Middle England**.

Wales

Beyond the Welsh border is another country, albeit a tiny one, with its own language and its own fierce national pride, expressed in heavenly choral singing and uninhibited rugby football. The Welsh will tell you in English that their tongue is older, indeed that it is the original language of Britain. The Welsh number fewer than three million, and there are twice as many sheep grazing on the wild and lonely hills. Although the capital, Cardiff, is less than two hours from London by high-speed train, Wales is still a mountain stronghold ringed with ancient castles, one of which is the official seat of the Prince of Wales. It also claims the industrial heritage of the coal-mining valleys of South Wales and the slate mines of North Wales, celebrated in marvelous museums at Blaenavon and Blaenau Ffestiniog. Every July the town of Llangollen attracts a gathering of singers, dancers, musicians, and poets for the *Eisteddfod* music festival. They come not just from Wales but from all over the world.

The North Country

In effect, the North of England is another country, too. The decline of its traditional heavy industries of coal, textiles, steel, and shipbuilding, and the consequent high levels of unemployment, widened what is known as the North–South Divide, although, unlike in the 1930s, the North suffered less than the South in the recession of the early 1990s. The barrier is emphasized by the fact that although the North Country does not have its own language, as Wales does, it does have a variety of dialects. The accents of the Liverpool Scouser and the Geordies of the Northeast might well sound foreign to the uninitiated, and Muslim immigrant communities in the old mill towns have added even more strands to an already colorful tapestry.

The black slag heaps that once disfigured so much of the landscape are now for the most part grassed over. Northerners are less reserved and standoffish than southerners, more outgoing, easier to talk to. It does rain often, but no more often than anywhere else in Britain, and just as unpredictably. The weather is the opening gambit in almost every casual conversation.

The North Country's Lake District has been attracting tourists ever since the English Romantics, led by William Wordsworth, made rugged scenery fashionable at a time when war in Europe made the Alps inaccessible. During the high season the pressure of crowds can become intolerable, even occasionally forcing the closure of Keswick to incoming traffic. The scenery in the Lake District *is* spellbinding, but no more so than areas of Northumberland, the North Yorkshire Moors, and the Yorkshire Dales, all also national parks. Spectacular stretches of heather-covered hillside and craggy fells, wooded valleys, rushing rivers and waterfalls, gray stone country towns, and immense red-brick viaducts and bridges characterize the North Country. And the Northumberland Coast from Newcastle to the Scottish border is among the finest to be found anywhere in Great Britain, its long sandy beaches fringed with ancient castles that are often all but deserted.

Tourists throng the great cathedrals of Canterbury southeast of London and, in the North, York, and justifiably so, but sometimes a small village church can provide just as much of a spiritual experience. In the depths of what was once the Durham coalfield, at Escomb, is the oldest Saxon church in Britain, built with stones from a ruined Roman fort nearby when, as Bishop Lightfoot points out, "England was not yet England, when Saxons had recently settled in the island, and Danes were beginning to harry the coasts and Normans were still undreaded, because unknown."

East Anglia

Another part of Britain that is all too often neglected by the visitor lies between Cambridge and the North Sea and up to the Wash: the East Anglia that Constable loved to paint. Inland from Aldeburgh, at the navigable limit of the River Alde, are the red-brick Victorian buildings erected to process barley and now famous throughout the world: Snape Maltings, where music is taught and an annual festival is held. Yet this is a secret coast of shingle and sand dunes, marshes and salt creeks, where fishing vessels and sailing barges bask at low tide. Its spacious landscape stretches from the Stour to the Wash, changing from wooded hills and lush meadows to the watery network of the Norfolk Broads, thronged with cruisers and yachts, to the fens and flat, fertile farmlands won back from the sea with dikes and embankments.

Islands off the Coasts

"This precious stone set in the silver sea," this England, has many facets and other smaller islands strung about it like a necklace, from the Isles of Scilly, 28 miles southwest of Land's End in Cornwall (our **Devon and Cornwall** chapter), to the Farnes, just off the northeast coast, where gray seals breed and seabirds fill the skies with their cries (our **North Country** chapter). There is a rare music from these unsung isles that calls people from the mainland. We have passed over other, larger offshore territories, such as the Channel Islands of Guernsey and Jersey, and the semi-independent Isle of Man, off the northwestern coast of England. The fact that we are obliged to omit such gems is a measure of the richness of the "sceptered isle." Britain's historical, literary, and cultural heritage is so diverse that it would be impossible to include everything worth seeing in one book. Our aim has been to select *some* of the rarer delights of "this other Eden, demi-paradise," as well as to guide you along the favorite and, therefore, more crowded paths.

USEFUL FACTS

When to Go

There is never an off-season for Britain. Although many people might prefer to come in May, when the azaleas and rhododendrons in some of the lovely gardens are in full bloom, others might prefer year-end holiday time, when they can enjoy a typically English Christmas, with all the trimmings of log fires and pantomimes.

Britain's major tourist season is July and August, and as a result hotels, restaurants, and theaters are often heavily booked then. The stately homes and gardens also have their full share of the tourist torrent. Spring and autumn are much better times to visit. The weather in Britain is entirely unpredictable, but these two seasons are also often the nicest. Spring can be wonderful, with mild, sunny weather and the trees coming into leaf. Autumn, with its glorious, hazy-sunny days, often lasts until Christmas. But England is, after all, an island, with a maritime climate subject to the winds and weather of the Atlantic.

What to Wear

If you come loaded with Burberry and thick sweaters, you may have three weeks in the 80s; of course, the reverse can also happen. The answer is to bring a little bit of everything. You are unlikely to need very dressy evening clothes, because, except for grand balls, the English tend not to dress up much; they underdress rather than over-dress and will go, for example, to the theater and even the opera in the clothes they wear to the office.

Getting In

Most international airlines serving Britain use London's Heathrow or Gatwick airports. Increasingly, a number of international carriers are also using the airports in Manchester and Birmingham, providing direct access to the Midlands. From North America there are now direct flights to London from Atlanta, Boston, Chicago, Dallas/Fort Worth, Los Angeles, Montreal, New York, San Francisco, Toronto, and other cities. Some of the many major airlines flying the North America–Britain route are Air Canada, Air India, American, British Airways, British Caledonian, Virgin Atlantic, and World. Qantas and British Airways fly the long route between Britain and Australia.

The London airports are well connected to the central city by public transportation. Heathrow is on the Underground (Piccadilly Line; 45 minutes from the airport to Piccadilly Circus), which is very convenient. However, if you are taking the Underground from the city center to Heathrow, it is essential that you know from which terminal you are departing. One Underground stop serves

Terminals 1, 2, and 3; another serves Terminal 4—and if you get off at the wrong stop, you will walk miles with your baggage.

You can also take a Flight Line 777 bus from Gatwick or Heathrow to Victoria Coach Station. London Transport's Express Airbus connects with Heathrow only and makes frequent stops throughout central London. The A1 Airbus goes to Victoria coach (bus) and railway stations; the A2 goes to Euston Station. The trip from Heathrow to central London usually takes less than an hour, and the fare is £5. Taxis take about the same time and charge about £38.

An efficient and much cheaper alternative is offered by London Airways Car Service (Tel: 071-403-2228; Fax: 071-403-5015), which charges a flat rate of £15 for a journey between any address in central London and Heathrow Airport and £25 to Gatwick, for up to four passengers.

The best way to get from Gatwick to London is by train. This extremely efficient service runs directly from the main terminal every 15 minutes, and trains reach Victoria Station in just 30 minutes. Hourly Flight Line 777 buses also connect Gatwick with Victoria Coach Station and take 80 minutes.

Ferries link Britain with dozens of ports on the Continent and in Ireland. The two major Continental lines are P & O, which serves Dover–Calais, Dover–Ostend, Felixstowe–Zeebrugge, Portsmouth–Cherbourg, Portsmouth–Le Havre, and Portsmouth–Bilbao (Tel: 0304-20-33-88 in Dover or 081-575-8555 in London), and Sealink Stena Line, which serves Dover–Calais, Harwich–Hook of Holland, Southampton–Cherbourg, and Newhaven–Dieppe (Tel: 0233-64-70-47). The trip across the Channel can take anywhere from a few hours to a full day or night, depending on your destination. The fastest crossing is by hovercraft with Hoverspeed, which makes the trip from Dover to Calais in just 35 minutes (summer only; Tel: 0304-24-02-41 in Dover or 081-554-7061 in London). P & O and Sealink, along with several other companies, also connect western England (Liverpool is the major port) with Ireland.

For those who enjoy a longer sea voyage, the Cunard line's *Queen Elizabeth II* makes the transatlantic crossing in style, from New York to Southampton, April through December.

Entry Documents

A passport is required of all travellers entering Britain, with the exception of citizens of other EC countries, who must present only an identity card. Citizens of the U.S., Commonwealth nations (Canada, Australia, and New Zealand), South Africa, and many other countries do not need a visa. Britain imposes strict anti-rabies measures, and all pets entering the country must be quarantined for a minimum of six months; unless you are moving to Britain, leave the pets at home.

Getting Around

British Rail, the national railroad network, serves some 2,500 stations throughout Britain. Major cities are connected by the extremely rapid (up to 125 m.p.h.) InterCity trains, and overnight trains (equipped with sleeping cars) run from London to the North of England, Wales, the west, and Scotland.

If you are travelling from London, be forewarned that there are many different train stations, each serving a different part of the country: Charing Cross serves southeastern England; Euston, northern Wales, the Midlands, northwestern England, and the west coast of Scotland; King's Cross, western Yorkshire, northeastern England, and the east coast of Scotland; Liverpool Street, East Anglia; Paddington, the south Midlands, the west Midlands, western England, and southern Wales; St. Pancras, the east Midlands and southern Yorkshire; Victoria, southern England; and Waterloo, southwestern England.

Several discount passes for train travel are available. The most popular is the BritRail Pass, available for both first-class and second-class travel, which allows holders unlimited travel through England, Scotland, and Wales for periods of 8, 15, or 22 days or for one month. The BritRail Pass is sold only outside of Britain, at British Rail offices or through travel agents.

National Express is Britain's nationwide bus network. Of special interest to overseas visitors is the Tourist Trail Pass, which provides unlimited travel for any consecutive period of 5, 8, 15, 22, or 30 days. Adult prices start at £65. Alternatively you may wish to consider buying a BritExpress card, which entitles you to a discount of 30 percent off all standard fares on every journey you make in any consecutive 30-day period; it costs £12. Tel: 730-0202.

Among the airlines connecting British cities are British Airways, Caledonian Airway, British Midlands, and Air UK.

Most major car-rental agencies have offices at airports and train stations in sizable cities. You must be 21 years of age (25 with some firms) and present a valid driver's license; an international driver's license is not required. Driving is on the left, and drivers from the United States and other countries where driving is on the right may have difficulty adjusting to this orientation. Be extremely careful. The same holds for pedestrians—remember to look both ways when crossing the street.

Barge trips along the canals of the North and Midlands are becoming another popular way to see the English countryside. For booking details see Overview, above.

Local Time

Britain observes Greenwich mean time (GMT), five hours ahead of the east coast of North America (excluding the Canadian Atlantic Provinces) and nine hours behind Sydney, Australia.

Telephoning

The country code for Britain is 44. When dialing from outside Britain, do not include the initial 0 in city codes. The London area has been split into two area codes: (071) for inner London and (081) for outer London.

To make a public-telephone call, put 10p (pence) into the coin slot in the telephone box if it has a *pink* band on the exterior. Dial the number you require and speak; when you hear an insistent beeping tone you will need to feed more money into the box to continue the call. For a box with a *green* band on the exterior you will need a green telephone card, which can be purchased at most newsagents. You insert the card into the slot and make your call. From either type, if you wish to speak to the operator, dial 100. For London directory inquries dial 142 (when you are in London), and for directory inquiries in other regions, dial 192.

Currency

The unit of currency in Britain is the pound sterling (denoted as £), which is divided into units of 100 pence. There are coins for 1p, 2p, 5p, 10p, 20p, 50p, and £1, and notes in denominations of £5, £10, £20, and £50. Check postings in banks and in daily newspapers for the current rate of exchange.

In the main hall at most airports there is a bank where you can change foreign currency into pounds and pence. Outside airports, banks are always open Monday through Friday between 9:30 A.M. and 3:30 P.M. Many branches are now open later, some until 5:00 P.M., and some also open on Saturday mornings. There are many bureaux de change around London, and most hotels will change money.

At press time, the English pound converted to the U.S. dollar at the approximate rate of £1.00 to $2.00.

Room Rates

Hotel room rates listed in this book are for double rooms, double occupancy. Rates are projections for 1994 and, for hotels outside London, include room and breakfast unless otherwise stated. As prices are subject to change, always double-check before booking. The rates given may or may not include service charges and taxes; be sure to inquire about these charges, as they can add a significant amount to the cost of a room.

You may want to ask about two- or three-day weekend and mid-week deals, or "breaks," which can reduce the cost of staying in some hotels considerably. Prices also may vary seasonally.

Business Hours

Most businesses in England are closed on Sundays. This is a day for strolling in the parks and going to church. Tourist areas aside, very few shops are open, many restaurants are closed, and even some museums don't open until 2:00 P.M. During the week most pubs now stay open from 11:00 A.M. to 11:00 P.M. On Sundays they open at noon and close from 3:00 to 7:00 P.M., then reopen until 10:30 P.M..

Shops generally open at 9:00 A.M. and close at 5:30 P.M., except for the one evening a week when shops in some districts of London stay open until 8:00 P.M.—Wednesdays in Knightsbridge and Kensington, and Thursdays on Oxford Street. Shops and banks are closed for bank holidays.

Holidays

Bank holidays are Christmas Day and Boxing Day (December 26), New Year's Day, Good Friday and Easter Monday, May Day (the first Monday in May), Spring Whit Bank Holiday (the last Monday in May), and August Bank Holiday (the last Monday in August).

Electric Current

Voltage in Britain is 220/240, 50 HZ, which means that an adapter or converter, plus an adapter plug, is necessary for North American appliances.

Information

Offices of the British Tourist Authority provide maps, booklets on sights and travel itineraries, accommodations listings, tips on travel passes and tourist discount passes, and a wealth of other information, and are located in cities and towns across Britain. BTA offices abroad are extremely helpful when you are planning a trip. Major offices are located at: Suite 701, 551 Fifth Avenue, New York, NY 10176 (Tel: 212-986-2200; Fax: 212-986-1188); Suite 1510, 625 North Michigan Avenue, Chicago, IL 60611 (Tel: 312-787-0490; Fax: 312-787-7746); Suite 450, 350 South Figueroa Street, Los Angeles, CA 90071 (Tel: 213-628-3525; Fax: 213-687-6621); Suite 470, 2580 Cumberland Parkway, Atlanta, GA 30339-3909 (Tel: 404-432-9635; Fax: 404-432-9641); Suite 450, 111 Avenue Road, Toronto, Ontario M5R 3J8 Canada (Tel: 416-925-6326; Fax: 416-961-2175); 123 Lower Baggot Street, Dublin 2, Ireland (Tel: 01-614-188; Fax: 01-785-280); Suite 305, 3rd Floor, Dilworth Building, Corner Customs and Queen Streets, Auckland 1, New Zealand (Tel: 09-303-1446; Fax: 09-377-6965); and 8th Floor, 210 Clarence Street, Sydney, N.S.W. 2000 Australia (Tel: 02-267-4555; Fax: 02-267-4442).

—*Paul Murphy*

BIBLIOGRAPHY

PETER ACKROYD, *Dickens' London*. Ackroyd sets the scene and then leaves it to Dickens's writings and to excellent photographs to bring Victorian London alive.

ALISDAIR AIRD, *The Good Pub Guide*. A Consumers' Association annual, this guide to the pub, that most British of institutions, gives clear descriptions of pubs and, where applicable, the food they offer.

THE AUTOMOBILE ASSOCIATION, *2000 Days Out in Britain*. A complete listing of places open to the public, with opening times and admission charges. Updated annually.

JOHN BETJEMAN, *Betjeman's Cornwall*. A celebration of the area in poetry and prose, illustrated with drawings by John Piper and photographs.

JANET AND COLIN BORD, *Ancient Mysteries of Britain*. Where standard guides offer strictly factual descriptions of ancient sites, the Bords explore them in terms of prehistoric religions and mystical forces.

EDITH BRILL, *Life and Traditions on the Cotswolds*. This book serves as a reminder that there is more to the Cotswolds than pretty scenery and picturesque villages. The area's sights are related to centuries of working life.

ANTHONY BURTON, *Cityscapes*. A fully illustrated guide to 18 British cities.

HUGH CASSON, *Hugh Casson's Cambridge*. A sketchbook by the eminent architect, who looks at the beauty of the famous colleges and also at the intimate, hidden corners of the city.

BARRY CUNLIFFE, *The City of Bath*. This illustrated book recounts the history of Bath from the Roman spa to the present day.

HUNTER DAVIES, *The Good Guide to the Lakes*. A guide to the Lake District, primarily intended for those who like exploring the countryside on foot rather than on wheels.

————, *A Walk Along the Tracks*. A guide to exploring the countryside by walking disused railway lines.

DANIEL DEFOE, *A Tour Thro' the Whole Island of Great Britain*. A fascinating glimpse of England before the Steam Age. Published in 1724 and recently reprinted in a new illustrated edition.

MICHAEL DE-LA-NOY, *Exploring Oxford*. A book for those who want something more than the bus tour. The reader is taken to city streets, pubs, and the riverside.

————, *Windsor Castle Past and Present*. Drawing on letters and memoirs of kings, queens, and courtiers, the author brings to life the 900-year history of the great castle.

MARGARET DRABBLE, *A Writer's Britain*. This is no mere catalog of places visited and described by famous writers but rather a survey of how authors have viewed the land. The photographs by Jorge Lewinski are excellent.

DAPHNE DU MAURIER, *Enchanted Cornwall*. The novelist used Cornish settings for much of her work, and this book is a personal view of all she loved in the county.

————, *Vanishing Cornwall*. More personal reflections on the places that inspired the novels.

DOROTHY EAGLE, HILARY CARNELL, AND MEIC STEPHENS, EDS., *The Oxford Illustrated Literary Guide to Great Britain and Ireland*. A guide to more than a hundred places associated with authors and their works.

DOUGLAS FERGUSON, DONA HAYCRAFT, AND NICK SEGAL, *Cambridge*. A fully illustrated account of the life of the university and city.

BRYN FRANK, ED., *The Good Holiday Cottage Guide*. A popular, annually updated collection of the best cottages and apartments to rent for vacations in Britain.

CHRISTINA GASCOIGNE, *Castles of Britain*. An evocative study of great medieval castles, illustrated with photographs.

MARK GIROUARD, *Life in the English Country House*. Stately homes appear on most visitor itineraries, and this brilliant and hugely enjoyable book links the architecture of the great houses to their social history.

PETER HARBISON, *The Shell Guide to English Parish Churches*. Describes 500 of the country's most beautiful churches; illustrated with photographs and maps.

CHRISTOPHER HIBBERT, *A Story of England*. A very readable acccount of the country's history from prehistoric times onward. Includes maps, tables, and genealogies.

SUSAN HILL, *Shakespeare Country*. The country of the title is the area around Stratford-upon-Avon. This book explores the landscape of the Bard's works, rather than merely listing places known to be associated with Shakespeare.

Historic Houses, Castles, and Gardens. (Published by Reed Information Services Ltd.) A guide, revised annually, to more than a thousand sites in Great Britain and Ireland that are open to the public. The sites are listed by county.

W. G. HOSKINS, *The Making of the English Landscape*. A classic work that traces how the English have shaped the landscape, both town and country, from ancient times to the present day.

HAMMOND INNES, *Hammond Innes' East Anglia*. A celebration by the well-known novelist of the secrets and delights of the region.

TOM JAINE, ED., *The Good Food Guide*. An annual review of more than 1,000 of the best restaurants in Britain, produced by the Consumers' Association.

BRIAN JOHN, *The Pembrokeshire Coast Path*. Part of the walking series published by Her Majesty's Stationery Office.

EDGAR JOHNSON, *Charles Dickens, His Tragedy and Triumph*. The definitive biography of Dickens, with evocative descriptions of the Medway towns and Broadstairs as Dickens knew them.

RUDYARD KIPLING, *Puck of Pook's Hill*. A eulogy of England and the English, especially those in Sussex.

RICHARD LLEWELLYN, *How Green Was My Valley; Up, into the Singing Mountain; Down Where the Moon Is Small;* and *Green, Green My Valley Now*. A charming series of novels set in Wales during the early 20th century.

DAVID W. LLOYD, *Historic Towns of South-East England*. The author describes more than 60 towns, from the obvious (such as Brighton) to the relatively unknown. He traces their history and explores their character with the help of excellent illustrations.

————, *The Making of English Towns*. A fascinating account covering 2,000 years of change from Roman settlements to present-day cities.

ARCHIE MILES, *The Malvern Hills*. The author, both poet and photographer, explores the area with a special emphasis on composer Edward Elgar, who lived in and loved the region.

KENNETH O. MORGAN, ED., *The Oxford Illustrated History of Britain*. This is a single-volume history of Britain, from the first Roman invasion to the present day, written by a team of experts who combine erudition with readability.

JAN MORRIS, *Oxford*. This is one of those rare books that has become a classic, a description of the city that combines a wealth of information with acute personal observation.

RICHARD MUIR, *The Shell Guide to Reading the Landscape*. A fascinating illustrated account of how the British landscape, town and country, has developed and changed over the centuries.

————, *The Coastlines of Britain*. An illustrated view of 3,000 miles of coast, looking at scenery, wildlife, and the human factor.

Museums and Galleries in Great Britain and Ireland. (Published by Reed Information Services Ltd.) A comprehensive guide, revised annually, to more than a thousand museums and galleries in Great Britain and Ireland.

IAN NAIRN, *Nairn's London.* The classic guidebook revised by Peter Gasson in a new Penguin edition.

Nicholson Guides to London. A series of slim guides, including Pubs, Night Life, and a London Shopping Guide and Streetfinder.

V. S. PRITCHETT, *London Perceived.* This is London as seen by an author who has lived in the city since the days of hansom cabs and gaslights. The approach is historical, but it is history firmly tied to the London of today.

CHARLES ROBERTSON, *Bath.* An illustrated guide that explores the city's architecture but manages to work in a good deal of history as well.

EGON RONAY, *Guide to Healthy Eating Out.* As the name suggests, a restaurant guide aimed primarily at the vegetarian, although it also lists places that cater to the carnivore.

———, *Just a Bite.* Essential reading for those looking for good, cheap meals, with the accent on "good." It is particularly useful for finding specialties, such as a genuine afternoon tea or a decent fish-and-chip shop.

PETER SNOW, *Oxford Observed.* A penetrating and witty account of the city in the 1990s, illustrated with photographs and line drawings.

EDWARD STOREY, *Spirit of the Fens.* This is an evocative study of this area of East Anglia that the author has known and loved all his life—an area that does not always easily reveal its charms to the casual visitor.

DYLAN THOMAS, *Under Milk Wood.* A dramatic work that is a joyful celebration of Welsh life, by the country's most famous writer.

NIGEL VINEY AND DAVID PIPER, *The Shell Guide to the Great Paintings of England.* Descriptions of the art masterpieces to be found in English galleries and collections.

ALFRED WAINWRIGHT, *Fell Walking with Wainwright.* Wainwright's guides to walks in Britain have become famous. Here he describes his favorites, illustrated with his own drawings and photographs by Derry Brabbs.

———, *A Pennine Journey.* Written at the time of the Munich crisis in 1938, this story of a 200-mile trek from Settle to Hadrian's Wall and back is also a revealing self-portrait of the author.

WILLIAM WORDSWORTH, *Guide Through the District of the Lakes.* First published in 1810, this is *the* Romantic view of the Lakes.

MARILYN YURDAN, *Oxford Town and Gown.* An exploration of the history of the city and the university, and the relationship between them.

—Anthony Burton

LONDON

By David Wickers

David Wickers, a longtime resident of London, is travel correspondent for the Sunday Times *of London, travel editor of* Marie Claire *magazine, and a regular contributor to several other magazines and newspapers in the United Kingdom. A member of the British Guild of Travel Writers, in 1992 he was named U.K. Travel Writer of the Year.*

When a man is tired of London, he is tired of life; for there is in London all that life can afford." Few writers on London manage to resist the temptation to bring the good Dr. Johnson into their prose. But an up-to-date version of his most famous and flattering compliment would soften the drastic course of action for men or women tired of London. Rather than giving up on life, they can merely shift their point of reference. When tired of one part of London, they can, nowadays, simply find another part more suited to their mood or circumstances.

Two hundred years ago, when Johnson was writing, "London" referred to a condensed commercial core huddled along the northern flanks of the Thames, a sordid ghetto defined by rows of unsanitary buildings fighting for light and breath. Beyond a scatter of surrounding villages lay folds of open countryside. London today is a motley urban patchwork of places. Unlike the majority of the world's capitals, London does not have an obvious downtown. Ask a Londoner to put you on the right bus or train for this mythical epicenter of urban activity and you will still be none the wiser about just where you want to go.

If you, the lost cause, happen to be dressed in a smart but drab suit and carry a briefcase, you'll probably be

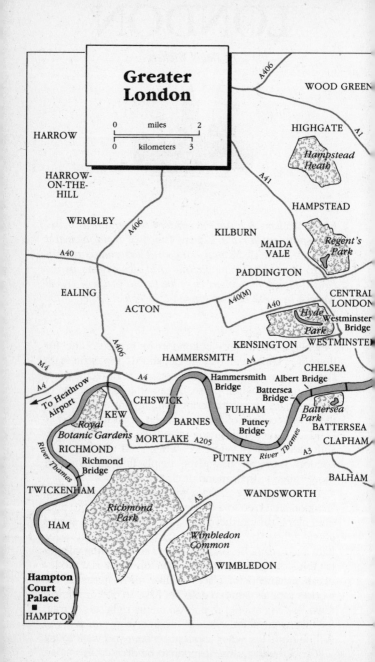

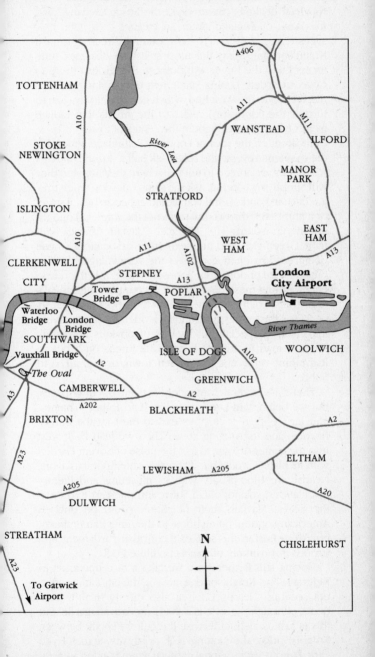

pointed toward the City, the hub of banking and other financial dealings centered on the Stock Exchange and the Bank of England. Wear an elegant dress with chic accessories, and you'll be politely directed toward Knightsbridge. Sport the most stylish of designer "uniforms," and the finger will point to the slickest route to Covent Garden. Look a shade less trendy, and you'll be dispatched to the West End, which geographically (just to further the confusion) refers to the streets that radiate from Oxford Circus, right in the center of town.

To broaden the idea of London's self-image, let us, for the moment, reverse the roles. Ask half a dozen residents when they are abroad to tell you where they live, and they will simply say London. Ask the same question when they are back in London, and you would expect to hear a street or a numbered district. But that's not the way it is. Londoners live in Notting Hill, Highgate, Mayfair, Chelsea, Fulham, Greenwich, and umpteen other destinations whose pedigrees are often rooted in the very villages that lay outside the London of Dr. Johnson's time. It is the differences among these districts that account for the capital's enormously rich diversity. It is not the city's museums, its parks, or the endlessly abundant evidences of yesteryear that make it special, but its lack of obvious definition. When a man is tired of London he jumps on a bus to Richmond, on a tube to Camden Town, or into a taxi to Soho.

There are several contenders for our opening pages, but we begin with London's river, "Old Father" Thames, and let the current carry us east to the City, the hub of finance, and its fringing areas. Then we leap back west into the center of town to feel the pulse of Covent Garden with its historic roots but distinctly contemporary flavors. Nearby are Bloomsbury with its museums and literary associations, cosmopolitan Soho, and the West End's major stores. Mayfair, their neighbor, could be dubbed American London, being home to the American Embassy, but Westminster, the seat of the British Parliament and various government offices, is undiluted U.K.

Moving still farther west, we take a turn upmarket to Belgravia and Knightsbridge, among the city's most affluent sections. Nearby Chelsea also means wealthy residents, although the style is a shade more avant garde. But this is just as well; otherwise the culture shock between Knightsbridge and Notting Hill, northwest across Hyde Park, famous for its annual carnival when London's Caribbean population takes to the streets in a pageant of calypso and reggae, would be hard to digest. Farther west still, both Richmond and Hampton Court, famous as the palace of King Henry VIII, are green gems. Not that the west enjoys a monopoly of urban greenery. In the north, Regent's Park, with its zoo, is one exception; it's close to both Madame Tussaud's Waxworks Museum and Camden Lock's weekend market, both major tourist pulls. Islington and Hampstead, farther north, are great places for a saunter around interesting small shops (Islington for antiques, Hampstead for clothes, though neither exclusively so). Hampstead also has the bonus of the best of London's open spaces, the rural landscapes of the Heath.

Back toward the east of the City is the epicenter of Cockney London, the East End, with its Jewish and, more recently, Indian and Pakistani populations. And nearby on the river is the new city of London, the Docklands area, a vast horizon of disused docklands that have been, and are still being, transformed into both residential and commercial properties. From this very latest of neighborhoods in London you can walk through a tunnel under the River Thames that will bring you face to face with Greenwich, one of the most historic.

MAJOR INTEREST

The Thames
A boat tour
Tower of London
South Bank Arts Centre

CENTRAL LONDON

The City
St. Paul's Cathedral
Museum of London
Fleet Street
The Strand
Courtauld Institute Galleries
Inns of Court

Covent Garden
Royal Opera House
Shopping

Bloomsbury
British Museum
Georgian squares

Soho
Ethnic restaurants
Chinatown
Jazz

West End
Oxford Street and Regent Street for shopping
Wallace Collection
Royal Academy
Piccadilly Circus
Theater

Mayfair
Grosvenor and Berkeley squares

Westminster
Buckingham Palace (Changing of the Guard)
St. James's Park
National Gallery
Cabinet War Rooms (Churchill's bunker)
Houses of Parliament
Westminster Abbey
Tate Gallery

LONDON WEST

Knightsbridge–Belgravia
Harrods and other shops
Hyde Park

Chelsea
Old houses of literary greats
Shopping on the King's Road

South Kensington
Victoria and Albert Museum and other museums

Richmond
Walks along the Thames
Kew Gardens

Hampton Court

Notting Hill
Annual Caribbean Carnival
Portobello Road market and art galleries

LONDON NORTH

Marylebone Road
Madame Tussaud's Waxworks Museum
Planetarium
Baker Street

Hampstead
Hampstead Heath
Highgate hilltop village

Camden Town
Camden Lock weekend market
Music venues and restaurants
London Zoo and Regent's Park
Nash terraces
Regent's Canal boat tours

Islington
Antiques shops and markets
Sadler's Wells Theatre

LONDON EAST

East End
Cockney ambience
Petticoat Lane market
Kosher and Indian food

Docklands
St. Katharine's Dock
New commercial and residential development
Docklands Light Railway
Canary Wharf

Greenwich
Maritime history
Old Royal Observatory

The Thames

Although there is no single London, there is a significant single divide between the north and the south: the River Thames. As you move upstream (west) from Tower Bridge, there are more than a dozen bridges that link its northern and southern banks. Despite the ease of transition, though, the emotional divide between north and south London is deeply rooted. While the south has always had its pockets of affluence in such places as Dulwich Village and Blackheath, joined now by Battersea, Greenwich, Clapham, and

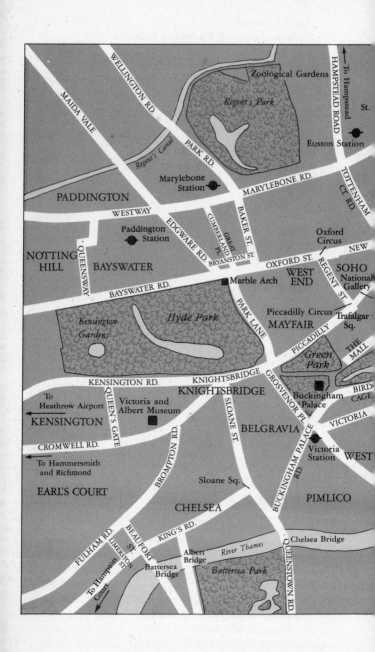

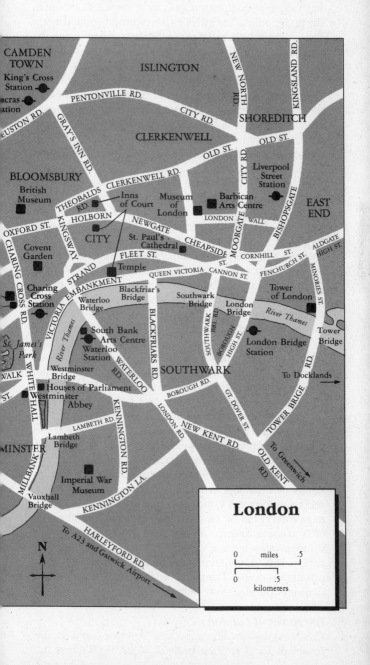

a block of other recently gentrified boroughs, the north has long enjoyed the monopoly on affluence. But more to the point, as far as the traveller is concerned, south London has relatively little to offer the tourist compared with the wealth of attractions—from stylish shops to seasoned sights—north of the river.

London happened because of its river. Its commercial significance was the city's raison d'être. Today, although the forest of masts and rigging, bustling warehouses, cranes, and general state of economic frenzy that dominated the area in the past have all but disappeared from the scene, the Thames is still the most essential element in London's chemistry.

Among the world's great rivers the Thames ranks very low. Its entire length runs only a little more than 200 miles, making it a mere stream in contrast to, say, the 4,000 miles of the Amazon or even Europe's 1,000-mile-long Rhine. And it is not always a pretty sight, especially at low tide when its muddy banks are exposed. But while a boat ride along the Seine may be hard to beat when it comes to romance, Paris's river cannot hold a candle to the Thames for the sheer interest sustained by the passing panorama. In the 1950s the Thames was so filthy that anyone who had the misfortune to fall in was rushed off to have his stomach pumped. Today, perch, trout, and even the occasional salmon have been fished from its waters. The Thames has been granted a new lease on life, one in which leisure has taken the place of commerce, and its importance as a focal point for the visitor is of greater significance now than it has ever been.

A sightseeing boat ride is the best way to enjoy the Thames. Starting from **Westminster Pier**, right beside Westminster Bridge on the opposite side of the road from the Houses of Parliament, you can travel on a regular number of sailings in either direction. You'll drift past several of the most important sights in the city, and while most will cry out for far closer scrutiny than from the rails of a passing launch, at least the ride—backed by a commentary—is an apt introduction to the London scenario. The commuter service called Riverbus runs catamarans on the Thames (see "Boat Excursions" in the Getting Around section, below).

The Tower of London

The most historically important riverside sight is the Tower of London. First built of wood by William the

Conqueror in 1067, then converted to stone a decade later, it protected the king's capital both from the invaders sailing upstream from the Channel and from conquered Londoners who might challenge his authority. Perhaps the tower's most famous historical role was as a prison to a score of leading figures, including the Little Princes (both allegedly murdered in the Bloody Tower), Thomas More, Anne Boleyn, Sir Walter Raleigh, Guy Fawkes, and, the last in the line, Rudolf Hess. Many were to pass through Traitors' Gate, the main water entrance, never to see daylight again.

Although the tower is one of those "obvious" sights that the majority of Londoners probably haven't visited since their childhood, its popularity with visitors is enormous. Apart from the impressive antiquity of the place, there are two other aspects of the tower visit that will linger in the memory long after the knowledge of the date of its foundations has faded. First is the **Crown Jewels**, which include the five-pound crown said to have been worn by all British monarchs, including Queen Elizabeth II, since Charles II (and maybe even earlier), and the crown of the Queen Mother, which incorporates the enormous Koh-i-Noor diamond.

The second memory will be of the **Beefeaters**—more officially, the Yeoman Warders—whose history dates from their role as bodyguards to Henry VII in the 15th century. You can see them at their most spectacular—though you need to make a written application to the Resident Governor of the Tower to do so—at the Ceremony of the Keys, the closing of the main gates of the tower every evening at 10:00. Before you leave the tower, be sure to count the ravens. There are always a minimum complement of six, and legend dictates that when they no longer flap about the place, the tower and England will fall.

Tower Bridge

Immediately in front of the tower is Tower Bridge, probably the single most widely recognized landmark in the entire city. Though your visit may not coincide with the impressive opening yawn of its road section—or bascules—as it only occurs roughly three times a week, the bridge nevertheless makes a stunning picture. It took eight years to build and was opened in 1894 with great pomp and ceremony by the Prince of Wales, later King Edward VII. At the time it was hailed as one of the great engineering wonders of the world. In its heyday, the bridge would open for passing business some 50 times a day and required a permanent staff of more than 100, including a few whose sole role was to collect the horse droppings (presumably so they wouldn't cascade down the opening bascules onto waiting traffic).

The bridge cost more than £1 million to build, and in the early 1980s £2.5 million was the price of converting it into a tourist attraction. Today you can make acquaintance with the bridge from the walkway, the topmost, latticed structure that links the two great Gothic towers. The walkway and several tower rooms constitute a **museum**, with exhibits illustrating the history of the bridge (including, for those who miss it, pictures of the bridge with its jaws wide open for passing ships; one photograph shows a bus that failed to stop and was caught straddling the gap). Best of all, the walkways afford one of the best views of the Thames to be had.

South Bank Arts Centre

The place in central London, however, that offers the most intimate relationship with the Thames is the South Bank Arts Centre, by Waterloo Bridge. In front of the **Royal Festival Hall**, built for the Festival of Britain in 1951, there is a broad promenade along which to stroll, lean, and watch the passing barge traffic or gaze across the river at the Houses of Parliament. The Royal Festival Hall is an architectural triumph of its time, but you may not feel that the same accolades can be applied to its neighbors. You will no doubt form a strong opinion about the newer buildings in the complex—stark, highly radical concrete presences that house the Queen Elizabeth Hall (staging a wide range of musical events from blues to classical concerts), the Purcell Room (a small theater used for recitals and chamber music), the Hayward Gallery (mounting major art exhibitions, contemporary and historic), the National Theatre, and the National Film Theatre.

The newest attraction, opened in 1988, is the **Museum of the Moving Image**, the largest museum in the world devoted to cinema and television. It traces the history of film from the Chinese shadow plays of 2000 B.C. to the latest in optical disc technology. Another new development is Gabriel's Wharf, next to the National Theatre, which features a colorful food market on Fridays, with some stalls open on Sundays.

A new section of walkway called (and signposted) the
Riverside Walk now allows pedestrians to walk from
County Hall, on the South Bank opposite the Houses of
Parliament, to beyond Tower Bridge with just a minor
detour. The walk passes the **Clink Museum**, displaying
torture instruments and other penal artifacts on the site of
a 15th-century prison, and the new **Hay's Galleria** shopping, office, and restaurant complex. From the walk you
can also gain access to the cruiser H.M.S. *Belfast,* a
decommissioned Royal Navy warship that saw action in
World War II.

Central London

St. Paul's Cathedral

Unmistakably, St. Paul's Cathedral *is* London. Designed by
Sir Christopher Wren, Britain's most highly regarded architect, the great 17th-century church now sits rather
uncomfortably in its surroundings, not unlike an aging,
rent-controlled tenant who occupies a prime parcel of
fast-appreciating real estate. Look at a selection of old
paintings of London, and St. Paul's, with its curvaceous
dome and squat twin towers, reigns magnificently over
the skyline. Even in pictures taken during the 1940s the
cathedral's environs lie around its ankles.

Today, the cathedral has been both hidden and dwarfed
by clusters of uninspired office buildings, all fed by reve-
nues from the City's commerce. Prince Charles has even
gone on record as decrying such works as "carbuncles."
Poor old St. Paul's looks pitiably ill at ease in this setting,
and, architectural gem though it is, it no longer works the
way Wren intended it to.

When you do occasionally catch a glimpse of the cathedral rising above the skyline of modern London—from
the southern bank of the Thames near Blackfriars Bridge,
for example, or looking along from Fleet Street or from a
riverboat—it is superb. The dome, a giant pewter tureen
from the outside, ornately painted within, is one of the
cathedral's most impressive features. Depending on
whether you are looking from within or without, the size
varies; the interior of the dome is actually a false ceiling.
The inside is best appreciated from a less neck-craning
perspective afforded by the famous Whispering Gallery,
named after its unique acoustics, which allow a *sotto voce*

murmur on the far side of the dome to be carried around the circumference and heard by an ear held beside the opposite wall.

Across the river, in Bankside, is Sam Wanamaker's ambitious project, the rebuilding of the **Globe Theatre**, due for completion in the mid-1990s. Built along traditional Elizabethan lines, the theater will hold 1,500 people for Shakespearean performances under open skies and natural light.

THE CITY

St. Paul's is arguably more a symbol of the City of London than of London the city, a confusing matter for first-time visitors but a double identity that is easy to explain. The City of London is both the oldest section of town and, as London's financial heart, the place that bore the brunt of 1987's Black October, when share prices plummeted. It is an official city-within-a-city. Its foundation was laid by the Romans in A.D. 43, when they built the first bridge over the Thames and declared the existence of Londinium, defending their new outpost with a wall. Fragments of their protective perimeter can still be seen today (next to the Museum of London, for example), while the names Ludgate, Aldgate, and Bishopsgate remain as testimony to the wall's existence.

The Museum of London

Visitors with more than a slight curiosity about precontemporary London should first stop by the Museum of London on the street evocatively called London Wall, which explains the capital's story from prehistoric times. It is an unprepossessing, modern building, its entrance opening directly onto the pedestrian walkway that connects the Barbican Centre (see below) with the rest of the City. But the building's youth lends itself to exciting, contemporary displays and light, airy galleries.

Pity the unfortunate person whose task it was to whittle down a potentially mammoth collection into a few choice exhibits that would best portray London's history. The galleries are open-plan and chronologically ordered, so it makes sense to start on the upper floor with The Thames in Prehistory, followed by Roman, Saxon and Medieval, Tudor, and Early Stuart London. Downstairs, mock shop fronts, transport exhibits, and video screens display Late Stuart, Georgian, Early 19th-century, Imperial, 20th-century, and Ceremonial London (the latter includes the

Lord Mayor's State Coach, built in 1757 and still used in the annual Lord Mayor's Show). Other galleries specialize in prints, drawings, and paintings of London, and costumes and textiles. Now move on to roam the streets.

Around in the City

In medieval times the City expanded to roughly a square mile (677 acres). Today British and other major banks, insurance companies, commodity exchanges, and other financial firms have their headquarters within the historic Square Mile originally bordered by the medieval wall. More than 300,000 people pour in during the day from suburbia, but walk these streets on weekends or at night and you will hardly meet a soul.

The Great Fire of 1666 (described so vividly in Samuel Pepys's *Diaries*), the wartime Blitz, and postwar redevelopment have proved to be in the worst interests of conservation. Evidences of old London are thin on the ground. If you're blessed with a sense of imagination, though, you can get a feeling for the City's past from present-day names. Cheapside was the site of a market in the Middle Ages, while nearby Poultry and Milk streets had more specific retail functions. And within the contemporary fabric of City life you will still find constant references to sheriffs, aldermen, and early trade guilds.

Signs that the City is a separate entity include the uniforms of local policemen, similar but not quite the same as those worn in the rest of London (they have red and white armbands, for a start), and various unique ceremonies, culminating in the Lord Mayor's Show to mark the annual election of the new top official. Even the Queen is traditionally escorted into the City by the lord mayor. And each December the Worshipful Company of Butchers presents a boar's head to the lord mayor in thanks for the City's giving the butchers access to the Fleet, once a tributary of the Thames, where they could clean the "entrails of beasts."

The **Barbican Arts Centre**, the City's newest grand-scale development, on Silk Street, grew out of an enormous hole in the ground, a 60-acre bomb site just to the east of the Museum of London. As well as its trade exhibitions, concerts (it's home to the London Symphony Orchestra), stage plays (many by the resident Royal Shakespeare Company), conferences, and art exhibitions, the Barbican is a place where some 5,000 people live. It is also a place that visitors love to hate not only for its out-of-the-way location

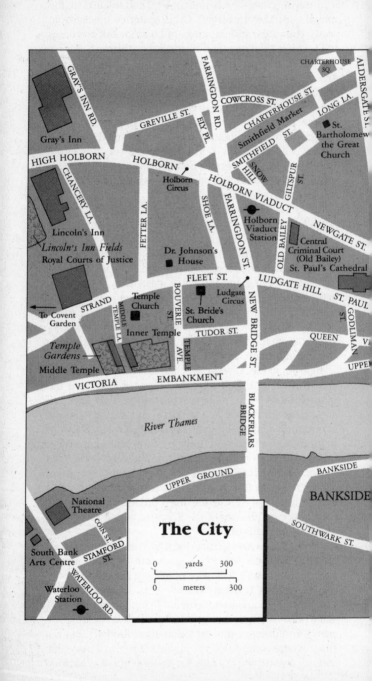

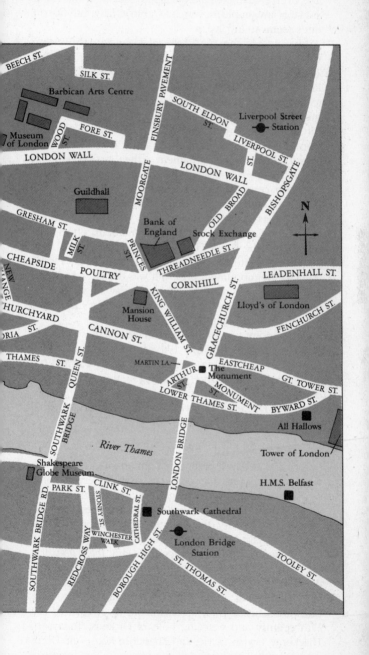

and overpoweringly harsh design but also for the confusion that any simple movement within its labyrinthine confines seems to involve.

Just outside the City's official boundary is **Wesley's Chapel** (see the map of Islington, later in the chapter). The chapel, "the mother church of Methodism," at 47 City Road, and John Wesley's house next door are both open to the public. Wesley is buried in the graveyard behind the chapel, for which he laid the first stone in 1777. Other City sights to see include the Bank of England, the Mansion House (official residence of the lord mayor), the Guildhall (site of the parliament of the City of London for almost 1,000 years, though the present building is mostly late 18th century), and the futuristic Lloyd's insurance building (built like the Centre Georges Pompidou in Paris with its insides on the outside). Just north of London Bridge, on Fish Street Hill, is the **Monument**, which commemorates the Great Fire (it started in a bakery that at 202 feet was situated as far from the base of the monument as the monument is tall). It was designed by Wren, who, were he to climb to the top today, might well be tempted to leap to the bottom after seeing the clutter around his more famous edifice.

At this point you might like to take a walk south over London Bridge—not the 19th-century version, which now stands in Arizona—and have a drink at the 17th-century pub **The George**, just along on the left down in a courtyard off Borough High Street. The pub, which appeared in Dickens's *Pickwick Papers* and *Little Dorrit,* is now owned by the National Trust.

FLEET STREET AREA

Before the redevelopment of London's Docklands you would have found the office of nearly every national newspaper somewhere along **Fleet Street**. Although the printing trade has been linked with it since the beginning of the 16th century, the high-tech machinations of the Docklands have milked Fleet Street of her successful sons (*The Times,* the *Sunday Times,* the *Daily Telegraph,* and the *News of the World* among them). No major newspapers are now located on Fleet Street, but the spirit of the past still resides in **El Vino**'s wine bar and **Ye Olde Cheshire Cheese** pub, a remarkable throwback to the 17th century and watering hole of Dickens, Tennyson, Thackeray, Conan Doyle, and Theodore Roosevelt. Don't ignore the street—one of its most beautiful landmarks is the Art Deco former *Daily Express* building at number 121, a world of glass and polished chrome—or its off-shoots either. Just behind the south side of Fleet Street, on the east side of Salisbury Court, is the church of **St. Bride**, known as the "wedding cake" and designed by Wren in 1701, with the tallest of his steeples.

St. Paul's, towering above Ludgate Circus, forms an impressive eastern tail to Fleet Street. Start walking the length of the street from there and, between the former homes of media giants, you'll come across traditional tobacconists, topsy-turvy Tudor gabled buildings, **Dr. Johnson's House** in Gough Square (open to the public), where the famous dictionary was written between 1749 and 1759, and several large outdoor clothing and sports stores. At the western, Strand end of Fleet Street, look for London's last surviving example in situ of a timber-framed Jacobean town house (number 17), known as **Prince Henry's Room**. Located within the Inner Temple gateway and containing an exhibition devoted to Samuel Pepys, the house has a Jacobean enriched plaster ceiling. It survived only because the Great Fire of 1666 stopped next door. Fleet Street now takes another sharp upturn in class as it becomes the Strand.

The Strand (or simply Strand) parallels the river (although its pedestrians cannot see the river), thus adding immense value to the buildings along its southern flank, most of which back onto the water. The ▶ **Savoy Hotel** is without doubt the grandest (try to have breakfast in its delightful **River Room**), though its neighbor on Tavistock Street, **Somerset House**, is a close competitor. Built in white Portland stone, Somerset House used to be the headquarters of the Registrar General of Births, Deaths, and Marriages; it now houses the less popular Board of Inland Revenue and the Probate Registry as well as the very popular **Courtauld Institute Galleries**, which recently moved here from Bloomsbury, where only a third of the collection could be seen at any one time. Painters who are represented in this rich collection include 19th-century masters—Bonnard, Degas, van Gogh, Seurat, Manet, Monet, Cézanne—as well as such other luminaries as Rubens, Michelangelo, Brueghel, Dürer, Tintoretto, Rembrandt, Gainsborough, Bellini, and Kokoschka.

Other worthy sights in the area include the Wren-designed **St. Clement Danes** church (the bells ring out the "Oranges and Lemons" nursery rhyme at 9:00 A.M., noon, 3:00 P.M., and 6:00 P.M. Monday through Friday, but the interior is of little interest to most visitors), the Royal

Courts of Justice (see below), the semicircular, traffic-ridden one-way street known as the Aldwych, with the BBC's Bush House, and the **London School of Economics** (officially the London School of Economics and Political Science) on Houghton Street. Just off the Strand, on Strand Lane, are the remains—their authenticity disputed—of the so-called Roman Baths, restored in the 17th century.

THE INNS OF COURT

Apart from its literary associations, Fleet Street (along with its offshoot, Chancery Lane) cuts through the heart of legal London. The "Big Four," all a short stroll from one another, are the four Inns of Court: Gray's Inn, Lincoln's Inn, Middle Temple, and Inner Temple (the last two are part of the Temple complex; the other two, separate from each other, are off to the north). Together, they have been the linchpins of Britain's closely knit legal community since the 14th century. A stroll through the cloistered courtyards of the Inns reveals a uniquely tranquil world of fine stone buildings, manicured gardens, and elegant quadrangles. In a few steps you can leave the traffic hubbub of Chancery Lane and find yourself in an atmosphere more like that of Oxford or Cambridge than the City.

Any tour of the area should begin with the **Temple**, accessible down one of the tiny side streets off the south side of Fleet Street, Middle Temple Lane. The college-like buildings of the Temple house the two older inns: the **Middle Temple** and the **Inner Temple**. An area called the Outer Temple has long since disappeared, but next to the Inner Temple is the 12th-century **Temple Church**, one of England's last remaining round churches. Originally home to the Knights Templars, a military order founded in Jerusalem in 1118, the Temple was built in the mid-12th century. In the early 14th century, the order was disbanded and the Temple was let out to students.

In 1292 King Edward I declared that the country's legal system was a mass of shortcomings. Until then all matters of justice had been dealt with by members of the clergy. They were undoubtedly the most literate members of society, but they were still laymen as far as noncanon law was concerned. Edward's desire to professionalize the legal system led to the recruitment of top students from the aristocracy. At first the students were scattered around the country, but within 100 years all barrister pupils were brought to London and accommodated in hostels, or "inns," including the former lodgings of the Knights Templars.

Today each inn is a self-contained, autonomous entity with its own chapel, library, and dining hall. The latter, a richly decorated room, has always been the focal point; Queen Elizabeth I and her courtiers, for example, were wined and dined in **Gray's Inn**, off High Holborn, on so many occasions that today's inmates still toast "Good Queen Bess" in a room adorned with relics of a vessel captured during the rout of the Spanish Armada. Shakespeare's plays were also acted at the inns; Gray's Inn members saw the first performance of *The Comedy of Errors* in 1594, while the magnificent Middle Temple Hall claims the same honor for *Twelfth Night* in 1602.

In Britain, unlike in the United States and most other countries, there are two distinct types of lawyer. Barristers represent the prosecution or defense in the high-ranking courts, whereas solicitors—who are forbidden to stand and be heard in these places—handle the nuts-and-bolts paperwork on a case and deal directly with clients. The barrister may never even meet those he represents in court. But the laws governing the law are beginning to change; in the near future solicitors are likely to be permitted to represent clients.

While the blustering pomposity of the TV character Rumpole of the Bailey is an exaggerated impression of British barristers, there is a great deal of snobbishness attached to the inns, and the members of each one adhere to a strict hierarchy. Their interiors are sacrosanct, as they contain the offices (or "chambers") of practicing barristers, whose names are listed beside each doorway.

Over the years these lists have read like the pages of *Who's Who*. Sir Thomas More and several other lord chancellors were members of **Lincoln's Inn**, the place where rival prime ministers Disraeli and Gladstone also qualified as barristers. Sir Francis Bacon was the most famous member of Gray's Inn, and Charles Dickens was apprenticed to one of its lawyers at age 15. Sir Walter Raleigh and Sir Francis Drake were both members of the Middle Temple (it's even rumored that a dining-hall serving table is made of timber from Drake's ship *Golden Hind*). John Dickinson, a Middle Templar, was the man who coined the phrase "no taxation without representation"; when the U.S. Declaration of Independence was drawn up, five Middle Templars signed the final document. Many prominent North Americans are still honorary members of the inns.

You will undoubtedly catch sight of barristers rushing to and from court in twos and threes, each clutching a bundle of "briefs." By tradition, they do not carry briefcases; all documents are carried openly and bound by a red ribbon (hence references to bureaucratic "red tape").

Royal Courts of Justice

Having prepared their cases, barristers have only a short walk to work. The Neo-Gothic Royal Courts of Justice on the Strand, home of the High Court and the Court of Appeal of England and Wales, pass judgment on the most important civil cases. The vaulted, cathedral-like Great Hall, supported by granite pillars and hung with oil paintings of former judges and coats of arms, echoes the hushed activity. Barristers, ticking on White Rabbit schedules, their black gowns bloated like the wind-filled sails of galleons and their frizzes (wigs) askew, emerge from one corridor, zip across the hall, and disappear into another. Don't even attempt to follow them; five and a half miles of corridors lead off the hall, and that's a lot of shoe leather if you get lost.

Members of the public whose cases are scheduled for judgment later in the day in one of the 64 courts stand huddled in earnest conversation with solicitors. All the day's cases are listed in showcases. To witness a trial involving murder, robbery, or other such heinous crimes, you have to make your way to Old Bailey Street at Newgate Street, northwest of St. Paul's, to the public gallery of the Old Bailey, the most famous criminal court in the world.

The Old Bailey

"Justice is not blind at the Old Bailey," declared the City of London Corporation 87 years ago when the Old Bailey (or the Central Criminal Court, to give it its proper name) was built on the site of Newgate Prison, demolished in 1902. To emphasize the point, they made sure that their version of the figure of Justice, the statue that sits on the building's green dome holding the scales of justice and the sword of retribution high above the traffic jams, was one of the only ones in the world without a blindfold.

Criminal justice in England and Wales focuses on the Old Bailey, and within the walls of its 19 courts you can

hear the verdicts of major trials, many of which are referred to the High Court judges as a last resort. The most
famous and most important cases are heard in the surprisingly small Court Number One, a wood-paneled court-
room whose dock floorboards have creaked under some
of the most notorious criminals in the history of 20th-
century Britain. These include American-born Dr.
Crippen, accused of murdering his wife, Belle Elmore,
and cutting her up into pieces before eloping with his
mistress. More recent trials have included that of the
"Yorkshire Ripper," the late-1970s murderer.

North of Lincoln's Inn, at 13 Lincoln's Inn Fields, visitors
can enter a time warp at **Sir John Soane's Museum.** Soane
(1753–1837), the architect of the Bank of England, stipu-
lated that his collections remain unaltered. As a result, a
fine house of the period, with an eclectic assortment of
fine art, antiquities, and furniture, remains as it was in
1813.

COVENT GARDEN

Cross busy Kingsway, walk down Great Queen Street past
the vast Masonic Hall, and you'll find yourself in London's
newest village (at least on the visitors' map), Covent
Garden. Within the space of a few years the city's old fruit-
and-vegetable market has been transformed into one of
the liveliest and loveliest urban centers in Europe.

In underground cellars once used to store bananas,
young sophisticates now pick cherries off the ends of tiny
paper parasols resting on the edges of cocktail glasses.
From stalls in the central Apple Market, where Granny
Smiths and Cox's Orange Pippins were once stacked,
shoppers now buy elaborately patterned sweaters and
scores of other products handmade by the craftspeople
who sell them. And in high-ceilinged warehouses that
once stored crates of carrots, parsnips, potatoes, and
other roots, Filofax clutchers now dine on nouvelle cuisine served by bow-tied waiters whose own social background would not permit them to take on such menial
and deferential roles anywhere else in Britain.

In an earlier incarnation Covent Garden was also a very
fashionable part of town. Inigo Jones designed **St. Paul's
Church,** popularly known as the actors' church, as well as
the Piazza on which it stands, just west of the market. The
story has it that the earl of Bedford (the original landowner) told Jones that his budget would only stretch to

cover a barn, so the architect promised the "most beautiful barn in the country." Completed in 1633 as part of London's first square, modeled after the Italian piazzas Jones had studied in his travels, the church was later destroyed by fire but rebuilt to its initial specifications.

The original Theatre Royal, where Nell Gwyn sold oranges, opened in 1662, and soon afterward the **Royal Opera House** opened its doors on Bow Street, off Long Acre. But the area's early elegance did not last long. The presence of the wealthy drew rogues—the poet Dryden was beaten up in an alleyway outside the Bucket of Blood pub, now the Lamb and Flag. It is no coincidence that London's first police force, the Bow Street Runners, was established just around the corner.

Attracted by the security of the strong arm of the law, a new wave of prosperity followed. The renaissance was marked by the construction of the Central Market buildings in 1830, when the duke of Bedford decided that something smarter was needed to replace the rows of shanty vegetable stalls that had stood their ground since the 17th century. Coffeehouses also flourished; Dr. Johnson first met Boswell in a small establishment, now fittingly called Boswell's, on Russell Street.

In 1974, after three centuries of trading, the market vendors moved out to modern premises across the River Thames at Nine Elms. They left behind a mass of grimy buildings, and an enormous debate began on just what to do with such a potentially prime site on the fringes of the West End. Restoration work on the old buildings was started, but the transition was not accomplished without opposition—mainly from neighborhood residents, who would have preferred to see the development of a simple residential community, not an upscale designer village.

The Shopping

The Covent Garden area offers some of the best of London's shopping, not for basics (there is only one butcher shop, and even that is mostly a purveyor of game) but for fashionable, boutique-type wares. Lots of old traders remain: for example, Anello and Davide, the theatrical shoemakers; the Drury Tea and Coffee Co.; and Stanfords, the map and travel book shop. Covent Garden itself and neighboring streets such as Long Acre contain scores of galleries and bookshops, clothing boutiques, epicurean and organic food stores, gift shops, and others whose products all bear a stamp of design that far exceeds the functional.

Many shop fronts are based on original designs, and in the north hall, site of the old Apple Market, a flavor of the old days remains. Forty original wrought-iron stands, salvaged from the Flower Market, are now rented to traders and craftspeople, who sell their goods beneath the magnificent glass roof. As for the Old Flower Market itself— on the eastern side of the Piazza, completed in 1872 and staffed entirely by women—it now houses the **London Transport Museum**'s collection of early buses and trams. The entrance to Britain's first **Theatre Museum** is around the corner on Russell Street, within walking distance of the Royal Opera House and many other theaters.

Every day at lunchtime you will find performances by buskers (street performers), all carefully screened by the Covent Garden management, in front of the portico of St. Paul's Church, the very spot where George Bernard Shaw's Eliza Doolittle first met Professor Higgins, and under the 1830s roof of the Apple Market.

At night the activity takes on a different rhythm. When the stores close—most not until 8:00 P.M.—people drift to the pubs and wine-and-cocktail bars, then on to restaurants. You can eat inexpensive but sometimes bland African fare at the **Calabash**, Italian at **Orso**, American at **Joe Allen's**, Chinese at **Poon's**, classic English at the **Opera Terrace**, French at **Mon Plaisir** or **Boulestin**, Japanese at **Ajimura**, and Mexican at **Café Pacifico**.

BLOOMSBURY

Sinatra's "foggy day in London town" reflects Bloomsbury, directly north of Covent Garden, in a surprisingly dramatic mood. The British Museum, he croons, has lost its charm, which is a curious attribute to apply anyway to such a hefty, solid chunk of masonry, even on the sunniest of days. And, just to correct those misconceptions, London's traditional pea-soup fog, in which Sinatra's lyricist was no doubt once engulfed, is now only to be experienced in ancient horror movies. In 1956 the Clean Air Act was passed, outlawing the use of coal and wood fires and regulating industrial emissions.

British Museum

The British Museum, with its magnificent colonnaded façade and entrance on Great Russell Street, is at the

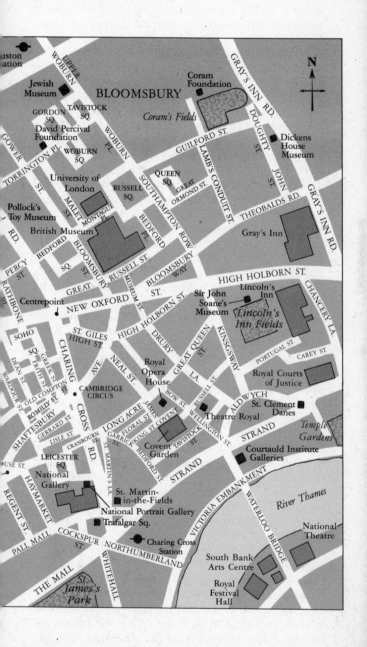

heart of Bloomsbury, a fitting edifice for this, the most cerebral area of town. The great repository of treasures, many blatantly stolen from Egypt and other lands at a time when Britain's imperialist arrogance, not to mention its archaeological light-fingeredness, exercised no ethical restraints on other peoples' property, is invariably among the top half-dozen priorities of overseas visitors to London (although most Londoners went there the first and the last time as children led by their teacher).

Construction of the present building, with its ancient Greek influences (rather ironic, considering the recent tussle over the fate of the Elgin Marbles taken from the Parthenon site), was completed in the middle of the past century. It displayed the grime of all those years, too, until a recent cleaning. The building houses a vast collection, spread among some 94 rooms, galleries, and landings. Museum freaks may feel the need to tackle the lot, devoting their entire vacation to poking around. Others will prefer to limit their visits to some of the essential viewings. These must, of course, include the **Elgin Marbles** (a set of sculptures and a frieze that were taken from the Parthenon in Athens by Lord Elgin in 1803), if only to see the cause of the dispute between the authorities in Britain and Greece concerning their permanent home. You'll find them displayed in the Duveen Gallery. The Library Galleries contain the **Magna Carta**, one of the most important documents in the history of democracy, while the prize in the Egyptian Sculpture Gallery is the **Rosetta Stone**. All these rooms are on the ground floor. In the Egyptian Gallery upstairs are the famous mummies, arguably the museum's most interesting exhibits. You can also have a brief look at the Reading Room, a stunning library in which rows of desks radiate out from a central area beneath a 40-foot dome. The library is scheduled for relocation to a site near St. Pancras railway station; the move, to begin in 1995, will take until 1999, perhaps longer. Meanwhile, visitors are allowed in at noon and 2:00, 3:00, and 4:00 P.M.

Other Museums

Other Bloomsbury museums include the **Percival David Foundation of Chinese Art**, on Gordon Square, which includes superb porcelains; the tiny one-room **Jewish Museum** on Upper Woburn Place, Tavistock Square; the **Dickens House Museum** at 48 Doughty Street; and **Pollock's Toy Museum**, at 1 Scala Street, with the original

"Penny Plain Tuppence Coloured" Toy Theatres as well as 19th- and 20th-century toys.

University of London

If the British Museum represents Bloomsbury's seat of knowledge, the University of London is its seat of learning. American visitors, in particular, will be surprised at the relatively small acreage that such an important educational institution appears to occupy. This is partly because there are no halls of residence as such, but also because several of the surrounding ordinary-looking buildings have been bought by the university for the use of individual faculties.

Located to the rear of the British Museum, on the southwestern side of Russell Square, the main part of the university is a relative newcomer to Bloomsbury—the tall Senate House was begun only in 1932—but because so many of its parts are found in older buildings, its geographical roots seem much older. Among the most important of the larger buildings are University College and, on the opposite side of Gower Street, University College Hospital.

Elsewhere in Bloomsbury

Sadly, the tallest building in Bloomsbury also happens to be one of the ugliest. West of Tottenham Court Road, the British Telecom Tower (also known by its former name, the Post Office Tower), which dominates London's skyline (it's the third-tallest structure in London, after Canary Wharf in the Docklands and the NatWest Tower in the City), is widely despised, though it has a good reason for being there, as its ungainly stature affords the necessary ground clearance for its communications functions.

There are, as in any section of any city, other monstrosities. But Bloomsbury is one of the corners of Georgian London that has survived fairly well, its leafy squares little changed since their drawing rooms witnessed the frantic exchanges of artistic, literary, and philosophical banter by the early-20th-century Bloomsbury Group. Most members of this circle (Virginia Woolf and her sister, Vanessa Bell, Rupert Brooke, D. H. Lawrence, art critic Roger Fry, Lytton Strachey, Clive Bell, Maynard Keynes, and E. M. Forster) didn't have far to travel when visiting—they lived on one or another of Bedford, Woburn, Russell, Gordon (Virginia Woolf lived at number 46 before she married), Tavistock, or Fitzroy squares. Bloomsbury Square has sadly lost all its original architecture; only **Bedford Square** and **Fitzroy**

Square are still lined with their vintage tall and extremely handsome mid-18th-century terraced houses. The core of most squares is still a quiet patch of green, though when in the shape of lush gardens they are usually closed to the public (the residents have keys).

Brunswick Square is the black sheep of Bloomsbury— its dimensions have narrowed and its beauty has disappeared since the construction of an ugly housing block, and a small, modern cinema, the Renoir, has been plunked in the center, alongside a Safeway supermarket and other commercial outlets.

With all its literary flowering, it's small wonder that Bloomsbury sprouted a spray of publishing houses, many now departed in the face of skyrocketing rents, however. And when you want to see what they've produced, try some of the area's many bookshops—**Dillons** is the largest, built to serve the university, its distinctive navy blue and gold window display hogging the northern end of Malet Street. For secondhand or more specialized tomes, head south of Russell Square to the network of narrow streets around Museum Street.

SOHO

Since the beginning of the century Soho has enjoyed a dubious reputation. The name still conjures up images of sleazy clubs, brothels, gambling parlors, and Mafia plots (both the Italian and Chinese varieties). It is a world where, by night at least, tourists once either feared to tread or did so with their adrenaline pumping.

Not so long ago one-third of all its houses were brothels and, although a great deal has been done to clean up the area, only recently have the authorities begun to stem the tide of sex shops and peep shows that blossomed in their place. Soho is not a no-go. It may not appeal to your taste, but, compared with most other sin centers of the world, it is relatively tame. In any case, it cannot be ignored. To do so would be to turn your back on the highest density of good dining to be found in the whole of London.

The area is anchored on the southeast by Leicester Square and bordered by **Charing Cross Road** (still famous for its bookstores—Foyle's, Zwemmer's, and others) and the shopping thoroughfares of Oxford and Regent streets. **Leicester Square** is a good place to begin a Soho saunter. It is difficult to imagine, despite the grass underfoot and the giddy heights of the plane trees, that in Henry VIII's time the area was at the heart of a royal hunting ground surrounded by open country and rural villages, with the City of London still a few miles off to the east. The very name Soho is derived from an old hunting cry, the contemporary equivalent being "tallyho."

The actual square, known originally as Leicester Fields, was named after the earl of Leicester, who built its first town house on what is now the site of the Angus Steak House, on the northern side of the square. Soon other houses went up in one of the country's earliest spates of property speculation. Once commoners moved in to occupy them, however, the earl moved out. Today the square is a bright-lights mecca that mainly entices out-of-towners in search of a newly released movie (there's also a ticket booth selling seats for same-day theater performances at half price; but don't expect tickets for smash hits—the system works best for second-rank shows and plays).

Many people regard **Soho Square**, in Soho's northeast corner near the intersection of Charing Cross and Oxford Street, as the heart of the area. It is certainly its greenest core, with a statue of King Charles II standing among the trees, holding what looks like a spout in one hand. It *is* a spout; the king used to be a fountain "powered" by a row of windmills along what is now Oxford Street. The square was once a garden for the exclusive use of residents, but they departed and the park became public, a popular summer retreat for lunchtime sandwich-eaters and more than a scattering of winos. A close inspection of the building that looks like a Tudor hunting lodge in the center of the square will reveal that it is mock Tudor, dating back to the 1930s but built as a replica of the type of lodges that used to be dotted around the royal hunting grounds in case of rain. It is now a tool shed.

Soho's social history is colorfully cosmopolitan. French Huguenots fleeing the consequences of the revocation of the Edict of Nantes, Greeks escaping the Turks, Swiss, Italians, Germans, Jews, and other refugees have all immigrated to Soho in large numbers, most sharing backgrounds of persecution in their home countries. By 1914, for example, one-third of the houses here were occupied by Jews, a figure that will come as a surprise to people who think of the East End as the traditional Jewish district in London.

Soho Restaurants

The cosmopolitan mix today is best seen in the enormous number of ethnic restaurants. Stand, for example, on the corner of Leicester Street (just north of the square) and Lisle Street, and you'll see Poon's Chinese restaurant virtually next door to Manzi's Italian fish restaurant, which, just to add to the confusion, used to be a German hotel whose visitors' book recorded Karl Marx and his wife and children as onetime guests.

Among the many echoes of the French accent in Soho is the **French House** at 49 Dean Street, a regular pub but one as close as you're likely to come to a French bar in London (although its characterful owner, Gaston, has retired). It is complete with photos of French boxers lining the walls and with not-too-distant memories of Charles de Gaulle, who, during the war, patronized the bar along with other members of the Free French movement. There's also the delightfully bohemian **Pâtisserie Valerie** on Old Compton Street and **Maison Bertaux** on Greek Street, perfect places to rest weary sightseers' feet over a coffee and croissant or *gâteau*.

If Londoners had to pick a single street that summed up the essence of Soho, the honors would go to **Old Compton Street**. No more than 200 to 300 yards long, it contains an Algerian coffee store, a French restaurant, a Spanish deli, an Italian pizzeria, a Malaysian restaurant, a Vietnamese restaurant, and, one of the most recent arrivals, an American diner called Ed's. The area's diversity is well represented by the newsagent called A. Moroni & Son, who sells just about every newspaper in the world (except for, surprisingly, the *New York Times*).

Chinatown

The last ethnic group to move into Soho in significant numbers have been the Chinese, from Hong Kong. It wasn't until 1981 that the area in which they settled, centered on the now pedestrianized **Gerrard Street**, became officially recognized as Chinatown. The Chinese have totally revitalized what used to be a run-down inner-city slum. Although London's Chinatown is far smaller than its counterparts in, say, New York City or San Francisco, the area's shops, restaurants, and overall atmosphere are almost completely Chinese, and, yes, the telephone boxes are shaped like pagodas.

Historic Soho

Soho has numerous blue plaques commemorating the famous as well as red lights announcing the presence of the infamous. No matter where you walk in Soho and no matter what ethnic stamp is currently on the street, evidences of its history abound. William Blake was born here, on Marshall Street; Hazlitt died here, on Frith Street. On Gerrard Street you'll spot a plaque that describes the time that John Dryden lived there. Just a few doors along the road, in the house now occupied by the Loon Fung restaurant, Edmund Burke resided. On the opposite side of the street you'll spot an original 18th-century building with a portico (now the Loon Moon supermarket) that is famous for a former occupant, the Turk's Head Tavern. The Turk, mentioned by Dickens and by Boswell in his biography of Johnson, was the great literati hangout of the day (interestingly, the current media hangout is the private club Groucho's, just around the corner on Dean Street).

The parish of Soho was once far grander in scale than it is now and claimed the church of St. Martin-in-the-Fields (at Trafalgar Square) as its parish church. As the area grew in popularity as a residential section of town, the scale became unmanageable, and the parish was split in two. St. Anne's was built as Soho's new parish church—but, since World War II, all that remains is a tower with a unique barrel-shaped clock, the only one in London. It is best seen from the corner of Romilly and Dean streets, where a new a community center represents the spirit of a newer, cleaner Soho, a phoenix rising from an image-poor past.

But back to the blue plaques. Casanova lived on Frith Street and also on nearby Meard Street, which still contains a row of mid-18th-century brick houses, among the oldest in the area. Chopin gave a recital in one. Jean-Paul Marat lived on Romilly Street in a house with a distinctive bay-window overhang, or "jetty." He came to London not as a revolutionary but as a doctor, writing a treatise on eye diseases.

Another unifying Soho theme, apart from history, sexual innuendo, and good eating, is music. In the 1950s Soho was famous for its coffeehouses, which spawned the U.K.'s first superstars of pop. Though all of the original venues are gone, Soho is still a place to hear music. **Ronnie Scott's** is the jazz epicenter, located, coincidentally, opposite a brick building where Mozart came to entertain at the age of eight. Just a few yards away, on the same side of the road at 47 Frith Street, yet another blue plaque marks the spot where, at the embryonic stage in the development of another branch of entertainment, John Baird demonstrated the first television set.

THE WEST END

Although visitors may find the nomenclature geographically confusing—it's in central, not western, London—Londoners never think twice about the West End's location. To them the West End means central shopping (and the theater). If you want to immerse yourself in the commercial heart of town, just mingle with the lunchtime office workers or weekend suburban pilgrims in the country's biggest stores here.

Oxford Street

Two miles of crowded sidewalks line Oxford Street, the West End's main artery, trampled daily from Marble Arch at its western end to the Centrepoint skyscraper at Tottenham Court Road. Its reputation has been carried to all corners of the globe, yet its days as London's premier shopping street seem numbered. There was a time when no self-respecting chain of stores would fail to open a branch on Oxford Street; without the address, a concern would hold little credibility in the retail hierarchy. Nowadays shoppers tend to give its stores a pass, preferring its more fashionable, polished rivals along Kensington High Street, in Covent Garden, and on Fulham Road in Chelsea.

Commercially, at least, it is still viable for a retail outlet to have at least one branch on Oxford Street—Saturday crowds justifying police megaphones to move them out of the way of oncoming buses cannot be bad for business. (There's even a regular shuttle-bus service that ferries shoplifters to the police station.) But the traditional Oxford Street names would probably be far happier if the tacky discount stores, furiously trying to unload cheap sweatshirts, plastic watches, tasteless imitations, and gimmicky paraphernalia, weren't their neighbors. Even offshoot Carnaby Street, a West End high spot during the swinging 1960s, is now surviving on reputation alone; in reality, its veneer is more than a trifle tarnished.

Largely it's the quality department stores (Selfridges, John Lewis, Marks and Spencer, C & A, Debenhams, and

British Home Stores) that keep the lunchtime, Saturday, and late-night Thursday shopping crowds flowing down Oxford Street. They have survived as the great British shopping institutions, giant magnets without which Oxford Street would have died.

Marking the street's Park Lane (western) extremity, **Marble Arch** deserves a brief mention. Built by George IV to celebrate England's victory over Napoleon, it originally stood outside Buckingham Palace. If Marble Arch figures high on the tourist's list of London sights, to native motorists it signifies little more than bumper-to-bumper traffic jams.

St. Christopher's Place, an alley so narrow you could easily miss it, leads off the north side of Oxford Street almost opposite New Bond Street and is lined with high-fashion, one-off boutiques, stores that sell just one example of a particular design. The Warehouse clothing store and the home-furnishing frippery store, the Reject Shop, are doing a roaring trade in the Plaza shopping mall. And running at a tangent to the mainstream traffic off the south side from the Bond Street tube station is super-chic **South Molton Street**, which is closed to vehicular traffic.

Manchester Square, north of Oxford Street behind Selfridges, contains the **Wallace Collection**. When the first marquis of Hertford started amassing 18th-century paintings and French furniture and artworks, the collection was housed in Paris, but by the time it was in the hands of Richard Wallace, five generations later, it was in England, opened to the public in 1900.

Regent Street

Take a sharp turn to the south at Oxford Circus, step down Regent Street, and you take a giant stride up the elegance scale. The street, laid out by John Nash in the early 19th century, was originally planned to run straight from the prince regent's home, Carlton House, north to the new Regent's Park, but Nash interrupted the tedium of the endless avenue approach with his unmistakable, lavishly expansive curves. Immediately attractive to the rich and famous (Nash himself lived at number 14; Lady Hamilton, Admiral Nelson's renowned mistress, resided down the road at number 25), Regent Street soon became an attractive proposition for shopkeepers, too.

Although large chunks have been reconstructed over the years, Regent Street, now controlled by the Crown Estates Commissioners, is enjoying a revival. The mock-

Tudor Liberty's and Dickins & Jones department stores, and the racks of trenchcoats at Burberry's on Lower Regent Street, for example, are still there, and the grim airline offices and fusty one-off stores are being gradually nudged out by a brigade of parquet-floored, marble-pillared designer newcomers like the U.S.–imported Gap, the middle-of-the-road Next, and the popular Laura Ashley fabric outlets.

Bond Street

Window-shop, if nothing else, on Bond Street (Old Bond Street to the south, running up from Piccadilly, and New Bond Street at the northern end up to Oxford Street). A jewelers' lair for decades, the street has retained its sumptuous image with sky-high rents and retail prices to match. The same applies to **Jermyn Street** just south of and parallel to Piccadilly—where it helps to be rich *and* male because a large proportion of shops (Bates, Harvie & Hudson, and Astley's, for example) cater exclusively to men with a whim for a jar of mustache wax or a badger-hair shaving brush.

The Piccadilly Area

Two of the West End's biggest shopping attractions are on Piccadilly: **Burlington Arcade**, built in 1818 as one of Britain's first covered shopping malls, for fine woollens, linens, jewelry, and the like, and the affluent **Fortnum & Mason** emporium. Even the royal family stocks up on groceries in its frogs'-legs-to-*fines-herbes* food hall. Weary shoppers who wander off in search of sustenance here can choose from two of London's most palatial afternoon tea haunts—the Soda Fountain in Fortnum & Mason and, a scone's throw away, down Piccadilly to the west, the Palm Court Room in the Ritz hotel. If they're both full, cross the road and listen to the harpist in the lounge of the Hotel Meridien.

Follow such heavenly delights with a visit to the **Royal Academy** in Burlington House, a close Piccadilly neighbor that is devoted mainly to temporary exhibitions. The grand courtyard, filled with snaking lines at peak visiting times (especially on Sunday mornings during the annual Summer Exhibition), fronts a Renaissance-style building. Inside is a grand, sweeping staircase and galleries of treasures, including Michelangelo's *Madonna and Child*.

At the back of Burlington House is the more modest, though equally Italianate **Museum of Mankind** (6 Burlington Gardens), whose exhibitions always focus on non-Western cultures. Within the same building is the British Museum's ethnographic collection, including a skull carved from a single piece of Mexican crystal.

London is at her most gaudy and flirtatious with tourists in **Piccadilly Circus**. Walls of neon lights flicker day and night here, captured by a million camera shutters. As part of the Circus's general face-lift, the aluminum statue of Eros (officially the Angel of Charity), once marooned in the tawdry center of the Circus, has been renovated and is now back in the limelight on the south side. Approval of his new good looks is welcome: When Eros was unveiled in 1893, *The Times* described him as the "ugliest monument in any European capital, more suited to the musical hall," while many simply frowned on his nakedness.

Piccadilly's newest brand of entertainment is the **Trocadero Centre** on Coventry Street. Featured at this youth-oriented mall is the excellent Guinness World of Records, an exhibit that derives from the world's best-selling book. The rest of the complex is devoted to noisy, touristy shops and restaurants and video games. Adjacent is the **London Pavilion**, a similar mall that hosts Rock Circus, the latest brainchild of Madame Tussaud's. As you admire the details of the wax renditions of your rock and pop favorites, your short-wave headphones pick up their greatest hits.

Theater District

The back doors of the Trocadero open onto Shaftesbury Avenue, the West End's evening breadwinner. More than 100 years old (its centenary was in 1987), the heart of London's theater district has six theaters and two cinemas. Shaftesbury Avenue was named after the 19th-century philanthropist the earl of Shaftesbury, who carried out much of his alms-giving work in this area; its construction actually resulted in the demolition of several squalid Dickensian slums. The first theater to go up along the new avenue was the Lyric, in 1888. The Royal English Opera House on Cambridge Circus followed, but demand for fine singing was slack. The music hall was in fashion, and the theater was renamed the Palace. Musicals are still the staple diet of London's theater, particularly if they're written by Andrew Lloyd Webber. The Palace, in fact, is currently owned by Lloyd Webber and once housed *Jesus Christ Superstar,* the second-longest-running musical in the history of British theater; the theater now has *Les Misérables,* which is in its seventh year.

The Apollo, the Globe, the Queen's, and the Shaftesbury complete the six. Originally the New Prince's theater, the Shaftesbury is most famous for its misfortunes: A gas explosion interrupted Fred and Adele Astaire's dancing in Gershwin's *Funny Face,* while later the musical *Hair* literally brought the house down when part of the ceiling collapsed.

MAYFAIR

Between the West End and, to the west, Hyde Park you'll find Mayfair. The small, appealing parts of Mayfair are the rows of elegant brownstones that were the original *Upstairs, Downstairs* houses of London's upper (and lower) echelons. Concentrated chiefly in Mayfair's two most famous squares, Grosvenor (home of the U.S. embassy) and Berkeley, these brownstones boast top-floor and basement former servants' quarters that today command some of the highest rents in town, while the mews houses, once the stable yards for the coach and horses (with upper-floor living accommodations for the driver), sell for small fortunes.

The essence of Mayfair is its elegant shops and squares, though working Londoners are also aware that the city's most prestigious office buildings tower above it. Window-shoppers and those with great amounts of money should head for Brook Street, South Molton Street (one of the city's most elite pedestrianized precincts), New and Old Bond streets, and Savile Row. Smaller showrooms and galleries are to be found on Dover Street, also home to ▶ **Brown's Hotel** at number 22, London's renowned "gentleman's" hotel, founded by the husband of Lady Byron's maid and now owned by Forte Hotels. The hotel has worked hard to preserve a sense of quietude and privacy, and it still attracts some of the city's most gentrified visitors. It also serves an excellent traditional tea.

Curzon Street, part residential (number 19 marks the spot where Disraeli died in 1881) and part commercial, backs onto **Shepherd Market** (the name belies its wealth), a delightful "village" of narrow streets, period houses, and pubs like the Bunch of Grapes (referred to as Ye Grapes), cafés geared for alfresco dining, and tiny courtyards—the whole linked by a series of archways. It is also noted for its prostitutes.

Thanks to the heavy traffic and plethora of motorcycle

messengers in central London, a quiet stroll around Berkeley Square is possible only on a Sunday morning. Nevertheless, it's not difficult to appreciate the grandeur of its 200-year-old plane trees (all that remain of Berkeley Woods), which shelter some of the city's most beautiful architecture. Two buildings to look out for are number 45, the former home of Clive of India (where in 1774 the career colonialist committed suicide, although he had been vindicated by Parliament's investigation of the "East India Company scandal"), and number 50, where **Maggs**, the antiquarian book specialists, is open to bibliophiles.

WESTMINSTER

Westminster is London wearing its most royal plumage and governmental robes. On the map, the area officially defined as the City of Westminster is vast, bordered by Camden on the north and the Thames on the south, but even Londoners rarely relate the name to its full territorial stake. The name really connotes the government buildings of Whitehall, the Houses of Parliament, Westminster Abbey, the Prime Minister's official residence at 10 Downing Street, and St. James's Park. Westminster is a residential borough, but its palaces and government offices, including the bulk of the ministry headquarters, overshadow the lives of its ordinary citizens.

Buckingham Palace

Buckingham Palace is Westminster's prize showpiece. It was built for the duke of Buckingham in 1703 and bought by King George III in 1761. John Nash played a part in the building's restructuring in 1825, although many of the trimmings that you see today were the result of a face-lift in 1913 by Sir Aston Webb. Today's palace is yesterday's Buckingham House, a beautiful pillared and porticoed mansion house carved in white Portland stone, overlooking a semicircular bow of manicured gardens. The grandeur continues inside, from the bedchambers to the state rooms; even the stable block is magnificent.

St. James's Palace, on Pall Mall at the foot of St. James's Street (south from Piccadilly), was the official royal residence before Queen Victoria moved to Buckingham Palace in 1837. The red-jacketed and bear-skinned guards in front of the palace in St. James's are much photographed. (See below for the Changing of the Guard ceremony.) St. James's Palace, Henry VIII's turreted gift to Anne Boleyn when they were first married, is now virtu-

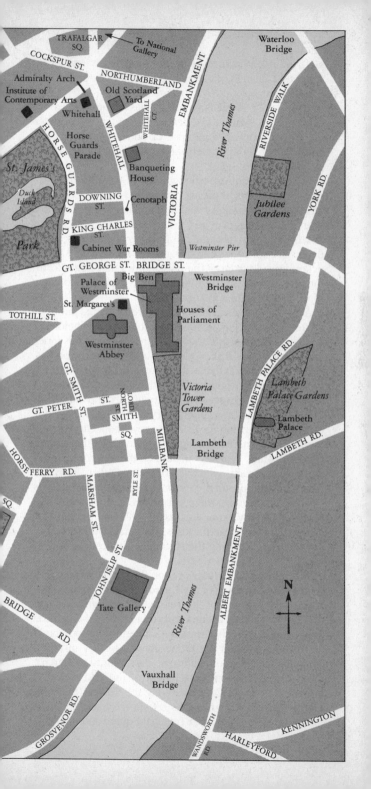

ally redundant as a royal house, though any announce-
ment of a change of ruler is traditionally made from its
Friary Court balcony.

If the gold Royal Standard flag is flying high above
Buckingham Palace, the Queen is in residence. Occasionally, you may catch a glimpse of one or another of the
royal family sitting rather anonymously in the back of a
sleek black Daimler.

For the first time in its long history, Buckingham Palace
opened its doors to paying visitors in 1993. For an eight-
week period in August and September for the next five
years, sightseers may buy tickets (£8 for adults, £4 for
children) for a tour of the public areas of the palace. Most
tickets are sold for same-day tours at the St. James's Park
ticket office in front of the palace; lines may begin forming as early as 7:00 A.M. Information is available from any
of the tourist offices in London.

A few thousand members of a more esteemed public—
aristocrats, sporting personalities, the higher echelons of
local government, and the like—are invited to this inner
sanctum for one of the Queen's summer garden parties.
The even luckier, if that is the right word, are summoned
here to investitures, when knighthood and other honors
are bestowed. The **Queen's Gallery**, just around the corner
in Buckingham Gate, is open every day except Mondays for
exhibitions of paintings from the royal collection. In the
Royal Mews, on Buckingham Palace Road, are the family's
Cinderella-like coaches, including the cherub-covered
Gold State Coach, which carried the Queen from the
palace to Westminster Abbey for her coronation. The Glass
Coach, which transports royal brides, is on show, as are
some vintage royal cars, such as the 1901 Daimler built for
Edward VII. Open Wednesdays, Thursdays, and some Friday afternoons during the summer; Wednesdays only in
winter.

Westminster is London's venue for pomp and circum-
stance. The **Changing of the Guard** at Buckingham Palace,
a military pageant of horse guards and infantrymen
dressed in black bearskins and red tunics, is the familiar
image most often chosen to depict London on postcards
and posters around the globe. At 11:00 every morning
between April and July (alternate days, August to March),
the St. James's Palace detachment of the Old Guard is
inspected in Friary Court. Carrying the Colour (the regimental flag), it then marches off via the Mall, the wide
formal boulevard between Trafalgar Square and Bucking-

ham Palace designed by Charles II. At Buckingham Palace the palace detachment is lined up and inspected. The St. James's detachment enters by the South Gate and together with the Buckingham detachment awaits the arrival of the New Guard (at 11:30). Led by a regimental band, the New Guard marches into the palace forecourt via the North Centre Gate, having earlier assembled at Wellington Barracks in Birdcage Walk along the southern side of St. James's Park. By 12:05 it's all over for another day (except for the duties of the street cleaner).

The **Institute of Contemporary Arts**, with often obscure and controversial items within its contemporary exhibitions, is in Nash House on the Mall. It features three galleries plus a cinema, a theater, and a restaurant.

St. James's Park and Green Park

For such a central city borough, Westminster supports a surprising abundance of greenery. Running along the south side of the Mall, with its fashionable promenades, lanes, and walkways, St. James's Park, the oldest royal park in central London, has been compared with Versailles. James I, a passionate lover of wildlife, stocked it with deer; Birdcage Walk, which runs along its southern flank, was named after a string of aviaries established by Charles II. The pelicans that reside in the park are descendants of a pair presented to Charles II by the Russian ambassador in 1665. Duck Island, in the middle of the curvaceous lake, is a private sanctuary for several species of birds. Stand on the small bridge that hoops over the lake and you could be in a Hans Christian Andersen story, as you look across the water at the turrets and minarets of St. James's Palace, surrounded by trees.

After a turn around St. James's Park, Charles II would habitually stroll up Constitution Hill, which cuts through neighboring Green Park north of Buckingham Palace. Although only the Queen Victoria Memorial comes between them and they both border on the Buckingham Palace grounds, Green Park has a completely different nature from St. James's. It's much smaller (53 acres in contrast to St. James's 93) and has rejected any attempts at floral trimmings, opting for just an ample ration of trees and grass. As its name suggests, it remains an expanse of simple, unadulterated green and is the optimal place to walk off a breakfast or a grander feast at the neighboring Ritz hotel up on Piccadilly, which is Green Park's northern boundary.

The quarter of **St. James's**, around St. James's Square east of Green Park and north of St. James's Park, is an almost exclusively male preserve, its domain defined by the entrenchment of some gentlemen's clubs, the most famous being Brooks's, Boodle's, White's, and the stuffy like. Walk down Pall Mall at night, for example, and you could be back in Georgian London. Step inside these inner sanctums of conservatism (subject to invitation, of course, and your sex), and the only event likely to disturb the status quo is the creak of a chubby leather-backed chair, the tinkle of ice against crystal, the rustle of the pink pages of the *Financial Times,* and the slow ticking of a grandfather clock. You can occasionally peek through the windows at such scenes, but only at that time of day when the inside lights have been fired and the curtains have yet to be drawn on the outside world.

Pall Mall, which runs from St. James's Palace east to Trafalgar Square, was also conceived by Charles II, in this case so that he could play *paille-maille,* a newfangled game he had discovered across the Channel that is similar to croquet. He leased a house here to Nell Gwyn, who poutingly insisted that she should own the freehold of the house—after all, her "services" to the Crown were given freely. Charles agreed, and 79 Pall Mall is still the only privately owned property on the broad avenue.

Trafalgar Square

The top (east end) of Pall Mall opens up into Trafalgar Square. Laid out by John Nash in 1820 as part of his grand design, the square is rather a hodgepodge of architectural styles. The focal point is its central area, with fountains by Sir Edwin Lutyens and the granite Nelson's Column by William Railton (with a statue of Lord Nelson on top by Edward Hodges Baily and four bronze lions by Sir Edwin Landseer forming the base plinth). Trafalgar Square is home to flocks of pigeons and is always the terminus of political rallies and demonstrations, the anti-establishment shade of which Nelson would no doubt disapprove. On December 31 the political causes give way to a raucous crowd in an alcoholic haze cheering Big Ben's midnight chimes.

The **National Gallery**, by far the most beautiful building in Trafalgar Square, is backed by the National Portrait Gallery. Climb the steps up to the National Gallery, a grande dame built in Classical style, and look back a second for a sweeping view of Trafalgar Square. Then get on with the art on the inside. The gallery was opened in 1838 to house the national collection of masterpieces (at the time the gallery shared its premises with the Royal Academy, but for reasons of space the latter has since moved to Burlington House, Piccadilly). All the great periods of European painting are represented in the National—works by Botticelli and Bellini hang in the Italian rooms, alongside Leonardo da Vinci's *Virgin and Child with St. Anne* and *St. John the Baptist.* Constable's *Haywain* and Gainsborough's *Mr. and Mrs. Andrews* are also here, as well as a copious number of Dutch and Flemish paintings. Recently opened (after ten years of controversy about its design) on the northwest corner of the square is the Sainsbury Wing, housing early Italian, Dutch, and German Renaissance paintings. The use of natural light in the bright, airy galleries provides an almost ethereal setting for the new wing's many treasures, and the brasserie and coffee shop afford superb views of Trafalgar Square.

The original aim of the **National Portrait Gallery**, around the corner in St. Martin's Place, was to portray Britain's history through paintings, sculptures, miniatures, and photographs of the country's historical personalities. With so many famous people now represented here, it has become a visual *Who's Who.* Start at the top and work your way down in chronological order.

At the northeast corner of Trafalgar Square is the church of **St. Martin-in-the-Fields**, the parish church of the sovereign and the best-loved work of Scottish architect James Gibbs. The first mention of it dates back to 1222, when it was a chapel serving Westminster Abbey. The present church was built between 1722 and 1724 and was originally designed as a round church. The tower, rebuilt in 1824, was controversial at the time, rising centrally from behind the huge Classical portico, but this design was soon used in many churches, particularly in the United States. The church is the venue for the St. Martin-in-the-Fields Sinfonia and also hosts free lunchtime concerts by various artists on Mondays, Tuesdays, and Fridays (Tel: 839-1930).

Whitehall

From the square, a stroll down Whitehall takes you past some of England's most prestigious civil-service departments, including the Treasury, the gigantic headquarters of the Home Office and the Foreign Office, and the stark new

Ministry of Defence building. On the left is the **Banqueting House**, a superb example of Palladian-style architecture built by Inigo Jones for James I in 1619 and still used for official receptions. Its ceilings are like miniature versions of those in the Sistine Chapel, decorated with nine remarkable paintings by Rubens (they brought £3,000 and a knighthood to the artist). Thirty years after the hall was built, Charles I stepped from one of its windows onto the waiting scaffold, where he was executed.

Great Scotland Yard (the former office of the Metropolitan Police, as seen in a thousand B-movies) is also off Whitehall, though the headquarters have since shifted to Victoria Street. A military presence is maintained at **Horse Guards Parade**, in the form of two Household Cavalry sentries who sit motionless, immune to the persistent flash of cameras (though they do change shifts every so often), and a ceremonial guard is mounted daily at 11:00 A.M. (Sundays at 10:00 A.M.). A few yards farther down Whitehall is the Cenotaph, the simple Lutyens monument commemorating Britain's war dead.

Britain's prime ministers have never had to walk far to work. Behind the famous black door of **10 Downing Street**, with its lion-shaped brass knocker, is an eight-room top-floor apartment; state rooms used for official receptions and banquets on the middle level; and Cabinet room, anterooms, and offices on the ground floor, opening onto private gardens. Downing Street is closed to pedestrians.

Winston Churchill's bunker, some 10 feet below Whitehall, the Cabinet's secret bombproof headquarters during World War II, opened its 16-foot-thick walls to visitors as the **Cabinet War Rooms** a few years ago (entrance adjacent to the park end of King Charles Street). Nothing has changed in this three-acre maze of rooms and corridors since the Blitz: According to the map room and various notices around the place, the war is still going on. Sir Winston's bed and the telephone cabinet from which he would phone President Roosevelt are just as they were.

Palace of Westminster (Houses of Parliament)
The Palace of Westminster, the official name of the Houses of Parliament, is an extravagant example of Gothic style. Its lean clock tower has four clock faces, each measuring 23 feet across, and its 13.5-ton bell, Big Ben, chimes on the hour. The palace is another one of London's most photographed sights; the familiar view is

taken from across the river. The public is admitted to the Houses of Parliament only to hear the debates in the Lords or the Commons (usually the livelier of the two). Visitors may enter the House of Commons starting at 2:30 P.M. Monday through Thursday, and at 9:30 A.M. on Fridays. Admission to the House of Lords begins at 2:30 P.M. Monday through Wednesday, 3:00 P.M. Thursdays, and 11 A.M. Fridays. On Tuesdays and Thursdays, Prime Minister's Question Time in the Commons is always popular and busy. You can avoid standing in line for these sessions by applying to your home country's embassy for tickets well in advance.

Westminster Hall is the oldest and most historic part of the parliamentary complex and home to the original law courts before they moved farther north to their present site around Chancery Lane. These courts witnessed the kinds of state trials that have made history, including that of Guy Fawkes, the man who attempted to blow up the Houses of Parliament with kegs of gunpowder in 1605 and whose effigy now sits atop thousands of bonfires every November 5. Within the Houses of Parliament are the Royal Gallery, the Prince's Chamber, the Lords' Chamber (where every bill passed by the Commons or initiated in the Lords has to receive the Peers' assent before becoming law), the Members' Lobby, and the royal throne in the Peers' Chamber. Those stationary figures in the Central Lobby are Prime Ministers Churchill, Lloyd George, Arthur James Balfour, Herbert Asquith, and Clement Attlee.

The highlight is the **House of Commons**, the arguments and debates of which are broadcast and now televised into British homes. This world of green leather benches (in contrast to the red of the House of Lords) seats 437 M.P.s plus 15 Commons officials at any one time. (There are fewer seats than M.P.s entitled to them; this is a deliberate policy—instigated during Churchill's time as prime minister—with the intent of increasing the sense of occasion when the House is full.)

In the Norman Porch you can see samplings from a collection of some two million parliamentary records, including the original copies of all acts of Parliament, dating as far back as the Middle Ages.

Westminster Abbey

Next door to Parliament stands Westminster Abbey. It is the royal church, where monarchs are crowned on the ancient coronation chair, a piece of furniture that has been serving its regal purpose of succession since Edward II's coronation in 1307.

The abbey was originally owned by a Benedictine monastery, one of the few that managed to escape Henry VIII's dissolution, which destroyed much of ecclesiastical England. Now more than three million people visit the abbey each year, so if you come in search of spiritual peace and sanctuary you'll be a shade disappointed. Even the burial space is overpopulated with kings and queens, from Edward the Confessor, who founded the abbey in 1065, to George II, the last monarch to be buried here, in 1760. Such historic literati as Chaucer, Tennyson, Dickens, Kipling, Hardy, and Browning are buried in the Poets' Corner; Ben Jonson was actually buried upright in the nave—by choice, as it happens, but it certainly made a contribution toward alleviating the space problem.

Tate Gallery

One can only praise the Classical-style Tate Gallery, near Pimlico tube station on Millbank, a section of the river's north shore upriver from Parliament between Lambeth and Vauxhall bridges. The gallery's origins date back to 1897, when the country was looking for a home for a national collection of British art. Sugar magnate Sir Henry Tate put forward the money, plus his personal collection of 64 paintings. Many a Londoner's Sunday afternoon is spent browsing its galleries. The original 64 paintings have been joined by continually changing exhibitions as well as a permanent collection of British works from the 16th to the early 20th century, Impressionist canvases, and, since 1916—when it was decided the Tate would not just be an extension of the National Gallery—many works of modern art from abroad. Matisse, Braque, Chagall, and Picasso share hanging space with Jackson Pollock, Henry Moore, Barbara Hepworth, and Alberto Giacometti. In its Clore Gallery, the Turner Bequest contains more than 300 oil paintings. The entire Tate collection has recently been rehung and rearranged in simple chronological order, and the results are impressive. The Tate has a good restaurant (lunches only, famed for its wine list) and a self-service cafeteria.

A minor detour across Lambeth Bridge to the south bank here (actually, at this part of the river the south bank is to the east) will bring you to **Lambeth Palace**, a medieval building and the London residence of the archbishop of Canterbury for more than seven centuries. It's open to groups on Wednesdays and Thursdays by prior arrangement (apply to the palace secretary, Tel: 071-928-8282).

London West

KNIGHTSBRIDGE – BELGRAVIA

Harrods

Think of Knightsbridge, and you think of Harrods. The two words seem to reinforce each other in a fragrant blend of high income and refined taste. No matter where in the world you normally do your shopping, Harrods, on Brompton Road, deserves a pilgrimage and at least a small spree.

In 1975, when he was governor of California, Ronald Reagan ordered a baby elephant from Harrods. Your own needs might be rather more basic, but whether you go to Harrods to buy or to browse, you can't fail to be bowled over by the sheer weight of style, let alone the store's contents.

Harrods, on Brompton Road, is the largest store in Europe. It has its own bank, and, just to reel off a few of its stock statistics, it sells 150 types of pianos, 9,000 ties, 450 kinds of cheese, 130 kinds of bread, 85 different brands of malt whisky, and more or less anything else made on the globe. If you want just a taste, head for the Food Hall, a palatial, beautifully tiled, magnificently stocked emporium. The store's own-brand items, often packed in distinctive green tins with the Harrods label, make easy and popular presents.

Other Shopping

Nearby at Knightsbridge and Sloane Street, the main intersection west of Buckingham Palace and the Palace Gardens, past where Piccadilly ends in a vast traffic interchange, is Knightsbridge's "other" department store, **Harvey Nichols**. Harrods may have its special Queen's entrance, but Harvey Nichols is the store where you're more likely to come across Princess Di casting an eye over the stock of designer labels. Apart from the main shopping arteries of Brompton Road and Knightsbridge proper, another shopping mecca that principally caters to the wealthy residents around and about is **Sloane Street**, which runs south from Knightsbridge Street at the Knights-

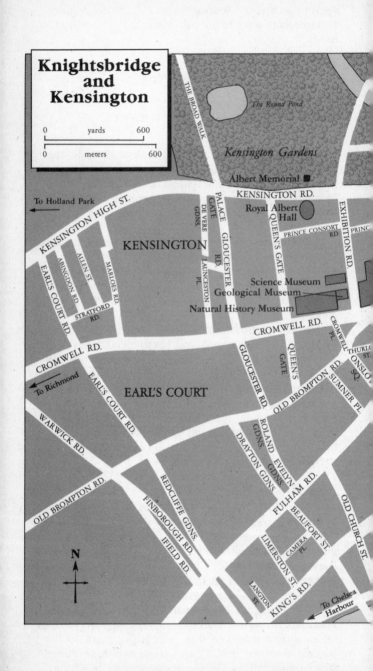

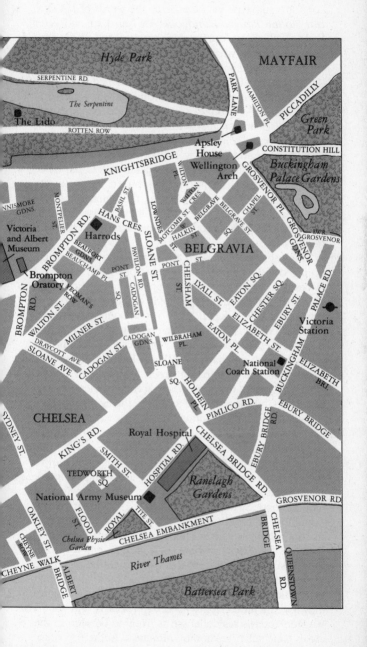

bridge tube station. The very name has spawned its own London social type whose style, in the words of *The Official Sloane Ranger Handbook* (by Ann Barr and Peter York), is all about "quality, conservatism, and classicism." And that's exactly what you can expect from the majority of stores on Sloane Street.

The tiny streets that lie in the elbow formed by Knightsbridge—the street as distinct from the environs—and Sloane Street constitute a neighborhood of expensive town houses and small, exclusive stores selling antiques, paintings, haute couture gowns, and pretty frippery. Cross Sloane Street, and Belgravia's **Halkin Arcade**, in particular, which spans Motcomb and West Halkin streets, has more priceless items in its windows than you'd come across in a sheikh's palace—which is, indeed, the ultimate destination of many of the pieces. This elbow is also home to many of London's finest small hotels; see Accommodations, below.

Knightsbridge is home to **Beauchamp Place** (pronounced BEE-cham), off Brompton Road west of Harrods. Contrary to recent shopping trends, Beauchamp Place has remained a refreshingly anachronistic oasis of small, primarily independently owned boutiques and restaurants (some of the most interesting of which are in unprepossessing basements). Originally a row of Regency houses, this narrow, 400-yard-long road has more variety than many shopping streets ten times the length. Its name recalls the time when French nobles took up residence in Knightsbridge to escape the egalitarian consequences of the Revolution.

Belgravia

Those in search of Belgravia won't find a sign, but they've found it once they're in Wilton Crescent, Belgrave Square, Eaton Place, or Eaton Square. Belgravia, lying just east of Sloane Street, was a neat, early-19th-century development later rebuilt in Classical style. Surprisingly, it is not the generously proportioned 18th-century Grosvenor Square, the Mayfair home of the U.S. embassy, but Belgravia's Chester Square that has earned the nickname "American Square in Mayfair," on account of its high proportion of expatriates in residence. In recent times they have included Henry Fonda, Tony Curtis, and Robert Wagner. Today's residents are as likely to be seen in the area's top Italian restaurant, **Mimmo d'Ischia** (on Elizabeth Street), presided over by the flamboyant Mimmo and his lively team of waiters, or on the opposite side of the street in the **Ebury Wine Bar**, which specializes in steaks, grilled before your eyes (if you sit at the counter, that is).

Hyde Park

Knightsbridge is not only an elegant place to shop but an elegant place to live as well. Even the Queen resides just around the corner, after all. The sweeping crescents, anonymous mews, and manicured squares—with their smart Rollers, Jags, Bentleys, and Daimlers patiently waiting like faithful retainers at the curbside—all lie within an easy stroll of quality shops and, to the north, Hyde Park, that vast, pool-table expanse of greenery (at 340 acres, the largest of central London's royal parks) surrounding the mile-long Serpentine lake, and the setting of Kensington Palace, the London home of Prince Charles and Lady Diana in **Kensington Gardens**, neighboring Hyde Park to the immediate west.

Hyde Park, along with Kensington Gardens, is London's equivalent of New York's Central Park, a place to let off pent-up urban steam by jogging or hiring a rowboat, or even a horse from Richard Briggs's stables on Bathurst Mews by Lancaster Gate station. If you opt for the latter, you can follow the hoofprints of the palace guards, who canter around a mile-long sandy track known as Rotten Row in the wee hours every morning. In addition to the before-work, after-work, and weekend activity, the park still lives up to its popular image: Nannies wheel perambulators along the Broad Walk; children throw crusts of bread to the ducks; model boats make their way sedately across Round Pond; brass bands play on Sundays; small-time politicos expound on a soapbox at Speakers' Corner (Britain's symbol of democracy, where anyone can express whatever opinion he or she may hold dear, within reason) in the northeast corner near Marble Arch; and spartan swimmers plunge from the Lido into the Serpentine at 5:30 A.M., sometimes breaking a layer of ice to do so.

CHELSEA

Like the Roman Empire, ancient Greece, and the Weimar Republic, Chelsea has already wallowed in its golden era. Its heyday in the annals of history is rooted not in its military supremacy or imperialistic acquisitiveness but in the ephemeral world of fashion. The Chelsea that attracted the attention of the world in the early 1960s was symbolized by the scantiest of all emblems: the miniskirt. Chelsea earned its place on the map by virtue of its highly talented designers, as well as the scores of artists, writers, and musicians who came to live within its geographical and emotional boundaries. It was the birthplace of "Swinging London," a notion born of an alchemy of coincidences—an enormously attractive environment, proximity to central London, and the then-low rents.

The decade of the 1960s was not Chelsea's only period of creativity. Scores of famous people, particularly in the arts and literature, have lived in the village, among them Charles Kingsley, Dante Gabriel Rossetti, Mark Twain, T. S. Eliot, Henry James, Oscar Wilde, and the so-called sage of Chelsea, Thomas Carlyle, whose Queen Anne house on Cheyne Row is open to view Wednesday through Sunday during the summer.

Chelsea, between Knightsbridge-Kensington and, to the south, the Thames, still merits a visit today, and not just to mourn its passing glory. Chelsea is a delightful place to live or, as a compromise, to visit. Its terraces and squares, studded with trees and lined by rows of pretty, pastel-painted town houses that look like outsize dollhouses, would seem more in keeping with a rural than an urban context. Chelsea's main street, **the King's Road**, named after the path that Charles II took as part of his private processional route to Hampton Court Palace—is still an interesting shopping street, even though its heyday was long ago. The retail action now stretches from Sloane Square in the east along the New King's Road continuation and onto Fulham Road, which is parallel to the King's Road to the north.

Once they lost their ability to shock, London's punks were adopted as a kind of tourist attraction, gracing many a postcard and poster. You can still see mohawks, safety pins, and studded leather on the King's Road on most Saturdays, though other members of the Saturday crowd sport Paul Smith and Armani suits. They spend small fortunes in interior-decor stores like Conran's near the South Kensington Underground station, then meet for lunch in the Habitat Café.

Clothing stores still predominate, but there are also plenty of antiques arcades and art galleries. If you happen to be partial to Victorian and Edwardian lighting, find your way to **Christopher Wray's** period light emporium at 600 King's Road. He stocks hundreds of models, mostly quality reproductions, some originals. The street is also heavily endowed with lighting stores of the modern-design type. **Antiquarius** is a covered, 200-stall antiques market selling Art Deco and Art Nouveau designs, English porcelain, watercolors, and period jewelry and clothing.

In between is a generous sprinkling of pubs and restaurants, many having occupied the same site for 20 years. The most famous pubs include the **Man in the Moon** and the **Markham Arms**; plant-filled and patioed, the latter witnesses an extensive sidewalk throng of lager drinkers in summer. the **Pheasantry**, a popular 1960s meeting place with an unusual arched entrance and a historic blue plaque, now houses a cocktail bar, a brasserie, and a nightclub.

Perhaps the busiest eatery of them all, on account of its minute proportions, is the **Chelsea Bun Diner**, tucked down a side road on Limerston Street. Arrive any time between 7:00 A.M. and 11:30 P.M. and you can be served a foaming cappuccino, a traditional English breakfast, a sandwich, or a burger. Everything's homemade, but the owners have no liquor license, so you must bring your own bottle.

Places of historical interest include the **Chelsea Physic Garden**, the second-oldest botanical garden in England. Its 5,000 plant species include—as the name suggests—the medicinal variety as well as Britain's biggest olive tree (there used to be cannabis, too, until 1982, when a dedicated home botanist jumped over the wall in the middle of the night and took the specimen); open Wednesday and Sunday afternoons in summer. The **National Army Museum**, which records the history of the British military, is also in Chelsea, as is the home of the Chelsea Pensioners, the **Royal Hospital**, originally founded by Charles II as a home for "men broken by war and old age." When Mary Quant designed the miniskirt, originally sold on the King's Road in her store Bazaar, those uniformed pensioners, sharing the frame with pretty girls with dead-straight hair, heavy eyes, and lots of leg, were the photographic cliché of London.

SOUTH KENSINGTON

You may feel that Chelsea falls short on serious culture, but neighboring South Kensington, roughly to the north, more than compensates for it. **Exhibition Road**, running north off Cromwell Road, a 20-minute walk to the north of Chelsea, was Prince Albert's special project. As Queen Victoria's consort he was able to wield the power to open the Great Exhibition in Hyde Park in 1851. It was such an immense success that in 1856 all profits were used to buy the Gore Estate, on which, he demanded, a collection of educational establishments should be built. Judging by the hordes of schoolchildren filing into the estate's grand collection of museums, which spill down Cromwell Road, his wishes have been well respected.

Victoria and Albert Museum

Queen of them all is the Victoria and Albert Museum, home to a vast collection of fine and applied art. It's the sort of museum best tackled by studying the plan, picking your favorite handful of "theme" rooms, and ignoring the rest. In fact, those who decide to "do" all the galleries would be wise to invest in a pair of hiking boots—they stretch a total of seven miles. At least the abundance keeps people coming back, discovering something new each visit. Don't miss the collection of Chippendale furniture, John Constable's English landscapes on the first floor, or the Jones Collection, a riveting display of French artistocratic interior decor, painting, furniture, ceramics, and other decorative arts, including examples of Marie Antoinette's lavish tastes. The Dress Collection contains one of the greatest clothing collections in the world, popular with pencil-wielding fashion students. The rest of the museum's collections can barely be listed: Japanese, Islamic, British art and music, Raphael cartoons. . . .

Natural History Museum

Just west on Cromwell Road is the Natural History Museum and its more specialized adjunct, the **Geological Museum**. From the outside the Natural History Museum resembles a grand sandstone church; the massive interior can be divided into five main departments: botany, entomology, mineralogy, paleontology, and zoology. It's one of the city's most popular museums; most Londoners, even if they haven't visited, have at least seen pictures of the skeletons of the *Brontosaurus rex, Tyrannosaurus rex,* and other dinosaurs, formerly housed in the magnificent central hall, now all except one located in the new Ronson Gallery (*Diplodoctus* remains in the central hall). After that, it's a question of which awe-inspiring sight to look for first. The ceiling of the Whale Hall in the west wing has to be seen to be believed: Skeletons and models of several species of mammals hang from it like spiders on webs. There are also fossil collections, galleries of birds, underwater creatures and coral, plants and minerals, plus a gallery devoted to simple ecology.

Science Museum

For fans of "hands-on" displays, the Science Museum, just north of the Geological Museum on Exhibition Road, is unbeatable, with knobs to twiddle, lights to flash, electric shocks to be administered, and plenty of bleeping sound effects. Children make up a generous proportion of the museum's devotees—there's even a Children's Gallery on the lower ground floor devoted to teaching simple scientific ideas using dioramas and working models. Older visitors, having mesmerized themselves with the Foucault pendulum that hangs near the entrance on the ground floor (its slow deviation proves that the earth does indeed rotate), usually head straight for the Apollo 10 space capsule and simulated moon base in the new Exploration of Space Gallery. But the museum also caters to steam engine buffs (Puffing Billy, the world's oldest-surviving locomotive, is in the road- and rail-transport wing) as well as lovers of astronomy, nuclear physics, modern technology (see the Challenge of the Chip display), photography, electricity, and navigation.

The **Royal Albert Hall** is also in this area, north of the Science Museum on Kensington Road, just across from Kensington Gardens. If it were in Spain you'd swear the hall was a bullring. A multipurpose venue, it hosts everything from regular Eric Clapton concerts to political conventions, graduation ceremonies of the University of London, and boxing matches, but is perhaps best known as the site of the summer Promenade Concerts, or "the Proms."

RICHMOND

Identifying Richmond on most maps of London has never been difficult. At the region's heart lies a gigantic green expanse, Richmond Park, seen at the map's bottom left-hand corner. If you fly into Heathrow from the east, the area will appear as a sea of green floating below the left-hand windows. Richmond is a prosperous borough that not only has more open spaces than any other in London but also has hundreds of listed buildings (because of their historical value they cannot be drastically altered or demolished)—and even the trees have preservation orders slapped on them.

Richmond-upon-Thames, to give the borough its full name and pertinent location, spans the banks of the river upstream from central London between Hammersmith Bridge and Hampton Court. Despite its proximity to central London, it's actually a borough of individual, small "villages": Barnes, Ham, Kew, Teddington, Twickenham, and Mortlake, all of which have managed to cling to significant shows of antiquity.

The name Richmond is inherited from a palace rebuilt by Henry VII, who had borrowed the name from his Yorkshire earldom. All that remains today of the original 12th-century building, whose foundations were laid by Henry I, is the **Gatehouse** just off Richmond Green (the Gatehouse is not open to the public). During the 15th century Richmond Palace was a favorite Tudor retreat. Later, Shakespeare staged performances of his plays here, while the wardrobe that Queen Elizabeth I stored in the palace—it contained well over 2,000 dresses—would put Joan Collins to shame. Both Henry VII and Elizabeth I died here. The palace's importance gradually declined until the structure was finally demolished in 1660, after the Restoration.

Despite its distinctive character, Richmond is just a half-hour Underground trip on the District Line from central London. You can also travel by British Rail from Waterloo Station in about 20 minutes. The most scenic way to approach Richmond is aboard one of the boats that chug up from Westminster Pier during the summer. Once you step ashore you'll find yourself in the middle of a completely self-contained village. There's likely to be a cricket match in mellow swing on the Green, the locals (anyone from barristers and bankers to writers and actors) to-ing and fro-ing, with liquid refreshments in hand, between their patch of spectator grass and the beery interior of the Cricketers pub.

Different styles of architecture jostle for position— Georgian, Palladian, Tudor, and Victorian—but the last definitely predominates. Minutes away are the Richmond Theatre and aging, narrow walkways and streets like Old Palace Lane, which runs from Trumpeters' Court to the river, and **Maids of Honour Row**. The latter is a famous row of four tall 18th-century houses, complete with wrought-iron gates and railings, on the Green, built in 1724 for the companions of Caroline, wife of the future King George II. But the name is now more synonymous with the **Maids of Honour Tearoom** on Kew Road near the famous Botanic Gardens. You can either line up for a table and wallow in the cottagey ambience, or take out a bag of scones, cakes, and Maids of Honour curd tarts (made from a secret recipe) and eat them at leisure down by the river. Closed Sundays.

Summer is the best time for a **riverside walk** (in spring and autumn, heavy tides have been known to flood the walkway). Low tide in hot, dry weather reveals the river's steep, sandy banks. Low-slung trees trail their leaves in the water, and ducks, swans, and moorhens rock along on the wash left by motorboats revving past. The most hectic time for the Thames here (not to mention its wildlife) is March, when the **Oxford and Cambridge Boat Race** is held. Cutting through the waters from Putney to Mortlake, this is an amateur race for rowing "eights" and an important competition for the two universities. The best viewing points are on the Surrey bank above Chiswick Bridge, Mortlake close to the finishing line, or anywhere else along the towpath. To show your allegiance, wear something of either light blue (Cambridge) or dark blue (Oxford).

Richmond's stretch of river is also active during **Swan Upping**, an ancient and rather curious pageant held in late July/early August. The Worshipful Companies of Vintners and Dyers spend one week rowing their half-dozen Thames skiffs upstream from Sunbury to Pangbourne, ceremoniously catching swans, counting them, and nicking the beaks of the year's new batch of cygnets. The tradition dates back to the Middle Ages; its original purpose was to establish the ownership of these then-profitable, prestigious, and tasty birds. The Crown can still lay claim to any unmarked swans. At present only some 200 swans are to be seen in the entire Lower Thames, and the Swan Upping ceremony has become a crucial census for ecological reasons.

Richmond Park

The least urban of London's boroughs, Richmond contains Richmond Park, the largest of the royal parks. It covers 2,500 acres and was first enclosed by Charles I as a deer sanctuary. In fact, you might pack a pair of binoculars so you can examine at close range the large herds of fallow and red deer that roam freely.

The park's woodland gardens and Isabella Plantation are at their best from mid-April to the end of May, when the azaleas and the rhododendron dell are in full bloom.

Historic buildings include the King's Observatory; the White Lodge, built in 1727 as a hunting lodge for King George II (open only in August); and Princess Alexandra's home, Thatched House Lodge. Stop for tea at **Pembroke Lodge**, a restaurant and café with its own garden and terrace, found in the west side of Richmond Park. This place, ideal for pensive reflection, was the childhood home of the philosopher Bertrand Russell.

Kew Gardens

For years it cost only two pennies to enter the turnstiles of the Royal Botanic Gardens, also known as Kew Gardens. The fee has now risen to £3.30. Originally made up from the grounds of Richmond Lodge (now demolished) and Kew Palace (a small Jacobean mansion that is the last of a group of royal residences), the 300 acres of landscaped gardens contain more than 25,000 species of plants from all over the world. The hurricane of October 16, 1987, wreaked havoc on Kew, toppling 800 trees and destroying in one night 150 years' careful nurturing. Happily, the gardens have been restored.

Aircraft destined for Heathrow fly overhead at the peak rate of one a minute, creating an incongruous din as visitors wander the paths through groves, woodlands, and rock gardens, stopping to visit the Orangery, the four temples, the tall red Pagoda, or one of the plant houses. These fine Victorian conservatories, with such names as Alpine House, Water Lily House, Temperate House, Palm House, and the new Princess of Wales Conservatory, are an architectural blend of cast iron and glass. The 17th-century Dutch House is one of the exceptions; this sturdy red-brick and gabled building by the main gate is all that remains of Kew Palace.

The Temperate House, one of the biggest hothouses, is dominated by a single giant palm whose towering leaves brush the ceiling. Visitors can walk along an upper balcony for aerial views of fountains and ponds full of ornamental fish. When visiting the houses be prepared for abrupt climatic changes—within the space of a few paces you can be transported from the tropical rain forests of South America to the arid desert of Arizona.

Richmond Environs

For the most delightful river walk to be had in these environs, head for the stylish Hammersmith Bridge and walk along the north bank toward Chiswick. The best time for such a walk is early on a summer's eve, when you can buy a glass of "bitter" (ale) in any (or each) of four charming pubs—the **Blue Anchor**, the **Rutland Arms**, the **Ship**, and the **Dove**—and sit and sup in the open with a friendly crowd, idly watching the scullers whose boat-houses line the banks below the bridge. **Hammersmith Terrace** is a delightful row of Georgian houses, several with their tiny gardens right above the river, separated from the homes by the towpath. William Morris used to live in Kelmscott House here. Just before you reach Chiswick Square, step into the churchyard of St. Nicholas, where the painters James Whistler and William Hogarth are buried. Beyond lies **Syon House**—most famous for Robert Adam's Great Hall—the London residence of the duke of Northumberland. The house is open to the public, although Syon is most famous for its gardens, the 18th-century handiwork of Capability Brown, who included a lake, conservatory, aviary, and aquarium in his designs. He had nothing, however, to do with the Heritage Motor Museum, which is also on the grounds and houses a collection of British cars from 1895 to the present day, nor with the London Butterfly House, which displays numerous species fluttering madly in a tropical greenhouse. More energetic walkers can cross Hammersmith Bridge and follow the south bank as far south as the **Bull's Head** pub in Barnes, a mecca for jazz fans.

A couple of miles south of Putney Bridge is **Wimbledon Common**, an open parkland with a distinctive windmill, and on nearby Church Road the **All England Club**, home of the lawn tennis championships played every year in June and July. Overlooking the Centre Court is a museum housing a vast historical collection of tennis fashions and associated trivia.

HAMPTON COURT

When Henry VIII made Richmond Park the place to hunt, outsiders built hunting lodges, and it became, at the same time, a popular stopping-off place for boats on their way upriver to Hampton Court Palace. Unlike other palaces, which have stood empty as museums, Hampton Court has been lived in continuously since it was built by Cardinal Wolsey, the lord chancellor of England, in 1515. George III was the last sovereign in residence; today, it is partly occupied by pensioners of the Crown, the "Grace and Favour" tenants. The palace is unique in that it represents the very best examples of English architecture of both the

16th and the early 18th centuries. And the location, hard on the Thames, is stunning.

In March 1986 a fire caused severe damage to the palace. Amazingly, although many works of art were destroyed or damaged, most of the palace's valuable contents, including the collection of 500 Renaissance paintings, were saved. The building itself, however, suffered enormously. The fire gutted the King's Audience Chamber, the Cartoon Gallery (named for the Raphael cartoons bought by Charles I and moved to the Victoria and Albert Museum more than a century ago), and State Apartments designed by Sir Christopher Wren for King William and Queen Mary. Restoration work is now completed; the King's State Apartments were opened by the Queen in July 1992.

Although inhabited by a succession of kings and queens, Hampton Court is probably best known for its associations with Henry VIII. When he became owner, he extended the palace in earnest, including the building of Chapel Court as a nursery for Prince Edward, his son and presumed heir. But by the time William and Mary came to the throne, the Tudor style was considered rather passé, and they commissioned Wren, the architect of St. Paul's Cathedral, to demolish the entire palace and build a new, more symmetrical, more spacious residence on a scale that would rival Versailles. Because the palace was fully inhabited, Wren could only work on a little at a time, and, mercifully for architectural posterity, the money ran out before he could implement his grand designs. Hence the uniqueness of Hampton Court: One of the most complete examples of a Tudor palace coexists harmoniously alongside buildings by England's greatest architect.

The most popular element of Hampton's horticulture is its **maze**, first planted in 1714. It may not look too challenging from the outside, but it can take up to an hour or more to get out of the half-mile of yew-hedge labyrinth. So don't postpone finding the way out till the main gates are about to close. Some visitors from abroad, it is said, have watched their homebound aircraft pass overhead, having taken off without them from Heathrow just down the road.

NOTTING HILL

The broad Bayswater Road, the continuation of Oxford Street that forms the northern boundary of Hyde Park, begins its westward journey at Marble Arch. Once past the park, it almost immediately becomes the southern boundary of Notting Hill, a much-gentrified, ethnic area of town. Increasingly, professionals gravitate here, unable to resist the combination of ethnic diversity in cafés and shops and the gentility of five-story houses on tree-lined avenues such as Elgin Crescent.

Notting Hill's August Bank Holiday Caribbean Carnival draws more than a million people into the area, in particular along Westbourne Grove and Ladbroke Grove. There are stalls, floats, and dancing in the streets to reggae and calypso. For a relief from the noise, walk south along Ladbroke Grove to find **Holland Park**, a delightful oasis of woods, a good café, and a new Japanese garden with a waterfall.

Saturdays at the **Portobello Road Market** (northwest of the Notting Hill Underground station), where you will find antiques, Victoriana, and a variety of secondhand items, are already on the tourist circuit. What you don't want to miss are the many small, specialized art and photographic galleries that have recently opened along Kensington Park Road, which is parallel to Portobello, and down various side streets.

If you'd like an American-style breakfast, start the day relaxing over your newspaper in the multilevel **Gate Diner**, also on Kensington Park Road. More serious eating, with a modern British approach to the cooking, takes place at **Leith's** at number 92. **192**, at number 192, is Italian with a new slant. **Julie's Wine Bar and Restaurant** opposite David Black Oriental Carpets on Portland Road also attracts the smart set; it serves an international cuisine but veers toward the highly traditional for its Sunday lunch. At the eastern end of Westbourne Grove, near the junction of Queensway, are a number of excellent and reasonably priced Indian restaurants, including **Khan's** (13–15), the **Standard** (21–23), and the **Kyber** (56). On Queensway itself the Edwardian department store called **Whiteley's** has been restored and transformed into a large mall with many individual stores, cafés, and a multiscreen cinema.

Chelsea Harbour, on the border with Fulham, upstream from Battersea Bridge, is a new development on the river distinguished by the Belvedere Building with its bright-red ball. On the site once occupied by an old coal depot there are now luxury flats, offices, shops, cafés, and restaurants, including **Deals**, which is partly owned by Lord Litchfield and Viscount Linley.

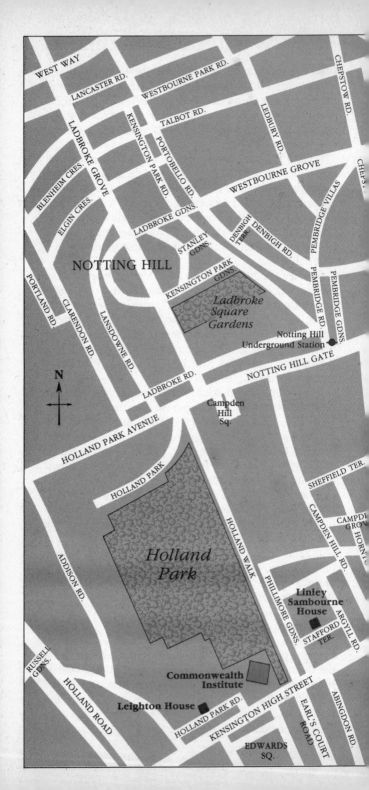

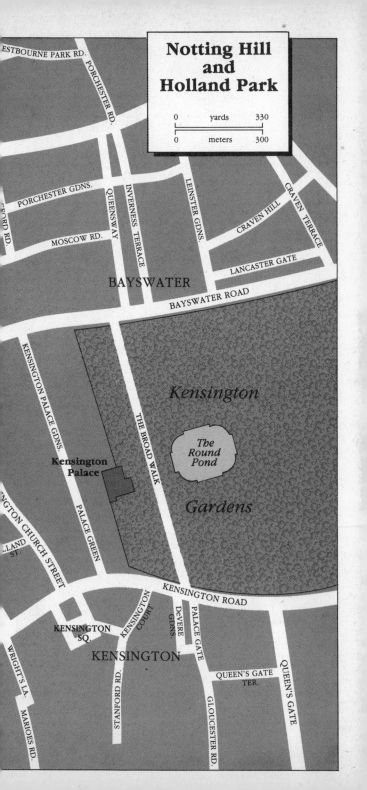

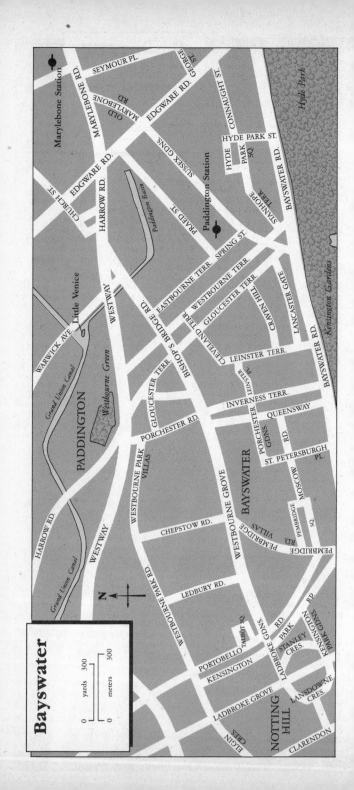

London North

MARYLEBONE ROAD

When Madame Tussaud, a French sculptor and one of King Louis XVI's tutors, arrived in London with a bizarre collection of wax facsimiles of heads that had rolled during the French Revolution, she could not have dreamed that **Madame Tussaud's Waxworks Museum**, the exhibition she established on the southern fringes of Regent's Park on the Marylebone Road in 1835, would eventually become London's most-visited admission-paid attraction. Today visitors line up far down the street to see lifelike figures of historical, political, royal, and show-business personalities. In the **Planetarium** next door, there are permanent constellation exhibitions plus, every evening from Wednesday through Sunday, laser shows accompanied by rock and classical music. Try to avoid the lines by going early and not on Saturdays, when the ranks of tourists are swelled by British out-of-towners.

Marylebone Road (originally St. Mary-le-bourne; *bourne* meant "river" in the 18th century) is long and busy. It is also the location of St. Marylebone Church, most famous for its tiered tower and cupola. The church is wedged into the opening of Regent's Park's York Gate, one of the main entrances to the park, built in 1817. Marylebone Road's offshoots (their northern reaches almost in Regent's Park, the southern almost in Oxford Street) include Harley Street, where the country's top physicians have clinics, and Wimpole Street, where Robert Browning courted Elizabeth Barrett. **Baker Street**, the biggest and longest, is most famous as the fictional address of detective Sherlock Holmes at number 221B. In his day, that part of Baker Street was known as York Place. Today, thanks to the renumbering of the street in 1930, the house at 221B is inhabited by the Abbey National Building Society, whose employees must every day reply politely to "Dear Sherlock Holmes" letters.

The more interesting and prettier **Marylebone High Street** is lined with shops and small cafés. **Maison Sagne**, at number 105, is one such refreshment house. This Swiss pâtisserie and bakery, established in 1921, is still concocting pastries and cakes on the premises. Antiquities can be found in **Blunderbuss** on Thayer Street (the southern continuation of the High Street). The eclectic shop is full of pistols, helmets, swords, and other military bric-a-brac.

Chiltern Street, parallel to and east of Baker Street, is interesting for its fashionable boutiques for men and women, its antiques stores, and its music and musical instrument shops stocking oboes, flutes, early-music instruments, and musical scores.

HAMPSTEAD

Hampstead Heath

Hampstead is London at its most rural. Drop strangers in the heart of the 800 acres of leafy, luscious Hampstead Heath, north of Regent's Park and Camden Town, and they will swear on oath that they have been abandoned in some remote English shire, a verdant, bushy-tailed wilderness far from the madding crowds. Only when their ears turn away from birdsong to the distant hum of metropolitan traffic will they accept the urban coordinates. Stuff them into a taxi and they can be in central London in 20 minutes.

As a place to live, Hampstead's tree-lined lanes and twisting alleys have long been prominent addresses in the pages of *Who's Who*. Early residents included Robert Louis Stevenson, D. H. Lawrence, John Keats, John Galsworthy, George Orwell, William Blake, and John Constable. By the early 1900s Hampstead had become London's Montmartre, full of painters and their contemporary equivalent of wanna-bes. Wander around the streets today and you'll see many of the distinctive blue plaques that denote the fame of an earlier inhabitant.

Hampstead Heath is one of the "lungs of London." Tranquillity and clean air (at least by city standards) are its stock in trade, and the lichen grows thick. Judging by the real-estate prices, which rank among the highest in the city, such virtues have much appeal today. Among the rich and famous current residents are Jeremy Irons, John Le Carré, and Glenda Jackson. Hampstead being what it is, no one bothers with a second glance after spotting a celebrity buying out-of-season asparagus at a local greengrocer, taking tea at **Louis Pâtisserie**, or sipping a slow cappuccino at the **Dome Café**.

A Walking Tour of Hampstead

Despite the massive Heath, the appeal of Hampstead is all too easy for the London visitor to miss. Emerge from the Hampstead Underground station onto a busy intersection lined with unexciting shops and you'll immediately wonder what the fuss is all about. Turn left down Hampstead High Street, though, and left again onto Flask Walk, and the prospect improves.

You'll want to slow your pace as you approach **The Flask**, one of Hampstead's many pleasant pubs. The very name Flask puts things into immediate historical context. It is derived from the bottles of medicinal waters that once were filled from nearby chalybeate springs and sold here. The shops now go in for Perrier and other variations on the *eau* theme, but several are well worth a browse. Follow Flask Walk onto Well Walk, another place with obvious watery associations, and pause at number 40, once the home of John Constable, England's finest landscape painter. From his house, after a couple more minutes, you should come face to face with the Heath.

Hampstead is the one place in London where a map and compass are more useful to the tourist than a handful of currency. To get the best of the greenery, you need to walk in, around, and through the Heath, and, with luck, return to the point where you started. Take heart in the knowledge that even locals go astray.

The point to head for, out of sight but likely to be known to passing strollers, joggers, dog walkers, bird watchers, and the like, is **Kenwood House**. A very large and very white house across the Heath, northeast from the general location of Constable's house, Kenwood is a classic example of the 18th-century species of gentleman's country home. First owned by Lord Chief Justice William Murray, who employed Robert Adam to enlarge and embellish the property, Kenwood is now a bequest to the nation. It contains a fine collection of paintings by Rembrandt, Vermeer, Rubens, and others. During the summer there is a series of open-air concerts on the grounds.

From Kenwood, walk through the rhododendron gardens, littered with the occasional piece of weathered sculpture, along the linden-shaded gravel path, and ask to be pointed to the Spaniards Inn, reputedly an old haunt of Dick Turpin, the highwayman. From there, through the still narrow gap between the inn and the tollhouse (both 18th century), head south along Spaniards Road (or, better still, follow a more rural course parallel to the busy thoroughfare) toward Whitestone Pond, whose dark waters mark the highest point in London (443 feet). Just before you reach the road, you will catch a glimpse of the

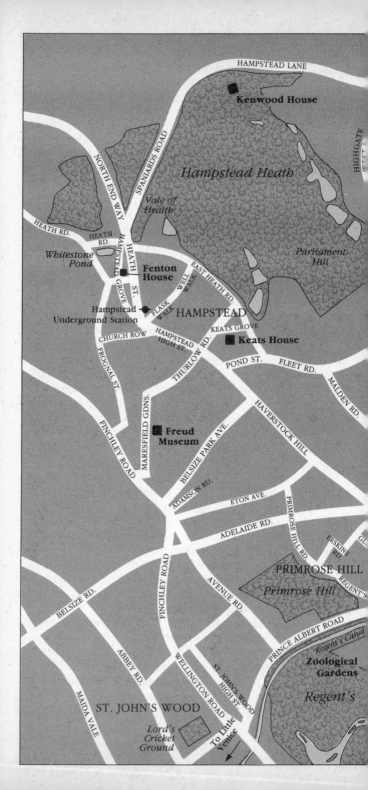

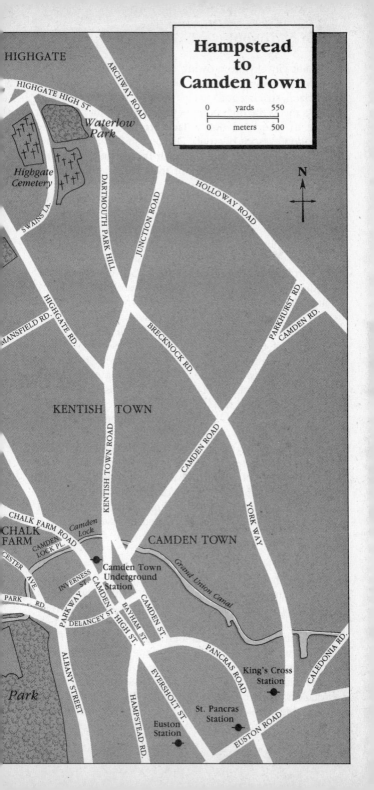

distant city skyline growing out of the Thames valley, a spectacular sight when the afternoon sun is low on the horizon, striking gold against the city structures.

As this is the high point of the walking tour, you might like to take time out at **Jack Straw's Castle**, a white wooden eyesore of a pub. Or you can follow North End Way to the popular **Bull and Bush Tavern**, built on the site of a 17th-century farmhouse that was briefly home to Hogarth.

Hampstead has a few other important landmarks, well worth a detour before you scurry back to more central parts of town. One is **Keats House** on Keats Grove (open to the public), set in the delightful garden where the poet composed *Ode to a Nightingale*. Another is the 17th-century **Fenton House** at Hampstead Grove, with an interesting collection of paintings, furniture, and ceramics, and a highly regarded collection of early keyboard instruments. A third landmark is the remarkable 18th-century terrace of "brownstones" along Church Row. With the Church of St. John's at the end of the row, which is planted with trees along its center, the scene is quintessentially English. Imagine it with a dusting of snow and you have the makings of a classic Christmas card.

If the day is fine, head northeast across the Heath toward the ponds to the hilltop village of **Highgate**. Close to another Flask pub (this one, with its large courtyard and outside summer tables, looks unmistakably rural) lies **Highgate Cemetery**. It is divided into two sections: The one to the east of Swains Lane is the newer half, containing the grave and bold bronze bust of Karl Marx; the one to the west is a tangled, overgrown, rather bizarre yet beautiful world of vaults and other monumental masonry.

CAMDEN TOWN

The charm of Camden Town, the lively, streetwise district bang in the center of north London (southeast of Hampstead and a ten-minute Underground ride due north of Tottenham Court Road), lies mainly in its social and cultural mishmash. Along Camden High Street, Chalk Farm Road, and Parkway, plant-filled wine bars and bistros, antiques shops, and smart clothing boutiques rub shoulders with disheveled discount stores, secondhand music retailers, and the pulpy droppings from the fruit and vegetable market on Inverness Street. Harmless down-and-outs, occupants of the Arlington Road shelter for the homeless, are deep in inebriated conference on most street corners.

The slightly jaded, hippie ambience of **Camden Lock's weekend market** is famous throughout London. Its scale is generous, spilling from the cobbled lockside area around the stagnant basin waters to Chalk Farm Road, almost as far as the former Roundhouse Theatre, located in an old brick-built railway locomotive shed. The blue-canopied stalls are surrounded by trendy shops and renovated haylofts and warehouses. The market has recently been significantly rebuilt, the central core now known as the New Market Hall.

Anyone wishing to sell his or her wares to the battalions of yuppies and punks lines up at nine in the morning and, if lucky, is allocated a stall. The market has everything from potted palms to pine furniture, handmade jewelry to Hawaiian shirts, posters to pure-wool sweaters, antiques and bric-a-brac to high-tech gift items.

Two French-inspired restaurants almost justify an excursion to the area: the **Brasserie** (for some of the best french fries in town) on Camden High Street just south of the market, and **Café Delancey** on Delancey Street, open from breakfast (check the daily specials blackboard). Both draw the arts and media clientele, many of whom saunter over from the futuristic television studios building, with its "egg cup" rooftop trimming, on Buck Street.

Camden Town is home to several music venues. The **Jazz Café** on Parkway often features visiting U.S. musicians, while the **Camden Palace** by Mornington Crescent as well as the **Electric Ballroom** on Camden High Street, just next to the Underground station, host up-and-coming rock bands. Many of the area's pubs, including the **Dublin Castle** (also on Parkway) and **Liberties Bar** (on Camden High Street), host live Irish music.

The 50 acres of **Primrose Hill**, an offshoot of Regent's Park to the west of Camden, are a voluptuous green hummock on an otherwise pancake-flat horizon. This area earned its name from its wildflowers, although in the 18th century the area blossomed with as many derelicts as blooms, and only the foolhardy would dare cross its boundaries once night had fallen. Today Primrose Hill's Regency terraces rank among the most salubrious and expensive in north London. On Sunday afternoons the grassy mound is busy with kite-flyers and walkers who climb to its summit to enjoy one of the best panoramas of London.

London Zoo

The purpose of the closest, most prominent structure on the southern horizon viewed from Primrose Hill would be impossible to guess. It is an aviary, designed by Lord Snowdon and standing within the London Zoo in Regent's Park, one of the city's biggest tourist attractions. Open seven days a week, the zoo was founded by Sir Stamford Raffles (a name more immediately associated with the hotel in Singapore, the British trading colony he founded).

Apart from the aviary, other highlights of the menagerie, which is home to more than 5,000 animals, include a tropical house, where hummingbirds freely commute between thick foliage and your head; an "open-plan" lion house; an insect and arachnid house; and a tigers' den, where only a pane of glass separates you from the toothsome beasts. There's also a rich-smelling elephant house, where the public can witness regular teeth-cleaning and toe-filing sessions; several high-octane monkey houses; and the Moonlight World, where nocturnal fauna are deceived into activity at hours to suit visitors.

Chalk Farm, the area tightly bordered by Primrose Hill, Regent's Park Road, and a main railway line, had been a fairly run-down precinct until gentrification occurred in the 1970s. The main thoroughfare here is Regent's Park Road; its lower portion is now a neighborhood of shops that seem to sell a blend of everything—wine and kitchen equipment included—that a wealthy community could possibly need. There's also a smattering of restaurants, including the refined **Odette's**, for modern international cuisine, and the nearby **Lemonia**, a classy Greek eatery.

Regent's Park

A large proportion of Camden is made up of parklands. During the British civil wars of the 17th century, the future of Regent's Park, arguably London's most urban park, looked gloomy, as most of its trees were razed to be used as firewood for the needy. It was John Nash who, at the end of the 18th century, backed by the prince regent, engineered today's pièce de résistance. Within the manicured hedges that line the Outer Circle road lie 500 acres of gardens, shrubbery, and bird life, all in a basic Victorian format, right down to an old-fashioned bandstand where tubas and trumpets entertain lunchtime and Sunday-afternoon picnickers.

More modern trappings include a boating lake (formed

by damming the River Tyburn), a children's boating pond, the zoo, and ornamental bridges. There's also an open-air theater, where the New Shakespeare Company performs throughout the summer. The glades and woods provide the perfect setting, and the audience, sitting on tiered seats exposed to the elements, can move around with the scenes when necessary, clutching plates of food and glasses of wine.

Once you are inside the Queen Mary's Gardens, within the park's Inner Circle road, the sounds of London are reduced to that of an occasional airplane. This fragrant enclave is a mass of perfumed rose bushes grouped around a landscaped rock pool on the site where Nash originally planned to build a royal palace for the prince regent.

The Outer Circle road is lined with **Nash terraces**— smart, cream-colored, porticoed and pillared buildings that nowadays function as fashionable offices as well as private homes. The houses were originally built to raise money for the Crown and attracted the well-known and well-to-do—Hugh Walpole lived at 10 York Terrace, for example; King Edward VIII's lover, Mrs. Simpson, was ensconced at 7 Hanover Terrace; and the author H. G. Wells lived at 13 Hanover Terrace.

The only significant dwelling within (as opposed to bordering) the park is Winfield House, once the mansion of Woolworth heiress Barbara Hutton. It is now the official London residence of the U.S. ambassador. You can view it only through the closely guarded gates at the bottom of the drive on the Outer Circle road. Almost opposite, straddling the south end of St. John's Wood High Street, is the Central Mosque, copper-domed and minareted, one of the most incongruous sights in the vicinity. At the end of the day, it can be mistaken for a mutant sun lowering its obese body below the skyline trees.

Just outside the park, on the corner of Wellington and St. John's Wood roads, is **Lord's Cricket Ground**, recognizable by its white sails on the Mound Stand, completed to celebrate the Marylebone Cricket Club's bicentenary in 1987. Guided tours include "the Ashes," a trophy symbolizing the first time the England team lost to Australia in 1882, and the famous Long Room gallery containing, among other memorabilia of the game, a stuffed sparrow killed by a ball powerfully struck by Pakistani batsman Jehangir Khan in 1936. Visits by appointment (Tel: 266-3825 or 289-1611).

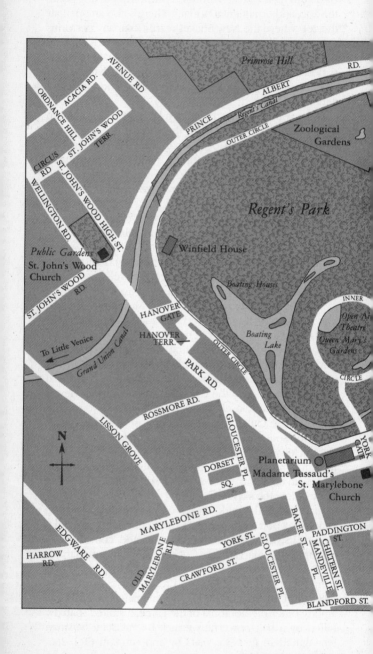

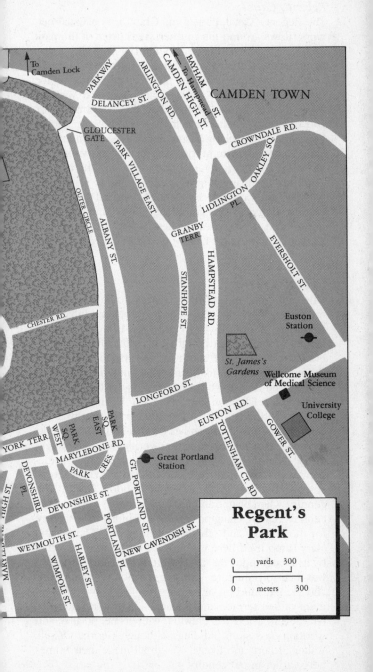

To Camden Lock

CAMDEN TOWN

PARKWAY

DELANCEY ST.

ARLINGTON RD.

CAMDEN HIGH ST.

BAYHAM ST.

To Hampstead

GLOUCESTER GATE

CROWNDALE RD.

OAKLEY SQ.

LIDLINGTON PL.

PARK VILLAGE EAST

OUTER CIRCLE

ALBANY ST.

GRANBY TERR.

STANHOPE ST.

HAMPSTEAD RD.

EVERSHOLT ST.

CHESTER RD.

Euston Station

St. James's Gardens

Wellcome Museum of Medical Science

University College

LONGFORD ST.

EUSTON RD.

GOWER ST.

YORK TERR.

PARK SQ. WEST

PARK SQ. EAST

PARK CRES.

MARYLEBONE RD.

Great Portland Station

TOTTENHAM CT. RD.

MARYLEBONE HIGH ST.

DEVONSHIRE PL.

DEVONSHIRE ST.

PARK

GT. PORTLAND ST.

WEYMOUTH ST.

HARLEY ST.

WIMPOLE ST.

PORTLAND PL.

NEW CAVENDISH ST.

Regent's Park

| 0 | yards | 300 |

| 0 | meters | 300 |

Regent's Canal

The Regent's Canal, part of the Grand Union Canal network, flows around the northern perimeter of the park (you can see some of the zoo animals from the water) before taking a dogleg up to Camden Lock. Its total length runs to eight miles, from the pretty core of **Little Venice** (west of the park and north of Bayswater near Warwick Avenue Underground station; see the Bayswater map, above) east to Limehouse in the Docklands. Several longboats operate regularly in summer between Camden and Little Venice (the round trip takes just under two hours), including the *Jenny Wren, Jason's Trip,* and the London Waterbus Company, which operates regular service on the Zoo Waterbus between Camden Lock and the zoo. *My Fair Lady* serves lunch and dinner; nondining passage is not offered. You can catch these boats near either the Warwick Avenue (near Little Venice) or the Camden Town Underground stations.

ISLINGTON

One of the first of London's "villages" to be gentrified—the prices of its rows of basic artisan dwellings inflated by an influx of middle-class residents—Islington, east of Regent's Park and north of the City, suffers from a proliferation of real-estate agents whose windows advertise "bijoux" properties with quarter-of-a-million-pound price tags for the tiniest. Well connected by the Underground (Highbury & Islington stop on the Victoria Line, the Angel on the Northern Line, a 15-minute ride northwest of central London), Islington has come a long way since its days as one of London's seediest working-class boroughs.

The Domesday Book records Islington as a small settlement within the Great Forest of Middlesex, a largely rural, dairy-producing district supplying London. In the 17th century, when plague and fire caused a mass exodus from central London, Islington became a fashionable residence for the nobility and otherwise well-heeled (Charles and Mary Lamb lived here in the 1800s), who were attracted by its health-inducing spas. By the 19th century Islington was a curious mixture—the construction of better roads and the introduction of railways resulted in the development of fine terraces and squares—but the central core had declined and was crawling with grime, poverty, and working-class slum buildings, although George Orwell, Walter Sickert, and Evelyn Waugh all made their homes here earlier in our century.

Today Islington is the undisputed territory of the intelligent socialist. Ruled by a council of liberal tendency, it's a borough that survives on meager finances but doles out welcome bowls of sympathy. Such a reputation has made it a place of refuge for struggling minority groups and has spawned countless voluntary self-help associations, among them the Islington Voluntary Action Council, designed to help those who would doubtless suffer discrimination elsewhere.

However, as with all deprived areas (Islington is the eighth-poorest borough in London), its low real-estate prices have attracted a plethora of the upwardly mobile. Rubbing shoulders with those relying on state support, the newcomers are buying the last of the borough's decaying properties and converting them into smart, terraced residences. And they buy all their fixtures and fittings on **Upper Street**, Islington's main thoroughfare, adrift in wine bars, restaurants, designer kitchen-accessories shops, and other late-20th-century paraphernalia.

Of course there are antiques stores. Islingtonians frequent **Camden Passage**, north of the Angel tube station, a narrow, flagstoned, pedestrians-only street behind the miniature Islington Green, where wrought-iron shop signs advertise numerous antiques emporiums: Franco's, the Furniture Vault, Gordon Gridley, Ark Angel, and Laurence Mitchell, to name a few, plus the **Angel Arcade**, a Gothic precinct of 20 shops selling silver, porcelain, rare books, and objets d'art. Finbar Macdonnell has a caged mynah bird whose chirruping will accompany your browsing through his old prints and engravings. And if you wind up in **The Mall**, on neighboring Islington High Street, you may never come out—it contains a bewildering 35 galleries of antiques and decorative arts. On Wednesday mornings and all day Saturdays there are also rows of antiques stalls in Camden Passage.

A large part of the borough of Islington is dominated by a district to the south called **Clerkenwell**, named after the Clerks' Well, which was discovered in 1924 in what is now the New Statesman/Society building. The well was christened after the medieval parish clerks of the City of London, who performed miracle plays near here on the banks of the River Fleet. The **Charterhouse**, a beautiful, towered building near the Aldgate Underground stop and the Smithfield market (see below), owes its foundation in 1371 to Sir Walter de Manney, who recognized its potential as a center of prayer and place of refuge for plague

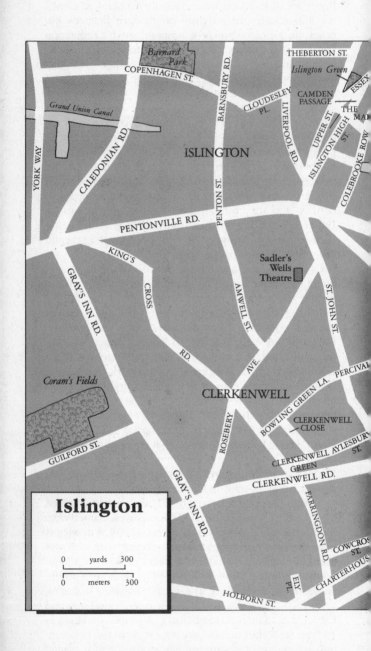

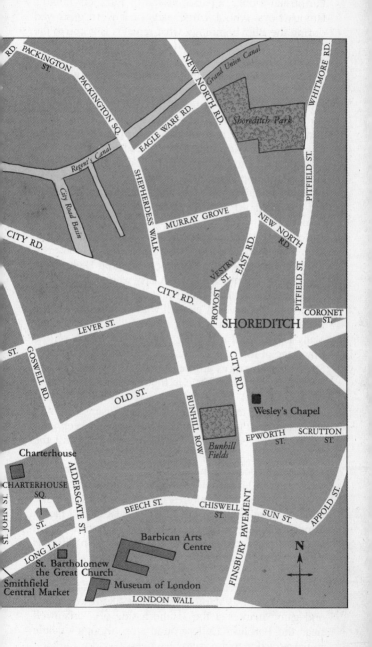

victims. Since then the Charterhouse has been home to Carthusian monks, a palace visited by Elizabeth I, and a famous boys' school. Large parts of it were destroyed during the Blitz bombings; what remains is home to the Charterhouse Pensioners and is open on Wednesdays for guided tours.

The fertile meadowland on which Clerkenwell was founded is alive with spouting wells. Some are still quite productive, like the one under the **Sadler's Wells Theatre** on Rosebery Avenue. The purity of the local well water attracted beverage makers such as Gordon's, famous for its gin distillery, and Samuel Whitbread; both still occupy their original sites. In fact, the Whitbread Brewery Shire Horses still clop along their morning delivery rounds to pubs in the City to the south and southeast and also turn out for the Lord Mayor's Show and other ceremonial occasions.

No wonder Islington's wine bars are so well stocked. **Mon Plaisir du Nord**, in The Mall, is a cool, conservatory-like brasserie. **The Dôme**, on Islington High Street, has a Parisian ambience, particularly when the windows are opened wide in summer and the smell of croissants drifts into the street. A glass of wine at these places is a good way to begin a night that may include theater: Many a West End box-office success has begun on the tiny stage at the back of the **King's Head** pub on Upper Street. Performances are held nearly every night. When the show ends, live music in the bar begins. The pub's old decor and gentrified spit-and-sawdust feeling is heightened by the staff's quaint habit of using a cash till that dates back to pre-decimalization days, so keep your currency converter handy or be prepared to trust the change.

After the theater you can squeeze into **Minogues** on the corner of Liverpool Road and Theberton Street, one of London's few Irish pub/restaurants, for flowers on the table and traditional dishes from the blackboard menu. **Young's** Chinese restaurant is a short distance away on Upper Street; the nearby **Upper Street Fish Shop** is bright, breezy, and a bit upscale, at least for a fish-and-chip shop.

You'll have to get up early to catch the market traders at **Smithfield Central Market**. This wholesale meat, poultry, and game market at the southern side of Clerkenwell near the Barbican Underground stop, though of little initial attraction to the visitor, has been a London tradition

since the 10th century (in those days the cattle were live).
Located on the site of Islington's old Caledonian livestock
market, it extends over ten acres, with 15 miles of rails
and the capability of hanging 60,000 sides of beef. Smithfield is active Monday through Friday.

The Norman **St. Bartholomew-the-Great Church**, one
of the oldest and most atmospheric churches in London,
lies a few minutes' walk to the east of the market. There is
a restaurant here, **Café du Marché**, that looks as if it
belongs on Paris's Left Bank. It's hard to find, though:
Stand on Charterhouse Square, look north, and you'll see
it tucked down a tiny alleyway.

London East

EAST END

London's East End is not an obvious goal for visitors. It is
far from refined, short on interesting shops, relatively
light on historic buildings, and lacking in greenery. But
for anyone interested in London as a sociological phenomenon, the East End—located at the eastern end of the
city, from about the Tower area onward, and hugging the
northern bank of the Thames—is an essential detour.

Although London has nowhere near the same melting-
pot alchemy that, say, New York does, it has certainly
welcomed its fair share of huddled masses. The first to
stake a claim were the Huguenots in the 16th century.
Close on their heels came Sephardic Jews, Irish Catholics
(who excavated the city's docks), Polish and Russian Jews
escaping the pogroms, and later, though less concentrated as a group in this particular section of town, thousands of Central European Jews fleeing Nazi persecution.

In 1887 a sociological study described Whitechapel,
the area between the City and the rest of the East End, as
simply the "dwelling place of the Jews," where they practiced tailoring and other traditional skills. To place yourself in this famous and still slightly raw and intriguing
corner of London, walk about half a mile north of the
Tower of London or due east from the Bank of London.
Today the East End is still steeped in Jewish history. For
example, Bevis Marks, near Aldgate Underground station,
is Britain's oldest surviving synagogue, built for the Sephardic community in 1701. Jewry Street is nearby, and
there is even a Jewish soup kitchen on Brune Street.
Cable Street is famous for the "battle" in which Jewish

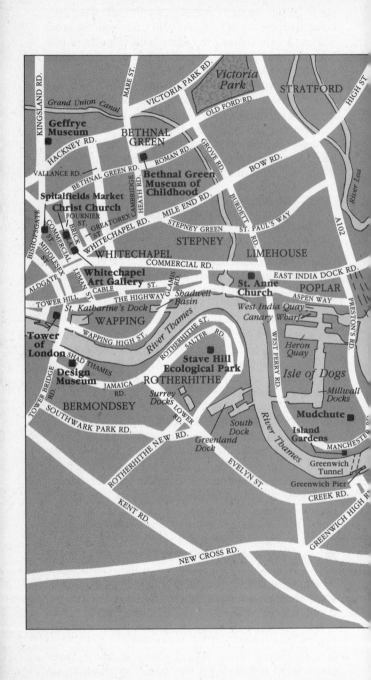

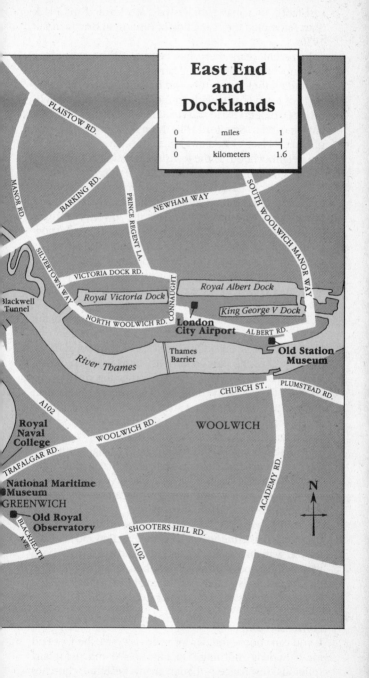

resistance to a march by Oswald Mosley and his Black Shirts stemmed the rising tide of Fascism in Britain in the 1930s.

In recent years there has been a shift in the ethnic makeup of the East End. Many Jews have moved out, upgrading their properties and buying in more desirable parts of town (particularly in the northwest London suburbs of Golders Green and Hendon; most of the Orthodox have moved to Stamford Hill). Even the Great Synagogue of Duke's Place closed in 1978, and so have ten others in the neighborhood, as the Jewish population has declined from 125,000 in 1900 to around 12,000 today.

Their places have been filled by a fresh wave of immigrants from the Indian subcontinent, notably Bengal and Bangladesh, who have taken over the lower-priced real estate as well as the traditional sweatshops. There are now as many *halal* butchers in the main shopping streets as there are kosher. On one street corner, where Fournier Street meets Brick Lane, a structure that was built as a Huguenot chapel later became a synagogue and is now a mosque.

The East End has always been on the "other" side of the tracks, a tough, working-class district of crowded row houses and flats, outside lavatories, and communal baths. At the end of the past century its slums were notorious. They inspired, among others, U.S. philanthropist George Peabody to finance the building of apartment blocks in an effort to alleviate the worst areas of overcrowding. Crime and prostitution flourished here, and this was the setting of the macabre deeds of Jack the Ripper.

To place yourself in this famous and still slightly raw and intriguing corner of London, walk about half a mile north of the Tower of London or due east from the Bank of England. Before you venture east, try to catch an episode of Britain's most successful soap opera, "Eastenders." The show may pay only lip service to the truth, but it will introduce you to the ambience of the East End and familiarize you with the Cockney dialect. It is said that anyone born within the sound of Bow Bells (the bells of St. Mary-le-Bow, on Cheapside) is a true Cockney, and most of the East End's places of interest lie within their decibel radius.

Petticoat Lane

If you can choose the day for your visit, save the East End for a Sunday morning. Do this not so much for any religious resonance—though many beautiful churches designed by Christopher Wren and Nicholas Hawksmoor lie within the area—but for its Petticoat Lane market. You won't find that name on a map, though; just take the tube to Aldgate and follow the crowds. If you prefer to trust a map, look for Middlesex Street and you'll find yourself in the heart of the action. (Less touristy but more ethnic and interesting are the Sunday-morning markets on Brick Lane, mainly devoted to used and secondhand goods, and Columbia Road, with flowers and plants.)

At Petticoat Lane there are a few antiques and bric-a-brac stalls, but nothing to compare with, say, Portobello Road or Camden Lock. In fact, the market's name hails from the days when it was predominantly a clothes market, but today's wares are as much the celebration of plastic and fly-by-night manufacturing as anything remotely tied to nostalgia. The pleasure of Petticoat Lane is in listening to the patter of the stall holders, barrow boys, costermongers, and fly-boys, the unlicensed traders who are always ready to flee at the first sign of a bobby. You should simply drift along with the crowd, soaking up the sheer vitality of the occasion. This is an extremely popular market, almost an institution among local residents, so you'll mingle with just about all of the Cockneys in London. Petticoat Lane is one of those classic markets where they say you can find whatever was stolen from you the week before. Don't trust the irresistible prices, explained away by an unfortunate accident whereby the merchandise just happened to fall off the back of a lorry, a popular Cockney euphemism for hot goods.

Elsewhere in the East End

In the shadow of the recently completed and massive Broadgate development, a complex of mostly offices plus shops at ground level, nestle some of the oldest and most atmospheric residential areas of London. In the area north of the now-closed Spitalfields Market are Folgate Street and Elder Street, with many beautiful 18th-century Georgian houses (number 18, furnished in the style of the period, has limited opening times; Tel: 247-4013). Behind **Christ Church**—Hawksmoor's masterpiece, now sadly run-down—is Fournier Street, with more, also often run-down, Georgian houses. To the south of Spitalfields are Artillery Row and Gun Lane; Jack the Ripper's last and most grisly murder took place in nearby White Row, off Crispin Street. For a by now much-needed drink, head for **Dirty Dick's** (202 Bishopsgate), previously a house where recluse Nathaniel Bentley stopped washing on the death of his fiancée. The pub has authentic-looking cobwebs and mouse skeletons.

Other interesting sights in the East End are worthy of higher cultural esteem. On Whitechapel High Street, the **Whitechapel Art Gallery**, one of the best in London with its renovated Art Nouveau façade, specializes in exhibitions devoted to modern visual art. Opposite the Whitechapel Underground is the London Hospital, most notably the home of John Merrick, better known as the Elephant Man. Beautifully located in early-18th-century ironmongers' almshouses shaded by plane trees, the charming **Geffrye Museum** on Kingsland Road displays a small collection of fine furniture in rooms arranged chronologically by period, from 1600 to 1939. A great favorite for a family outing is the **Bethnal Green Museum of Childhood** on Cambridge Heath Road, with collections not only of children's toys but also of costumes and furniture; it lies a short walk north of Bethnal Green Underground station.

With all its ethnic origins, you won't go hungry in the East End, but you may have to abandon your food prejudices. **Tubby Isaacs'** seafood stall on Greatorex Street is just one of the area's institutions, a place to buy a small plate of jellied eels, whelks, cockles, and winkles. The fine range of Indian and Bangladeshi restaurants, from small cafés to more upmarket establishments catering to nearby City gents, include **Nazrul** and **Clifton**, both on Brick Lane and both inexpensive. **Bloom's**, on Whitechapel Road, the East End's main artery, is London's best kosher restaurant. Take-out sandwiches or borscht followed by pastrami is the order of the day here.

DOCKLANDS
Visitors to London beware. The capital is changing faster than any other city in the world except perhaps Paris, Hong Kong, or Tokyo. But stick to the familiar haunts of the City and the West End, visit only such popular landmarks as Westminster Abbey, the Houses of Parliament, St. Paul's Cathedral, and Buckingham Palace, and you won't notice a thing. Even many Londoners are none the wiser—their typical reaction, when shown what's happening on their very doorstep, is amazement at just how much has already been altered.

Venture just five minutes or so east from the Tower of London and you'll come across the fringes of a London that is undergoing massive redevelopment on a scale

seen only on two previous occasions—after the 17th-
century Great Fire and during the 1950s, when the city
repaired the ravages of war. Although work began here
only in the early 1980s, the Docklands is on the way to
becoming one of the most important and exciting inner-
city developments in Europe.

The area destined to become the new London is the
old docks, a vast acreage of basins, locks, and canals
where, during the peak of the country's imperial power,
raw materials were unloaded from the colonies and
manufactured goods were exported to the rest of the
world. But with the gradual loss of empire and the under-
mining of England's commercial supremacy, as well as
the growth of containerized traffic, the docks gradually
dwindled in importance. Decline led to decay, and the
vast landscape became a giant urban wasteland.

Canals in the Docklands, filled in during the 1960s—
having ceased to function as commercial arteries—are
now being dug out for purely aesthetic considerations.
With its eight miles of River Thames and 460 acres of
retained water, the Docklands has been compared with
Amsterdam and Venice, which is where several architects
have looked for inspiration.

Top names in architecture, both British and foreign,
have been recruited to renovate the area's structures
(some of which survive from the 1790s, although most
are from the 19th century) and design new residential
and commercial buildings. In a location as big as central
London itself (a land area equivalent to that stretching
from Marble Arch to the Tower of London and from
Waterloo to Euston), old warehouses—some still smell-
ing of the spices they once stored—are now being transformed slowly into chic stores, wine bars, restaurants,
exhibition centers, craft workshops, art galleries, museums, and hotels.

Immediately east of the Tower is **St. Katharine's Dock**.
In this restored Docklands area you may still occasionally
see a historic Thames sailing barge. Modern yachts anchor in a basin surrounded by arcaded warehouses constructed by Scottish engineer Thomas Telford, and the
Dickens Inn, a wooden warehouse now converted into a
pub with a sawdust floor and two restaurants.

On the other side of the river, a short but breezy walk
south across the Tower Bridge, is **Butler's Wharf**. Sir Terence Conran, fresh from revitalizing the high streets of
Britain, has turned this outstanding remnant of original

19th-century riverside warehouses (Quilps' Wharf, in Dickens's *Old Curiosity Shop,* was sited nearby) into shops, homes, restaurants, offices, and, notably, the excellent **Design Museum**. Established by the Conran Foundation, this collection of everyday objects explores why they look the way they do. Two new restaurants well worth considering here are the **Blueprint Café**, for modern British cooking and for outstanding views of the river (on the first floor of the Design Museum), and the even more stylish, modern French **Le Pont de la Tour** in the renovated wharf.

The Docklands Light Railway Route

The Docklands Light Railway (DLR) serves the new breed of residents, workers, and visitors some 20 feet above street level, using many of the original Victorian viaducts. It runs from the Tower of London through a series of stations to the Isle of Dogs (see below), east along the Thames to the London district of Stratford, and now extends to Beckton, near the City Airport. (DLR operates only Monday through Friday; on weekends a bus runs along a similar route.) The best way to see the Docklands is to jump aboard one of the brightly colored, driverless trains at either the Bank or Tower Gateway stations (by Tower Hill, just opposite the Tower of London). The **Green Line**, which runs through Canary Wharf to Island Gardens, is of most interest to visitors: for the passing sights, which include historic churches, Victorian industrial scenery, and futuristic architecture; and because it terminates at the foot tunnel that leads under the Thames and emerges in Greenwich.

An early landmark to spot from the train's right-hand window—get off at Shadwell if you are a fan of ecclesiastical architecture—is Hawksmoor's **St. George in the East** on Cable Street. Trained by Wren, Hawksmoor would surely be shocked to his quills by the restored, modern interior; the original church was severely bombed in 1941.

Shadwell is also your stop if you want to enjoy two of London's best riverside pubs. The **Town of Ramsgate** on Wapping High Street is where the notorious "hanging" judge George Jeffreys was arrested in 1688 when the political tide turned against him (just along the river is Execution Dock, where various pirates were hanged). Though there is no access across the river at this point, on the opposite bank, on Bermondsey Wall (from Shadwell take the East London Underground Line two stops to

Rotherhithe), is the **Angel**, a 16th-century pub where diarist Samuel Pepys paused, lingered, procrastinated on his way to Deptford Dockyard, his place of employment. The *Mayflower* is also on the southern shore, on Rotherhithe Street, near where the Pilgrims set sail in 1611.

On the north bank, a half mile or so walk through renovated warehouses, is the **Prospect of Whitby** on Wapping Wall. It is often crowded and, sadly, altered through renovation, but its wonderful terrace overlooks the river. Samuel Pepys, Charles Dickens, and the artist J. M. W. Turner all supped here.

Limehouse Station is the stop for Hawksmoor's **St. Anne** church, topped by the highest church clock in London. Walk down to the river and Narrow Street for **The Grapes**, a small pub immortalized by Dickens as the Six Jolly Fellowship Porters in *Our Mutual Friend*. It has a fine view, and a good fish restaurant upstairs.

After Westferry Station the tracks take a swing to the right to enter the **Isle of Dogs**, so called because Henry VIII kept his hounds in kennels here when the area was a bushy wilderness. The "isle" is in fact a kind of peninsula formed by an enormous U-bend in the river. You can hardly miss Olympia & York's **Canary Wharf**, the giant but financially troubled pride of the area's redevelopment, with its 800-foot tower capped by a silver pyramid, at night lit from the inside as a beacon dominating the new East London skyline. Most floors of the building (designed by Cesar Pelli) are devoted to offices, while at its base is **Cabot Place**, with shops, cafés, an exhibition, and often musicians entertaining passersby. Cabot Square, just outside, is the largest square built in London since Trafalgar was completed in 1850.

The train passes over two of the large basins of the West India Dock; at South Quay you can get out and wander along the quaysides. At Limeharbour you'll find the Docklands Visitors Centre, with lots of information on the various attractions in the area. Nearby, the **Island History Trust**'s photographic display shows what life was like in the area during the 1880s. The Trust is at Island House on Roserton Street (afternoons only, Tuesday, Wednesday, and Friday; Tel: 987-6041).

Next stop is Mudchute, a 32-acre working farm with riding stables for local residents, created from the first dredgings of the docks in 1802. The end of the tracks is at Island Gardens opposite Greenwich—a view painted by Canaletto.

The DLR **Red Line** extends north to the London district of Stratford (no connection with Shakespeare and of no tourist interest). From here you can change for British Rail's North London Line, which heads southwest to London's City Airport. Just 15 to 20 minutes after collecting their baggage, less than half the time it takes to journey out to Heathrow, arriving travellers can be in the heart of the City, making the airport an ideal gateway for financiers and other businesspeople. From the City Airport, shuttle buses connect with Riverbus service at Canary Wharf.

From the visitor's point of view the most exciting aspect of the Docklands may be not what's new but what's old. Again, you can take the DLR Red Line north to Stratford and change for the BR North London Line to reach, at the end of the line (just past the City Airport), the North Woolwich **Old Station Museum**. Restored to its period glory, the Old Station, with its old flagstone floors, exhibits railroad memorabilia in the Booking Hall, the Ticket and Parcels Office, and the Ladies and General Waiting rooms. The museum's pride and joy is the lovingly restored "Coffee Pot" saddle-tank engine, the only survivor of a class of engines formerly used to shunt goods about the area. The neighboring Woolwich Ferry, still a free ride across the Thames, affords a fine view of the **Thames Barrier,** a remarkable work of engineering consisting of steel plates that lie flat on the riverbed but pivot up to a vertical position when a flood threatens, reaching as high as a five-story house. An excellent visitors' center (access via the south bank) features audiovisual displays and scale models, plus cruises around the Barrier.

What's best about the Docklands is that this is a living environment, not an artificial stage set manicured for tourists. When the Docklands really was docks, high walls kept Londoners from seeing, let alone enjoying, their backyard acres of water. Today, with the building of scores of walks along the Thames and canals, an entire waterscape is opening up before their eyes.

GREENWICH

Greenwich, the historic maritime heart of London, lies some five miles east of the center of town, on the southern shore of the Thames, opposite the Isle of Dogs. Because its maritime traditions still shape its present-day appeal, it is especially fitting to arrive in Greenwich by boat from Tower Pier, Westminster Pier, or Charing Cross

Pier (behind Charing Cross Station). Step off the pier at Greenwich and, within a few paces, you can be mounting the gangplank of the *Cutty Sark,* a magnificent clipper that plied 19th-century trade routes carrying cargoes of tea, the brew that oiled the cogs of an empire.

Within a few yards, dwarfed by the soaring masts of the *Cutty Sark,* is the tiny *Gipsy Moth IV,* the yacht that carried Sir Francis Chichester on his solo circumnavigation of the globe in 1966 and 1967. Nearby is the Royal Naval College, inspired by Wren, Hawksmoor, and Sir John Vanbrugh, and, just across the main road, the **National Maritime Museum**, which brings Britain's rich seafaring heritage vividly alive. Housed in a grouping of some of the country's finest 17th-century buildings, the museum displays paintings, models, and real-life boats, as well as exhibits that evoke some of the country's great naval battles and the voyages of discovery by Captain Cook and other adventurers. Within the museum is Inigo Jones's **Queen's House**, restored by the National Maritime Museum and opened by the Queen in 1990. It was once home to Queen Henrietta Maria, wife of Charles I.

After exploring these sights, take a climb through Greenwich Park to the top of the hill where, from the ankles of the statue of General Wolfe, you'll enjoy a grand view of the river. Try to time your climb so you are at the summit at 1:00 P.M., when the famous ball drops from the top of the **Old Royal Observatory**. The moment marks the correct Greenwich mean time. The observatory, part of the Maritime Museum, houses the largest refracting telescope in the U.K. as well as an extensive collection of historical timepieces and astronomical instruments. A plaque marks the Greenwich Meridian, the spot that defines the zero line of longitude—stand astride it and you'll have one foot in the Orient, the other in the Occident.

An interesting alternative return route to central London is to follow the **foot tunnel** beneath the Thames from Greenwich to the Isle of Dogs. Built in 1902 to carry workers from south London into the docks, the tunnel is 1,200 feet long. From Island Gardens on the Isle of Dogs you can catch the Docklands Light Railway (on weekdays; a bus on weekends) back to the Tower.

GETTING AROUND

The telephone area code for inner London (roughly anywhere within a four-mile radius of Trafalgar Square) is, with one or two exceptions, (071). The area code for outer London is (081). Throughout this chapter we have given the area code only if it is (081); if it does not appear, you can assume that the area code is (071).

Main Airports

Heathrow (Tel: 081-759-4321; British Airways, 081-897-4000) is 15 miles west of the city and can be reached in 50 minutes on the Piccadilly Underground Line from central London (one stop before the last for Terminal 4, last stop for Terminals 1, 2, and 3); trains run every five minutes, starting around 5:30 A.M. Monday through Saturday and finishing around midnight. On Sundays the first train is around 7:00 A.M. and the last around 11:00 P.M. Airbuses pick up at several points throughout the main hotel areas of central London. **Gatwick** (Tel: 081-668-4211) is around 30 minutes from Victoria Station by British Rail Gatwick Express (every 15 minutes from 5:30 A.M. to midnight, hourly service throughout the night). Combined Gatwick Express/Underground tickets are available from any Underground station.

British Rail

London is served by several railway stations whose lines fan out like spokes on a wheel to various destinations of day-trip interest to the visitor. The best single source of information is the **British Travel Centre** at 12 Regent Street; open Monday through Friday, 9:00 A.M. to 6:30 P.M., Saturdays and Sundays, 10:00 A.M. to 4:00 P.M., with extended summer hours; Tel: 730-3400, calls accepted only Monday through Saturday. Inquiries about specific services can be directed to the various stations: Charing Cross (Tel: 928-5100); Euston (Tel: 387-7070); King's Cross (Tel: 278-2477); Liverpool Street (Tel: 283-7171); London Bridge (Tel: 928-5100); Marylebone (Tel: 262-6767); Paddington (Tel: 262-6767); St. Pancras (Tel: 387-7070); Victoria (Tel: 928-5100); Waterloo (Tel: 928-5100). (For all of these numbers, a central stacking system ensures that phone calls are answered in strict rotation, so be patient and wait for a reply.) For information on the area of Britain each station serves, see Useful Facts at the front of this book.

Visitor Information

The most detailed sources of information for visitors to London are the weekly listing magazines *Time Out* and

What's On, of which *Time Out* is by far the better. These come out on Wednesdays and are sold at all newsstands. *The Evening Standard,* London's weekday evening newspaper, is also a useful source of information, particularly on entertainment. Major tourist-information centers include:

London Tourist Board and Convention Bureau, 26 Grosvenor Gardens, London SW1W ODU (enquiries by mail only); **London Tourist Information Centre** at the following locations: Victoria Station Forecourt, open daily 8:00 A.M. to 8:00 P.M., with reduced winter hours; Selfridges department store (basement), Oxford Street, open 9:30 A.M. to 6:00 P.M. Monday through Saturday, except Thursdays, when it's 9:30 A.M. to 8:00 P.M.; Liverpool Street Underground station, open Mondays 8:15 A.M. to 7:00 P.M., Tuesday through Saturday 8:15 A.M. to 6:00 P.M., and Sundays 8:30 A.M. to 4:45 P.M.; Heathrow Terminals 1, 2, and 3 Underground station, open daily 8:00 A.M. to 6:30 P.M.; **British Travel Centre**, 12 Regent Street, near Piccadilly Circus, open Monday through Friday 9:00 A.M. to 6:30 P.M., Saturdays and Sundays 10:00 A.M. to 4:00 P.M., with extended summer hours (Tel: 730-3400, Monday through Saturday). There are also Tourist Information Centres in Bloomsbury, Croydon, Greenwich, Harrow, Hillingdon, Kingston-upon-Thames, Lewisham, Redbridge, Richmond, Tower Hamlets, and Twickenham, as well as in St. Paul's Churchyard in the City of London. The offices that carry the most comprehensive selection of booklets, maps, and the like are those in the Victoria Station Forecourt and on Regent Street near Piccadilly.

The hall porter of your hotel is also probably a good source of information.

Guided Tours

London Transport (Tel: 222-1234) operates half- and full-day tours from Victoria Coach Station, Buckingham Palace Road. For information, maps, and brochures visit the British Travel Centre, 12 Regent Street, Piccadilly Circus. Other tours are operated by **Cityrama** (Tel: 720-6663), **Evan Evans** (Tel: 930-2377), **Harrods** (Tel: 581-3603), and **Frames Rickards** (Tel: 837-3111). Both *Time Out* and *What's On* give details of the numerous independent lecturers and walking tours available. There are also taxi guide services; details are available from Tourist Information Centres.

Underground (Tube) and Buses

London Transport has a 24-hour travel-information telephone service (Tel: 222-1234; English only) and also operates **Travel Information Centres** at the following stations: Euston (BR concourse), Heathrow terminals 1, 2, and 3 Underground stations (and all airport terminals), King's Cross, Liverpool Street, Oxford Circus, Piccadilly Circus, St. James's Park, and Victoria (BR concourse).

The first trains run from around 5:30 A.M. (7:00 A.M. on Sundays) and the last at approximately midnight (11:00 P.M. on Sundays). Children under five ride for free, and those under 14 ride at reduced fares, as do 14- and 15-year-olds with a Child Rate Photocard (available from post offices in the London area; be sure the child has a passport-size photo and proof of age). Free maps of tube and bus services, a huge number of ever-changing leaflets describing various fares, and special passes are available at Underground and bus stations. The map of the city bus network is posted on tube station platforms, bus shelters, and main bus stations. Individual bus routes are detailed at bus shelters.

Fares on both tube and bus are computed according to stages and zones; therefore, a relatively short bus ride crossing three fare zones costs the same as or more than a much longer ride within a single zone.

Tourist Passes

The **London Visitor Travelcard**, available only outside Britain through British Rail offices or a travel agent, offers more or less unlimited use of the Underground, all London red buses (except sightseeing tours), the Docklands Light Railway, and British Rail within London and suburban zones for three-, four-, or seven-day periods. The card also comes with discount vouchers for a number of tourist attractions, such as Madame Tussaud's.

Available only in Britain is a one-day Travelcard; it can be purchased from London Transport offices in Underground stations.

Taxis

London's black cabs (a few are maroon or some other color) are rated the best in the world. Any cab with its yellow "For Hire" sign lit should stop if you flag it, and, provided your journey is under 6 miles (10 km) and within the borders of London, the cab must take you where you want to go. Tip 10 to 15 percent. You may telephone **Radio Taxis** for a black cab (Tel: 272-0272, round the clock).

A second form of taxi is the minicab. Unlike black cabs, drivers need no special qualifications and cars are generally unmetered with the fare being agreed upon in advance. Minicabs cannot be hailed in the street, and you should avoid drivers soliciting business, as this is illegal. (Less scrupulous drivers may not even be insured to carry fare-paying passengers.) However, over long distances a minicab may be cheaper than a black cab. Two reputable 24-hour companies are **Atlas Cars** (Tel: 602-1234) and **West One** (Tel: 560-5346).

Driving in London

Do not drive in London unless it is absolutely necessary: Traffic is extremely dense, traffic jams are the norm, and parking places—if you can find one—are expensive. **National Car Parks** has several locations throughout London; two of the more central ones are on Cavendish Square (Tel: 629-6968) and on Brewer Street near Piccadilly Circus (Tel: 734-9497). The NCP at the National Theatre, Southbank (Tel: 928-3940), is less expensive. A free list of locations is available from NCP, 21 Bryanston Street (Tel: 499-7050). The North and South Circular ring roads of London are easily accessible from the city center (though generally very busy) and link up to all major motorways around London.

Rental Cars

Budget: central reservations (Tel: 0800-181-181; toll free); **Avis**: central reservations (Tel: 081-848-8733); **Europ Car InterRent**: central Reservations (Tel: 0532-42-22-33 or 081-950-5050); **Hertz**: central Reservations (Tel: 081-679-1799). It is best to pick up a car at one of the London airports, which has the added advantage of getting you familiar with driving on the left before you hit the traffic in central London.

Boat Excursions

In summer boats leave from Westminster Pier and travel regularly up the Thames to Kew from 10:15 A.M. to 3:30 P.M.. Trips upstream to Hampton Court leave at 10:30 A.M. and noon (Tel: 930-4712). **London Waterbus Company** runs trips to London Zoo and along the Regent's Canal, which depart from Little Venice, near the Warwick Avenue/ Camden Town tube stations (Tel: 482-2550); **Jason's Trip** also offers cruises along the canal from Camden Town tube station (Tel: 286-3428). Riverboat Information Service, a recorded message giving the times and routes of river trips, can be reached at (0839) 123-432.

Riverbus service operates high-speed catamarans every 20 minutes (on weekdays) from Chelsea Harbour to Greenwich via Cadogan Pier, Charing Cross Pier, Festival Hall, Swan Lane Pier, London Bridge City Pier, St. Katharine Pier (convenient for both Tower Bridge and the Tower of London), Canary Wharf, and Greenland Pier, with a shuttle bus connection to the City Airport from Canary Wharf. Riverbus Explorer tickets also entitle the holder to discounts at selected riverside attractions. Riverbus is primarily a commuter service and originally ran only on weekdays. However, there was some (limited) weekend service during the summer of 1992, and this may continue in future years. Fares depend on the length of your journey; Tel: 512-0555.

Bus Excursions

Green Line buses leave from Victoria Coach Station for various places of interest in the surrounding area. For information on routes and fares (including the Diamond Rover tickets, valid for one to three day's unlimited travel on the network) call 081-668-7261. Several companies also offer one-day tours, including **Frames Rickards** (Tel: 837-3111) and **Evan Evans** (Tel: 930-2377).

ACCOMMODATIONS

Part of the pleasure of visiting London is staying in a hotel that is typically and eccentrically British. London is rich in just such places. Many London hotels occupy converted town houses full of hidden corners and great charm. Others are refurbished Victorian and Edwardian hostelries in which no two rooms are alike. Even new hotels in London often try to make each room different from the others.

The following list is far from comprehensive, but it includes some of the best ones in different price ranges. The rates given are projected 1994 prices for a double room without breakfast, unless otherwise stated. As prices are subject to change, you should always double-check before booking. Keep in mind that London is crowded with visitors year-round, so it is always best to book well in advance. Also, as London is such a huge city, you should decide upon the area in which you wish to stay before you make your booking; there is no point in saving money on a hotel only to spend it on travelling to and from the places you wish to visit.

The telephone area code for inner London, including all accommodations listed here, is (071).

Tower/City

▶ **Tower Thistle Hotel**. Despite its ugly modern exterior and out-of-the-West End location next to Tower Bridge, this hotel does have its pluses: a most wonderful position on St. Katharine's Dock, unmatched views, and attractive rooms.

St. Katharine's Way, E1 9LD.. Tel: 481-2575; Fax: 488-4106; in U.S., Tel: (800) 847-4358, Fax: (402) 398-5484. £135–£165.

Whitehall/Strand

▶ **Royal Horseguards Thistle Hotel**. Large but cozy, this pleasant hotel has much to offer, including location. It is within walking distance of most of Westminster's historical sights, and it occupies the elegant quarters of the old National Liberal Club, between the War Office and Victoria Embankment. The coffee shop serves light meals all day, and the cocktail bar also offers an inexpensive menu at lunchtime. There is a business-services center and, of course, 24-hour room service.

2 Whitehall Court, SW1A 2EJ. Tel: 839-3400; Fax: 925-2263; in U.S., Tel: (800) 847-4358, Fax: (402) 398-5484; in Canada, (800) 448-8355; in Australia, (008) 22-11-76. £110–£155.

▶ **Savoy Hotel**. Built on the site of the medieval palace of Savoy, this is probably London's best-known luxury hotel and is doubtless the one with the most fascinating history. It was built by the brilliant impresario Richard D'Oyly Carte out of the profits he made on his productions of the operettas of Gilbert and Sullivan, which were performed at his Savoy Theatre next door. When he took his productions of Gilbert and Sullivan to America, he was so impressed by the standards of the luxury hotels there that he decided to build a comparable one in London. He certainly succeeded: The Savoy was the first hotel in Britain to provide private bathrooms and the first hotel in London to have elevators. Another notable point, but nothing to do with Mr. D'Oyly Carte, is the hotel's association with the 99.9 percent perfect dry martini. You can enjoy one in the **American Bar**. Next to this popular gathering spot is the **Savoy Grill**, a favorite place for after-theater suppers.

The Strand, WC2R 0EU. Tel: 836-4343; Fax: 240-6040; in U.S. and Canada, (800) 63-SAVOY; in New York State, (212) 838-3110; in Sydney, (02) 233-8422; in the rest of Australia, (008) 22-20-33. £195–£260.

Bloomsbury

▶ **Hotel Crichton.** This 19th-century house across from the British Museum in Bloomsbury is well-run and under-standably popular. The large breakfast (included in the price of the room) is a good start to a day of sightseeing.

36 Bedford Place, WC1B 5JR. Tel: 637-3955; Fax: 323-0018. £46–£48.

Radisson Kenilworth Hotel. This recently refurbished hotel on the edge of Bloomsbury and close to the British Museum caters to business meetings and small confer-ences. Even so, it's well equipped for tourists, too, and is a good value.

97 Great Russell Street, WC1B 3LB. Tel: 637-3477; Fax: 631-3133; in U.S., (800) 447-7011; in Canada, (800) 333-3333; in Australia, (008) 22-11-76. £145–£186.

▶ **Euston Plaza Hotel,** opened in the early 1990s, is close to the major railway stations of Euston, King's Cross, and St. Pancras—convenient if you are travelling to the north. It is large and beautifully decorated in the Scandi-navian manner, and the rooms are well-appointed. The winter garden conservatory, The Terrace, offers light food all day, while the restaurant serves a wider choice during normal dining hours. A health and leisure area offers Jacuzzi, solarium, and saunas.

17–18 Upper Woburn Place, WC1H 0HT. Tel: 383-4105; Fax: 383-4106. £129–£147.

North of Oxford Street

▶ **Berners Park Plaza Hotel.** This large and highly deco-rated Victorian hotel, which recently has been upgraded, is situated in the heart of rag-trade land, just north of Oxford Street and close to Soho. Its splendid marble entrance hall is a popular meeting place for Londoners.

10 Berners Street, W1A 3BE. Tel: 636-1629; Fax: 580-3972; in U.S. and Canada, (800) 448-8355; in Australia, (008) 22-11-76. £130.

▶ **Dorset Square Hotel.** This small, attractive hotel occu-pies several 19th-century town houses on the corner of two-and-a-half-acre Dorset Square, just to the southwest of Regent's Park (the site of the original Lord's Cricket Ground, created by Thomas Lord in 1787 and a mecca for cricketing fans from all over the world). Despite the discreet town-house atmosphere, the Dorset Square offers all the most up-to-date facilities: state-of-the-art security systems, 24-hour room service, and secretarial services.

39-40 Dorset Square, NW1 6QN. Tel: 723-7874; Fax: 724-3328; in U.S., (800) 543-4138. £110–£165.

▶ **Mandeville Hotel.** Tucked away in Marylebone north of Oxford Street near Wigmore Street, Wigmore Hall, and the Wallace Collection, this attractive hotel is a favorite of busy executives who make use of its restaurant, coffeehouse, two bars, and comprehensive business services.

Mandeville Place, W1M 6BE. Tel: 935-5599; Fax: 935-9588; in U.S. and Canada, (800) 44-UTELL; in Australia, (02) 419-7111. £122 (including Continental breakfast).

▶ **Mostyn Hotel.** Relaxing comfort is what the Mostyn is all about, a welcome relief from the bustle of Marble Arch and Oxford Street. In 1740 Lady Black of George II's court commissioned John Adam to build her a grand house. Her home, which is now listed by the Historic Buildings and Monuments Commission as being of national importance, has been skillfully incorporated into the rest of the present building, but you can see part of the original structure as you enter the restaurant and cocktail bar. The grand staircase, superbly molded ceilings, wall paneling, and handsome fireplaces all show the airy spaciousness of the 18th century. Price includes full English breakfast.

Bryanston Street, W1H 0DE. Tel: 935-2361; Fax: 487-2759. £130–£142.

▶ **Savoy Court Hotel.** In a quiet mews just moments from the noise and bustle of Oxford Street sits this small, unpretentious hotel. Maybe its greatest asset is that it is almost next door to one of the biggest Marks and Spencer stores in Europe, as well as being one minute from Selfridge's. If you are intent on shopping, this is a wonderful site, with a cocktail bar and restaurant to revive you when you return exhausted with your purchases.

19–25 Granville Place, W1H 0EH. Tel: 408-0130; Fax: 493-2070; in U.S. and Canada, (800) 333-3333. £111–£118.

Mayfair

▶ **Brown's Hotel.** In 1830 James Brown, a gentleman's gentleman who was married to Sarah, the lady's maid to

Lady Byron, bought the first of the large Mayfair houses that make up this most understated but elegant hotel. Over the next 150 years another 11 houses on Dover Street and Albemarle Street were acquired, making the hotel a veritable rabbit warren but in no way detracting from the impeccable service that makes this one of the most civilized places to stay in London. The cozy, paneled public rooms are crammed every afternoon as people enjoy the delicious afternoon tea for which Brown's is famous. It was in this hotel, in 1876, that the first successful telephone call was made in Britain—between the youthful inventor Alexander Graham Bell and the young son of the landlord, Henry Ford. It was also from this hotel that Theodore Roosevelt walked to his wedding at St. George's Church in Hanover Square, and just a few years later Franklin and Eleanor Roosevelt spent several days of their honeymoon in the same suite.

Albemarle and Dover streets, W1A 4SW. Tel: 493-6020; Fax: 493-9381; in U.S. and Canada, (800) 225-5843, Telex: 6852554; in Australia, (008) 22-24-46, Telex: AA 121448. £205.

▶ **Chesterfield.** Created from a gracious town house in the heart of Mayfair, close to Berkeley Square and Curzon Street, the Chesterfield is a gracious hotel. Named after the fourth earl of Chesterfield, who was a local landowner, this hotel has an affiliation with the English Speaking Union, whose headquarters, Dartmouth House, are next door. The interior is warm and inviting, and the staff is very friendly and helpful. There's also an attractive interior terrace where tea can be taken.

35 Charles Street, W1X 8LX. Tel: 491-2622; Fax: 491-4793; in U.S. and Canada, (800) 44-UTELL; in Australia, (02) 419-7111. £150–£170.

▶ **Claridge's.** This wonderful hotel in the heart of Mayfair, near New Bond Street, may remind you of the great transatlantic liners, and the service is comparable, too. Quite simply, Claridge's is the ultimate in London luxury and discreet service, which is probably why guests of the royal family are frequently put up here. The rooms are among the most comfortable and best equipped anywhere, yet they still retain the grace and style of another era. During World War II, Claridge's became a haven for exiled royalty and heads of state. The story is told of a diplomat who telephoned Claridge's and, asking to speak to the king, received the reply, "Which king?"

Brook Street, W1A 2JQ. Tel: 629-8860; Fax: 499-2210; in

U.S. and Canada, (800) 223-6800; in New York City, (212) 838-3110; in Australia, (008) 222-033. £270–£329.

▶ **Connaught**. This establishment is more like a very select club than a hotel; most of the guests have been staying here—and eating at the renowned **Connaught Grill**—for years. The high standards maintained at this hotel, near the U.S. embassy, are all the more appreciated these days, when they are so rare. Most of the staff has been here for years, providing impeccable service. Book well in advance for both the hotel and the grill.

16 Carlos Place, W1Y 6AL. Tel: 499-7070; Fax: 495-3262; in U.S. and Canada, (800) 223-6800; in New York City, (212) 838-3110; in Australia, (008) 222-033. £270.

▶ **Delmere Hotel**. Close to Paddington Station and Bayswater, this is the best choice on a street of small hotels. With 40 rooms, which were attractively converted from a large town house, it caters not only to the vacationer but also to the business traveller, offering all the usual support services, including fax machines.

130 Sussex Gardens, W2 1UB. Tel: 706-3344; Fax: 262-1863. £91–£102 (includes Continental breakfast).

▶ **London–London Hotel**. This newly opened hotel has high standards, with all the usual facilities. Converted from several large houses in a quiet London square, it is close to Paddington Station, which serves the west of England as well as some of the nearer out-of-town tourist destinations such as Windsor. The hotel is also close to the Bayswater district north of Hyde Park, and, for those who like to shop, Oxford Street is a reasonable walk away. Thatchers, the hotel restaurant, specializes in vegetarian food.

2–14 Talbot Square, W2 1TS. Tel: 262-6699; Fax: 723-3233. £95.

St. James's

▶ **Dukes Hotel**. This small and attractive hotel is hidden discreetly in a courtyard brimming with flowers. With service that matches its comfort, no wonder it is recommended by regulars who wouldn't stay anywhere else.

35 St. James's Place, SW1A 1NY. Tel: 491-4840; Fax: 493-1264; in U.S. and Canada, (800) 525-4800; in Australia, (008) 80-25-82. £220–£290.

▶ **Ritz**. This is where the word "ritzy" originated, and everything about it is just that—from the service to the decor, from the opulent public rooms, the most beautiful in London, to the elegant guest rooms and suites. The

Palm Court is probably the best place in London for afternoon tea; the magnificent, gilded dining room looks out onto Green Park. The Marie Antoinette Suite, next to the dining room, is where Winston Churchill, General Eisenhower, and General de Gaulle planned the invasion of Normandy.

Piccadilly, W1V 9DG. Tel: 493-8181; Fax: 493-2687; in U.S. and Canada, (800) 525-4800. £220–£280.

▶ **Stafford Hotel.** Reached from St. James's Street through a cobbled mews (although there is a more conventional entrance in the front of the hotel), this is one of London's treasures. The smallish hotel occupies two converted 19th-century town houses just to the east of Green Park. Public rooms are formal but welcoming, and attention to detail is in evidence everywhere— comfort even extends to a tunnel leading from the hotel beneath nearby buildings into the park. The restaurant is expensive but excellent. In the cellars, hidden away among the bottles of wine, is a small, private, and fascinating museum of wartime memorabilia, complete with sandbags and posters of the period. During World War II this was a bomb shelter for the U.S. and Canadian officers who used the hotel as a club.

16-18 St. James's Place, SW1A 1NJ. Tel: 493-0111; Fax: 493-7121; in U.S. and Canada, (800) 525-4800; in Australia, (008) 22-74-95 or (02) 954-5255. £220–£235.

Sloane Square/Victoria Station

▶ **Eccleston Hotel.** Within easy walking distance of Victoria Station and its trains to Continental Europe and Gatwick Airport, as well as Victoria Coach Station and the Underground, both with their links to Heathrow, this large and efficiently run hotel is an ideal location for the business traveller or for the vacationer who will be doing a lot of moving around. The Eccleston offers most of the facilities you would expect to find in a more expensive hotel. Office facilities can be organized.

82-83 Eccleston Square, SW1V 1PS. Tel: 834-8042; Fax: 630-8942; in U.S., (800) 223-6764 or (617) 581-0844; in Canada, (800) 223-6764. £78–£89.

▶ **Elizabeth Hotel.** Situated on one of the many garden squares of London, only a few doors away from one of the former residences of Sir Winston Churchill, this small hotel has a loyal following among travellers. Full English breakfast is included in the price. An unexpected bonus is that residents may use the tennis court in the communal gardens.

37 Eccleston Square, SW1V 1PB. Tel: 828-6812. £60–£80.

▶ **Goring Hotel.** This, perhaps London's best small hotel, is still owned by the same family that built it in 1910. (The Goring claims to be the first hotel in the world to have central heating *and* private bathrooms in every room.) Much loved by regulars, it occupies a quiet position by the Royal Mews of Buckingham Palace and is close to Victoria Station. Many of the rooms, as well as the comfortable and pleasantly seedy lounge and bar, overlook a garden. The motto of this hotel is "There is no longer a Mr. Claridge at Claridge's, there is no longer a Mr. Brown at Brown's, but there will always be a Mr. Goring at Goring's!"

15 Beeston Place, Grosvenor Gardens, SW1W 0JW. Tel: 396-9000; Fax: 834-4393; in U.S., (800) 323-5463. £200.

▶ **Royal Court Hotel.** Location is this hotel's appeal—on Sloane Square in the heart of Chelsea, between Peter Jones, one of London's very best department stores, and the Royal Court Theatre, renowned for producing avant-garde plays, and near all the shopping on the King's Road. Despite its location it is surprisingly peaceful, and justly popular. The restaurant offers good international cuisine. Also on the premises are the Old English Tavern and Court's Café Bar, both very popular. There is 24-hour room service.

Sloane Square, SW1W 8EG. Tel: 730-9191; Fax: 824-8381; in U.S. and Canada, (800) 44-UTELL; in Australia, (008) 22-11-76. £145.

▶ **Rubens Hotel.** Built at the turn of the century to serve Victoria Station, this hotel, situated opposite the Royal Mews, has recently been refurbished. It is attractively decorated, with large public rooms. Included in its many facilities are five meeting rooms that can be rented for conferences or social occasions. Located close to excellent Underground and bus services, as well as the major trains of Victoria Station, the Rubens is particularly convenient.

39–41 Buckingham Palace Road, SW1W 0PS. Tel: 834-6600; Fax: 828-5401; in U.S. and Canada, (800) 424-2862. £123.

▶ **St. James's Court.** Originally built at the turn of the century as grand apartments, by London standards this hotel is huge, with 390 bedrooms—but this does not mean it is without character; far from it. Recently upgraded, the St. James's is built around a landscaped central courtyard with a magnificent fountain. The building boasts an enormous brick frieze, which depicts scenes from Shakespeare, but for more modern taste the facilities also include three very good restaurants, a health and leisure center, and a large business center. It is located south of Buckingham Palace and close to St. James's Park.

Buckingham Gate, Westminster, SW1E 6AF. Tel: 834-6655; Fax: 630-7587; in U.S., (800) 458-8825. £152–£188.

Knightsbridge/Kensington

▶ **Astor House Hotel.** Yet another of the small hotels in Sumner Place, Kensington, this one is very much family-run by Mr. and Mrs. Peter Carapiet. They stress that you are a guest in their home, with your own front-door key. Most of the rooms have been nicely refurbished and have private facilities. Breakfast, included in the price, is served in the newly built and attractive Orangery. There is also a garden. This is a no-smoking hotel.

3 Sumner Place, SW7. Tel: 581-5888; Fax: 584-4925. £68–£85.

▶ **Basil Street Hotel.** This wonderfully old-fashioned and eccentric hotel has a large clientele who wouldn't stay anywhere else. In an excellent position in Knightsbridge off Sloane Street, it is perfect for shoppers and is very popular with affluent women from the country who come to London to shop. In fact, the whole hotel has a very clubby atmosphere and is furnished throughout with comfortable chairs and writing desks. The staff-client ratio is one of the highest in London, and the staff tends to stay.

8 Basil Street, SW3 1AH. Tel: 581-3311; Fax: 581-3693; in U.S. and Canada, (800) 44-UTELL; in Australia, (02) 419-7111. £156.

▶ **Beaufort.** On a cul-de-sac of very large, terraced houses near Harrods, this small hotel is privately owned and attractively decorated in country-house style. Guests are given their own key to the front door when they arrive, so you come and go as though the hotel were your own home in London. Continental breakfast is served in your room or in the small sitting room, and there is a complimentary 24-hour bar and snack menu as well as use of a health club. Closed Christmas and New Year's.

33 Beaufort Gardens, SW3 1PP. Tel: 584-5252; Fax: 589-

2834; in U.S., (212) 682-9191; in Canada, (416) 598-2693; in Australia, (02) 957-4511. £150–£220.

▶ **Berkeley**. This modern luxury establishment, close to Hyde Park and the shops of Knightsbridge, has all of the old-fashioned values you expect from a great London hotel. Unusual for London, though, are its penthouse swimming pool, beauty and health center, and a basement garage (a great plus in a city where parking is such a problem). There are secretarial and valet service and 24-hour room service.

Wilton Place, SW1X 7RL. Tel: 235-6000; Fax: 235-4330; in U.S. and Canada, (800) 63-SAVOY. £270–£310.

▶ **Capital Hotel**. Small, quiet, and beautifully decorated, and just around the corner from Harrods and the bustle of Knightsbridge, this hotel is a gem. The restaurant (one of the best in London) is a favorite of gourmets.

22–24 Basil Street, SW3 1AT. Tel: 589-5171; Fax: 225-0011; in U.S. and Canada, (800) 926-3199 or (800) 223-5695. £210–£260.

▶ **Cranley Gardens Hotel**. Among London's less expensive hotels, this one shines like a beacon. Converted from four attractive adjoining houses, it overlooks a private garden square in one of the most popular areas of the city. It is beautifully decorated, in both its public rooms and bedrooms, and members of the staff are pleasant and helpful. Continental breakfast is included in the price. In fact, the small restaurant serves *only* breakfast, but the area abounds with dining establishments of all types.

8 Cranley Gardens, SW7. Tel: 373-3232; Fax: 373-7944; in U.S. and Canada, (800) 44-UTELL. £89–£99.

▶ **Eleven Cadogan Gardens**. There is no sign on the door of this small hotel off Sloane Street south of Harrods to suggest that it is anything other than a private house. Nor is there a reception desk or a restaurant—just a visitor's book and room service. Ring the bell next to the front door, and a manservant will let you in. Created from several Victorian houses, this hotel is much favored by diplomats and art dealers. Room service provides light meals, but for anything more substantial just venture down the road, where you'll find plenty of excellent restaurants.

11 Cadogan Gardens, SW3 2RJ. Tel: 730-3426; Fax: 730-5217. £132–£172.

▶ **Gore Hotel**. This pleasant small hotel across from Kensington Gardens, west of Royal Albert Hall, is very quiet yet close to all the activity of South Kensington. It has a pleasant lounge and a bistro that serves light meals, as well as one of the most popular restaurants in this corner of London, **One Ninety Queen's Gate**.

189 Queen's Gate, SW7 5EX. Tel: 584-6601; Fax: 589-8127; in U.S. and Canada, (800) 528-1234; in Australia, (02) 954-8111. £142–£197.

▶ **L'Hotel**. This delightful small hotel on the street behind Harrods has an air of the country about it, perhaps because it is frequented by people who come up from the country to shop or attend meetings and who neither want nor need all the services of a larger hotel. The guest rooms are simple, but they are most attractive, with pine and brass fittings. There are no public rooms, but the bistro in the basement, **Le Metro,** is very popular with hotel guests and neighborhood residents alike. L'Hotel is a sister hotel of the Capital Hotel next door.

28 Basil Street, SW3 1AT. Tel: 589-6286; Fax: 225-0011; in U.S. and Canada, (800) 223-5695 or (914) 833-3303. £125 (includes Continental breakfast).

▶ **Hotel George**. This attractively decorated and spacious hotel has grown over the years until it now occupies almost an entire terrace of 19th-century houses. Its position is marvelous, close to Earl's Court, one of the main Underground junctions, and the noisy cosmopolitan shops of Earl's Court Road. The excellent facilities include a fitness center with swimming pool, sauna, spa, and a garden and free parking—rarities in London hotels.

Templeton Place, Earl's Court SW5 9NB. Tel: 370-1092; Fax: 370-2285. £79–£95 (including Continental breakfast).

▶ **Hyde Park Hotel**. At 10:30 every morning you can see the Horse Guards riding past this stately hotel, one of London's oldest, on their way from the Horse Guards Barracks next door to the Changing of the Guard at Whitehall. Many debutantes' parties are held here, maybe because the young Guards officers are close at hand to act as escorts. With a lovely dining room overlooking Hyde Park, and several bars and lounges, this member of the Forte Hotels group is a favorite meeting place for Londoners and visitors alike. All rooms have recently been redecorated and are furnished with antiques.

66 Knightsbridge, SW1Y 7LA. Tel: 235-2000; Fax: 235-4552; in U.S. and Canada, Tel: (800) 225-5843; Telex: 6852554; in Australia, (02) 299-7224. £277–£356.

▶ **Knightsbridge**. This is a small, cozy, unpretentious

place, and one of the least expensive of several small hotels on this quiet cul-de-sac just west of Harrods, off Brompton Road. Don't expect much more than a bed, Continental breakfast, and a front-door key. Spend your money instead in the delightful restaurants on nearby Beauchamp Place.

10 Beaufort Gardens, SW3 1PT. Tel: 589-9271; Fax: 823-9692. £50–£90.

▶ **Lanesborough Hotel.** Following its opening in the early 1990s, this hotel quickly assumed a place in the top echelon of hotels worldwide. The magnificent building, constructed at Hyde Park Corner as one of London's major hospitals in 1828, has been completely restored and renovated with style and attention to detail. The great conservatory at its heart has become a popular lunchtime meeting place, as has the library bar. The dining room is elegant—and expensive. Each room has two personal direct-dial telephones as well as a fax, VCR, compact disc player, and safe. Every floor has a butler who ministers to the guests and their special requirements, which are recorded for future visits. Attractive rooms are available for guests who wish to give parties.

1 Lanesborough Place, SW1X 7TA. Tel: 259-5599; Fax: 259-5606; in U.S., Tel: (800) 999-1828; Fax: (800) 937-8278. £258.

▶ **Number Sixteen.** Built in 1848, these four intercon-necting and charming town houses create a most agree-able ambience. The hotel is very well placed in South Kensington, too. It has two drawing rooms, one of which provides tea and coffee throughout the day; the other is a delightful conservatory drawing room overlooking the attractive walled garden.

16 Sumner Place, SW7 3EG. Tel: 589-5232; Fax: 584-8615. £85–£135 (includes Continental breakfast).

▶ **Pelham Hotel.** This hotel is a hidden treasure situ-ated in South Kensington, a very popular corner of Lon-don that is close to many important museums, as well as to the shops and restaurants of Knightsbridge. Like nu-merous other London hotels, the Pelham comprises two very large converted houses, but the standard to which they have been converted is extraordinary. It is owned by Kit and Tim Kemp, who also own the Dorset Square Hotel (see above in the North of Oxford Street section), and their attention to detail is exceptional.

15 Cromwell Place, SW7 2LA. Tel: 589-8288; Fax: 584-8444; in U.S., (800) 553-6671. £150–£180.

▶ **Swiss House**. A small and inexpensive family-run bed-and-breakfast hotel, the Swiss House is situated in the heart of South Kensington, close to the Gloucester Road Underground station. There are just 16 rooms, 12 of which have private facilities. This attractive house, its frontage covered in trailing ivy and flower-filled window boxes, is a winner of the Best Value Bed and Breakfast award. Continental breakfast is included in the price.

171 Old Brompton Road, SW5 0AN. Tel: 373-2769 or 373-9383; Fax: 373-4983. £50–£60.

North and West of Hyde Park

▶ **Abbey Court**. Newly and very elegantly converted from a large town house, this small hotel offers very personal and friendly service. Snacks and drinks are available around the clock and a full English breakfast can be served in your room every morning, though it's not included in the room rate. This area of London (Notting Hill, just west of Bayswater and north of Kensington Gardens) abounds with restaurants of every kind for other meals.

20 Pembridge Gardens, W2 4DU. Tel: 221-7518; Fax: 792-0858. £130–£160.

▶ **Garden Court Hotel**. This family-run hotel is usefully situated close to Queensway, a busy and cosmopolitan street with two adjacent Underground stations, Queensway and Bayswater. There are many restaurants of various types in the area. The hotel, which is in the process of being upgraded, has comfortable rooms and a pleasant and helpful staff. Not all rooms have private facilities. Breakfast is included.

30–31 Kensington Gardens, W2. Tel: 229-2553; Fax: 727-2749. £39–£52.

▶ **Halcyon Hotel**. Converted from two large houses on the corner of Holland Park (west of Hyde Park/Kensington Gardens), the Halcyon is popular with theater people. No doubt they are drawn here by the greenery beyond the front door and the tastefully decorated rooms, designed to make you feel like a guest in a country house. The restaurant is highly regarded.

81 Holland Park, W11 3RZ. Tel: 727-7288; Fax: 229-8516; in U.S. and Canada, (800) 457-4000. £235–£250.

▶ **Holland Park Hotel**. This hotel in Notting Hill has 24 rooms, two of which are for families. Although small, the rooms are individually furnished and have en-suite facilities. There is an attractive sitting room with a fireplace, adjacent to a pleasant garden where tea or Continental breakfast, included in the price, can be taken in the summer.

6 Ladbrooke Terrace, W11 3PG. Tel: 792-0216 or 727-5815; Fax: 727-8166. £63 (including breakfast).

▶ **Pavilion Hotel**. Sussex Gardens is an area known for its small, and mostly cheap, hotels. Sadly, we can recommend few of these. An exception is the Pavilion, which has a slightly idiosyncratic but attractive atmosphere. The rooms have fairly basic en-suite facilities, and, because the hotel has no dining room, the Continental breakfast is served in the guest rooms.

34–36 Sussex Gardens, W2 1UL. Tel: 262-0905. £50.

▶ **Portobello Hotel**. Media people tend to frequent this easygoing hotel in a hard-to-find corner of Holland Park, within a stone's throw of Portobello Road market and all the fun shops and restaurants of this corner of town, west of Hyde Park/Kensington Gardens. The bar/restaurant is open to guests 24 hours a day. Rooms range in size from a ship's cabin to very large, but they all have the necessary amenities. The hotel is equipped with a special clean-air system pioneered in Scandinavia.

22 Stanley Gardens, W11 2NG. Tel: 727-2777; Fax: 792-9641. £100–£120 (includes full English breakfast).

▶ **Westminster Hotel**. Occupying several large converted houses in Leinster Square close to the Bayswater and Queensway Underground stations, this hotel is in an interesting area: slightly raffish, with a cosmopolitan feel and restaurants of every type close at hand. The hotel's helpful staff create a friendly atmosphere, and the pleasant public rooms are popular with businesspeople. The bedrooms are adequately furnished and have en-suite facilities. Breakfast is included.

16 Leinster Square, W2 4PR. Tel: 221-9131; Fax: 229-3917. £92–£114.

▶ **Whites Hotel**. Looking like a beautiful white wedding cake, this recently restored large hotel is in a wonderful position, with views over Kensington Gardens and Bayswater. On weekends, the railings of the park become an open-air picture gallery where artists hang their paintings in the hope of making a sale. The public rooms are most attractive, and the bedrooms have been decorated in an unusual and luxurious style, with all comforts included. Office facilities can be arranged.

90-92 Lancaster Gate, W2 3NR. Tel: 262-2711; Fax: 262-2147. £170–£210.

Apartments

For those who want to look after themselves when they come to London, the answer is to rent a serviced apartment, of which there are many. Although they are not necessarily cheaper than hotels, you do get more space for your money. Here are some of the best.

▶ **Dolphin Square**. Not far from the Tate Gallery, this was the largest apartment complex in Europe when it was built in 1937, and it offers the biggest range of apartments. They are perfectly adequate but definitely not in the luxury class, although the in-house facilities make up for this. There is a shopping arcade with butcher, grocer, ticket agency, two licensed bars, gym, squash and tennis courts, and a very good restaurant of the brasserie type that overlooks the large swimming pool. There is also a large central garden.

Chichester Street, Pimlico, SW1V 3LX. Tel: 834-3800; Fax: 798-8735. £115 per night.

▶ **Draycott House**. Just off Sloane Square, these exceedingly well designed apartments—always very popular—are temptingly close to the shops and restaurants of Knightsbridge and the King's Road in Chelsea.

10 Draycott Avenue, SW3 3AA. Tel: 584-4659; Fax: 225-3694; in U.S., (800) 448-4852. £840–£2,174 per week.

▶ **Durley House**. These excellently placed apartments, on Sloane Street between Chelsea and Knightsbridge, were taken over in 1989 by the ubiquitous Kemps of Dorset Square and Pelham Hotel fame, who are fast becoming the leading entrepreneurs in the small-hotel world of London. Refurbished to their usual high standard with exquisite taste, the formerly ramshackle Durley House is no longer recognizable. The only drawback to this sort of makeover is that such excellent service and comfort don't come cheap. (But included in these rates is the use of the tennis courts in Cadogan Square Gardens.)

115 Sloane Street, SW1X 9PJ. Tel: 235-5537; Fax: 259-6977; in U.S., Tel: (800) 553-6674. One bedroom, £195–£300 per night; 2 bedrooms, £275 per night.

▶ **47 Park Street**. This is the place for those looking for unabashed luxury and privacy. Although Mayfair is synonymous with elegance, these sumptuous serviced apartments are the top of the tree. The entrance hall is commanded by a concierge who will look after you down to the smallest detail, and the in-house restaurant is none other than Michelin-starred **Le Gavroche**. Even breakfast, served in your suite, is a gastronomic delight.

47 Park Street, Mayfair, W1Y 4EB. Tel: 491-7282; Fax: 491-7282; in U.S., Tel: (800) 845-6636. £284–£499 per night (suites only).

▶ **In the English Manner.** This firm offers more than 50 luxurious apartments in various areas and price ranges, in and around London. All are attractively furnished, and on arrival fresh flowers and breakfast provisions await you.

Lancych, Boncath, Pembrokeshire SA37 0LJ. Tel: (02) 397-7444; Fax: (02) 397-7686; in U.S., Tel: (800) 422-0799, or (213) 629-1811, Fax: (213) 689-8784; in Australia, (02) 957-4511. £500–£1,750 per week.

—Katie Lucas

DINING

There is no single gourmet area in London, although Soho, shedding its red-light image, is becoming increasingly well endowed with decent eateries. Covent Garden, on the other hand, has more than its share of mediocre establishments that service a fast turnover of tired shoppers and hungry theatergoers.

Some of Britain's best chefs are firmly ensconced in the top hotels; others move around, taking with them a steady band of dedicated followers to unlikely backwaters of London. And while the city's ethnic restaurants have always been its most inexpensive, a number of Indian, Japanese, Chinese, Thai, and Lebanese establishments now offer some of the best food in the capital in fashionable designer settings.

As a rule, it is necessary to make reservations for good restaurants. In a difficult economic period when it has been easier to list restaurants that have closed than to find new openings, some of the most expensive seem to be recession-proof. Top-line establishments such as Le Gavroche and One Ninety Queen's Gate, where you expect to pay £80 and £100 per person, respectively, are sometimes booked up two, three, even six weeks ahead. However, cancellations tend to come through on the afternoon of the day itself.

The recession and fluctuations in currency exchange rates have made even more problematic the always difficult task of categorizing eating establishments by price. While prices at many London restaurants may seem unbelievably high, our categories reflect the way the British view the cost of dining out: A meal for one person (cover charge, appetizer, main course, dessert and coffee, tax and tip, but not wine) is "inexpensive" if the bill is less than £20; £20 to £40 is "moderate," and more than £40 is "expensive."

The following section describes London restaurants in all price ranges, serving all types of ethnic food, in all of London's diverse neighborhoods.

English

Restaurants that look and feel like dining rooms of private homes are very much in vogue in London these days. **Launceston Place** (sister of Kensington Place; see below), on a quiet street of the same name behind Gloucester Road in South Kensington, achieves a candlelit intimacy in a crowded couple of rooms full of fine oil paintings and mirrors. The moderately priced menu here is decidedly British—roast beef and Yorkshire pudding on Sunday evening, and a groaning cheese board—as is most of the clientele. Closed Sunday lunch; Tel: 937-6912.

At 21 Romilly Street in Soho, the **Lindsay House** attempts to make you feel as if you are a guest in a private town house: You ring the bell to enter, drink an aperitif in front of an open fire in the downstairs sitting room, and eat upstairs among drapes, flounces, and flowers from an elaborate and moderately priced 18th-century English menu that includes traditional English puddings. Even so, the place hasn't quite managed to exorcise the ghost of the Chinese restaurant that occupied these quarters before it. Prix-fixe lunch from 12:30 to 2:30 P.M. and dinner from 6:00 P.M. until midnight, 7:00 to 10:00 P.M. on Sundays. Tel: 439-0450. The **English House** (on Milner Street, off Cadogan Square) and the **English Garden** (on Lincoln Street, off the King's Road) are similar and both moderately priced.

Leith's occupies three Victorian houses knocked into one at 92 Kensington Park Road. Prue Leith, the talented principal of Leith's School of Food and Wine, owns this establishment, equipped with French silver, English bone china, and Dartington glass. Swivel chairs make for relaxing dining, spotlights ensure that you can see how good the food is, and the Wagons Leith, trolleys for hors d'oeuvres and desserts, are outstanding. Dishes include charcoal-grilled rib of beef, ox tongue, and their unfussy like. There are also English cheeses, and herbs and vegetables from Prue's own farm in Gloucestershire.

Prices are moderate to expensive. Dinner only. Tel: 229-4481.

A Leith by-product with prices in the inexpensive to moderate range is the reopened **New Serpentine Restaurant**, an ideal rustic setting for a fine-weather meal near the bridge in Hyde Park. Tel: 402-1142.

The grill and the main restaurant in the **Connaught Hotel** (on Carlos Place in Mayfair) continue to serve excellent traditionally British food in an Edwardian setting that never seems to change. The grill is closed on weekends. Expensive; Tel: 499-7070.

Brasseries and Cafés

Brasseries and cafés are usually cheaper than more formal restaurants, and many serve meals—which tend to lean toward French—all day from breakfast onward.

Currently popular with Londoners is **Kensington Place** at 205 Kensington Church Street, the noisy Continental sister of the more formal Launceston Place. Revolving doors lead to a high-tech, glass-fronted brasserie that concentrates on exciting and unfussy European dishes with the freshest of ingredients. It is inexpensively priced and always crowded. Open every day from noon to midnight. Tel: 727-3184.

The Continental-style **Soho Brasserie** at 23 Old Compton Street serves typically French dishes such as fish soup, as well as snacks at the long bar (which is a popular drinking venue). On summer evenings when the restaurant gets crowded, the full-length doors are opened and patrons spill out onto the sidewalk. Open noon until 11:30 P.M.; special oyster offer Sundays. Inexpensive/moderate; Tel: 439-9301.

At 48 Greek Street in Soho, the street-level brasserie **L'Escargot** is a favored lunch place for members of the media who don't belong to the Groucho Club around the corner on Dean Street and who prefer not to pay the higher prices upstairs (a restaurant for more than 100 years). The brasserie menu offers modern English dishes, and the wines are celebrated. You can only make reservations for the evening. Lunch is served Monday through Friday from noon on, and dinner Monday through Saturday from 6:30 to 11:15 P.M.; closed Sundays. Moderate/expensive; Tel: 437-2679.

Off Piccadilly, **Langan's Brasserie** on Stratton Street is always crowded (but it's big so you can usually get in). The two floors (upstairs is quieter, but they don't serve the famous spinach soufflé up there) are jammed with splendid paintings, lots of large round tables, and a regular influx of conversation stoppers, including the occasional entertainer (Michael Caine is one of the owners). The long menu offers dishes, including daily specials, of variable quality, and the tab can be moderate if you watch what you order, expensive if you don't. Service may be interminably slow, but you can't come to London without eating here. Open Monday through Friday 12:30 P.M. to 2:45 P.M. and 7:00 P.M. to 11:45 P.M., Saturdays 8:00 P.M. to 12:45 A.M. Live band in the bar after 9:00 P.M. Tel: 491-8822. Booking ahead up to six weeks is encouraged, but you may be able to get in due to a same-day cancellation.

Le Caprice on Arlington Street in Mayfair is chic, stylish, and frequented by stars. Reserve well ahead, unless your name will get you in. The decor is black, white, and chrome, with photos on the walls. Simple snacks and meals for the diet-conscious are served from noon to 3:00 P.M. and 6:00 P.M. until midnight; brunch on Sundays until 3:00 P.M. Open every day of the year, including bank holidays. Expensive; Tel: 629-2239.

Joe's Café, on Draycott Avenue at Brompton Cross, opposite the Conran Shop, is frequented by well-dressed people from the fashion and pop worlds, and is about as far removed from a café as you can get. Waiters sport black waistcoats and white shirts that match the black-and-white decor and black-and-white tagliatelle. The lunch menu includes salads, bagels, and a few hot dishes, while evening meals are more formal, though still quite inexpensive. The bar is open weekdays from 6:00 P.M. to 9:00 P.M.; otherwise, you have to eat. They also serve Saturday breakfast and brunch on Sundays. Moderate; Tel: 225-2217.

If you're shopping in Knightsbridge, the **Emporio Armani Express** at 191 Brompton Road (Tel: 823-8818), one of the smartest cafés in town, is convenient. It looks a bit like a railway carriage and serves modern Italian dishes as well as cakes and espresso during store hours: Monday through Saturday 10:00 A.M. to 6:00 P.M.; 7:00 P.M. on Wednesdays. **Casper's Restaurant** at 6 Tenterden Street off Hanover Square (Tel: 493-7923) is part of a chain that includes **Tall Orders** on Soho's Dean Street at 2 St. Anne's Court (Tel: 494-4941) and has a gimmick that works. Modern European food is served warm (not hot) in Chinese-style wicker *dim sum* baskets stacked high. Dishes here include grilled swordfish with white beans in virgin olive oil, and salmon carpaccio with guacamole.

Prices are moderate, and there is an animated, lively atmosphere as well as music (although the din often drowns it out). Open seven days a week from noon to midnight.

French

A few of London's French restaurants regularly receive the highest accolades from food critics. Three are particularly outstanding (note that they are all very expensive in the evening and closed on weekends): **Le Gavroche**, at 43 Upper Brook Street (Tel: 408-0881), is owned by one of London's best-known chefs, Albert Roux, and offers a lunchtime menu and dishes that range from the simple to the sophisticated; expensive. **La Tante Claire**, 68 Royal Hospital Road in Kensington (Tel: 352-6045), boasts chef Pierre Koffmann, who is renowned for his pig's trotters dish, and a good-value set lunch menu. **Chez Nico**, 35 Great Portland Street in the heart of the garment district, but a stone's throw from Oxford Street near Oxford Circus, is owned by Nico Ladenis, whose largely classical French menu has been satisfying his discerning followers for years. The food is simply outstanding and presented immaculately; each meal is almost a theatrical experience. Expensive; Tel: 436-8846.

Nico's old premises at 48A Rochester Row are now **Simply Nico**, which offers an informal brasserie-style experience with a reasonably priced set menu. Open every day except Sundays with lunch from noon to 2:00 P.M. and evening meals from 7:00 P.M. (no lunch on Saturdays). Tel: 630-8061.

The **Bistro Carapace** was until recently Le Mazarin. It consists of a series of alcoves leading off a main dining area in an elegant pink basement at 30 Winchester Street, just beyond Victoria Coach Station. The new owner has retained some of the former kitchen staff, who prepare exquisite sauces from quality ingredients and accentuate the bistro presentation with a Mediterranean style. The menu has been tapered, reducing prices now to a moderate range. Closed Sunday evenings; Tel: 828-3366.

The French food at the **Auberge de Provence** brings the cooking of the south of France into a somewhat drab restaurant in the St. James's Court Hotel. As at the Oustaù de Baumanière in France, on which it is modeled, cloches are lifted to reveal colorful Provençal ingredients skillfully combined. Vegetarians are well catered to, and the wine list is carefully chosen. The excellent prix-fixe lunch menu attracts local businesspeople. South of Buckingham Palace at Buckingham Gate. Inexpensive/moderate; Tel: 821-1899.

The south of France atmosphere also prevails in Pierre Martin's group of fish restaurants. Popular among celebrities who don't mind rolling up their sleeves and tucking in to the vast *plateau des fruits de mer* is the simple, crowded **Le Suquet** at 104 Draycott Avenue at Brompton Cross. Moderate; Tel: 581-1785.

La Croisette, 168 Ifield Road (running past the cemetery into the Old Brompton Road—look for the awning), was the first of Martin's chain to open, in 1975. Ring and you will be ushered into a crowded basement where London's French come for the fixed menu and to socialize over the enormous cork platters loaded with crab, langoustines, winkles, oysters, and mussels. La Croisette is 100 percent French, down to the youthful staff in Cannes tee-shirts, the paintings of the Mediterranean, and the unsalted butter; a trio strums guitars on some nights. Closed Sunday, Monday, and Tuesday. Moderate; Tel: 373-3694.

At Martin's **Le Quai St. Pierre**, 7 Stratford Road just off the Earl's Court Road, you can sit at the counter under a huge umbrella or at a table in the only slightly more formal dining room up the spiral staircase. What this place lacks in finesse it makes up for in atmosphere. Closed all day Sunday and Monday lunch. Moderate; Tel: 937-6388.

La Croisette is best for an intimate evening, Le Quai St. Pierre more fun if you're in a party, Le Suquet if you like star-spotting. All are excellent value for the money.

In Knightsbridge are the two inexpensive to moderately priced St. Quentin restaurants, which are owned in part by the Savoy Group. The **St. Quentin**, a bustling, elegant French establishment on two floors (opposite the Brompton Oratory) at 243 Brompton Road, serves a reasonable prix-fixe lunch. Open daily; Tel: 589-8005. The **Grill St. Quentin** occupies a huge, bright, and warmly lit basement reminiscent of La Coupole in Paris at 2 Yeoman's Row off Brompton Road. Closed Sundays; Tel: 581-8377.

Bernard Gaume at the Hyatt Carlton Tower at 2 Cadogan Place in Knightsbridge is well respected for his French (but not nouvelle) cuisine in the **Chelsea Room**. The restaurant has a sunny conservatory from which you can see the gardens of Cadogan Place; there are deep settees on which to relax over a drink in the adjoining bar; and the moderate, prix-fixe lunch menu includes a half bottle of wine—unusual for London. The **Rib Room** downstairs offers fine grills and seafood. Tel: 235-5411.

Other excellent hotel restaurants include the intimate **Le Soufflé** on the ground floor of the Inter-Continental in Hamilton Place (on Hyde Park) and the opulent **Oak Room** on the ground floor of the Meridien in Piccadilly. At Le Soufflé, Peter Kromberg is at the helm, offering imaginative soufflés and a consistently high standard of French cuisine. There is a short set menu at lunch, five courses in the evening, and Sunday brunch (closed Saturday lunch). Tel: 409-3131. The decor couldn't be more different in the grand gilt-and-mirrored Oak Room, though the food is similarly acclaimed. Tel: 734-8000. Closed Saturday lunch and Sundays. Both are expensive.

The **Four Seasons**, at the Inn on the Park hotel on Park Lane, is a palm-filled room in which the esteemed young Bruno Loubet offers *cuisine du terroir* (classical bourgeois cooking) as well as dishes that are low in cholesterol. Although the dinner menu is expensive, there is a reasonable *menu du jour* at lunch. Tel: 499-0888.

You can eat inexpensive French food in London's numerous brasseries (see Brasseries and Cafés).

Indian

Some of London's best Indian restaurants are unpretentious places, but those of the new school have turned up the lights, spruced up the decor, and begun to offer cocktails as well as beer with their curries. Leading the band of these upscale Indian restaurants are **The Last Days of the Raj** at 22 Drury Lane (Tel: 836-5705) and **Lal Qila**, at 117 Tottenham Court Road (Tel: 387-4570). All are moderately priced and offer North Indian cuisine. At the **Bombay Brasserie** adjoining Bailey's Hotel on Courtfield Close (140 Gloucester Road in South Kensington), the decor is impressively colonial in style—chandeliers, ferns, a conservatory, paddle fans, and a white piano. You can sample food from all over India; here, as at many Indian restaurants, the buffet lunches are good value. Tel: 370-4040.

For inexpensive South Indian dishes in simple surroundings it is hard to beat a new arrival, the **Ragam**, at 57 Cleveland Street, which runs parallel to and west of Charlotte Street. Tel: 636-9098.

Far Eastern

London's Chinatown is in Soho. Most of London's best Chinese restaurants are here, south of Shaftesbury Avenue on and around Gerrard Street. **Fung Shing** on nearby Lisle Street (Tel: 437-1539) and **Wong Kei** on Wardour Street (Tel: 437-8408) are authentic old-school Cantonese establishments where you can eat cheaply and well.

You can get some of London's best wind-dried food (a Chinese process of hanging out food to dry naturally) at the ever-popular **Poon's** at 4 Leicester Street (Tel: 437-1528) as well as at the vast **Chuen Cheng Ku**, 17 Wardour Street (Tel: 437-3433), and **New World**, on Gerrard Place (Tel: 437-0396). **Yung's** on Wardour Street is open from 4:00 P.M. until 4:00 A.M. (Tel: 437-4986).

London's first formal Chinese restaurant was Ken Lo's **Memories of China** on Ebury Street, Victoria (Tel: 730-7734). A second branch, **Memories of China Chelsea**, overlooks the boats in Chelsea Harbour and, unlike most other Chinese restaurants, offers a menu that roams the regions, an inexpensive brasserie, and Sunday brunch. You can arrive by river boat (from the Embankment) or approach by land via Lots Road. Two floors, with "Ming dynasty" gold and blue decor. Tel: 352-4953.

For beautifully presented Chinese food and a backdrop of water cascading down the walls, try **Zen** in Chelsea Cloisters on Sloane Avenue (Tel: 589-1781) or **Zen Central** at 20 Queen Street off Curzon Street in Mayfair (Tel: 629-8089). Both are moderately priced and attract a fashionable clientele, including Chinese.

It's well worth the journey out to the Fulham Broadway for a meal at the **Blue Elephant** restaurant, almost opposite the Underground station at 4–6 Fulham Broadway. Here, in an exotic jungle of ferns and bamboo, an ever-smiling staff exquisitely presents moderately priced Thai dishes and beautifully sculpted fruit (Tel: 385-6595). Popular Thai restaurants in Soho are **Chiang Mai** at 48 Frith Street (closed Sunday lunch; Tel: 437-7444), and the rather gloomy **Bahn Thai**, almost opposite on the same road, where there is a choice of hundreds of dishes (Tel: 437-8504).

Some of London's most expensive Japanese restaurants are in the City near St. Paul's. **Miyama** on Godliman Street (Tel: 489-1937) caters to businesspeople on expense accounts and is closed on weekends. Elsewhere in London, the expensive **Suntory** at 72–73 St. James's Street (south of Piccadilly) is popular among discerning Japanese (Tel:

409-0201); the **Miyama** at 38 Clarges Street (closed Sundays and Saturday lunch; Tel: 499-2443) off Piccadilly near Green Park is much less expensive, especially at lunchtime; the prix-fixe meals at **Shiki Restaurant**, 27 Davies Street in Mayfair (closed on weekends; Tel: 409-0750), are also good value. The basement **Ikkyu**, 67 Tottenham Court Road near Goodge Street Underground station, is handy for shoppers. Closed Saturdays and Sunday lunch; Tel: 436-6169.

Mediterranean and Middle Eastern

The Lebanese **Al Hamra**, 31 Shepherd Market, Mayfair, offers sophisticated Middle Eastern fare. The tables are close together, so if you're not sure what to eat, follow the example of a neighboring diner. You are sure to be safe if you stick with the hot and cold starters (wiped up with pita bread) and the salads, which come in huge baskets and include plenty of chunky raw vegetables. Open until midnight every day. Tel: 493-1954. Insomniacs can find Middle Eastern solace and vegetarian comfort at **Al Maroush II**, 38 Beauchamp Place, off Brompton Road, until 4:30 A.M. (Tel: 581-5434), and at **Al Maroush**, 21 Edgware Road near Marble Arch, until 1:00 A.M. Tel: 723-0773. **Al Maroush III**, nearby at 62 Seymour Street, is open until 12:30 A.M. Tel: 724-5024. All are moderately priced.

Of Jewish places, there is no question which name reverberates most familiarly in kosher quarters: **Bloom's**. There are actually two, both at the heart of Jewish enclaves. In the East End, the waiters at Bloom's, 90 Whitechapel Road, dispense chicken soup and gefilte fish with the minimal grace that suggests they know they themselves are indispensable; Tel: 247-6001. In the Jewish residential headquarters, Golders Green, find the other Bloom's, 130 Golders Green Road, open 9:30 A.M. to 11:30 P.M., purveying *latkas* and pot roast. Inexpensive/moderate; Tel: (081) 455-3033.

Turkish cooking entered the consciousness of London diners when the **Topkapi**, 25 Marylebone High Street, won a Restaurant of the Year Award in 1984. They still celebrate the win with their chicken breast (secret recipe). The spitted *doner* kebab turning in the window and the row of tall-hatted Turkish chefs tell you that you've arrived; the long list of *mezeler* (hors d'oeuvres) and general theatricality of the bistro beyond communicate that you may as well settle in. Moderate; Tel: 486-1872.

Greek

Greek restaurants aren't currently in vogue in London, but the old standbys do a brisk business, among them the **White Tower,** 1 Percy Street, Tel: 636-8141 (closed weekends). The less expensive **Beotys,** 79 St. Martin's Lane (near the theaters) has been around for more than 40 years; it starts serving pre-theater dinners at 5:30 P.M. (closed Sundays; Tel: 836-8768). For a livelier atmosphere you can watch plates being thrown around and dance on the tables in **Anemos,** 32 Charlotte Street; Tel: 636-2289. Still lively but a bit less raucous is the crowded and candlelit **Kalamaras** on Inverness Mews, an alley behind Queensway, in the area just north of Hyde Park. This is authentic Greek food, not Cypriot, as in most of the city's "Greek" restaurants; open until midnight. Closed Sundays and at lunch; Tel: 727-9122.

American

If you're in the mood for a special hamburger, the place to go is the **Hard Rock Café,** at the Hyde Park Corner end of Old Park Lane—that is, if you can stand loud music and don't mind sharing a table or lining up to get in. In Soho, **Ed's Easy Diner,** a small, neon-lit café wedged into the corner of Old Compton Street and Moor Street, serves quick, sit-at-the-chrome-counter, 100 percent additive-free burgers and soda. In the jukeboxes on the counter, 5p buys 1950s rock and roll. There is also a branch on the King's Road at number 362. **Joe Allen's,** in a brick basement at 13 Exeter Street just behind Covent Garden, livens up with a theatrical crowd late at night; Tel: 836-0651. The **Rock Island Diner** on the top floor of the London Pavilion at Piccadilly Circus is a huge 1950s-style eatery with a Chevy suspended over the bar. The DJ plays period music, there's sometimes a roller-skating mâitre d', and food is of the meatloaf and steak-sandwich variety, plus milkshakes and cocktails. Open seven days a week, 11:00 A.M. to 11:30 P.M. No need to reserve ahead, but you may have to stand in line. All the above are inexpensive. Definitely expensive, however, is **Christopher's—The American Grill,** opened in 1992 by an Englishman with a passion for New England food, so that Maine lobster, clam chowder, and "New England Boiled Dinner" of salt beef and vegetables are permanent features on the menu (18 Wellington Street; Tel: 240-4222).

Italian

Orso at 27 Wellington Street in Covent Garden is currently trendy. Decorated in 1930s style and sister to Joe Allen's, its regularly changing menu includes pizzas and pasta. Open noon to midnight; Tel: 240-5269. Rivaling it in popularity is the inexpensive **Cibo** at 3 Russell Gardens (off Holland Road—use the Kensington Olympia Underground station), with authentic peasant food served against a backdrop of modern art. Tel: 371-6271; closed Sunday evenings.

It's well worth the journey to the **River Café**, Thames Wharf, Rainville Road, between Putney and Hammersmith bridges. Converted from an old warehouse, it has splendid Thames views, simple, white decor, and authentic regional Italian food with the emphasis on Tuscany. The proprietors even grow their own herbs. The menu changes twice daily, and you can dine outside in summer. Open weekdays for lunch and dinner, for lunch only on weekends, with last orders at 9:30 P.M. Inexpensive; Tel: 381-8824 or 385-3344.

At **Kettners**, a reasonably priced eatery in Soho at 29 Romilly Street, you may feel like lingering longer. Despite the refined Edwardian atmosphere, though, Kettners is actually a branch of Pizza Express, and it serves hamburgers, too. The Champagne bar, a fashionable Soho meeting place, is open until 11 P.M. There is a cocktail pianist every evening and on Thursdays and Fridays at lunch; reservations not accepted.

Going up in price: **San Lorenzo**, just past Harrods at 22 Beauchamp Place, attracts a steady band of devotees (including the rich, the royal, and the famous) who eat pasta among the potted plants (closed Sundays; Tel: 584-1074). **Santini**, at 29 Ebury Street near Victoria Station, attracts businesspeople at lunch. It is quiet and airy, and the menu hovers around specialties of the Veneto; Tel: 730-4094. The owners' newest restaurant, the fashionable and moderately priced **L'Incontro** at 87 Pimlico Road, also specializes in dishes of the Veneto. There is a pianist every evening except Sundays. Closed Sunday lunch; Tel: 730-3663.

Scandinavian

You can get an authentic lunchtime Scandinavian smorgasbord in the comfortable **Causerie** at Claridge's, where you may find yourself in the company of royalty. Closed Saturdays; lunch from noon to 3:00 P.M., dinner from 5:30

to 11:00 P.M. Also has pre- and post-theater menus. Expensive; Tel: 629-8860.

Eclectic

Several London restaurants include English dishes on an eclectic menu. One of London's most accomplished yet modest chefs is Alastair Little, who runs a stylized, simple, monochrome café to which he's given his name. With its black lacquered tables, bright lighting, and rather stark decor, at first glance **Alastair Little's**, on Soho's Frith Street, looks like a Japanese restaurant. Actually, you might get something vaguely Chinese from the menu . . . or French, or Danish, or British: whatever takes the chef's fancy. Little changes his menu twice daily, and his imaginative dishes are recognized as being some of the most exciting in London. Lunch from 12:30 to 2:30 P.M.; dinner from 7:30 to 11:30 P.M. Closed Saturday lunch and Sundays. There's also a small downstairs bar (no reservations accepted for dinner) for fish, including sushi, and cold dishes. No credit cards. Expensive; Tel: 734-5183.

Sutherlands, on neighboring Lexington Street, is more formal than Little's: a tiny, serious, stylish restaurant on street level, serving some of the best food in London. Tel: 434-3401. Closed Saturday lunch and all day Sunday and Monday.

Clarke's at 124 Kensington Church Street also takes its name from its enterprising owner. You don't get a choice on the evening menu (you do at lunchtime), but don't let that put you off. Whatever comes out of the basement kitchen (which you can view from the dining room) is good. The menu roams through Italy, France, and California, although Sally Clarke also regularly offers English cottage-made cheeses and homegrown vegetables and fruits. The menu changes nightly; closed weekends. Moderate; Tel: 221-9225.

Renowned chef Simon Hopkinson, who has no patience with nouvelle cuisine, is at the helm of the spacious, bright dining room of **Bibendum**, on the first floor of the Michelin Building on Fulham Road. Elegant and fashionable, Bibendum attracts serious food lovers and celebrities. The menu is mostly expensive (though lunch is more of a bargain—try the fish and chips) and spans France, Italy, and Britain. Tel: 581-5817.

South of the Thames and a bit off the beaten track, **Harvey's** at 2 Bellevue Road, overlooking Wandsworth Common, is an outstanding restaurant owned by the talented chef Marco Pierre White, who offers inspired food at moderate prices, especially at lunchtime. Worth travelling out of your way for. Closed Sunday and Monday. Tel: (081) 672-0114.

Early and Late

Apart from brasseries, which serve meals all day, most London restaurants don't start serving until 7:30 P.M. and stop at 11:00 P.M., so you have to make plans if you want to eat before or after the theater, unless you fancy Chinese or other ethnic food (many places for which are open after midnight).

Some theaters and concert halls have their own restaurants. These include **Ovations**, with meals before and after performances in the South Bank complex (Tel: 928-3531), the Mermaid, the Barbican, the Palace Theatre, the Young Vic in Lambeth, and the Camden Arts Centre. Theater meals can be inexpensive, though there is scope enough in their menus to build up an impressive bill. Many theaters have sandwiches and coffee available in the bar, and the Royal Opera House offers moderately priced buffets when the curtain comes down.

In Covent Garden, the French **Café du Jardin** at 28 Wellington Street serves a pre- and post-theater supper from 5:30 to 11:30 P.M. Royal Opera House patrons, rather more formally attired than the rest of the clientele, wander in clutching their programs, and waiters wend their way between tables balancing trays of Cognac. Sit at ground level to be seen, downstairs to get on with it. The food, though inexpensive, is as erratic as the service. Tel: 836-8769.

Magno's, around the corner on Long Acre, is rather more formal but also relatively inexpensive, and its pre-theater menu of simple, quick dishes that change weekly is an especially good buy. Closed Sundays; Tel: 836-6077.

Rules, at 35 Maiden Lane, just north of the Strand, serves traditional English food in a decor to match and is open from noon to midnight. Moderate; Tel: 836-5314.

The **Savoy Grill**, in the famous luxury hotel off the Strand, is within walking distance to the theaters and offers a moderate to expensive pre-theater menu. After the show, you can go back for dessert and coffee in the Thames Foyer. Jackets and ties are required in both places. Closed Sundays; Tel: 836-4343. If you don't meet the dress code at the Grill, **Upstairs at the Savoy** will serve you relatively inexpensive snacks, oysters, Champagne, and vintage wines by the glass noon to midnight weekdays and 5:00 P.M. to midnight Saturdays (closed Sundays). You can sit at the marble counter or at one of the tables along a narrow corridor, from which you have a fascinating view of arrivals at the front entrance. They also offer a breakfast buffet on weekdays (8:00 to 10:00 A.M.).

One of London's best-loved oyster and Champagne bars, **Green's**, at 36 Duke Street in St. James's (near Jermyn Street), starts serving at 5:30 P.M. The atmosphere is formal (regulars include royalty) but some of the traditional English dishes, including kedgeree and bangers and mash, most certainly aren't. Moderate to expensive. Closed Sundays; Tel: 930-4566.

Le Caprice, on Arlington Street in Mayfair, is open from 6:00 P.M. to midnight daily, even on public holidays, as is Kensington Place (see Brasseries, above). **The Causerie** at Claridge's has an early buffet supper from 5:30 P.M. You can get reasonably priced snacks at **Fields**, a huge restaurant/coffee bar in the crypt of St. Martin-in-the-Fields church (near Charing Cross Station) until 8:30 P.M.

The **Terrace Garden** at the Meridien, Piccadilly, is open every day from 7:00 A.M. to 11:30 P.M. for an inexpensive breakfast, lunch, dinner, a light French snack, or tea. In this spectacular conservatory overlooking Piccadilly, a pianist plays most evenings.

Across the river on the South Bank, **RSJ**, behind the National Theatre at 13A Coin Street, is a restaurant in a converted hayloft offering imaginative French dishes. Prix-fixe menu or à la carte. Open for lunch and from 6:00 P.M. with last orders at 11:00 P.M.; closed Sundays. Moderate; Tel: 928-4554.

—Susan Grossman and Alex Hamilton

PUBS AND BARS

PUBS

Publicans know a lot about beer, rather less about spirits, and hardly anything about wine, which probably reflects the proportions they sell of each. The majority of pubs are owned by breweries, giving them an overwhelming influence on the pub's stock, appearance, and staff. "Tied houses," as they are known, principally sell the beers from the brewery that owns them. The rest, offering a fine miscellany, are known as "free houses."

A recent change in the law allows pubs to set their own open hours between 11:00 A.M. and 11:00 P.M., except on Sundays, when hours are reduced to 12:00 to 3:00 P.M. and 7:00 to 10:30 P.M. The practical effect, born of competition, is that most pubs feel obliged to stay open all that time, and the round-the-clock drinker can seem as much a fixture as the sign warning minors (under 18) off alcohol.

There are between 5,000 and 6,000 pubs to serve London. The visitor should be aware that some popular pub names are adopted many times over. In London there were at last count 25 pubs called the King's Head and 12 the Queen's Head; there are 22 Railway Taverns; the emblem of spring, the Green Man, is used 19 times. Likewise the George, the Coach and Horses, the Crown, the Rising Sun, the Red Lion, and the Blue Posts are each to be found in all sorts of incarnations. So, in asking directions or instructing a taxi, it is wise not only to give the name of the pub but also to specify the street.

Beer drinkers keen to extend their knowledge can do so in the **Sun**, opposite the Children's Hospital on Great Ormond Street in Holborn, which has the largest selection of cask-conditioned ales in the world—187 at the last tally, with oddities such as Oy Vay, weissbier (a grain), Merrie Monk, and Old Scrap Cyder. (An early evening tour of the 1688 cellar to see how beers are prepared can be arranged by calling the landlord; Tel: 405-8278.)

Pubs change, if slowly. Fine summers prompt the managements to set out tables and chairs on the sidewalks in Continental style. The big difference in London, though, is the gradual blurring of distinctions between the plush saloon bar and the more basic and lower-priced public bar.

Central London

Just as time begins for the British at Greenwich, so distances are measured from Trafalgar Square. (The precise center of the universe is the statue of Charles I at the entrance to Whitehall.) Appropriately, one of the pubs against which others could measure themselves can be found at one of its corners, where St. Martin's Lane leaves it, a dart's throw from the statue of poor Edith Cavell, shot as a spy in 1915. This is the **Chandos**—spacious, good beer, quick service, and a slightly more dashing menu than most that includes such items as beef olives, steak-and-pepper pie, and smoked mackerel. The pub is very much a meeting point, with six ground-floor cubicles, like little chapels with their stained-glass windows looking onto the square, and the Opera Lounge upstairs (the English National Opera is housed a few doors up the road), with deep leather armchairs and blessed freedom from Muzak.

Farther up St. Martin's Lane, past an eclectic shopping alley called Cecil Court, which travellers should note as the collectors' hub for original Baedeker guides, are two curious places. The **Green Man & French Horn** is very long and thin, like a cul-de-sac with a ceiling, the result of joining two pubs together. Victorian prints on the walls here illustrate the gloomy story of the decline of a drunkard and his family. Opposite, the **Salisbury** is much more ample, an island bar set in an ocean of rococo decoration and kitsch.

Among the plethora of pubs around Piccadilly Circus and the great shopping arteries (the electronics of Tottenham Court Road, the rag trade and shoe leather of Oxford Street, and the travel, fashion, ceramics, and silver of Regent Street) it is hard to finger many of real distinction. But there are a few shining exceptions. On Beak Street, on the Soho (east) side of Regent Street, the **Old Coffee House**, with its burnished brass and copper fittings, comfortable furniture, and crimson carpet, has a relaxed ethos and an amiable staff serving a wide range of bottled and hand-pumped beers.

Carnaby Street, that magnesium flare of the Swinging Sixties, offers the **Shakespeare's Head** at the corner of Great Marlborough Street, with wooden floors, good hot food, and an upstairs restaurant, but otherwise nothing to write home about. In Soho, choose the **Dog & Duck** on Bateman Street (a small street between Dean and Greek streets). Go not for food but for the company of the flotsam and jetsam of bohemian society, a contrast with the monogrammed gear of the staff. Small and rowdy, the D & D has an upstairs snug (a small private room) with saucy cartoons and postcards and cozy casement tables from which to look down on the street action. The **French House** on Dean Street, with a somewhat raffish clientele and a staff that knows more about wine than most, has a reputation that dates from World War II, when it was the off-duty rendezvous of the Free French Forces in Britain.

If you penetrate the hinterland north of Oxford Street into Marylebone, you will see great swarms of young office workers drinking on the sidewalks, men and women alike in uniform charcoal-gray suiting, gathered like colonies of seals outside such places as the **Lamb & Flag** on the corner of James and Barrett streets.

But the year-round special in Marylebone is the **Prince Regent** on Marylebone High Street. The portrait of the prince himself is a complete fantasy, not the corpulent Prinny we think of but a handsome Young Lochinvar. The pub has a strong miscellany of local regulars, drinking under cartoons and prints, and enjoying its celebrated collection of cheese dishes.

And on cobbled Weymouth Mews, parallel to Portland Place, is one of the oldest pubs in London, the **Dover Castle**, a coaching inn where horses were changed on the first stage from the City en route to Oxford. The lounge and pleasant back room of this house are very busy at lunch and early evening with a crowd of media, design, and advertising people. After 25 years, a change of management at the **Queen's Head**, on the corner of Wheatley and Westmoreland in the Marylebone district, opposite the old Heart Hospital, has freshened up this attractive small pub, which succeeds in the art of being lively and unpretentious, busy but relaxed.

Go east from Tottenham Court Road and cross Gower Street to find the **Museum Tavern**, standing opposite the British Museum on Great Russell Street. With so many scholars and literati restoring their parched gray cells here, plus the pub's eccentric practice of serving afternoon tea, it is not surprising that a neighboring publisher has produced an account of its history, which dates from 1723.

Heading north and east across Southampton Row, stop for a quick one at the **Queen's Larder** in the alley leading into Queen Square (there are hospitals of all sorts in this area and therefore doctors and nurses too) on the way to the always fashionable **Lamb** on Lamb's Conduit Street, where you'll find hospital people at midday, theater people at night. Brass rails around the tables stop the drinks from falling off; strange, old pivoting panels at the bar were apparently devised to prevent the staff from hearing private conversations. A rare feature is a nonsmokers' cubbyhole. On the walls are rows of faded sepia pictures of theatrical divinities, with Hogarth prints and *Vanity Fair* cartoons.

The City
A jungle by day, a desert by night, the City has always had different hours and rules for its pubs—and its own police

force to see them observed. The tendency is to close by 8:00 P.M., and not to open at all on weekends. In the shorter time frame, however, the old, heavy-beamed pubs like **Olde Wine Shades** on Martin Lane and **Ye Olde Mitre** on Ely Place off Holborn Circus do brisk enough business with the stockbrokers, financiers, and conveyancers to compensate. The beer fancier curious to know what happens when a pub brews its own stuff can try the **Market Porter** on Stoney Street south of the Thames across London Bridge and off Borough High Street.

This last pub's name suggests the great wholesale food markets that once pulsed within the City precincts and enjoyed special indulgences for thirsty early-morning traders. The last significant example of these, still on its original site, is the Central Market, which has stood at Smithfield since the tenth century. The license to operate from 5:30 A.M. is still exercised by some pubs here; two in particular are recommended for the opportunity for lively, humorous trader talk and a hearty breakfast with ale. The **Cock Tavern** is in a basement down steps from the second archway; the **Fox & Anchor** is adjacent to the entry to serene Charterhouse Square. Market porters critical of the beef served in local cafés have sometimes taken their own steak in to fry, but that is not necessary in the Fox & Anchor.

The southern neighbors of Smithfield are St. Bartholomew, London's busiest hospital, and the Old Bailey, the central criminal court. Opposite St. Bart's is the **White Hart**, a serviceable and friendly establishment. The **Magpie & Stump**, formerly a ferment of gossip and good low-life stories spun by a clientele composed largely of lawyers and journalists, was dissolved in redevelopment for three years but has emerged in renewed, smart guise in a corner of a giant new building, still opposite the Bailey, still ready to lubricate wagging tongues.

A find north of Smithfield is the **Crown**, a 17th-century inn on an attractive small square called Clerkenwell Close. The square's great feature is the Marx Memorial Library, a mass of socialist literature from seething tracts and compassionate novels to stolid economic analysis assembled to honor the author of *Das Kapital,* who labored at the British Library nearby on his seminal work. Apparently apolitical, the pub nevertheless still separates the plusher saloon area from the public bar; it also has a backroom restaurant.

Chelsea

The King's Road and those that lead off it are well provided with pubs. The **Chelsea Potter**, a great source for the gossip columnists, has a very young clientele that chatter like starlings, though the pub is so dark it looks closed from the outside.

The Six Bells by the Town Hall (on the King's Road) has been renamed **Henry J. Bean's** ("But his friends all call him Hank") and transformed into a cocktail zoo with heavy-metal sounds, fast food, and fancy drinks. The hundreds of customers in this grand old barn average age 19, but the big garden in the rear remains a great, if crowded, romantic asset. At the **Cadogan Arms** on the corner of Old Church Street you'll find another young and lively but less frantic crowd, a jeans-and-sweaters bunch swarming on split levels. From here on east the pubs have lately taken to offering breakfast from 9:00 A.M. and sometimes earlier—the full-scale bacon, eggs, sausage, tomato, toast, and marmalade meal. At the end is the **Man in the Moon**, a free house with heavy maroon drapes, caramel-colored lighting, throbbing music, and its own theater club upstairs (see Fringe Theater, below).

WINE BARS

The closer association of Britain with Continental Europe has not yet, from the wine drinker's point of view, had any very noticeable effect on prices, but the reductions must surely come when the European Community drops trade barriers. Knowledge and appreciation of wines and places dedicated to their drinking have already improved, resulting in an increase in the number of wine bars, which have been taking some business away from the pubs.

The expansion has had two styles: the masculine and the contemporary. The older is the masculine manner, leaning heavily on tradition and characterized by oak beams and counters like ramparts, clumsy, comfortable furniture—big casks often standing in for tables—a sprinkling of sawdust on the stone floors, typically, a full-dress battalion of high-quality Champagnes such as Veuve Clicquot, and a cumulus cloud of cigar smoke. Many of the best examples of this are to be found among the 40 owned by Davys, as well as among the chain run by Balls Brothers. There is naturally a strong concentration in the City, among which the **Bottlescrue** in Bath House on

High Holborn, the **Pulpit** on Worship Street (north of the Liverpool Street station), and the **Boot and Flogger** on Redcross Way (in Southwark south of the Thames) provide a dark and dignified atmosphere suitable for conversation about the bottom line.

The ancestor of them all is the **Olde Wine Shades**, on Martin Lane off Cannon Street, opened in 1663 and the only such establishment to survive the Great Fire three years later. Its owners run another, even more celebrated, place, **El Vino's** on Fleet Street, which proffers a similar choice of fine wines, Port, and Sherries drawn from a great parade of casks. Although the national newspapers are now scattered away from Fleet Street, something of the former mood persists, with old fire-brigade journalists reminiscing about their best stories. The rule here barring women has been abrogated, but it is still preferred that women sit at a table rather than stand at the bar and wear skirts rather than trousers. The dress rule for men at the Olde Wine Shades and El Vino's is particularly strict: In the absence of jacket and tie you will be asked to leave. (A few doors down, opposite the ancient and also vinous **Olde Cheshire Cheese** pub, is a Tie Rack shop.)

An entrepreneurial New Zealander, Don Hewitson, has established himself with a slightly lighter version of this style, putting French art posters on the walls and white cloths on the tables, and offering tasty meals at around £10. His little empire comprises **Shampers** on Soho's Kingly Street (parallel to Carnaby Street); the **Cork and Bottle**, in a cramped basement on Cranbourn Street (the continuation of Long Acre near Covent Garden); and the much ampler flagship, the award-winning **Methuselah's** on Victoria Street, which is much liked by younger people (and not merely the trendies).

The contemporary style in wine bars has had a variable pattern, shifting to adapt to designer-fashion currents, merging at the one end with restaurants, like the Soho Brasserie, at the other with cocktail bars like the Long Island Iced Tea Shop on Cranbourn Street, or with tourist-oriented places that have exotic themes, such as the Spanish *tapas* bar whirl of **Brahms and Liszt** in Covent Garden. Generally they do not serve beer but offer a wide range of wines, among them French, Alsatian, German, Italian, Spanish, and occasionally Australian vintages, with prices starting at £7 a bottle and commonplace Champagnes at £17 to £20.

There is no such phenomenon in London as the American singles bar scene, but it is fair to say that some, like **Le Cochonnet** in outlying Maida Vale (northwest of Paddington), which has a wine list as long as a telephone directory, are chummier than others. Among a relaxed miscellany that stand out for amiability are **Morgan's** on Soho's Ganton Street, for its reasonably priced meals and a barman with both a genuine delight in wine lore and a wish to lead his patrons in the right direction; **Volkers**, handily sited on the Haymarket, for its excellent stock and the unique opportunity to drink pink Champagne from a bottle clamped in a pewter cuirass while you are sitting at the bar on a copper milk churn filled with Champagne corks; and **The Metro** by Clapham Common Underground station, a great meeting point with a glass roof like a conservatory's that the neighborhood cats frequent.

COCKTAIL BARS
American bars and cocktail bars are as close to being synonymous in the British mind as Coke and Pepsi. An excellent choice with discretion and style, where a woman on her own may pause without discomfort, is the bar in **Brown's Hotel** on Albemarle Street. On the same wavelength, with senior barmen who know what goes into a daiquiri or a Tom Collins, a whiskey sour or a planter's punch, are the nookeries of **Durrant's** on George Street in Marylebone, the **Connaught** on Carlos Place in Mayfair, and, through a door on an inner courtyard off St. James's Street, the **Stafford** on St. James's Place—all have the pukka tone (meaning they're first-class).

The dazzling white counter and Art Deco of the **Savoy Bar** conjures up the spirit of 60 years ago, when the creative barman Harry Craddock developed and expanded the cocktail range way beyond the confines of its original definition—a concoction of any spirit with water, sugar, and bitters. The period design persists, though the menu lacks imaginative spring. Nevertheless, with its Champagne cocktails, sharp old-fashioneds, Moscow mules, and some knockouts like the brandy Alexander and the black Russian for nightcaps, the Savoy keeps the faith. Expect to find similar standards at the Ritz and Claridge's.

The luxurious old favorites just mentioned have their counterparts in new branches of several chain hotels—the Hilton, by the BBC on Portland Place, which opened in 1991 as the Langham; the Mayfair; and St. George's Hotel, opposite the new Hilton, with a bar on the 15th floor high above the spire of All Souls Church—but the character of the bars in these latter-day establishments fluctuates with the changing tides of customers.

Vogue curiosities include the basement art gallery effect of **Freud's** at the High Holborn end of Shaftesbury Avenue and—a common phenomenon—the bar that suddenly changes its style on the whim of the owner, one example being **Efes II**, formerly the Manhattan, on Great Portland Street. The bar now looks down on a kebab restaurant. It still serves the cocktail that has lately been mandatory, and after which another busy house on Cranbourn Street, with live music, has renamed itself: the **Long Island Iced Tea Shop**.

—*Alex Hamilton*

ENTERTAINMENT AND NIGHTLIFE

THEATER

Periodic crises threaten to darken one theater or another as developers encroach or the art houses find their subsidy inadequate even when they are booked solid. Not too long ago the old Savoy was burned out. Nonetheless, nearly 50 commercial playhouses soldier on. The **Royal Shakespeare Company** performs in the Barbican complex in the City, home also of the London Symphony Orchestra. The **Royal National Theatre** in the South Bank Arts Centre comprises three separate stages: The whole complex includes the Royal Festival Hall, Queen Elizabeth Hall, the National Film Theatre, and the Museum of the Moving Image. And that other stalwart of the classical repertory, the **Old Vic**, lies just south of Waterloo Bridge. The vehicle of much serious modern work, the **Royal Court Theatre**, dominates Sloane Square in Chelsea. In the summer, defying the vagaries of the weather, the **Open-Air Theatre** in Regent's Park has mounted a Shakespeare repertory season every year for 60 years. The citadels of entertainment are **Drury Lane Theatre** (musicals) and the **London Palladium** in Soho (celebrity shows). Wembley Stadium is the venue not only for major sporting events but also for gigantic concerts by rock stars and other popular performers.

Newspaper listings are rarely comprehensive enough to satisfy either cinema or theatergoers. Better service is provided by three weekly guide magazines: *Time Out* (the best, published every Wednesday), *What's On* (Wednesday), and *City Limits* (Thursday); these publications also include information on productions at outlying theaters.

The largest ticket-selling organization in Britain, for live events and sporting occasions as well as theater, is the Keith Prowse agency, a victim of recession in 1991 after 200 years of trading, but restored now as a property of Wembley Holdings, which gives them access to major pop concerts and sporting events as well. For half-price tickets (plus booking fee) to same-day performances in West End theaters with seats to spare, apply to the **ticket booth on Leicester Square** between 2:30 P.M. and 6:30 P.M. Ticket limit of four seats per customer; cash only. Turning this half-price idea on its head, a charity venture with impeccable theatrical sponsorship, **West End Cares**, sells tickets at twice their face value for the best seats in the house at sold-out smash hits (Tel: 976-6751). Between 11:00 A.M. and 6:00 P.M. **Theatre Tonight** makes late bookings at major West End theaters without extra charge (Tel: 753-0333).

Fringe Theater

Innumerable elements make up the lively phenomenon of the London fringe theater: one-act plays, satirical revues, stand-up comedy, bravura solo acts, dramas that passionately argue political causes, expressionistic shows with no discernible argument, a local playwright working the parish pump, and a foreign import in translation for the first time. The fringe is a sprawling network that includes the by-products of established theaters near the middle of town, like the **Theatre Upstairs**, part of the Royal Court Theatre on Chelsea's Sloane Square, as well as very successful venues that, properly speaking, are not in London at all, like the **Warehouse** at Croydon, which has a strong attraction for London audiences.

Among the many, some of which have a transient, fitful career, half a dozen are worth distinguishing. In Islington they are the **King's Head** and the **Old Red Lion**; in Hammersmith the **Lyric Studio**; in Chelsea, at the far end of the King's Road from the Royal Court, the **Man in the Moon**; at Shepherd's Bush Green the **Bush**; and in

Notting Hill the **Gate**. One of the longest-established fringe theaters with a consistently high standard is the **New End** in Hampstead.

The Gate is particularly loved by the critics for its habit of introducing unknown foreign plays, but as a rule fringe managements do not have settled policies of commitment and prefer a varied diet. However, the **Drill Hall** in Camden prides itself on supporting gay and lesbian culture, and the **Tricycle** in Brent on backing new plays by black and Irish writers. The fact that many are advertised as clubs does not often limit entry. Election to membership can generally be achieved almost instantaneously, and the fee is rarely a serious deterrent. Comfortable seating is not the strong point of such theaters; people like them who are interested in discovering new talent and in enjoying the camaraderie that can form in their casual atmosphere.

Children's Theater

Aside from the pre-Christmas season when the playhouses break out in a rash of pantomimes, not a great deal is done on the London stage for children. However, a few specialists fill their schedules with a range that runs from classics to mixed-media entertainments involving slides, film, modern rap, and music hall. The principal pillars are the **Unicorn Theatre** at Great Newport Street (September through June) and the **Polka** on the Broadway, Wimbledon, the only theater in Britain designed specifically for children. The **Little Angel Marionette Theatre**, on Dagmar Passage off Cross Street in Islington, puts on performances for the very young as well as older kids, and in the same line there is the **Puppet Theatre Barge**, moored in Little Venice. Some public libraries have also taken to putting on children's shows, notably Willesden Green Library. Children's cinema, incidentally, can be found at the Barbican. **Theatre Line** advises on the availability of children's shows on the day of performance (Tel: 0836-43-09-63).

CLASSICAL MUSIC, BALLET, AND OPERA

From cinema to theater to concert hall to opera house the prices rise in geometric progression, and at the top end patrons could feel themselves under pressure to make a commensurately heavy investment in their personal wardrobes. However, neither tickets nor clothes need be too extravagant in the "gods," or highest seats, of the showcase of opera, the **Royal Opera House**, Covent Garden (but demand heavily exceeds supply). The classic repertory is sung in translation at the London Coliseum on St. Martin's Lane, home of the **English National Opera**. Both of these regularly include ballet in their schedules, but the heart of the balletomane lies in **Sadler's Wells**, a cultural enclave as remote as a desert fort at the northern end of Rosebery Avenue north of Farringdon Road in Islington (it can be reached on the number 38 bus from Piccadilly; the nearest Underground stop is the Angel).

The principal concert halls are those in the **South Bank Arts Centre**: Purcell Room, Queen Elizabeth Hall, and Royal Festival Hall, overlooking the River Thames. There is also the **Royal Albert Hall** in Kensington (where the annual Promenade Concerts are held) and the **Barbican Arts Centre** in the City. At the same level of intimacy as the Purcell, the **Wigmore Hall** on Wigmore Street in the Marylebone district schedules recitals and chamber music. In the summer, St. John's in Smith Square, off Millbank, offers a huge daily variety of lunchtime and evening recitals and concerts.

Also in summer, open-air concerts, some with fireworks, are held by the lake on the grounds of **Kenwood House** on Hampstead Heath. Take a blanket, a thick sweater, and picnic (proper plates and glasses, please). No other prescriptions on dress are needed for audiences of serious music; the majority of listeners at the great concert halls tend to dress formally but not competitively.

JAZZ

London is not Copenhagen or Chicago for jazz. **Ronnie Scott** seems to have propped it up in his club on Soho's Frith Street since almost before the big band became obsolete, distributing the foreign strains through an unrivaled sequence of eminent player-guests (Tel: 439-0747). More recently arrived, but thoroughly established among addicts for its nightly variety as well as quality, are the **Bass Clef** on Coronet Street, Islington, and the **100 Club** at 100 Oxford Street. After the **Pizza Express** on Dean Street and the **Dover Street Wine Bar**, the dilettante is clutching at straws of the Sunday Jazz Brunch at the Hotel Russell kind, which must be a contradiction in terms, but farther out there are a couple of good jazz pubs, the **Bull's Head** at Barnes, a Thames-side district in the west of London, and the **Prince of Orange** on the Mile End Road. Some 25 years ago Philip Larkin suggested that as jazz increasingly became a composer's art, it would move from the club to the concert hall, but that transition has not yet been realized in London.

The newly developed complex at Chelsea Harbour by the Thames has been encouraging jazz on weekends, but until the Harbour itself gathers strength, it's likely to remain a thin strain.

DISCOS AND LIVE MUSIC

Believe no disco recommendation until you're in. Being admitted to a disco is generally a matter of matching its style and paying its admission price, but in the case of a few, whose attraction for an older set is their exclusivity, introduction by a member is needed and a hefty entrance fee is exacted. When a place makes it into print, one part of the crowd is ready to say it's history. **Annabel's**, on Berkeley Square, has lasted a few years and is entitled to be called semi-permanent. It is notorious for its undisco-like patrons, entry fee of £25, and annual membership (via an introduction) of £500. **Stringfellow's** on Upper St. Martin's Lane is another place for the affluent, with a £300–£1,000 annual membership, and nonmembers introduced at £8–£15 per session.

Coming off this high plateau, the **Café de Paris** on Coventry Street (off Piccadilly Circus) and the **Hippodrome** on Charing Cross Road seem to get the most repeat business, and kind words for their music and pace. The **Hammersmith Palais** has been here forever, opening at least 20 years before Granddad came here to jive during World War II; now restyled, it is a good, modern disco near the Hammersmith Broadway tube station. The **Wag Club** on Soho's Wardour Street has a truly young crowd at the leading edge of streetwise.

But, while **Gossips** on Dean Street in Soho, **Limelight** on Shaftesbury Avenue, and the cheerfully extroverted biggie on Leicester Square, the **Empire Ballroom**, all have their regulars and deserve them, some of the best disco action is a movable feast, like the crap games immortalized by Damon Runyon. Look for the strangely dressed sidewalk line, buzzing with anxiety as they hope to impress the men at the door with their street smarts and rightness for this evening's session.

Country-and-western music has its own special havens, most often arts centers or pubs like the **King's Head** out at Crouch End (in north London beyond Islington), the **White Horse** at Hampstead, and the **Swan** at Stockwell (south of the river and east of Clapham). Its temple is the old Art Deco **Astoria Theatre** on Charing Cross Road, where people can also dance on the two floors that once were the stalls and the dress circle.

CLUBS, CABARET, AND CASINOS

The term "clubs" covers a multitude of sins and, no doubt, as many virtues. There are three main types, in addition to the residential kind that are run by the social, political, sporting, and artistic networks of the country and are joined only through introductions, and then generally for life, such as the Oxford & Cambridge, the Travellers, White's (Tory politics), the Garrick (publishers and literary intellectuals), and the Caledonian (Scottish regiments).

The first kind of club is of the same caliber as those mentioned above but is open to all or has reciprocal arrangements with certain clubs overseas, such as the American Club in Piccadilly or the Royal Overseas League on St. James's Street. The Sloane Club on Sloane Street, Knightsbridge, was founded as a ladies-only club but now accepts men as well. Peter de Savary's St. James's Club is also unrestricted in its membership, but a night there can be as expensive as a life subscription to many other clubs.

The second kind of club is the nonresidential members' club, often with a restaurant and spacious bar, such as the Groucho Club, a media enclave on Dean Street, and the ad world's rendezvous, the Moscow Club on Frith Street. (If you want to join either of these you must be nominated by a member.)

The third kind usually switches on after nightfall. It may be quite demure, like the **Spanish Garden Club** off Maddox Street, or somewhat raunchy, like the **Pinstripe** on Beak Street, where drinks are served by topless French maids. Women accompanying men into cellar drinking clubs with topless entertainers such as are found in the **Gaslight Club** on Duke of York Street must be prepared for basilisk stares from the regulars.

Two clubs that depend on old-fashioned "glamour," with cabaret, sophisticated trappings for food and drink, and hostesses (but with an easy welcome for couples) are **Churchill's** by the Royal Academy in Piccadilly, and the **Director's Lodge** in Mason's Yard off St. James's. Both have erotic cabaret as a staple, but licensed striptease clubs with pretentions at a Continental level are few—girls with bodies that seem to have been turned on a lathe show them off on the stage of Raymond's durable **Revuebar** on Brewer Street in the 30-years-and-counting Festival of Erotica. The same Raymond also runs the adjoining **Madame Jo Jo's**, a campier and more louche venue.

The **Clubman's Club** on Albemarle Street (Tel: 493-4292) offers membership to selected clubs all over Britain for an annual subscription.

Casinos

The style of London gaming houses is quite unlike anywhere else. You must apply for membership 48 hours in advance, so don't leave a flutter until your eve of departure, and the dress code of suit and tie for men is strictly enforced. There are no cabaret and no drinks, nor tips at tables. The settings, however, are generally grand, the meals good, and the level of play interesting to international gamblers. The picture cards, so to speak, are **Crockford's** (Tel: 493-7771) and **Aspinall's** (Tel: 629-4400), both on Curzon Street. Less exalted but still useful cards are the **London Park Tower Casino** (Tel: 235-6161) and the hotel casinos of the Ritz and the Hilton.

There are some 20 casinos in London, and the **British Casino Association** (Tel: 437-0678) in Leicester House on Leicester Street will provide callers with venues, rules, and regulations.

DINNER AND DANCING

Ballroom dancing has become more of a sport or a hobby these days than a social accomplishment, but the traditional dance rhythms are still to be heard accompanying diners in the great hotels, particularly at the Savoy, the Ritz, and the Park Lane Hilton. However, there are a number of ethnic restaurants—Greek, Italian, Spanish, Portuguese—with small dance floors and live music where couples who are a little rusty on the steps and use a pump-handle action with their arms will not feel shamed by their performance. Among these are **Barbarella 2** (Italian) on Thurloe Street in South Kensington, **Costa Dorada** (Spanish) on Hanway Street in the West End, the **Grecian Taverna & Grill**, also in the West End, on Percy Street, and **Os Aquanos** (Portuguese) on Porchester Road in Bayswater. In the discos, Latin American rhythms such as the salsa and the samba, formerly the taste of more mature dancers, are now being discovered by the young.

THE RIVER

When the legendary stacks of gold coins of the working city are transformed by night into reflections on the river of the lights of the buildings, the Thames takes on a different character. Many people like to take a dinner cruise or hitch up to one of the many pubs that give on to the water. The stretch involved is essentially between Greenwich to the east and Kew Gardens to the west, and the cruise departure point is most often Westminster Pier. Which direction the boat travels varies and is generally the decision of the captain on the day. **Catamaran Cruises** sails into (or away from) the sunset every evening except Saturdays (Tel: 839-3572). **Romance of London** operates three-hour cruises only on Sundays (Tel: 620-0474). **Tidal Cruises** offers a disco with supper (Tel: 839-2164).

Because there is no company as yet that sets passengers down at any of the river pubs, you will have to reach them by road. Those that are particularly worth the effort include the 18th-century **Dove Inn** in the Upper Mall, an interesting walk beside lovely old houses between Hammersmith Bridge and Chiswick (the nearest Underground stations are Hammersmith and Ravenscourt Park); resonant with echoes of Dr. Johnson, the restored 18th-century **Anchor Inn**, itself replacing a 15th-century original, on the south bank of the Thames in Clink Street (next to Cannon Street railway bridge) between Southwark Bridge and London Bridge; and the medieval **George Inn** (just off the London Bridge end of Borough High Street), whose cobbled yard is the set for Morris dancing and Shakespearean plays (the nearest Underground station for both is London Bridge). On the opposite bank. **The Dickens Inn by the Tower**, beside St. Katharine's Dock, is a lively and popular place in this blossoming area.

GOING HOME

The last Underground trains run out of central London on weekdays at varying times between 11:30 P.M. and 1:00 A.M. (the Piccadilly Line) but midnight is the safer average, and 11:30 P.M. on Sundays. In the larger railway terminals the next day's newspapers begin to go on sale around 10:00 P.M.. Night buses use Trafalgar Square as their hub—look for the prefix N on the number and on the bus stop. (Note: The one-day and multizone London Transport bus passes are not valid on N buses.) About a third of London's 16,000 taxis are in action on the night shift, which is considered anything from 8:00 P.M. onward. The worst times for finding cabs are around 7:00 P.M. (when the day shift is going home and the night shift is not yet on the scene, and they are wanted by workers leaving the office and others going out to dinner and the theater) and 11:00 P.M., when there is a general exodus from theaters, pubs, and restaurants. But at 1:00 A.M. there is often quite a fair supply, particularly near bridges where cabs are coming back into the center (such as Parliament Square or the Aldwych). Oddly enough, although there is a small supplement after 8:00 P.M., the fare at night tends to be lower because of the relatively traffic-free streets. The law now requires passengers to use rear seat belts where provided. The police do not enforce this rigorously, but it is worth remembering that the penalty is £100.

—*Alex Hamilton*

SHOPS AND SHOPPING

London's wide and colorful array of shopping areas—each with its special sightseeing and dining possibilities—offers a very enjoyable, if expensive, experience. The city remains one of the world's great trading centers and many of its stores can boast, without exaggeration, "You name it, we sell it." Finding it and buying it may be quite another story, however.

Credit cards are widely accepted everywhere here except in street markets, but traveller's checks are not always welcome at the smaller shops. Most large stores have a system for foreign visitors to combat that blight on shopping, the unpopular 17.5 percent Value Added Tax (VAT) that is included in the selling price of most goods. Take your passport with you, fill in a form, get it stamped by Customs on departure (have the goods with you), and mail it back to the store where you bought the goods. It will then send you a refund. You should be aware that some stores set a minimum price below which the plan doesn't operate, usually about £200 for visitors from countries in the European Community and lower, around £40, for Americans. Always ask before you buy whether the store will ship or mail items to your home address without the VAT. Some very expensive items such as motor vehicles and boats are outside the scope of these various schemes; in these cases you'll want to consult the supplier about separate arrangements.

Recent additions are the Europe Tax-Free Shopping

booths at all terminals of London's Heathrow and Gatwick airports. On presenting the relevant vouchers, departing visitors can reclaim VAT paid on purchases in Britain and in Europe if their travels have taken them there also. The refund may be in cash (sterling) or by check (in any one of 11 different currencies) or as a credit to the traveller's credit-card accounts. The booths, to be found near Customs and Excise points, are open from 6:00 A.M. to midnight.

Most shops give a receipt when you buy something. If not, simply ask for one. All reputable shops will either exchange the goods or give a cash refund or credit slip. Remember, you are entitled to ask for a cash refund instead of a credit slip.

The best bargains in London are to be found at the twice-yearly sales: from mid-June through August and from late December through late January, though during the recession sales have been running virtually year-round.

If you are here only for a short stay and have a lot of specialized shopping to do, it might pay to engage the services of a resident expert. Most of the shopping-service organizations provide escorts. They know where to buy exactly what you want, at the right price. Charges vary according to the service required. Details can be obtained from Universal Aunts, 250 King's Road SW3 (Tel: 738-8937), or British Tours, 6 South Molton Street W1 (Tel: 629-5267).

You need to be as careful in London as in any other major city. Avoid carrying large amounts of cash and beware of pickpockets. The best way to ensure that you are not ripped off is to stick to recognized markets and shopping areas and steer clear of casual street traders.

If you want something guaranteed "made in England," try the **Design Center** shop at 28 Haymarket, just off Piccadilly Circus. The center has a permanent exhibition of the latest and best of British design, and all the merchandise is for sale.

In general, London shops are open from 9:00 A.M. to 5:30 P.M., Monday through Saturday, and closed on Sundays. Shops in the West End stay open until 8:00 P.M. on Thursdays. In Knightsbridge, Sloane Square, and on the King's Road in Chelsea, the late shopping night is Wednesday. Suburban stores have similar hours, but some close one afternoon a week, usually Wednesday or Thursday, varying from area to area. Many shops in Covent Garden and other new malls are open until 8:00 P.M. most evenings.

London's shopping is extensive enough to fill a guide-book on its own. The following is a roundup of the main shopping areas and recognized street markets.

Oxford Street

Although it has seen better days, Oxford Street is still the mecca for thousands of shoppers. Unable to afford the high rents, many small traders were forced out in the late 1980s. The empty shops, some occupied by squatters, create an air of tackiness, but there are many more still doing good business and offering the cheapest prices in London, although not necessarily the best quality.

It is on Oxford Street that you'll find the major depart-ment stores, as well as more than 30 different shoe shops. Buses stop at regular intervals along the street, which also has access to four Underground stations: from west to east, Marble Arch, Bond Street, Oxford Circus, and Tottenham Court Road. In addition, it has two branches of **Marks and Spencer** (the ubiquitous M & S or "Marks and Sparks," as it is playfully called), whose flagship store is at Marble Arch. Good-quality clothing at very reasonable prices is the hallmark of this chain, but until recently fitting rooms were not provided. Returning items here can be a chore as well, although company policy allows for ready exchange upon production of a receipt. And when hunger strikes, the Marble Arch M & S has an excellent food hall.

Selfridges' imposing building, with flags flying, is an enduring landmark on Oxford Street. It is worth braving the inevitable crowds in the large food, kitchenware, and cosmetics departments for the sheer quantity and variety of goods. Moreover, Selfridges guarantees to refund the difference if you find the same item cheaper elsewhere.

At 363 Oxford Street, near the Bond Street tube station, **HMV**, claiming to be the largest record store in the world, has a mega-selection of records, tapes, and compact discs suiting every conceivable taste to back up its boast. (Rich-ard Branson's **Virgin Megastore** at the far end of Oxford Street near the Tottenham Court Road tube station retali-ates by claiming to be the *best* record store in the world.)

Behind Bond Street and running diagonally south off Oxford, **South Molton Street** is reserved for pedestrians and is home to top hairdressers and expensive designer boutiques for men and women. For high fashion, **Browns** must be the first stop for labels such as Gaultier, Conran, Hamnet, Christian Lacroix, and Rifat Ozbek. Prices are very high, so if money is an issue, wait for the sales.

Butler & Wilson has an enormous selection of fashion jewelry. **Gray's Antique Market**, the covered emporium on the corner of Davis Street, offers a wide choice of jewelry and small items from individual collectors; closed weekends.

Back across Oxford Street, on the same side as Selfridges, **St. Christopher's Place**, another traffic-free haven, is easy to miss but worth a visit for its affordable boutiques. **Whistles** stocks a combination of inexpensive and designer women's clothing, including maternity wear. Look for the labels of Lolita Lempica, Ghost, and knitwear by Artwork.

Continuing the detour north along **Thayer Street**, where an intriguing little shop called **Blunderbuss** sells all kinds of antique military uniforms, helmets, swords, and small arms, you'll come in a few steps to **Marylebone High Street**, which, although in the heart of the West End, could be the main street of any English country town—except that famous faces are twopence a dozen here (unlike the exotic fruits sold at the greengrocers). **Maison Sagne**, at number 105, sells (and serves at table) delectable Swiss pastries.

A few blocks west of Marylebone High Street is **Chiltern Street**, with interesting boutiques, antiques stores, fabric shops, and musical instrument makers and sellers.

Back on Oxford Street, the department store of **John Lewis** ("Never knowingly undersold") excels in reasonably priced and attractive household goods. The quality generally is excellent, but don't expect to find any innovations in fashion. Between John Lewis and Oxford Circus, a large branch of BHS (**British Home Stores**) specializes in inexpensive but fashionable clothing for men, women, and children. Household light fittings and fixtures are especially good buys here.

From Oxford Circus east to Tottenham Court Road the sidewalks of Oxford Street are narrower and the crowds even more oppressive. There is little to attract the shopping visitor at this end of the street.

Regent Street

Regent Street still retains the curving Classical lines of the noble thoroughfare that John Nash designed and named for the prince regent in the early years of the 19th century. At Christmas its festive lights and decorations attract throngs of shoppers, and in summer its lampposts are adorned with hanging baskets of flowers. Most of the shops (as well as numerous large airline and tourism offices) are located on Regent Street between Oxford Circus and, to the south, Piccadilly Circus. These are also the names of the tube stations at either end, and there are a number of bus stops between the two "Circuses." The volume of traffic makes crossing the road an undertaking in itself.

At the junction of Regent and Oxford streets is the delightful **Wedgwood Gift Center**, selling the latest examples of the style of pottery that was first created by Josiah Wedgwood in the 18th century, as well as fine porcelain and glassware. Export service is available on the premises. Heading south from Oxford Circus on the east side of the street you arrive almost immediately at **Laura Ashley**, with its wide range of distinctive and stylish ladies' and children's wear as well as fabrics. A step or two farther south and you can't miss the large mock-Tudor building first opened as a store in 1875 by Arthur Lasenby Liberty, an entrepreneur with a passion for the Orient. Inside, carved wood paneling adorns the elevators and galleries line the main shopping floor. **Liberty** is justly famous for Tana Lawn and Varuna wool, silk scarves and neckties, clothes, fabrics, furnishings, fine crystal, and antiques, as well as for merchandise from the Far East.

Next up is **Hamleys**, "the biggest toy shop in the world"—although New York City's FAO Schwarz might dispute the claim. Six floors here are crammed with models and gadgets, toy boats, planes and trains, cuddly stuffed animals, electronic games, and all the latest trends of the toy world. A **Disney Store** has opened at 140 Regent Street just in case you can't find that Mickey Mouse cuddly toy elsewhere. To the left of Hamley's in the direction of Piccadilly, **Garrard**, the Queen's jeweler, makes it seem a privilege to be allowed through the door. The window displays alone are breathtaking. Garrard is noted especially for clocks of all descriptions. **Aquascutum**, that most British of fashion stores, is virtually next door on the opposite side of Glasshouse Street, and between that and the Quadrant Arcade the choices range from Mitsukiku's Japanese shop and Waterstones the booksellers to the Scotch House, which is jammed with woollens.

On the other side of the street, **Austin Reed** is the best-known men's tailor this side of Savile Row (which is actually a back street just a few blocks to the west), without the astronomical prices. **Burberry's**, farther up on the left heading back toward Oxford Circus, will sell you one of its famous raincoats for around £300, as well as a brolly, a scarf, a hat, gloves, shoes, children's wear, and much else besides. It's a bargain hunter's paradise at sale time.

St. James's and Piccadilly

St. James's is a small, exclusive area south of Piccadilly that has yet to be spoiled by developers and where a number of Victorian-fronted shops boast the Royal Warrant, which means they are suppliers to the Queen and her immediate family. Shops in St. James's specialize in fine toiletries and high-quality English tailoring. All sizes and shapes are fitted out, and customers ared accorded V.I.P. treatment.

At 6 St. James's Street, **James Lock & Company** (established 1676) will mold a hat to the exact shape of your head, which they measure with a strange contraption invented in Victorian times. Lock invented the bowler hat that used to be the badge of the respectable London City businessman but is rarely seen today. **Crabtree & Evelyn**, also on St. James's Street, displays beautifully packaged preserves, herbs, and soaps on delightfully old-fashioned wooden counters, while **J. Floris** has been selling fragrant soaps, bath oils, pomanders, and English flower perfumes at 89 Jermyn Street since 1730. Jermyn Street has an array of such stores appealing to the upper crust, and is especially noted for made-to-measure gentlemen's clothing and shoes. A narrow thoroughfare, it runs parallel to Piccadilly.

Piccadilly originally took its name from a tailor who specialized in making pickadils, the frilly lace collars worn by fashionable Elizabethans. Today much of it is occupied by hotels, airline offices, and car showrooms. It still has plenty to offer the shopper, however, from great department stores like **Simpson's** for fashion and **Lillywhites** in Piccadilly Circus, which has every type of sports equipment and clothing, to **Fortnum & Mason** farther west, which lends impeccable style to the world of groceries. Provision merchants by royal appointment and still going strong after two and a half centuries, it stocks everything and anything from bags of potato chips to a jar of the finest Sevruga caviar. The celebrated Fortnum's hamper, costing about £80 for four people, turns a picnic into a banquet—but you must telephone a day in advance to have one prepared for pickup or delivery (Tel: 734-8040). Likewise, the Fountain restaurant at Fortnum's has long been a rendezvous for afternoon tea or a light pre-theater supper, and is open until 11:30 P.M.

On the opposite side of Piccadilly is **Airey & Wheeler**, a classy gents' outfitter famous for well-cut shirts. **Hatchard's** is a bookselling chain, and its premises on Piccadilly have one of the best and widest stock of books to be found anywhere, along with a knowledgeable and helpful staff. Even out-of-print books can be ordered here.

Among the arcades and covered shopping malls off Piccadilly, the early 19th-century **Burlington Arcade** (parallel to Old Bond Street) is the most elegant, exclusive—and expensive. A full-time beadle is employed to make sure no one whistles or runs or otherwise disturbs the peace in this Old World enclave. The Prince of Wales and his father, the duke of Edinburgh, get their Hammam Bouquet cologne from **Penhaligons**, and the tiny **Irish Linen Company** shop sells beautiful household linens. Elsewhere in the arcade you will find jewelry and accessories, fine woollens and cashmere sweaters and scarves, leather goods, rare pipes, tobaccos, and cigars, and a range of other items suitable as gifts or souvenirs. But whatever you do, don't whistle.

The **Trocadero**, also on Piccadilly Circus, with access from Coventry Street and Shaftesbury Avenue, is quite another cup of tea. Reopened in 1984 as an exhibition-cum-shopping center, cheap souvenir shops, loud boutiques, and restaurants now occupy this three-floor tower. The **London Pavilion**, around the corner at the bottom of Shaftesbury Avenue, is a covered shopping area worth visiting.

Jermyn Street

This narrow thoroughfare running just south of and parallel to Piccadilly is the haunt of affluent shoppers who want only the best and know where to find it. **Church's Shoes** (number 112) and **Turnbull & Asser** (number 70) may not be household names, but for the discerning customer they are *the* places to buy, respectively, shoes and shirts. Jermyn Street is also the home of **Floris** perfumes; **Dunhill** tobaccos, pipes, and leather goods; and the specialist cheesemonger **Paxton & Whitfield**.

Bond Street (Old and New)

There are in fact two Bond streets, Old and New, which meet at the junction with Burlington Gardens. "New" in this case has become something of a misnomer, as it was built around 1721 and contains some of London's most elegant and fashionable shops, a window-shopper's paradise. Old Bond Street, a short continuation of New Bond Street, stretches south from Burlington Gardens into Piccadilly.

Asprey doesn't boast, but with its glittering showcases of rare and beautiful jewelry, gold, silver, and antiques, it has to be one of the finest shops in the world. There's more of the same at Cartier, fine porcelain at Georg Jensen, high fashion at the houses of Chanel, Lagerfield, and St. Laurent, as well as magnificent leather goods at Gucci. If you're looking for distinctive notepaper, stop in at **Smythson**, suppliers of stationery to the Queen, and for any kind of musical instrument, try **Chappells**.

Fenwicks, the only department store on New Bond Street, offers an extensive range of lingerie and fashion wear, mostly for women and in all price brackets.

Admiral Lord Nelson once lived at 147 New Bond Street (which today houses **Wildensteins**, traders in fine paintings and drawings). The fine art gallery of **Ackermann & Johnson** deals in and publishes sporting prints spanning the past three centuries, but the flagship of the street is probably the auction house of **Sotheby's**. Viewing, usually for three days before a sale, is from 9:00 A.M. to 4:30 P.M. The actual sales take place at 11:00 A.M. Although bids running into millions attract the headlines, many of the sales are quite modest. (The other famous London auction houses are **Christie's** on King Street near the Green Park tube station, **Phillip's** on nearby Blenheim Street, and **Bonham's** on Montpelier Street over in Knightsbridge.)

Tottenham Court Road

Before (or perhaps instead of) heading west from the so-called West End to the lush pastures of Knightsbridge and Kensington, you might take a look at some of London's other lively central shopping areas. Tottenham Court Road can hardly be described as a shoppers' paradise (nor is it exactly pleasing to the eye), but it is the center for sound systems and electrical equipment of all kinds. With so many shops selling similar items in such a small area it is easy to compare prices and shop for the best value.

Tottenham Court Road is also the place for stylish furniture in the showrooms of **Maples and Heals**, with

Habitat specializing in the latest trends at everyday prices. **Paperchase** is a super shop in which to browse and buy wrapping paper, gift tags, unusual greeting cards, and many other paper items.

Bloomsbury

This is not a great shopping area, with one exception: Museum Street, opposite the British Museum, the place to go for shops specializing in old prints and secondhand books. Visit **Bloomsbury Rare Books** at number 29 and **The Print Room** at number 37 next to the Museum Tavern. The quality Scottish woollens at **Westaway and Westaway** on Great Russell Street are an especially good buy. Within walking distance on Gower Street (to the south) is the enormous, efficiently run bookshop of the University of London, **Dillons**. The British Museum itself has a small shop that sells reproductions of Roman and Greek jewelry as well as prints and books.

Charing Cross Road

Although it features in the title of a successful play, Charing Cross Road has none of the outward glitter and glamour of the West End, yet it remains a magnet for bookworms. **Foyles** here claims to stock every British book in print, but its staff doesn't always give the impression of being all that well informed about where to find what. **Waterstones**, nearby, is a newer bookstore, with a very helpful staff and wide-carpeted aisles between the shelves. It stays open late, too. **Zwemmer**, at number 76–80, is noted for books on art and architecture. The charm of Charing Cross Road for those with a nose for a rare book is the number of shops where it's still possible to browse among second-hand volumes, most long out of print.

Soho

West of Charing Cross Road, Soho is one of the capital's older immigrant quarters, noted for its ethnic shops and restaurants and also as a favorite haunt of writers, artists, and show-business personalities. There is no principal shopping street in Soho. Berwick Street houses one of the best fruit-and-vegetable markets in London, and is noted for its many fabric shops, of which **Borovicks** is the best known. The latter is stacked with extravagant materials and boasts a gallery of signed photographs of the circus and theater stars who have worn costumes made from them. The staff is likewise animated and helpful. On

Beak Street, **Anything Lefthanded** sells just that, from pens to cooking utensils. On Golden Square, **Bennett's Cashmere House** has been in business for more than 30 years.

Soho includes London's Chinatown on Lisle Street, Gerrard Street, and part of Wardour Street, and the area is especially crowded on Sunday afternoons with Chinese families. **Loon Fung supermarket** here offers an excellent selection of pretty dishes and unusual cookware amid shelves piled with noodles, dried fish, sweets, and spices. Old Compton Street is full of exotic shops; one of them, the **Pâtisserie Valerie**, is worth a visit just to sample its heavenly chocolate truffle cake.

Covent Garden

East of Charing Cross Road lies Covent Garden, for 300 years the distribution center for fruit and vegetables brought into the capital from the rest of the country and the world. Then, in 1974, the wholesale fruit, vegetable, and flower market was moved to a new site south of the river, and after much controversy and local community action the abandoned warehouses were saved from demolition and turned into small galleries, workshops, studios, and offices.

The addition of cafés, boutiques, crafts shops, and market stalls of all kinds, and the revival of street theater and entertainment (much as it would have been in the 18th century), have created a draw for tourists as well as Londoners. You can buy affordable garments at the branches of many of London's best-known fashion shops here, or choose from an amazing variety of handicrafts and specialty items in the smaller shops that have sprung up in the surrounding streets.

Neal Street has more than its share, with the Copper Shop, the Tea House, and the Kite Store (names that speak for themselves) among the best. **Neal's Yard**, just off Neal Street, caters to health-conscious shoppers with a whole-foods warehouse, farm shop, bakery, and Neal's Yard Apothecary, where old-fashioned remedies can be made up to suit individual requirements. **New Row** is worth looking into for **Naturally British**, which offers gifts, clothes, toys, and furniture of good quality, though the prices are rather high; and **Scottish Merchant** for knitwear, especially Fair Isle sweaters. If maps fascinate you, don't miss **Stanford's Map Shop** on Long Acre, another good street for strolling and window-shopping. If you're into astral travel, **Mysteries** on Monmouth Street, London's largest psychic shop, sells everything from tarot cards to astrological charts.

The **Museum Store** at Covent Garden has collectibles from galleries and museums around the world. If you're shopping for children or have them in tow, head for the tiny **Doll's House Toys Ltd.** on the ground floor of the main market building. It is crammed with miniature British structures, from Elizabethan cottages to Victorian shops. **Pollock's Toy Theatres** and the **Puffin** bookshop, both upstairs, are also worth a visit. On the corner of King and Bedford streets is **Hackett**, the gentlemen's outfitters.

There is late-night shopping in Covent Garden six nights a week (until 8:00 P.M.), and there are open markets for antiques on Mondays, and crafts Tuesday through Saturday, from 9:00 A.M. to 5:00 P.M.

Knightsbridge

An improbable version of how this fashion-conscious area got its name is that two knights on their way to the Crusades fought to the death on a bridge that once stood here. Be that as it may, there is no doubt that Knightsbridge is where the fashionable people shop. In fact, if there is such a thing as a neighborhood shopping area for the royal family, this is it. The tall, attractive blonde with the shy smile at the glove counter could be you-know-who, always escorted by a plainclothes detective.

The stylish shops extend into dozens of side streets and cul-de-sacs, but it is **Harrods**, of course, that dominates the scene. *The* Knightsbridge store is not actually on the street that bears the name but on the Brompton Road, but who is arguing? There is only one Harrods, famous throughout the world. No matter what you're looking for it has it, or can do it: Arrange your travel, rent a house, send anything anywhere. (It once dispatched a baby elephant to Ronald Reagan.) Throughout its many departments retailing every conceivable kind of merchandise, quality and service are of the highest, although the same, happily, cannot be said of its prices. There are bargains to be had at Harrods, especially during the legendary sales, when long queues form at the doors well in advance of opening.

Harrods apart, at sale time one favorite Knightsbridge store is the nearby **Harvey Nichols**, known to its devotees as Harvey Nicks. If you have seen what you want in a glossy magazine, this is the most likely place to find it, among racks packed with high-fashion names such as Helen Storey, Byblos, and Nichole Farrhi. The range of fashion accessories here is just as wide, and it is fun to visit the store's fashion shows. (Top cosmetics houses often give demonstrations with "free gifts" to tempt buyers.)

Knightsbridge is packed with fashion and shoe shops, Rayne, Bally, and Charles Jourdan among them. The **Scotch House** on the corner displays fine woollens, including cashmere, and (naturally) tartans of all clans, while famous names in jewelry are represented in the area by **Kutchinsky** and **Mappin & Webb**.

On Sloane Street, running south into Chelsea and "Sloane Ranger" country, you will find much sought after machine-knitted sweaters and skirts and hand-knitted sweaters with tiger motifs for around £300 at **Joseph Tricot**. Nearby, **Katharine Hamnett's** shop—with an aquarium in the window—offers everything from quietly understated fashions for men and women to dramatic creations studded with leather.

For its range of products and sheer style, shopping on the Brompton Road is hard to beat. **Episode** (number 13) is a store where style is allied to the purest of natural fibers; the emphasis is on classic good looks rather than passing fashion. Next door **R. M. Williams** sells durable equestrian and country wear that draws cunningly on the company's roots in the Australian Outback.

Beauchamp (pronounced BEE-cham) **Place**, off the Brompton Road a bit west of Harrods, is an enclave of smart fashion houses and restaurants in what used to be residential terraces. The windows lining the narrow street have displays to dazzle young female followers of fashion under such names as Janet Reger, Caroline Charles, Whistles, and Bruce Oldfield. Appealing antiques shops are interspersed with the street's boutiques; the **Map House** is the place to go if you are looking for genuine antique or reproduction maps and prints.

The Brompton Road continues into the Fulham Road, less aristocratic than Knightsbridge but with a growing reputation for both antiques and fashion. The former Michelin Tire Company building overshadowing the intersection known as Brompton Cross houses the **Conran** shop with its range of reasonably priced designer furnishings and fabrics, books, Italian cookware, English preserves, teas, and much more. If you are feeling drained and need a rest, under the same roof is a Champagne-and-oyster bar and the **Bibendum** restaurant.

King's Road, Chelsea

The king after whom this street is named was Charles II. One theory holds that it was the quickest route from Whitehall Palace to the house of his mistress Nell Gwyn in Fulham. Much more recently, Mary Quant invented the miniskirt and sold it on the King's Road, which went on to achieve a reputation as the heart of the swinging London of the sixties. This faded as fashions changed—but not totally, as was unfortunately the case of Carnaby Street, now merely a tacky backwater off Regent Street. Especially on Saturdays, the King's Road still attracts the young and fashion-conscious across a broad spectrum, from smart to eccentric and even bizarre. Boutiques and antiques shops of every kind abound.

Designers Sale Studio, at number 14, concentrates on famous labels' end-of-lines and canceled orders, so you can pick up Byblos, Krizia, or Ralph Lauren women's wear here at unbelievably low prices. **Antiquarius Antique Market**, opposite the cinema, has 200 stalls displaying fine arts, silver, antique jewelry, Edwardian silk blouses, period furniture, and all kinds of bric-a-brac.

West of the World's End pub, where the King's Road leaves Chelsea and enters Fulham, there are fewer fashionable boutiques and bistros, but still more antiques shops. One of the best known is **Christopher Wray's** period lighting emporium at number 600, with its huge stock of Victorian and Edwardian lampshades and fittings. The **London and Provincial Antique Dealers Association** has its headquarters at 535 King's Road, where it represents 225 dealers in the London area. Its directory, *Buying Antiques in Britain,* is a useful guide, and the association will arbitrate on any complaints that cannot be settled directly with the individual trader. Look for its sticker (LAPADA) in shops that are members.

Kensington High Street

As on any other High Street, you will find on Kensington High the branches of such well-known British chains as Marks and Spencer, British Home Stores, Next, and C & A. But this street runs through one of the most expensive residential districts of the capital, and the stock of these stores reflects this. You can step off the Underground train at High Street Kensington directly into a shopping arcade dominated by M & S.

Aside from the chain stores, upscale outlets of Benetton and Laura Ashley can be found alongside Kensington Market, which has seen better days but still offers the occasional bargain in denim or leather as well as second-hand clothes. Behind the large white statues, **Hyper-Hyper** displays the work of 70 young British fashion designers. If you have children in mind or in tow, walk farther west to the Early Learning Center, the Young World Toy and Children's Book Center, and the Tree House for gifts.

Kensington Church Street, heading north from the High Street by St. Mary Abbots Church, is lined with dozens of antiques shops all the way up to Notting Hill Gate. Notable among these are **Robert Hales** for swords and other militaria, **Pamela Teignmouth** for 18th-century furniture, and **Rafferty** for clocks and watches.

One stop east from Notting Hill Gate on the Central Line brings you to Queensway, a lesser-known shopping area that stays open late. The star attraction here is **Whiteleys**, whose Edwardian building has been renovated and redeveloped into a precinct with numerous shops, restaurants, cafés, and a multiscreen cinema. It is a relatively calm place to shop under one roof, and is just dying to be rediscovered.

Tobacco Dock

Tobacco Dock, east of the City in former docklands behind Wapping High Street, is a huge new development that is waiting for liftoff with the end of recession. The shops (open daily until 8:00 P.M., 10:00 P.M. on Fridays) and restaurants are converted Victorian warehouses and restored Georgian vaults. Entertainers, themed attractions (including two full-size sailing-ship replicas), and craft stalls, open from Wednesday through Sunday, aim to give the place a village atmosphere. There is plenty of car parking. Otherwise take the Docklands Light Railway or Docklands Minibus from Tower Gateway to Shadwell or Wapping. From there it is a five-minute walk, which is signposted.

Street Markets

New shopping precincts and malls have killed off many of the street markets that were once such a feature of London, but some still survive. If you visit one and—sadly—don't find a bargain, at least you will get some free entertainment listening to the patter of the stallholders. Avoid fly-boys, those unlicensed traders who work out of suitcases and are ready to snap them shut and run at the sight of a policeman.

Middlesex Street (better known as Petticoat Lane), between the Aldgate and Aldgate East Underground stations, is the most famous (or notorious) of the Sunday markets in the East End, open from 9:00 A.M. to 2:00 P.M. Its stalls are filled with fun junk, fashions, household goods, and an impressive array of leather goods. There is little hope of understanding the fast-talking market traders' spiel, and goods offered at ridiculously low prices have probably "fallen off the back of a lorry." **Petticoat Lane Designer Fashion Market**, a covered mall between Middlesex and Goulston streets, is open on Sundays from 9:00 A.M. to 2:00 P.M. except Easter Sunday.

On Saturdays from 8:00 A.M. to 5:00 P.M. **Portobello Road**, near the Notting Hill Gate and Ladbroke Grove tube stations, is crammed with antiques dealers lying in wait for innocent tourists, although it *is* possible to pick up interesting pieces here at fair prices. The numerous small galleries in the side streets are a better bet for a bargain. At all costs avoid the booths exchanging foreign currency. The serious buyer would be well advised to visit any of the 90 antiques and art shops during the week, when it is easier to park and the dealers can give customers personal attention.

North London's premier weekend market is **Camden Lock**, open Saturdays and Sundays from 9:00 A.M. to 6:00 P.M. and all bank holidays except Christmas Day. The variety of merchandise here and the characters who sell it attract large crowds. Anyone wishing to trade lines up in the morning and, if lucky, is allocated a stall. Alongside the market there are several crafts shops in converted canal warehouses, with canal boat trips and restaurants nearby. **Camden Passage**, off Islington High Street, is another good open market for bric-a-brac and antiques and is open on Wednesdays as well as Saturdays (when trading is at its peak). The nearest Underground station for Camden Lock is Camden Town; for Camden Passage, it's the Angel.

Greenwich isn't on the tube but can be reached by overground train, bus, or riverboat; if you happen to be visiting this center of Britain's maritime history on a weekend don't miss the open-air market. Open from 8:00 A.M. to 4:00 P.M. on Saturdays and Sundays, it is the best market south of the river or, according to some, in the whole of London. Look for the wonderful hat stall (as there is only one small mirror, you might get jostled while you're trying on the merchandise). Oriental china and pottery are sold here at very reasonable prices. The bookstalls are a delight, too, especially for old poetry.

The best advice if you are visiting markets is to get there early. Not only are the best bargains still available, but the traders will be in a better humor.

—*Catherine Connelly*

DAY TRIPS FROM LONDON

OXFORD, CAMBRIDGE, WINDSOR, BRIGHTON

By Anthony Burton and Frank Victor Dawes

Oxford

Visitors to Oxford, 59 miles northwest of central London, tend to arrive with a ready-made image in mind: Matthew Arnold's description of "that sweet City with her dreaming spires." That is not always what they find, particularly if they arrive by public transportation. Emerging from the railway station, passengers are confronted by a brewery and an old jam factory. The latter, once the source of Oxford's famous marmalade, now houses an antiques market where the atmosphere is friendly and there are bargains to collect. Bus travellers are dropped in one of the city's more nondescript quarters. The dreaming spires, however, are not far away. The city center is still dominated by the colleges that together make up the university, a few uncompromisingly modern but most still proudly displaying their medieval origins in their ancient stones. The University of Oxford is not some distant institution drawing its academic skirts away from the life of the city but is very much at the heart of it.

The best way to get an instant feel for Oxford is to find

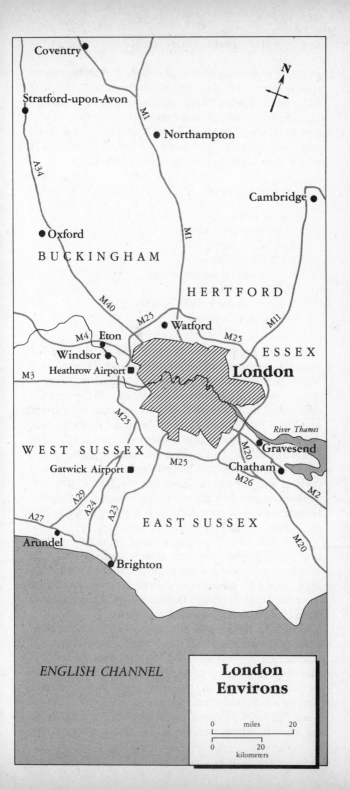

a vantage point with an overall view, and a literally central spot is where the main streets converge, at Carfax. The 14th-century **Carfax Tower** (all that remains of St. Martin's Church, which was demolished in 1896) is open to visitors who, when they have wound their way up the spiral stairs, will find all Oxford laid out before them. This is where you should begin your tour of Oxford.

MAJOR INTEREST

Carfax Tower
The University colleges
Radcliffe Square
Bodleian Library
Bookstores on Broad Street
Sheldonian Theatre
Museum of the History of Science
Ashmolean Museum

To the east, High Street—always known as "the High"—curves away to the distant hills. To the north is Cornmarket Street. Between these two streets is an enticing array of domes, pinnacles, and towers. St. Aldate's, to the south, is dominated by the ornate Tom Tower, marking the entrance to Christ Church College. Beyond it is the Thames, or (as it is more popularly known in its passage through Oxford) the Isis. To the west are sadder sights. Queen Street leads to a mishmash of modern shopping areas and parking lots. The old castle lies this way, but the romantic battlements are now the site of the local jail, and all that remains of the Norman fortress is a grassy mound—the old "motte," still a very distinctive landmark.

From the Carfax Tower, the areas of rewarding exploration are apparent. The rich golden stones of the old, which on a sunny day seem to glow with their own inner light, offer a far greater lure than the neon and plastic of the new. Thus, visitors to Oxford are drawn to the city's main claim to fame, its ancient university.

Travellers here frequently ask to be directed to the university, only to be told that it is all around them—as you can clearly see from the top of Carfax Tower. The university is made up of 35 separate colleges, each with its individual history and traditions, yet all growing from a single root. To understand the system you must step back some 700 years. Medieval learning drew its strength from the church, which was the major center of study and which controlled virtually all forms of education. By the 13th century Oxford was home to a guild of teachers, the Universitas, whose students were housed in communal halls. From these grew the colleges, each with its chapel for prayers and its quadrangles, around which were grouped rooms for students and teachers. Common facilities, such as libraries, soon developed to serve all the colleges. But the heart of the teaching system remained the tutorial, the meeting of teacher and student in the comfortable, informal surroundings of a college room.

Great variety exists among the colleges, certainly in appearance. There are grand colleges, with architecture so classically formal it approaches pomposity, and others where you might feel you had strayed into the garden of some old country mansion. To understand the colleges, it may help to take a little time at the beginning of the tour and look at one in detail.

CHRIST CHURCH COLLEGE

As you descend Carfax Tower and walk south on St. Aldate's, the first college you come to is Christ Church. The site originally held an Anglo-Saxon nunnery, but the church was rebuilt several times before the Norman church of St. Frideswide was begun here in the 12th century. In 1525 Cardinal Wolsey arrived with typical bravado and plans to demolish all that was old and raise a new college with a new chapel. The cardinal's fall brought a change of plans and patrons. Henry VIII took over, and Cardinal College became Christ Church. In the process, St. Frideswide's was saved, first as the college chapel, later as **Oxford Cathedral**.

Given its powerful patronage, the college was inevitably built on a grand scale and improved and developed over the centuries, with much of its present formal beauty due to the influence of the architect Sir Christopher Wren. The grand entrance, topped by the tall **Tom Tower**, is intended to impress the visitor, and it does. Each evening during term time the great bell in the tower tolls 101 times, once for each member of the original foundation of the college. Once inside the quad you are in an enclosed space, the self-contained world of the college. All around are the buildings that house students and dons, but the sheer size of the open grounds prevents any sense of claustrophobia. Meanwhile, the eye is drawn to the tower and spire of the cathedral. Thus, the architecture expresses the college's religious and scholarly heritage. Christ Church has an air

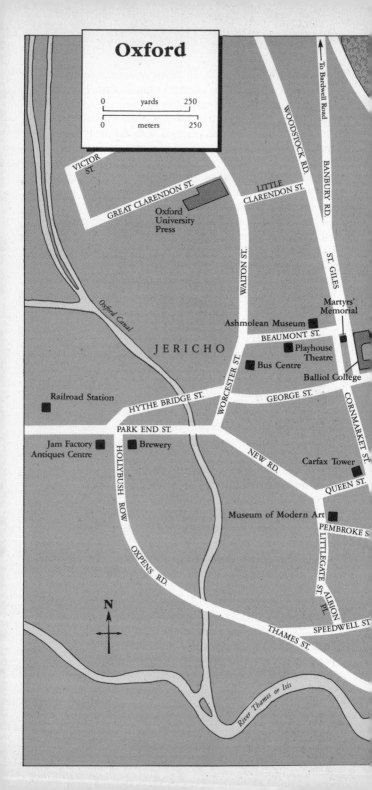

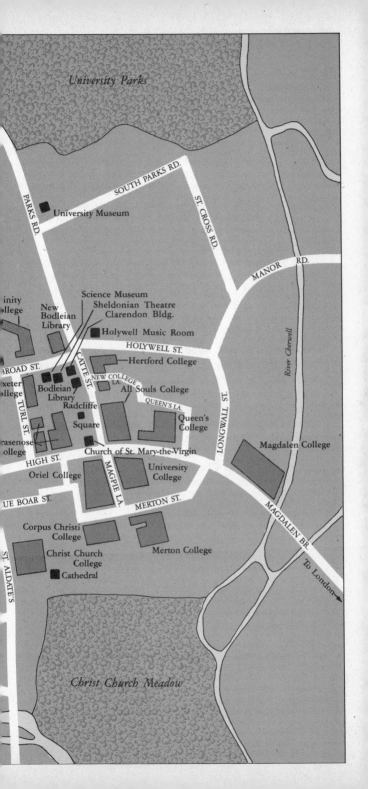

of spaciousness, fronting a wide street with the open green of Christ Church Meadow alongside. Beyond the main quad are subsidiary quads and such important buildings as the college kitchens.

Famous alumni of Christ Church include the mathematics tutor C. L. Dodgson, better known as Lewis Carroll. He might have been amused by some of the antics of the 20th-century undergraduates: A swan was once discovered languishing in Tom Quad, formally attired in black bow tie; on another occasion, when Dean Lowe of Christ Church landed in Christ Church Meadow in a helicopter, he was greeted by a choir of undergraduates singing "Lo, he comes in clouds descending."

Christ Church creates its own unmistakable atmosphere, just as every other college at Oxford does, and if it can boast of former members as illustrious as Lewis Carroll, William Penn, and W. H. Auden, so can they.

OTHER COLLEGES AND LANDMARKS

If you go back up St. Aldate's and then take a stroll down Blue Boar Street, a quite different sense of space and time develops. The noise of traffic recedes, and the narrow lane briefly opens out into Oriel Square, bounded by the **Peckwater Quad** of Christ Church and Oriel and Corpus Christi colleges. What is at once so striking is that Oxford really is a mixture of quite disparate styles: **Oriel** is grandly Jacobean, with its strong rhythms of shaped gables, while **Corpus Christi**, altered and enriched though it has been over the years, has a feel of almost domestic intimacy. It is typical of Oxford that there should be curiosities to look for, such as Corpus Christi's pelican sundial with its strange perpetual calendar.

Beyond the square, the way continues its ever more secretive path up cobbled Merton Street, past **Merton College**, which received its first statutes (the laws for governing the college) in 1263 and is generally regarded as the oldest of the colleges—though the claim is strongly contested by two others, Balliol and University. Merton can at least claim to have some of Oxford's oldest buildings, and nowhere can you feel closer to the medieval heart of the university than in **Merton Chapel**, with its beautiful stained glass.

Merton Street bends through a right angle, and the mood changes again, quite dramatically, for there at the end is the High, dominated by colleges and two churches set among many old houses of character (virtually all now converted to shops). To the west are crowded city streets, to the east openness and light—no accident but a reflection of the fact that the former lay within the old city walls, the latter outside them. To the east the view is dominated by **Magdalen College** (pronounced MAUD-lin), its elaborate stonework gleaming from a recent cleaning. It is the focal point for one of Oxford's most popular traditions. Each May Day morning at 6:00, a hymn is sung from the tower, signaling the start of a pre-breakfast round of roistering that fills the surrounding streets, not to mention the surrounding pubs, which are opened early specially for this one day of the year. From here you can hire punts to explore the River Cherwell. A favorite excursion is to punt down to the **Victoria Arms**—universally known as the Vicky Arms—for a well-earned pint of beer on the lawn. It takes approximately two hours from Magdalen Bridge. A shorter, one-hour trip is possible by hiring a punt upstream at Bardwell Road.

As you head west toward the city center down the High, the scene is one of rather formal grandeur, with the classicism of **Queen's College** setting the dominant note. But to reach the core of the university complex you must turn off the High onto Catte Street to **Radcliffe Square**. An urban space that captures the imagination, the square owes its impact to the genius of the architect Nicholas Hawksmoor, who suggested that the library, the **Radcliffe Camera**, be built as a rotunda. His own design was not used, however, and the work was given to James Gibbs, though both men received fees. It sits there like the hub of a wheel, positively inviting you to look outward to the splendors on every side.

To the south is the **Church of St. Mary-the-Virgin,** with its tall tower. The main body of All Souls College comes into view to the east, and Brasenose College is to the west, while to the north is the Bodleian Library. But it is not just the magnificence of the buildings that gives the square its special character. The Camera is the principal undergraduate library, so it is constantly surrounded by a clutter of bicycles and a whirl of students who are there to work, not merely to gaze.

Bodleian Library

The Bodleian Library is rather more solemn, a research library used by scholars from all over the world. Statistics, for once, do give some notion of scale: five million volumes, spread along 81 miles of shelving, with seating for

2,078 readers. What statistics cannot do is convey the air of antiquity of a library whose heart is now four centuries old. Modernization has been slow. Heating was introduced only in 1821, which is why the oath all new readers must take includes a vow "not to bring into the Library or kindle therein any fire or flame." Visitors who want to see the oldest part of the library must make arrangements in advance, but it is well worth the effort. Visitors should call the Bodleian (Tel: 0865-27-71-65) and book a tour; there are four a day on weekdays, starting at 10:30 A.M., and two on Saturdays (except for degree days), from mid-March to the end of October, with limited visits in winter. No children under 14 permitted; admission by ticket.

BROAD STREET

Opposite the Bodleian is New College Lane, spanned by Oxford's version of the Bridge of Sighs, which unites the two parts of Hertford College.

Those tempted to explore will find ever more secluded alleyways that end surprisingly at a country-pub-come-to-town in the shape of the thatched **Turf Tavern**. Just around the corner at the end of Broad Street is one of the undergraduates' favorite pubs, the **Kings Arms**, where you can choose between the big open bar at the front and the cozy paneled back bar, which until very recently was exclusively a male preserve. Still reserved for men is the famous bathing spot on the Cherwell, Parson's Pleasure, where gentlemen may bathe in the nude. Those who prefer wider vistas will certainly find just that in Broad Street. Close at hand is the **covered market**. Stalls originally cluttered and blocked the surrounding streets before they were moved into this specially built market hall. Here the colleges buy their provisions; many of the vendors sell very traditional English food—from the specialists in game, whose stalls, in season, are festooned with pheasant and partridge, to the sellers of English cheeses. But Broad Street caters to a quite different need: For book lovers, it is as close to heaven as they are ever likely to get. Here virtually anything can be found, from the most esoteric textbook to the latest paperback. There are shops specializing in art books, children's books, and even antiquarian books. Trinity, Balliol, and Exeter colleges manage to squeeze in among the booksellers and still leave space for a small group of historic buildings.

The **Sheldonian Theatre** was designed not as a theater in the modern sense but as a site for ceremonials. The first work of Sir Christopher Wren ("the first" in the sense that it was the first to be begun; Pembroke Chapel at Cambridge, though completed earlier, was started later) soon found other uses. Home for a time to the University Press, it later became a concert hall and remains one today. The Sheldonian and the delightful little **Holywell Music Room** up Holywell Street are part of Britain's musical history—Haydn performed here and so did Handel. In July there is the Handel in Oxford Festival; hearing the composer's works in the ornate setting of the Sheldonian is not unlike hearing Mozart in Salzburg.

Broad Street is a cheerful place, but it has had its moments of horror. A cobblestone cross in the road and a metal plaque outside Balliol marks the spot where the Protestant martyr Thomas Cranmer, archbishop of Canterbury, was burned at the stake in 1556, and an old gate in Balliol Quad is still said to show the scorching of the flames. Bishops Hugh Latimer and Nicholas Ridley were also burned nearby, and all three are commemorated in the Martyrs' Memorial in St. Giles.

The Ashmolean and Other Museums

Broad Street has one more building of note, not perhaps the grandest but one that has a fascinating history. The tiny **Museum of the History of Science**, which holds an array of beautiful old scientific instruments, began life in the 17th century as home to Elias Ashmole's Cabinet of Curiosities, the world's first public museum. The Ashmolean collection outgrew its old quarters and found a new, classically styled home in Beaumont Street—it is not unlike a British Museum in miniature. The **Ashmolean Museum** today covers a wide range of exhibits from Egyptian mummies to 19th-century paintings. The ceramics are particularly fine, and among the gems of the art collection are a number of beautiful, haunting paintings by Samuel Palmer. Opposite the museum is the **Playhouse Theatre**. For many years it was the University Theatre, and among those who returned to perform here, after achieving fame and fortune, was Richard Burton. It closed for a number of years but has reopened as an independent theater and a new lively center for the arts.

During the mid-19th century, Oxford decided it needed a natural history museum, and again a new style was pioneered, an almost riotously elaborate Gothic, using the new building materials of iron and glass. This, the **University Museum**, is on Parks Road. As well as housing the natural history collection, it is home to the Pitt-Rivers Collection of ethnography, an extraordinary assemblage of objects from around the world, including such bizarre items as shrunken human heads. The 20th century abandoned elaboration, and the **Museum of Modern Art** on Pembroke Street is housed in a converted warehouse—very bare, very austere, but a perfect setting for its constantly changing exhibitions. The restaurant in the basement is a popular place for a lunchtime snack, when the diners are often as colorful as the pictures on the walls.

A relatively new addition to the Oxford scene, opened in spring 1988, combines something of the museum world with a good deal of show business and high-tech wizardry. At **The Oxford Story** on Broad Street, visitors follow the evolution of the university and meet some of the great thinkers and personalities who have been "up at Oxford."

THE OTHER OXFORD

University Oxford is what most visitors rightly wish to see. There is another city, too, however—the one where William Morris began making motorcars. Car making has now moved out to new works at Cowley to the east of the city, but evidence of its old industrial life remains, nearer the center. A pleasant way to catch a glimpse of this other world is to stroll along the towpath of the Oxford Canal from Hythe Bridge. The canal that once carried coal from the collieries round Coventry and Birmingham now carries people on vacation, enjoying a gentle cruise through the countryside. The canal threads its way past little cottages and grander houses, many with gardens stretching down to the water's edge. Eventually it runs along beside Port Meadow, an area of grassland that stretches across to the Thames. This is still common land, where local people turn ponies out to graze. The energetic can walk all the way to Wolvercote, a distance of 2 miles (3 km), and reward themselves with a drink at the **Plough**. The less energetic can turn off at one of the many bridges along the way to explore the area known as Jericho. This maze of narrow streets was once home to the working-class families of Oxford but has now become fashionable. The past is still preserved, however, in simple pubs such as the **Bookbinders Arms** on Victor Street—a reminder that the Oxford University Press is not very far away. Oxford is still a city where town and gown both have important parts to play.

STAYING AND DINING IN OXFORD

Opposite the Martyrs' Memorial on Beaumont Street is Oxford's best-known hotel, the stately and very traditional ▶ **Randolph**. Those looking for somewhere less overwhelmingly grand to stay need only walk up St. Giles to the ivy-covered ▶ **Old Parsonage** at the end of Banbury Road. Good, cheaper accommodations can be found a little farther afield, at hotels such as the ▶ **Westgate** on Botley Road, eight minutes from the city center, near the railway station; and the ▶ **Courtfield Private Hotel**, on a tree-lined road close to the River Thames and picturesque Iffley village.

Along Banbury Road are two of Oxford's favorite, if contrasting, restaurants. **Brown's** has good food at reasonable prices and is invariably bustling, noisy, and crowded but full of atmosphere. **Gee's Brasserie**, at 61 Banbury Road, is very different: Housed in an elegant Victorian conservatory, it boasts one of the best and most sophisticated menus in the country—modern English with Mediterranean influences (Tel: 0865-535-40). Another popular restaurant in this area is **Munchy Munchy** at 6 Park End Street. Its plain appearance gives no hint of the exotic flavors of Ethel Ow's authentic Indonesian cooking; reservations needed for four people or more (Tel: 0865-24-57-10). Equally exotic is **Al-Shami** at 25 Walton Crescent, which specializes in Lebanese cooking, complemented by a Lebanese wine list (Tel: 0865-31-00-66).

—Anthony Burton

Cambridge

In the perpetual pairing of Cambridge with Oxford, Cambridge always comes second. It is Oxford and Cambridge, or even Oxbridge, but never the other way around, except perhaps in the specialized world of the scientist. This may be a reflection of history, for the university at Cambridge began with an exodus of scholars from Oxford after a quarrel between town and gown at the beginning of the 13th century. Yet, paradoxically, Cambridge contrives to appear the older city, more closely tied to its medieval past. Here, the influence of the university is overwhelming; it is an inescapable presence in a way that

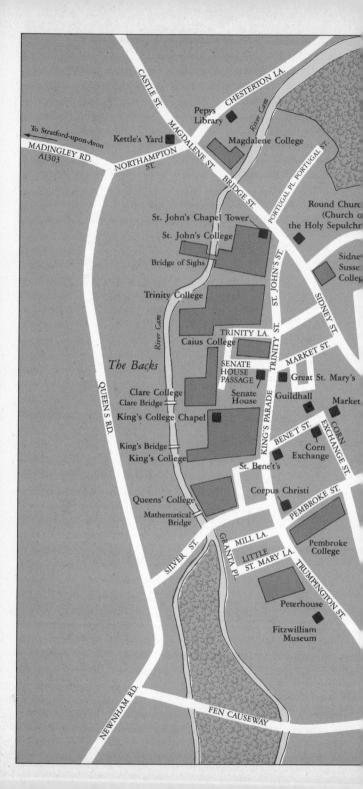

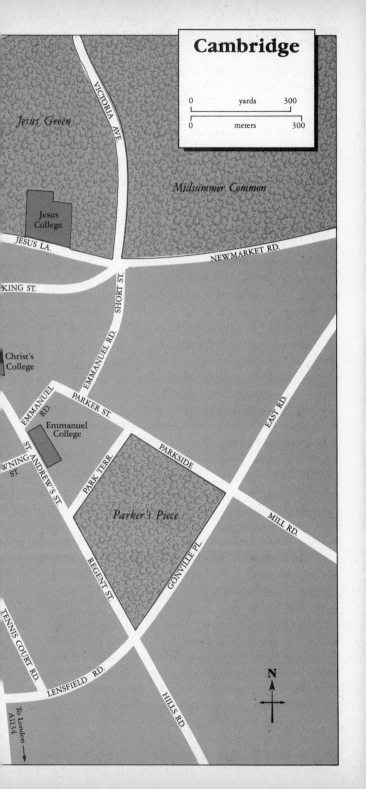

is never quite the case at Oxford. But if it is the university that has made Cambridge the fascinating and beautiful place it is today, it is the River Cam that first brought the city into being. It was at the crossing of the river that the settlement of Cam-bridge grew, and it is the river that today threads together the different parts of the city's past to make a coherent whole.

MAJOR INTEREST

The Backs
University colleges
Kettle's Yard
Round Church
King's College Chapel
Fitzwilliam Museum

From the river, the visitor passes **the Backs**, which are exactly what the name suggests—the green space in back of the colleges, along the river's edge. But the unimaginative name gives no notion of the enchantment here, where the stone towers and turrets of colleges and chapels are reflected in the quiet waters of the Cam. By far the best way to take in this view is from a punt, the traditional narrow, flat-bottomed boat propelled by pole. These can be hired either by the bridge at Magdalene Street or by Mill Lane. It is possible to take "chauffeured punts" and let someone else do the poling. Those who choose to be punted rather than punt may fancy themselves in some English Venice, a feeling reinforced as you pass under Cambridge's bridges, particularly the local version of the **Bridge of Sighs** at St. John's College. The oldest bridge, at Clare College, was built in the 1630s, and the oddest is the Mathematical Bridge at Queens' College. A shapely wooden arch, it was constructed entirely without nails, from straight timbers that notch together like a Chinese puzzle. It was certainly a puzzle that proved too complex for generations of drunken undergraduates. They were capable of dismantling it, but putting it together again was quite beyond them. Eventually, authority had to step in, and the bridge sections are now bolted together.

The views of the colleges from the Cam include what is perhaps the city's most famous—**King's College** and its **chapel** (see below). The latter is on every tourist itinerary and deservedly so, for it is one of the great buildings not just of Cambridge but of the world. Its majesty is apparent from the outside, but its true glory is its interior. It was begun in the 15th century but not completed until the 16th, by which time Gothic architecture was at its most flamboyant. We should be grateful for the delays, for without them the building would never have been given its glorious, fan-vaulted ceiling.

Cambridge University is, like Oxford, the sum of its colleges, and while there are many similarities in organization, there are subtle differences as well. Colleges in both universities are usually built around squares, but what is a quad at Oxford is a court at Cambridge, and undergraduates here never have tutorials—they go for "supervisions" instead. For visitors, however, the most obvious difference lies in building materials: Whereas in Oxford stone rules, here warm red brick dominates. Most of the colleges are open to visitors except during the examination period, which runs from early May to mid-June. But even when they are closed, much of the colleges' magnificence is on display. Indeed, it is the cumulative effect of college architecture that gives Cambridge its unique atmosphere and that visitors tend to remember far more clearly than any nice points or fine details.

The geography of Cambridge is comparatively simple. Starting in the north, below the river crossing of Bridge Street, the main road divides. One branch becomes Sidney Street, changing to St. Andrew's Street and continuing as Regent Street. The second branch, starting as St. John's Street, continues on as Trinity Street, King's Parade, and Trumpington Street. Both these routes are lined with colleges, and the space between is given over to town affairs, to the Guildhall, the Corn Exchange, and the still-flourishing market—a proper market with stalls selling everything from fresh meat to fine books.

EXPLORING THE COLLEGES

Magdalene College

Beginning a tour of Cambridge on the far side of the Cam, at Magdalene Bridge (originally Great Bridge), the spot where the Roman road crossed the river, you come first to Magdalene College (pronounced MAUD-lin), founded in 1542. Although it is not one of the grander colleges, the splendor of its Renaissance gateway can be admired, while the extremely Gothicized church can be left to those with enthusiasm for heavy-handed Victorian restoration. The college has much of interest besides its architecture. The **Pepys Library** contains Samuel Pepys's bequest, which includes the famous diaries written in the author's unique shorthand and the more easily deciphered pocket book of Sir Francis Drake. In the 17th century there was a strong Puritan element in the college, and one member who left for the New World, Henry Dunster, went on to become the first president of Harvard College.

Magdalene and its immediate surroundings show how rich and diverse the charms of Cambridge can be. You could spend a contented day without straying more than a few hundred yards from here. Magdalene Street itself has a wealth of ancient buildings. Look, for example, at number 25, now a shoe shop but basically a timber-framed medieval building with an upper story jutting outward and embellished with lovely, ornate carving. Just north of the crossroads, in the corner between Northampton Street and Castle Street, is one of the city's most surprising finds, known somewhat prosaically as **Kettle's Yard**. Here is the house of the art collector Jim Ede, who died in 1990. Nothing on the outside prepares you for the interior. This really is a home, not a museum, so arranged that the visitor feels the owner might turn up at any moment to resume residence. Ede bought the then-unfashionable and unwanted work of his contemporaries—from Gaudier-Brzeska to Ben Nicholson—and he had special affection for the "primitive" paintings of Cornish artist Alfred Wallis.

Across the bridge, visitors who enjoy exploring back streets will find an area that once housed college servants but now comprises what the local real-estate agents would call "desirable residences." It also has its oddities and surprises. On the corner of Portugal Street, an aged police notice announces that hand carts and trolleys are not allowed in, while nearby Portugal Place has a genteel terrace that ends with the High Victorian Gothic of St. John's chapel tower. Back on Bridge Street is the popular student pub the **Baron of Beef**, and just a little closer to the city center is another of Cambridge's more pleasing oddities. The church of the Holy Sepulchre is usually known simply as the **Round Church**, for the very good reason that it is indeed round. Originally built in the 12th century, it contains a ring of stone heads—from fiercely mustachioed warriors to even fiercer demons—that stare down at the visitor.

St. John's College

The Round Church stands by the point where Bridge Street and St. John's Street diverge, at St. John's College, which boasts one of the most attractive and ornate gatehouses of all the colleges. Typical of many, it was built of both red brick and stone. In addition to a statue of the saint, the gatehouse bears a variety of heraldic emblems, from Lancastrian roses to mythical creatures with horns and tusks known as yales. They are the emblems of Lady Margaret Beaufort, under whose will the college was founded in the 16th century. These you might expect, but the builders had a sense of humor. A field of marguerites makes a visual pun on the founder's name, and among the daisies is a rabbit hole with a fox disappearing down one end and a rather smug rabbit popping out the other.

Trinity College

St. John's Street leads to Trinity Street and Trinity College, where you might notice that the heraldic ornaments on the great gate are the same as those at St. John's—not surprising, since Henry VIII was Lady Margaret's grandson. The statue of Henry clutches an orb in one hand and—thanks to generations of undergraduates—a chair leg in the other. (The king originally held a scepter, but as it was relentlessly removed and replaced by a chair leg, eventually the authorities abandoned the struggle and the chair leg remains.) Trinity's **Great Court** is the largest in Cambridge, and college athletes test their prowess by attempting to run a circuit while the clock is striking 12:00—as depicted in the film *Chariots of Fire.* The apple tree on the lawn is descended from one that stood in the garden of a former member of Trinity, Sir Isaac Newton.

Gonville and Caius College

Trinity Lane is one of those curved, narrow ways that promise fresh delights just around the corner. Here it leads on to Gonville and Caius College, begun by Mr. Gonville and enlarged by Dr. Caius and usually known simply as Caius (pronounced "keys"). It has three gates: The undergraduate enters in Humility to Tree Court, passes through Virtue to Caius Court, and leaves the college via Honour. The lane leads on past Senate House Passage and the 18th-century classical formality of Senate House itself, where university degrees are conferred in a ceremony that, because of the numbers involved, takes two days. After that comes Clare College, closely followed by King's.

King's College and Queens' College

King's is a delight, but the **King's College Chapel** is the inevitable focus of attention. Seen across from the Backs it is majestic; up close the detail is revealed; and inside the full splendor appears. It might never have been so splendid but for the turbulence of medieval life. The chapel was begun in the reign of its founder, Henry VI, but the long and bloody Wars of the Roses caused numerous interruptions, and it was completed by Henry VIII. His devices— the Royal Arms, portcullis, Tudor rose, dragon, and greyhound—can be seen everywhere in the building. More important, English architecture had reached a period of great elaboration; hence we have what is literally the chapel's crowning glory, the intricate tracery of the beautiful fan-vaulted roof. The chapel's proportions are noble, and the vast areas of stained glass send a warm light washing over the intricate details of carving and tracery. If you left Cambridge having seen nothing else, you would go away content.

King's has an appropriate companion in nearby Queens' College, named after its two founders, Margaret of Anjou and Elizabeth Woodville. Where the former college is all grandeur, the latter has a feeling of pleasant domesticity, with buildings of mellow brick that could be part of a country house.

King's Parade and Trumpington Street

Back on Trinity Street, now become King's Parade, the clock on **Great St. Mary's Church** rings the hours with a familiar chime, for it is the same as Big Ben's at Westminster—although first struck at St. Mary's. Church bells are also cause to visit St. Bene't's [i.e., Benedict's] Church, where modern bell-ringing, or change-ringing, was begun. There are two ways of ringing bells. The simplest is one in which the bells play a melody. In change-ringing, however, the bells ring peals, compositions—often quite lengthy—that may not appear to the uninitiated to have any melodic basis. Each peal is differentiated from the next by the order in which the bells are rung. It is a system of great, almost mathematical, complexity whose nearest musical equivalent might be a Bach fugue. Change-ringing, still widely practiced in English churches, was invented by a parish clerk at St. Bene't's named Fabian Stedman. Another reason to visit the church: It boasts a Saxon tower, the city's oldest building.

Where King's Parade becomes Trumpington Street, water courses run down deep gulleys on either side. These once brought drinking water to the city's center, and the man largely responsible was Thomas Hobson, who owned extensive livery stables. His customers were forced to take whichever horse was nearest the door, a practice that gave rise to the expression "Hobson's choice."

Off Trumpington Street is Pembroke College, with a **chapel** by Sir Christopher Wren, the first of his architectural works to be completed—giving Cambridge a Wren "first" to set beside Oxford's Sheldonian Theatre. Nearby **Peterhouse**, the oldest of the colleges, dating to 1281, has a famous curiosity. Looking up at the top of the building near the church, you can see an iron bar across a window. The poet Thomas Gray had it placed there to anchor a fire-escape rope. This proved too tempting for his fellow undergraduates, who put a tub of water at the bottom and yelled "Fire!" He was so upset by the experience that he packed his bags and moved to Pembroke College.

Trumpington Street leads on to the **Fitzwilliam Museum**, which has the solemn appearance associated with much Victorian architecture, having been built in 1848. Once past the somewhat dourly tiled entrance, rather reminiscent of a grandiose public lavatory, you will find a fine collection of art and antiquities, with the work of French and English Impressionists doing a great deal to lighten the overall sense of darkness that seems to pervade the university museum. There are temporary exhibitions mounted throughout the year.

STAYING AND DINING IN CAMBRIDGE

If you are tempted by the thought of afternoon tea, then the thing to do is to leave the Fitzwilliam for **Fitzbillies**, Cambridge's most famous tea shop, at 52 Trumpington Street, or, if the riverside still exerts its appeal, then the ▶ **Garden House Hotel** in Granta Place for cream tea on the lawn stretching down to the water. The Garden House is also recommended for an overnight stay. The ▶ **University Arms** on Regent Street is another excellent accommodation. The hotel is 150 years old and features a paneled restaurant with stained glass windows of college crests. The recently enlarged but old, established ▶ **Lensfield Hotel** is a friendly, relaxed, family-run place; centrally located, it is within walking distance of colleges, shops, and the river. A mile from the city center and a few minutes from the railway station, the ▶ **Helen Hotel** has an Italian-style garden; owners Gino and Helen Agodino specialize in Italian cuisine.

Those on the lookout for something equally traditional but a little stronger than tea might care to sample the beer at the 17th-century coaching inn the **Eagle** on Benet Street. And if a full-scale meal is in order, there is no shortage of restaurants. You might try the imaginative menu at **Twenty Two** on Chesterton Road, where offerings range from cold ginger-and-melon soup to lamb with rhubarb, or the hustle and bustle of popular **Brown's** on Trumpington Street, with generous portions of pastas, salads, pies, and grills, among other English, Continental, and American fare. **Midsummer House** on Midsummer Common has a distinctly metropolitan air, which extends from its elegant setting to its international cuisine (Tel: 0223-692-99). Fine though international restaurants are, visitors to Cambridge are more likely to be wanting something as English as a punt on the Cam, and what could be more English than a cricket pavilion? **Hobbs Pavilion** restaurant on Parker's Piece is just that, though the proprietors cannot guarantee you will have any cricket to watch.

—*Anthony Burton*

Windsor

From a plane approaching London's Heathrow Airport, or across the fields from a car on the M 4, the crenellated walls of Windsor Castle and its one big, round, hollow tower topped by a crown look like a child's dream of a heavenly sand castle. Sadly, in 1992 fire destroyed a large part of the castle buildings, including the Great Hall.

Closer, from the three-mile-long double avenue of trees called Long Walk, it seems to belong in Camelot rather than in this world of airports and freeways. Yet Windsor Castle, just 21 miles west of London on the banks of the River Thames, is uniquely a part of both: the home and fortress of nine centuries of English monarchy and of the present helicopter-hopping, polo-playing royal family.

MAJOR INTEREST

Windsor
Royalty and Empire Exhibit
The Guildhall (Wren, royal portraits)

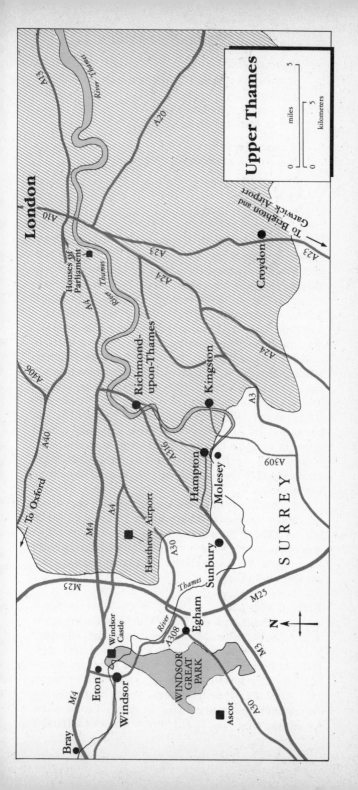

Upper Thames

miles

kilometers

London

Houses of Parliament

River Thames

A13

A20

A10

A4

A406

A40

To Oxford

M4

A4

Heathrow Airport

A30

Richmond-upon-Thames

A316

A24

A23

Kingston

A3

Hampton

Molesey

A309

Sunbury

M25

SURREY

A3

M25

Thames

Egham

A308

River Thames

Windsor Castle

Windsor Great Park

WINDSOR GREAT PARK

Ascot

A30

Eton

Windsor

Bray

M4

Croydon

To Brighton and Gatwick Airport

A23

A24

N

The Castle
St. George's Chapel (Chapel of the Order of the
   Garter)
The State Apartments
Queen Mary's dollhouse

Windsor Great Park
The Royal Mausoleum at Frogmore House

Around Windsor
Eton College
Runnymede

When Queen Elizabeth I commanded William Shakespeare to write a play for her court, this town of red-roofed houses became the setting for *The Merry Wives of Windsor,* his only domestic comedy. The **Garter Inn** pub stands on the site of the very inn where Sir John Falstaff and his cronies roistered (rebuilt much later as the Harte and Garter). At the Victorian (1849) Central Railway Station, the **Royalty and Empire Exhibit** evokes a later period: the precise moment on June 19, 1897, when Queen Victoria stepped off the train with her entourage in readiness for the celebration of her diamond jubilee the following day. **The Guildhall** is a handsome 17th-century colonnaded building designed by Sir Thomas Fitz and completed by Sir Christopher Wren. It houses a small museum of local history, but its main attraction is its collection of royal portraits. Next to the Guildhall, the Elizabethan Market Cross house leans as perilously as the Tower of Pisa.

Visited by nearly three million people each year, Windsor cannot begin to provide parking for them all. Go by bus, by train, or, even better, by boat. The royal borough is overshadowed by the huge castle perched on its chalk ridge above the River Thames and dominating the approaches from London.

THE CASTLE

It is not difficult to picture Henry VIII, bloated with excess and age, dragging his ulcerated leg through the cloisters of Windsor, where courtiers plotted and whispered of heresy and treachery. It's said that his halting steps can still be heard there. It was to Windsor that Henry fled in August 1517, when the "sweating sickness" struck the capital. But the epidemic followed the king, carrying off some of the royal pages who slept in His Majesty's chamber. Henry's coat of arms, along with the Tudor rose and the pomegranate of his first wife, Catherine of Aragon, are engraved in stone above the entrance gate named after the king. But Henry is only one of 41 monarchs who have added to and altered the castle that William of Normandy began just four years after he defeated Harold at the Battle of Hastings. Henry II's Round Tower, which surveys the Thames as it winds through its green valley, is surrounded by other towers, walls, courts, lodges, and chapels built by successive royal dynasties. Plantagenets, Tudors, Stuarts, and Hanovers have added to the castle over the years. (The only interruption in the near millennium of royal residence at Windsor was the bitter decade of the Civil War in the 1640s.) The most recent occupants, the Windsors, so renamed their House of Saxe-Coburg and Gotha in 1917, when anti-German feeling was high. A new addition to the grounds is the Tudor-style mansion that the duke and duchess of York designed for themselves after their marriage in 1986.

Tradition rules here at Windsor, the heart of the system that from an island of warring barons created a nation and an empire upon which, it was said, "the sun never set." British tradition is glorified every morning from Monday through Saturday at 11:00 with the elaborate rituals of the changing of the guard. Soldiers in their red tunics and black bearskin helmets stamp their boots and make the ancient walls ring. The same troops, in flak jackets rather than scarlet, are available for action in NATO or trouble spots farther abroad. At Combermere Barracks on St. Leonard's Road, just a few blocks from the castle, is the **Museum of the Household Cavalry**. The Household Cavalry can also be seen mounting the guard daily at the Horse Guards opposite Whitehall in London. The museum tells the story of the Blues (who, confusingly, wear red plumes in their helmets) and the Life Guards (white plumes) from 1685 to the present. The two regiments are being merged in a reorganization of defense forces.

Chapel of the Order of the Garter

Also known as St. George's Chapel, this is the first building you see when you pass through the Henry VIII Gate. Carved choir stalls in the chapel include those of the Knights of the Garter, an order that, according to romantic legend, Edward III founded in 1348 after he picked up a garter the countess of Salisbury dropped while they were dancing. He rebuked the tittering courtiers with the words *"Honi soit qui mal y pense"* ("Evil be to him who evil thinks"), and this is the motto inscribed in gold letters on the dark blue velvet garter that to this day members wear beneath the left knee.

Edward IV began building the present chapel where the processions and ceremonies of the Knights of the Garter are enacted. Their banners are hung in the choir. The chapel was completed by Henry VIII, who shares a tomb there with Jane Seymour, his favorite among his many wives. The body of Charles I, beheaded after the Civil War and brought secretly to Windsor, was found nearby in the chapel vault when it was opened by George IV in the early part of the 19th century. Apart from Henry and Charles, eight other kings of England, including three from the present century, rest in peace beneath the chapel's fan-vaulted ceiling.

The State Apartments

When, in 1820, George IV came to the throne late in life (he was prince regent for years during his father's madness), he transferred the family apartments from the dank north wing to the southern and eastern sides of the castle. He built the Grand Corridor to connect them with the State Apartments. These richly furnished quarters are used for royal ceremonies and receptions but are otherwise open to the public. The Queen's Presence Room is still as Charles II decorated it, commissioning the Neapolitan artist Antonio Verrio to paint the ceiling. The walls are adorned with late-18th-century Gobelins, other tapestries, and royal portraits. In the sequence of rooms with majestic titles there are carvings by Grinling Gibbons, etchings by great masters, priceless porcelain and furniture, and paintings by Rubens, Rembrandt, Van Dyck, Canaletto, Dürer, Holbein, Reynolds, and others. The aptly named Grand Staircase is dominated by a vast, gleaming suit of armor made to measure in 1540 for gouty Henry VIII. The Waterloo Chamber, created by George IV as a memorial to those who brought down Napoleon, has a carpet 80 feet long and 40 feet wide without a seam in it. It was made in India for Queen Victoria and is probably the largest example of its kind in the world.

Everything in Windsor Castle is on a regal scale—everything, that is, except the **dollhouse** presented to

Queen Mary in 1923 by the architect Sir Edwin Lutyens. It is on a scale of 12:1, and so is everything in it, including works of writers such as Chesterton and Kipling and paintings of Orpen and Munnings, down to electrical and plumbing fixtures of Lilliputian proportions. Like the State Apartments nearby, it is open to the public.

WINDSOR GREAT PARK

The 4,800-acre park, lying on the far side of the castle in a wide loop of the River Thames, was a hunting ground for William the Conqueror. Herds of deer roam here still. At the farthest end of Long Walk from the castle is the Copper Horse, an equestrian statue of George III dressed as a Roman emperor—a suitably sardonic memorial to the king who lost the American colonies.

On the grounds of Frogmore House, a royal residence dating from 1697 in a quiet corner of the park, is the **mausoleum**. A masterpiece of mosaic and monumental masonry, it is a reminder of the Victorian way of death, open to visitors only on occasional days in May. Victoria, the Widow of Windsor, had it built for her beloved consort, Albert, whom she mourned for 40 years before she joined him. In the burial ground outside lie the remains of the king of the briefest reign, Edward VIII, and the woman for whom he gave up the throne of England, Wallis Simpson.

ETON AND RUNNYMEDE

Eton College, that oldest of old schools that molded no fewer than 18 British prime ministers, stands modestly beside the High Street of the little town from which it takes its name, just across the river from Windsor. Some of the buildings, including the exquisitely painted Chapel, date from the school's founding in 1440 by Henry VI when he was only in his late teens. A tower completed by Roger Lupton in 1520 looks down on the cobbled schoolyard and the playing fields beyond, on which, according to the duke of Wellington, himself an old Etonian, the Battle of Waterloo was won. There is a wall against which a game peculiar to Eton is played annually. The younger boys still wear the inimitable Eton jacket and stiff collar, and the "Eton Boating Song" is still sung. Ask at the Tourist Information office about when the school can be visited.

One fine summer's morning in 1215 King John and his entourage rode out from Windsor Castle to meet the king's disaffected barons, assembled on Runney Mede, and to put his seal to the Magna Carta. All English-speaking peoples, including those who went to America, have benefited from this charter of liberty. The water-meadows of **Runnymede** beside the Thames, 2 miles (3 km) northwest of Egham on A 308, remain virtually untouched by the passing centuries. A small Classical-style temple was erected in 1957 by the American Bar Association, and nearby a memorial to President John F. Kennedy stands at the foot of Cooper's Hill. At the summit is another memorial, commemorating the 20,456 Allied airmen who died in World War II and have no known graves. Their names are recorded in the cloister.

ROYAL WINDSOR HORSE SHOW

The Royal Windsor Horse Show is held in Home Park in mid-May. Members of the royal family play an active part, whether it be show jumping or driving. The best way to see the show, which is done while drinking Champagne and eating smoked-salmon sandwiches, is to become a member. Write to the Secretary, Mews, Windsor Castle, Berkshire. Royal Ascot, immortalized in Lerner and Loewe's *My Fair Lady,* takes place in June on the racecourse south of Home Park. For those who would rather listen to Baroque music than compare the finer points of horse-flesh, the Windsor Festival runs from late September through October.

DINING IN WINDSOR

A good place to dine in Windsor is **The Castle**, a Georgian coach inn opposite its namesake that offers a plain à la carte menu. However, to escape the crowds it is worth taking a half-mile walk across the pedestrians-only bridge to the town of Eton. **Christopher**, on Eton's High Street (closed Saturday lunchtimes and at Christmas), is fashionable and not terribly expensive. If you want to splurge and sample some of the finest food in Britain, go six miles upriver to Bray for a meal at the **Waterside Inn**. The restaurant, run by the celebrated Roux brothers of France, has views of smooth lawns and summerhouses, weeping willows, boats, and swans on the river. Book in advance; Tel: 0628-206-91.

—Catherine Connelly and Cathy Bartrop

Brighton

Queen Victoria was not amused by Brighton; George IV, as Prince of Wales ("Prinny" to fashionable Regency society), adored the place, which he first visited one Sunday in September 1783 when it was just a small fishing town called Brighthelmston.

Brighton is a town built on misbehavior. Prinny installed his morganatic wife, Mrs. Maria Fitzherbert, here in a house he built for her in Old Steine, a triangular garden at the center of Brighton. Today the house is a YMCA hostel. In less permissive times it was an open secret that unmarried couples, or at least couples who were not married to each other, slipped down to Brighton for an illicit weekend of pleasure. Titled men kept their actresses here. Brighton was known as early as the mid-18th century, when a local doctor published a pamphlet recommending the "oceanic fluid" as a curative, to be taken both by bathing and by drinking.

Fifty years ago Graham Greene used the resort as the backdrop for *Brighton Rock,* a novel about sleazy crime amidst the seaside trippers and at the racetrack in the hills above the town. The "rock" of the title is not a geographical feature but a stick of rainbow-hued candy, very hard on the teeth, with "Brighton" spelled out in red sugar all the way through its white core. Greene's boy-gangster, Pinkie, would have no difficulty in recognizing Brighton—and its rock—today.

Less than an hour from London by train, and easily within commuting distance, Brighton is nonetheless a smart place to live, much favored by creative people such as the late Lord Olivier. Apart from Greene, Terence Rattigan and Noël Coward found inspiration here. Not so long ago, kippers could be had for breakfast on the Pullman service to town, but, alas, the *Brighton Belle* is no more. Frankly, the steeply shelved beach of large round pebbles is nothing to write home about, except that a section of it just west of the marina is reserved for nudists. But Brighton still revels in naughtiness and is always fun to visit, even for a day—though it has enough to keep you entertained and occupied for much longer.

MAJOR INTEREST

Royal Pavilion and the Dome
The Lanes (antiques shopping)

Palace Pier views of the coast
The Aquarium
Volk's beachside railway

THE ROYAL PAVILION

Trim suburbs climbing inland up the grassy slopes of the Downs, manicured public lawns, and bright ribbons of flowers give no hint of the centerpiece that, when revealed, hits the visitor smack in the eye. It is a palace from the hills of northern India, complete with minarets and onion domes, magically transported and set down in the midst of an English garden. The Royal Pavilion was built not by a Mogul emperor but by the extravagant, debauched, lecherous, eccentric George IV. About the time of his father's terminal bout with madness, George hit upon the idea of transforming the mansion he had built in Brighton into an Eastern fantasy palace. His architect was John Nash, who laid out London's Regent's Park and Regent Street and redesigned Buckingham Palace. No expense was spared. The result, the Royal Pavilion, convinced some people that the family insanity was hereditary. Among some of the more polite remarks were these: "This potbellied palace, this minaret mushroom, this gilded dirt pie, this congeries of bulbous excrescences . . ."

The interior was no less exotic than the exterior, satisfying the prince's taste for chinoiserie, which can still be viewed today, together with marvelous Regency furniture, porcelain, glass, silver, and gold plate. Many of the pieces are on loan from Queen Elizabeth II. The lavishly decorated Music Room is where the 70 members of a royal orchestra played while Prinny sang a popular song called "Life's a Bumper." Gutted by a fire in 1975, the room was expensively restored, then wrecked again when a three-ton minaret crashed through the roof during the great windstorm of 1987, which also devastated the lovely central parks of Brighton. Once again, the Music Room has been returned to its original splendor. So has the Banqueting Room, which is still used for entertaining and looks much as George IV would have seen it on his last visit in 1827.

By the time the pavilion was completed, the prince regent had become king and lost interest in it. But the fashion he had started rolled on. **Regency Square**, just across the promenade from West Pier and planned as the Royal Pavilion neared completion, provides the grandest example of the genre of bay windows, balconies, and wrought-iron tracery in the houses that line it.

Before he built the Pavilion, George commissioned William Porden to build stables and a riding school in the style of a Muslim mosque. Today the **Dome** is the home of the Brighton Philharmonic Orchestra and is also used for events as varied as rock concerts, trade-union conferences, and the degree-conferring ceremonies of Sussex University, whose campus, designed by Sir Basil Spence in the 1960s, is high on the Downs out of town. The adjoining stables fronting Church Street serve as Brighton's public library, art gallery, and museum.

THE LANES

Nowhere is the atmosphere of Brighton, a heady mixture of colorful history and present glamour, more in evidence than in what remains of Brighthelmston, a square mile of small weatherboarded houses and twisting alleyways called the Lanes. Book and antiques shops, jewelers and junk dealers, pubs and restaurants are crammed into these pedestrians-only byways, the entrances to which are clearly marked in the wider streets surrounding them.

At the center of this medieval enclave is **Brighton Square**, a 20th-century traffic-free shopping precinct; open-air cafés give it a Continental feel. Certainly you will hear a variety of European tongues here, and not only from tourists—Brighton is a busy center for English-language schools.

There is no need to confine your shopping to the Lanes, of course—Gardner Street bric-a-brac market is nearby and Brighton has more than its share of stylish emporia, which have helped it earn its reputation as "London by the sea." Among the many fine stores in North Street, the department store **Hannington's**, the oldest (1808), prides itself on its knowledgeable and courteous staff. **Wyn Gillett**, at 34 Upper North Street, sells antique linen and lace in pristine condition. **Graham and Jo Webb**, at 59 Ship Street, specializes in antique music boxes, some of which play whole operatic overtures. Even farther off the well-beaten tourist track, in a narrow lane off Gloucester Road near the railway station, is **Pyramid** (at 9A Kensington Gardens), which has a wide range of Art Deco pieces, from tea services and lampshades to telephones and mahogany-cased radios.

THE ESPLANADE AND PIERS

It would be unthinkable to visit Brighton without taking a sniff of sea air and a stroll along "the front," which is as gaudy as the promenade at any other popular seaside resort. Between Brighton's two piers are fast-food joints, fish-and-chip cafés, cockles-and-whelks stalls, amusement arcades, bumper cars, paddling pools, putting greens, and sleazy shops selling a range of awful kitsch. Among the crowds taking the air are the inevitable dropouts, eccentrics, and aging punks, whose purple hair and safety-pin adornments have become as passé as bell-bottom jeans.

The view from the end of **Palace Pier**, stretching a third of a mile into the sea from Grand Junction Road and Marine Parade, takes in a wide section of English Channel coast, including the beginning of the white cliffs to the east. Admission and deck chairs are free, and the amusements offered (including karaoke in the Offshore Bar and video games in the Palace of Fun) are a matter of individual taste. Although it celebrated its centenary in 1991, this is the younger of the two Victorian piers. Local enthusiasts saved the **West Pier** from demolition, but it is, alas, no longer open for visitors to enjoy the slot machines that were shown in Richard Attenborough's satiric film *Oh, What a Lovely War*. Built in 1866 by Eugenius Birch when the English seaside pier was at the zenith of its popularity, this is a Victorian masterpiece in form, style, and elegance of proportion. Today it has an air of ravaged beauty, but the Brighton West Pier Trust plans to restore it to its original glory by the end of 1999. Brighton and adjoining Hove, incidentally, were a center for movie-making before Hollywood set eyes on its first hand-cranked camera.

Brighton's **Aquarium**, next to Palace Pier, is well past its centennial and still displays sea lions, seals, and turtles, as well as thousands of fish. Also at hand is Britain's first public **electric railway**, Volk's. Opened in 1883 and travelling for a mile along the edge of the beaches (including the one for nudists), it carries passengers in little yellow wooden cars with open sides. The service runs from Easter to October and is inexpensive. At the farthest end of Brighton is one of the town's newer attractions, the largest yachting marina in Europe, opened by the Queen in 1979.

THE BRIGHTON INTERNATIONAL FESTIVAL

In 1967 Lord Olivier brought this arts festival to his home town. Held every year through most of May, it is now one of Europe's liveliest, rivaling the more famous one in Edinburgh. It encompasses theater, jazz, classical music, big bands, opera, rock, cabaret, poetry, fireworks, and such eccentric experiments as a conducted tour of the sewers and the world's smallest theater—an actor on a motorbike with an audience of one in the sidecar.

On the first Sunday in November, fans turn out for the London-to-Brighton Veteran Car Run.

DINING AND STAYING IN BRIGHTON

The best-known seafood restaurants in Brighton are **English's** and **Wheeler's**. Lesser known, and less expensive, is **D'Arcy's** on Market Street, where the plaice and other fish are fresh from the Channel. The **Eaton Garden Restaurant** in Eaton Gardens, Hove (which adjoins Brighton on the west), also serves excellent fish and good old-fashioned English fare such as steak, kidney, and mushroom pie. For those seeking a traditional English tea, the **Mock Turtle Restaurant** at 4 Pool Valley serves a good pot of tea with lashings of homemade cakes and jams on Wood's willow blue-and-white china. Brighton has numerous first-rate French restaurants, too, among them **La Marinade** in Kemp Town and **Le Grandgousier** on Western Street, where rich sauces, garlic, and *l'escargot* provide a whiff of the land just across the Channel. New restaurants open as others fade away.

Between the Lanes and the sea is the newly built ► **Hospitality Inn Brighton**, boasting a four-story plant-filled atrium, two restaurants, and a fully equipped health club and swimming pool. It sits in stark contrast to its neighbor, the ► **Old Ship Hotel**, which is more than four centuries old. Thackeray stayed at the Old Ship while writing *Vanity Fair,* Charles Dickens gave public readings of his works in the ballroom, and Paganini gave a recital here in 1831. More recently the late poet laureate Sir John Betjeman was a habitué. Locally caught seafood is a specialty, and the cellars are extensive. Less historic but just as convenient and comfortable is the ► **Royal Albion**, located in the heart of Brighton between the Royal Pavilion and the seafront.

Just a short walk westward along King's Road, facing the sea, are Brighton's fanciest hotels: the ► **Brighton**

Metropole and the ▶ **Grand**. Stately neighbors, they have been extensively renovated and both feature indoor swimming pools. Accommodation in either one includes well-appointed suites as well as rooms with all modern facilities. For less expensive lodgings, the Brighton Accommodation Bureau is available to help; Tel: (0273) 327-560.

ARUNDEL

A pleasant 20-mile (32-km) drive west of Brighton on the A 27, Arundel has both a fine castle, the ancestral home of the dukes of Norfolk, and a Roman Catholic cathedral (see the Literary Southeast chapter).

—Frank Dawes

GETTING AROUND

Oxford

Oxford, 59 miles (94 km) northwest of London, is reached by rail from Paddington Station, by bus from Victoria Coach Station, and by road via A 40 and M 40.

Cambridge

Cambridge, 55 miles (88 km) north of London, is reached by rail from Liverpool Street Station, by bus from Victoria Coach Station, and by car via M 11.

Windsor

By car, leave London through Hammersmith and follow the M 4 to Junction 6. Windsor is 39 minutes by train from London's Paddington Station to Windsor and Eton Central; the trip takes 55 minutes from London's Waterloo to Windsor and Eton Riverside. You can also reach Windsor by Green Line bus from Victoria Coach Station.

Brighton

By car, Brighton is just 53 miles (85 km) south of London on A 23, a section of which becomes motorway M 23. From London's Victoria Station, Brighton is reached in a mere 51 minutes by express trains, which run hourly. National Express buses make the trip from Victoria Station in two hours. Gatwick Airport lies midway between London and Brighton.

ACCOMMODATIONS REFERENCE

Rates are projected 1994 prices for a double room with breakfast, unless otherwise stated. As prices are subject to change, always double-check before booking.

Oxford

▶ **Courtfield Private Hotel.** 367 Iffley Road, **Oxford** OX4 4DP. Tel: (0865) 24-29-91. £38–£42.

▶ **Old Parsonage Hotel.** 1 Banbury Road, **Oxford** OX2 6NN. Tel: (0865) 31-02-10; Fax: (0865) 31-12-62. £125–£190 (includes Continental breakfast).

▶ **Randolph Hotel.** Beaumont Street, **Oxford** OX1 2LN. Tel: (0865) 24-74-81; Fax: (0865) 79-16-78; in U.S. and Canada, (800) 225-5843; in Australia, (008) 22-24-46. £150 (breakfast not included).

▶ **Westgate Hotel.** 1 Botley Road, **Oxford** OX2 0AA. Tel: (0865) 72-67-21; Fax: (0865) 72-20-78. £41–£52.

Cambridge

▶ **Garden House Hotel.** Granta Place, Mill Lane, **Cambridge** CB2 1RT. Tel: (0223) 634-21; Fax: (0223) 30-04-83. £125–£170 (includes Continental breakfast).

▶ **Helen Hotel.** 167–169 Hills Road, **Cambridge** CB2 2RJ. Tel: (0223) 24-64-65; Fax: (0223) 21-44-06. £45–£50.

▶ **Lensfield Hotel.** 53 Lensfield Road, **Cambridge** CB2 1EN. Tel: (0223) 35-50-17; Fax: (0223) 31-20-22. £60.

▶ **University Arms.** Regent Street, **Cambridge** CB2 1AD. Tel: (0223) 35-12-41; Fax: (0223) 31-52-56. £115–£120.

Brighton

▶ **Brighton Metropole.** King's Road, **Brighton** BN1 2FU. Tel: (0273) 77-54-32; Fax: (0273) 20-77-64. £156–£164.

▶ **Grand Hotel.** King's Road, **Brighton** BN1 2FW. Tel: (0273) 32-11-88; Fax: (0273) 20-26-94. £168–£236.

▶ **Hospitality Inn Brighton.** King's Road, **Brighton** BN1 2GS. Tel: (0273) 20-67-00; Fax: (0273) 82-06-92; in U.S., (212) 689-9284; in Canada, (800) 668-1513; in Australia, (008) 22-11-76. £145–£165.

▶ **Old Ship Hotel.** King's Road, **Brighton** BN1 1 NR. Tel: (0273) 32-90-01; Fax: (0273) 82-07-18. £75–£135.

▶ **Royal Albion.** 35 Old Steine, **Brighton** BN1 1NT. Tel: (0273) 32-39-72; Fax: (0273) 239-72. £115.

THE LITERARY SOUTHEAST
KENT, SUSSEX, SURREY

By Frank Victor Dawes

Within a chalk oval formed by the hill ranges of the North and South Downs between London and the English Channel, many of England's great writers took root. Inside that oval lies the Weald (pronounced wheeled), the old Saxon word for wood. Across the North Downs to Canterbury in the east winds the Pilgrims Way trod by Chaucer. The chalk oval meets the Channel in a series of cliffs, a bastion against would-be invaders of the island; and folds itself away inland into the open plains that stretch, prairie-like, westward toward the mysterious circle of Stonehenge, older than the pyramids, marking the calendar of the seasons since prehistoric times (covered in our Cotswolds to Winchester chapter).

This is Dickens and Kipling country and the favorite retreat of the Bloomsbury writers Virginia Woolf and E. M. Forster. Others identified with the area—from Kent through Sussex to Surrey—include 17th- and 18th-century poets, diarists, travellers, and thinkers such as William Cobbett, Jonathan Swift, John Evelyn, Thomas Paine, and Daniel Defoe, as well as more contemporary literary figures such as A. A. Milne, Henry James, H. G. Wells, and Winston Churchill (who, though primarily thought of as a statesman, was awarded the Nobel Prize in literature in 1953).

Our perceptions of the landscape, towns, and villages of this small corner of England encompassing the counties of Surrey, East and West Sussex, and Kent—all of them only an hour or two's drive south of London—have been shaped by the words of this celebrated company. Who can drive the byroads of the Southeast, winding through green meadows and woods and over gentle hills, without remembering Chesterton's lines: "Before the Roman came to Rye or out to Severn strode, the rolling English drunkard made the rolling English road"?

The rivers of the Southeast, once navigated far inland, ripple down to the sea, providing sport for anglers and canoeists: the Cuckmere, Ouse, Arun, and Adur in Sussex and Kent's Medway, dallying through orchards and hop fields to its confluence at the sea with the greatest British waterway of all, the Thames. Norman churches, castles, ruined abbeys, stately homes, and country houses, Tudor beams and thatch, clapboard inns and oasthouses, bluebell woods and gardens laid out centuries ago can be discovered along these riverbanks and in the narrow country lanes.

Most of this part of England was covered in forest when the Normans invaded in the 11th century, and a few places still are, even though 15 million trees, mostly beech and oak, were knocked down by 100-mile-per-hour winds in October 1987. (Six of the seven oaks planted at Sevenoaks in Kent to mark the coronation of King Edward VII in 1902 were blown down.) There had been nothing like it in the Southeast since the Great Storm of 1703, when Daniel Defoe noted 17,000 uprooted trees in Kent alone before he gave up counting. The climate here may be notoriously unpredictable, but it is not usually given to such extremes. Like the English people, the gentleness of the landscape can be deceptive; history has shown that both are tough enough to survive almost anything.

MAJOR INTEREST

Westerham and the Weald
Chartwell (Churchill)
Great houses of Kent
Sissinghurst Castle (the Nicolsons)
Royal Tunbridge Wells (E. M. Forster, Thackeray)

Pilgrims Way (North Downs Way)
Canterbury

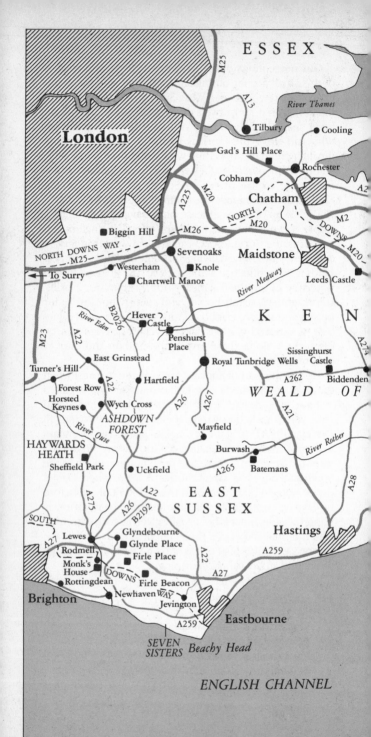

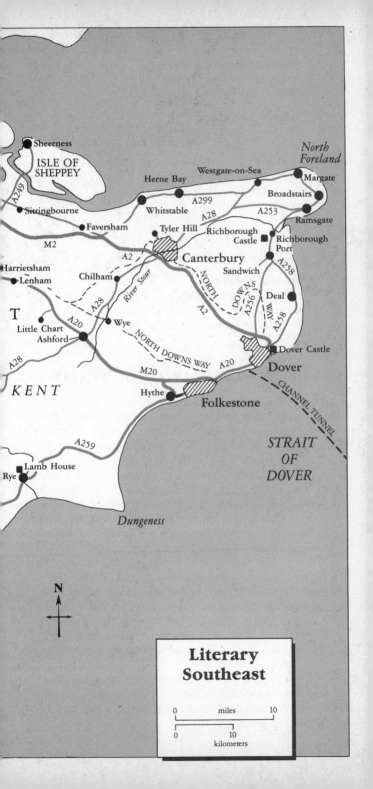

Dickens Country
Medway towns and Broadstairs
The Channel coast

Literary East Sussex
Winnie-the-Pooh country (A. A. Milne)
Charleston and Monk's House (Virginia Woolf
   et al.)
Batemans (Kipling)
Rye (Henry James, E. F. Benson)
South Downs Way

Surrey
Abinger Hammer (E. M. Forster)
Hog's Back and Devil's Punch Bowl

Hampshire Borders
Chawton (Jane Austen)
Selborne (Reverend Gilbert White)
Arundel and Amberley castles

WESTERHAM AND THE WEALD

A few miles east of Gatwick Airport on M 25, the motorway that orbits London, signs indicate the turning-off
point for Chartwell Manor and Hever Castle, a convenient
gateway to the Weald of Kent, which Winston Churchill
loved so much. Chartwell, where Churchill lived for
more than 40 years, lies among the wooded hills 2 miles
(3 km) to the south of **Westerham**, a country town to
which peace has returned now that much of the heavy
traffic bypasses it on the motorway. William Pitt the Younger used a timbered cottage on the outskirts of Westerham as a summer home. General James Wolfe, who died
at age 32 on the Plains of Abraham at Quebec in 1759
while wresting control of Canada from the French, spent
part of his childhood in the town, in a gabled 17th-
century house that is now a museum of this epic expedition. Mementos of his life can be seen among the fine
paintings, furniture, tapestries, and china. General Wolfe's
statue shares the town square with another, of Winston
Churchill.

Three miles (5 km) north of the town on A 233, which
scales the steep bank of the North Downs, is Biggin Hill,
one of the airfields from which Churchill's Few took off
in their Spitfires and Hurricanes to do battle with the

Luftwaffe in the skies over Kent in the summer of 1940. Biggin Hill was also the control center for Sector "C" of the Royal Air Force Fighter Command during the Battle of Britain and, as such, came under heavy air attack. A chapel stands on the site of one of the bombed hangars, in commemoration of pilots and ground crew who lost their lives. Immaculate replicas of a Hurricane and a Spitfire guard the main gate. The aerodrome is still in use for commercial flying and is not a museum.

CHARTWELL MANOR

Churchill bought this old manor house, riddled with dry rot, in 1922 for the marvelous views from its hill down to the wooded valley. The Churchills moved in two years later, after it had been reconstructed with a new wing (which the young statesman called "my promontory") and many French doors, making house and garden one. It was now a fine mansion with five reception rooms, 19 bedrooms and dressing rooms, eight bathrooms, and three cottages on 80 acres. "Winnie" dug out ornamental ponds, lakes, and a heated, floodlit swimming pool. He created waterfalls and erected a brick wall around the kitchen garden with his own hands—for which he was invited to become an "adult apprentice" in the builders' trade union; he accepted.

Between the ages of 55 and 65, Churchill produced a stream of books, including *My Early Life: A Roving Commission,* with its nostalgia for a glorious past when Britannia ruled the waves; *World Crisis,* a history in several volumes of World War I and a vindication of his own part in it; *Thoughts and Adventures,* a collection of his best newspaper articles; *Great Contemporaries,* biographical essays; and, most ambitiously, a multivolume life of his ancestor, the duke of Marlborough. His *History of the English-speaking Peoples,* begun in 1938, was interrupted by World War II and was completed and published in four volumes after it, together with his entirely subjective account, *The Second World War.*

Most of this work was done at Chartwell, hardly the lonely writer's garret. Churchill commanded large fees, and he employed a researcher and a whole team of secretaries whom he worked at a ferocious pace, starting when he sat up in bed early in the day and finishing at three or four the following morning as he paced up and down, still dictating (the track worn across the carpet in his study is visible). The rooms still seem to echo with

Churchill's voice and the laughter and conversation that animated the dinners attended by a continual flood of visitors, from government officers and academics to foreign statesmen, newspaper owners, and celebrities such as Charlie Chaplin.

House and garden were a source of delight to Churchill through all the years he lived there, until his death at the age of 90. A bronze statue of Sir Winston and Lady Churchill was unveiled in 1991 by Her Majesty Queen Elizabeth, the Queen Mother. It looks up the valley over the garden, much of which was designed by Lady Churchill.

HEVER CASTLE

From the summit of Crockham Hill near Chartwell, the Weald spreads out in green and brown patchwork south and southeast to the horizon. There are so many fine historic houses within the area that it would take a week to visit them all. Hever Castle, 5 miles (8 km) south of Chartwell and up a small lane off B 2026, or an hour by train from London to the tiny local Hever station, should not be missed. In Tudor times it was the home of the Bullen (or Boleyn) family, and it was here that Henry VIII wooed Anne Boleyn. The original moated manor, dating from the 13th century, was bought by William Waldorf Astor in 1903, restored, and surrounded by a newly built village in mock Tudor style. Astor created an Italian garden with classical statues and sculptures, including a carved marble relief that was part of the triumphal arch erected by Rome's Emperor Claudius in A.D. 51 at Richborough on the Kent coast to mark his conquest of Britain. This treasure, one of only two surviving remnants of the arch (the other is in the Louvre in Paris), is now displayed inside Hever Castle. Its American owner took British citizenship and became the first viscount Astor of Hever. The Astors still live at Hever Castle.

PENSHURST PLACE

An old stone bridge crosses the River Eden at Hever. A few miles downriver, where the Eden flows into the River Medway, is Penshurst Place, which can be reached either on B 2176 or, if you can read an Ordnance Survey map, through a variety of delightful but unclassified lanes that play hide-and-seek with the river among the woods and meadows. The stately edifice where the Elizabethan soldier, poet, and statesman Sir Philip Sidney was born is entered through Leicester Square, named after the earl of

Leicester. The Great Hall, with its minstrels' gallery and armor, goes back to the 14th century. Penshurst is the ancestral home of the Sidney family, and Viscount de L'Isle (who died in 1991) continued the family tradition as a soldier (he won the Victoria Cross at Anzio), a diplomat, and a landowner.

The Spotted Dog at Smarts Hill, half a mile south of Penshurst off B 2188, on an unclassified country lane, is a charming old Kentish clapboard pub with a terrace looking over the Weald. A traditional Sunday lunch is served in the low-beamed bar, and a variety of tasty pub food, including local Speldhurst sausage (a rich mix of pork, spices, and herbs), is available at all times. The pub is very popular with locals, so it is advisable to book in advance for sit-down meals in the restaurant (Tel: 0892-87-02-53).

KNOLE

Another ancestral home, begun in the middle of the 15th century by the archbishop of Canterbury and given by Queen Elizabeth I to courtier-poet Thomas Sackville in 1603, is Knole, on the outskirts of the country town of **Sevenoaks** on A 225, 12 miles (19 km) north of Penshurst. The Sackville-Wests still live there, although the mansion and its furnishings, tapestries, silverware, and paintings, including portraits by Reynolds and Gainsborough, have been given to the National Trust. Knole, which stands in a great park where deer roam freely, was described by Virginia Woolf in her novel *Orlando* as "a town rather than a house," a fitting description of a building that covers three acres and has seven courtyards, one for each day of the week; 52 staircases, one for each week of the year; and 365 rooms, one for every day of the year. Virginia Woolf's friend Vita Sackville-West, also a writer, grew up here.

LONG BARN AND SISSINGHURST CASTLE

Vita and her husband, the diarist, biographer, diplomat, and politician Harold Nicolson, created two other notable houses and gardens in the Weald. Two years after their marriage in 1913 they bought 15th-century Long Barn, where printing pioneer William Caxton is said to have been born. They extended and developed it, and laid out a garden with the help of Edwin Lutyens. It is 2 miles (3 km) south of Sevenoaks, off A 21, but it is not open to visitors.

In the 1930s the Nicolsons bought and restored Sissinghurst Castle (just off A 262 near the village of Biddenden), creating a series of gardens "furnished" in contrasting colors and styles. Visitors can see the first-floor room of the Tudor gatehouse in which Vita Sackville-West wrote her poetry, with a view of the garden, and also her library, as well as the original Hogarth handpress on which T. S. Eliot's *The Wasteland* was printed. Sissinghurst is richly furnished with polished oak and Persian carpets, and its gardens are still acclaimed as some of Britain's finest. As visitors arrive at the rate of some 200,000 per year, the numbers allowed in sometimes have to be controlled. On busiest days timed tickets are issued and you may have to wait.

Royal Tunbridge Wells

This characterful town, perched among the great sandstone outcrops of the Weald of Kent with 250 acres of gorse-covered green commonland at its heart, was long associated with crusty retired colonels who wrote letters to *The Times* signed "Disgusted, Tunbridge Wells." As the county's center of commercial and cultural life, it deserves a better image because it is an interesting place to visit. The Wells, fed by an iron-impregnated spring deep in the rocks, were discovered in 1606 by Lord North as he was out riding. They soon attracted the attention of fashionable society and the stamp of royal approval. As a young princess, Victoria "took the waters" every day during her visit to the town in 1834 and referred to it as her "*dear* Tunbridge Wells." But it was not until her son Edward was on the throne that the "Royal" prefix was formally given, in 1909.

E. M. Forster grew up in Tunbridge Wells, and William Makepeace Thackeray lived for a time in a plain, square Regency house on London Road. It is still there, defying the traffic and serving a good purpose as a reputable restaurant called, simply and appropriately, **Thackeray's House**. Go there for good-quality English food, but not on Sundays and Mondays, when it is closed.

The original spring that gave birth to Tunbridge Wells is found in a corner of the **Pantiles**, a tree-shadded, paved square next to the Common that was laid out during the reign of Queen Anne three centuries ago. The Bandstand is regularly used for performances of everything from

New Orleans jazz to military marches, and **Binns** is the place to go for a traditional English afternoon tea. The Pantiles had begun to look shabby, but a major redevelopment in the late 1980s gave it a new lease on life, with a modern shopping and entertainment complex that retains the period façades of the Corn Exchange, the Assembly Rooms, and the Royal Victoria Inn. In this lively center a permanent exhibition called "A Day at the Wells" recreates with high-tech skill the sedan chairs and powdered wigs, the coffeehouse gossip, the balls, and the gaming halls of Georgian Tunbridge Wells, where master of ceremonies Beau Nash built on his social triumph at Bath.

No visit to Tunbridge Wells would be complete without a walk around **Calverley Park**, where the great Georgian architect Decimus Burton was commissioned to design a new town. He used blocks of the local Wealden stone to create a Greek Revivalist classic: Calverley Park Crescent rivals anything to be found in Bath or around Regent's Park in London. Calverley Park is near the train station, with the Pantiles and the Common just a short walk away, but Tunbridge Wells is very hilly and long treks cannot be recommended for the not-so-fit.

SHOPPING IN ROYAL TUNBRIDGE WELLS

Tunbridge Wells is a great place for shopping or just browsing, with several multistory parking garages convenient for the pedestrians-only Calverley precinct, Mount Pleasant Road, and the High Street. The **Great Hall** is a restored glass-roofed arcade with furniture shops, boutiques, and a branch of Hatchards, the London bookshop. Tunbridge Ware, a distinctive type of inlaid woodwork, is something to watch for in the antiques shops that abound, along with secondhand bookshops and art galleries, in Chapel Place, Nevill Street, and along Camden Road.

STAYING IN ROYAL TUNBRIDGE WELLS

For those who want to extend their visit or use Tunbridge Wells as a base for exploring the Weald of Kent, the ▶ **Spa** is a very comfortable hotel with an indoor heated swimming pool, tennis courts, and a children's play area. What was formerly the rather drab Wellington has been transformed by extremely colorful fabrics and furnishings and is now the ▶ **Periquito**. Despite this exotic name, it retains its original Regency woodcarving and staircase, large sash windows, and high ceilings, together with an air of period charm.

THE PILGRIMS WAY

"He knew the tavernes wel in every toun," wrote Geoffrey Chaucer in the prologue to his *Canterbury Tales,* and 600 years after the words were written, there are as many old villages and pubs along the Pilgrims Way. To follow the route taken by the medieval pilgrims across the shoulder of the North Downs from Winchester, the ancient Saxon capital, to Canterbury still calls for good boots and a stout heart, but the way is marked. For much of its length, the Pilgrims Way crosses open country, over fields and through woods that have never known tarmacadam or concrete. The nearest modern roads heading in more or less the same direction are the M 25 London Orbital, which passes just north of Sevenoaks at Junction 5, and the M 20 motorway.

Beyond Maidstone, the Pilgrims Way passes near **Leeds Castle**, built in the twelfth century from the original ninth-century fortress in the middle of a lake, and still in use for high-security summit meetings. Henry VIII converted it into one of his many royal palaces, and later Lord Culpepper, who was the governor of Virginia from 1680 to 1683, used Leeds Castle as his English country seat. It contains superb medieval accoutrements, French and English furniture, tapestries, and Impressionist paintings, and has a maze of 3,000 yew trees planted by the present owners in the mid-1980s; the maze features as a centerpiece an underground grotto decorated with seashells, statues, and fountains, as well as a 90-foot "secret" tunnel.

Ringlestone, one of those marvelous inns that Chaucer would recognize, with its blackened beams, brick floors, and a fireplace with an inglenook, is a mile or so farther along A 20 at **Harrietsham**. If you are looking for a simple place to stay the night, as well as good food and wine, ▶ **The Harrow** at Warren Street, just off A 20, was once a forge and a resting place for pilgrims going to Canterbury. Nowadays the fare it serves is far from simple—venison in cherry and wine sauce or beef and pheasant casserole, for instance—and it uses local produce. There are just seven bedrooms, four of which have private baths.

▶ **Eastwell Manor**, on the other hand, offers elegance

in its oak-paneled bar and baronial dining room. A period mansion on 3,000 acres of private parkland just outside Ashford, it was completely rebuilt in the 1920s. The bedrooms are huge and the bathrooms sumptuous. The ▶ **Ashford Post House** on the Canterbury Road at Ashford incorporates a 15th-century manor house with a 17th-century barn converted into a restaurant. **Ashford**, an old cattle-market town and railway center, has been given a new lease on life as the focal point for rail passengers and road freight using the Channel Tunnel.

In the surrounding countryside, timeless villages with broad greens where cricket is played on weekends, oasthouses with white cowls where hops are dried for the breweries, and apple orchards that burst into oceans of pink and white in May slumber on. They are the stuff of H. E. Bates novels. Bates made his home at **Little Chart**, a few miles west of Ashford, the site of a large green (known in these parts as a *forstal*) where cattle were penned or forestalled before going to market in Ashford.

A few miles northeast of Ashford on A 28 is **Chilham**, a village dating from medieval times, where a "pilgrims' fayre" is held on spring bank holiday, with local people in costume setting up market stalls. The main street leads past a carved-timber Wealden house to the ▶ **Woolpack Inn**, where the oak-beamed bar is hung with hop vines and ancient pews are arranged around the inglenook fireplace. Roast beef and steak, Guinness, and oyster pie are served. There are 14 bedrooms, three in converted stables, eight in a separate building across the courtyard, and the remainder in the original inn.

Canterbury

From Chilham, it's 6 miles (10 km) north on A 28 to Canterbury, whose splendid cathedral tower, "Bell Harry," can be seen from afar across the Garden of England (so called for its acres of orchards, hopfields, and market gardens), whether you approach from inland or from the white cliffs that guard the coast. The cathedral has been the mother church of English Christianity since Pope Gregory sent Saint Augustine here in A.D. 597. Saint Augustine (not the Augustine of the *City of God*) founded the abbey that bears his name outside the city walls and started another church on what is believed to be an earlier Roman site beneath the nave of the present Norman cathedral. Six hundred years later an event occurred that was to make Canterbury a center of pilgrimage and inspire great writers: murder in the cathedral. On December 29, 1170, Archbishop Thomas à Becket was waylaid and assassinated by four knights who had overheard King Henry III cry out in frustration, "Who will deliver me from this turbulent priest?"

The response of Rome was to make Becket a martyr-saint and start the procession of pilgrims, which continued over the next 400 years until Henry VIII, breaking with Rome, denounced Becket for "treason, contumacy, and rebellion." The pilgrims came to pray at two hallowed places—the spot in the northwest transept where the knights cut Becket down, and his tomb in the crypt. Vials containing watered-down drops of Becket's blood were sought as relics and charms because it was believed he had died in the name of Jesus and in defense of the Church.

Soon after Becket's murder, a fire destroyed the Norman choir and the chapel beneath which his tomb lay. Stone was shipped across the Channel from Caen in Normandy up the River Stour to William of Sens, who created an early Gothic cathedral and shrine of St. Thomas the Martyr on the site. When William was crippled after falling from scaffolding, William the Englishman took over and completed Trinity Chapel. The feet and knees of pilgrims wore grooves in the mosaic tiles in this holy place; not even Henry VIII could erase these marks of devotion. Nor did Henry destroy the chapel's 12 inspiring stained-glass windows showing the miracles of Christ and some of the cures attributed to the murdered archbishop. These windows represented to unlettered pilgrims a "Poor Man's Bible."

Parts of the city are still enclosed within medieval walls, and the keep of the ancient castle survives, together with the ancient buildings lining the narrow streets that defied the ravages of the Luftwaffe. The King's School, clustered around Green Court behind the cathedral, numbers among its former pupils the Elizabethan dramatist Christopher Marlowe (who was born, the son of a shoemaker, in Canterbury) and Somerset Maugham. The University of Kent, founded in 1961, surveys the panorama of history from a hill named after Wat Tyler, who led the Peasants' Revolt 600 years ago.

CANTERBURY EXHIBITIONS

An exhibition in the medieval **Church of St. Margaret**, a short walk from the cathedral gatehouse, employs the latest visual, aural, and olfactory technology to give 20th-century visitors a taste of what it was like to be a pilgrim in Chaucer's time and travel on foot from the Tabard Inn at Southwark in London to the martyr's tomb. The work of Heritage Projects, which created the Jorvik Viking Centre (see the York chapter), it re-creates Chaucer's band of travellers: the Reeve, the "verray parfit gentil Knight," the beery, blowsy Wife of Bath, and others—warts and all—including a drunken reveler with pockmarked face recalling "So was hir joly whistle wel y-wet." Whether or not you approve of Chaucer's masterpiece being turned into a "pop-up book," the project should help spread appreciation of Chaucer's work and the story of Becket.

Holograms and computers play a part in the City Council's **Canterbury Heritage** exhibition in the 13th-century Poor Priests' Hospital, on the banks of the Stour just off the High Street. The visitor is conducted on a walk through time, viewing silver spoons left by the Romans, *mazers* (drinking bowls) from medieval hospitals, a fully threaded loom of the Huguenots, who made Canterbury famous as a weaving town, and a re-creation of the firebomb Blitz of 1942, which destroyed a quarter of the city.

STAYING AND DINING IN CANTERBURY

There are numerous old Canterbury inns that the pilgrims knew, but none is more welcoming than the ▶ **Falstaff Hotel**, in St. Dunstan's Street beside West Gate. It was built in the 15th century and, despite modernization of its 24 bedrooms, has preserved its oak beams and paneling. The inn serves hearty, old-fashioned English food such as steak-and-kidney pudding. The ▶ **County Hotel** in High Street is the most central choice, and its restaurant, **Sullys**, is recommended. But for the region's finest English and French cooking (duck roasted with apples and served with a brandy sauce, perhaps) and a wine list of impressive variety, drive 10 miles (16 km) out to the **Wife of Bath Restaurant** in Wye, off A 28 in the direction of Ashford.

DICKENS COUNTRY

North of Maidstone, the Pilgrims Way loops across the River Medway by the same bridge that carries the modern M 2 motorway toward the Channel ports. The Romans came this way after invading the Kent coast at Richborough and put up a bridge downriver from the modern motorway. The town the Romans established here, Durobrivae, now **Rochester**, grew as a staging post on Watling Street, the great highway across England. When the Normans invaded, they too grasped the strategic situation of Rochester and built a castle, the keep of which survives. In due course they replaced the adjacent Saxon church, the second-oldest bishopric in Britain (after Canterbury), with a building that forms the core of the existing modest cathedral. In the south transept there is a brass memorial to Charles Dickens, who spent the impressionable years of his childhood and the later part of his life in or near this city, and used it in several of his novels.

When Dickens lived here, between the ages of five and ten, Rochester had already merged with its bustling neighbor, Chatham, a dockyard with a long history of building warships, from those that defeated the Spanish Armada to H.M.S. *Victory,* the flagship at Trafalgar. Indeed, a young midshipman named Horatio Nelson joined his first ship, H.M.S. *Raisonnable,* here. Today the fleet has gone, and **Chatham Historic Dockyard**, with its 18th-century ropewalk and the mid-Victorian steam sloop H.M.S. *Gannet,* has become England's fastest-growing heritage attraction.

Charles Dickens was born at Portsmouth in a little terraced house on Old Commercial Road, now a museum. His father was a navy pay clerk who sometimes took his son with him as he went about his official business. Charles watched the ropemakers and smelled the tar, stood under the wooden walls on the slips amid oak chips and wood shavings, an experience vividly re-created in the popular Wooden Walls exhibition in the Mast House and Mould Loft at the Dockyard. It shows the construction of H.M.S. *Valiant* through the eyes of an apprentice shipwright starting out in 1758. Dickens senior and son often sailed down the river to Sheerness and the Thames, passing the black hulks where convicts awaited transportation to Botany Bay. Red-coated soldiers paraded in Chatham Lines on the hill above the town, and in the High Street was Simpson's coach office, operating the Blue-Eyed Maid along the old Roman road to London. The massive square **keep of Rochester Castle** offered then, as now, captivating views of the Medway estuary, the North Downs, and the cathedral to anyone willing to climb the 150 steps to the top.

The Bull Inn, where Mr. Pickwick stayed, and the Blue Boar of *Great Expectations* were, and are, none other than the ▶ **Royal Victoria and Bull**, a 400-year-old coaching inn that is still open as a hotel and that serves good plain English food, in the High Street. The rooms retain Dickensian decor accompanied by modern conveniences such as TV, central heating, and *en suite* bathrooms. Miss Havisham's haunting, cobwebbed Satis House is in reality the 16th-century Restoration House in Maidstone Road, but it is not open to visitors.

On rural outings, with Father orating all the way, the Dickenses went as far as **Cobham** on the Dover–London road (A 2) and visited the church of **St. Mary Magdalene** (boasting the finest collection of medieval brass memorials to knights in armor and their ladies in England) and the half-timbered **Leather Bottle Inn**, still open for drink and food, which later became a setting in *Pickwick Papers*. **Cobham Hall**, an Elizabethan red-brick manor with a broad colonnaded front, is today a girls' school, but it is open to visitors at certain times during school breaks. Its octagonal corner towers and array of chimneys remain as they were when father and son admired them on their walks, before entering the shadowy glades of Cobham Wood to come out, two miles farther on, by Gad's Hill, where Falstaff waylaid travellers. Here the boy feasted his eyes on the white portico of an ivy-fronted rose-brick mansion overlooking the valley of the Medway—**Gad's Hill Place**—where John Dickens told his son that he might one day live if he worked very, very hard. Indeed, after using many of the images planted in his head as a child in his brilliantly successful novels, Dickens bought Gad's Hill and lived there for 14 years until his death.

Gad's Hill Place is not open to the public, but the Swiss chalet that Dickens installed on the grounds has been moved to the **Dickens Centre** in Eastgate House on High Street in Rochester. Eastgate House figures in his last, unfinished work, *The Mystery of Edwin Drood,* as the Nun's House, Cloisterham. Dickens, who loved dramatics and reading his own works on stage, would surely approve of the theatrical display of some of his unforgettable characters at the center, which uses a sound-and-light show to bring them vividly to life.

The Lonely Shore

To the north of Rochester and Chatham, between the estuaries of the Medway and the Thames, is a mysterious area of creeks and marshes, ditches and mud flats, where herons fly over the ancient Hundred of Hoo and there are no major roads (the "Hundred" is the name formerly given to a subdivision of a county in England). Tankers, container ships, and the occasional passenger liner pass by on their way to and from Tilbury. Oil refineries glow on the Essex shore across the Thames estuary, and the long pier of Southend-on-Sea can be seen in the distance on a clear day, but it is hard to believe that this desolate place is a mere 40 miles from central London.

In the churchyard at **Cooling**, 13 stones mark the graves of the children of the Comport family from Decoy Farm who died from marsh fever. Dickens, venturing out from Gad's Hill Place in search of atmosphere, found it here and described it in the opening chapter of *Great Expectations,* when young Pip startles Magwitch, an escaped convict hiding among the gravestones. The place has lost none of its atmosphere of brooding isolation, especially when the wind is sighing through the reeds. Cooling was the setting of Joe Gargery's forge. As you go eastward from Rochester and Chatham, along the northern edge of Kent, the scene is altogether more hospitable, more as Mr. Jingle described in *Pickwick Papers:* "Kent, sir—everybody knows Kent— apples, cherries, hops, and women." The M 2 dashes on, but several delightful places may be reached via the old Roman road to Dover. These include **Sittingbourne**, where ocher-sailed, tarred Thames barges can be admired at the Dolphin Yard, and **Faversham**, where Shepherd Neame has been brewing ale from local hops since the 16th century.

A branch (A 299) off the old Dover Road brings you to the seaside town of **Whitstable**. Sample the "Whitstable Natives" (oysters) at **Wheeler's Oyster Bar**, with views across the bay to the Isle of Sheppey. Next are Herne Bay, Westgate-on-Sea, and Margate. As you follow A 299 around the headland of North Foreland, where for nearly five centuries a light has warned ships of the treacherous Goodwin Sands just offshore, you come to Broadstairs. This is the resort where Dickens spent many of his summers, writing feverishly and enjoying the "rare good sands," as he called them, and the brisk and bracing air.

Broadstairs

According to Dickens, Broadstairs at the North Foreland "beat all other watering places." When Dickens first took his wife and infant son here for a long summer holiday in 1837, it was little more than a fishing village at the edge of the chalk cliffs. "I have walked upon the sands at low-water, from this place to Ramsgate," Dickens wrote in a letter at the time, "and sat upon the same at high-ditto till I have been flayed with cold. I have seen ladies and gentlemen walking upon the earth in slippers of buff, and pickling themselves in the sea in complete suits of the same. I have seen stout gentlemen looking at nothing through powerful telescopes for hours."

Dickens was 25 and already famous for *Pickwick,* which was into its final installments. *Oliver Twist* was pouring out of him, and in the following year he would undertake his investigation of the notorious Yorkshire schools that led to *Nicholas Nickleby.* He wrote the last lines at two o'clock on the afternoon of September 20, 1839, and immediately dashed off to Ramsgate to send the copy to the printers in London.

Among the places he rented here were 37 Albion Street and Lawn House, and while the family members were getting "as brown as berries" and Broadstairs filled with his friends, *The Old Curiosity Shop* and *Barnaby Rudge* flowed from his writing table. He wrote most of *David Copperfield,* his "favorite child," in an airy little room at the top of a house built like a fort on the cliff overlooking Viking Bay. Now known as **Bleak House**, it is privately owned but open to visitors and full of fascinating memorabilia of the author, including "the mirror that many times reflected the face of Charles Dickens," his inkstand and pen, corrections he made to proofs, and his pocket knife. Indeed, there are reminders of Dickens at every corner of this charming town, with its little harbor and sandy beach protected by a small pier from Peggotty's Launderette to the "What the Dickens" café.

The Channel Coast

It is possible to walk, as Dickens did, from Broadstairs south to the busy harbor of **Ramsgate** along the sands at low tide. From here all the way south along the Channel to Hythe the coast is at once a fortress and a gateway to the Continent, which can be seen in clear weather across the narrow **Strait of Dover**. The **North Downs Way**, a trail 141 miles in length across Surrey and Kent from Farnham to Dover, crosses rivers and highways. It is intended mainly for walkers, but some sections are open to cyclists and horse-riders. The middle part of it follows the Pilgrims Way, but it loops beyond Canterbury just south of

Dover Harbor to the sea at Shakespeare Cliff, a massive chalk headland 300 feet high with a dizzying view over the Channel that is described in *King Lear* and beneath which the tunnel link with the continent of Europe now runs.

Until now, this natural ditch has been England's bastion against invasion since the Normans came, and it was reinforced by formidable castles at Dover, Walmer, and Deal. The ruined castle at **Richborough** (just south of Ramsgate and Pegwell Bay), the main landing place for the invading forces of Emperor Claudius in A.D. 43, was last used for coastal defenses in World War II—when soldiers on guard duty reported seeing whole cohorts of ghostly Roman legions marching into the sea. There are traces of the foundations of the enormous triumphal arch that would have been visible for miles out to sea (a fragment of it is kept at Hever Castle), and ancient coins, ornaments, and weapons are displayed in the museum on the site.

Momentos of the more recent struggle when invaders were kept at bay may be found along Aerodrome Road off the A 260 just north of Folkestone at Hawkinge, a former Royal Air Force base where fighter pilots waited to "scramble" against German bombers in the summer of 1940. The guardhouse, armory, and control tower survive together with a Spitfire, Hurricane, and Messerschmitt Bf109 used in the film *Battle of Britain.* Hawkinge, which played a frontline role, is now the **Kent Battle of Britain Museum**. On a far more ambitious scale and using all the resources of video-age technology, the *White Cliffs Experience,* a new permanent exhibition on the Market Square in Dover, at the site of important archaeological remains, brings together the major events in the town's history, from the landing of the Roman legions to the air raids of the 1940s. It is really 13 interactive exhibitions, specifically designed to stimulate the interest of children. A three-floor museum, fully accessible to disabled visitors, is an integral part of the *White Cliffs Experience.*

The North Downs Way runs along the top of the White Cliffs, skirting the vast new Folkestone Terminal where vehicles will be loaded on and off the Channel Tunnel trains. Despite this competition, large vehicle-carrying ferries will still shuttle back and forth across the Channel from **Dover** and **Folkestone**, the twin gateways in the wall of chalk. Between these and Ramsgate there is a long stretch of sand dunes that forms a 700-acre wild-bird reserve, the Sandwich Bay Nature Reserve, and provides the setting for three championship golf courses: the Royal Cinque Ports, Royal St. George's, and Prince's. Ian Fleming, the creator of James Bond, liked to relax here, and he used the background for 007's game in *Goldfinger*.

LITERARY EAST SUSSEX

Within commuter reach of London yet still relatively unspoiled countryside, East Sussex has acquired a reputation of being Volvo heartland, a place of expensive oasthouse conversions and green "Wellies" (rubber boots). Whatever the truth of this, the country is even richer in associations with the great and the good of English literature than any other part of the Southeast. Kipling, Henry James, A. A. Milne, and Virginia Woolf (not to mention the rest of the Bloomsbury set) lived here and adored it. It is easy to get to and full of delightful surprises, as well as excellent places to eat and stay.

ASHDOWN FOREST

The pretty road from London toward Lewes (A 22), easily accessible from Gatwick Airport and the M 25 orbital motorway, runs through East Grinstead, near which are several notable hotels in substantial grounds. Two, ▶ **Alexander House** and ▶ **Gravetye Manor**, are historic houses with lovely gardens (those of the latter were created by the horticulturist William Robinson when he owned the estate). Expect to pay for haute cuisine served in a gracious style. ▶ **Effingham Park** is on 40 peaceful acres only five minutes from Gatwick Airport. Its amenities include a leisure club, a nine-hole golf course designed by Francisco Escario, and a collection of vintage and classic cars.

From East Grinstead the A 22 road continues through Forest Row, a country town, and Ashdown Forest, a remnant of the Roman forest of Anderida, once a center of the Wealden iron industry. This is A. A. Milne and **Winnie the Pooh country**. Just outside the village of Hartfield, a couple of miles to the east of Forest Row, is the 100-acre wood Piglet's Quarry and, hidden up a trail, Pooh Bridge, from which you can drop sticks in the rushing stream and then race them. The "enchanted place" of *The House at Pooh Corner* is Gills Lap, at the very top of the forest, from where you can see "the whole world spread out until it reached the sky." A little shop called **Pooh Corner** in the village of Hartfield sells all kinds of mementos of the lovable bear, while the **Anchor Inn** serves satisfying meals as well as real ales. ▶ **Bolebroke Mill**, with its Domesday Book pedigree, is an unusual place to stay, provided you are agile enough to climb the stairs to the bedrooms among the rafters.

At Wych Cross, the right fork (A 275) goes via Sheffield Park and its magnificent gardens with five lakes laid out by Capability Brown. This is one end of the Bluebell Railway, which makes a seven-mile run through lovely countryside toward East Grinstead. The A 275 continues to Lewes.

LEWES

The steep, narrow streets of this town, which can be reached by rail from London via Haywards Heath in one minute over the hour, are paved with literary and historical associations. **Southover Grange** in Keere Street, part of Anne of Cleves's divorce settlement with Henry VIII, was once the home of the diarist John Evelyn, "a studious decliner of honours and titles," and the 16th-century, white-painted ▶ **White Hart Hotel** on High Street was where Thomas Paine held the debating club that he was later to call the cradle of American independence. The White Hart offers present-day debaters 48 bedrooms and a restaurant where its coaching-inn reputation for good food is maintained. It also serves Harveys real ale. ▶ **Shelleys Hotel** nearby, in a 17th-century manor with private gardens, is a superior and rather more expensive alternative. Lewes is a lively, sturdy place set in a hollow of the Downs and a convenient base for attending open-air opera at Glyndebourne and exploring the countryside that some of the most influential figures in post-Victorian arts made their own: Virginia Woolf and her husband, Leonard, the critic Clive Bell, and the biographer Lytton Strachey; painters such as Duncan Grant, Vanessa Bell, and Roger Fry (who was also an art critic); and the economist John Maynard Keynes. Most of them had known one another at Cambridge before they lived and loved together in Bloomsbury and here in East Sussex.

CHARLESTON

Virginia Woolf discovered this 18th-century farmhouse in the shadow of Firle Beacon, the highest point on the Downs east of Lewes, before the period between the wars when she wrote her seminal novels. Several fine houses lie in the shelter of the steep north-facing slope, including Firle Place, the home of the Gages, one of whose ancestors, General Thomas Gage, was commander-in-chief of the British forces at the outset of the American Revolution; the 16th-century Glynde Place; and nearby **Glyndebourne Manor**, famed for its summer opera season. (Glyndebourne is closed this year for construction of a new, larger theater; performances at this British Bayreuth will resume in 1994.) Just north of here toward Uckfield on the A 26 is ▶ **Horsted Place**, an outstanding Tudor/Gothic-style Victorian mansion where Queen Elizabeth was often a houseguest. It is now a really grand hotel with 14 superb suites and just three bedrooms, all with views across the Downs. The gardens, open to visitors, are full of specimen shrubs and trees, including a myrtle grown from a sprig that was part of Queen Victoria's wedding bouquet.

Virginia Woolf was so much taken with Charleston that she told her sister Vanessa and her sister's husband, Clive Bell: "If you lived there you could make it absolutely divine." The Bells took her advice and moved in, together with Duncan Grant, painting every surface—fireplaces, bedsteads, bookcases, tables—with loose swirls and messy colors in divine inspiration. The walled garden is filled with sculpture and mosaics as much as with flowers and shrubs. A restored Charleston is now open to the public, echoing with the voices of T. S. Eliot, Lytton Strachey, the Bells, and the Woolfs.

MONK'S HOUSE

Leonard Woolf bought this modest house near the church in the village of Rodmell, 4 miles (6½ km) southeast of Lewes (on A 275 where it is crossed by the South Downs Way) for £700 just after World War I ended. It is now owned by the National Trust but can admit no more than 15 people at a time. Although this was a retreat from the Woolfs' Georgian town house in Tavistock Square, London, in a sense Bloomsbury came with them—so many of their friends had houses or cottages in the area. Virginia spent the summer of 1924, as she did many summers, writing at Monk's House: "a very animated summer." She was on the threshold of confirming her own "queer individuality" as a novelist with the experimental *Mrs. Dalloway;* women, as she remarked later in *A Room of One's Own,* were not supposed to compete with Shakespeare or to write novels. Seventeen years later, depressed perhaps by the bombing of her beloved London, she drowned herself, not far from Monk's House, in the Ouse, which flows through Lewes and down to the sea at Newhaven; her ashes were scattered in the garden of the house. Her husband stayed on at Monk's House until his death in 1969.

Kipling Country

Rudyard Kipling brilliantly fused the present and the past of Sussex in *Puck of Pook's Hill,* when two children act out their version of *A Midsummer Night's Dream* as Puck conjures a Roman centurion, Viking raiders, a Norman knight, a Renaissance craftsman, and smugglers. Kipling loved Sussex so much—"Yea, Sussex by the sea!"—that he spent the second half of his life here, between world travels.

The Elms, where Kipling lived with his wife and three young children at the turn of the century, is perched on the cliff top at **Rottingdean** just east of Brighton, with the Downs behind it. It faces the village green and duck pond near the Plough Inn. **The Grange**, next door, is a museum of Kipling letters, manuscripts, and books. Kipling scoured East Sussex with his wife in one of the early automobiles (which often broke down) looking for a country seat. They found what they were looking for, among the "trees and green fields and mud and the gentry," just outside the village of **Burwash**, about halfway between Eastbourne on the coast and Royal Tunbridge Wells to the north.

Batemans, the solid Jacobean mansion built by a 17th-century ironmaster, lies at the end of a lane that Kipling described as "an enlarged rabbit hole." He bought Batemans in 1902 and lived there for the next 34 years. It is half a mile off A 265, the way clearly marked by signs. The hedgerows are trimmed back, but otherwise it is as Kipling left it. His 1928 Phantom I Rolls-Royce stands in the garage. A short walk through the garden and over a stream brings you to the ancient water mill mentioned in *Puck of Pook's Hill* and restored by Kipling to provide electricity for his country estate. Beside it, one of the oldest water-driven turbines in the world now stands idle, but once a week the great spur wheel and hurstings (grinding machinery) still produce whole wheat flour for sale to visitors.

Kipling and his wife laid out the formal garden, beyond which—over a hedge clipped into the shape of battlements—are the meadows, streams, and woods he so lovingly described. The views are framed in the mullioned windows of the gabled stone house, in which a timber staircase leads to a book-lined study and the French walnut table "ten feet long from north to south and badly congested" at which Kipling wrote *If* and *Puck*.

The exit road from Batemans emerges at the end of the tile-hung and weather-boarded High Street of Burwash. Among the inscriptions on the village war memorial is "Lieut. John Kipling, 2nd Irish Guards, killed 29 September 1915, aged 18." Kipling never wholly recovered from the loss of his only son on the field of Flanders.

STAYING AND DINING
IN KIPLING COUNTRY

Opposite the war memorial and the Norman Church of St. Bartholomew is the 17th-century ▶ **Bell Inn**, where apple logs burn in the grate, pints of Harveys and King & Barnes are drawn by hand pump, and the accents around the dart board are distinctively Sussex. There are five simple yet comfortable guest bedrooms, one of them so old that the floor slopes beneath the low oak beams. Even older, and boasting oak carvings by Grinling Gibbons, is the ▶ **Middle House Hotel** in the nearby village of Mayfield on what used to be the London-to-coast road (A 267). Good food is served in comfortable surroundings, and there are seven rooms, furnished in traditional style but equipped with TV and telephones.

Rye

Kipling often drove down the road that winds along the border between East Sussex and Kent and along the River Rother to Rye at the coast southeast of Burwash to visit Henry James at **Lamb House**. Stephen Crane, who settled nearby at Hastings, and H. G. Wells would drop by, too, and talk away sunny afternoons in the walled garden of the unpretentious two-story red-brick house that stands on a bend of West Street leading out of Church Square. E. F. Benson, whose Mapp and Lucia novels are set in Rye, lived in the house later, under the name of Tilling. The Garden Room, where James wrote *The Ambassadors, The Wings of the Dove,* and *The Golden Bowl,* was wrecked during a World War II air raid, and there is little physical evidence of his tenure from 1898 to 1914. But out of season, when what he called the "various summer supernumeraries" have gone, it is still easy to see why, having been to the far end of Florida, the writer preferred this far end of Sussex.

The town of Rye is guarded by a 14th-century gateway in its walls and sits on the only hill in an otherwise flat, marshy landscape. The outer edge of the chalk oval shows itself again in white cliffs flanking the seaside towns of Hastings and Eastbourne, with their piers, promenades, and bandstands, and reaches a magnificent crescendo in the Seven Sisters and Beachy Head. The **South Downs Way** begins its long haul west to Hampshire across wide tracts designated officially as an Area of Outstanding Natural Beauty. The bridleway section of the South Downs Way, open to cyclists and horse-riders, runs through Jevington while the footpath section for walkers only goes around the cliff tops. The cliffs stand between the open sea and the wide expanse of what Kipling called "our blunt, bow-headed, whale-backed Downs."

STAYING AND DINING IN RYE

The ▶ **Mermaid Inn** here in quaint, cobbled Mermaid Street (rebuilt in 1420) contains priest holes, where persecuted Catholics could hide. A secret staircase is located behind a bookcase in Dr. Syn's bedchamber, named for the fictional hero of Russell Thorndike's saga of the nearby Romney Marshes. Queen Elizabeth really did sleep here—in 1573. The rooms have sloping floors but every modern convenience and are mercifully free from traffic noise. An even better bet, just down the street, is ▶ **Jeake's House**, once the home of American poet Conrad Aiken, now a cozy bed and breakfast. Built in 1689, it it stuffed with books, antiques, and paintings, and has genuine period character.

On High Street, opposite the old grammar school that figures in Thackeray's *Denis Duval,* the ▶ **George Hotel** keeps up the coaching-inn tradition of comfortable rooms and good food, especially with fish delivered fresh from nearby Hastings. The banquet hall has a minstrels' gallery, and logs blaze in cavernous fireplaces. The George contains timber from one of Drake's "wooden walls," or wood-built ships, broken up at Rye after the defeat of the Spanish Armada. The sea is now two miles away, but Rye has managed to stay active.

Six miles (10 km) inland from Eastbourne by A 259 and B 2105, signposted to Jevington, is the **Hungry Monk**, a secluded restaurant in extended Elizabethan cottages serving sublime food and wines at very reasonable prices. It is open for dinner only and Sunday lunch, and advance booking is essential; Tel: (0323) 48-21-78.

SURREY-HAMPSHIRE BORDER

The two halves of the chalk oval discussed earlier converge inside the Hampshire border in the direction of Salisbury Plain, which E. M. Forster considered to be the "heart of our island," and which we cover below in the chapter The Cotswolds to Winchester. He wrote in *The Longest Journey:* "The Chilterns, the North Downs, the South Downs radiate hence. The fibres of England unite in Wiltshire, and did we condescend to worship her, here we should erect our national shrine." His home, West Hackhurst, is at **Abinger Hammer** in Surrey, near the North Downs Way.

The curious name of this hamlet derives from an iron-forging hammer of the 16th century, which was powered by the fast-flowing stream that now feeds watercress beds. A clock overhanging the Dorking–Guildford road (easily reached from M 25) marks the site of the old forge, and the figure of a smith strikes the hours on the bell with a hammer. Abinger Hammer was one of the last places where the Surrey iron industry survived, but its origins go back to the Stone Age settlement excavated on the grounds of the Manor House in the 1950s.

Six miles (10 km) to the north in Stoke d'Abernon (near the junction of A 3 and M 25) is an opulent 19th-century mansion that formerly belonged to the Bryants, a family that made its fortune in the match industry. The house has now been expensively restored as the ▶ **Woodlands Park Hotel**. Edward VII and Lillie Langtry were often house-guests here when it was a private residence.

Beyond the old posting town of Guildford (another ornate clock overhangs its Georgian High Street), the road to Winchester (A 31) runs along a ridge known as the **Hog's Back**. Frensham Great Pond, one of the largest lakes in southern England, and the **Devil's Punch Bowl**, a depression scoured out of the landscape by running water, lie to the south, flanked by the Portsmouth road (A 3). ▶ **Frensham Pond Hotel** at the water's edge has an air of

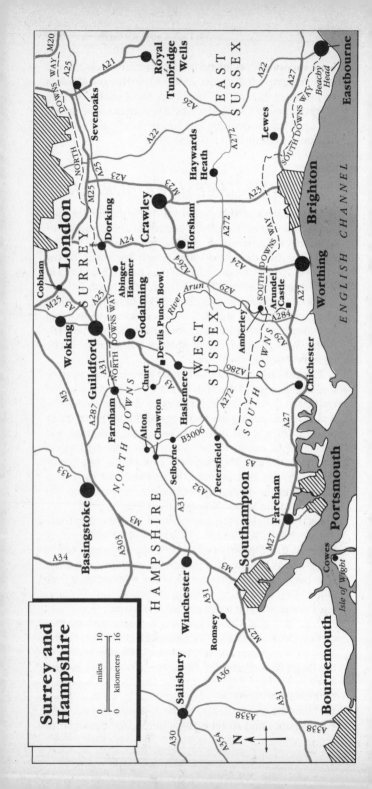

quiet exclusivity. Its amenities include an indoor swimming pool and squash courts. The country here is a mixture of woodland and wide expanses of heather that you can roam at will while admiring the distant views.

The **William Cobbett Inn**, a pub at **Farnham**, a Georgian red-brick country town of unsullied charm off A 31 west of Guildford, was formerly the Jolly Farmer. It was renamed in honor of the celebrated author of *Rural Rides,* who was born here in 1763. Cobbett, the son of a farmer, served in the army in Canada and worked as a teacher in the United States before coming home to start a weekly paper, the *Political Register.* An out-and-out radical, he championed the cause of farm laborers.

Cobbett is not the only literary figure connected with Farnham. Jonathan Swift wrote *Tale of a Tub* when he was secretary to Sir William Temple at Moor Park, which stands on the outskirts of the town. "Good God! What a genius I had when I wrote that book," he said later. At Moor Park he began his friendship with Hester Johnson, the subject of his *Journal to Stella,* published long before *Gulliver's Travels.*

Jane Austen Territory

The North Downs Way begins (or ends, depending in which direction you are walking it) at Farnham. Just out of town, A 31 leaves Surrey and crosses the rolling plain to the Hampshire town of Alton. A mile beyond is the village of **Chawton**, where Jane Austen spent the last eight years of her life. The two-story red-brick building here, originally an inn, was where she put the finishing touches to *Pride and Prejudice* and wrote in quick succession *Emma, Mansfield Park,* and *Persuasion.* The building is now a museum, furnished in early-19th-century style and containing personal effects such as a patchwork quilt that Jane made with her mother and her desk, bureau, and music books. In the bakery is the cart that the family hitched to a donkey for the short trip into Alton. Just outside the garden wall, beside the Winchester road, are two oak trees planted by Jane in 1809 when the family moved in. She wrote at the time that the cottage "when complete, would all other houses beat." Although her brother Edward inherited a fine manor house in a wooded park outside the village, Jane lived happily in the brick cottage and anonymously published her acutely observant novels of middle-class provincial society. She is buried in the cathedral at Winchester, near Saint Swithun, who, according to local legend, governs the summer rainfall.

A mile or two south of Chawton on B 3006 is the village of **Selborne**, whose natural history was chronicled by the Reverend Gilbert White in his classic work *Natural History and Antiquities of Selborne,* published in 1789. His house, **The Wakes**, which stands near the church and village green, is now a museum and library dedicated to White and to Captain Lawrence Oates, who died with Robert Falcon Scott on an expedition to the South Pole. White was born and died in this village, which remains virtually as it was. From the village, the Zig-Zag Path climbs to the top of a beech-covered hill called the Hanger, where White made many of the notes for his book. From this vantage point, he could see the slopes of the South Downs rolling away toward the southeast into West Sussex. The South Downs Way, which is accessible to horseback riders and cyclists as well as hikers, runs over Harting Downs nearby with famous views across the western end of the Weald toward the North Downs. It is just 75 miles (120 km) east by this trail, along the crest of the hill range that forms the bottom half of the chalk oval, to the sea at the white cliffs of Beachy Head on the south coast. If you head west the South Downs Way continues another 24 miles (38 km) to Winchester; most of this section is for walkers only.

Arundel Castle

A splendidly impressive Norman castle in a wooded park towers above the medieval town of Arundel on the River Arun 20 miles (32 km) west of Brighton on A 27. **Arundel** is the seat of the dukes of Norfolk, England's foremost Roman Catholic family, and the castle has a notable collection of paintings, including works by Van Dyck, Gainsborough, and Reynolds. The collection, along with apartments in the castle, may be toured by visitors.

The dukes also built the Gothic-style Roman Catholic cathedral of St. Philip Neri, the second-most imposing feature of this small country town. **Pogey's** on Tarrant Street offers a complete contrast to the medieval and Gothic surroundings with its Art Deco interior and inventive menu, which ranges from moderate to expensive.

Another historic castle (in the village of Amberley on the South Downs Way outside Arundel) became a hotel and restaurant in 1988. Its great walls, battlements, and oak portcullis are intact, yet every room (each named after a different Sussex castle) has its own Jacuzzi. ▶ **Amberley Castle** was attacked by Cromwell and twice visited by King Charles II. The barrel-vaulted dining room contains a fine Restoration mural of him and Catherine of Braganza. Some 36 acres of former chalk pits in the pretty thatched village have been turned into an open-air museum with its own narrow-gauge railway and a collection of industrial steam and diesel engines dating from 1880. The water meadows of the River Arun, habitat for a great variety of flora and fauna, including Bewick swans that fly in from Siberia every winter, are in the care of the Wildfowl and Wetlands Trust. There are seven hides (blinds), all of them suitable for disabled visitors, and wheelchairs can be borrowed without charge. In spring dozens of families of tiny ducklings wander about. Arundel and Amberley can be reached easily by rail from London's Victoria Station, or on A 29.

GETTING AROUND

All the places mentioned in this chapter are within an hour or so of central London by rail or road. The two major international airports of the region, Heathrow and Gatwick, are linked by the London Orbital Motorway (M 25) and provide convenient gateways for exploring the Southeast without becoming entangled in London traffic. The channel ports of Dover, Folkestone, and Newhaven are the entry points for those arriving from Europe, while Southampton (see the following chapter) handles the few long-distance passengers arriving by sea aboard the *QE2* and other liners. Most major car-rental companies have facilities at these ports and airports.

ACCOMMODATIONS REFERENCE

Rates are projected 1994 prices for a double room with breakfast, unless otherwise stated. As prices are subject to change, always double-check before booking.

▶ **Alexander House**. Fen Place, **Turners Hill** RH10 4QD. Tel: (0342) 71-49-14; Fax: (0342) 71-73-28; in U.S., (800) 848-1004. £165–£210.

▶ **Amberley Castle**. **Amberley**, near Arundel BN18 9ND. Tel: (0798) 83-19-92; Fax: (0798) 83-19-98; in U.S. and Canada, (800) 525-4800. £130–£225.

▶ **Ashford Post House**. Canterbury Road, **Ashford** TN24

8QQ. Tel: (0233) 62-57-90; Fax: (0233) 64-31-76; in U.S., and Canada, (800) 225-5843; in Australia, (008) 22-24-46. £41.50–£49.50 (breakfast not included).

▶ **Bell Inn**. High Street, **Burwash** TN19 7EH. Tel: (0435) 88-23-04. £35.

▶ **Bolebroke Mill**. Edenbridge Road, **Hartfield** TN7 4JP. Tel: (0892) 77-04-25. £48–£63.

▶ **County Hotel**. High Street, **Canterbury** CT1 2RX. Tel: (0227) 76-62-66; Fax: (0227) 45-15-12. £70–£100.

▶ **Eastwell Manor**. Eastwell Park, **Ashford** TN25 4HR. Tel: (0233) 63-57-51; Fax: (0233) 63-55-30; in U.S. and Canada, (800) 525-4800; in Australia, (008) 80-25-82. £120.

▶ **Effingham Park Hotel**. West Park Road, **Copthorne**, West Sussex RH10 3EU. Tel: (0342) 71-49-94; Fax: (0342) 71-60-39. £108–£128 (breakfast not included).

▶ **Falstaff Hotel**. 8–12 St. Dunstan's Street, **Canterbury** CT2 8AF. Tel: (0227) 46-21-38; Fax: (0227) 46-35-25. £85–£95.

▶ **Frensham Pond Hotel**. **Churt**, near Farnham GU10 2QB. Tel: (0252) 79-51-61; Fax: (0252) 79-26-31. £90.

▶ **George Hotel**. High Street, **Rye** TN31 7JP. Tel: (0797) 22-21-14; in U.S. and Canada, (800) 225-5843; in Australia, (008) 22-24-46. £84 (breakfast not included).

▶ **Gravetye Manor**. Vowels Lane, near **East Grinstead** RH19 4LJ. Tel: (0342) 81-05-67; Fax: (0342) 81-00-80. £154–£180 (breakfast not included).

▶ **The Harrow**. Warren Street, near **Lenham**, Maidstone ME17 2ED. Tel: (0622) 85-87-27; Fax: (0622) 85-00-26. £45.

▶ **Horsted Place**. Little Horsted, **Uckfield** TN22 5TS. Tel: (0825) 75-05-81; Fax: (0825) 75-04-59; in U.S. and Canada, (800) 525-4800. £99–£115.

▶ **Jeake's House**. Mermaid Street, **Rye** TN31 7ET. Tel: (0797) 22-28-28; Fax: (0797) 22-26-23. £39–£55.

▶ **Mermaid Inn**. Mermaid Street, **Rye** TN31 7EU. Tel: (0797) 22-30-65; Fax: (0797) 22-50-69; in U.S., (800) 843-1489. £98–£130.

▶ **Middle House Hotel**. High Street, **Mayfield** TN20 6AB. Tel: (0435) 87-21-46; Fax: (0435) 87-34-23. £60–£82.

▶ **Periquito**. Mount Ephraim, **Royal Tunbridge Wells** TN4 8BU. Tel: (0892) 54-29-11; Fax: (0892) 53-75-41. £37.50–£64 (breakfast not included).

▶ **Royal Victoria and Bull Hotel**. 16–18 High Street, **Rochester**, Kent ME1 1PX. Tel: (0634) 84-62-66; Fax: (0634) 83-23-12. £45–£65.

▶ **Shelleys Hotel**. High Street, **Lewes** BN7 1XS. Tel:

(0273) 47-23-61; Fax: (0273) 48-31-52; in U.S. and Canada, (800) 44-UTELL. £99 (breakfast not included).

▶ **The Spa.** Mount Ephraim, **Royal Tunbridge Wells** TN4 8XJ. Tel: (0892) 52-03-31; Fax: (0892) 51-05-75; in U.S. and Canada, (800) 528-1234. £88–£110 (breakfast not included).

▶ **White Hart Hotel.** 55 High Street, **Lewes** BN7 1XE. Tel: (0273) 47-66-94; Fax: (0273) 47-66-95; in U.S. and Canada, (800) 528-1234. £76.

▶ **Woodlands Park Hotel.** Woodlands Lane, Stoke d'Abernon, **Cobham** KT11 3QB. Tel: (0372) 84-39-33; Fax: (0372) 84-27-04; in U.S. and Canada, (800) 637-7200. £30–£170 (breakfast not included).

▶ **Woolpack Inn.** High Street, **Chilham** CT4 8DL. Tel: (0227) 73-02-08; Fax: (0227) 73-10-53. £45–£57.

THE WESSEX SHORE

WEST SUSSEX, HAMPSHIRE, DORSET

By Frank Victor Dawes

You will search in vain for the name Wessex on any modern map, but when the Normans crossed the Channel to invade England in 1066, this Saxon kingdom—extending inland from the south coast and the Isle of Wight and with its capital at Winchester (see The Cotswolds to Winchester)—was at the height of its power. Nine centuries later the same coast, stretching west from Sussex across Hampshire to Dorset and on to Devon, was the scene of preparations for a massive movement of Allied troops in the opposite direction to liberate Nazi-occupied France. Operation Overlord, the code name for the landings in Normandy on June 6, 1944, is commemorated by the Overlord Embroidery in the D-Day Museum at Portsmouth, an even more monumental piece of needlework than the medieval Bayeux Tapestry that records William the Conqueror's triumphant expedition.

The Dorset coast is one of the magnificent views from cliffs of chalk, sandstone, and limestone along crescent beaches ranging from golden sand to shingle to giant's pebbles. Other broad vistas open up inland, the folds of a cataclysmic convulsion millions of years ago, golden with gorse in spring and purple with the heather of late summer when rare species such as the brown-and-black Lulworth Skipper butterfly can be spotted. This is Thomas Hardy country. On Bulbarrow Hill, he wrote,

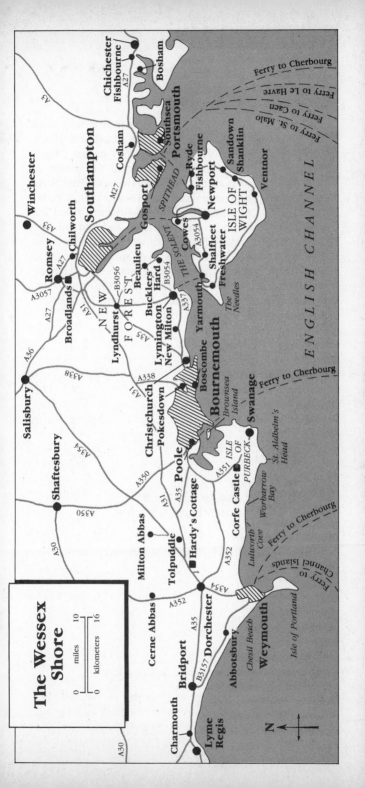

The Wessex Shore

| miles | 0 | | 10 |
| kilometers | 0 | | 16 |

N

> There are some heights in Wessex,
> Shaped as if by a kindly hand,
> For thinking, dreaming, dying on . . .

And this is as true today. Visitors come from every part of the globe to see for themselves the places that Hardy describes in his novels under fictitious names. "Sandbourne" is parvenu Bournemouth, still the queen of south-coast resorts as it was in Victorian times. East along the coast the great natural harbors of Southampton, Portsmouth, and Chichester, from which Britannia ruled the waves, are now given over to leisure and tourism, like that offshore chunk of England across the tidal Solent, the Isle of Wight. New industries have sprung up around these conurbations, whose housing estates spread farther and farther afield, but the 90,000 acres of the New Forest, so called by the early Norman kings who used it as a hunting ground, remain inviolate.

MAJOR INTEREST

Chichester
Roman palace
Cathedral

Portsmouth
Historic ships
D-Day Museum

Southampton
Queen Elizabeth II home port
Broadlands stately home

Isle of Wight
Cowes Regatta (birthplace of *America*'s Cup)

New Forest
Wildlife, walks

Bournemouth
British seaside at its best

Dorset coast
Unspoiled scenery, wildlife, Coast Path

Dorchester
Thomas Hardy country

THE HARBOR CITIES

CHICHESTER

A 16th-century market cross neatly marks the intersection of two straight Roman roads at the heart of this ancient city, 10 miles (16 km) west of Arundel (see Literary Southeast). Chichester was originally surrounded by a wall, parts of which, both Roman and medieval, survive. The largest **Roman palace** uncovered in Britain (excavated in the 1960s) is at Fishbourne a mile to the west; it boasts 12 recently uncovered mosaic floors and a museum. The **cathedral** in the city center is Norman, with a 15th-century detached bell tower, the only one of its kind in England, and a slender Victorian-era spire (replacing the original one, which was blown down in a storm in 1861) that can be seen from afar at the western end of the South Downs Way (see previous chapter). Among the cathedral's other notable features are an altar cloth by John Piper and windows by Marc Chagall. The buildings on the largely pedestrians-only streets around it are well-preserved Georgian.

Chichester is famed today for the annual summer drama season in its Festival Theatre, sited in a 40-acre park on the outskirts of town. The theater offers four plays a year from May to September that run the gamut from classical to modern and star such luminaries as Glenda Jackson and Vanessa Redgrave.

Chichester Harbour, reached from the town center by winding roads or canal, is a wide, landlocked lagoon divided by peninsulas with tidal creeks running off in all directions. It's a mecca for sailors, water-sports enthusiasts, anglers, and bird-watchers. One of the prettiest of the villages on its shores is **Bosham** (pronounced bozzam), where King Canute is reputed to have ordered the tide to reverse to prove to his courtiers that he wasn't as powerful as they thought. The tide, invincible as ever, is apt to submerge the cars of visitors who ignore warning notices.

Staying in Chichester

On North Street, near the cathedral, is ▶ **The Ship**, where General Dwight Eisenhower dined on the eve of D-Day. Originally built as a house for one of Nelson's admirals, it has 36 rooms for guests who like its casual Georgian style. Somewhat larger and updated with all the late-20th-century amenities is the ▶ **Dolphin & Anchor**, which faces the cathedral yet has parking.

PORTSMOUTH

The A 27, skirting Chichester Harbour inland, crosses the Hampshire border west to Portsmouth, whose harbor has been the home base and fortress of British sea power since the 15th century. It has been known to generations of sailors as "Pompey," but today there are fewer warships to be seen than ever before and interest is focused on relics. It was Henry V who built the Round Tower at the Point, guarding the narrow entrance to Portsmouth Harbour from Spithead, the channel between Portsmouth and the Isle of Wight. In 1545 Henry VIII watched his fleet engage the French from the battlements of his newly built castle at nearby Southsea, which can still be walked by visitors today, overlooking a large green and the promenade of a popular seaside resort (see below). At this spot Henry recoiled as his pride, the **Mary Rose**, suddenly keeled over for no apparent reason and went down with all hands. Four centuries later Prince Charles, having served at sea in the Royal Navy, led a remarkable salvage operation to raise the *Mary Rose* from the seabed, and today its Tudor timbers are preserved for all to see under a fine spray of water inside a special hall that is the centerpiece of **Her Majesty's Dockyard** (entered through Victory Gate). Alongside the *Mary Rose* are Admiral Nelson's flagship, *Victory,* and *Warrior,* the world's first iron-clad warship, dating from 1860 and restored to its former glory as the showpiece of Queen Victoria's navy. The First Fleet to the convict colony of Australia sailed from Portsmouth in 1788; today's voyages from the ferry terminal are to the nearer destinations of Le Havre and Cherbourg, Caen and St. Malo, and Guernsey and Jersey.

Portsmouth Museums

Portsmouth is rich in naval and military museums—the **Royal Naval Museum**, in a Georgian warehouse in the dockyard; the World War II submarine *Alliance* at Gosport, on the opposite side of the harbor mouth (crossed by ferry at the Hard, a boarding point near the Portsmouth railway station); at Southsea Castle, mentioned above; and at the Royal Marines' Eastney Barracks in Southsea, where the splendidly ornate Victorian officers' mess is on view. The seaside promenade here has a newer attraction in the **D-Day Museum**, which includes reconstructions and films of the invasion in which a million and a half Americans, British, and Canadians were transported across the Channel, as well as numerous exhibits and a gallery containing the **Overlord Embroidery**. It took 20 needlewomen five years to reconstruct this saga of our times in 34 panels (41 feet longer than the famous tapestry at Bayeux). Even the museum in the house at 393 Old Commercial Road, where Charles Dickens was born in 1812, has a military connection, because his father was a navy pay clerk, although it now contains Dickens memorabilia. Old Portsmouth is best explored on foot, as its streets are quite narrow and twisting.

Dining and Staying in Portsmouth

Three pubs you might stop in at for drinks or a bar lunch are the **Lively Lady**, the **Seagull**, and the **George Tavern**. This last, on Queen Street near the dockyard gates, dates to 1781 and specializes in dessert puddings.

The ▶ **Portsmouth Marriott**, a newish hotel of 170 rooms with full facilities, stands alongside North Harbour at Cosham, nearly 4 miles (6½ km) from Old Portsmouth. The ▶ **Posthouse Hotel**, just as large and well equipped (including an indoor swimming pool), with rooms reserved for nonsmokers, is only a mile away overlooking the promenade at Southsea.

SOUTHAMPTON

Three gentle Hampshire rivers—the Test, Itchen, and Hamble—flow into the tidal Southampton Water, which is next door to Portsmouth Harbour and, until the advent of mass air travel, was the major gateway to Britain for those crossing the Atlantic. The *Queen Elizabeth II* and other ocean liners can still be seen arriving and departing on a double tide that first flows in from the Solent, the channel separating the mainland from the Isle of Wight (see below), and then two hours later from Spithead, the Solent's eastern extension. Southampton Docks isn't what it was in its heyday, and the city fathers have been looking to their history to boost tourism revenue. The *Mayflower* set sail for the New World from Southampton in 1620, a fact that is emphasized by the Pilgrim Fathers Memorial near Royal Pier. Another memorial (in East Park) commemorates a later and less propitious maiden voyage from Southampton—that of the *Titanic*. Unfortunately, much of old Southampton was flattened by bombing during World War II, but substantial sections of the medieval walls and the old northern gate to the city (the Bargate) survived and are incorporated in the Town Walk Walkway, a signposted tour (brochures are available at the Visitors Centre). Imaginative use has been made of the few surviving buildings of antiquity; some are museums, while others have been developed as new marinas and shopping centers such as Ocean Village and Town Quay. They made an ideal setting for the television soap opera "Howard's Way," which restored some of the glamour lost when Greta Garbo last walked down the gangway of the *Queen Mary.* The Southampton International Boat Show in September is said to be the biggest of its kind in Europe. This is only one of many annual events here, which also include a Balloon and Flower Festival (July) and a Jazz Festival (November), as well as the Sailing Regatta (August) and the Powerboat Grand Prix (end of September).

Broadlands, "one of the finest houses in all England," according to Lord Palmerston, who once lived there, lies just 8 miles (13 km) north of Southampton on the A 3057 outside the country town of Romsey. In more recent times Queen Elizabeth and Prince Philip began their honeymoon there, an example followed in due course by their son Prince Charles when he married Lady Diana, now the princess of Wales. It would be hard to think of a more romantic place than this mid-Georgian mansion set in gardens landscaped by Capability Brown beside the River Test. Both garden and house, packed with paintings by Van Dyck and others, fine china, and furniture and mementos of Lord and Lady Mountbatten (whose last home it was), are open to summer visitors.

Dining and Staying in Southampton

Southampton has a surprising variety of cuisines from which to choose. **Pearl Harbor**, at 17 Above Bar, does Chinese quite well, and **Kuti's**, at 70 London Road, is for those who like subtly flavored Indian curries. Three choices in the Ocean Village complex are **Dolphin's** (American food and cocktails), **Los Marinos** (Spanish), and the **Village Pâtisserie** (cakes and tea). For plain English cooking, try **Brown's Brasserie** at Frobisher House, Nelson Gate, but not on a Sunday, when it's closed.

Large new hotels have mushroomed all over at Southampton. The pick of the crop has to be the ▶ **Hilton National** at Chilworth, next to the junction of the major routes A 33 and M 27. Its facilities include an indoor swimming pool, sauna, and fitness center. ▶ **Southampton Moat House** in Portswood is smaller and more intimate, although also new. It has a small gym and sauna, and the rooms are executive class. A favorite remains the ▶ **Dolphin**, which has been a landmark in the High Street for years with its bow windows, archway, and wrought-iron traceries. Jane Austen often attended fashionable balls here with her mother and her sister Cassandra, and Thackeray wrote part of *Pendennis* while staying at the hotel.

THE ISLE OF WIGHT

A network of ferries, Hovercraft, catamarans, and hydrofoils carries passengers and cars the four miles across the water from Southampton to this island that in prehistory was joined to the mainland. From Southampton you can catch the ferry at the terminal near the Royal Pier; there are also ferries from Portsmouth and Lymington.

The Isle of Wight was already an island when Vespasian conquered it for Rome in A.D. 43 and called it Vectis, meaning "separate division." Despite modern transport, the Isle of Wight is still a land apart, indefinably different from the county of Hampshire "over the water." It isn't large (23 miles from end to end), and its safe, sandy beaches, often reached by gentle wooded ravines known as "chines"—Shanklin Chine, Brook Chine, Whale Chine, and Blackgang Chine (the last named after notorious smugglers)—have made it a longtime favorite for family holidays. There's a coastal footpath around the whole island, and walking is rewarded by marvelous views of sea and landscape and a rich variety of flora and fauna.

Behind the seaside towns of Ryde, Sandown, Shanklin, and Ventnor on the east coast the green downs, where sheep graze, rise to a height of 787 feet, meeting the English Channel on the south shore in a series of chalk cliffs that culminate at the western point in the **Needles**. These three gleaming white 100-foot-high escarpments reach out to the lighthouse that warns ships to keep clear. Alum Bay here is noted for the varying colors of its sands.

Historic buildings on the island open to visitors include **Carisbrooke Castle**, parts of which date from the 12th century and where Charles I was a prisoner, and **Osborne House**, the Italianate villa built by Queen Victoria as an escape from the cares of ruling an empire and where she died in 1901. On the grounds is the Swiss Cottage given to the Queen by the Swiss people in 1853 and recently restored to its original condition. It was used by the royal children for their games and hobbies. A horse-drawn carriage ferries visitors the half-mile from house to cottage. Both Carisbrooke Castle and Osborne House are within easy reach of **Newport**, the sleepy capital, which lies inland on the River Medina on the north half of the island, and **Cowes**, which spans both banks of the same river where it enters the Solent on the northern shore. It was the Royal Yacht Squadron at Cowes that in 1851 offered a 100-guinea trophy for a race around the island; won by the schooner *America* for the New York City Yacht Club, the award has ever since been known around the world as the *America*'s Cup. Cowes is to yachting what Wimbledon is to tennis or Ascot is to racing; each August, boats of every description, from dinghies to the royal yacht *Britannia,* descend on the little town for the regatta known simply as Cowes Week. The atmosphere is as bubbly as the Champagne that flows freely.

Cowes, Ryde, and Fishbourne are the gateways for visitors crossing by ferry from Portsmouth and Southampton, but the shortest route is at the western end of the island between Yarmouth, another yachting center on the estuary of the River Yar, and Lymington, on the mainland between Bournemouth and Southampton.

Staying and Dining on the Isle of Wight

Near Freshwater Bay, just east of the Needles, is ► **Farringford**, where the poet Alfred Lord Tennyson lived for nearly 40 years. It's now a hotel with 20 bedrooms and self-catering cottages. Facilities include an outdoor swimming pool, croquet lawn, and a nine-hole golf course. Tennyson Down is named after the poet, who said the air was "worth sixpence a pint," and a monument to him crowns the summit. The ► **Albion Hotel** at the water's edge shares the views and offers comfortable accommodation (most of the rooms have sea views from south-facing balconies) and good food.

A nice place to stop for lunch is the **New Inn** in Shalfleet on the road between Yarmouth and Newport. This pub specializes in fresh fish, conger eels, and mussels in garlic; try any of these with Pompey Royal Ale (made in Portsmouth) in the pub's garden.

THE NEW FOREST

LYMINGTON AND ENVIRONS

Lymington, at the southern approaches to the New Forest, southwest of Southampton, is an attractive sailing and fishing resort with chandlery stores and tackle shops lining the busy jetties. You can rent a boat to fish for bass in the Solent or buy a day ticket to cast for trout on the River Lymington. And if you are looking for somewhere to stay, you will have a hard time choosing from among the many pleasant hotels in and around the New Forest. West of Lymington on the A 337 toward Christchurch is ▶ **Chewton Glen**, one of the finest country-house hotels in England, standing in 30 acres of private parkland. Facilities include a heated outdoor pool, tennis, golf, croquet, and, indoors, billiards and snooker. Captain Frederick Marryat (1792–1848), the author of *Mr. Midshipman Easy* and *Children of the New Forest,* stayed here in the early 19th century, and the period suites are named after characters from the latter book. The food is excellent— haute French cuisine in an elegant atmosphere—and the prices reflect this. More moderately priced, but still very comfortable, is the ▶ **Montagu Arms**, part of which dates from the 18th century but most of which is sturdily built 1920s mock-Tudor. Sited among wooded hills on the Beaulieu River, it offers excellent food and wine and traditional individual rooms with full facilities, including log fires in winter. (Guests are expected to dress smartly for dinner.) Nearby are the ruins of **Beaulieu Abbey**, founded in 1204, and the adjoining **Palace House**, the ancestral home of the Montagus of Beaulieu and open to visitors. The present Lord Beaulieu runs the **National Motor Museum**, located on his grounds. It tells the story of motoring from 1899 onward with a comprehensive display of historic vehicles and Disney World–style "time journeys." Transport around the park is by monorail, miniature train, and veteran open-topped London bus.

Just over two miles downriver (there is a marked trail along the bank), where the Beaulieu widens to meet the Solent, the village of **Bucklers Hard** recalls the days when the great oaks of the forest were carted or rolled here to be hewn and shaped into men-of-war for the British fleet. A substantial number of the ships that defeated the French at Trafalgar came from these slipways. There's a maritime museum and the historic ▶ **Master Builder's House**, a quiet, 23-room hotel with beguiling views of the estuary and sailing-ship pictures and models in its beamed bars— all that remain of shipbuilder Henry Adams's original home. Rooms range from solidly traditional in the main building to brightly functional in the modern extension.

In the opposite direction from Beaulieu village on the B 3056, Beaulieu Road Station, a stop on the railway line from Southampton to Bournemouth, is the annual scene on five widely separated days of the **New Forest Pony Sales**. The ponies can be seen roaming freely together with deer and other wildlife in the 90,000 acres of un-spoiled heath, bog, and woodland glades, through which the B 3056 continues northwest to Lyndhurst, the capital of the New Forest and crossroads of most of the routes through it.

LYNDHURST
There are several parking lots in the beech and oak forest around Lyndhurst, which is at the heart of the forest. You'll find leaflets describing various nature walks here or at the Forestry Commission Office in town. As you explore the forest along these trails, watch for fallow and roe deer, buzzards and other birds of prey, and a great variety of bird life attracted by the bogs and marshes.

Lyndhurst is the seat of the Verderers' Court, which meets six times a year at Queen's House for the business of protecting and maintaining the forest entrusted to it 600 years ago (and that's the estimated age of the Knight-wood Oak, which grows to the west of town and mea-sures more than 21 feet in girth). The Court's orders are carried out by mounted rangers. The residents retain the rights granted them in the Middle Ages to cut turf, gather firewood, and feed their pigs on forest acorns. These days, however, citizens concentrate on catering to visitors with hotels and guest houses, pubs and tearooms, and antiques and souvenir shops.

Staying and Dining in Lyndhurst
If you can brave the traffic in the High Street, the ▶ **Crown Hotel** is an inviting, Old World establishment that offers the charm of a timbered, ivy-clad façade, a wood-paneled bar, cozy lounges, and 43 well-kept rooms. The 300-year-old **Waterloo Arms Pub** on Pike's Hill offers reasonably priced meals in a building crammed with souvenirs and artifacts from around the world, ranging

from a boomerang to a stuffed crocodile. The **Castle Inn** is a thatched 17th-century pub with a terraced garden. As you appreciate the nooks and crannies indoors and out, you can sip from a wide range of beers, from Devenish Dark Mild to Great British Heavy.

THE DORSET COAST

The Dorset towns of Christchurch, Bournemouth, and Poole have merged in recent years into a coastal conurbation separated from Southampton by the wild spaces of the New Forest.

CHRISTCHURCH

Christchurch takes its name from its parish church, the largest in England with the two oldest bells, which were cast in 1370. The town's origins go back to Saxon times when it was one of King Alfred's fortresses against the marauding Angles and Danes. It appears later in the Norman Domesday Book as Twynham, or "town between two waters," because it stands at the confluence of the Rivers Stour and Avon (not to be confused with other Avons to the north). These waterways are a peaceful retreat for anglers, and the harbor is often full of yachts.

BOURNEMOUTH

Bournemouth begins as you head west out of Christchurch on A 35, although the city center is 6 miles (10 km) down the sandy beach. In 1989 its long-held reputation as the Queen of the South Coast was reinforced when it was named Resort of the Year by the English Tourist Board. It was a certain Dr. Granville in the mid-19th century who first recommended Bournemouth's mild and bracing air for those "in delicate health." Villas sprouted among the heathland and pinewoods through which the "chines," or valleys, descended to the shore on either side of the Bourne valley. In *Tess of the D'Urbervilles,* Thomas Hardy calls the town "Sandbourne" and describes its two new railway stations, gaslit piers, and promenades as "a glittering novelty." Robert Louis Stevenson wrote *Kidnapped* and *The Strange Case of Dr. Jekyll and Mr. Hyde* during the 1880s in a house on the avenue now named after him. Surprisingly, the graveyard of St. Peter's Church contains the heart of Percy Bysshe Shelley, which was brought back from Italy in 1822 by a companion; the rest of Shelley's ashes stayed in Rome. The only museum devoted to the poet's life and work is at **Shelley Park** on Beechwood Avenue in suburban Boscombe, which was formerly the home of his son, Sir Percy Shelley.

The city has six entertainment centers attracting top talent in summer, and its own symphony orchestra. Sporting activities range from ten-pin bowling and ice skating to cricket, golf, tennis, fishing, sailing, and powerboat racing.

Staying and Dining in Bournemouth

Prime Minister Benjamin Disraeli stayed at the ▶ **Royal Bath Hotel** for the sake of his health, and he might have benefited still more from the pool, sauna, and gymnasium provided there today. He might not, however, have approved of the Bournemouth Casino, which operates separately but on the same premises as the hotel, whose 124 rooms and seven suites, all with full facilities, are maintained in immaculate traditional style. Competing with the town's oldest hotel, the new ▶ **Norfolk Royale** offers comparable health and fitness facilities and 95 rooms with commodious bathrooms en suite, reserving a percentage of them for nonsmokers and women guests only. ▶ **Langtry Manor** capitalizes on the fact that it was built by the future King Edward VII as a love nest where he could be with his mistress Lillie Langtry; it offers four-poster beds and six-course Edwardian dinners. The ▶ **Carlton**, which stands on the cliff top, has a reputation for friendliness as well as five-star status. Many of its well-appointed 62 rooms and eight suites enjoy the sea view, which is shared by guests dining in the highly rated Grill Room. The facilities include sauna, an outdoor heated pool, and well-tended gardens, with sandy beaches at the bottom of the cliffs immediately below.

Bournemouth offers a huge selection of hotels. The Tourist Information Centre on Westover Road operates a special Accommodations Desk to assist visitors in making a choice and booking; Tel: (0202) 78-97-89. Among the more moderately priced hotels, ▶ **Marsham Court** has a quiet location overlooking the sea yet is only minutes from the city center. All its 80 rooms have either bath or shower and standard facilities such as TV and direct dial phones; there is an outdoor heated pool. ▶ **Chinehead** is much smaller—only 21 rooms, but most of them with a bath, TV, and phone. Its main appeal lies in the availability of delightful walks through the pinewoods round about, with the shops and the sea only a few minutes away.

Crust, on the town square, once Bournemouth's most acclaimed restaurant now serves snacks in addition to full meals in a setting of potted palms and cane furniture. The mantle of the town's finest has now passed to the long-established **Sophisticates**, smaller and 1 mile (1.5 km) from the city center on Charminster Road. It maintains its style with an ambitious menu that includes both European and Oriental dishes. Advance booking necessary; Tel: (0202) 29-10-19. **Chez Fred**, on Seamoon Road, Westbourne, was voted Britain's Fish 'n Chip Shop of the Year in 1991. It's not just a take-out but a proper restaurant, too, with its own label, Chez Fred wine!

Shopping in Bournemouth

Bournemouth has some of the best shopping outside London, with antiques, Victoriana, and Art Deco specialties in its Boscombe and Pokesdown suburbs. The main shopping area, with all the major stores represented as well as the local, family-run department store **Beales**, is around the square in the city center. The beach has a European Community "Blue Flag" for cleanliness, and the parks and gardens are kept in immaculate condition by a regiment of 230 municipal gardeners, earning it the title of Floral Capital of Britain in 1991's annual Britain in Bloom competition.

POOLE

With a population of 150,000 and still growing, blooming Bournemouth has all but engulfed Poole, its neighbor to the west. But this ancient port, which once traded with Newfoundland and the other colonies of the New World, jealously preserves its Georgian Custom House, Guildhall, and various harbor buildings. **Purbeck Pottery** on the Quay is a good place to buy reasonably priced examples of this local stoneware, glazed in off-white and shades of blue-gray, green, and brown. Poole Harbour, from which cross-Channel ferries operate to Cherbourg, is an enormous area of water crammed with all kinds of leisure craft and protected by a narrow spit called Sandbanks, whose beaches live up to its name.

Inside the harbor is the island where the Boy Scout movement was founded with a summer camp held in 1907 by Lord Baden-Powell. **Brownsea Island**, a 500-acre tract of wild heath and woodland, is now the property of the National Trust, which runs a shop here selling books about the Scout movement. The island can be reached by ferry from Sandbanks or Poole Quay from April to September. A new **Waterfront Museum** in medieval cellars and an 18th-century warehouse on Poole Quay has a section devoted to the Scout movement as well as a fascinating display on a Spanish galleon sunk off the town in Studland Bay in Tudor times.

Overlooking the harbor from Canford Cliffs is **Compton Acres**, seven gardens landscaped in various styles from around the world, including Japanese, Italian, and Roman schemes, with a subtropical woodland glen.

Swanage to Weymouth

SWANAGE

Swanage is a quiet little seaside town on the Isle of Purbeck (an island in name only) to the south of Poole Harbour. Its most notable features—the Wellington Clock Tower and the carved stone façade of the town hall—both came from London, but there is also a 13th-century parish church next to the Millpond and a local museum in the Old Tithe Barn. Nearby is the village of **Worth Matravers**, famous for centuries for the quarrying of the dark-gray Purbeck marble that went into the building of churches and cathedrals, including Salisbury, up and down the country. The ruins of **Corfe Castle** dominate the *corfe* (Anglo-Saxon for "pass" or "cutting") through the Purbeck Hills. Both the castle and the village that grew up around its domed green hill are entirely of gray Purbeck stone.

From here westward is the least touched stretch of the south coast, in marked contrast to that running eastward from Bournemouth. The southern shore of Poole Harbour is almost entirely given over to nature reserves, where adders and lizards as well as wildfowl may be encountered. A mile from the village of Studland is the **Agglestone**, a huge triangular chunk of ironstone that, it's claimed, the Devil planned to drop on Salisbury Cathedral—but its weight proved too much for him. There are other interesting natural formations at the sea's edge: Old Harry and Old Harry's Wife, off the Foreland, are pillars of chalk named for the Devil. The

Great Globe in Durlston Country Park near Durlston Head is man-made, however, from Portland stone.

THE DORSET COAST PATH

The Dorset Coast Path follows the cliff tops along the coast around St. Aldhelm's Head, where no main roads run and where guillemots and razorbills wheel around a Norman chapel perched on the headland as a marker for vessels in the Channel.

Since World War I, a great slice of the coast inland from oyster-shaped Lulworth Cove and Worbarrow Bay has been reserved for military use as a tank-training course and firing range. Ironically, this has preserved it from the worse depredation of "development" that has turned so much of Britain's coast into a ribbon of highways and housing, marinas, trailer parks, power stations, pylons, container ports, and drilling rigs. Wildlife, undisturbed by the gunfire, flourishes in the 7,000 acres of the range, and access on the Coast Path is allowed to visitors on most weekends and during public holidays. Barn owls nest in the rafters of the village of Tyneham, abandoned to the military in 1943. An exhibition in the church relates the long history of the valley in which it stands. Another piece of nature's sculpture to be seen from the Coast Path as it continues west toward Weymouth is Durdle Door, an arch of limestone jutting out into the sea from a sandy beach.

WEYMOUTH

Weymouth, at the western end of this stretch of coast, is an elegant resort of porticoed Georgian buildings that owes its legacy to George III himself, the first monarch to use a bathing machine, during a visit to the town in 1789. (A bathing machine is a changing room on wheels invented for modesty's sake; a bather entered it, wheeled down to the water, changed into swimming clothes, and slipped into the ocean without anyone seeing.) The **Gloucester Hotel** was formerly the king's summer home. His statue overlooking the promenade and the sands, put up in 1810 for his golden jubilee, is now one of the sights of the town. Another is the brightly painted clock tower erected on the promenade for Queen Victoria's similar anniversary in 1887. As Weymouth is a port, the harbor at the mouth of the River Wey is busy with small boats and ferries and hydrofoils on their way to and from Cherbourg and the Channel

Islands. (The hydrofoil to the Channel Islands runs only in summer.) To the south, the Isle of Portland reaches out toward Portland Bill with its attendant lighthouse and the Victorian Trinity House Tower.

The ▶ **Portland Heights Hotel** has 66 rooms, all with bathrooms and furnished in standard modern hotel style. It combines fine views over the "island" (it is, in fact, joined to the mainland by a causeway next to the final stretch of Chesil Beach) with squash and swimming in a heated pool. Portland is the "Isle of Slingers" in Hardy's novels, and prisoners used to break rock in its quarries. Portland stone went into many buildings, not the least of which is Buckingham Palace.

CHESIL BEACH
Chesil Beach, stretching in a ten-mile crescent from Portland west to Abbotsbury, is one of Britain's most unusual natural phenomena. This barrier of shingle, up to 40 feet high, encloses a lagoon called the Fleet. The pebbles on the beach are graded larger and larger toward Portland, but no one has been able to explain why. The stories of Chesil are of sailing ships driven by gales into the shingle and of hundreds of lives lost. Sixteenth-century ▶ **Moonfleet Manor**, overlooking Chesil Beach and the sea 5 miles (8 km) west of Weymouth, features in John Meade Faulkner's Victorian smuggling saga *Moonfleet*. It is now a 38-room hotel with lawn bowling, three squash courts, tennis, snooker, indoor swimming pool, and bowling green. The rooms are commodious, all with baths, and 12 are for families.

ABBOTSBURY
Abbotsbury has one of England's largest tithe barns, where the church gathered its share of the harvest crops from tenant farmers. This thatched 15th-century structure is complemented by a swannery started in the 11th century by Benedictine monks who reared the birds for meat. Today the abbey is no more, yet the only nesting colony of mute swans in Britain survives, ranging from 500 in summer to a thousand in winter. They feed on the rare eelgrass that grows around the Fleet. The ▶ **Ilchester Arms** is a comfortable, low-beamed, and inexpensive place to stay in this delightful village of thatch and orange-colored stone. It has just ten rooms, all named after wildflowers and all decorated with bright fabrics; some have four-poster beds. Advance booking is advised.

HARDY COUNTRY
Dorchester

The Hardy Monument that stands on gorse-covered Black Down just inland from Abbotsbury is not in memory of the famous novelist, as might be supposed, but of Thomas Masterson Hardy, the captain of the *Victory* at Trafalgar, to whom Nelson addressed his dying words, "Kiss me, Hardy." The gallant captain, who went on to a vice-admiralship and a knighthood, lived in Portisham at the bottom of the hill. By coincidence, the 1840 birthplace of the other Thomas Hardy is just a few miles away on the other side of the county-market town of Dorchester, which is directly north of Weymouth. The small thatched cottage in the woods at Higher Bockhampton ("Upper Mellstock" in his novels), just ten minutes from a parking lot, is in the care of the National Trust and open to visitors.

The A 35 leads on to Dorchester through Tolpuddle, the village of the trade-union-movement martyrs, and Puddletown ("Weatherbury"). If Hardy visited Dorchester today he would instantly recognize the town that he describes in *The Mayor of Casterbridge* and where he spent most of his life. He would also recognize the accents of the farmers bargaining over cattle and crops in the market and drinking locally brewed ale in the pubs.

Dorchester's handsome main street is lined with solid buildings of Portland stone; the Antelope Hotel, where "hanging judge" George Jeffreys sentenced 74 men to be hanged and quartered for joining the duke of Monmouth's rebellion of 1685, and the Shire Hall, where the Tolpuddle Martyrs were sentenced to transportation to Australia in 1834, are unaltered. So, too, are the 15th-century St. Peter's Church, which Hardy as a young architect helped to restore, and Max Gate (just outside the town), the house he designed and in which he spent his last years as a rich and famous author. It is, alas, undistinguished and not open to visitors.

However, the Dorset County Museum in Dorchester contains a reconstruction of Hardy's Max Gate study, including the pen with which he wrote *Tess of the D'Urbervilles*, his spectacles, violin, cello, and favorite walking stick. Hardy's tomb in the churchyard at Stinsford is midway between Max Gate and Higher Bockhampton. His heart is buried there, but the ashes of the rest of his body lie in Westminster Abbey. In this small country church-yard Hardy claimed to have seen and spoken to a ghost in 18th-century dress on Christmas Eve 1919. "Thrown aside as dead" as a baby, Hardy nonetheless lived to be 87 and "a miserable old fellow," as far as Dorchester folk were concerned. Certainly his statue, just off High West Street (unveiled in 1931, three years after his death, by his friend the playwright Sir James Barrie) wears a melan-choly expression.

In High East Street are two comfortable places to stay: the ▶ King's Arms, with 31 rooms, a restaurant, and parking facilities, which maintains the solid tradition of the country-town coaching inn, with up-to-date facilities, and the much smaller ▶ Casterbridge, which has no restaurant but is a charmingly furnished Georgian house with a conservatory for afternoon tea. Either makes a convenient base for exploring winding Wessex lanes in-land "far from the madding crowd" and for visiting thatched villages such as the model Georgian Milton Abbas and Cerne Abbas, which incorporate an early word for "abbey" in their names and are among the most idyllic in England. Civilization in this area goes back thousands of years. The evidence can be seen in the earthen ram-parts and ditches at Maiden Castle and South Cadbury, just south of Dorchester. There were hill forts here in the Iron Age (see Chronology).

The county isn't large; it is only 27 miles (43 km) northeast to Shaftesbury, the hilltop town to which Hardy gave its old name of Shaston in the Wessex novels. You can see the window from which Sue in *Jude the Obscure* jumps on her wedding night, and if you need a cream tea after that excitement, you will find it under the gnarled beams and old cider flagons in King Alfred's Kitchen here. The views from the 700-foot-high plateau over the Blackmoor Vale of "little dairies" (as Hardy described the area in *Tess of the D'Urbervilles*) are worth a detour, as are the abbey ruins and a fascinating local museum at the top of cobbled Gold Hill.

Abbotsbury to Lyme Regis

The coast is as lovely and untouched to the west of Wey-mouth and Dorchester as it is to the east. The extremely wide streets of **Bridport** ("Port Bredy" in several Hardy novels) are evidence of its long history of ropemaking, for this is where workers twisted the strands of hemp in straight lines a thousand or more feet long; these were called ropewalks. Indeed, it's claimed that the cultivation of hemp and flax was first introduced here by the Romans. Certainly, in the days of sail, to say that someone had been "stabbed by a Bridport dagger" meant he had been hanged. Today the old ropewalks are long gone, but nets are still made for fishing. There is a museum and art gallery and an open-air market on Wednesdays and Saturdays.

Great golden cliffs stretch west around the bay to **Lyme Regis**, which owes the second word of its name to a charter from King Edward I, who used its harbor to send ships out to fight the French in the latter part of the 13th century. Three centuries later ships sailed from here against the Spanish Armada, and in 1685 the duke of Monmouth raised his standard on the beach west of the harbor where he had landed to launch his ill-fated rebellion against his uncle, James II.

The 18th-century ▶ **Alexandra Hotel**, set in spacious gardens overlooking Lyme Bay, with 27 rooms and a sun lounge, is a pleasant place to stay in this colorful small resort. The stone breakwater called the Cobb that protects the harbor achieved unexpected international fame in the early 1980s when the actress Meryl Streep, mysteriously cowled, posed on it during the filming of the novel *The French Lieutenant's Woman*. Its author, John Fowles, lives locally and is something of an authority on the fossils from the cliffs that are displayed in the museum, some of which date from 200 million years ago. The first major discovery—of the complete 21-foot-long skeleton of an ichthyosaur in the cliffs of Black Ven near where the River Char enters the sea—was by Mary Anning, the 12-year-old daughter of a carpenter, in 1811. The area is now a nature reserve.

The cliffs of sandstone topped with bright yellow gorse climb from Charmouth to 618 feet at Golden Cap, the highest point on England's south coast. This 2,000-acre estate embracing farmland, woods, cliffs, and glorious beach is regarded as the crowning achievement of the National Trust's Enterprise Neptune, which, since 1965, has fought to protect coastline not already spoiled. There are 15 miles of footpath (including the Dorset Coast Path) for exploring places with intriguing names like Cain's Folly, Doghouse Hill, and the Saddle. The fields have not been turned over to prairie, and in the hedgerows yellowhammer and wren can be seen and heard and wild-flowers such as agrimony, spear, and stemless thistle grow vigorously.

GETTING AROUND
As in the Literary Southeast, most of the places in this chapter are easily reached from central London by road and rail within a couple of hours. Gateways to the main routes are provided by the London Orbital Motorway (M 25), which also links the major international airports of Heathrow and Gatwick. The Wessex Shore is especially convenient for those arriving by sea at Southampton aboard the *Queen Elizabeth II* and other ships. Local ferries make the crossing to the Isle of Wight in 30 minutes to an hour from Portsmouth, Southampton, or Lymington, the Hovercraft in 10 minutes from Southsea, and the hydrofoil almost as speedily from Southampton.

ACCOMMODATIONS REFERENCE
Rates are projected 1994 prices for a double room with breakfast, unless otherwise stated. As prices are subject to change, always double-check before booking.

▶ **Albion Hotel.** Gate Lane, Freshwater Bay, **Isle of Wight** PO40 9RA. Tel: (0983) 75-36-31; Fax: (0983) 75-52-95. £79.

▶ **Alexandra Hotel.** Pound Street, **Lyme Regis** DT7 3HZ. Tel: (0297) 44-20-10; Fax: (0297) 44-32-29. £70–£100.

▶ **Carlton.** Meyrick Road, East Overcliff, **Bournemouth** BH1 3DN. Tel: (0202) 55-20-11; Fax: (0202) 29-95-73. £150.

▶ **Casterbridge.** 49 High East Street, **Dorchester** DT1 1HU. Tel: (0305) 26-40-43; Fax: (0305) 26-08-84. £48–£60.

▶ **Chinehead.** 31 Alumhurst Road, **Bournemouth** BH4 8EN. Tel: (0202) 75-27-77; Fax: (0202) 75-27-78. £47.

▶ **Chewton Glen.** Christchurch Road, **New Milton** BH25 6QS. Tel: (0425) 27-53-41; Fax: (0425) 27-23-10; in U.S., (800) 344-5087. £187–£280 (breakfast not included).

▶ **Crown Hotel.** High Street, **Lyndhurst** SO43 7NF. Tel: (0703) 28-29-22; Fax: (0703) 28-27-51; in U.S. and Canada, (800) 528-1234; in Australia, (008) 22-21-66. £92–£105.

▶ **Dolphin.** 35 High Street, **Southampton** SO9 2DS. Tel: (0703) 33-99-55; Fax: (0703) 33-36-50; in U.S. and Canada,

(800) 225-5843; in Australia, (008) 22-24-46. £68 (breakfast not included).

▶ **Dolphin & Anchor.** West Street, **Chichester** PO19 1QE. Tel: (0243) 78-51-21; Fax: (0243) 53-34-08; in U.S. and Canada, (800) 225-5843; in Australia, (008) 22-24-46. £85–£100 (breakfast not included).

▶ **Farringford.** Freshwater Bay, **Isle of Wight** PO40 9PE. Tel: (0983) 75-25-00. £47–£92.

▶ **Hilton National.** Bracken Place, Chilworth, **Southampton** SO2 3UB. Tel: (0703) 70-27-00; Fax: (0703) 76-72-33; in the U.S., (800) 445-8667; in Canada, (800) 268-9275. £75–£95 (breakfast not included).

▶ **Ilchester Arms.** 9 Market Street, **Abbotsbury** DT3 4JR. Tel: (0305) 87-12-43. £60.

▶ **King's Arms.** 30 High East Street, **Dorchester** DT1 1HF. Tel: (0305) 26-53-53; Fax: (0305) 26-02-69. £45–£90.

▶ **Langtry Manor.** 26 Derby Road, East Cliff, **Bournemouth** BH1 3QB. Tel: (0202) 55-38-87; Fax: (0202) 29-01-15. £79–£149.

▶ **Marsham Court.** Russell Cotes Road, East Cliff, **Bournemouth** BH1 3AB. Tel: (0202) 55-21-11; Fax: (0202) 29-47-44. £58–£93.

▶ **Master Builder's House.** Bucklers Hard, Beaulieu SO42 7XB. Tel: (0590) 61-62-53; Fax: (0590) 61-62-97. £80–£95.

▶ **Montagu Arms.** Palace Lane, **Beaulieu** SO42 7ZL. Tel: (0590) 61-23-24; Fax: (0590) 61-21-88. £96–£110.

▶ **Moonfleet Manor.** Near **Weymouth** DT3 4ED. Tel: (0305) 78-69-48; Fax: (0305) 77-43-95. £76–£86.

▶ **Norfolk Royale.** Richmond Hill, **Bournemouth** BH2 6EN. Tel: (0202) 55-15-21; Fax: (0202) 29-97-29. £90–£130.

▶ **Portland Heights Hotel.** Yeates Corner, **Portland** DT5 2EN. Tel: (0305) 82-13-61; Fax: (0305) 86-00-81. £55–£60.

▶ **Portsmouth Marriott.** North Harbour, Cosham, **Portsmouth** PO6 4SH. Tel: (0705) 38-31-51; Fax: (0705) 38-87-01; in U.S. and Canada, (800) 228-9290. £105–£115 (breakfast not included).

▶ **Posthouse Hotel.** Pembroke Road, Southsea, **Portsmouth** PO1 2TA. Tel: (0705) 82-76-51; Fax: (0705) 75-67-15; in U.S. and Canada, (800) 225-5843; in Australia, (008) 22-24-46. £53.50 (breakfast not included).

▶ **Royal Bath Hotel.** Bath Road, **Bournemouth** BH1 2EW. Tel: (0202) 55-55-55; Fax: (0202) 55-41-58; in U.S., (800) 762-1003. £131–£147.

▶ **The Ship**. North Street, **Chichester** PO19 1NH. Tel: (0243) 78-20-28; Fax: (0243) 77-42-54. £66–£80.

▶ **Southampton Moat House**. Highfield Lane, **Portswood** SO9 1YQ. Tel: (0703) 55-95-55; Fax: (0703) 58-39-10; in U.S. and Canada, (800) 448-8355; in Australia, (008) 22-11-76. £63.50.

THE COTSWOLDS TO WINCHESTER

By Bryn Frank

Bryn Frank is the author of several books about Britain, including Discover Scotland, Everyman's England, *and, most recently,* Short Walks in English Towns. *He is a regular contributor to* British Heritage *and* In Britain *magazines, and he writes occasionally about travel in the U.K. for the London* Evening Standard.

Neither Oxford nor Bath would demean themselves by wearing the label "gateway to the Cotswolds," but, as they are respectively at the extreme eastern and the extreme western edge of the region, each makes a convenient springboard. Nor do they feel peripheral; on an early summer evening, with the sun on the golden stone, they could be in the Cotswold heart. Between the two cities lies one of southern England's best-kept secrets: lonely rolling uplands bordered by prosperous arable farms, ancient forests, and the still-tangible remains of prehistoric settlements, which indicate that what we now know as Wiltshire (around Salisbury Plain) was once highly populated.

The M 3 motorway is one of the country's best landscaped: On it you reach Winchester and, beyond that, across a swath of little-known, deeply rural countryside, Salisbury and its cathedral, which boasts the tallest spire in England. Cathedral aside, Salisbury has remained intact and charming despite the vicissitudes of the late 20th century.

Northwest of Salisbury and west of Bath, the cities of Britsol and Wells provide a study in contrast, the first an important commercial and shipping center since the Middle Ages, the latter a quiet market town that boasts one of the most beautiful cathedrals in the land.

MAJOR INTEREST

The Cotswolds: charming country towns and inns
Bath: Roman Baths, Royal Crescent, Pulteney Bridge
Bristol: maritime heritage
Wells: cathedral, Bishop's Palace
Glastonbury
Stourhead House and gardens
Salisbury Cathedral
Stonehenge
Winchester Cathedral
Avebury Stone Circle, Silbury Hill, White Horse Hill

The Cotswolds

North of the M 4, which runs due west out of London to Bristol near the top of Salisbury Plain, the Cotswold hills are rural England at its best. Largely unspoiled, they are almost too good to be true. Even the name, which confuses foreigners and even the English who claim to know this exquisite corner of the country, is a charmer. It comes from an amalgam of two Anglo-Saxon words meaning "sheepfold" and "open, uncultivated uplands."

Hard to define geographically, the Cotswolds stretch very roughly from Cheltenham in the west to Oxford in the east, from near Evesham (southwest of Stratford-upon-Avon) in the north to Cirencester in the south. You can choose Bath at their far southwest as a base for a Cotswold exploration, though Cirencester and Cheltenham, which offer a good choice of hotels, would also serve. If, as many do, you'd prefer to be based in a smaller town with a good choice of accommodations, consider Stow-on-the-Wold, Burford, and Chipping Campden. As-

sume that the best of the Cotswolds covers an area of
about 40 miles east to west and 25 miles north to south,
and that a fairly central point will make most parts of the
region accessible. A circular tour is possible, but you will
find yourself crisscrossing on the same roads, which can
be confusing.

Whether you plan a circular or a "follow-your-nose"
route, or choose a particular town or village as a base, a
good road map—some larger gasoline stations and most
large newsagents' shops have a wide selection—is essential in the Cotswolds. With the exception of half a dozen
picturesque villages and small towns, the best of the
region is hidden from view. Even so, country buses are
adequate, and rural taxis are accustomed to transporting
people fairly long distances; no part of the Cotswolds is
dramatically remote.

For accommodations in addition to those cited in the
following descriptions of the nicest Cotswold villages and
towns, see the end of this section.

ULEY
Some of the villages and hamlets on the extreme edges of
the Cotswolds are the ones that keep most to themselves.
Try Uley, southwest of Stroud (itself south of Gloucester),
in the heart of the country where Laurie Lee set his
perennial best-seller *Cider with Rosie*. He describes the
region as "a mystery land of difficult hills and deeply
wooded valleys." Nearby ▶ Owlpen is dominated by a
fine, sprawling Tudor manor house with a church and a
steep hillside behind. Accommodations are available in
the cottages on the estate. Another self-catering accommodation is ▶ Langford House Cottages, owned by Lady de
Mauley, on A 361 in Little Faringdon near Lechlade.

GREAT TEW
At roughly the opposite edge of the Cotswolds, near
Chipping Norton, northwest of Oxford, is Great Tew, until
recently so run-down and neglected that it seemed ready
to crumble into dust. But this slice of English village life
has been reprieved and is now undergoing renovation
without detriment to its original charm.

WITHINGTON
Just south of the busy A 40 road that links Cheltenham
and Oxford lies Withington, one of those villages that
even people who claim to know the Cotswolds may not

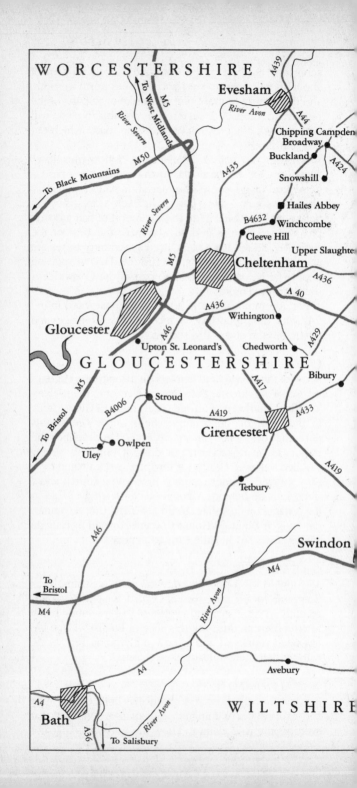

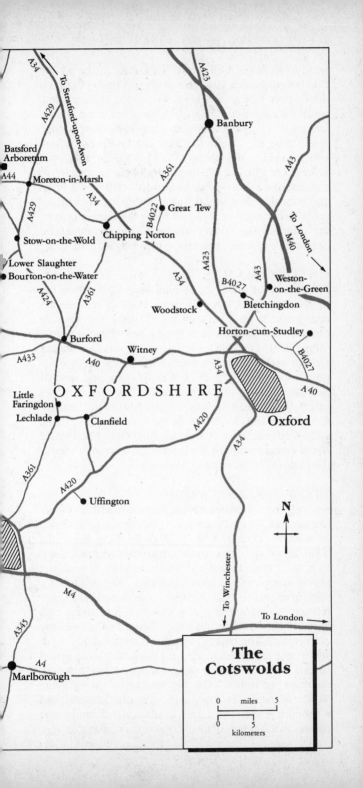

The Cotswolds

be able to place. Well worth the detour is the nearby **Chedworth Roman Villa**; go east about 3 miles (5 km) via the country lane from Withington toward Yanworth, and watch for signs to the villa. (Because of the tortuous local lanes, the village of Chedworth itself, while close enough as the crow flies, is not the most convenient point from which to get to the Roman Villa.) Visiting the villa, built around A.D. 150, you will need only a little imagination to translate the mosaics and the painted walls into a warm and habitable dwelling. It was probably built not by Romans at all but by locals (most likely the ancient Dubonnic tribe) in the Roman style. A highly recommended detour, it is in a fine, peaceful, partly wooded setting.

CHELTENHAM

For those who prefer a less rural base, Cheltenham can be recommended. It has some fine Regency architecture, dating from its days as a spa town. "Healthy" springs were discovered during the 18th century, and when George III sampled them in 1788 the town became very fashionable. Elegant architecture followed. There is excellent shopping, especially for clothing and antiques, and in early July the Cheltenham International Festival of Music takes place. Also, there's the Cheltenham Festival of Literature in October and, for horse racing fans, the Cheltenham Gold Cup meeting in March; after the Grand National at Aintree, near Liverpool, the latter is the most important of the National Hunt, or jump, meetings.

STOW-ON-THE-WOLD

Among other Cotswolds towns, Stow-on-the-Wold (east of Cheltenham) is exceptional. It is high-lying, surrounded by windswept countryside. "Stow-on-the-Wold, where the wind blows cold," runs an old adage. Its marketplace, as if to protect itself against the winter weather, is enclosed almost completely by inns and shops, including a hardware store and newsagent of the old-fashioned kind: Courtesies of "Good morning" and "Good evening" still prevail here. There is a cozy tea shop, **Edward's Café**, on the marketplace. The church is probably most famous as the site where Cromwell, during the Civil War, incarcerated several hundred Royalist troops, shooting two *"pour encourager les autres."* On the outskirts of Stow-on-the-Wold, on the A 424 road, is the pleasant, low-ceilinged ▶ **Unicorn Hotel**, featuring especially a few charming attic rooms. In the center of town is the very comfortable, very traditional ▶ **Grapevine Hotel**. Another good lodging in Stow is the ▶ **Wyck Hill House**, with spacious bedrooms and a cedar-paneled library, and a comfortable bar with leather armchairs downstairs.

BOURTON-ON-THE-WATER

Just southwest of Stow-on-the-Wold, Bourton-on-the-Water is smaller and different: Unashamed commercialization meets the "olde world" here. The village is an essential stop on day trips by bus that aim to capture some of the Cotswolds' flavor and also offer the chance to spend money on knickknacks. Don't miss the model village; of course, you can also purchase a model of the model village. Here and elsewhere in the Cotswolds, portable antiques are a good buy. They are not particularly cheap, but the quality is good, and browsing for them is a pleasure.

BURFORD

Set on a steep hill, Burford is a fairly short, easy side trip west on A 40 from Oxford. It is a busy place, well served by coaching inns, a couple of them of great character. The ▶ **Bull Hotel** is handy for a drink or a bar meal (the steak-and-kidney pie is recommended) and offers old-fashioned, low-ceilinged but comfortable rooms. **The Lamb** restaurant serves much-admired bar meals and more formal fare, with charming candlelight in the dining room proper. The ▶ **Bay Tree Hotel**, more quietly situated off the High Street, has deep leather armchairs, flagstone floor, and big, open fires. The **Tolsey Museum**, on the High Street, gives useful insight into the town's social and industrial past.

CHIPPING CAMDEN

Northwest of Stow-on-the-Wold, Chipping Campden is more low-lying and a little quieter, though equally popular with tourists. Its covered market building, constructed in 1627 "for the sale of cheese, butter and poultry," is a picture-postcard classic. (*Chipping* means "market"; the town was the center of the region's medieval wool trade.) There is a small rural museum here and, on the outskirts, an impressive "wool church," whose construction was financed by money made from the Cotswolds' famous sheep. Chipping Campden also has two fine inns. The modest ▶ **Noel Arms** dates from the 14th century; the cozy ▶ **Cotswold House Hotel and Restaurant** is known

for its food and the care and attention given to its guest
rooms: Each one has its own theme. A few minutes' drive
from Chipping Campden is ▶ **Charingworth Manor**, a
quiet country-house hotel full of antiques. Charingworth
has a fine leisure spa opened in the spring of 1992
(indoor heated pool, sauna, steam room, and billiards
room) that complements the new all-weather tennis
court. Clay-pigeon shooting can be arranged at 24 hours'
notice.

BROADWAY
The ▶ **Lygon Arms**, in the town of Broadway itself, is
one of the best-known country hotels in Britain. Many a
hunting scene has been painted or photographed outside its mellow exterior. If you take a suite, you can have
your own log fire. For energetic guests there are archery
ranges and an all-weather tennis court on the grounds,
and golf (with lessons if desired) at an excellent nearby
club. Broadway itself is an elongated "street village." As
one of the two or three most popular destinations in the
Cotswolds, it can be very crowded with people and cars.
But the rich, golden-stone cottages and shops are much
admired, and Broadway is an essential stopping point at
less busy times—during the winter, for example, when
it functions as an ordinary working village. Up Fish Hill,
on the outskirts of the village, is the very welcoming
▶ **Dormy House Hotel**, with especially pleasant dining
rooms. ▶ **Buckland Manor**, a few miles out of town in
an exquisitely pretty village of the same name, is a fine,
partly 12th-century manor house that has been impecca-
bly converted; its restaurant is also highly regarded.
Broadway has several antiques shops, art galleries, and
print and antiquarian bookshops.

Cotswold Castles and Houses
The Cotswolds region is not rich in castles and houses,
but there are a few fine and much-photographed exceptions. Among these is **Sudeley Castle**, once the home of
Henry VIII's last wife, Catherine Parr. Set in superb gardens, it is conveniently and attractively located on the
edge of the underrated (and less touristy) town of Winchcombe northeast of Cheltenham. You should go there
near the end of the day and hang back so you can appreciate the atmosphere without being jostled by too many
tourists. The ▶ **Sudeley Castle Cottages**, located effectively within the castle grounds, include a few old proper-

ties skillfully renovated to late-20th-century standards and a number of brand-new but nevertheless harmonious holiday homes, every bit as comfortable as permanent ones. **The Corner Cupboard Dining Room**, in a Winchcombe pub, is very cozy, with a skillfully executed short menu.

About 4 miles (6½ km) to the north is **Hailes Abbey**, the substantial excavated remains of a Cistercian abbey founded in 1246. **Snowshill Manor**, a small, unassuming manor house 3 miles (5 km) due south of Broadway and northeast of Cheltenham, contains eclectic artifacts collected by a previous owner, of which Japanese armor and penny-farthing bicycles are just two examples. Gardeners will appreciate **Hidcote Manor Garden** (4 miles/ 6½ km northeast of Chipping Campden via the unclassified road for Hidcote Boyce, then look for signs), considered by many to be the most influential example of English landscape architecture of this century. Created by U.S. Major Lawrence Johnston in 1913, it took 30 years to complete. It features some remarkable topiary and many irresistible alleyways. If you enjoy Hidcote, you'll appreciate **Batsford Arboretum** to the south, about a mile and a half (2 km) from Moreton-in-Marsh, eastward on the Evesham road and then north on an unclassified road. Its 50 acres contain more than 1,200 species of trees. About 20 miles (32 km) south, **Arlington Row** in Bibury, east of Cirencester, is a classic: a line of graystone wool-workers' houses dating from the early 17th century and now owned by the National Trust.

Cotswold Walks

This is some of the finest walking country in England, but until you get out and walk, you won't realize just how high some of the terrain is. **Broadway Hill** (1,025 feet), immediately southeast of Broadway, and **Cleeve Hill** (1,083 feet), near Cheltenham, are the two highest points in the Cotswolds. Both are accessible to reasonably energetic walkers, who will be rewarded on clear days with spectacular views. Broadway Hill offers views as far west as the Black Mountains of mid-Wales and as far north as the Wrekin, another distinctive outcrop, in mid-Shropshire. Dedicated walkers should pick up the **Cotswold Way**, a clearly signposted walking route of about 100 miles that connects Chipping Campden and Bath. Another point of interest for moderately ambitious walkers are the **Rollright Stones**, located and signposted 4 miles (6½ km) south of Chipping Norton, on the Oxfordshire side of the Cotswolds, off A 34. This circle of about 70 stones is said to represent a king, five knights, and a number of men at arms. As with Stonehenge, it is said to be impossible to count all the stones and come up with the same number twice.

STAYING AND DINING ELSEWHERE IN THE COTSWOLDS

(Note that many hotels and restaurants are recommended in the descriptions of villages and towns, above.)

If you are looking for a metropolitan base, the ▶ **Queen's Hotel** in Cheltenham is smart and central. It is used mainly by businesspeople on weekdays, but travellers appreciate its weekend package deals. The ▶ **Golden Valley Thistle Hotel** on the outskirts of town is also smart, modern, and very well appointed. Both have good and comfortable restaurants. The ▶ **Plough at Clanfield**, on the Cotswolds' southernmost edge near Lechlade, is a well-maintained Elizabethan manor house with a stylish restaurant and whirlpool baths. The ▶ **King's Head Hotel** at Cirencester is a coaching inn of great antiquity, a major attraction in this golden-stone market town near the southwestern corner of the region. The ▶ **Hatton Court Hotel** at Upton St. Leonard's (just south of Gloucester) is very stylish; the bar and restaurant are particularly spacious and welcoming. The ▶ **Lords of the Manor**, at Upper Slaughter near Bourton-on-the-Water just southwest of Stow-on-the-Wold, is yet another of the region's fine, high-ceilinged country houses that will transport you miles away from everyday cares—except perhaps when it comes time to pay the bill (though that can apply to many top-of-the-range country-house hotels if you are not careful to take advantage of the special weekend or mid-week packages many of them offer). It has a formal restaurant with elaborate classic dishes as well as innovative ones.

▶ **Lower Slaughter Manor**, a fine renovation of an imposing family house, is in the lovely village of Lower Slaughter. The stroll uphill through the woodlands to Upper Slaughter is delightful. ▶ **Studley Priory Hotel**, at Horton-cum-Studley, is another rambling, historic stone building. As is so often the case with older and larger hotels, rooms vary in size and appeal. Try particularly to secure one of the large double rooms overlooking the rear garden. Those who have seen the film *A Man for All Seasons* might recognize that garden as the setting of a crucial scene in the film. In Woodstock the ▶ **Feathers Hotel** and the ▶ **Bear Hotel** are accommodations of great character, the former superbly restored, with a much-admired color scheme, antiques, open fires, and an elegant restaurant, the latter a coaching inn with paneled bars, low ceilings, and lots of atmosphere. Neither of these hotels is cheap, but special weekend deals can bring prices down substantially. This is not the best part of Britain for inexpensive small hotels and quality guest houses. ▶ **Tall Trees**, a quiet bed and breakfast on the outskirts of Temple Guiting, is better than most. The village, clearly signposted, lies 1 mile (1½ km) south of the B 4077, east of Stow-on-the-Wold.

The Cotswolds are also superb picnic country, or you can wash down your bread and cheese or your game pie and salad with a pint or two of ale from a low-ceilinged pub that still sells beer from one of the local breweries. Look out for pubs that display signs for Donnington and Hook Norton ales.

Blenheim Palace

As a memorial to Britain's successes at war, Blenheim Palace is unequaled. Located near the village of Woodstock, some 10 miles (16 km) southeast of Chipping Norton on the A 34, Blenheim was built as the gift of Queen Anne to John Churchill, first duke of Marlborough, after his spectacular defeat of the French at the battle of Blenheim in August 1704. The architect of this immense palace, John Vanbrugh, was hired by the duke but always considered the building to be "more as an intended Monument of the Queen's glory than a private Habitation for the Duke of Marlborough."

It is in fact difficult to imagine Blenheim as a family home. Most of its interior is devoted to a series of magnificent State Rooms, sumptuously furnished and decorated and containing an impressive series of tapestries depicting Marlborough's most important victories.

The land given for the site was that of a royal hunting lodge—the royal Manor of Woodstock—and the palace was built between ▶ 1705 and 1722 on 2,200 acres. In the 1760s, the fourth duke commissioned landscape architect Capability Brown to completely redesign the park, changing its formal structure to conform with the newly fashionable "natural" look. The result is a pair of shimmering lakes separated by Vanbrugh's fine arched bridge and combined with a sweep of lawns and parkland, often said to be the finest view in England. More recently, the ninth duke added a series of fine Italianate water terraces.

Today's visitors can view the modest room where Sir Winston Churchill was born and see some Churchill memorabilia. Outside they can take a boat ride on the lake, board the narrow-gauge railway, or picnic in the park.

Bath

Bath has so much going for it that it doesn't bother to claim a Cotswold pedigree, but it is nicely situated on the outermost southern fringes of the area. If you are travelling by road from the Cotswolds proper, you can slip down into Bath via A 46. The ancient city is also just an hour and a half by train from London's Paddington Station.

It is said that around 875 B.C. Bladud, the father of King Lear, allowed a herd of sickly pigs in search of acorns to wallow in mud that seemed to cure them of all known ills. Thus were Bath's spa waters discovered. (If you visit the Circus, note the acorn motifs on top of the terrace of houses.)

The Romans rediscovered the health-giving waters after their invasion of Britain in A.D. 43, and in this comparatively balmy and prosperous part of the country, they found reasonably acquiescent local tribes and relaxation from the more strenuous and warlike northern border of the empire straddled by Hadrian's Wall. They built a series of **baths** and a temple to Sulis Minerva: Sul was an ancient Celtic deity, and Minerva, the Roman goddess of healing. The settlement was known as Aquae Sulis (waters of Sul). They also built a swimming pool, a feature not usually included in a Roman spa (in England, apart from Bath, only Wroxeter, near Shrewsbury, is known to have had one).

The baths were similar to today's Turkish baths and were as much a place to gossip and relax as to get clean. Bathers had to wash without soap, which had yet to be invented. Instead, dirt was literally scraped off, and bath oil was much in evidence. A large part of the original structure remains (though the "Roman" statues that look down into the Great Bath are Victorian embellishments). As you peer around columns into the green water you can easily imagine the scene nearly 2,000 years ago.

After the Roman occupation, Bath continued as an important center. In the tenth century the foundations of the many-windowed abbey (it became known as the "lantern of the west") were laid. In 973 the coronation of Edgar, the first English king, took place here. The abbey is the focal point of **Abbey Church Yard**, a spacious, traffic-free open area abutting the Pump Room and the entrance to the baths. Buskers and other street entertainers perform in the open air in summer; it is a delightful place to watch the world go by.

James I's Queen Anne put Bath's supposedly restorative waters back on the map in 1707. Taking the waters became *de rigueur,* but not in the Roman bath; that was not discovered until 1878. Instead, a five-minute walk away, Cross Bath and the Royal Baths were built in the 18th century and used throughout the 19th. Unfortunately, the restoration of these baths that was begun more than five years ago has been suspended, and they can be seen only from the outside; go via the Tourist Information Centre. The 18th-century architects who re-created Bath, rendering it among the finest cities in all of Europe, showed little interest in the Romans' achievements. Supreme among the architects were Yorkshire-born John Wood and his son, also named John. The former's greatest lifetime project was the **Circus**, a symmetrical circle of fine terraced houses, in the center of which are massive plane trees planted by the Victorians; that of the younger Wood was the **Royal Crescent**, an elliptical terrace of very imposing, mainly privately owned properties. Seldom do the outskirts of a city have such a focal point. The Scottish architect Robert Adam built the **Pulteney Bridge** (1769–1774), a classic piece of neo-Palladian design. Do not miss this. It is the second-oldest surviving bridge in England to have houses and shops built on it (only Lincoln's High Bridge is older).

Jane Austen—who actually disliked the city for its stuffiness and the garishness of its newly quarried stone (now beautifully mellowed)—described it in her novels. The early- and mid-18th-century entrepreneur and fashion arbiter Beau Nash turned Bath into a city of elegance and charm. To get a little closer to this remarkable man, you can have a meal at **Popjoy's** on Sawclose, in the last house in Bath to be occupied by Nash. He probably would have approved of the elaborate, rich cuisine: good fish with sometimes exotic sauces, game, and well-aged beef, old-fashioned creamy puddings.

The Victorians almost ruined the city center—one of

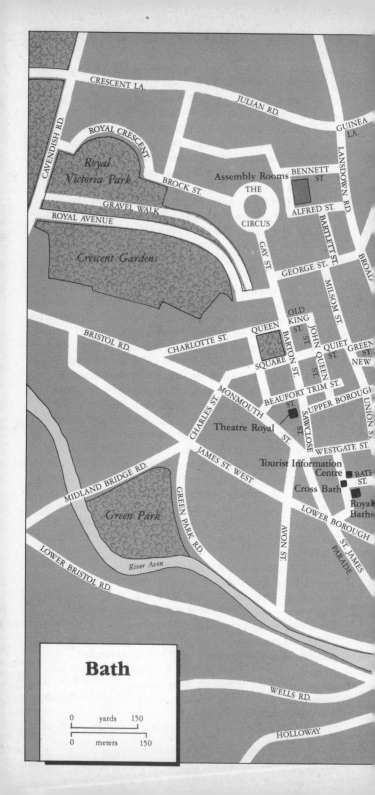

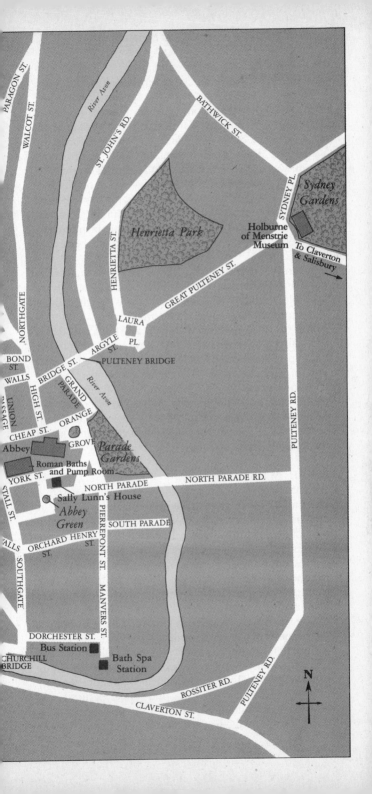

their worst excesses involved planting trees in squares and precincts never intended to have them.

Over the centuries, as now, the springs have gushed forth about 240,000 gallons of water a day, at a constant 116 degrees F. But you will not be able to bathe at all, because of the discovery, years ago, of an amoeba in the water. You *will* be able to drink the water in the **Pump Room**, water that Sam Weller in Charles Dickens's *Pickwick Papers* described as "having a wery strong flavor o' warm flatirons." While a venue of the same name existed early in the 18th century, the present Pump Room was built in 1796; some, though not the main, Roman remains had been discovered, and the Pump Room became a social center.

When you visit the Roman baths, take advantage of the guided tour; some of the guides are exceptionally witty and informative. You'll see the Romans' original limestone paving, the layout of the several baths, decorative stonework, many excavated artifacts, and the spring that is the source of the water, said to come from deep in the Mendip Hills, about 20 miles southwest of Bath. At the end of the tour you may opt for morning coffee or afternoon tea in the Pump Room, accompanied by the strains of a resident string trio. To see the rest of the city center, walk to the tourist information center at the Colonnades, on Bath Street, for information on joining one of the excellent guided tours.

BATH MUSEUMS
Bath has such a rare and impressive link with the past that its handful of exceptional museums constitutes almost an embarrassment of riches. One of the best in the entire west of England is **Number 1 Royal Crescent**. Few of the houses in the Royal Crescent are still complete private homes, but Number 1 comes surprisingly close to capturing the atmosphere of a family house of the late 18th century (Bath's heyday), with exquisite antique furniture, a fine staircase, even a sedan chair parked in the hall. The dining room is laid out exactly as it would have been for a dinner party of 200 years ago, with real food.

The 18th-century Assembly Rooms—a charming and spacious setting—epitomize what Beau Nash wanted to achieve, a genteel and cosmopolitan venue for "society," in which dances and gambling and supper parties could be held. The building also houses the **Museum of Costume**, said to be the world's largest collection of fashion through the ages. In low lighting designed to reduce fading, you can see some extremely rare 16th- and 17th-century apparel, as well as costumes up to the present day. Every year a leading fashion writer is invited to choose a representative contemporary outfit as an addition to the collection.

The **Holburne of Menstrie Museum of Art** is worth the picturesque half-mile walk over the Pulteney Bridge and along Great Pulteney Street. Built in the 18th century as a hotel, it is both a fine house and a repository of old masters, rare books, gold, and silverware. The museum is becoming increasingly well known for its Crafts Study Centre's concerts, lectures, exhibitions, and classes; these activities are especially popular with single travellers. Even by Bath standards—the city is famous for its tearooms— the teahouse in the grounds is renowned for its home-made cakes.

If the walk to the museum is too long, a highly recommended open-top bus (pick it up at any of a dozen or more convenient points) stops at the museum's entrance. This open-top tour, run by Guide Friday, is a happy marriage of rural and urban sightseeing. Looking down on the city as the bus makes its way across the surrounding hills is a treat. On the route, 2 miles (3 km) from the city center, is the early-19th-century **Claverton Manor**. This American Museum is unique in Britain, having been created in 1961 by two antiques collectors, one an American, to help improve understanding between two increasingly distinct cultures. Among the exhibits is a collection of traditional quilts and a special reconstruction of aspects of the opening of the American West. The reconstructed Conkey's Tavern contains, along with an open fire and home-baked gingerbread, artifacts of about 1776. Winston Churchill gave his first political speech at Claverton at a fête on July 26, 1897.

STAYING AND DINING IN BATH

Until recently there was a dearth of good hotels in Bath; now there are several. The modern ▶ **Hilton National**, on the banks of the River Avon close to Pulteney Bridge, was once considered an architectural blot on the horizon. It has now settled more happily into its surroundings, and, with smallish but plush and comparatively quiet rooms, it is much used by groups on the better bus tours, as well as businesspeople. More recent still is the ▶ **Bath Spa Hotel**, ten minutes' walk from the city center in a restored 19th-century mansion, all Grecian pillars, fine plaster ceilings, tiled floors, and modern chandeliers. Guest rooms are plush and pretty, with elegant bathrooms.

Guest rooms at the ▶ Royal Crescent are sumptuous, many with four-poster beds, all with fine paintings and antique furniture. The hotel's location is exceptional: right in the center of the Royal Crescent, overlooking Royal Victoria Park. (A memorable anecdote is told about the future Queen Victoria visiting this part of Bath as a young girl. A gust of wind blew up her skirts, after which she was known locally as "bandy legs." Deeply offended, she never came here again.)

A short stroll away along Gravel Walk and then across Queen Square is the comfortable ▶ Francis Hotel. Part of the extensive Forte Hotels chain but with more character than many in the group, it is popular with overseas visitors. The softly lit, very large restaurant of the hotel overlooks the square, another open space designed by the elder John Wood. The hotel was one of the buildings destroyed in this part of the city during a raid by the Luftwaffe in 1942. As rebuilt it fits attractively into its surroundings. The ▶ Priory Hotel has a feeling of the country, though it's just a mile from the city center. It dates from 1835 and has a fine restaurant that emphasizes imaginative game dishes in season. This is a connoisseur's establishment, very discreet and comfortable. The quiet ▶ Paradise House, in a Georgian building across Churchill Bridge, features Laura Ashley decor. A mile or so from the city center on Newbridge Hill lies the highly regarded ▶ Apsley House Hotel, a William IV mansion. There are only seven large bedrooms, and a much-admired restaurant.

Good bar lunches are to be had in the Crystal Palace pub in Abbey Green and at Sally Lunn's, known for its traditional teas and "Sally Lunn" buns—a sweetish bread similar to a French brioche and adaptable to sweet or savory toppings—but also a fine example of late-17th-century architecture. Sally Lunn's also serves candlelit dinners; Tel: (0225) 46-16-34. A popular, sometimes crowded, wine bar with a proper restaurant as well is The Moon & Sixpence, at 6A Broad Street. The newly enlarged conservatory is especially pleasant in the evening; Tel: (0225) 46-09-62 and 46-08-14.

Garlands (7 Edgar Buildings, George Street; Tel: 0225-44-22-83) proffers ambitious dishes and good sweets.

Woods (9–13 Alfred Street; Tel: 0225-31-48-12) skillfully offers bistro-style food in one part of the restaurant and more traditional fare in another, but still bustling, ambience. A few minutes' drive east of Bath on the A 4, in the village of Box, Wiltshire, is **Box House**, which provides a gourmet experience in very elegant surroundings; Tel: (0225) 74-44-47.

People who like their travels to have a focal point should visit the Bath Antiques Fair (May) or the Bath Festival (first half of June).

Bristol

Silver coins were minted in Bristol as early as the tenth century. Later the city's importance as a center of commerce was bolstered by its geographical position; about 120 miles due west of London and 10 miles northwest of Bath, it functioned as a gateway to the New World. Over the centuries Bristol's prominence as a port was ensured by its situation just 6 miles inland from the River Severn on the easily navigable Rivers Avon and Frome. Its natural basin was enhanced in the early 19th century by construction of the **Floating Harbour**, a series of docks built off a waterway that thrusts into the heart of the city.

Though there are several places from which to begin an exploration of the city (best done on foot), **Neptune's statue**, which looks southward over a short south–north spur of the harbor, is a favorite focal point. Stand beside the statue, close to a plaque that commemorates the exploits of the explorer John Cabot, and you are at the southwest corner of the ancient core of Bristol as it developed with increasing prosperity during the 17th and 18th centuries.

A few steps south of the statue, on Neptune's left, is the Tourist Information Centre, on Narrow Quay. The abundant literature available here provides details about Bristol's contemporary importance as a commercial center. It is known today particularly for its aircraft production (the British Airways Concorde was built here), the insurance business, and the modern docks complex to the northwest at Avonmouth, where freighters as long as many a village high street have to a considerable extent stolen the limelight from the smaller craft at anchor in the Floating Harbour.

MARITIME BRISTOL

When diarist Samuel Pepys visited Bristol on June 13, 1668, he declared it "in every respect another London." By the standards of the time the city had been rich and prosperous for more than two centuries; it was from Bristol that John Cabot had sailed in 1497 to land in Newfoundland and Nova Scotia. Even while Pepys was in Bristol people were setting off to make a fresh start in the New World, and many of the foodstuffs and other imports he and his contemporaries enjoyed were being unloaded and prepared for transportation to London: spices, tobacco, sugar, wine, Port, Sherry, olive oil, and soap. Although neither during Pepys's time nor later would slaves have actually been seen on the dockside, around 50 Bristol ships were involved in transporting Africans from the Gold Coast to America.

In the late 18th century Bristol's port went into decline. Despite extensions to the docks that were completed in 1809, the city's maritime trade was overtaken by Liverpool. Improvements in the road system, however, saved the day, mainly because they encouraged the gifted engineer Isambard Kingdom Brunel to come to Bristol to build the *Great Western*—launched in 1838, it was one of the first steamships to cross the Atlantic under its own power—and then the SS **Great Britain**, the first steamship built of iron and the first with a screw propeller. Now docked in the harbor, the *Great Britain* has become a symbol for Bristol. Along with the adjacent **Maritime Heritage Centre**, the ship, open to the public, is a focal point in Bristol. The *Great Britain* literally came home on July 19, 1970, an anniversary of her first plates being laid in Bristol in 1839 and of her launch there in 1843. For more than 30 years she sailed between Bristol and America and later Melbourne, Australia, and although even first-class passengers were expected to help man the capstans to lift the heavy anchor and to put up with the company of live sheep, pigs, geese, and turkeys, standards of comfort were comparatively high. After a disaster in 1886 (by now she was a cargo ship) off Cape Horn, the *Great Britain* was towed to Port Stanley in the Falklands; nearly a century later, she was brought back to Bristol. On an uncrowded day, as you explore the partly restored innards of the ship and stroll on deck, you will appreciate the genius of Brunel. Leave time for the video that describes the rescue and restoration of the ship and (adjacent to the Maritime Heritage Centre) the good **café**.

The most appropriate and convenient way to get to the *Great Britain* and the Maritime Heritage Centre is by a boat that docks opposite the entertainment and shopping venue called the **Watershed**, adjacent to Neptune's statue. You can get off for sightseeing at any of three or four stopping points and then rejoin the boat at a later time; for details, Tel: (0272) 27-34-16. A longer and more comfortable water-borne journey takes visitors around the whole of the docks complex. The Bristol Packet company operates boats with live commentary, some with bar and live music, including an evening tour of several dockside pubs. Most popular of all Bristol water tours is the Avon Gorge cruise, on which you travel via the Floating Harbour, under the suspension bridge built by Brunel (see below), and into the Bristol Channel; for details, Tel: (0272) 26-81-57 or 73-53-15.

CLIFTON

From the deck of the *Great Britain* you can see, to the north, one of the finest suburban skylines in Britain: the university quarter and the handsome, largely unspoiled 18th- and 19th-century buildings of the part of the city known as Clifton, not so much a neighborhood of Bristol as a community in its own right. (From Neptune's statue, you can walk to Clifton up the Park Street hill, though taking a bus as far as the university will save your calf muscles.) The pleasures of Clifton are not just architectural; this district is also known for its cozy pubs, reasonably priced boutiques, snack bars, and jazz clubs. Hardy visitors can go even higher, to the top of **Cabot Tower** on Brandon Hill, for incomparable views of the city.

From the tower it is a short distance to the pedestrian walkway over the **Clifton Suspension Bridge**, built by Brunel between 1831 and 1864 and linking central Bristol (via Clifton) with the west, including the holiday resorts of the Bristol Channel. The bridge spans the Avon Gorge at a height at high water of 245 feet above the Lower Avon (or Bristol Avon), the most tidal river in Britain. From the suspension bridge you will have a bird's-eye view, at low tide, of high-sided gleaming mudbanks that look like melted chocolate; the rise in tide here can be 40 feet.

TEMPLE MEADS STATION

If you travel to Bristol by train you will arrive at elegant Temple Meads Station, another of Brunel's still-functioning creations. The station lies about as far (20 to 25

minutes' walk) to the southeast of Neptune's statue as
Clifton and the Suspension Bridge are to the northwest.
Linked then as now with London's Paddington, the station
was not considered to be the end of the line: romantically, Brunel and others thought of the "Great Western
route" across the Atlantic to North America as simply an
extension of the Great Western Railway (once known
colloquially as God's Wonderful Railway), which he conceived in the 1830s and which ran first to Bristol and then
to Plymouth.

Though the area north and west of Temple Meads can
be dominated by fast-moving traffic on arterial roads, it is
well worth seeing the 14th-century church of **St. Mary
Redcliffe**, on Redcliffe Way. Avoid the worst of the traffic
by approaching the church from the city center via
Redcliffe Street, which runs due south off Victoria Street.
Among the church's many admirers was Elizabeth I, who
described it as ''the fairest, goodliest and most famous
[church] in the kingdom.'' St. Mary's superb Perpendicular architecture, its medieval glass, and its thirteen mellif-
luous bells have made it so dear to the citizens of Bristol
that it tends to overshadow the cathedral, impressive
though that structure is (see below).

BROAD AND CORN STREETS

Northwest of the church, back across the Floating Harbour, lies another historic neighborhood, comprising imposing 18th- and 19th-century buildings on and around
Broad Street and Corn Street; a pleasant approach from
Redcliffe Way is to cross Redcliffe Bridge and proceed
northward via Welsh Back. A stroll down Cornhill, with a
detour onto Broad Street, will give you a chance to admire solidly built bank buildings and lawyers' offices,
enhanced by many gleaming brass plaques. **Cadwallader's Coffee Shop**, on Corn Street, is a handy stop for
footsore sightseers.

If you walk downhill to the southwest along Corn
Street and onto Clare Street, you will arrive at the appro-
priately named Broad Quay and, parallel with that, St.
Augustine's Parade. Follow your nose: The tang of the sea
and the sight of dockyard cranes will draw you toward
Neptune's statue and the Floating Harbour.

PARK STREET

As you walk from Neptune's statue westward via College
Green toward Park Street, you pass the Swallow Royal

Hotel (see below), and, also on your left, **Bristol Cathedral**. Though overlooked by many visitors in favor of St. Mary Redcliffe, Bristol Cathedral is worth popping into to absorb the solid Norman ambience and to see the beautifully carved 16th-century choir stalls and the 14th-century Jesse window, inspired by the descent of Jesus from Jesse, father of King David.

The **City Museum and Art Gallery**, at the top of the Park Street hill, is set back from the road and is frequently taken to be part of the adjacent university. Easily the largest of its kind in southwest England, the museum is probably best known for its paintings of Bristol, its delftware, and its chinoiserie.

A short walk away, on the corner of Great George Street and Hill Street, is the **Georgian House**, an exquisite survivor of its period, sometimes called the best townhouse museum in the country. Downhill from the City Museum on Park Row is the **Red Lodge**, dating from about 1590, "modernized" in about 1730 and furnished in the style of that period. A commercial museum inextricably linked with Bristol and its wine trade is the **Harvey's Wine museum**, housed in 15th-century cellars on Denmark Street, to your left as you walk west from St. Augustine's Parade; it includes a rare collection of 18th-century drinking glasses.

CULTURAL EVENTS IN BRISTOL

Bristol offers a wide variety of cultural events, particularly musical ones, which are held in some of the finest auditoriums in the country. These include concerts in St. George's Church, on Brandon Hill, which are frequently broadcast by the BBC; music in the cathedral—mainly choral chamber music and jazz—and music of all kinds in Colston Hall; and live theater at the Bristol Old Vic, the Theatre Royal, the Hippodrome, Clifton's Redgrave Theatre, and a number of venues associated with the university. There is also lively jazz, rock, and folk music in pubs, notably the Old Duke, on King Street, and at the Watershed. The fortnightly publication *Venue,* which also covers Bath, is a useful guide to what's on in the city; pick it up at the Tourist Information Centre. Consult the local newspaper, the *Evening Post,* for up-to-the-minute listings.

STAYING IN BRISTOL

Reopened in the summer of 1991, though a hotel since 1863, the ▶ **Swallow Royal Hotel** is notable for its fine marbled entrance hall and skillfully restored Victorian palm court. Rooms are mostly large and nicely lit, with attractive drapes and, in many cases, antiques. The Swallow Royal is located west of Neptune's statue, near the cathedral. A few doors from Neptune's statue on Prince Street is the ▶ **Unicorn Hotel**. Recently completely refurbished, with a friendly staff, it has smallish, well-carpeted rooms, some with a view of the Floating Harbour.

On Broad Street is the 178-room ▶ **Grand Hotel**, spacious and imposing, with a plush and wood-paneled interior. Rooms vary in size and level of comfort; the best doubles are large and elegant. A note to those looking for absolute peace and quiet: As one of the premiere hotels in Bristol, the Grand is often busy with conventions and social gatherings.

Two good hotels, the ▶ **Bristol Holiday Inn Crown Plaza** and the ▶ **Bristol Hilton Hotel**, are located just to the west of Temple Meads Station. Their considerable comforts compensate for their distance from the center of the city. While the Hilton's rooms are quite small, they are quiet and comfortable. Designed mainly for businesspeople, the Hilton often has a family clientele on weekends. Similarly, the Bristol Holiday Inn Crown Plaza is geared to businesspeople but benefits other visitors when, on weekends, prices are lower. Its large, plush rooms are cool and abstract in design.

Among smaller, less expensive hotels with a following among regular visitors are the ▶ **Alandale Hotel** (smallish but fairly comfortable rooms) in Clifton and, 6 miles (10 km) west of the city, in the small town of Saltford off the A4 road to Bath, ▶ **Brunel's Tunnel House Hotel**, a classically proportioned Georgian building once owned by the great man himself. The double rooms are spacious and full of character.

Wells

While the cathedral city of Wells, 20 miles (32 km) south of Bristol, makes a natural excursion from Bath, the lack of a railway connection can make it seem rather off the beaten track, although good local bus connections are available. Wells seems to labor under the weight of the label "city"—"cathedral town" would seem more appropriate. It began as a holy place and today is still dominated by its exceptionally pleasing and harmonious cathedral, which is further enhanced by the huge adjacent

Bishop's Palace, whose grounds embrace the freshwater springs, or wells, that give the town its name.

Sadler Street and the High Street run dogleg-style through the town. To the east of the corner where they meet, Market Place is bustling during the day but tranquil during the evening, and the well-laid-out walkways beside the palace create a magnet for local people as well as visitors. Much smaller than Bristol and all of a piece, Wells makes a peaceful contrast with that major and modernized city.

And as you sweep down into Wells from the northeast via the A 39, with distinctive Glastonbury Tor (see below) in the middle distance to the left, you will see the three towers of Wells Cathedral rising ahead of you. Look left as you reach, on your right, the deceptively plain exterior of the Swan Hotel on Sadler Street. This is the best position from which to admire the cathedral's incomparable west front (though it *has* been compared with that of Chartres), which incorporates sculpture that provides a rare insight into the genius of medieval craftsmen. (More about the cathedral below.)

Golden-stone **Market Place**, is notable for its antiques shops, a National Trust shop (selling quality souvenirs, books, and gifts) on the corner that leads into the cathedral green, an elegant post office façade, and—watch where you walk!—open culverts that carry fresh spring water throughout the city from wells on the grounds of the Bishop's Palace, where water bubbles up at the rate of 40 gallons a second.

WELLS MUSEUM

Don't miss the Wells Museum on the north side of the cathedral green. Partly 14th, partly 16th, partly 18th, partly 19th century, the building lacks the gloss and razzmatazz of more modern, "themed" museums, but is all the more charming for that. Up a wooden staircase there are views of the back garden and landings crammed with such artifacts as a bizarre collection of pipe stuffers used to tamp down stray tobacco. Part of the fossil collection for which the museum is probably best known used to reside in the cathedral's west cloister, but the present labyrinthine premises are a better, more intimate, home. There are several paintings of Wells at different periods in its history and occasional exhibitions of local art on the ground floor. Also displayed are Roman and pre-Roman artifacts discovered in the dramatic underground caverns at Wookey Hole (see below). Among the most memorable exhibits, courtesy of a taxidermist, is a swan. It was the first of many that have learned to ring—for food—the little bell still attached to the gateway to the Bishop's Palace that straddles as handsome a moat as you will find in Britain. The tradition continues, though it's a lucky visitor who catches the swans in the act.

BISHOP'S PALACE
The Bishop's Palace, south of the cathedral, is impressive, not least for the approach over the moat, which can be crossed either from the cathedral green or from Market Place. Check on opening times with the Tourist Information Centre (Tel: 0749-67-25-52). Once through the 16th-century gatehouse and the unusual drawbridge that leads into an attractive greensward, follow the path through another gate, hugging the curtain wall of the palace alongside the moat. This route brings you to the **wells** that gently erupt from the sandy bottom of a pool and that give the city its name.

WELLS CATHEDRAL
Most visitors to Wells Cathedral enter via the west door. (You will be discouraged from walking around the interior if a service is in progress.) The present cathedral, using some of the stones of the original seventh- and eighth-century church, was begun in about 1180 and was completed more than 150 years later. The massive west front, a great masonry screen whose design is carried across the flanking towers and which originally carried 386 brightly colored sculpted figures, is the forerunner of the great Gothic façades of many European cathedrals. Among the many interior features that make the cathedral worth exploring are the ancient stone steps leading to the Chapter House and, across the nave, an impressive swirl of arches that was fashioned soon after the central tower was erected, to keep it from falling.

Certain humorous details also enliven the interior, such as a dozen carvings in the south transept of people suffering from toothache, and four scenes of an old man being punished for stealing fruit. In the north transept is the most memorable exhibit of all, a moving clock of 1390; every 15 minutes a round of horsemen appear in a mini-tournament, and at each rotation the same knight is knocked off his horse. Pause in the octagonal Lady Chapel for a look at the Golden Window (1339), beautifully composed of fragments of colored glass. The library, constructed in 1425 and believed to be the largest medieval library in Britain, contains archives from the tenth century onward.

STAYING AND DINING IN WELLS

The ▶ **Swan Hotel** is a historical gem, with carefully preserved oak paneling, gleaming silver, crackling log fires, and four-poster beds in many rooms. Its restaurant serves excellent traditional English food. The Swan is just one of a half-dozen ancient hostelries that sit comfortably within the heart of the city. Among the other exceptional places to stay are the ▶ **Crown**, the ▶ **Red Lion**, the ▶ **Star**, and the ▶ **White Hart** (none is more than three minutes' walk from any other, so intimate is the center of Wells); all have been brought sympathetically into the 20th century without losing their low-ceilinged, historical character.

One of the rooms in the ▶ **Ancient Gate House Hotel** sits over a 14th-century stone gate through which you enter the cathedral green, obliquely to the left of the magnificent west front. This hotel is widely known for **Rugantino's**, the Italian restaurant it incorporates. A particularly inexpensive weekday lunch is available at the restaurant, though prices are higher in the evening. The painstakingly run ▶ **Bekynton House** guest house, with rather cottagey, quiet, slightly old-fashioned rooms, is in the part of Wells dominated by the several separate buildings of the Wells Cathedral School. With more than 700 pupils, the school feels to the visitor more like an ancient university than a modern school. To absorb some of the atmosphere, walk up St. Andrew's Street alongside Cathedral Green, turning left into College Lane, Mountroy Lane, The Liberty, Back Liberty, Canon's Street, and Vicar's Close.

Around Wells

Several important sights near Wells add extra luster to the city's charms.

GLASTONBURY

Glastonbury is 5½ miles (9 km) southwest of Wells via the A 39. One of the most ancient settlements in Britain, it is cited as the cradle of European Christianity. Legend has it that in A.D. 60 Joseph of Arimathea stuck his staff into the ground here, where it sprouted and flowered. A church was built on the spot. The tree-fringed abbey ruins are a second focal point for the thousands of pilgrims (as many tourists would style themselves) who annually come to see nearby **Glastonbury Tor**, all that remains of a church that stood more than 500 feet above sea level and was destroyed by an earthquake in 1275. The site affords an impressive view of Glastonbury, Wells, and the Bristol Channel.

The ▶ **George and Pilgrims Hotel** on Glastonbury's High Street was founded during the reign of Edward III (1327–1377). Much admired for its intricately carved exterior, mullioned windows, and stained glass, it is said— perhaps not surprisingly—to have a ghost. Opt for one of the old rooms to enjoy the hotel's character. Immediately next to the abbey, the elegant Georgian ▶ **No. 3 Hotel and Restaurant** has a countrywide reputation for its good food and comfortable bedrooms.

WOOKEY HOLE

About a mile (1½ km) northwest of Wells, Wookey Hole is known for caves carved in the limestone of the Mendip Hills by the underground River Axe. They were occupied by prehistoric people and are open to the public, though visitors drawn by reports of beautiful stalagmite and sta- lactite formations and the slow-moving turquoise-green River Axe should note that modern amusements, includ- ing waxworks, have been installed. Eight miles (13 km) northwest of Wells and about 12 miles (19 km) north of Glastonbury is **Cheddar Gorge**, one of the most impres- sive natural fissures in Britain. Stone- and iron-age tools found here are displayed in a museum at the gorge. (The village of Cheddar, at the mouth of the gorge, is where the now widely imitated cheese of the same name was first produced.)

Salisbury Plain

From Bath it is a quick trip east on A 4 to Avebury (of the Stone Circle), which we cover after Winchester and Marl- borough below; or it is only 15 miles (24 km) south on A 36 to Warminster, on the westernmost edge of mysterious Salisbury Plain. If you tell someone in any of the local pubs around the plain that you've seen a flying saucer, you will not be laughed at. More UFOs have been sighted here than anywhere else in Britain—especially in the

1960s, when hardly a month went by without news of something extraterrestrial being spotted on a hillside. Doubters attribute the sightings to the presence of nearby military installations, and to the romantic associations of Salisbury Plain itself. On these lonely, windswept uplands, imaginative walkers may fancy they see the ghosts of Celtic and Saxon farmers and warriors. On frosty winter nights little affected by urban streetlights, the stars seem close, too, and can be viewed with great clarity.

Salisbury Plain is just one part of the chalky upland that dominates much of rural Wiltshire. It has been described as a rumpled plateau surrounded by steep slopes, and though it is on average just 500 feet above sea level, it seems higher. It appears soft and pleasant enough on a summer afternoon, but when the wind moans across the grassy, uninhabited hills it is a different proposition. For many centuries this has been a military testing ground. The Romans crisscrossed it, and army maneuvers first took place here during the Napoleonic Wars. Most notable are the region's remnants of never-quite-forgotten tribes of 3,000 to 4,000 years ago: Stonehenge (which we cover below, after the town of Salisbury) and the even more mysterious and romantic Avebury Stone Circle.

BRADFORD-ON-AVON

You can also make the trip from Bath to Salisbury by train; the route is comparatively roundabout but scenically pretty: mainly farmland with, occasionally, sprawling villages. Best of all, the line passes through Bradford-on-Avon, an exquisite town that is known for its antiques shops, as well as an art gallery in the public library that welcomes browsers. There is also Elms Cross Vineyard, open to visitors, about a mile from the town center. Something of a poor man's Bath, Bradford-on-Avon has, among other attractions, a Saxon church and a 14th-century tithe barn. (Tithe barns existed to store goods paid in kind as rent by tenants of church-owned land.) The town's prosperity came, not untypically, from wool production, but the last mill closed in 1905. A day-return ticket between Bath and Salisbury costs about £9, and you can stop to shop in Bradford-on-Avon without extra charge. If you're looking for a meal, two miles (3 km) away in the village of Avoncliff you will find the charming 17th-century inn called the **Cross Guns**—all low ceilings, horse-brasses, and oak beams. The inn, open for lunch and dinner seven days a week, serves inexpensive tradi-

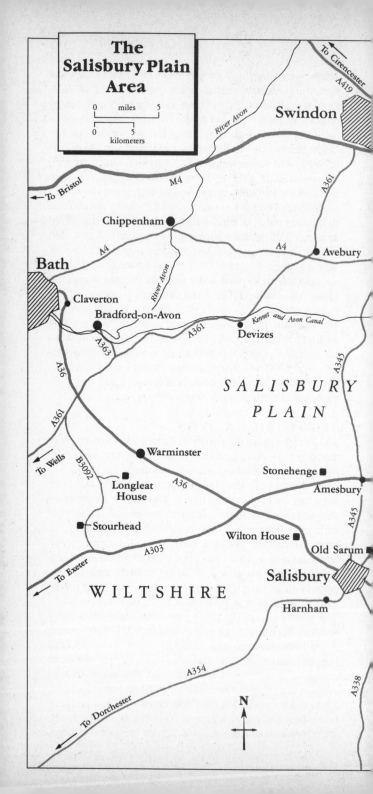

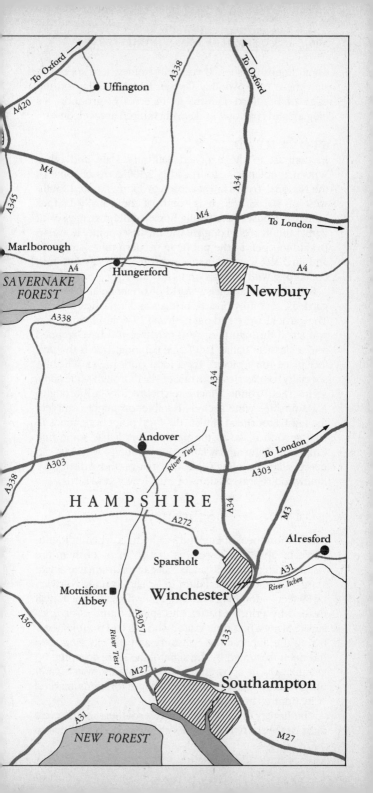

tional English dishes. If you want somewhere special to stay, there is ▶ **Woolley Grange Hotel** standing on the edge of Bradford-on-Avon in 14 acres of grounds. It's elegant and spacious, and small children are welcome.

STOURHEAD

In contrast to the exposed Salisbury Plain and other Wiltshire uplands—Stourhead is 2,500 acres of some of the National Trust's finest garden property. Located southwest of Warminster, it is south of the equally famous **Longleat House**—the family home of the marquesses of Bath, built in 1580. Longleat was the first country house in Britain to open to the public in modern times (in 1949) and, in 1966, was the first of many to create a safari park containing wild animals on its grounds.

Stourhead is a fantasy world of ornamental lakes and gardens, set off by bizarre bridges and a classical temple. The gardens were laid out between 1741 and 1780, and as you stroll through them you may feel you have stepped into a classical Italian landscape painting. This is the perfect place for a picnic: Try a local pork pie (a Wiltshire specialty) or pastries from one of Marlborough's fine pâtisseries. (See Around Winchester, below, for Marlborough.) A Hampshire wine such as Hambledon might complete the feast. **Stourhead House**, the focal point here, tends to take second place to the gardens, yet it has some fine Chippendale furniture, landscape paintings, works by old masters, and Grinling Gibbons carvings (those distinctive limewood representations of fruit, leaves, and birds).

Salisbury

Part of the appeal of England's cathedrals, whether identifiable by spires or towers, is that so many of them are visible from a great distance. Salisbury's distinctive single spire—at 404 feet the tallest in Britain, beating Norwich by 89 feet—dominates the city. Following a recent appeal headed by Prince Charles, the spire's future is now assured. Many a first-time visitor who has had trouble negotiating the approach to Salisbury and the city ring road has been frustrated by the sight of the spire cropping up tantalizingly in apparently different places. Watch carefully when approaching roundabouts for signs marked "City Centre" or "Cathedral."

The history of Salisbury, which is southeast of the great mass of Salisbury Plain, is closely interwoven with that of the cathedral. Neatly extending beyond the boundaries of the cathedral's close—perhaps the most harmonious and beautiful in the country—the town has retained its original medieval layout. It is graced by a huge marketplace, a 13th-century poultry cross, an exceptional parish church that was a "chapel of ease" to the cathedral, and a handful of highly evocative and historic coaching inns that seem to have materialized straight out of the pages of Dickens's *Pickwick Papers*.

Southwest of the city, the **water meadows**, from which John Constable painted several pictures of the cathedral, have been jealously guarded, with no building allowed. The walk across them to Harnham Mill—now incorporating a small hotel, a restaurant, and a café on the edge of the small village of Harnham, onto which Salisbury proper has never encroached—is recommended. The river that tumbles beside Salisbury's town mill and meanders toward Harnham in the shadow of the cathedral is a tributary of the Salisbury Avon, not to be confused with the Avon that flows through Shakespeare's Stratford. The name *Avon,* by the way, is derived from the Celtic word for "water."

It is entirely characteristic of Salisbury that the **Salisbury Arts Festival** is low-key and little known beyond a certain radius (and so less crowded as well). It takes place each September.

SALISBURY CATHEDRAL

Salisbury Cathedral, and thus most of the city we see today, was built on virgin land. Until 1219 Salisbury's cathedral stood at Old Sarum, on high ground two miles north of Salisbury, but this was impractical and a new cathedral was built. **Old Sarum**, a very worthwhile detour for visitors who want to explore Salisbury's origins, was probably occupied during the Iron Age. The Romans had a defensive fort here called Sorbiodunum. In the Domesday Book, the settlement appears as Sarisberie. Due to a lack of fresh water, Bishop Poore, incumbent at the original cathedral, requested papal permission in about 1220 to build a new cathedral. Those are the facts. The legend has it that Poore fired an arrow into the air, vowing to build wherever it landed. A good way to see Old Sarum is to attend the open-air plays (often Shakespeare) performed here in summer.

The new cathedral was consecrated a remarkably brief 38 years after the first foundation stone was laid. The first half of the 13th century saw a magnificent surge of Gothic architecture (Amiens and Lincoln cathedrals were created at roughly the same time). Even so, Salisbury is memorable, with a long nave—second only to Winchester's—that can be taken in at one glance. The cathedral is full of unique architectural detail: rare 13th-century stone friezes in the octagonal Chapter House and a clock mechanism of 1386—the oldest piece of machinery still working in the country, perhaps even in the world. Also contained in the cathedral is the best preserved of the four extant copies of the Magna Carta. This has been safely contained within the building since 1225, except between 1940 and 1945, when it was hidden in a nearby quarry to protect it from German bombing. The famous spire—so often pictured on chocolate boxes and calendars—was not part of the original cathedral plan but was begun in about 1330.

The earliest houses in the cathedral close were built partly from stones brought from Old Sarum, and these early remains can be detected alongside state-of-the-art Georgian red brick and later stucco that make the close a paragon of domestic architectural harmony. The close is, literally, an enclosure, as the four gates through which most visitors pass are closed at night, continuing a centuries-old curfew.

The easterly **St. Ann's Gate**, perhaps the most exciting approach to an English cathedral precinct, visually closes off St. Ann's Street. The gate, attractive and intriguing in itself, effectively divides the workaday streets of the town from the rarefied setting of the cathedral. In a room above, it is said, the young George Frederick Handel gave his first public recital in England. Beyond the close, the simple arrangement of houses and streets that followed immediately in the wake of the construction of the cathedral comprised neighborhoods that were known as "chequers," usually taking their name from inns. So there were precincts known as the White Hart Chequer, the Black Horse Chequer, and the **Cross Keys Chequer**, the last of which survives in the heart of the city, a few yards from the Guildhall, where a small shopping precinct still carries the name.

No transport is needed within this compact city, which has no hills to discourage the stroller. **St. Ann's Street** might appear on the map as an unlikely detour, but it is worth the short walk. This street is a microcosm of the best of several centuries of English domestic architecture. Walk up the street—it is a dead end—and then retrace your steps; it makes a fine approach to the cathedral, whose spire is visible as you walk along. Joiners' Hall, now owned by the National Trust, was once the guildhall of the Joiners' Company (carpenters skilled in structural work), which was created in 1617.

SALISBURY MUSEUMS

The most popular of the city's museums is the **Salisbury and South Wiltshire Museum**, beautifully situated in the Close, within the cathedral precinct. It is especially strong on archaeological finds tracing the prehistory of Wessex, which was one of Britain's most advanced and populous regions long before the Roman invasion. Better still, artifacts from Stonehenge are included, so this makes an excellent appetizer if you are en route to that monument. And not just artifacts: A collection of pictures of Stonehenge includes several watercolors by J. M. W. Turner.

A few doors along, at 58 The Close, is the **Duke of Edinburgh's Royal Regiment Museum**, with uniforms, pictures, weapons, and a display of the regiment's Victoria Crosses.

Mompesson House, in Choristers' Green, on the northern side of the Close, is one of the finest of the National Trust's urban properties. It is a recently lived-in house overlooking the northern flank of the cathedral with a warm and harmonious interior of about 1740. Also worth seeing from the outside, although its interior is closed to the public, is the **College of Matrons**—dating from 1682 and originally founded as a home for widows and unmarried daughters of clergymen—near High Street Gate and Malmesbury House, one of the finest houses in the close.

EXPLORING SALISBURY

St. Thomas's Church holds its own even against the cathedral, and parts of it are older. Just 100 yards from Market Square, it commands the commercial quarter. The church houses a famous painting known colloquially as *Doom,* an impressive medieval work depicting both highborn and common men and women emerging from a graveyard on their way to either heaven or hell.

You can finish off your visit to St. Thomas's by stopping at nearby **Snell's**, a stylish coffee room/delicatessen that is renowned for its handmade chocolates and other confectioneries.

Markets are held in Salisbury on Tuesdays and Saturdays. The Tuesday charter was granted in 1227, but the practice gradually became daily until neighboring towns objected. Thus the twice-weekly compromise. Above the library at one side of the marketplace is a clock celebrating the Queen's 1977 silver jubilee. Another royal event recalled here is the coronation of Edward VII, in celebration of which 4,000 people sat down to roast beef and a choice of dessert. At the southeastern corner of Market Square is the mainly 18th-century Guildhall, and just across Queen Street, which runs past it, is the Cross Keys Chequer shopping precinct.

A few yards beyond the Cross Keys Chequer is the house of John A'Port, a wool merchant and six-time mayor of Salisbury. The house is now a china and glass emporium called **Watson's** in which visitors are encouraged not just to browse among the crystal and Wedgwood but also to look at a cutaway section of the first floor's original structure, as well as a series of before-and-after photographs of the restoration. Another remarkable city-center building is the Hall of John Halle, which dates back to about 1479 and is now the lobby of the Odeon movie theater.

Salisbury has a well-known inn—the ► **Red Lion**, the original coaching yard on Milford Street, with a bright red stone lion on which children like to sit and have their photographs taken. In the heyday of the coaching era this was the starting point for the "Salisbury Flying Machine," which departed for London every night at 10:00. The public rooms of the Red Lion have resisted late-20th-century tarting up and remain oak-paneled, labyrinthine, and full of nostalgia, but bedrooms are modern and fairly comfortable. If you pop in here for a drink you half expect an ostler to emerge touching his forelock or a serving maid to come to your table bearing a jug of ale made on the premises. Walking south from the Red Lion along Fish Row and Butcher Row— clues to the nature of commercial life in Salisbury 400 or 500 years ago—you'll come to Poultry Cross, a small stone shelter that originally served as a marketplace and has stood here for about 600 years. It is one of only four of its kind in the country. Directly opposite is the ancient **Haunch of Venison** pub, a beautifully preserved, traditional chophouse. Good, inexpensive bar meals, as well as traditional roasts, are served in this low-ceilinged, bustling place, and a bizarre tale is still told of a mummified hand found in the dark recesses of the pub in 1905. Very close to the St. Ann's Gate entrance to the cathedral precinct, the **King's**

Arms, on St. John Street, exudes history and serves good bar food.

For unusual souvenirs try **Beach's Bookshop** on High Street, a large secondhand emporium in which the assistants wear uniforms. It is very good for books on local topography and history. Directly across the road from Beach's is **Mitre House**, now a tearoom and shop selling teas. Bishops were traditionally robed here before their enthronement. The National Trust shop on High Street sells things like needlepoint kits, luxury soaps, embroidered and printed tea towels, coffee-table books, commemorative plaques, and a traditional run of portable souvenirs—all displayed in a genteel environment. From Beach's it is just a few hundred yards to the Old George shopping mall. There is also a fine antiques shop on St. Ann's Street: **Ian Hastie**. At 37 Catherine Street is the **Antique and General Trading Centre**, a three-story antiques and bric-a-brac emporium.

DINING AND STAYING IN SALISBURY

Salisbury has no restaurants of national renown, and its ethnic restaurants (Indian and Chinese) tend to be of the friendly neighborhood variety, with no pretensions—just filling meals at good value. Salisbury seems best for solid pub fare: game in season, locally made meat pies, fish and chips. There is a large and popular fish-and-chip shop, **Stoby's**, between Fish Row and Market Square. The ▶ **White Hart** on St. John Street—also a hotel—serves good, hot bar lunches, and you will rub shoulders with comfortable solicitors in Harris tweed and ladies in Pringle sweaters. In the hotel foyer residents will be waiting for friends behind their *Daily Telegraph*s. Regular visitors tend to prefer rooms in the main building, but all rooms are of a good size and are well appointed. The 13th-century ▶ **Rose & Crown Hotel** also serves traditional English food and has lots of atmosphere. There's good, unpretentious English food at **Harper's**, just off the Market Square. Local people greatly praise the beefsteak casserole with dumplings and the rich bread-and-butter pudding. For something different, at a very reasonable price, try **Mo's** on Milford Street, suitable for vegetarians. An alternative on a pleasant summer day would be to buy some fruit and cheese from the market and eat it in the shade of the Poultry Cross. (See also the descriptions of the Haunch of Venison and the King's Arms pubs, above.)

Stonehenge

Just to the north of the city is Salisbury Plain, where thousands of the sheep that made Salisbury so prosperous once grazed. Of all the tangible reminders that in prehistoric times this was a popular and comparatively sophisticated patch of England, none is better known than Stonehenge.

Stonehenge, at the southern edge of the plain just eight miles north of Salisbury, is probably bigger in your imagination than in its actual physical presence. As has often been pointed out, its 162 stone blocks—unadorned, undressed, and only about 35 steps from one side to the other—would fit within the Library of Congress rotunda or within the dome of St. Paul's Cathedral. Nonetheless, each year it inspires approximately three quarters of a million people to go on a pilgrimage. These numbers are swollen by modern-day Druids and latter-day hippies who crowd onto Salisbury Plain for the summer solstice. It is mainly on account of these celebrants that Stonehenge is now subject to a four-mile "exclusion zone" that applies not only during the summer solstice but for several days around it.

This most famous of all Britain's stone circles is one of Europe's greatest enigmas. A thousand years before the Egyptians built the pyramids, Neolithic farmers lived on the windswept chalk plateau. There was little wood and less stone, but they built burial chambers around which Stonehenge eventually grew—first as a cemetery, then as a temple. Over the years it was put to many uses, which is one of the reasons Stonehenge has so puzzled later generations.

As trade routes became busier and the population increased, Stonehenge and similar burial grounds took on the role of meeting places, not only for traders but also for participants in seasonal fertility rituals.

Among the earliest visitors to Stonehenge were the Druids, Celtic priests who came over from the Continent about 300 B.C., when Stonehenge had lain abandoned and unused for more than 1,000 years. They took it over for ceremonial purposes (though not, as used to be fancifully supposed, for ritual slaughter).

In 1130 Henry of Huntingdon, a dean at Lincoln Cathedral, was commissioned to write a history of England, and he included Stonehenge. He borrowed from an even earlier chronicle—largely fictitious—that claimed Merlin, seer and prophet to King Arthur, had the stones removed from Ireland and reconstructed on Salisbury Plain.

Charles II was among the "great and good" to be fascinated by Stonehenge, and he commissioned Inigo Jones, the superb architect of St. Paul's, Covent Garden, and the Banqueting House in London, to solve the mystery. Jones concluded that as "those ancient times had no knowledge of public works, either sacred or secular, for their own use or honour of their deities, they could not be responsible for such an impressive structure." It must, ergo, have been Roman in origin.

Samuel Pepys took a day trip from Salisbury but found the cost of his party's saddle horses rather high. Of the site he was characteristically blunt: "Worth going to see. God knows what their use was." James I was utterly intrigued and commissioned John Aubrey, best known for his *Brief Lives,* to produce a thorough survey. But Aubrey was much more impressed with nearby Avebury Stone Circle, and his work at Stonehenge was skimpy. Among all the dross was the correct suggestion that this was a residential site of early British tribes.

People seem to have great difficulty counting the stones. There was even a legend from Elizabethan times that no ordinary mortal could count the stones twice and arrive at the same figure. Jonathan Swift, the author of *Gulliver's Travels,* and Celia Fiennes, the late-17th-century traveller and diarist, were among those who made a stab at it. Each came up with a different number, and Swift hedged his bets—"either 92 or 93."

THE LAYOUT OF STONEHENGE

As you approach Stonehenge, you first come upon a ditch and a bank about 100 feet from the first stones. Inside this are the 56 Aubrey holes, found to contain remains of cremated human beings, and what is effectively a gateway to the site known as the slaughter stone, now fallen. The Heel Stone, a so-called sarsen stone, stands outside the entrance. (The word *sarsen* probably comes from *saracen,* or, simply, "strange" or "alien"; the term "Heel Stone" is derived from a mark on the surface that resembles a man's heel.) The Heel Stone is the only one to have survived from the first circle of stones that appeared here around 1800 B.C. It was erected exactly in line, with other stones, with the point at which the sun rises above the horizon during the summer solstice.

Between 1700 and 1600 B.C. the construction of the second stage of Stonehenge began. Blue stones were transported from Wales and erected in two concentric circles. This was the work of the Beaker Folk, farmers from the Continent whose name derives from their excavated drinking vessels. The construction of Stonehenge III began after 1600 B.C., when the blue stones were moved and 80 huge sarsen stones were transported here from the Marlborough Downs. These were formed either into a ring of upright stones, connected by carved lintels, or an inner horseshoe shape.

Later (also part of Stonehenge III) an oval arrangement of blue stones was erected within the sarsen horseshoe, and a block of sandstone, also from Wales, was erected in the center. It became known as the Altar Stone. Finally, in about 1300 B.C., the residents rearranged 19 blue stones into their current configuration.

A word of advice: Try to visit Stonehenge when the rest of the world has decided to miss it. Dull, even rainy, days are good; misty or foggy ones are better still. It all helps to get the imagination working. Even when the site is closed, it is possible during daylight hours to see a certain amount of Stonehenge from the road.

Mottisfont Abbey

A visit to Salisbury and Winchester cathedrals has been called the best day's outing in southern England. And Mottisfont Abbey, set in a gentle valley by the River Test (famous for its trout fishing), is almost exactly midway between the two, making for an added bonus. It lies about a mile west of the A 3057 and approximately a mile north of the small town of Romsey. The abbey takes its name from the Saxon *moot* (council) once held on the site, and from a nearby spring, or font. In the 18th century the abbey became a country house, and it is now owned by the National Trust. The house is open only at limited times, but the lovely gardens are more frequently accessible and are delightful for picnicking. Mottisfont is a rural interlude between the two inevitably bustling and well-trodden tourist hot spots. Highly recommended for a light lunch or afternoon tea are the Post Office tearooms in the village center.

Winchester

When the Romans reached this part of the south of England, Winchester was well established as the most important city in the land. The Normans adopted it as their capital after the 1066 invasion, and Winchester almost became the English capital for all time. But London's geographical advantages, particularly its position on the Thames, were too strong to ignore.

Winchester's spectacular cathedral, which has the longest nave of any in England, was begun in 1079 and not completed until 300 years later. The presence of this mighty church—certainly more than the effective status as capital—made Winchester the most important market town in Wessex.

The town is comparatively small and intimate, though you might not think so on a hot day as you try to escape into the air-conditioned comfort of the larger-than-average branch of Marks and Spencer. On such a day be sure to stroll along the bank of the River Itchen, close to the spacious grounds of Winchester College on your right. To experience the medieval aspect of town, walk along the back lanes leading to and around the school.

Much medieval prosperity derived from wool, and Winchester enjoyed its share of this wealth. The bishops of Winchester held the charter for a great annual wool fair, and funds from this enabled Bishop William of Wykeham in 1382 to found **Winchester College**, possibly the oldest of the country's "public" schools (although this claim is disputed by King's School in Canterbury). The school offers occasional organized tours to the public, and its buildings are just several among many that make Winchester worth visiting on its own account and not just for the cathedral. The grounds and buildings are lovely, reminiscent of some of the larger Oxford and Cambridge colleges. Other essential sights include the **Castle Hall**, which is all that remains of the Norman castle that was largely destroyed by Cromwellian troops in 1651. Here you'll find "King Arthur's Round Table," but do not assume Arthur or Merlin (elusive figures at best) ever sat at it: It has been scientifically dated at around 1400. It is interesting to compare the Purbeck marble pillars in Castle Hall with those in Salisbury Cathedral. Nearby, there is a small museum in the Westgate, one of two surviving gateways from about 1200.

The truth about King Arthur, who he was and where he held court, is unclear, but there is no doubt that King Alfred, much ahead of his time, created a powerhouse of culture in fertile Wessex. He died in 899, after fortifying 20 or more towns and translating Latin texts into the vernacular Saxon. He also wrote the very first English history. His statue, erected in 1901 to mark the 1,000th anniversary of his death (two years too late) stands in Winchester's main street, Broadway.

Rarely crowded but exceptionally interesting are the military museums contained within the **Peninsula Barracks,** off the Romsey Road. These comprise the Gurka Museum (commemorating, for example, 26 holders of the Victoria Cross), the Royal Green Jackets Museum, the Royal Hussars Museum (55 VCs), plus, in a separate building, the Museum of the Royal Hampshire Regiment.

If you are really adventurous, you may apply for the wayfarer's dole of bread and ale at the **Hospital of St. Cross,** founded in 1137 by Henri de Blois, a grandson of William the Conqueror. Note the plain, smock-like gowns of the pensioners who reside at the hospital, uniforms designed in the 12th century by the founder. Only a tiny token of bread and ale is now available, but at least you become part of an 800-year-old tradition. (There has been a charge for the food and drink, currently £1.50, since 1911.) You can also make a literary pilgrimage of sorts in Winchester. Jane Austen and Izaak Walton both died here—Austen in 1817 in a house on College Street, Walton in 1683 in a house on Dome Alley (a cul-de-sac at the end of St. Swithun's Street) in the cathedral precinct, although neither house is open to the public. Finally, in your wanderings around Winchester, do not miss **Kingsgate Street.** Running due south from Kingsgate, on the south side of the cathedral, it is almost in the same league as Salisbury's St. Ann's Street, a rare example of harmonious domestic architecture.

While not a world-beater in terms of visitor centers, the Winchester Heritage Centre, at 52–54 Upper Brook Street, is a useful introduction to the city. There is, for example, a 20-minute audiovisual display.

WINCHESTER CATHEDRAL
This is the longest medieval church not only in England but in the whole of Europe. Part of the foundations, discovered during excavations in the 1960s, date from about 645, though the earliest stone most visitors see is

from the 11th century. The cathedral close, while not in the same class as Salisbury's, has some special buildings, including some dating from the 13th century.

For all the cathedral's rare and beautiful tombs and its outstanding collection of antechapels and chantries, the tomb of the ninth-century bishop Saint Swithun is the most popular attraction. Swithun was a man of such sincere humility that he refused to allow his own burial in the church proper. It is said that when his bones were brought into the cathedral to be reinterred on July 15, 971, it rained heavily for 40 days. Legend now holds that if it rains on July 15, it will do so at least in part for each of the next 40 days.

Among the details some visitors miss is the Winchester Bible, an illuminated 12th-century volume housed in the oldest book room in Europe, dating from about 1150. And in one transept are two wooden benches thought to be Norman—they are certainly the oldest pieces of oak furniture in the country. There are also several chests said to contain the bones of Saxon kings, including Canute and Ethelwulf. Jane Austen is commemorated by a stone in the floor of the nave, but no direct reference is made to her novels in the inscription. Most recent among things to see is the cathedral's Triforium Museum—sculpture, wood, and metalwork reflecting 1,000 years of the building's history.

SHOPPING IN WINCHESTER

Like Salisbury, Winchester has an abundance of second-hand bookshops. The long-established **Wells** is small but charming and sells prints too, at the cathedral end of Kingsgate Street. It has a new-books branch in College Street. A bigger secondhand bookshop is **Gilberts** in The Square—excellent browsing. For a variety of interesting antiques, try **Blanchards** on Jewry Street. This street is filled with antiques and bric-a-brac shops.

DINING AND STAYING
IN WINCHESTER

There are fewer well-known restaurants in Winchester than pubs, which offer a wide range of hot and cold bar lunches. The **Royal Oak**, off Royal Oak Passage, is one of several contenders for the title of the oldest drinking spot in Britain; it is part Saxon. Another small pub near the cathedral, the **Eclipse**, was originally the rectory for the little church of St. Lawrence, and it predates the cathedral itself. It offers traditional English food such as toad-in-the-hole (sausage cooked in batter) and kedgeree (fish, rice, eggs, and spices). For Itchen trout or pork in cream and cider sauce, with a better-than-average glass of (pub) wine, look for the **Wykeham Arms** pub on the corner of Kingsgate and Canon streets. Among local people, **Nine, The Square** restaurant and wine bar (9 Great Minster Street) has a good reputation; reserve for the restaurant (Tel: 0962-86-40-04).

You may be lucky enough to find local venison—from New Forest deer—in some of the restaurants in and around Winchester; the spacious and well-run restaurant of the Forte Crest, considered Winchester's best hotel, is one such source. If you decide to stay at the ▶ **Forte Crest Hotel,** be sure to request a room with a cathedral view. When Forte Hotels put up the hotel in the 1960s, it was considered an eyesore, but now it seems to have settled into its city-center background. Another nice place to stay is the ▶ **Lainston House,** just west of town in the village of Sparsholt (a short taxi ride from Winchester). This luxurious retreat, popular with a well-heeled clientele, occupies a 17th-century country house surrounded by many acres of grounds. You do not have to be a guest of the hotel to enjoy its inexpensive and elegantly served table d'hôte lunch.

Around Winchester

Just 6 miles (10 km) to the east of Winchester on A 31, **Alresford,** sometimes called New Alresford, is a comparatively unspoiled market town of 18th-century coaching inns and wide, tree-lined streets.

From Winchester, Newbury and the A 4 lie about 25 miles (40 km) due north. Close to workaday Newbury, and westward along A 4 (which is dotted with old coaching inns) are the historic towns of **Hungerford** (famous for its antiques shops) and **Marlborough,** where another famous public school, Marlborough College (former poet laureate John Betjeman was one of its pupils), offers residential summer courses for outsiders. Try to visit Marlborough on a Saturday, when the open-air market is held under multicolored awnings. It has just enough of the atmosphere of bygone centuries to add spice to your trip. Good, old-fashioned pubs and tea shops are a bonus. In warm weather a stroll from the elegant, mainly red-brick High Street down to the cool and shady riverside is pleasant.

Known mainly to local people but highly recommended for a change of pace are the cool and dappled glades of **Savernake Forest**, a short drive to the east of Marlborough. Its Grand Avenue of beeches is four miles long.

AVEBURY STONE CIRCLE

A few miles to the west of Marlborough are partly intact prehistoric settlements that some feel surpass the magic of Stonehenge. The Avebury Stone Circle is impressive: Its massive boulders today surround a substantial village. The circumference of the earthwork encloses 30 acres, ten times the space occupied by Stonehenge. But even less is known about Avebury than Stonehenge. It has been called "all things to all men": Military experts have tended to label it a military camp; sociologists think it was a gigantic market and meeting place; astronomers assume it was devised to predict a cosmic event.

SILBURY HILL AND
WHITE HORSE HILL

Silbury Hill, within walking distance of the Avebury Stone Circle, is even more intriguing. This unlikely, entirely man-made conical mound, which stands by a Roman road, may have been a burial chamber. Silbury Hill is railed off, but White Horse Hill, near the village of Uffington—birthplace of Thomas Hughes, the author of *Tom Brown's School Days*—is not. It lies northeast of Swindon. A not-too-difficult climb from the village, it offers superb, panoramic views and a close-up look at what some people say is a Neolithic cutting of a horse, from which the hill gets its name. (Recent research indicates that it was cut between the first century B.C. and A.D. 871.) It is probably best seen from the village of Uffington.

GETTING AROUND

The best way to see rural England is by rental car, and this is especially true in the Cotswolds. In summer you can also rent a bicycle. There are cycle shops in the larger towns, such as Noah's Ark in Cirencester, Thames and Cotswold Bikes in Tetbury, and Jeffrey's Toy Shop in Moreton-in-Marsh.

This region of the south of England is relatively free of traffic congestion so driving here is reasonably pleasurable. However, beware of traffic problems in larger cities and towns. Cities such as Oxford, Bath, Salisbury, and Winchester are not too bad for drivers, though Salisbury's ring road can leave you looking for a way into the very center; watch for signs for "City Centre" or "Cathedral."

Oxford lies just off the M 40 motorway from London. Bath is just a few miles off M 4; Winchester is easily reached from London via M 3. A good way to see the Cotswolds by car is to leave A 40 near Burford and drive northwest through Burford to Broadway and then southwest on B 4632 through Winchcombe toward Cheltenham and Cirencester.

To get to Oxford and Swindon by train, travel from London's Paddington Station. Salisbury, Winchester, and Bath are all easily accessible from London—Bath from Paddington Station and Salisbury and Winchester from Waterloo.

Country buses fan out from the larger towns to the rural villages, but sometimes they run only on market days or on market days and Saturdays. Sunday travel by public transportation can be well-nigh impossible. Train service survives in the Cotswolds, even in the face of government equivocation, but really only on the idyllically pretty line from Oxford to Worcester and between Swindon and Gloucester.

Wells has no train station. The most efficient way to get there from London is by train to Bath and then by bus—number 173 from Bath bus depot, 200 yards from the train station. To avoid retracing their steps, visitors wanting to take in Bath, Wells, and Bristol are advised to travel to Bristol from Wells or vice versa. Those not returning via the well-used east-west corridor that links London and Bristol will find good train (and bus) connections between, for example, Bristol, the Midlands, and the North of England. National Express bus service direct from London to Wells takes approximately three hours.

Even the M 4 motorway and the short M 32 spur that runs south from it into the heart of Bristol are no match for the excellent train service from London—just 1¾ hours at best from Paddington. National Express buses from London's Victoria Station reach Bristol in 2½ hours.

ACCOMMODATIONS REFERENCE
Rates are projected 1994 prices for a double room with breakfast, unless otherwise stated. As prices are subject to change, always double-check before booking.

▶ **Alandale Hotel.** 4 Tyndalls Park Road, Clifton, **Bristol** BS8 1PG. Tel: (0272) 73-54-07. £46–£49.

▶ **Ancient Gate House Hotel.** Sadler Street, **Wells** BA5 2RR. Tel: (0749) 67-20-29. £65.

▶ **Apsley House Hotel.** 141 Newbridge Hill, **Bath** BA1 3PT. Tel: (0225) 33-69-66; Fax: (0225) 42-54-62; in U.S. and Canada, (800) 323-5463 or (708) 251-4110. £80–£110 (includes Continental breakfast).

▶ **Bath Spa Hotel.** Sydney Road, **Bath** BA2 6JF. Tel: (0225) 44-44-24-; Fax: (0225) 44-40-06; in U.S. and Canada, (800) 225-5843; in Australia, (008) 22-24-46. From £170 (breakfast not included).

▶ **Bay Tree Hotel.** Sheep Street, **Burford** OX18 4LW. Tel: (0993) 82-27-91; Fax: (0993) 82-30-08; in U.S., (800) 437-2687. £110–£205.

▶ **Bear Hotel.** Park Street, **Woodstock** OX7 1SZ. Tel: (0993) 81-15-11; Fax: (0993) 81-33-80; in U.S. and Canada, (800) 225-5843; in Australia, (008) 22-24-46. £115–£130 (breakfast not included).

▶ **Bekynton House.** 7 St. Thomas Street, **Wells** BA5 2UU. Tel: (0749) 67-22-22. From £40.

▶ **Bristol Hilton.** Redcliffe Way, **Bristol** BS1 6NJ. Tel: (0272) 26-00-41; Fax: (0272) 23-00-89; in U.S., (800) 445-8667; in Canada, (800) 268-9275; in Australia, (008) 22-22-55. £90–£115 (breakfast not included).

▶ **Bristol Holiday Inn Crown Plaza.** Victoria Street, BS1 6HY **Bristol.** Tel: (0272) 25-50-10; Fax: (0272) 25-50-40; in U.S. and Canada, (800) 465-4329; in Australia, (008) 22-10-66. £105.

▶ **Brunel's Tunnel House Hotel.** High Street, **Saltford** BS18 3BQ. Tel: (0225) 87-38-73; Fax: (0225) 87-48-75. £55.

▶ **Buckland Manor. Buckland,** near Broadway WR12 7LY. Tel: (0386) 85-26-26; Fax: (0386) 85-35-57. £145–£270.

▶ **Bull Hotel.** High Street, **Burford** OX8 4RH. Tel: (0993) 82-22-20. £47–£57.

▶ **Charingworth Manor. Charingworth,** near Chipping Campden GL55 6NS. Tel: (0386-78) 555; Fax: (0386-78) 353; in U.S. and Canada, (800) 525-4800; in Australia, (008) 802-582. £115–£220.

▶ **Cotswold House Hotel and Restaurant.** The Square, **Chipping Campden** GL55 6AN. Tel: (0386) 84-03-30; Fax: (0386) 84-03-10; in U.S., (818) 981-6177. £95–£148.

▶ **Crown Hotel.** Market Place, **Wells** BA5 2RP. Tel: (0749) 67-34-57; Fax: (0749) 67-97-83. £50–£60.

▶ **Dormy House Hotel.** Willersey Hill, **Broadway** WR12

7LF. Tel: (0386) 85-27-11; Fax: (0386) 85-86-36; in U.S. and Canada, (800) 323-5463 or (708) 251-4110. £104–£135.

▶ **Feathers Hotel**. Market Street, **Woodstock** OX20 1SX. Tel: (0993) 81-22-91; Fax: (0993) 81-31-58. £99–£135.

▶ **Forte Crest Hotel**. Paternoster Row, **Winchester** SO23 9LQ. Tel: (0962) 86-16-11; Fax: (0962) 84-15-03; in U.S. and Canada, (800) 225-5843; in Australia, (008) 22-24-46. £89 (breakfast not included).

▶ **Francis Hotel**. Queen Square, **Bath** BA1 2HH. Tel: (0225) 42-42-57; Fax: (0225) 31-97-15; in U.S. and Canada, (800) 225-5843; in Australia, (008) 22-24-46. £108 (breakfast not included).

▶ **George and Pilgrims Hotel**. High Street, **Glastonbury**, BA6 9DP. Tel: (0458) 83-11-46; Fax: (0458) 83-22-52. £60–£75.

▶ **Golden Valley Thistle Hotel**. Gloucester Road, **Cheltenham** GL51 0TS. Tel: (0242) 23-26-91; Fax: (0242) 22-18-46; in U.S., (800) 847-4358; in Canada, (800) 448-8355; in Australia, (008) 22-11-76. £95 (breakfast not included).

▶ **Grand Hotel**. Broad Street, **Bristol** B51 2EL. Tel: (0272) 29-16-45; Fax: (0272) 22-76-19. £80–£95 (breakfast not included).

▶ **Grapevine Hotel** (Best Western). Sheep Street, **Stow-on-the-Wold** GL54 1AU. Tel: (0451) 83-03-44; Fax: (0451) 83-22-78; in U.S. and Canada, (800) 528-1234; in Australia, (008) 222-166. £98–£138.

▶ **Hatton Court Hotel**. Upton St. Leonard's, **Gloucester** GL4 8DE. Tel: (0452) 61-74-12; Fax: (0452) 61-29-45; in U.S. and Canada, (800) 437-2687. £90–£125.

▶ **Hilton National**. Walcot Street, **Bath** BA1 5BJ. Tel: (0225) 46-34-11; Fax: (0225) 46-43-93; in U.S., (800) 445-8667 in Canada, (800) 268-9275; in Australia, (008) 22-22-55. £105 (breakfast not included).

▶ **King's Head Hotel**. Market Place, **Cirencester** GL7 2NR. Tel: (0285) 65-33-22; Fax: (0285) 65-51-03; in U.S. and Canada, (800) 624-3524; in Australia, (008) 132-400. £67.50–£75.

▶ **Lainston House Hotel**. Sparsholt, Winchester SO21 2LT. Tel: (0962) 86-35-88; Fax: (0962) 776-72. £120–£240 (breakfast not included).

▶ **Langford House Cottages**. Little Faringdon, **Lechlade** GL7 3QN. Tel: (0367) 25-22-10; Fax: (0367) 25-25-77. £157–£472 per week (self-catering).

▶ **Lords of the Manor**. Upper Slaughter, near Bourton-on-the-Water GL54 2JD. Tel: (0451) 82-02-43; Fax: (0451)

206-96; in U.S. and Canada, (800) 525-4800; in Australia, (008) 802-582. £120–£195.

▶ **Lower Slaughter Manor. Lower Slaughter**, near Bourton-on-the-Water GL54 2HP. Tel: (0451) 82-04-56; Fax: (0451) 82-21-50. £160–£215.

▶ **Lygon Arms**. High Street, **Broadway** WR12 7DU. Tel: (0386) 85-22-55; Fax: (0386) 85-86-11; in U.S. and Canada, (800) 223-6800; in Australia, (008) 22-20-33. £153–£180 (includes Continental breakfast).

▶ **Noel Arms**. High Street, **Chipping Campden** GL55 6AT. Tel: (0386) 84-03-17; Fax: (0386) 84-11-36; in U.S. and Canada, (800) 528-1234; in Australia, (008) 22-21-66. £78.

▶ **No. 3 Hotel and Restaurant**. 3 Magdalene Street, **Glastonbury** BA6 9EW. Tel: (0458) 83-21-29. £75.

▶ **Owlpen Manor. Owlpen**, near Dursley GL11 5BZ. Tel: (0453) 86-02-61; Fax: (0453) 86-08-19. £42–£176 (self-catering cottages).

▶ **Paradise House**. 86-88 Holloway, **Bath** BA2 4PX. Tel: (0225) 31-77-23; Fax: (0225) 48-20-05. £50–£68.

▶ **Plough at Clanfield**. Bourton Road, **Clanfield** OX8 2RB. Tel: (0367) 812-22; Fax: (0367) 815-96; in U.S. and Canada, (800) 437-2687. £80–£95.

▶ **Priory Hotel**. Weston Road, **Bath** BA1 2XT. Tel: (0225) 33-19-22; Fax: (0225) 44-82-76; in U.S., (800) 322-2403. £158–£205.

▶ **Queen's Hotel**. The Promenade, **Cheltenham** GL50 1NN. Tel: (0242) 51-47-24; Fax: (0242) 22-41-45; in U.S. and Canada, (800) 225-5843; in Australia, (008) 22-24-46. £119.

▶ **Red Lion** (Best Western). Milford Street, **Salisbury** SP1 2AN. Tel: (0722) 32-33-34; Fax: (0722) 32-57-56; in U.S. and Canada, (800) 528-1234; in Australia, (008) 22-21-66. £80–£110.

▶ **Red Lion**. Market Place, **Wells** BA5 2RG. Tel: (0749) 67-26-16; Fax: (0749) 67-96-70. £55.

▶ **Rose & Crown Hotel**. Harnham Road, **Salisbury** SP2 8JQ. Tel: (0722) 32-79-08; Fax: (0722) 33-98-16. £100–£115.

▶ **Royal Crescent**. 16 Royal Crescent, **Bath** BA1 2LS. Tel: (0225) 31-90-90; Fax: (0225) 33-94-01; in U.S. and Canada, (800) 457-4000. £168–£205 (includes Continental breakfast).

▶ **Star Hotel**. High Street, **Wells** BA5 2SP. Tel: (0749) 67-05-00; Fax: (0749) 67-26-54. £48–£60.

▶ **Studley Priory Hotel. Horton-cum-Studley** OX33

1AZ. Tel: (0865) 35-12-03; Fax: (0865) 35-16-13; in U.S. and Canada, (800) 437-2687. £98–£150.

▶ **Sudeley Castle Cottages.** Sudeley Castle, **Winchcombe** GL54 5JD. Tel: (0242) 60-41-03 or 60-23-08; Fax: (0242) 60-29-59. £170–£577 per week (self-catering).

▶ **Swallow Royal Hotel.** College Green, **Bristol** BS1 5TA. Tel: (0272) 25-51-00; Fax: (0272) 25-15-15; in U.S., (800) 444-1545. £124.

▶ **Swan Hotel.** Sadler Street, **Wells** BA5 2RX. Tel: (0749) 67-88-77; Fax: (0749) 67-76-47; in U.S. and Canada, (800) 528-1234; in Australia, (02) 212-6444. £83–£90.

▶ **Tall Trees. Temple Guiting** GL54 5RP. Tel: (0451) 85-04-67. £33.

▶ **Unicorn Hotel.** Prince Street, **Bristol** BS1 4QF. Tel: (0272) 23-03-33; Fax: (0272) 23-03-00; in U.S. and Canada, (800) 223-5560 or (914) 631-2005. £87.

▶ **Unicorn Hotel.** Sheep Street, **Stow-on-the-Wold** GL54 1HQ. Tel: (0451) 83-02-57; Fax: (0451) 83-10-90; in U.S. and Canada, (800) 225-5843; in Australia, (008) 22-24-46. £87 (breakfast not included).

▶ **White Hart Hotel.** 1 St. John Street, **Salisbury** SP1 2SD. Tel: (0722) 32-74-76; Fax: (0722) 41-27-61; in U.S. and Canada, (800) 225-5843; in Australia, (008) 22-24-46. £90–£105 (breakfast not included).

▶ **White Hart Hotel.** Sadler Street, **Wells** BA5 2RR. Tel: (0749) 67-20-56; Fax: (0749) 67-20-56. £50–£60.

▶ **Woolley Grange Hotel.** Woolley Green, **Bradford-on-Avon** BA15 1TX. Tel: (0225) 86-47-05; Fax: (0225) 86-40-59; in U.S., (800) 848-7721. £95–£168.

▶ **Wyck Hill House.** Burford Road, **Stow-on-the-Wold** GL54 1HY. Tel: (0451) 83-19-36; Fax: (0451) 83-22-43. £95–£170.

DEVON AND CORNWALL

AND THE
ISLES OF SCILLY

By Ken Thompson

Ken Thompson is a newspaper and broadcast journalist who has lived in Cornwall for more than 30 years. His vacation guide, Discover Cornwall, *has won national acclaim. For 12 years, until 1987, he was Cornwall's chief tourism officer.*

Devon and Cornwall have a certain magical quality. Perhaps it is the magnificence of 650 miles of coastal scenery, which is unsurpassed in either England or Wales. Or maybe it is the unhurried pace of life in the relaxing and mild climate of this far southwesterly corner of Britain. Perhaps it is the delight in discovering why the Isles of Scilly will forever be known as the Fortunate Isles. Whatever it is, Devon and Cornwall offer an attractive combination of scenic beauty and historical and cultural interest.

MAJOR INTEREST

Seaside villages, art colonies
Mild climate
Celtic culture

Devon
Exmoor National Park

Clovelly
Exeter Cathedral
Dartmoor National Park
Buckfast Abbey
Dart Valley Steam Railway
English Riviera resort area
Buckland Abbey
Plymouth Hoe
The Barbican and the Mayflower Steps

Cornwall
Tintagel Castle
Trerice Manor
Land's End
St. Michael's Mount
Truro Cathedral
Polperro

Isles of Scilly
Uncrowded beaches
Sea life
Tresco Abbey and Gardens

DEVON

Whether you enter the county from Somerset to its north or from Dorset to its east, it scarcely requires a frontier post to proclaim that you have reached the geographical gateway to southwest England: Devon. Gone are the familiar English villages with their houses and shops grouped around a proud, Gothic country church. Instead, white-washed, cob-walled farm cottages with reed-thatched roofs punctuate the landscape alongside fields of rich red soil, lush green hillsides, and combes (or coombs), the short valleys climbing inland from Devon's famed seacoast.

This ancient Celtic kingdom, once called Dumnonia, boasts 2,000 square miles of some of the finest and most varied scenery in Britain. At its heart is the hauntingly beautiful Dartmoor National Park, the last largely unspoiled wilderness left in England. Here you will find granite tors and sweeping moorland, sparkling streams and wooded valleys, ancient stone circles and clapper (wooden) and packhorse (stone) bridges, historic towns and charming villages around which wild ponies graze placidly.

Devon has two fine cities: Exeter, with its 14th-century cathedral and historic Guildhall, and Plymouth, the great naval port from which Sir Francis Drake sailed to defeat the Spanish Armada 400 years ago and that will forever be associated with the Pilgrims. Fleeing religious persecution, they sailed from here in 1620 and subsequently founded the township of Dorchester in Massachusetts.

Devon, like Cornwall, has two contrasting coastlines. Overlooking the Atlantic to the north are the rugged cliffs and great expanses of sand called the "golden coast." In the south are towering red sandstone cliffs that slip down into river estuaries and palm-fringed bays, a surprising touch of the tropics.

When driving down to Devon from points north, you can leave the M 5 at Bridgwater and take A 39 toward the coast road and Minehead; this route gives you the option of exploring Exmoor, a park that Devon shares with neighboring Somerset. Or you can exit the M 5 at junction 27 (Tiverton) to join the newly opened North Devon Link Road, which closely follows the line of the former A 361.

DUNSTER

It would be uncharitable not to mention an architectural gem you will encounter while crossing Exmoor en route for North Devon: the historic market town of Dunster, although geographically speaking it belongs to neighboring North Somerset. Dunster Castle, built on the site of a Saxon fortress, dominates the High Street. The town also features an octagonal 17th-century Tudor yarn market, once used for the sale of locally woven cloth. The High Street is perhaps the best surviving example of life in medieval England and should not be missed. While in Dunster, you might visit the **Tea Shoppe** at the lower end of the High Street to sample the delicious home cooking of Pam and Norman Goldsack. The Tea Shoppe was voted one of the Best Country Restaurants in Britain in 1992, and the Goldsacks have twice received the Tea Council's Award for Excellence. Lunch and cream teas are served from March through the end of October. Dunster lies just south of the A 39 road inland from the coastal resort of Minehead.

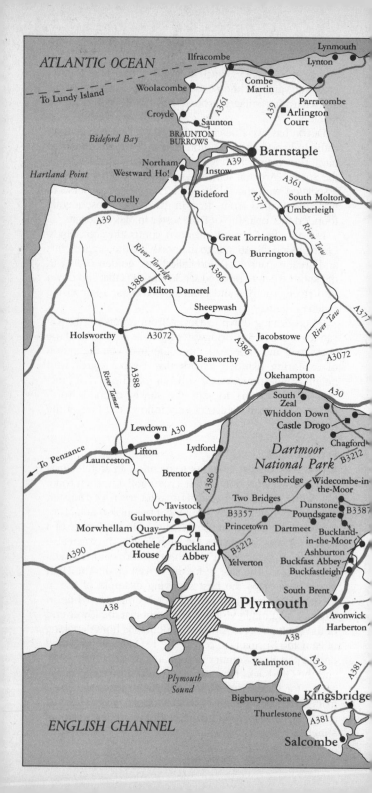

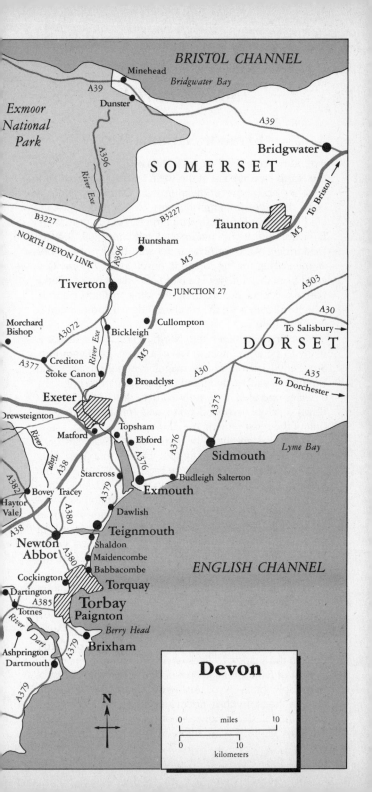

NORTH DEVON

Exmoor National Park

Extending from the Quantock Hills on the eastern side to the North Devon coast at the west, Exmoor National Park is softer and more undulating than Dartmoor and has been described by English poets as "The Little Switzerland of England" for its springtime carpets of primroses. It is not difficult to understand why, in 1869, Richard Doddridge Blackmore chose the wild beauty of Exmoor as the setting for his romantic novel *Lorna Doone*. Rescued from the clutches of a band of outlaws by John Ridd, Lorna was shot during their wedding in **Oare Church**, which still stands on the northern edge of Exmoor and is worth visiting.

Your first encounter with North Devon after Exmoor is likely to be at the twin towns of **Lynton** and **Lynmouth**. Since 1890, Lynton, with its magnificent hilltop views, and Lynmouth, with its delightful harbor, have been linked by a water-operated cliff railway that descends 500 feet down a steeply wooded valley and remains to this day one of the most remarkable railways in the world.

While you are here be sure to visit Watersmeet, a much-photographed beauty spot that lies in a deep, tree-lined gorge at the point where Hoar Oak Water joins the East Lyn River on its way down to the sea at Lynmouth—hence the name Watersmeet. From Lynmouth take the A 39 Watersmeet road toward Barnstaple. After 1½ miles (2½ km) you can drive to within a few hundred yards of Watersmeet. This is superb walking country, best visited after a spell of rain, when the rivers and waterfalls are full and running fast.

Before leaving Exmoor, visit the **Brass Rubbing Center** in Lynton on Queen Street. You might then head for the **Exmoor Bird Gardens** at Parracombe on your way west to Combe Martin and Ilfracombe. Incidentally, there's an interesting inn at Combe Martin— the **Pack o' Cards**, built in the shape of a deck of playing cards.

West of Exmoor, in steep wooded country northeast of Barnstaple on A 39, is **Arlington Court**, an early-19th-century house with a fascinating assemblage of objets d'art, model ships, pewter, costumes, and furniture of the past century. The stables contain a collection of horse-drawn vehicles, and Shetland ponies and Jacob sheep graze in the surrounding parkland. The late Sir Francis Chichester, that remarkable seafarer who single-handedly circumnavigated the globe, once lived here; now both house and gardens are in the care of the National Trust.

STAYING NEAR EXMOOR

There's a great deal to see in this part of Devon, quite enough to justify an overnight stop, and a good place to stay is the ▶ **Rising Sun**, a 14th-century thatched smugglers' inn alongside Lynmouth's tiny harbor and the East Lyn salmon river. Full of character, it is only a few miles from the Brendon (Doone) valley, which features in *Lorna Doone;* Blackmore wrote part of the book during his stay at the Rising Sun. One feature of the hotel is the cottage in which the poet Percy Bysshe Shelley and his bride, Harriet, spent their honeymoon in 1812. The cottage has lost none of its romance. Guests sleep in the same four-poster bed once occupied by the poet and his young bride.

An alternative base from which to explore this area is the ▶ **Woodlands Hotel**, a country guest house at Lynbridge in Lynton. It stands in an acre of grounds running down to the West Lyn River and has private fishing rights that guests are encouraged to use.

The North Devon Coast

The town of **Ilfracombe**, North Devon's premiere resort, grew up around its old harbor; it nestles in a valley surrounded by spectacular cliffs and rolling countryside. From a small fishing village, Ilfracombe emerged to be an extremely select resort in the Victorian era, when the advent of the railways first made seaside vacations practical.

On the seafront is the Victoria Pavilion theater, focal point of Ilfracombe's Victorian Week in June, when the resort re-creates the atmosphere of the 1880s and hundreds of the townsfolk don period costumes. A lasting tribute to Victorian ingenuity are the famous tunnels excavated through the cliffs to reach safe and sheltered sea-bathing areas among the tidal rock pools. Make a point of visiting **Chambercombe Manor**, a 16th-century house 2 miles (3 km) southeast of Ilfracombe. Built in 1500, it contains an interesting collection of Tudor and Jacobean furniture and Cromwellian armor.

The North Devon coast is incomparable where Exmoor meets the sea, and nowhere is this more apparent than at Woolacombe, Croyde, and Westward Ho!, three resorts with fine beaches much sought after by surfers. **Croyde** is a particularly attractive village of thatched and color-washed cottages at the foot of steep, grassy downs, just north of Saunton Sands and Braunton Burrows.

STAYING AND DINING ON THE NORTH DEVON COAST

You will have no difficulty finding a hotel in this area. There is a wide choice, ranging from the sumptuous ▶ **Saunton Sands**, overlooking five miles of unspoilt beaches and a championship golf course, to the Old World ▶ **Kittiwell House**, at the eastern end of Croyde, with its Elizabethan restaurant. Kittiwell may offer 20th-century comforts, but you can still ask for a room with a four-poster bed. Just across the estuary of the Taw and Torridge rivers and overlooking the superb waterfront stands the ▶ **Commodore**, a three-star hotel popular with the yachting set and midway between the towns of Barnstaple and Bideford. The Commodore provides an exceedingly comfortable base from which to explore North Devon.

Tarka Country

Inland from here you will enter a different world: "Tarka Country," the countryside of the two rivers, the Taw and the Torridge, which Henry Williamson immortalized in his nature classic, *Tarka the Otter*.

Close to the mouth of the River Taw stands the ancient market town of **Barnstaple**, reputedly the oldest borough in England, having been granted its royal charter by Queen Elizabeth I in the 1580s. Barnstaple has been a major seaport and commercial center since the Middle Ages; five ships sailed from here in 1588 to help Sir Francis Drake defeat Spain's Armada.

Be sure to visit the Pannier (basket) Market on Tuesdays, Fridays, and Saturdays (the market dates to 1714); St. Peter's Church, with its twisted spire; and the Old Quay. You should also cross the Long Bridge, with its 16 arches spanning the River Taw. The bridge is one of the oldest structures in the town and easily the most impressive.

One of the most exciting ideas of recent times here is the development of the **Tarka Trail**, a long-distance footpath that follows in the footprints of Tarka the Otter, as described in Williamson's book. The route also incorporates one of the loveliest train journeys in England—the Tarka Line—which runs from Barnstaple along the banks of the River Taw and on to Exeter.

If you have a day or two to spare, you can explore the Taw, Torridge, and other Tarka Country landmarks with Trevor Beer, a writer and wildlife artist (Tel: 0271-735-20).

The ancient port and market town of **Bideford** is rich in history. Two fine ships were sent from here to help Sir Francis Drake defeat the Spanish Armada, and the J. Hinks and Son boatyard on the Torridge still builds replicas of these historic vessels. The most notable was a copy of Drake's legendary ship the *Golden Hind,* which crossed the Atlantic to America.

The **Torridge** is a spate river; the chance of catching a salmon here depends on the height and color of the water. The river is also known for the large sea trout that travel it as early as April and May; the main run, however, begins in June, and July and August are the best months for the angler. If you want to fish the river, stay at the ▶ **Half Moon Inn** at Sheepwash near Beaworthy, where Water Authority licenses are issued and they know all about the sport.

Before reaching Hartland Point, and Devon's northern boundary with Cornwall, you should stop at **Clovelly**, a colorful fishing village clinging dramatically to a steep hillside over the sea, with quaint cobbled streets that can be negotiated only on foot. Animal lovers will be glad to know that a Land Rover has replaced the donkeys that were formerly the only other means of transportation back up the hill.

STAYING AND DINING
IN TARKA COUNTRY

There is an excellent choice of hotels in this area, including the highly rated ▶ **Park Hotel** overlooking the river in Taw Vale (formerly the North Devon Motel, it was totally refurbished in 1990), and the ▶ **Royal & Fortescue**, a charming old coaching inn that was patronized by Edward VII, prince of Wales, and has kept its character and charm. In neighboring Bideford, the ▶ **Royal Hotel** successfully combines 400 years of history with every modern comfort. The Kingsley Room retains the plaster ceiling designs originally imported from Venice.

The ▶ **Woodford Bridge Hotel** at Milton Damerel, on

A 388 between Bideford and Holsworthy, is a superb thatched and whitewashed 15th-century coaching inn (its roof is the longest thatched one in England) set in 20 acres of attractive gardens. The hotel has an excellent bistro.

South from the Coast

Heading south down A 386 from Bideford toward Oke- hampton you will encounter **Great Torrington**, the home of Dartington Glass, where you can watch skilled workers dressed in period costumes demonstrating the art of glassblowing.

In Torrington there's an interesting place to eat, **Rebecca's** in Potacre Street. Unfortunately, it is closed on Sundays, but on the other six days of the week they will cook to order any English dish you choose from the menu. Rebecca's comes highly recommended—even by the Queen's youngest son, Prince Edward.

Before heading south toward Exeter, it would be worth making a slight detour to visit **Quince Honey Farm** on A 361 at South Molton, a market town known for its numerous antiques shops. The farm is hailed as the world's most important honeybee exhibition; in the 25,000-square-foot apiary you can actually open the hives at the press of a button and see the colonies at work.

As you continue southeast along the A 373 you encounter the B 3137 just before you reach the market town of Tiverton. Turn south here, following the line of the River Exe for 3 miles (5 km), to the A 396 toward Bickleigh. Here you'll find the **Devonshire Craft Center** with its superb working watermill, craftsmen's workshops, and heritage farm. They also offer horse-drawn barge trips on the Grand Western Canal.

STAYING AND DINING
EN ROUTE TO EXETER

Just off the newly constructed North Devon Link Road at South Molton, below the southern slopes of Exmoor, stands enchanting ▶ **Whitechapel Manor**, a country-house hotel par excellence. Within this listed building (which means it is covered by a preservation order), the entrance hall contains a perfect Jacobean carved-oak screen, and the house is adorned throughout with William and Mary plasterwork and paneling, complete with painted overmantels. The international cuisine at White-chapel has won wide recognition.

For mild eccentricity ▶ **Huntsham Court Country House**, an impressive Gothic mansion near Tiverton, is hard to beat. The hotel is as relaxed as the land around it and prides itself on a country house-party atmosphere. It is stuck in a Victorian time warp, with its 15 guest bedrooms all named after composers, so you may find yourself keeping company with Mr. Beethoven or Mr. Brahms. There's also a great place to eat in Tiverton—**Henderson's** on Newport Street, highly regarded for its organic cuisine.

This area abounds in country-house–type hotels. If you are looking for an overnight stop here, a slight detour from Tiverton toward Crediton along unclassified lanes (drive west 13 miles/21 km on the A 373 before turning south toward Morchard Bishop) will bring you face to face with history. After travelling through tiny villages with unlikely sounding names like Puddington and Black Dog, you will find picturesque ▶ **Wigham**, a 16th-century thatched longhouse about a mile and a half outside Morchard Bishop. Surrounded by woods and farmland, Wigham has five en-suite rooms, two beamed sitting rooms with huge fires, and a snooker lounge. Dinner is available if requested.

EXETER

Exeter was originally settled by the Celtic people of Devon and Cornwall, the Dumnonii. The city, standing at what was then the head of the navigable waters of the River Exe, was later used as an administrative center by the Romans.

In the third century A.D. Exeter was fortified by a massive stone wall, and parts of this defense system can still be traced in town at Rougemont Gardens, Southernhay, and below South Street. An early Norman tower can also be seen at Rougemont, as can the remains of a Norman keep.

For over 600 years **Exeter Cathedral** has been standing much as it appears today, but its history goes back more than 1,000 years. It had three predecessors on the same site: a Saxon church rebuilt in 1050 to become the first cathedral, a Norman cathedral with north and south towers built to the east of it in 1160, and a larger cathedral incorporating the best of its predecessors into a Gothic-style structure in 1270. The nave was completed in 1370 and the West Front, with its wealth of sculpture and 300-foot-long stone vaulting—considered among the finest of its kind in Europe—a few years later. The Chapter House, built originally in 1224 but reconstructed in the early 15th century, should also be visited if only to view sculptures of the stages of the Creation as told in both the Old and New Testaments. Installed in 1974, they are the work of local sculptor Kenneth Carter.

Exeter has a great deal from its historic past to show the visitor. On the busy High Street is the 14th-century Guildhall, from which the city has been governed since Saxon times. It is one of the oldest municipal buildings in the country and is still in use. Not far from it is the entrance to the Underground Passages, Exeter's medieval aqueducts, which can be toured between 2:00 and 5:00 P.M. Tuesday through Saturday.

St. Nicholas Priory, a medieval building containing period furniture, is in fact the restored guest wing of a Benedictine priory founded in 1070 by monks from Battle Abbey in Sussex, which itself was founded by William the Conqueror. The surviving features include a Norman undercroft (underground chamber), a 15th-century guest hall, and the kitchen.

The **Royal Albert Memorial Museum**, named in 1868 in memory of Queen Victoria's consort, houses a collection of paintings by well-known British artists, including many who lived and worked in Devon. Also on display is Exeter silver, pottery, porcelain, and glass. The important **Rougemont House Museum of Costume and Lace** on Castle Street displays fashions through the ages in a series of period rooms in an attractive Regency house overlooking the castle and Rougemont Gardens.

Since 1981 the Exeter Ship Canal and Quay Development Trust has been revitalizing the quay, which is becoming an important center for leisure activities. High on the city's list of tourist attractions is the **Exeter Maritime Museum**, down by the River Exe. There are boats from Arabia and China, Africa, the Americas, Britain, and the Mediterranean on display; nowhere else in the world can you inspect such an amazing collection of canoes, punts, coracles, rowboats, and steamers—afloat, indoors, and ashore.

As you might expect, the quay has always played an important role in the lives of Exeter's citizens, but never more so than in the days of the prosperous wool trade. Cloth exported from here brought wealth to Exeter during Tudor and Stuart times. Today, in the Quay House Interpretation Center, you can see displays relating to the use of the river and riverside areas throughout history.

STAYING AND DINING IN EXETER

Exeter has a wide choice of accommodations. Foremost among them, overlooking the cathedral, is the ▶ **Royal Clarence**, which was the first inn in Britain to receive the title "hotel." This elegant Georgian building, richly furnished in Tudor, Georgian, and Victorian styles that reflect its colorful history and sense of tradition, once played host to Admiral Lord Nelson and Czar Nicholas I. The 56 bedrooms have recently undergone restoration.

Gourmet weekends are a specialty of the ▶ **St. Olaves Court Hotel**, a Georgian house in its own walled garden in Mary Arches Street, also overlooking the cathedral. The hotel, which keeps collecting awards for its exciting cuisine, offers special packages for two that include candlelit four-course dinners and full English breakfasts. St. Olaves has undergone a major transformation since Raymond Wyatt and his wife, Ute, bought it in 1991 and recruited as executive chef David Mutter, a Scotsman whose meals are as delightful to the eye as they are to the taste buds.

A mile from the city center, out along the Topsham road and set in its own attractive landscaped gardens, stands ▶ **Buckerell Lodge Hotel and Restaurant**, once the home of a Regency squire. Convenient to the M 5 motorway, the hotel provides an ideal base from which to explore Dartmoor and Exmoor. It enjoys an excellent reputation for traditional food and service, and is popular with the business community.

Restaurants abound, but for impressive ambience we suggest you try the **Tudor House**, in Tudor Street, which dates from the 15th century. One of the oldest buildings in Exeter, it has elegantly beamed parlors and bars, and has received the coveted European Heritage Award. You'll find it at the bottom of Fore Street, just minutes away from the House That Moved (a house that was lifted intact and wheeled to a new location during recent city-center development). Also highly recommended are the **Cloisters** restaurant in Broadgate, just off Cathedral Yard and located in yet another historic building; **Mad Meg's**, a medieval-style restaurant in Fore Street; and the **Ship Inn** in Martins Lane, which specializes in pub food and bar meals.

Around Exeter

Killerton, an 18th-century house at Broadclyst on the road out of Exeter to Cullompton, is the administrative headquarters of the National Trust in Devon. Dating back to the Civil War, Killerton was substantially rebuilt in 1778. It houses the **Paulise de Bush Costume Collection**, which traces 200 years of fashion in a series of period rooms and stands in 15 acres of gardens containing many rare trees and shrubs.

Staying near Exeter

A convenient base from which to visit Exeter is the ▶ **Devon Motel** at Matford (close to junction 31 of the M 5 motorway), which provides a unique blend of Georgian elegance and modern-motel amenities for the travelling motorist. The smaller ▶ **Ebford House Hotel**, near Topsham and also convenient to the city, is a lovely Georgian country-house hotel that has managed to retain a homey atmosphere. To reach it, leave M 5 at junction 30 and follow the signs for Exmouth (A 376).

WEST OF EXETER

Four miles (6½ km) west on the Exeter to Okehampton road (A 30, signposted to Crockernwell) you will find **Castle Drogo**, sitting 900 feet above a wooded gorge of the River Teign and commanding views across the eastern slopes of Dartmoor National Park. This granite-faced masterpiece, completed in 1930, is the work of architect Sir Edwin Lutyens. Despite its medieval appearance, it has such modern amenities as its own hydroelectric system. Castle Drogo is a family home cared for by the National Trust but is open to visitors daily except Fridays, from April to November. The gardens are also worth seeing.

Head out of Exeter along A 30 toward West Devon and the historic market towns of Okehampton and, via the southern leg of the A 386, Tavistock (see below). About halfway between the two towns you will come to **Lydford**, with its famous gorge. The gorge is a deep ravine scooped out by the River Lyd, which plunges into a succession of whirlpools, among them the awesome Devil's Cauldron, and culminates in the 90-foot-high White Lady waterfall.

STAYING AND DINING
WEST OF EXETER

It follows that in an area of such outstanding beauty there must be a range of hotels to match. The two-star ▶ **Lydford House Hotel**, near the gorge, has four-poster beds and its own riding stables to boot. In the delightful village of South Zeal (on the south side of A 30 near South Tawton and 17 miles/27 km from Exeter) you will come across a 12th-century inn, the ▶ **Oxenham Arms**, and a thatched cottage, ▶ **Poltimore**. Both accommodations serve good food and are ideal stopping points if you are overnighting on your way to Dartmoor. Westward along the A 30, and before you descend to Dartmoor, is Lewdown, with its roadhouse and gas station. Just to the south of the village is ▶ **Lewtrenchard Manor**, a stone manor house built in 1600 and today a luxurious hotel combining all the attributes of an English country house with the highest standards of comfort and cuisine. Most noteworthy of its former owners is the Rev. Sabine Baring Gould, a cleric best remembered for writing the hymns "Onward Christian Soldiers" and "Now the Day Is Over." He left his mark on Lewtrenchard with ornate ceilings, paneling, and carvings.

A hotel of exceptional character and charm is the ▶ **Arundell Arms** at Lifton, on A 30 from Okehampton toward Launceston. It is England's best-known fishing hotel and controls 20 miles of salmon, trout, and sea-trout fishing on the River Tamar and four tributaries. Here a leading young English chef, Philip Burgess, prepares traditional English and French dishes with an imaginative touch.

Dartmoor National Park

Dartmoor National Park, which occupies some 365 square miles, is an area of exquisite beauty, peace, and tranquillity where Bronze Age people made their home thousands of years ago. It consists chiefly of two high plateaus that rise in places to 2,000 feet. There are also areas of moorland, enclosed farmland and wooded valleys, sparkling streams and rivers, and great granite tors, weathered into curious shapes by exposure to the elements.

Whether you join one of the many organized walks or venture out onto Dartmoor alone, make sure you are well equipped to withstand sudden changes in the weather. The villages on and around the moor are a delight; watch for the wild ponies that are allowed to wander at will across the open land and through village streets.

Take time to visit **Tavistock**, the market town on the western edge of Dartmoor where Sir Francis Drake was born. Largely Victorian in character, it reflects the copper bonanza of the late 19th century. Or go over to **Okehampton**, widely regarded as the "capital" of the Northern Moor, and see what remains of its Norman castle, built as a stronghold from which to subdue the rebellion that broke out in the southwest following the Battle of Hastings.

Dartmoor's loveliest villages include **Widecombe-in-the-Moor**, the much-photographed cottages that cluster around **Buckland-in-the-Moor**, and **Postbridge**, where you can see the best example of a clapper bridge on Dartmoor. Down from the heights, on the western and northern fringes of the national park, respectively, are the legendary hilltop church at **Brentor** and the cob-and-thatched village of **Drewsteignton** in the Teign valley. (The roofs of the cottages are thatched with reeds and straw, and their dry-stone cob walls are made with a composition of clay, stone, and straw.) And be sure to sample a Devonshire cream tea at the **Badgers Holt Café** in Dartmeet.

When **Dartmoor Prison** was built at Princetown in 1803 to accommodate the growing number of French prisoners taken during the Napoleonic Wars, it's doubtful anyone guessed that nearly 200 years later it would become an object of curiosity for tourists, who often pose for photographs in front of its forbidding gates.

On the southeastern edge of Dartmoor stands **Buckfast Abbey**, a Benedictine monastery in the valley of the River Dart, off the Exeter–Plymouth road (A 38). Here monks have restored a medieval monastery to its former splendor. The abbey restoration, completed in 1938, took four monks 31 years to accomplish. It contains many art treasures, including stained-glass windows made in the abbey workshops, and is open to visitors.

DINING AND STAYING ON DARTMOOR

There are many places to dine and to stay on Dartmoor, and the challenge is to select the most interesting. Take, as an example, the **Horn of Plenty** restaurant at Tamar View House, Gulworthy, near Tavistock, where the international cuisine of Sonia Stevenson is exceptional. Be-

sides the classical menu, there are regional menus that
change monthly, and in 22 years the proprietors of the
Horn of Plenty have concocted 130 menus without ever
once repeating themselves.

The ▶ **Cherrybrook Hotel** at Two Bridges in the center of the Dartmoor National Park is an ideal touring base.
To reach this small hotel, exit the Exeter–Plymouth road
(A 38) at Ashburton. You will find it cozy and moderately
priced, with a low-beamed lounge/bar and good home
cooking. You can arrange for dinner and breakfast or for
lodging. Another hotel of distinction occupying a singu-
larly romantic and secluded position between Ashburton
and Two Bridges on the southern fringe of Dartmoor is
the ▶ **Holne Chase Hotel and Restaurant**, a former Georgian hunting lodge set on 26 acres of parkland and overlooking the valley of the River Dart, where the hotel has
about a mile of salmon fishing. The proprietors, Kenneth
and Mary Bromage, really do care about food, drink, and
comfort.

TOWARD THE ENGLISH RIVIERA

When you leave the hilly uplands of Dartmoor, you have a
choice. You can either set off to the southeast to Torquay,
Devon's premier south coast resort and self-styled "Queen
of the English Riviera," or set course for Plymouth, to the
southwest of the moor.

Torbay—the coastal metropolis created by Torquay,
Paignton, and the fishing port of Brixham—is a good
choice, and for a change it is possible to leave the strain
of driving and join the **Dart Valley Steam Railway** at
Buckfastleigh southeast of Buckfast Abbey. The seven-
mile journey follows the River Dart to **Totnes** (just west of
Torbay), a royal borough in Saxon times that still contains
many historic and interesting features.

In Totnes's narrow streets and alleyways you can see a
thousand years of history. Especially worth visiting are the
16th- and 17th-century houses on High Street and Fore
Street, now largely rebuilt following a devastating fire in
1990. From early May to the end of September, try to be in
town on a Tuesday morning, when the townsfolk dress in
period costume and hold an Elizabethan market day. Also
visit the 14th-century castle and its circular keep. At Totnes
station you can leave behind steam-train nostalgia by join-

ing the less romantic British Rail diesel railcar for the short ride into Torbay, or take the local bus, which operates frequently between Totnes, Paignton, and Torquay.

Before you visit palm-fringed Torbay, you may want to spend a day farther north along the coast toward Exeter at **Exmouth**, a traditional resort with a two-mile-long esplanade. Unspoiled **Budleigh Salterton** nearby is the site of Bicton Park's 50 acres of enchanting gardens— Italian, American, Oriental, and Hermitage styles—and a host of additional attractions, including falconry displays. Farther east of Exmouth, elegant **Sidmouth**, with its Georgian and Regency architecture, annually plays host to the International Folk Dance Festival, which attracts colorfully costumed performers from all over the world. It's usually held in August.

Reference is made in the section on West Cornwall to the fact that the famous potter Bernard Leach established his studio at St. Ives, which can be seen to this day. It is worth noting on your travels through Devon that his son, **David Leach**, is now practicing the skills that Japanese potters taught his father. David Leach's studio is in Bovey Tracey at the extreme eastern slopes of Dartmoor.

STAYING AND DINING
EN ROUTE TO THE ENGLISH RIVIERA

There's a wide selection of accommodations in this part of South Devon, but little to surpass the four-star ▶ **Victoria Hotel**, which welcomed its first guests during the last year of Queen Victoria's reign. The hotel is adjacent to the property that was once Queen Victoria's official Sidmouth residence. If you are looking for a simple bed-and-breakfast establishment, try ▶ **Willmead Farm** in Bovey Tracey, near Newton Abbot (north of Torbay), a thatched house built around 1450. If you prefer the coast to the country on your visit to the Torbay area, comfortable accommodation can be found at the ▶ **Thomas Luny House** on Teign Street at Teignmouth. Built in the late 18th century by the well-known marine artist Thomas Luny, this Georgian house stands in an attractive courtyard not far from the fish quay. You can be assured of a friendly welcome, good food, and an atmosphere of quiet informality.

Highly recommended as a place to stay in this part of South Devon is the historic ▶ **Waterman's Arms** at Bow Bridge, Ashprington, near Totnes, a prison during the Napoleonic Wars but today as quaint an inn as you could ever wish for. With only eight bedrooms, it's small, comfortable, and welcoming. To find the Waterman's Arms, follow the signs from Totnes toward Kingsbridge.

THE ENGLISH RIVIERA

Although it may seem unlikely, there is such a place as the English Riviera. It consists of 22 miles of unspoiled coastline around Torbay in South Devon. There are three major resort areas and 18 beaches and secluded coves, all in a unique environment of exotic plants and palm trees, beautiful gardens, and salty harbors.

Fashionable **Torquay**, with its large, modern hotels, has been compared to Cannes; Paignton's long, safe bathing beaches are perfect for family holidays; and Brixham is a thriving little fishing port steeped in history. It was 300 years ago that William of Orange landed at Brixham to claim the throne and become King William III of England. Paignton, too, is not without its history. **Oldway Mansion**, built in 1871 for sewing-machine millionaire Isaac Singer, is well worth a visit; his son, Paris, extensively altered the mansion in the style of the great palace at Versailles.

Torbay

Torquay's palm trees, exotic flowers, and shrubs give the resort a Mediterranean atmosphere. While there, make sure to visit the completely thatched village of Cockington, with its famous forge, and include Kent's Cavern and the Model Village at Babbacombe in your tour of the town, as well as the Aircraft Museum on the road (A 385) to Totnes. Agatha Christie was born in Torquay in 1890. The Agatha Christie Room at the Torre Abbey mansion displays some memorabilia relating to her.

Adjoining Torbay are the popular holiday resorts of **Teignmouth** and **Shaldon**, set on the estuary of the River Teign and linked by bridge and passenger ferry. Close by, northeast of Teignmouth, is the equally attractive resort of **Dawlish**, where a stream and colorful gardens dominate the town center.

STAYING AND DINING
IN AND AROUND TORBAY

For accommodations around Torquay, a few miles inland, try the enchanting ▶ **Cott Inn** (circa 1320) at Dartington, one of the five oldest inns in England. The roofing thatch is 187 feet long. While in Torquay visit the elegant **Boulevard Restaurant** on the waterfront overlooking the international yacht marina, and the fashionable Fleet Walk restaurant and shopping complex.

In the village of Harberton, near Totnes, is the 17th-century ▶ **Ford Farm House**, where you can be assured of a warm welcome from Sheila Edwards.

Just 3 miles (5 km) from Torquay is the ▶ **Orestone Manor House**, a country-house hotel at Maidencombe that was once the home of John C. Horsley, an artist and the brother-in-law of the engineer Isambard Kingdom Brunel (see Plymouth, below), who lived close by. Rudyard Kipling lived for a time next door.

Toward Plymouth

Tucked in between Torbay and Plymouth is yet another attractive part of Devon known simply as the **South Hams**. Here, beyond Berry Head, you will find the historic port of **Dartmouth**, with its strong maritime associations, including the Britannia Royal Naval College; the sailing center of Salcombe; and the busy little market town of Kingsbridge. It would be difficult to imagine a more idyllic setting for a restaurant than the promenade at Dartmouth overlooking the picturesque River Dart. There on the South Embankment at the sign of the **Carved Angel**, you will find Joyce Molyneux serving freshly caught salmon—from the Dart, naturally—in a Champagne sauce, or grilled lobster with tarragon butter. Don't be surprised to find Mediterranean overtones and liberal use of the finest olive oils.

STAYING AND DINING
EN ROUTE TO PLYMOUTH

There are some remarkably interesting hotels in the South Hams district: All 14 rooms at the ▶ **Soar Mill Cove Hotel** rest at ground level but enjoy sea views. National Trust beach and cliff walks are popular, but dinner becomes the main event, ordered in advance from the rooms. The menu gives prominence to lobsters, king crabs, sea bass, and brill, as well as Devon beef and local lamb. The ▶ **Tide's Reach**, another privately owned and run luxury hotel, nestles in a tree-fringed sandy cove on the Salcombe Estuary in an Area of Outstanding Natural Beauty. Guests praise the superb food and friendly service, along with the extensive indoor leisure facilities. In the same category are

the highly regarded ▶ **Thurlestone Hotel** near Kingsbridge and ▶ **Piper's Bench** at Thurlestone, a colonial-
style hotel that specializes in golfing holidays. With seven
double bedrooms, Piper's Bench preserves an individual
style and country-house atmosphere.

If you would like to turn back the clock 70 years and
spend your vacation in the manner of the 1920s, you can
do just that at the ▶ **Burgh Island Hotel**. This "great white
palace" of a hotel on Burgh Island, just off the coast at
Bigbury-on-Sea, has been lovingly restored and reopened
in true Art Deco style by London fashion consultants Be-
atrice and Tony Porter. You can occupy a suite used by
Agatha Christie during one of her working holidays here
(one of 14 distinctive suites); dine in the restaurant once
patronized by Edward VIII, who brought Wallis Simpson to
Burgh Island to escape the attention of the press just prior
to his abdication; and dance the night away under the
Peacock Dome as Noël Coward did on many occasions.
The remarkable thing—and this is what makes the Burgh
Island Hotel so special—is that nothing has changed; it
remains exactly as it was in the jazz-crazy 1920s.

PLYMOUTH

You could spend a week in and around the city of Plymouth and still not see everything, but wherever you look
the sea has created history. Sir Francis Drake, greatest of
all Elizabethan seafarers, sailed from here aboard the
Golden Hind in 1577 to circumnavigate the globe. When
he returned three years later, he became Plymouth's
mayor. Drake bought **Buckland Abbey**, north of Plymouth
near Yelverton, from Sir Richard Grenville. Here you can
actually inspect "Drake's Drum," which accompanied him
on all his voyages and notably when he set sail to do
battle against Spain's Armada, which he defeated in 1588.
Since his death the legend has grown that should England
ever again face mortal danger, unseen hands will once
more beat the drum, calling Drake back from the grave to
rise up in his country's defense and rally the fighting
qualities of Englishmen everywhere.

On **Plymouth Hoe**, a promontory where he calmly
finished a game of bowls before setting out to engage the
Spaniards, Drake's immense contribution to England's
maritime history is marked by an imposing statue. While
on Plymouth Hoe be sure to see the latest addition to the

city's attractions—**Plymouth Dome**, an award-winning exhibition center overlooking world-famous Plymouth Sound. In 14 separate viewing areas the fascinating history of Plymouth unfolds.

Sir Walter Raleigh, born at Hayes Barton near Budleigh Salterton, also sailed from Plymouth to North Carolina in 1584, where he "discovered" the tobacco leaf and brought it back to England with him.

Today Plymouth Sound is still busy with ships. Be sure to visit the **Barbican**, the old Elizabethan quarter, with its lively fish quay surrounded by restaurants, antiques shops, and inns with names that have a salty tang. Across the road from the fish market is the **Island House**, where the Pilgrim Fathers, their names listed on an outside wall, spent the night before they left from the **Mayflower Steps** in 1620 on their perilous voyage to America. More by chance than design, their ship, the *Mayflower*, landed at a place called Plymouth on an earlier map, and they retained the name. Once in the New World, the Pilgrims became the "founding fathers" of Dorchester in Massachusetts.

Other plaques commemorate the return of the Tolpuddle Martyrs (six agricultural workers who dared to form Britain's first trade union) from Australia in 1838 and the first seaplane flight across the Atlantic in 1919. Up a narrow cobbled street (inappropriately named New Street) an Elizabethan house (circa 1584) is one of many old buildings preserved around the Barbican.

Visit the **Royal Citadel**, a 17th-century fortress alongside the Hoe, to look far across Plymouth Sound; while there, climb **Smeaton's Tower**, the first true lighthouse, which John Smeaton designed and built on the Eddystone Rock, 11 miles off Plymouth. Smeaton's 22-foot tower set the standard by which all stone lighthouses were subsequently built. After four hazardous years under construction on the storm-lashed Eddystone Rock, it was lit for the first time in 1759. After resolutely withstanding angry waves for 123 years, it was finally undermined by the sea and had to be demolished in 1882. Two years later it was re-erected on Plymouth Hoe.

Three miles (5 km) east of the city center toward Kingsbridge is **Saltram**, a remarkable George II mansion with its original contents, situated in a landscaped park and administered by the National Trust. Watch for two important rooms designed by Robert Adams that contain fine period furniture, china, and paintings, including many portraits by Sir Joshua Reynolds. Saltram, open to

visitors Sunday through Thursday from April to the end of
October, is 3½ miles (almost 6 km) east of Plymouth city
center. It can be reached by the A 38 Exeter road or by the
A 379 Kingsbridge road (turn off at the Marsh Mills roundabout for Plympton).

Find time while you are in Plymouth to inspect the
Tamar Road Bridge, which links the city with Cornwall to
the west. When it opened in 1962 it replaced a steam-
driven chain ferry. Take an even closer look at the railway
bridge alongside it and marvel at the engineering skill of
Isambard Kingdom Brunel, who built it in 1859 to carry
the Great Western Railway from Plymouth into Cornwall.

STAYING AND DINING IN PLYMOUTH

Plymouth offers an exciting range of first-class hotels,
mostly situated on the Hoe and affording breathtaking
views across Plymouth Sound. They include the multi-
storied ▶ **Forte Posthouse** and the ▶ **Plymouth Moat
House**, the city's only four-star hotel. Both are tailored to
meet the needs of the business traveller, yet they are at
the center of things for the visitor. Keeping them company is the quiet Victorian elegance of the ▶ **Grand
Hotel**, built more than a century ago but now restored to
the highest standards for business and pleasure; it occupies a site on the Hoe to rival any in Europe. Conveniently situated on the A 38 two miles (3 km) from the
city center, a modern ▶ **Novotel** set in landscaped gardens makes an excellent base for exploring Devon or
Cornwall.

New to Plymouth is the 135-room ▶ **Copthorne Hotel**,
opened in 1987. On a central site on Armada Way and with
two restaurants, **The Burlington** and **Bentleys**, which have
quickly achieved recognition, the Copthorne has brought
international standards of excellence to Plymouth.

CORNWALL

Cornwall, whose mild climate and great natural beauty
are perhaps its main attractions, is virtually an island. It is
distanced from the neighboring county of Devon, particularly on the south coast, by the River Tamar, which for all

but a few miles forms a natural border "with England," or so native Cornish men and women will have you believe. Throughout history Cornwall's sons and daughters have behaved as if theirs is a land apart, and in certain respects you will find yourself agreeing with them.

Kernow is the name the Cornish proudly attribute to their Celtic homeland. Once across the fine modern road bridge that carries you into Cornwall by the southern route (A 38) and through a newly completed tunnel under the town of Saltash, just west of Plymouth, you will notice the many Celtic place names, similar to those found in Scotland, Wales, Ireland, Brittany, and the Isle of Man. You can recognize them by the prefixes Tre (farm or village), Pol (anchorage), Pen (head or end), Ros (heath or spur), Res (ford), Kelly (grove), and Car (camp or fort). These prefixes extend to Cornish surnames as well. As the saying goes: "By Tre, Pol, and Pen, you may know the Cornish men."

Cornwall also has its own language, though it is seldom spoken today except by students encouraged to keep it alive by the Cornish Language Society. Similar to the Welsh language, it remained Cornwall's mother tongue until the 18th century, when it was superseded by English, save in a few fishing villages around Penzance. Dolly Pentreath, who died in 1777 at Mousehole, in West Cornwall, is reputed to have been the last native speaker of the Cornish language. (You can still see her house in Mousehole.)

Counting all the inlets, creeks, and river estuaries, Cornwall is gifted with England's longest and most inspiring coastline, 326 miles, bounded on the north and west by the Atlantic Ocean and on the south by the English Channel. Along its northern shoreline, from Bude to Land's End, majestic cliffs brace themselves against the sea, interspersed with steep-sided valleys formed by fast-flowing rivers and streams. This coast contains some of Europe's finest surfing and bathing beaches—magnets that attract three million visitors to Cornwall annually, mostly in July and August. By contrast, along its southern English Channel shore from Plymouth Sound to Land's End, Cornwall presents a softer picture, one of less rugged cliffs; instead, headlands reach out to sea to form magnificent bays, estuaries, and creeks that draw an admiring yacht set.

Inland, Cornwall exchanges the grandeur of its coastal scenery for rugged moors, the best example being **Bodmin Moor**, in the county's craggy uplands, where the landscape resembles Dartmoor. The highest points on Bodmin Moor are Brown Willy (1,375 feet) and Rough Tor (1,311 feet), near Camelford.

Not every visitor falls under the spell of Cornwall's beautiful and varied scenery. Many are drawn to the county instead by its wealth of archaeological and historic sites—dolmens and stone circles from the Stone Age, Bronze Age burial chambers, Iron Age hill forts, castles, keeps, and coastal fortifications.

In addition to numerous hill forts and cliff castles, the Iron Age Celts left behind fascinating villages like **Chysauster**—already in existence for two centuries before the Romans arrived—and **Carn Euny**, both near Penzance. The two villages are now in the care of English Heritage and are open to visitors.

Celtic saints, who came to Cornwall mainly from Wales and Ireland in the sixth and seventh centuries, are venerated in the names of many Cornish villages, such as St. Ives, St. Ewe, St. Issey, St. Tudy, St. Breward, and St. Madron. The father of Cornish saints was Saint Petroc, who established monasteries at Padstow and Bodmin. Then there was Saint Piran, patron saint of tin miners, whose ancient oratory lies buried beneath the sand dunes near Perranporth. Saint Piran's cross (a white cross on a black background, symbolizing white metal being extracted from the black tin ore) has been adopted as Cornwall's emblem.

The Romans came here seeking tin; so too did the Phoenicians. Disused winding-engine houses punctuate the landscape in parts of the county, reminders of the fact that tin was once the lifeblood of the Cornish economy. Winding engines are impressive relics of the tin mining industry. These great beam engines (one at Pool, near Redruth, has a cylinder 7½ feet in diameter) were once used for pumping water from more than 2,000 feet down and for winding men and tin ore from the bottom of the mine to the surface. They exemplify the use of high-pressure steam patented by the Cornish engineer Richard Trevithick in 1802. The industry was revived in the early 1970s, when tin again became profitable to mine. The market subsequently collapsed, enjoyed a brief recovery from 1988 to 1989, but early in 1990 received another setback when falling tin prices forced the £6 million Wheal Jane mine near Truro to close, causing the loss of 150 jobs. The mine was later abandoned; when the pumps

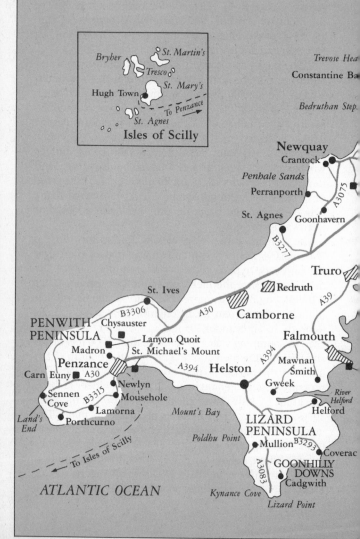

Cornwall

0 miles 10
0 10 kilometers

ATLANTIC OCEAN

Isles of Scilly

Bryher
St. Martin's
Tresco
Hugh Town
St. Mary's
St. Agnes
To Penzance

Trevose Hea
Constantine Ba

Bedruthan Step.

Newquay
Crantock
Penhale Sands
Perranporth
St. Agnes
Goonhavern
A3075
B3277

Truro
Redruth
St. Ives
A30
Camborne
A39
PENWITH
PENINSULA
Chysauster
B3306
Lanyon Quoit
Madron
St. Michael's Mount
Falmouth
Penzance
Carn Euny
A30
A394
Helston
Mawnan
Smith
Gweek
Sennen
Cove
Newlyn
B3315
Mousehole
Land's
End
Lamorna
Porthcurno
Mount's Bay
River
Helford
Helford
LIZARD
PENINSULA
Poldhu Point
Mullion
B3293
Coverac
GOONHILLY
DOWNS
Cadgwith
A3083
Kynance Cove
ATLANTIC OCEAN
To Isles of Scilly
Lizard Point

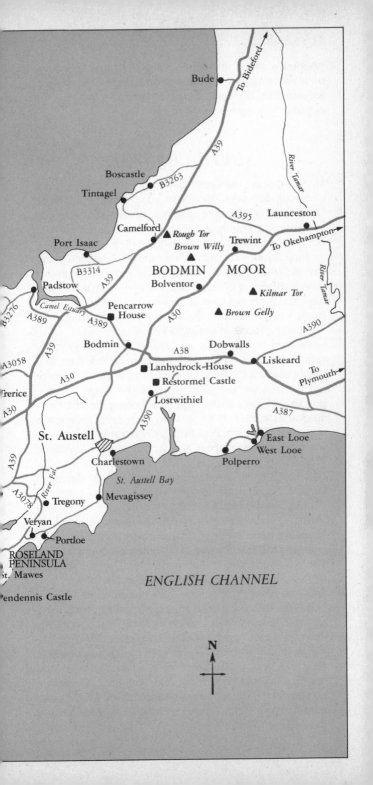

stopped working, it became flooded. China-clay extraction, almost unique to Cornwall and parts of Devon, is an industry that, like agriculture, fishing, and tourism, is still of prime importance to the region.

NORTH CORNWALL

Many overseas visitors take the northern route (A 39) into Cornwall, following the coast road down from North Devon after stopping at Lynton, Lynmouth, and Clovelly, and enter the county at the aptly named Welcome Cross, not far north of the holiday resort of Bude.

"King Arthur's country" is the romantic label tied to this part of North Cornwall, which incorporates the charming coastal villages of Boscastle and Tintagel. From **Boscastle**'s tiny quay there is a view of 14th-century cottages clinging to the steep wooded hillsides above a fast-flowing river. The harbor is one of Cornwall's most picturesque.

Tintagel is famed for its 12th-century cliff-top castle ruin, in which the legendary folk hero King Arthur, who fought the Saxons, is said to have been born. Whether or not this is true, the gaunt shell of the castle, perched precariously on a rocky ledge overlooking the Atlantic, is an evocative sight (but you need to be fairly agile to get up there). Dozmary Pool on nearby Bodmin Moor is the legendary resting place of King Arthur's sword, Excalibur.

While visiting Tintagel it would be a pity to miss the Old Post Office, a 14th-century building in the main street; it is a photogenic monument to the past.

Inland from Tintagel and Boscastle, and well worth seeing, are Launceston's ruined Norman castle with its imposing keep; Methodist John Wesley's cottage at Trewint, and the **Jamaica Inn**, at Bolventor on Bodmin Moor. The slate-hung pub is immortalized in Daphne du Maurier's novel of the same name, with its tale of wrecking and smuggling. The Jamaica Inn, like so many Cornish buildings, has roof slates hanging vertically down the top half of its exterior walls, matching those on the roof. This lets heavy rain run off the building rather than be absorbed into the dry-stone cob walls (composed of stone, clay, and straw). Tiles also are used in the same way, hence the terms slate-hung and tile-hung. Recent improvements to the A 30 now require the motorist to take the slip road, signposted Bolventor, to visit the Jamaica Inn and John Wesley's cottage.

Just a short distance from Port Gaverne is **St. Enodoc Churchyard**, wherein former poet laureate Sir John Betjeman is buried. He spent childhood holidays in this area and was greatly influenced by Cornwall in his writing. If you've time for a round of golf, the excellent course at Trevose Head is only just across the Camel estuary. Find time to stroll around the busy little harbor at **Padstow**, where the quayside architecture owes much to the Flemish influence and where every May Day morning the residents take part in the oldest dance festival in Europe, the 'Obby 'Oss (Hobby Horse).

Inland again from here is **Lanhydrock**, an imposing mansion near Bodmin, set in acres of parkland and colorful gardens. Originally built in the 17th century, it was largely rebuilt in the grand Victorian manner following a fire in 1881. This great house, cared for by the National Trust, awaits your arrival as if time had stood still. To reach Lanhydrock, which lies 2 miles (3 km) southeast of Bodmin, turn south off the A 30 to join up with the A 38 Bodmin–Liskeard road. At the point where the two roads meet, the direction to Lanhydrock is well signposted. Back toward the coast on the A 389, and still family owned and occupied, is **Pencarrow**, a stately home that contains period furniture and a collection of fine paintings by Sir Joshua Reynolds.

STAYING AND DINING IN NORTH CORNWALL

An ideal base from which to explore this part of North Cornwall is the lovingly restored ► **Port Gaverne Hotel**, a 17th-century inn nestled in a fishing cove near Port Isaac. The fact that since 1969 the 18-room hotel, which has an international clientele, was owned by genial Americans Fred and Midge Ross was an added attraction for the many U.S. visitors who stay here. Sadly, Fred died in 1992 but Midge carries on the business they built up together. The hotel is recognized for its good dining; the restaurant specializes in freshly caught local seafood.

Two other hotels in this area command attention. Originally a Customs and Excise building, the two-star ► **Old Custom House Inn**, which has occupied a prime site on the quayside at Padstow since the early 1800s, is now listed as a property of historical interest. The inn has 25 bedrooms, all with private bathrooms, and a restaurant that specializes in locally caught seafood. The ► **Treglos Hotel** is a quiet, 44-bedroom country house set in three acres of gardens overlooking unspoiled Constantine Bay and Trevose Head golf course. The owners and staff pride themselves on the fact that they still clean your shoes, carry your luggage, turn down the beds at night, and serve you early-morning tea.

Visit the **Seafood Restaurant** on the riverside at Padstow for a memorable dining experience. Owners Rick and Jill Stein have created a delightful spot alongside the sea to sample the bounty of those waters. Whet your appetite with freshly caught fish soups and stews, and conger eel and oysters; then proceed to the succulent grilled lobster.

MID-CORNWALL

Cornwall's premier resort, **Newquay**, which grew from a tiny fishing port, has seven miles of the finest coastline and beaches in Europe. The incredibly beautiful **Bedruthan Steps**, just to the northeast, are large black rocks in the sand that are said to have been used as stepping stones by Bedruthan, a legendary local giant. Drop in at the **Old Albion Inn**, a pub that was once a smugglers' haunt at Crantock, and at **Trerice**, an Elizabethan manor house built in 1571 and now preserved by the National Trust.

St. Agnes, a former tin-mining village southwest of Newquay, rose to prominence with the television serialization of Winston Graham's best-selling *Poldark* novels. Many of the scenes were shot in the Trevellas valley on the outskirts of the village. There are at least two other reasons for going there: "Cornwall in Miniature," and "The World in Miniature," at nearby Goonhavern, remarkable theme parks featuring authentic models of favorite landmarks in Cornwall and the rest of the world.

STAYING AND DINING IN MID-CORNWALL

An overnight stop at Newquay's ▶ **Headland Hotel**, which occupies a ten-acre natural headland and is surrounded on three sides by the sea, could prove one of the high points of your visit to Cornwall, especially if you are here during one of their hot-air balloon festivals. A large hotel, the Headland caters to all tastes, from murder-and-mystery weekends to wildflower painting.

Two country-house hotels in this area are also worth considering. ▶ **Rosemundy House**, a delightful Georgian residence at the center of the unspoiled village of St. Agnes, has 43 rooms and a reputation for good home cooking. ▶ **Rose-in-Vale Country House Hotel** at Mithian, near St. Agnes, lies secluded and peaceful in its own 11-acre wooded valley; fresh seafood is prominent on the menu, and all produce comes directly from the owners' family farm.

As you continue west along the north coast toward St. Ives you will pass the town of Redruth. Worth a stop here is the **Chart Room**, a restaurant housed in the Inn for All Seasons on the inner bypass road. Its imaginative menu changes weekly, and map charts adorning the walls create an elegant and warm atmosphere.

WEST CORNWALL
St. Ives

This once-small fishing port, with its maze of cobbled streets and stone cottages clustered around the picturesque harbor, has changed little through the centuries. Here among the narrow streets, alleyways, and court-yards—bearing such improbable names as Teetotal Street and Upalong and Downalong—fish cellars and shops jostle with craft workshops, art galleries, and sail lofts turned into studios. There has been an artists' colony in St. Ives for close to 100 years, and as a center for the arts the resort enjoys an international reputation, so much so that London's famed Tate Gallery has opened the **Tate Gallery of St. Ives** on a site overlooking Porthmeor Beach, to house a collection of 300 works produced by the St. Ives School of artists in the late 19th and early 20th centuries.

Of foremost interest is the **Barbara Hepworth Museum and Sculpture Garden**, another outpost of the Tate Gallery that has on permanent display sculptures by the late Dame Barbara Hepworth, whose home this was. She did some of her best work here between 1949 and 1975, when she died tragically in a fire. It was also in St. Ives that Bernard Leach revived the potter's art during the 1920s, and his work can be purchased in the pottery shop on the road called the Stennack. (His son is also a potter; see the Toward the English Riviera section, above.)

DINING AND STAYING IN ST. IVES

The **Sloop Inn** on the harbor wall is a favorite pub with fishermen and artists, but if you have in mind to stay a while, the 50-bedroom ► **Porthminster Hotel**, which looks down over the harbor, will give you an excellent base from which to explore Land's End peninsula. From most of the rooms you can look out across St. Ives Bay as far as Godrevy Lighthouse. The Porthminster is one of the larger hotels in St. Ives. Although it has been catering to guests for nearly a hundred years, it offers a range of modern facilities for relaxation and leisure.

Land's End

Land's End is to Cornwall what Jerusalem is to the Holy Land, the saying goes, and indeed it remains today one of the most important and best-loved landmarks in Britain, with a million visitors making the annual pilgrimage to this most westerly location in England.

Since August 1991 Land's End has been owned by Nycal, Inc., of Washington, D.C., a conglomerate with interests in oil and property. Prior to that time, it was privately owned by entrepreneur and *America's* Cup challenger Peter de Savary, who has been retained by Nycal as the Master of Land's End. Under de Savary's leadership, the Land's End Experience was created. The centerpiece of this multimillion-pound tourism development is the legendary Last Labyrinth, an electronic theater attraction that tells the story of Land's End with the aid of stunning special effects. Other high-quality attractions include exhibitions of the sea and ships, play areas, and craft shops.

Leaving Land's End by the B 3315, travelling northeast toward Penzance, you'll come across many more of Cornwall's treasures. At Porthcurno, for instance, you can visit the unique open-air Minack Theatre, on a craggy cliff high above the sea. Here, in the summer months, touring theater companies stage a variety of live entertainment, ranging from Greek tragedy to drawing-room comedy, with the English Channel as a backdrop.

You may want to make stops at Lamorna, a tiny cove approached through a narrow valley blooming with wild flowers, and at **Mousehole**, with its diminutive harbor and wild-bird hospital. Take refreshment here at the **Ship Inn**, where Dylan Thomas enjoyed a drink while in Cornwall. During December, taste the specialty of the house, "starry gazy pie"—a pie containing seven different species of fish, with pilchards' heads and tails poking up through the pastry . . . if you dare.

STAYING AND DINING AT LAND'S END

The formerly unpretentious Land's End Hotel has been redesigned and upgraded and has now emerged as the ▶ **State House**, which bills itself as the First and Last Hotel in England. Here, for a moderate outlay, you can occupy one of its 34 luxuriously appointed rooms with four-poster beds and en suite facilities. From its cliff-top position the hotel commands unrivaled views of the Longships Lighthouse and the Isles of Scilly beyond. You can dine in the hotel's **Observatory Restaurant** and enjoy its romantic backdrop of ocean and sky.

An interesting stopover at Cornwall's western extremity would be the 17th-century fishing inn ▶ **Old Success**, nestling down in Sennen Cove. Old Success offers excellent accommodations, including three suites, two of them with four-poster beds. The inn retains the robust seafaring flavor of a maritime village. Fresh fish dishes are available throughout the day, as are "proper" Cornish pasties—a taste of the true Cornwall.

It used to be said that the Devil never visited Cornwall for fear of being made into a pie. Cornish women have always had plenty of original ideas for pie fillings—limpets, figs, sweet herbs, pilchards, you name it. Most famous of them all is, of course, the Cornish pasty (pronounced with a short *a*, as in "map") made from chopped beef steak, diced potatoes, turnip or rutabaga, and onion. The ingredients are placed in the oven encased in a strong pastry shell crimped along the top edge to enclose the meat and vegetables. A complete meal in itself, the pasty is thought to have originated in the tin-mining communities of Cornwall where, it was claimed, the pastry shell had to be unbreakable in case it was accidentally dropped down a mineshaft. Pasties can vary enormously in quality and flavor. Buy them from small bakery shops where they are made on the premises.

Penzance

From Mousehole it is just a short drive along the south coast road to Penzance. You will pass Newlyn, home port of Cornwall's largest fishing fleet.

West Cornwall is packed with ancient sites and monuments and is, in fact, a living museum. You can meet girls turned to stone for dancing on a Sunday (the Merry Maidens, a Bronze Age stone circle near Lamorna) and climb through a holed stone reputed to cure your back-ache and other ailments (Men-an-Tol, on the moors between Madron and Morvah near Penzance).

Among the most ancient objects are the great quoits (large flat stones raised above the ground atop standing pillars of granite, like a miniature Stonehenge) and cairns (ancient burial chambers), built between 4,000 and 6,000 years ago. The biggest of the quoits, Chun, is at Zennor, but **Lanyon Quoit**, between Madron and Morvah near Penzance, is the most famous and more easily reached.

Penzance, boasting the only promenade in Cornwall, is the major town on the Land's End peninsula. It is the administrative center for West Cornwall, the district describing itself as Penwith, a Cornish word meaning "extreme end." The town is full of historical and archaeological interest.

It lies on the sheltered curve of Mount's Bay, which takes its name from the island castle of **St. Michael's Mount**, rising 238 feet above the sea a mile offshore. At low tide the castle is linked to the mainland at Marazion (which in the Middle Ages was a Jewish settlement) by a granite causeway over which it is possible to walk to the mount, but at high tide the only way to get there is by boat. It was originally the site of a Benedictine monastery established by Edward the Confessor. From the highest point on the romantic island castle (which has a "twin" in Mont-St-Michel on France's northwest coast near Avranches) there are, on a clear day, uninterrupted views that take in the Lizard, as this part of the Cornish peninsula is called, to Land's End.

STAYING AND DINING IN PENZANCE

There's a splendid view of St. Michael's Mount from the intimate ▶ **Camilla Hotel**, a small Regency house adjacent to the promenade, where you'll find a really homey welcome plus good food, comfort, and excellent advice about travelling around the Land's End peninsula. The folks at the Camilla will even book you on board the *Scillonian* for your visit to the fortunate isles.

If you are interested in antiques, you will love the ▶ **Queen's Hotel**, an elegant Victorian property on Penzance's promenade. Every room is different, and many of them are furnished with genuine antiques. The hotel has long been renowned for its collection of fine art, prints, and originals from the Newlyn School of Art—and for the finest of freshly caught fish from nearby Newlyn Harbor.

For good measure, the Queen's Hotel has recently opened **Gino's Spaghetti House**, a restaurant with a super-informal atmosphere and decor that includes traditional Cornish granite warmed by pine gazebos, rich fabrics, brass, and polished-wood surfaces.

Before leaving Penzance, walk up Chapel Street behind the parish church. There you will discover, tucked away amid the Regency and Georgian town houses, the **Dolphin Tavern**, in which Judge Jeffries, nicknamed "the Hanging Judge," held court; the ornate Egyptian house, the ground floor of which is now a National Trust shop; the **Turk's Head**, an inn dating from 1233, when Turks visited Penzance during the Crusades; and the **Admiral Benbow Coffee Tavern**, decked out like an old sailing ship.

Following the road out of Penzance to Madron, stop at Trengwainton to see the magnificent subtropical gardens filled with fuchsias, exotic magnolias, rhododendrons from Nepal and Assam, and rare maples from China and Japan.

The Lizard Peninsula

We're fortunate that there is one district of Cornwall that, even today, remains largely undiscovered—the Lizard Peninsula, the most southerly point in England. You really do need a car to see it properly.

This region affords some of the finest coastal scenery in Cornwall, including Lizard Point, Church Cove, Kilcobben Cove, and Mullion Cove, in addition to the much-admired villages of Coverack and Cadgwith. Kynance Cove, with its craggy green serpentine stone cliffs carved out by the crashing waves, is especially worth a visit. While you're there walk down to the lighthouse for staggering views.

At its head is the quaint old town of **Helston**, where every year, on or about May 8, elegantly dressed couples dance in and out of the houses and shops in the ancient Furry (or Floral) Dance—a delightful spectacle. Should you happen to be near Helston at the time, and not mind crowds, you might join the 10,000 people who attend every year. If you're feeling peckish, the most popular Cornish pasties hereabouts can be found at **Ann's—The Lizard Pasty Shop**. Ann makes especially good pasties but, since the shop is open only three days a week, it's best to call her and order them specially made up for you; Tel: (0326) 29-08-89.

GOONHILLY DOWNS

Goonhilly Downs is the Lizard Peninsula's wildest part—
a heathland area considered of special scientific interest
for the unique plant life that grows there. A profusion of
wildflowers found nowhere else in the British Isles is
responsible for the Downs being designated a conservation area. You can see tomorrow's world today at **Goonhilly Earth Station** (built in 1961 at the request of NASA),
which provides a fascinating glimpse into the science of
satellite communications. Here, at the heart of one of
England's oldest nature-conservation areas, is one of the
most complex pieces of high technology in the world, its
vast, saucer-shaped aerials looming large against the skyline, a familiar landmark. In its control center you can see
pictures beaming in from all corners of the world.
Through Goonhilly, millions of telephone conversations,
facsimile calls, and television transmissions pass each
year. It is a far cry from the day when Marconi, from this
same spot, bridged the Atlantic by sending out the first
radio signals from Poldhu Cove. The Earth Station is 7
miles (11 km) from Helston on B 3293.

There are other tourist attractions on the Lizard Peninsula. **Flambards**, Cornwall's leading theme park, features
an authentically reconstructed, life-size Victorian village
complete with shops, carriages, and costumes, and there
is a **seal sanctuary** at Gweek.

THE FALMOUTH
SOUTH COAST AREA
Falmouth

From here it is but a short ride to Falmouth, gem of the
Cornish Riviera, which has the third-largest natural harbor in the world and, it follows, a great maritime history,
dating back to the era of the post office sailing packets,
the tea clippers, and windjammers—great square-riggers
from sailing's glory days.

Today Falmouth is a very fashionable holiday resort, yet
it is largely unspoiled. As you might expect with such a
large harbor, Falmouth offers an exciting range of water
sports and activities. Sea and river trips are popular.
Inquire at the Prince of Wales Pier in Falmouth about a
boat trip up the River Fal, landing at Truro, if tidal condi-

tions permit. It is a beautiful ride. Subtropical gardens and coast walks around Falmouth itself also hold great appeal. A unique annual festival held every April and May opens to visitors some 70 gardens, many of world renown. Among the superb gardens open to the public is **Glendurgan**, near the Helford River, with a laurel-hedge maze laid out in 1833. Be sure to visit **Pendennis Castle** and its twin **St. Mawes Castle** (one mile across the estuary from Falmouth), both built on the instructions of Henry VIII to guard the entrance to the harbor against marauding pirates. Both castles contain exhibitions of arms and armor.

STAYING AND DINING
IN THE FALMOUTH AREA

If you want to be pampered during your stay in Cornwall, then make for the ▶ **Budock Vean Golf and Country House Hotel**. It's set in 65 acres of subtropical gardens at Mawnan Smith, between the River Helford and Falmouth, and provides its own private golf course, a spectacular indoor swimming pool, and championship-standard all-weather tennis courts. The hotel's **Duchy Restaurant** has a growing reputation for its cuisine, which includes the famous Helford oysters.

Enjoying an unusual position at the water's edge, the ▶ **Greenbank Hotel**, with 60 bedrooms, has been an important landfall for the world's seafarers since Falmouth was England's principal post office packet station in the days of sail. Sailors still regard the Greenbank as their safe haven at the end of epic Atlantic voyages. Among such guests was the late Robert Manry of Cleveland, Ohio, who in August 1965 singlehandedly brought his 13-foot sailboat, *Tinkerbelle,* from Falmouth, Massachusetts, to the very door of the hotel. It was while he was a guest at the Greenbank that Kenneth Grahame wrote a number of letters to his young son ("Mouse") that were later to form the basis of the classic *The Wind in the Willows.* Throughout a long and fascinating history, the Greenbank has maintained standards of excellence.

Another local hotel of distinction is the three-star ▶ **Green Lawns Hotel**, with 40 bedrooms and convenient to both town and harbor. If you should find stairs a problem, the hotel offers ground-floor rooms. Dining in the Garras Grill is the high point of a stay at the Green Lawns, with steaks and fresh local seafood as the specialties.

When the 80-bedroom ▶ **Falmouth Beach Hotel** was

built in 1984, overlooking the resort's main beach, the owners wanted to provide style without ostentation, friendliness without familiarity, and to be, at the same time, homey. And that's exactly what they've achieved. Also prominent on the seafront a short, level walk from the town and harbor of Falmouth stands the ▶ **Royal Duchy Hotel**, only 100 yards from the beach. This first-class hotel enjoys a reputation for comfort and the quality of its cuisine.

Another good choice for dinner is **Livingston's**, which commands superb unobstructed views across Falmouth Bay from its position above the Seahorse Inn overlooking Maenporth Beach on the outskirts of Falmouth. Livingston's is an excellent restaurant, offering a sophisticated and airy decor and a very warm, relaxed atmosphere for diners. The chef was formerly at the London nightclub Annabel's. You may need to reserve; Tel: (0326) 25-02-51.

In the tiny granite town of Penryn, 2 miles (3 km) upriver from Falmouth via the A 39, Jack and Jean Hewitt welcome visitors to ▶ **Clare House**, a 17th-century building in the center of town. Lovingly restored and tastefully furnished, the delightful small guest house has three guest bedrooms where travellers can spend the night in comfort and then awake to a sumptuous full English breakfast, all at an affordable price.

Not far from Penryn you can find "the best pub food in Britain" at one of Cornwall's most famous establishments, **The Pandora**. On the banks of Restronguet Creek near Falmouth, this thatched and whitewashed inn dating to the 13th century specializes in seafood meals. At the bar you can order such tasty items as Moules Marinieres (local mussels steamed in white wine, garlic, and herbs) and Restronguet Fish Pie (whitefish, prawns, eggs, onions, and parsley in a cream sauce, topped with a potato and cheese crust).

Roseland Peninsula

It is only 20 minutes' drive from Falmouth north to **Truro**, the commercial and administrative center of Cornwall. A fine Gothic-style cathedral dominates the city center. The latest addition to Cornwall's wide range of lodgings is the ▶ **Alverton Manor Hotel**, standing in six acres of parkland in the center of Truro and providing gracious country-house living at its best. The 150-year-old building is interesting both historically and architecturally and has been restored to incorporate every modern comfort. The suites have been individually designed. The food, too, is of a high standard, prepared under the supervision of a chef direct from London's Dorchester Hotel.

Another 20-minute drive, this time from Truro up the A 390 toward St. Austell (take the B 3287 turnoff to Tregony and then the A 3078 St. Mawes road), will lead you to **Portloe**, the living reality of a true Cornish fishing village. Little has changed in the last hundred years to destroy the timelessness of this, the most picturesque cove on the Roseland Peninsula. Dominating the cove is the ▶ **Lugger Hotel**, originally a 17th-century inn that lost its license in the 1890s when the landlord was hanged for smuggling. With 20 bedrooms and now a modern hotel in every sense, the Lugger nevertheless offers an escape from the hurried pace of contemporary life. There's room in the cove for half a dozen fishing boats to be winched in and out of the emerald sea, and naturally the pick of the catch goes directly to the hotel.

Close to Portloe is the village of Veryan, with its five "round houses," each with a thatched roof and surmounted by a cross. They date back to the early 19th century. It is said that superstitious Cornish folk built them to prevent the Devil from hiding in the corners.

On your way south to **St. Mawes**, at the tip of the Roseland Peninsula and facing Falmouth across the estuary (where the average winter temperature is only five degrees cooler than in the south of France), be sure to visit the 13th-century church at **St. Just-in-Roseland**, a village that stands at the head of a lovely creek.

An American, Harley Moseley, then owner of the ▶ **Idle Rocks Hotel**, which sits astride the harbor wall at St. Mawes, came up with the idea that made the hotel internationally famous: He offered guests free bed and breakfast if more than an inch of snow settled in St. Mawes during their stay. With such an agreeable climate he was seldom called upon to honor his promise, and today the hotel's new owners continue to give top priority to the comfort of their guests. The hotel restaurant is rated one of the best in Cornwall.

THE SOUTH COAST TOWARD PLYMOUTH

If you retrace your steps from St. Mawes, the next port of call is the much-photographed fishing port of **Mevagissey**, with its picturesque harbor. Take the A 3078 until you see the sign for Veryan; then follow the narrow coastal lanes to Portholland, Gorran Haven, and finally Portmellon before reaching Mevagissey. The same winding coastal lanes—signposted but not numbered—will bring you to Pentewan, Porthpean, and then Charlestown, with its **Shipwreck Centre** and **Heritage Museum**, in St. Austell Bay. Rejoining the main road (A 390) near Lostwithiel, which has 800 years of history, pause to visit **Restormel Castle**, former home of the first duke of Cornwall, the Black Prince. It is one of the oldest and best-preserved Norman motte-and-bailey castles in Cornwall.

Still to be enjoyed (especially for railroad buffs) is the **Dobwalls Family Adventure Park** in the eastern half of Cornwall, at Dobwalls, near Liskeard, adjoining the A 38. There is a host of attractions here, including replicas of the Rio Grande Western Railroad and the Union Pacific Railroad of America. Nowhere else will you find superb working, passenger-hauling models of both of the world's largest steam and diesel locomotives—Big Boy William Jeffers and Centennial. You can also enjoy an Edwardian experience by strolling down a lantern-lit London street, faithfully reproduced, or through the Highlands, taking in the largest and most important collection of paintings by Britain's greatest natural-history artist, Archibald Thorburn. This is a truly outstanding theme park.

Your next stop should be the showpiece harbor at **Polperro**, one of the prettiest villages anywhere. The author Sir Arthur Quiller-Couch (or "Q" to his friends and readers) lived in Polperro. The main attraction here is the "House on the Props," supported above the ground in the manner its name suggests.

Before retracing your steps east back into Devon across the Tamar Bridge, take a stroll around **Looe**. In reality, it is East Looe and West Looe, two ancient boroughs separated by a narrow tidal river and united by a seven-arched stone bridge. Together they form a popular resort of a quaintness and charm found only in communities whose sea-directed history goes back hundreds of years.

STAYING AND DINING ON THE CORNISH RIVIERA

The ▶ **Carlyon Bay**, near St. Austell, is the most prestigious hotel on the Cornish Riviera. Standing in 250 acres, much of which is given over to subtropical gardens, it has its own championship 18-hole golf course and a large leisure complex with both indoor and outdoor heated swimming pools.

An exciting new "Taste of Cornwall" menu is attracting diners to **The Well House** in the village of St. Keyne, between Liskeard and Looe (B3254) in the east of the county. Under proprietor Nick Wainford business is flourishing and the restaurant is catering to a truly international clientele. Featured on the menu is wild boar, hand-reared on his farm at Cardinham on Bodmin Moor. Some restaurants serve feral pig as wild boar, but in the case of The Well House it is the genuine article. To the unitiated wild boar tastes like a combination of succulent pork and tender young veal and is very slightly "gamey." Head chef David Woolfall offers diners medallion of wild boar served with roast potatoes and spinach, or, casserole of wild boar complemented with celeriac chips, a root vegetable that tastes like celery. For reservations, Tel: (0579) 34-20-01.

ISLES OF SCILLY

From the bridge of the steamship *Scillonian III* the view is breathtaking: nearly 100 heather-clad islands and islets rising from the Atlantic depths as if pushed above the surface by an unseen force from the legendary, submerged land of Lyonesse. No matter in which direction you look as you approach the Isles of Scilly, the sea dominates the landscape, and it is the relationship between the sea and the land that makes the archipelago so attractive. Yet only five of the islands are inhabited: St. Mary's and the "off-islands" of Tresco, St. Martin's, St. Agnes, and Bryher. The *Scillonian* makes one trip daily each way between Penzance and St. Mary's (two and a half hours one way).

St. Mary's, the commercial and social center of Scilly,

is home to most of the 2,000 Scillonians. The capital, Hugh Town, is little more than a village by mainland standards. Even so, there is a good selection of hotels, guest houses, restaurants, and inns, and there are two banks and a post office.

Tresco contains the famous **Abbey Gardens**, created in 1834 by Augustus Smith, in which exotic plants and shrubs from all over the world flourish. Also worth visiting is the **Valhalla Maritime Museum**, containing a collection of figureheads salvaged from ships wrecked on the rocky shores of Scilly.

St. Martin's, noted for its flowers and white sandy beaches, has a population of 83 and a school with just a handful of pupils. **St. Agnes**, the most southwesterly community in the British Isles (population: 65), is surrounded by deep, clear water. It is joined to the still smaller island of **Gugh** (pronounced goo) by a sandbar that is covered at high tide. From here you can gaze upon the infamous Western Rocks, the graveyard of many fine ships.

Bryher, a favorite with many tourists, has the smallest population (56) of the inhabited islands. It is wild and rugged in the north but to the south has a sheltered bay around which are grouped guest houses and a few shops and cafés. The islanders are hospitable and their island beautiful.

During the main season local boatmen arrange trips from the quay at St. Mary's and other islands to Samson, Nornour, St. Helen's, and Tean, all of which are uninhabited; visitors go there to view seal colonies, seabirds, and lighthouses.

Scilly, low in the sea, fails to trap weather fronts, which explains why these "fortunate" islands enjoy more hours of summer sunshine than mainland Britain and are a good deal warmer. Frosts seldom occur here in winter, and this has enabled the islanders to become Britain's leading producers of naturally grown narcissus and daffodils, including the well-known Soleil d'Or variety. Growers start picking them as early as November, but generally they are exported to the mainland in bud from December onward.

The same favorable climate ensures that early (new) potatoes grown on Scilly reach market that much sooner than supplies from either the Channel Islands or mainland Cornwall. However, to balance its economy, Scilly has come to rely increasingly on the influx of summer visitors, and tourism is today the chief preoccupation of many islanders. During the peak months of June, July, and August upward of 2,000 tourists descend on Scilly every week, a number equal to the islands' entire resident population (hence the need to book well in advance if you are planning to stay here in high season).

Exploring the Islands

Ask any visitor what he likes most about Scilly and he will probably list peace, quiet, tranquillity; the absence of traffic, urban stress, pollution, and commercialization; the seclusion, the uncrowded beaches, the natural beauty, the wildlife, the Old World charm and hospitality. In short, the islands comprise a paradise where one can escape the pressures of modern living and find a sense of timelessness and open-handed friendliness.

The mile-long walk around Garrison Hill on St. Mary's is an unforgettable experience, providing superb views of the "off-islands" and a chance to inspect an Elizabethan fort, ▶ Star Castle, built of stone in 1593 to guard the island against pirates and the threat from Spain. The inner building is now a hotel (extensively modernized for guests' comfort), the dungeons a bar. The 26-room Star Castle, which still forms part of the Royal Garrison property on St. Mary's and as such is part of the Duchy of Cornwall, boasts that every subsequent heir to the English throne has stayed here, from Charles I to the present Prince of Wales. The sharp-eyed might get a glimpse of Tamarisk, the royal bungalow owned by Prince Charles, duke of Cornwall.

When the feet begin to tire, you can board a bus outside the Town Hall (and Tourist Information Centre) in Hugh Town for **Vic's Tour** of the island. It takes just over an hour, covers seven miles, and is accompanied by informative and highly entertaining commentary from the driver. The trip was devised in 1947 by local wit Vic Trenwith. Today his nephew Ron Perry carries on the family tradition of a side-splitting tour of St. Mary's.

You can visit what are known to Scillonians as the "off-islands." Dolphins, porpoises, and whales are regularly sighted here; giant turtles are occasionally seen. Chief interest, however, lies in the colonies of the Atlantic grey seal, which breeds within the outer reefs. Bird watchers will be fascinated by the sight of puffins, shearwaters, petrels, and roseate terns.

The pollution-free atmosphere and frost-free climate of

Scilly combine to create conditions that support a range of very rare plants, including more than 250 varieties of lichen. Plants introduced from the Mediterranean and other subtropical regions to the famous **Tresco Abbey Gardens** have spilled over to bring further color to the natural flora of all the islands.

Generations of Scillonians have kept watch for ships in distress in the rock-infested seas around the islands, and there are museums on St. Mary's that tell the maritime story of Scilly. **Hugh Town Museum** has on permanent display artifacts salvaged from wrecks together with a collection of coins brought up from the ocean floor. The **Longstone Heritage Center,** about a mile from Hugh Town, houses a collection of coins and priceless porcelain salvaged from a Dutch East Indiaman, together with ancient cargoes and brass bells from ships that centuries ago found a watery grave off these islands. More recently, in March 1967, the 61,000-ton Italian super-tanker *Torrey Canyon* struck the Seven Stones reef, northwest of Scilly. Her crew was saved, but 119,000 tons of crude oil polluted the sea on both sides of the English Channel, killing thousands of seabirds and devastating marine life (the area has since recovered).

STAYING ON THE ISLES OF SCILLY
Outstanding among places to stay on Scilly is the ▶ **Island Hotel** on Tresco, which is the first choice of an international clientele. Typical of the guest houses on St. Mary's is ▶ **Westford House** on Church Street. Like so many Scillonians, proprietors Tim and Barbara Simpson are extraordinarily accommodating. They walk down to the cobblestoned quay to meet guests disembarking from the *Scillonian* and arrange for luggage to be delivered to the door. Hotelkeeping on this level is a very personal business.

GETTING AROUND
The introduction and completion of the motorways network and major road improvements in the southwest have made the journey to Devon and Cornwall by road from London, the Midlands, and the North of England simplicity itself. Bus travel is growing in popularity, and the fares are relatively inexpensive.

In 1992 National Express introduced direct Rapide bus service between Cornwall and London's "third airport,"

Stansted, in Essex. Passengers are offered a choice of travelling by day or overnight. Journeys are timed to coincide with a growing number of flight arrivals and departures from this expanding airport. Rapide service provides hostess-served refreshments, reclining seats, and toilet facilities. The bus reaches Truro in the center of Cornwall in under six hours.

If you are driving a car, an alternative route from London is by way of the M 3 motorway and subsequently the A 303 or A 30 to Exeter. Traffic does build up at the approaches to Devon and Cornwall on the peak Saturdays of the holiday season—generally the last two Saturdays in July and the first two Saturdays in August. During the summer, Holiday Routes, clearly marked "HR," are introduced. They use a network of minor roads, taking a less busy and more leisurely route to your destination. Maps showing the Holiday Routes can be obtained from tourist boards, information centers, and motoring organizations.

Devon and Cornwall are served by fast, direct, and frequent rail service from London, the Midlands, and the North. Intercity expresses operate from London's Paddington Station to Exeter in two hours, Plymouth in three hours, Truro in four and a half hours, and Penzance in five hours. They include the famous Cornish Riviera express, which now has a full Pullman car service.

If you are planning to arrive at Heathrow or Gatwick, Railair Link buses now operate to Reading, where you can connect with British Railways' high-speed InterCity express trains and reach Exeter in just under two hours, and arrive in Penzance at the end of the line in under five hours.

Those in a hurry to reach Devon and Cornwall can take advantage of the West Country's own airline, Brymon, which in 1992 merged with the West Midlands carrier Birmingham European to form Brymon European. They can fly you from Gatwick to Exeter, from Heathrow to Plymouth or Newquay via Plymouth, on a 50-seater turbo-prop De Havilland Dash 7 or Dash 8.

Exeter Airport is becoming recognized as a gateway to Devon, handling traffic from Gatwick, Belfast, Dublin, the Channel Islands, and the Isles of Scilly. It connects to Dinard (France) and Paris, and a service is being introduced linking Plymouth, through the new London City (Docklands) Airport, to Paris, Brussels, and Amsterdam.

From Plymouth's City Airport at Roborough, Brymon

operates direct services to Heathrow, London City, Gatwick, Newquay, the Isles of Scilly, Jersey, Guernsey, Cork, and Aberdeen.

The Isles of Scilly

The Isles of Scilly Steamship Company provides ferry service between Penzance and St. Mary's. Boats leave from Penzance daily at about 9:15 A.M. and return from St. Mary's at about 4:15 P.M.; the crossing takes about two and a half hours each way; Tel: (0736) 620-09. The company also operates a Skybus between Land's End Airport and St. Mary's, making about 12 flights each way daily during July and August, fewer at other times of the year; from May through September, Skybus service to and from St. Mary's is available from Exeter Airport and Newquay Civil Airport. British International Helicopters has approximately hourly service from Penzance to St. Mary's and Tresco during the summer season; Tel: (0736) 638-71. You can reach the Isles of Scilly from either Penzance Heliport or Land's End Airport in 20 minutes. Local companies provide frequent boat service between the isles.

ACCOMMODATIONS REFERENCE

Rates are projected 1994 prices for a double room with breakfast, unless otherwise stated. Price ranges span the lowest rate in the low season to the highest in the high season. As prices vary according to season and are subject to change, always inquire about current rates before booking.

▶ **Alverton Manor Hotel.** Tregolls Road, **Truro** TR1 1XQ. Tel: (0872) 766-33; Fax: (0872) 22-29-89. £99–£105.

▶ **Arundell Arms Hotel.** Fore Street, **Lifton** PL16 0AA. Tel: (0566) 78-46-66; Fax: (0566) 78-44-94; in U.S. and Canada, (800) 528-1234; in Australia, (008) 222-166. £75–£90.

▶ **Buckerell Lodge Hotel and Restaurant.** Topsham Road, **Exeter** EX2 4SQ. Tel: (0392) 524-51; Fax: (0392) 41-21-14; in U.S. and Canada, (800) 528-1234; in Australia, (02) 212-6444. £71–£91.

▶ **Budock Vean Golf and Country House Hotel.** Mawnan Smith, near Falmouth TR11 5LG. Tel: (0326) 25-02-88; Fax: (0326) 25-08-92. £100–£140.

▶ **Burgh Island Hotel.** Bigbury-on-Sea, South Devon TQ7 4AU. Tel: (0548) 81-05-14; Fax: (0548) 81-02-43. £166–£200 (includes breakfast and dinner).

► **Camilla Hotel.** Regent Terrace, **Penzance**, West Cornwall TR18 4DW. Tel. and Fax: (0736) 637-71. £30–£38.

► **Carlyon Bay Hotel.** St. Austell, **Cornwall** PL25 3RD. Tel: (0726) 81-23-04; Fax: (0726) 81-49-38. £128–£167.

► **Cherrybrook Hotel. Two Bridges**, Dartmoor, Devon PL20 6SP. Tel: (0822) 882-60. £46–£60.

► **Clare House.** Broad Street, **Penryn**, near Falmouth TR10 8JH. Tel: (0326) 37-32-94. £36–£40.

► **Commodore Hotel.** Marine Parade, **Instow**, North Devon EX39 4JN. Tel: (0271) 86-03-47; Fax: (0271) 86-12-33. £85–£100.

► **Copthorne Hotel.** Armada Center, Armada Way, **Plymouth** PL1 1AR. Tel: (0752) 22-41-61; Fax: (0752) 67-06-88; in U.S. and Canada, (800) 448-8355. £103–£119 (breakfast not included).

► **Cott Inn. Dartington**, Totnes, Devon TQ9 6HE. Tel: (0803) 86-37-77; Fax: (0803) 86-66-29. £55–£65.

► **Devon Motel.** Matford, **Exeter** EX2 8XU. Tel: (0392) 592-68; Fax: (0392) 41-31-42. £37–£53.

► **Ebford House Hotel.** Exmouth Road, Ebford, **Exeter** EX3 0QH. Tel: (0392) 87-76-58; Fax: (0392) 87-44-24. £62–£80.

► **Falmouth Beach Hotel.** Seafront, **Falmouth** TR11 4NA. Tel: (0326) 31-80-84; Fax: (0326) 31-91-47. £51–£70.

► **Ford Farm House.** Harberton, near **Totnes** TQ9 7SJ. Tel: (0803) 86-35-39. £35–£40.

► **Forte Posthouse Hotel.** Cliff Road, The Hoe, **Plymouth** PL1 3DL. Tel: (0752) 66-28-28; Fax: (0752) 66-09-74; in U.S. and Canada, (800) 225-5843; in Australia, (008) 22-24-46. £45–£56 (breakfast not included).

► **Grand Hotel.** Elliott Street, The Hoe, **Plymouth** PL1 2PT. Tel: (0752) 66-11-95; Fax: (0752) 60-06-53. £72–£102.

► **Greenbank Hotel.** Harbourside, **Falmouth** TR11 2SR. Tel: (0326) 31-24-40; Fax: (0326) 21-13-62. £105–£138.

► **Green Lawns Hotel.** Western Terrace, **Falmouth** TR11 4QJ. Tel: (0326) 31-27-34; Fax: (0326) 21-14-27. £64–£96.

► **Half Moon Inn. Sheepwash**, Beaworthy, Devon EX21 5NE. Tel: (040-923) 232 or 376. £54–£65.

► **Headland Hotel.** Fistral Bay, **Newquay**, Cornwall TR7 1EW. Tel: (0637) 87-22-11; Fax: (0637) 87-22-12. £68–£90.

► **Holne Chase Hotel and Restaurant.** Tavistock Road, **Poundsgate**, near Ashburton Newton Abbot, Devon TQ13 7NS. Tel: (036-43) 471; Fax: (036-43) 453. £85–£115.

► **Huntsham Court Country House. Huntsham Valley**, near Tiverton, Devon EX16 7NA. Tel: (039-86) 365; Fax: (039-86) 456; in U.S., (415) 453-9689. £105–£131.

▶ **Idle Rocks Hotel**. Harbourside, St. **Mawes**, Cornwall TR2 5AN. Tel: (0326) 27-07-71; Fax: (0326) 27-00-62. £90–£136.

▶ **Island Hotel**. **Tresco**, Isles of Scilly TR24 0PU. Tel: (0720) 228-83; Fax: (0720) 230-08. £147–£230 (includes breakfast and dinner).

▶ **Kittiwell House Hotel and Restaurant**. St. Mary's Road, **Croyde**, **North Devon** EX33 1PG. Tel: (0271) 89-02-47; Fax: (0271) 89-04-69. £73.

▶ **Lewtrenchard Manor**. **Lewdown**, near Okehampton, Devon EX20 4PN. Tel: (056-683) 256 or 222; Fax: (056-683) 332; in U.S. and Canada, (708) 954-2944. £98–£135.

▶ **Lugger Hotel**. **Portloe**, Truro, Cornwall TR2 5RD. Tel: (0872) 50-13-22; Fax: (0872) 50-16-91. £100–£120.

▶ **Lydford House Hotel**. **Lydford**, Okehampton EX20 4AU. Tel: (082-282) 347; Fax: (082-282) 442. £64.50.

▶ **Novotel**. Marsh Mills Roundabout, 270 Plymouth Road, **Plymouth** PL6 8NH. Tel: (0752) 22-14-22; Fax: (0752) 22-14-22; in U.S. and Canada, (800) 221-4542. £39.50 (breakfast not included).

▶ **Old Custom House Inn**. South Quay, **Padstow** PL28 8ED. Tel: (0841) 53-23-59; Fax: (0841) 53-33-72. £42–£79.

▶ **Old Success Inn**. **Sennen Cove**, Land's End, Cornwall TR19 7DG. Tel: (0736) 87-12-32. £66–£88.

▶ **Orestone Manor House**. Rockhouse Lane, Maidencombe, **Torquay**, Devon TQ1 4SX. Tel: (0803) 32-80-98; Fax: (0803) 32-83-36. £90–£140.

▶ **Oxenham Arms**. **South Zeal**, Okehampton, Devon EX20 2JT. Tel: (0837) 84-02-44; Fax: (0837) 84-07-91. £40–£50.

▶ **Park Hotel**. Taw Vale, **Barnstaple** EX32 8NJ. Tel: (0271) 721-66; Fax: (0271) 785-58. £37–£53.

▶ **Piper's Bench**. **Thurlestone**, near Kingsbridge, South Devon. TQ7 3NG. Tel: (0548) 56-01-57. £50.

▶ **Plymouth Moat House**. Armada Way, **Plymouth** PL1 2HJ. Tel: (0752) 66-28-66; Fax: (0752) 67-38-16. £99.

▶ **Poltimore**. Ramsley, **South Zeal**, Okehampton, Devon EX20 2PD. Tel: (0837) 84-02-09. £44–£50.

▶ **Port Gaverne Hotel**. Near **Port Isaac**, North Cornwall PL29 3SQ. Tel: (0208) 88-02-44; Fax: (0208) 88-01-51. £82.

▶ **Porthminster Hotel**. The Terrace, **St. Ives**, Cornwall TR26 2BN. Tel: (0736) 79-52-21; Fax: (0736) 79-70-43; in U.S. and Canada, (800) 528-1234; in Australia, (008) 222-166. £90–£110.

▶ **Queen's Hotel**. The Promenade, **Penzance**, West

Cornwall TR18 4HG. Tel: (0736) 623-71; Fax: (0736) 500-33. £66–£90.

▶ **Rising Sun Hotel.** Harbourside, **Lynmouth**, Devon EX35 6EQ. Tel: (0598) 532-23; Fax: (0598) 534-80. £79–£95.

▶ **Rose-in-Vale Country House Hotel. Mithian**, St. Agnes, Cornwall TR5 0QD. Tel: (0872) 55-22-02; Fax: (0872) 55-27-00. £59–£79.

▶ **Rosemundy House Hotel.** Rosemundy, **St. Agnes**, Cornwall TR5 0UF. Tel: (0872) 55-21-01. £44–£68.

▶ **Royal Clarence Hotel.** Cathedral Close, **Exeter**, Devon EX1 1HD. Tel: (0392) 584-64; Fax: (0392) 43-94-23. £79–£140.

▶ **Royal Duchy Hotel.** Cliff Road, Seafront, **Falmouth**, Cornwall TR11 4NX. Tel: (0326) 31-30-42; Fax: (0326) 31-94-20. £81–£138.

▶ **Royal & Fortescue Hotel.** Boutport Street, **Barnstaple**, North Devon EX31 1HG. Tel: (0271) 422-89; Fax: (0271) 785-58. £37–£53.

▶ **Royal Hotel.** Barnstaple Street, **Bideford**, North Devon EX39 4AE. Tel: (0237) 47-20-05; Fax: (0237) 47-89-57. £45–£55.

▶ **St. Olaves Court Hotel.** Mary Arches Street, **Exeter**, Devon EX4 3AZ. Tel: (0392) 21-77-36; Fax: (0392) 41-30-54. £55–£90.

▶ **Saunton Sands Hotel.** Near **Braunton**, North Devon EX33 1LQ. Tel: (0271) 89-02-12; Fax: (0271) 89-01-45. £116–£198.

▶ **Soar Mill Cove Hotel. Salcombe**, South Devon TQ7 3DS. Tel: (0548) 56-15-66; Fax: (0548) 56-12-23. £134–£153.

▶ **Star Castle.** St. **Mary's**, Isles of Scilly TR21 0JA. Tel: (0720) 223-17; Fax: (0720) 223-43. £60–£100.

▶ **State House Hotel. Land's End**, Cornwall TR19 7AA. Tel: (0736) 87-18-44; Fax: (0736) 87-15-99. £49–£130.

▶ **Thomas Luny House.** Teign Street, **Teignmouth**, South Devon TQ14 8EG. Tel: (0626) 77-29-76. £60.

▶ **Thurlestone Hotel. Thurlestone**, Kingsbridge, South Devon TQ7 3NN. Tel: (0548) 56-03-82; Fax: (0548) 56-10-69. £124–£197.

▶ **Tide's Reach Hotel.** South Sands, **Salcombe**, South Devon TQ8 8LJ. Tel: (0548) 84-34-66; Fax: (0548) 84-39-54. £80–£150.

▶ **Treglos Hotel. Constantine Bay**, near Padstow, North Cornwall PL28 8JH. Tel: (0841) 52-07-27; Fax: (0841) 52-11-63. £96–£126 (closed November through February).

▶ **Victoria Hotel.** The Esplanade, **Sidmouth**, South Devon EX10 8RY. Tel: (0395) 51-26-51; Fax: (0395) 57-91-54. £100–£170.

▶ **Waterman's Arms.** Bow Bridge, **Ashprington**, near Totnes, Devon TQ9 7EG. Tel: (0803) 73-22-14; Fax: (0803) 73-22-14. £58–£68.

▶ **Westford House.** Church Street, **St. Mary's**, Isles of Scilly TR21 0JT. Tel: (0720) 225-10. £41–£44.

▶ **Whitechapel Manor. South Molton**, North Devon EX36 3EG. Tel: (0769) 57-33-77; Fax: (0769) 57-37-97. £98–£160.

▶ **Wigham. Morchard Bishop**, near Crediton, Devon EX17 6RJ. Tel: (036-37) 350. £80–£115.

▶ **Willmead Farm. Bovey Tracey**, near Newton Abbot, South Devon TQ13 9NP. Tel: (064-77) 214. £42–£46.

▶ **Woodford Bridge Hotel. Milton Damerel**, near Holsworthy, North Devon EX22 7LL. Tel: (0409) 26-14-81; Fax: (0409) 26-15-85. £75.

▶ **Woodlands Hotel.** Lynbridge, **Lynton**, North Devon EX35 6AX. Tel: (0598) 523-24. £56–£60.

EAST ANGLIA
SUFFOLK AND NORFOLK

By Katie Lucas

Katie Lucas, a well-known travel writer who specializes in Britain, has lived in Suffolk for 27 years. Her London-based company, Grosvenor Guide Service, organizes tours of Britain for individuals and small groups.

The charms of East Anglia have been immortalized over the centuries by the many renowned artists who have lived in this remote and beautiful corner of England. The huge skies and the gently rolling fields, bordered by ancient hedgerows, with perhaps a flint church tower betraying a village tucked away in the valley, are for many people the quintessential England. The mysterious, haunting quality of this ancient landscape creates a distinctive culture and atmosphere.

Although it is barely 60 miles from the noise, bustle, and bright lights of London, the county of Suffolk, the center of East Anglia, could be in another world. (The other counties of East Anglia are Essex—from London up to Colchester—and, north of Suffolk, Norfolk, of which only Norwich and King's Lynn are covered in this chapter.) Perhaps because it is situated on the easternmost point of Britain, it has, until very recently, stayed aloof from the vagaries of fashion and modernization. The people of East Anglia seemed content with a bad road system from London because they felt it kept intruders out; only the hardy, that is, got through. Natives of Suffolk and Norfolk turned their faces toward the sea, rather than to the rest of Britain.

But everything changes. With the advent of the Common

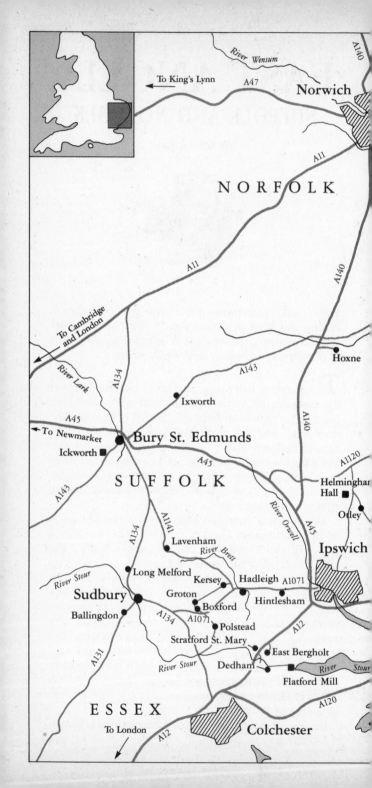

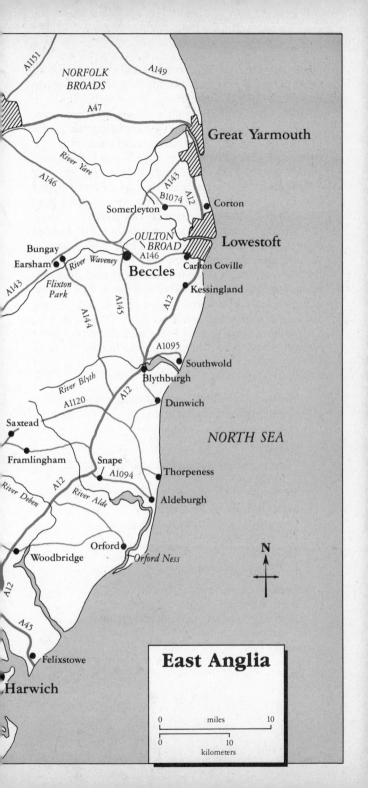

Market and the near demise of the London docks, the East Coast ports have come to prominence because they are numerous (Suffolk is a maritime county with 45 miles of coastline) and efficient, with excellent labor relations. Therefore the roads to London are improving fast, which, in turn, has brought light industry and electronics concerns to the area. Until very recently, laborers in these parts could expect to work on the land for their entire lives. But as farm mechanization increased and production dropped to fit in with the new Common Market agricultural quotas, the pool of the unemployed grew. This unexpected spurt into the 21st century by this most agricultural of counties could not have come at a better time: Today Suffolk has one of the lowest unemployment rates in the country. And because intervening stages have been bypassed, the development in Suffolk could well serve as a model for the rest of Britain. Most of the horrors perpetrated in the 1960s and 1970s by planners with grandiose ideas have passed it by, and modernization seems to have been carried out more sympathetically here than elsewhere in Britain.

MAJOR INTEREST

Tranquil, unspoiled medieval villages with small inns and magnificent churches
Haunting seacoast marshlands

Suffolk
Churches at Lavenham, Framlingham, and Blythburgh
Medieval village of Kersey
Abbey at Bury St. Edmunds
Ickworth art collection
Orford Castle ruins
Otley Hall
Framlingham Castle ruins

Norfolk
Norfolk Broads
Norwich: Norman castle, Bridewell Museum, cathedral
King's Lynn

SUFFOLK

East Anglians as a race, and Suffolk people in particular, are very hardy, having fought with, and learned to live with, the wild North Sea over the centuries. They are independent and private people, and they have an honesty that is very appealing. It is no accident that most of the great dissenters in British history have come from East Anglia. They also have one of the most attractive dialects in Britain, with almost every sentence ending in the interrogative. In the midst of Suffolk, you still meet people whose accent is so strong that it is almost impossible to understand them.

Suffolk has a rich racial heritage. In A.D. 43 the Romans came and made Colchester in Essex their capital city. From this base, which they called Camulodunum, they dominated the local Celtic tribes—the Iceni and the Trinobantes—establishing camps all over East Anglia. But by the fifth century their lines of communication to Rome had been stretched too far, so they departed, leaving the native Celts prey to the next invaders, the Anglo-Saxons. Like their successors, the Anglo-Saxons came over the North Sea; their intention was not to pillage and plunder, however, but to make their home here. They were basically village people who lived in small communities but who liked independence and self-sufficiency—characteristics they have passed on to their Suffolk descendants of today.

The Vikings, who crossed the North Sea in their longboats, were the next to land on these shores. They mixed with the local population, and their descendants are very visible today. Many Suffolk place names also show a Nordic influence.

After the Vikings came the Normans, in the Conquest of 1066. They themselves were Vikings who had settled earlier in Normandy and adapted themselves to the French culture and language. The Normans were great castle and church builders, and most of the castles you see today in Suffolk are Norman. Although many are in ruins, enough still stand to show how impressive these magnificent structures must have looked to the downtrodden Anglo-Saxon population.

The Flemish were another major influence in Suffolk.

They left Flanders in the 1330s because of restrictive guild practices and brought their technology, which was weaving, to Britain at the invitation of Edward III. They created great wealth in the area. Until the 18th century Suffolk was famous for its wool trade; it produced almost all the worsted used in England and nearly a third of the woollen cloth. The result of all this money and energy can be seen in the area's magnificent churches, built by rich men in gratitude to a munificent God. It can also be seen in the wool towns, many of which are gems of medieval architecture, with their half-timbered buildings a riot of color, ranging from a gentle shade of cream through pink and orange to a rather violent reddish-dung hue. These colors are actually all variations on a theme: The daub covering the wattle between the timber frames is a mixture of horsehair or cow dung, plaster, lime, and varying amounts of oxblood. Although the paint is now manufactured in a factory, an attempt is still made to emulate the color; in fact, you'll find Suffolk Pink listed in any paint catalog.

Of course, the traffic has not been entirely one-way. Early in the 17th century a group of Puritans set forth from the Suffolk coast for the New World. The best known of all the ships that sailed to America, the *Mayflower,* started her journey in East Anglia. The Puritans were the first of many dissenters to sail to America and found colonies. They named their new towns and villages after the ones they left behind, and the surnames of many of the eminent citizens on the east coast of America were originally surnames from the east coast of England.

As the North Sea borders East Anglia on the east and the north, the winds can be very bracing: East Anglians call it healthy. But the antidote to this is more sun than anywhere else in the British Isles. This fact, and the comparative flatness of this large area of eastern England, with its close proximity to Europe, made it ideal for laying airfields during World War II. Where sugar beet and wheat had grown in this excellent agricultural land, more than 70 airfields created what the locals called "the Unsinkable Aircraft Carrier." As a result, the last invasion of this area, in 1942, was a friendly one, by half a million American servicemen who joined the RAF in supporting and flying round-the-clock bombing missions.

At first there was suspicion by the English, but gradually friendships developed, many of which, after half a century, are still strong. In 1992, the 50th anniversary was celebrated, with many veterans returning to take part in commemorative events and activities.

Suffolk is a large and currently underpopulated county, although at the time of the Domesday Book in 1086 it had the densest population in Britain. But since the mid-1960s the population has grown by a third. Fortunately, the landscape has remained unspoiled and the pace of life gentle. Suffolk is expansive and beautiful in a quiet, understated way. High Suffolk, which runs from Cambridgeshire in the west to about ten miles inland from the coast, is rolling and fertile: a domestic landscape of fields and hedgerows, isolated and often moated farmhouses, and remote and beautiful flint church towers—far too many, it would seem, for the sparse population. There is a timeless and ancient feeling to this land.

Nearer the sea, where many estuaries punctuate the coastline, Suffolk feels untamed and wild. As you look across reed-fringed marshes, with the curlews wheeling overhead through the huge East Anglian skies, you will sense the mysterious quality of this area.

Over the centuries this conjunction of space and light has given rise to the greatest concentration of English artists in the country. Constable came from Dedham, Gainsborough from Sudbury, and Turner painted Orford. This still holds true, although now other kinds of artists—composers, musicians, novelists, and craftspeople—are represented as well. One of the best-known music festivals in Britain is the Aldeburgh Festival. Founded just after World War II by the composer Benjamin Britten, it is held for two weeks every June in churches, village halls, and maltings near the coast at Aldeburgh. (Maltings are large buildings where barley was malted for brewers. Now they frequently serve as concert halls.)

But don't assume that this most culturally oriented of areas has no outdoor life. On the contrary, this is one of the great sailing—as well as walking, hiking, and bicycling—areas of Britain. Horse-riding is also very popular, and several livery stables hire out horses.

June is a wonderful time to be in Suffolk, particularly with the festival to enjoy. But Suffolk is beautiful throughout the year, and there is always plenty to see and do whatever the season. In fact, it is difficult to write about Suffolk without constantly using superlatives. It generates them.

THE IPSWICH AREA
Stratford St. Mary

The entry to Suffolk could scarcely be more dramatic. A few miles northeast of Colchester on the London road, A 12, you descend Gun Hill into Dedham Vale, and there, on the far side of the River Stour, lies gently rolling Suffolk. It is unmistakable because it has hardly changed since John Constable immortalized it in his paintings.

The first group of villages you come to are all connected with Constable. The first of these is Stratford St. Mary, which was a Roman settlement called Ad Ansam. It has an attractive winding main street, bordered by a lovely stream and lined with interesting timbered houses and inns. The biggest is the **Swan**, a former coaching inn with stabling for 100 horses that was a main staging post on the road to Ipswich. Most of the pubs in Stratford St. Mary serve food at lunchtime, and the Swan has a garden beside the stream where you can eat and drink on sunny days. Like those in most towns and villages in Suffolk, many of the pubs here offer bed-and-breakfast accommodations, although the Swan does not.

The A 12, which used to be a meandering street, now runs between the village and its impressive flint church, which can be reached via an underpass at the end of the street. You often see this church in the paintings of Constable, and inside you will see reproductions of some of his works.

The church, **St. Mary's**, was built mostly in the 15th and 16th centuries by prosperous cloth merchants, although it was added to and restored by the Victorians. On its exterior there are some interesting flushwork inscriptions (flint and freestone decorations are called flushwork). These include the letters of the alphabet, which were probably used by passersby as an aid to prayer. The interior of the church is lofty, with a finely crafted 16th-century angel roof, a wooden roof in which angels are carved on the hammer-beams (short beams that project from the wall at the foot of the main rafters).

STAYING AND DINING
NEAR STRATFORD ST. MARY

If you wish to go no farther on your first night in Suffolk, you will find the ▶ **Maison Talbooth** at Gun Hill in nearby Dedham to be one of the best hotels and restaurants in the area. The hotel is a converted country house set in its own grounds, and very comfortably appointed. The restaurant, a beautiful medieval house, sits apart from the main building on the banks of the River Stour. If, rather than stay the night, you would rather carry on into the depths of Suffolk but would first like a civilized meal, this is definitely the place for you. Having a drink on the terrace by the river while watching the swans drift past will introduce you to the joys of Suffolk at the outset of your adventure.

East Bergholt

East Bergholt (just east of Stratford St. Mary), whose name in Old English means "wooded hill," stands on a south-facing slope on the Suffolk side of Dedham Vale. It is an unusual village: long and rather straggly, with six distinct settlements. Several contain modern housing built to cope with the rise in population that this area's easy access to London, Ipswich, and Colchester has prompted over the past 20 years. The heart of the village embraces the church, the post office, and several pubs.

From the 13th to the 16th century East Bergholt was an important cloth-making center. As a result, there are many imposing timber-framed houses that were built by wealthy cloth merchants (although several of these homes now have brick façades that were added in the 18th and 19th centuries). The **Hare and Hounds** pub on Heath Row is a good example of this, and it also serves a delicious and inexpensive lunch. While ordering in the bar, be sure to look up at the elaborate ornamentation on the Tudor plaster ceiling. If you wish a more leisurely meal, the **Fountain House**, right in the heart of the village, serves good English food.

East Bergholt must be one of the most often painted villages in the world. Constable, who was born here in 1776, depicted it many times; 21 of these paintings hang in the Victoria and Albert Museum in London. Constable was the son of a prosperous mill owner who wanted him to enter the family business. He actually did work at Flatford Mill for a short time, but fortunately he was allowed to follow his own desires. Although his birthplace no longer survives, there is a plaque on the original railings by the church to commemorate the site. His first studio, a small cottage in the center of the village, has survived and is also marked by a plaque. It is now part of the local gas station.

In the church of **St. Mary the Virgin** there is a monument to Constable's wife, Maria Bicknell, who was the granddaughter of the rector, Dr. Rhudde, and in the churchyard are the graves of the artist's parents. (He was not buried in Suffolk but instead in Hampstead parish church in London.) The church is imposing, even though the west tower was not completed when the church was built in the Early Tudor period. There is a legend that at the end of each day the Devil undid the work the builders had just done. Eventually they gave up and built a wooden cage in the churchyard in which the five bells are hung upside down. These are rung by hand, and it is fascinating to watch the bell ringers at work on Sundays.

Down on the banks of the Stour at Flatford stands one of East Bergholt's best-known houses—**Willy Lott's cottage**, which is instantly recognizable to anyone familiar with Constable's painting. Willy Lott worked as a millhand for Constable's father at **Flatford Mill**, and he lived in the cottage for 88 years. Constable also painted the mill several times. Built in 1733, it is now a field-study center owned by the National Trust; for information on forthcoming courses, Tel: (0206) 29-82-83. Other buildings on the old mill site house two museums, one with displays on the life of Constable and the other showing agricultural artifacts. There is also a tea shop.

If, after all the walking you have done, you feel like sitting down, you will find your opportunity here, for beside the little wooden bridge over the Stour is a mooring where you can rent rowing boats by the hour. Drifting along the water will give you another view of this beautiful river that has inspired so many great paintings.

Sudbury

Sudbury (northwest of East Bergholt, at the intersection of A 131 and A 134) is very ancient and the largest of the wool towns. It is a center for the surrounding villages and hamlets, and on market days, which are Thursday and Saturday, the hill in front of St. Peter's church is covered with stalls and thronged with people. People come not only to buy the fresh produce, clothing, kitchen utensils, and even car seats that are on sale but also to meet family and friends from the other villages in the pubs and tea shops. An added attraction on Thursday mornings is the livestock market in Burkitts Lane, and in the afternoon there is a secondhand goods and antiques auction. This market has been in existence since Saxon times and is noted in the Domesday Book of 1086.

Sudbury is an attractive town situated in a loop of the Stour. It has beautiful **water meadows** on three sides, which are traversed by well-signposted walks. These water meadows are unique in an ancient borough like this—in most prosperous towns any land with navigable water running through it is swallowed up for building. But in the 13th century the Freemen of Sudbury were given the ancient hereditary grazing rights to the common lands, which still afford grazing—and wonderful walks for everyone to enjoy.

The river saved Sudbury from the decline of the wool trade that hit the other towns in the area at the end of the 16th century. At the beginning of the 18th century improvements in river transport made the North Sea just 15 hours away by barge. Although the land distance involved is only 20 miles, the roads at the time were so appalling and unsafe that the river trip was infinitely preferable. At the same time Sudbury's quay and warehouse were built in Quay Lane. With the coming of the railways in 1850, however, these buildings gradually fell into disrepair, and it is only recently that restoration has begun. The **Sudbury Quay** has been imaginatively restored by the Sudbury Dramatic Society, who reopened it in 1981 as an arts center, with a cinema, a theater, and a restaurant and bar with tables on the riverbank. While this conversion was taking place, the River Stour Trust dredged the channel and rescued a Stour lighter, one of the barges that plied its trade on the waterway, and it can be seen at the quay at any time.

Ironically, the railways that replaced the river have in turn gone into decline, and there is now infrequent train service to the south and none at all to the north. The track that went to Bury St. Edmunds has been lifted altogether, and the two-and-a-half-mile **Valley Walk** to Long Melford now runs along it. The station buildings have been turned into the town's museum.

The Market Hill, St. Peter's church (now redundant—that is, no longer needed by the parishioners and under the care of the Redundant Churches Fund), and a statue of Thomas Gainsborough are at the center of town. Roads radiate from here; on the roads to the west, particularly, there are several very fine timbered houses, notably the

Chantry and the Salter's Hall on Stour Street and the 15th-century Priory Gate (all that remains of the 13th-century Dominican priory) on Friars Street.

The wealth of Sudbury came not only from the wool trade but also from silk weaving. The town still has rows of three-storied silk weavers' cottages, with large first-floor windows where the loom stood. Even today fine silk is woven here, including that used to make the wedding dress of the current Princess of Wales.

Thomas Gainsborough was born in Sudbury in 1727 on what is now called Gainsborough Street. **Gainsborough's House** is actually two 15th-century cottages, but two years before Thomas was born his father connected them with the red-brick façade we see today. The house has been turned into a museum, with a permanent display of some of Gainsborough's work, including a marvelous and recently discovered painting of Hadleigh Church that he did when he was only 15 years old.

Past Gainsborough's House, the road turns right to **St. Gregory's Church**, the mother church of Sudbury. Part of this handsome structure may date back to the eighth century, although Simon of Sudbury, named archbishop of Canterbury in 1375, was responsible for much of the building we see today. This remarkable local man became chaplain to Pope Innocent VI in Rome, then papal nuncio to Edward III, before becoming chancellor of England in 1380. One of his acts was to impose a poll tax of three groats per head. The downtrodden and poverty-stricken peasants, led by Wat Tyler, responded with the Peasants' Revolt in 1381. They marched on London, extracted Simon from the Tower of London, where he had taken refuge, and beheaded him on Tower Hill. Then they displayed his head on London Bridge. His body was buried in Canterbury Cathedral, but his head is contained in the vestry of this church and can be seen upon request.

Near the entrance to the churchyard is a small green. There is a touching memorial here to the 486th Bombardment Group of the U.S. Air Force, which flew 191 combat missions over Nazi-occupied Europe from May 1944 to July 1945. During World War II many U.S. forces were stationed in Suffolk because it was flat enough for airfields and near the Continent. Several USAF bases remain here.

STAYING AND DINING IN SUDBURY

Where there is a river, there is often a mill with its millpond; Sudbury is no exception. But when the mill here ceased to be used for milling, it was imaginatively converted into a hotel, the ▶ **Mill Hotel**. Extensively refurbished recently, this hotel still retains much of its original character. The Meadow Bar boasts two blazing log fires and is separated by the 103-year-old mill wheel, which still works, from the restaurant, which is itself the miller's house, now 300 years old. The hotel has fishing rights to the adjacent stretch of the River Stour.

Beside the Priory Gate on Friars Street is the oldest inn in Sudbury, the 400-year-old **Ship and Star**. This was probably the priory's guest house for pilgrims, but it is now an interesting pub and a good spot for lunch. If you wish to have something more substantial, **Friars Restaurant**, just a few yards away, serves British food in its 15th-century establishment.

Long Melford

Long Melford (north of Sudbury on A 134) is aptly named. The beautiful tree-lined main street is more than a mile long, and it is one of the widest in Suffolk. It has an attractive mixture of shops and houses, mostly timber framed, though many were refronted in the 18th and 19th centuries. Many of the shops sell antiques; Long Melford is in fact one of Britain's most important antiques centers. Under the west side of the High Street is one of the largest Roman settlements discovered in Britain.

After the road crosses the bridge, at the mill ford, the village opens up into a huge village green; it is triangular in shape and one of the largest in Suffolk. On the edge of the green stands **Melford Hall**. This imposing, turreted, red-brick house, set behind a high wall and an interesting gatehouse, was built in the 16th century and is where Queen Elizabeth I began her Suffolk perambulations in 1578. It is now administered by the National Trust and is open to the public.

The other large house in the village is a moated Elizabethan house, **Kentwell Hall**, which is approached down a long avenue of lime trees planted in 1678. This house had become derelict, but in 1970 the new (and present) owners began a careful restoration of it. It is open to the public. On several weekends a historical re-creation of the Tudor period takes place here, with the staff dressing, talking, and behaving as they would have in Tudor times.

Long Melford Church has been called the jewel in the crown of Suffolk; it can certainly lay claim to being the most beautiful of the county's 500 churches. It stands on the highest point of the green, behind the Holy Trinity Hospital almshouses, and in appearance is more like a cathedral than a church. As with so many other churches, the previous church on this site has been incorporated into the present 15th-century structure. Inside the church the overwhelming impression is of incredible light, particularly on a fine day, when the sunlight pours through the clerestory windows. In all, there are 100 large windows.

Like many churches in Suffolk, this one suffered both during the Reformation and at the hands of General Dowsing, the parliamentary commissioner for Oliver Cromwell, who was put in charge of removing, by whatever means he had at hand, any popish imagery he could find. This included stained glass, font covers, bench ends, and, of course, commemorative brass. His soldiers shot at the decorative glass and angel bosses (highly colored plasterwork or wooden angels) in the roofs; with their swords they would slash bench ends; and it was not unknown for them to stable their horses in the naves of churches.

Fortunately, though, a great deal of the medieval glass was spared here and can be seen in the windows commemorating the Clopton family, who were great benefactors. In the Clopton Chapel, through the door on the left at the east end of the church, is one of the most important pieces. It is a tiny lily window that represents the Holy Trinity. The corresponding chapel on the other side of the high altar is the Lady Chapel; its entrance is outside the church, through the door near the porch. It was used as a schoolroom in the past, and there is still a multiplication table on the wall.

STAYING AND DINING
IN LONG MELFORD

There are so many pubs, hotels, and restaurants in Long Melford that it is difficult to choose where to eat. The picturesque coaching inn, the ▶ Bull Hotel, serves all types of food and has rooms available. It is owned by Forte, with the standards of service one gets from such an enormous chain. But the building is beautiful, with low ceilings, beams, and log fires, and the rooms comfortable, with en-suite facilities. For a more personal ambience, as well as very good food, the ▶ Black Lion Hotel and Countrymen Restaurant on the green is the place to go. The Black Lion is owned by Stephen and Janet Errington;

staying here is like spending time in an English country house. Quite apart from charming bedrooms with en-suite facilities, there are maps and reference books to help you enjoy your stay in the area, and games to play on the few rainy days. For a cozy and simple lunchtime pub, the **Crown Inn**, opposite the Bull, fits the bill nicely.

Lavenham

Lavenham (northeast of Long Melford on A 1141) is one of the finest medieval towns in England, and it is the most famous of the wool towns. So picturesque is it that the local inhabitants have to suffer not only tourists but regular invasions by film and television companies as well. It is not uncommon to arrive in Lavenham and find the whole of the wonderful market square filled with actors in historical costumes, horses, carriages, and all the paraphernalia of filmmaking.

The town is built on a hill, with its triangular market square at the top. In the center is the **Guildhall**. This magnificent building was erected by the Guild of Corpus Christi—the guild of the cloth workers—in 1520, and it is now a museum showing the rise and fall of the wool trade. For at least 500 years wool was Lavenham's main source of wealth; indeed, during the reign of King Henry VIII, this was the 14th-wealthiest town in England. From the market square, streets run higgledy-piggledy down the contours of the hill, and each is lined with superb half-timbered houses and cottages.

A rich wool town would be expected to have a magnificent church, and Lavenham does: The **Church of Sts. Peter and Paul** is among the finest in Suffolk. It sits, dominated by its massive tower, on another hill to the south of the town. It has very elaborate flushwork, and the heraldic devices of the de Veres, earls of Oxford, and the Spryngs, a rich clothing family, appear many times. The heraldic device of the Tudors, the Tudor rose, is also much in evidence. John de Vere, who was the 13th earl of Oxford, was captain-general to Henry Tudor. He was with Henry on the battlefield of Bosworth when Henry picked the crown of England from a thornbush where it had fallen after Richard III died, placed it on his own head, and became the first Tudor king, Henry VII.

To the earl, the wealthy town of Lavenham was the obvious place to build a grand new church upon the accession of the Tudors to the throne. He approached the townspeople, who were enthusiastic about the idea, and over the next 40 years most of the old church, apart from the chancel, was pulled down and the present glorious church built.

The tower is 141 feet high, and it contains eight bells. One, cast in 1625, has been described as the finest-toned bell in England and probably in the world. From the interior the tower arch is very beautiful, as is the west window beyond it. Yet until 100 years ago it was obscured by the organ and the choir loft; then the organ was moved to the Branch Chapel. The bellows of the organ had to be pumped by hand, and, indeed, the handle is still there in case of emergencies. During World War II, however, the 487th Bombardment Group of the U.S. Air Force generously paid for an electric blower, which still happily puffs away.

STAYING AND DINING IN LAVENHAM
At the corner of Lady Street is the beautiful 14th-century ▶ **Swan Hotel**. This is every visitor's idealized English hostelry—basically a jumble of interconnecting houses, all beamed, all on different levels, and all with log fires. It is also owned by Forte, who own so many picturesque coaching inns. During World War II, the bandleader Glenn Miller had his last drink here before flying from the local U.S. Air Force base, and on the walls of the Old Bar there are many signatures and squadron badges left by U.S. airmen of the 487th Bombardment Group, which was based here. There is a memorial to them in the town.

Opposite the Swan is the **Priory**, which was the home of Benedictine monks until Henry VIII dissolved the monasteries in 1536. It then became the home of a clothier, and the original Lavenham wool mark remains on the outside wall. This is a magnificent building that, after years of neglect, has recently been restored and is now open to the public. Buffet lunches, as well as coffee and tea, are served in the priory refectory. Another good place to have lunch is the **Greyhound Inn**, a small and cozy pub close to the Swan.

Kersey

If Lavenham is a most perfect medieval town, then Kersey, 8 miles (13 km) to the southeast, must claim to be a most perfect medieval village. Kersey is set on two steep hills; its main street starts at the top of one, by the church of St.

Mary, and runs down to a water splash, where ducks have the right of way. The street then climbs the next hill. For most of its length it is lined with a picturesque jumble of weavers' cottages, pubs, and merchants' houses, outside one of which hangs the sign of a horse's tail, the symbol of a veterinarian.

Because of its commanding position the tower of the church is visible for miles around, and it is well worth climbing to the top to see its spare, simple interior. The oldest part dates back to the 12th century.

Groton

There is no village of Groton as such, just a series of small hamlets 3 miles (5 km) southwest of Kersey, a church, and, of course, a pub. Were it not for the Winthrop connection, one would drive through Groton without noticing it.

Adam Winthrop, a rich clothier from Lavenham and the grandfather of John Winthrop, was granted Groton manor in 1544 by Henry VIII. John Winthrop, who was born in 1588, inherited the lordship of the manor and was made patron of the church when he was 30. Twelve years later, in 1630, he led the Great Puritan Emigration to New England, setting sail with 15 ships and nearly 1,000 emigrants. He subsequently became the first governor of Massachusetts.

The old manor house where he lived no longer exists, but the mulberry tree under which he played as a boy can still be seen, as can the imposing church, with its many Winthrop memorials and tombs, including those of John Winthrop's father and grandfather and his first two wives.

The charming village of **Boxford** lies between Sudbury and Kersey, just south of Groton, in the valley beside the River Box. It was here that travellers forded the river on their way south to Essex or on to Sudbury. This village has a sleepy quality; there is a feeling here that little has changed in hundreds of years. Although this was an important wool town from the 15th to the 18th century, it was also important as a brewing town, and there was a sizable brewery behind the White Hart Inn, along with a large malting. All that is left now of this industry and activity is the pub. (Milling was the other big local industry.) Across the bridge is the lovely 14th-century church of **St. Mary**.

Hadleigh

Hadleigh, set east of Boxford in some of the finest countryside in Suffolk, is a beautiful, bustling market town. For centuries it was one of the richest of the cloth towns; now it is a thriving center of both commerce and small industry. It is also one of the 51 English towns listed by the Council for British Archeology as having special historical and architectural importance.

As is true of most Suffolk towns, its most noticeable feature as you approach is the church. But this church, **St. Mary's**, is different from others in the region because it has a large, lead-covered spire. The church and churchyard are part of a magnificent complex of medieval buildings, including the enchanting 15th-century **Guildhall**, which has, oddly, two overhanging upper stories, and the 15th-century Deanery Tower. The Guildhall was the home of the five Hadleigh guilds, which were social and religious organizations. The relatively large number of guilds reflects the importance of this town. The Deanery Tower served as the gatehouse to the now-demolished rectory. In Gainsborough's House in Sudbury there is a painting of this group of buildings as they looked in 1748.

St. Mary's is the fourth-largest church in Suffolk. Over the centuries, as the town became richer, the church was enlarged. But the tower is actually part of the earliest structure and is therefore narrower than the rest of the church. The spire was added in the 13th century, along with the Angelus bell, one of the oldest bells in the country. As you enter St. Mary's, you will be exhilarated by its loftiness, light, and immense feeling of space. Although General Dowsing and his gang of gun-happy Puritans did their work here, there are still plenty of treasures to see.

The town, like the church, is full of treasures, one being the High Street. Many of the shops show signs of their historic past, such as 17th-century pargeting, a form of ornamental plasterwork in which a pattern or design is applied to the building.

On Market Street there are many more delights. The tiny 19th-century Corn (i.e., grain) Exchange, built in Neoclassical style, stands next to the flamboyant 19th-century Town Hall, which bears a fine coat of arms depicting sheep and wool sacks—the source of the town's wealth in the past. In front of the Town Hall is a most attractive cast-iron pump, which is also decorated with the town coat of arms. The final building at the bottom of Market Street is 17th-century Toppesfield Hall. Although it is not particularly interesting in its own right, you should stop here awhile because this is the headquarters of the East Anglian Tourist Board. Although the parish churches are normally the best places to find the most comprehensive guides to towns and villages, it is also worthwhile to browse through the leaflets and pamphlets available here.

From Toppesfield Hall a lane leads south to the lovely River Brett. Spanning the river at this point is ancient **Toppesfield Bridge**, which was built in the 14th century. In 1591 it was judged "decayed and ready to fall down"— but it still stands.

DINING AND STAYING IN HADLEIGH
Among several pubs in the town to be recommended for both lunch and dinner is the **Eight Bells Inn** on Angel Street. It has a very clubby atmosphere; although everyone seems to know everybody else, you will be made to feel welcome. Just out of town, on the road to Ipswich, is ▶ **Hintlesham Hall**. This spectacular house, most of which dates from 1570, is an excellent hotel and restaurant, one of Britain's best. Expensive but justifiably so, a meal here (or, better still, a stay in one of the beautifully decorated and very large rooms) is memorable. Set in 175 acres of rolling Suffolk countryside, it offers a host of leisure facilities, including an 18-hole golf course, clay-pigeon shooting, trout fishing, croquet, tennis, and snooker and pool.

Ipswich

Although most streets in Ipswich (east of Hadleigh, and the largest town in Suffolk) have evocative names from the past, the past they evoke is getting harder to recognize as more and more of this country town is swept away in the name of progress.

By the seventh century, Ipswich, situated on the River Orwell, was one of the largest ports in Britain. It remained so until the 18th century, when it went into a period of decline. It was rescued by the Industrial Revolution and more recently by the European Community, which has thrust it (and its coastal neighbors Felixstowe and Harwich) into the forefront of trade with the rest of Europe.

In the center of town are a civic center (which houses

the local information office), a theater, several cinemas, and the town's current pride and joy—a leisure pool, with waterfall, fountains, and wave machines. Ipswich has a red-brick Victorian museum (on Museum Street), which shows mainly archaeological and geological artifacts. Close to it, in lovely Christchurch Park, is **Christchurch Mansion**. This E-shaped Elizabethan house, where Elizabeth I stayed in 1561, is now open to the public. Another interesting building is the 15th-century Ancient House in Butter Market. Now a bookshop, it is worth going to see for the magnificent pargeting and plasterwork.

Although Ipswich was a walled town, nothing now remains of the walls but the names of some of the streets in which the gates were situated, such as Northgate and Westgate streets. But the medieval street pattern survives in the center of the town, as do some medieval houses and shops. Some of the most distinguished of these are near the docks.

In East Anglia it is never easy to get away from Henry VIII, and Ipswich is no exception: This is the childhood home of his lord chancellor, Cardinal Wolsey, who was the son of a local butcher. On Silent Street a plaque on one of the houses notes this. In Wolsey's day the spiritual life of the town was well served by its many medieval churches. These still stand, along with one of the country's first Nonconformist chapels, opened here in 1700 following the Toleration Act of 1689. This lovely and very peaceful building, the **Unitarian Chapel** on Friars Street, is full of delights: The original box pews and gallery and an elaborate carved pulpit, which is probably the work of the master wood-carver Grinling Gibbons, are among them. It is situated next to one of the most improbable buildings in Suffolk, a reflective black glass structure that has won many architectural awards but does rather lack charm, particularly when compared with its next-door neighbor.

DINING AND STAYING IN IPSWICH

Like most ports, Ipswich has many pubs; one of the better ones for an inexpensive lunchtime meal is the **Swan** on King Street. Alternatively, for a more ambitious meal of fresh fish, go to **Mortimer's Fish Restaurant**, hidden away on an interesting corner of the docks on Wherry Quay. Nearby is the Old Custom House, a distinguished building of 1845. It was constructed at the same time as the 26-acre Wet Dock, which was once the largest in Europe.

For a port as large as Ipswich, there are surprisingly few hotels. So if you wish to stay, follow in the footsteps of Charles Dickens and Admiral Lord Nelson and go to the ► **Great White Horse Hotel** on Tavern Street. As coaching inn to the town, it has been looking after wayfarers for hundreds of years. The building was refronted in 1815, but the 16th-century structure remains behind it, although, like the town, it is getting harder and harder to recognize. The hotel, which boasts most facilities, has recently been refurbished.

CENTRAL SUFFOLK
Bury St. Edmunds

Just a country market town in size, **Bury St. Edmunds** (30 miles/48 km northwest of Ipswich on A 45) is nonetheless the second-largest town of Suffolk and very important in England's history. It has all the dignity and elegance of the Georgian age, but that is just a façade, because it is really a great deal older. The Normans laid out the town in a grid pattern that still exists, an unusual scheme in England, where roads tend to meander all over. Although the town's buildings are largely medieval and even Norman, many were refronted in the 18th century, giving Bury St. Edmunds an intangible aura of Georgian balls and assemblies (social gatherings).

At the heart of the town are the ruins of the great **abbey.** This was founded in 633 when King Sebert (or Sigebert) built a church on this spot in what was then the Anglo-Saxon settlement of Bedericksworth. It was burned down by the Danes but rebuilt in 903 to hold the body of the martyred King Edmund. Young Edmund had been crowned king of East Anglia on Christmas Day 856, but he was cruelly murdered by the Danes just 14 years later, on November 20, 870, because he refused to renounce his Christian faith. The Danes tied him to a tree at nearby Hoxne and used his body for target practice with their arrows, then beheaded him and left his body in a thicket. A wolf led the English to his remains, and this is why the town's coat of arms shows a wolf holding a human head.

In 1095 a stone church replaced the chapel. It was huge—more than 500 feet long—because the saint's body had become an object of pilgrimage. Many miracles are said to have occurred at the church until it was closed by King Henry VIII at the dissolution of the monasteries.

But even more important than the miracles was the meeting in this abbey church, in front of Saint Edmund's tomb, of the barons of England on November 20, 1214. At this meeting they swore to obtain the ratification of the Magna Carta from King John; just a few months later—on June 15, 1215, at Runnymede near Windsor—they did. Among the ruins at the site of the high altar are two plaques commemorating this important historic event; one lists the barons who were present. The motto of Bury St. Edmunds is "Shrine of the King, Cradle of the Law."

The monastery here was one of the most important and powerful in the land. Judging by the remains, the abbey must have been enormous. At least once, in 1327, the townspeople rebelled against its tyranny and destroyed the great abbey gate. The present gate was completed in 1347 and is a fortress as well as a gate. The area inside is a pleasant place in which to stroll, with gardens planted among the gray-stone remains and a bowling green and a tennis court on the greensward that leads down to the River Lark. Spanning the river is the attractive 12th-century Abbot's Bridge; nearer the gate is the Old English Rose Garden. This was given to the people of Bury by John T. Appleby of the United States, who was stationed here during World War II. It is a memorial honoring the men of the U.S. Air Force who died from these shores.

The **Cathedral Church of St. James** dates mainly from the 16th century, although some parts are much older. It became the cathedral church of St. Edmundsbury and Ipswich in 1914, making Bury St. Edmunds the cathedral town of Suffolk. The imposing west front is richly carved with the emblems of Saint James and Saint John. The interior is lofty and painted white.

Close to St. James is the **Norman tower**. This impressive building dates from 1148 and is one of the finest examples of Norman architecture in Britain. It is now used as the belfry for the cathedral, with a peal of ten bells. It was originally designed to be the gateway to the massive abbey church, whose west front is across the churchyard. The west front is 250 feet wide, which gives some indication of the size of the church. This is the oldest surviving part of the abbey; three arches, into which houses have been built, are still visible.

Nearby is the 14th-century **Chapel of the Charnel**. The entrance to the crypt of this chapel was undiscovered until 1844; when opened it was found to be filled with bones to a depth of two feet.

On the far side of the churchyard stands **St. Mary's Church**. This lovely church is one of the largest in England. It was built in 1433 and is the fifth on this site. The nave has a magnificent angel roof; of particular note is the chantry chapel of John Baret, a wealthy clothier who died in 1467. Its decorations include 100 stars, all of which have looking-glass centers to reflect the light. In this church is the grave of Mary Tudor, onetime queen of France, and sister to the king of England, Henry VIII.

On the west side of the abbey gates is Angel Hill, a large open space that was very attractive before it was converted to a parking lot. Every Georgian town has an assembly room, and Bury St. Edmunds is no exception: On Angel Hill stands the Athenaeum, which was the social hub of the town. Not only were balls and masques held here, but famous actors and authors of the day gave readings of their works. Among their number was Charles Dickens, who stayed next door in the ▶ **Angel Hotel**. This attractive privately owned hotel, with its Georgian frontage, is still the best place to stay here. The public rooms are comfortable, the bedrooms are stylishly and individually decorated, and it is the meeting place of the town, so there is plenty of activity. Its cellars, which date from the 13th century, have been converted into an atmospheric restaurant.

Another attractive Regency building is the **Theatre Royal**, one of only three remaining Regency theaters in the country. It was designed by William Wilkins, the designer of the National Gallery in London, in 1819. Subsequently it fell into disrepair and became a brewery warehouse for the local concern Greene King. It was restored in the 1960s and is now very much used by the town.

Suffolk brewers generally make very good beer, and Greene King is no exception. You should sample their wares while in town, possibly at the **Nutshell**, the smallest pub in England. It is situated at the junction of Abbeygate Street and the Traverse. While it's definitely worth one glass just to say you've been there, only 100 yards away, on Whiting Street, is the **Mason's Arms**, an excellent and cozy pub. The landlord looks after his guests, and the food is good.

After you leave the Mason's Arms, continue down Whiting Street until you reach Churchgate Street. This was designed by the abbots to be a kind of triumphal avenue to the abbey church and was laid out so that one could look straight down, through the Norman arch and the west doors, right to the high altar. Unfortunately, the townspeople foiled this plan by slanting the street slightly away from the gate. If you look at the town map, you will see that the same thing has happened to Abbeygate Street.

Turn right on Churchgate Street and you'll come to Guildhall Street. The oldest part of the **Guildhall** here dates from 1250, but it was refronted in 1809, and the entrance porch is early Tudor—quite a hodgepodge. Continue up to Butter Market and to possibly the oldest example of domestic Norman building in East Anglia—**Moyses Hall**. This fascinating 12th-century building may have been a Jewish merchant's house, but he couldn't have stayed there long, because the Jews were expelled from Bury St. Edmunds in 1190. After many vicissitudes, including a term as the house of correction, Moyses Hall became the town museum in 1898. As such, it is interesting and well laid out, and it has good temporary exhibitions from time to time.

Ickworth

Just 3 miles (5 km) southwest of Bury St. Edmunds stands Ickworth, the home of the marquess of Bristol. This magnificent house is more than 600 feet long, has an impressive 100-foot-high central dome, and stands in a deer park. Although the land has been in the family since 1485, the present structure was built in 1800 to house the splendid collection of works of art amassed by the fourth earl, who was also the bishop of Derry and a man of outstanding wealth. Sadly, the bishop died before the house was completed, and his collection was captured in Rome by the French. But other members of the family were also notable collectors, so the imposing state rooms are opulently decorated and filled with a fine assortment of furniture and paintings, and an outstanding collection of silver. Ickworth is open to the public and worth seeing.

Newmarket

The approach to Newmarket (west of Bury St. Edmunds on A 45) is unmistakable. On each side of the road are more than 50 stud farms and racing stables, in which trainers keep and work with up to 100 horses at a time. Beyond the stables lie the heaths, where horses can be seen exercising from very early in the morning, a magical sight.

Newmarket has been the capital of English horse racing since King Charles II established it as the headquarters of the sport during his reign (1660–1685). He loved the town and was a regular visitor. In the 1750s the Jockey Club on the High Street was founded for gentlemen interested in the sport, but it soon developed into the racing world's administrative authority, and any raffish connotations it may have had in the past certainly don't apply today. It is very grand and respectable.

Horse racing is the main industry of Newmarket. Each year there are about 30 racing days on two lovely courses, the Rowley and the July, and on these occasions this sleepy little town bursts at the seams with people pouring in for the great contests such as the Two Thousand Guineas in the spring, and for the less august but equally enjoyable events at which winning and losing money adds to an afternoon's excitement. The Newmarket Sales are run by Tattersalls auctioneers several times a year and usually coincide with the race meetings. These sales draw horse buyers from around the globe.

STAYING AND DINING IN NEWMARKET

The town itself is basically one straggly main street, in the center of which is the ▶ **Rutland Arms Hotel**, built in the shape of a horseshoe. An attractive Georgian building that has provided hospitality to race-goers for 200 years, the hotel really comes to life during the race meetings, when its slightly raffish atmosphere comes into its own. It is possible to eat at the bar or the restaurant, or stay the night.

Close to the hotel is the **National Horseracing Museum**, definitely worth a visit. It tells the history of racing from Roman times to the present day.

UP THE COAST
Woodbridge

Woodbridge (northeast of Ipswich on A 12) is an old market town of great character set in the valley of the River Deben. This is a short, very beautiful river that offers excellent sailing, as it is only a few miles from the North Sea, as well as pleasant riverside walks for the landlubber. In the Middle Ages Woodbridge was a thriving commercial port, and a maritime atmosphere lingers still. It continues to thrive partly because of its geographical position, which makes it both a sailing and a holiday center, and also because it is a shopping and administrative center for the surrounding villages.

The railway line divides the town from the river. To arrive here by rail (take the East Suffolk line from Ipswich) is a great joy because the last mile of the journey runs along the water to the ramshackle station. On the far side of the river is the site of the **Sutton Hoo burial**, one of the greatest Anglo-Saxon treasures ever found in Britain. In 1939 archaeologists discovered the magnificent regalia of a seventh-century East Anglian king in one of the 11 boat graves that lie on the high land beside the Deben. That treasure can now be seen in the British Museum in London.

Beside the station is the newly restored Riverside Theatre/Cinema, which has a very good bar and restaurant. Behind this, on the quay, is the 18th-century **tide mill**. This stands on the millpond, which, when the mill was in operation, would fill up at high tide. The gates would then be closed, and the water would flow back to the river through a channel cut beside the tide mill, turning the mill wheel as it did. This is an unusual system, and there were few like it in the country. The first tide mill here was built in 1170; the present one, built in 1793, was in use until 1956, the last working tide mill in the country. The machinery has now been restored, and the mill is open to the public. The millpond has been given new life as a marina for yachts.

From the quay several charming roads and lanes lead up into the town. They are all lined with a wealth of interesting buildings, many of which date back to the 15th century. The main shopping street in Woodbridge is the Thoroughfare, and from it runs Church Street, which leads up to Market Hill. This street and Market Hill are lined with antiques shops (Woodbridge is an important antiques center) and picture galleries. In the center of the market square stands the **Shire Hall**. This elegant building, with its Dutch gables, is basically Elizabethan and serves as the magistrates' court every second Thursday, when bewigged barristers can be seen climbing the external double staircase to plead the cases of their clients inside.

In a Georgian house on the south side of the square is the **Woodbridge Museum**. Quite apart from providing a great deal of information about Woodbridge, this small, well-laid-out museum tells the story of the Sutton Hoo burial in an interesting way. Behind the museum is St. Mary's Church. Its massive 15th-century flint tower stands 108 feet high and provides a useful guide for yachters as they return to harbor.

STAYING AND DINING IN WOODBRIDGE

At the entrance to the market square is the ▶ **Bull Hotel**. Edward FitzGerald, translator of the *Rubáiyát of Omar Khayyám,* used to meet his friends in this 16th-century coaching inn. Tennyson and Thomas Carlyle, both of whom made the journey to Woodbridge to see FitzGerald, stayed in the Bull while they were here. It is a comfortable, but by no means grand, family-run hotel, in a wonderful location overlooking the Shire Hall. The public bar, much frequented by locals, serves simple food, while its restaurant offers a more extensive menu. Twenty-three of the bedrooms have baths en suite.

On the other side of the Bull is New Street, now a total misnomer, as can be seen by the great age of many of its buildings, including the timbered pub, **Ye Olde Bell and Steelyard**. The Steelyard was a lever machine for weighing carts and their loads. Last used in 1880, it can still be seen on the exterior of this fascinating building, which is a good stopping place for lunch, unless you wish to follow in the footsteps of the literary giants of the past and lunch at the Bull Hotel.

If you prefer grander surroundings, the ▶ **Seckford Hall Hotel**, in the country outside Woodbridge just 1 mile (1½ km) from Market Hill, is the place. Thomas Seckford was the local landowner after whom one of the streets leading out of Market Hill was named. He built the lovely red-brick almshouses on that street in 1587, as well as much of the chancel in St. Mary's Church. Seckford Hall was his family home. Sitting in extensive grounds, it is a beautiful, soft-red brick building, with a large terrace overlooking a lake. There is lots of atmosphere here, with everything one expects of a Tudor building, such as wood paneling and sloping floors. The rooms, some with four-poster beds, are large and very comfortable. Recently an adjacent farmhouse and barn were converted into suites and a leisure center, with swimming pool, spa bath, exercise machines, and solarium; there is also a nine-hole golf course.

Orford

The small and enchanting red-brick village of Orford (east of Woodbridge) is remote. It is bordered by the remnants of an ancient oak forest, and some of the trees that line the road are 1,000 years old. The present village is all that remains of a very much larger medieval port, evident from the ruins of the castle and the church. Over the centuries the river silted up, and the great shingle bank formed by the tides opposite the harbor mouth, Orford Ness, cut off direct access to the sea. Access is now 4½ miles along the spit, which makes it a very safe passage into a calm mooring and therefore a popular sailing center.

Although fishing and farming are its main industries, Orford is also a favorite vacation village. Possibly because of this, it has one of the best and simplest fish restaurants in Britain—the **Butley Orford Oysterage**. It specializes in smoked fish (which the proprietors smoke themselves) and oysters from its own beds in the adjoining Butley Creek. All three pubs in the village serve food of varying types; the most simple and most fun pub is the ▶ **Jolly Sailor**, down near the quay. It also offers bed-and-breakfast accommodation. The village pubs date from the days when the port was flourishing, as do the lovely fishermen's cottages on Quay Street.

All that is left of **Orford Castle** is the keep, the final stronghold in times of siege. It is well worth the climb to the top of this imposing 90-foot building because the views out to sea and of the surrounding countryside are spectacular. The castle was built in 1165 by Henry II to keep the rebellious Baron Bigod at bay. (The Bigods, the earls of Norfolk and a powerful Norman family, were among the nobles elected to maintain the terms of the Magna Carta. Over the generations, they participated in a number of rebellions against the English monarchy as the kings sought greater control.) Orford Castle was the only royal stronghold in East Anglia at the time, and it is the oldest castle in England for which pipe rolls (the building and financial records from the King's Exchequer) exist, as well as lists of the provisions needed to supply the castle's garrison. The castle must have been huge, judging by the remains of its fortifications, which can be seen in the form of small hills around the keep. This is a perfect place for a picnic: Children and dogs can safely run up and down the hills.

St. Bartholomew's Church, on the far side of the market square from the castle, is a massive structure whose tower echoes the castle keep. In the churchyard, at the eastern end of the church, are the remains of what must have been a superb Norman edifice. The early-14th-century tower of the present church collapsed in 1830 (it was partially rebuilt in 1971). As you enter the church, you will see three of the bells to the left, as well as the old village stocks, which, when in use, would have stood in the market square to detain offenders. Although General Dowsing visited this church and removed many of the memorial brasses, 11 remain. After a visit to the vicarage, and payment of a small fee, brass rubbings may be taken. In June of every year operatic concerts and performances of the Aldeburgh Festival are held at St. Bartholomew's. The composer Benjamin Britten performed his church parables here, including the first performances of "Noye's Fludde" and "Curlew River."

The **King's Head**, which is next to the church, was the coaching inn of the village; now it is a restaurant serving good food. The attached coach house is a well-stocked craft shop. The inn was also the distribution center for smugglers and pirates who plagued this coast from the 17th to the 19th century. Next to the Oysterage in the Market Square is a small and reasonably priced antiques shop; it's fun to prowl around it after lunch.

Apart from Havergate Island, a reserve owned by the Royal Society for Protection of Birds where it is possible to bird-watch with a permit, most of Orford Ness (the promontory opposite Orford) has been taken over by the Ministry of Defence. Although a ferry temptingly runs from the quay to the ness, the public is not permitted (but see Dunwich, below, for information on obtaining a bird-watching permit).

Otley

Just a few miles northwest from Woodbridge lies the straggling village of Otley. Although it is not scenically interesting, it has great historical importance. In 1602

Bartholomew Gosnold set off from Otley Hall for the New World in a 56-foot-long vessel called the *Concord*. After 49 days at sea he reached Massachusetts, landing at Cape Cod, which he named Gosnold's Hope. However, because his sailors caught many cod when they were fishing, he renamed it. Gosnold named Martha's Vineyard after his two-year-old daughter Martha, who had died just prior to his departure. When Gosnold and his crew returned home they were in better health than when they had left, so Gosnold decided, with Captain John Smith (of future Pocahontas fame) and several other East Anglian entrepreneurs, to return and found a permanent settlement in the New World. On December 20, 1606, a flotilla of three boats—the *Susan Constant,* the *Discovery,* and the *Godspeed,* which was under the command of Gosnold—left England. After a far more difficult voyage than expected, they reached what is now the state of Virginia and sailed up a majestic river, which they named the James River, after the king. There they settled on May 23, 1607, and built a township called James Towne. Sadly, on August 22, Gosnold died of swamp fever.

It well shows the adventurous spirit of the Elizabethan age that Gosnold left home at all, because his house, **Otley Hall**, nestled in the countryside near Woodbridge, is so beautiful that it is hard to imagine anyone forsaking it. The Gosnolds had acquired the property in 1450 but, because of their failing fortunes, were forced to sell the estate in 1674. For the next 250 years it was leased by absentee owners to local families, who retained its important historical features.

Today Otley Hall is owned by John Mosesson, who has restored the house and garden most charmingly and in keeping with the period. As Mr. Mosesson is very aware of its historical importance, he opens the house to the public on selected days. North Americans, as you might expect, are particularly welcome (Tel: 0473-392-64). The house has marvelous woodwork, oak beams, linenfold paneling, and a moat. It is altogether delightful.

The nearby ▸ **Otley House** offers comfortable bed-and-breakfast accommodations, with a charming hostess and delicious food.

Helmingham

Helmingham is just 1 mile (1½ km) northwest of Otley. Most of the village is owned by one family, the Tollemaches, and it is their house, **Helmingham Hall**, that sits in an ancient deer park amid large herds of both red and fallow deer. The family has owned the house since it was built in 1480. It is surrounded by a wide moat, over which a drawbridge is raised every night. The house is not open to the public, but the park and gardens are open on Sunday afternoons for enjoyable strolls along herbaceous borders and through immaculate kitchen gardens.

Framlingham

As you approach Framlingham (about 7 miles/11 km northeast of Otley) you will see three buildings that dominate this little market town. At the top of the slope on which the town is built stand Baron Bigod's castle and the large and beautiful church of St. Michael the Archangel. In the flat meadowland below is the huge red-brick Victorian school. Stroll up the hill and you will pass many more buildings of great character. Among them is the ▶ **Crown Hotel**, the old coaching inn where the mail coach would have called with travellers and the mail. The interior is cozy and beamed, and bar meals are served, as well as meals in the restaurant. The atmosphere is leisurely except on Saturdays, which are market days, when the whole town bustles and the triangular marketplace outside is full of stalls. The Crown has 14 bedrooms, one of which has an enormous four-poster bed.

Roger Bigod's Castle, which was started in 1100 by Roger Bigod, has an interesting history. The Howards, who became the dukes of Norfolk and the premiere Roman Catholic family in England, lived at Framlingham until 1555. During the reign of Henry VIII the family suffered greatly. Although the third duke successfully promoted the interests of his two nieces with the king, the results were disastrous: Both Anne Boleyn and Catherine Howard became queens, but Henry sent them to the block. Then the duke's son and heir, the poet earl of Surrey, was taken off to the Tower of London and beheaded. The third duke himself almost suffered the same fate, but Henry died the night before the duke was due to go to the block. The fourth duke was beheaded by Henry's second daughter, Elizabeth I. It is strange indeed that the family endured such hardship, because Henry's illegitimate son Henry Fitzroy, duke of Richmond, was betrothed to the daughter of the third duke.

Edward VI, the only legitimate son of Henry VIII, died

when he was sixteen. During his brief reign, however, he gave Framlingham to his half-sister, Mary, daughter of Catherine of Aragon. When he died in 1553, Mary sought refuge at Framlingham while she prepared to do battle with her cousin, Lady Jane Grey, who had usurped her throne. Nine days later she was proclaimed Queen Mary I here. In 1555 the Howards moved to Arundel Castle in Sussex. Eventually, the estate was bought by Sir Thomas Hitcham, who willed it to Pembroke College, Cambridge, still the lords of the manor today.

Apart from one dwelling house, no other building remains within the castle's curtain wall. It is still possible, however, to climb the staircase in one of the 13 towers in the wall and enjoy the magnificent views of the surrounding countryside from the top of the castle.

The **Church of St. Michael the Archangel** is a short stroll from the castle; indeed, it once had a private entrance for nobility from the castle. As you can imagine, the magnificence of the Howards is reflected in the church, and the Howard tombs are particularly outstanding. The third duke ordered the old chancel to be pulled down and a new one built as a mausoleum for the family. Even Henry Fitzroy lies here.

Most of the church was built between 1350 and 1555, although the chancel arch certainly dates from the 12th century. The chancel is unusually large compared with the small nave, but it is balanced by the majestic 96-foot-high square tower. In the nave, at the entrance to the tower, is an organ built by Thamar of Peterborough in 1674. It is the only complete one left (both the case and pipes remain), all the rest having been destroyed during the Commonwealth. As a result, it is much in demand by organists from around the world. The final treasure here is *The Glory,* the mystical painting at the center of the church's reredos, which dates from 1720. *The Glory* is depicted as a flame-colored circle surrounded by clouds and symbolizes looking through the veil into eternity. It is truly magnificent.

Just a mile to the west of Framlingham, on Saxtead Green, stands a fine example of a Suffolk **post mill** still in working order. This windmill dates from 1796, although records of mills on this site date back to 1309. It is open to the public.

Aldeburgh

The fame of Aldeburgh (east of Framlingham on A 1094) is disproportionate to its size. Composer Benjamin Britten and singer Peter Pears came to live here in 1946; in 1948 they founded the **Aldeburgh Festival**, one of the most famous music festivals in Britain. Over time the increasingly prestigious event outgrew the small seaside town that spawned it. Several years ago the Aldeburgh Festival managed to acquire the Maltings at Snape, a few miles inland, and convert them into a magnificent concert hall with adjoining rehearsal rooms and master class studios.

In 1745, the poet George Crabbe was born here while his father was the local customs and excise officer—probably a fairly thankless task because of all the smuggling along the coast at that time. Crabbe wrote about his hometown in a poem called "The Borough," and one of the characters in it was the fisherman Peter Grimes; Benjamin Britten turned this tragic story into his first great opera.

Aldeburgh is also famous for having a lazy wind—one that blows through, not around, you. But on a sunny summer day, this is the most enchanting of English seaside towns, and even on a bleak winter day it has a unique fascination.

Although Aldeburgh is the home of many writers, musicians, and artists, it is also very much a fishermen's town, from the fishing boats pulled up on the shingle beach to the huts where the catch is sold. And when the festival-goers leave the **Cross Keys** pub on Crag Path, it reverts to the locals, many of whom are fishermen. This atmospheric pub serves a very good lunch. On a sunny day you can sit outside, watch the seaside activity, and admire the lifeboat that stands on the shingle at the station of the Royal National Lifeboat Institution, just behind the pub.

From the 15th to the 17th century this town was a prosperous port. But as with many towns on this part of the East Coast, much of Aldeburgh has disappeared under the sea over the centuries. In the past 400 years alone at least half the town has vanished. In the old council chamber of the town, the Tudor **Moot Hall**, which stands on the edge of the sea, there is a small museum of local history; among the interesting artifacts on display are two maps, one showing the Moot Hall in its present position on the edge of the sea and the other showing it as it was in the past, standing in the center of town. Just south of the town, the former village of Slaughden disappeared within the last century. All that remains is the Martello Tower, standing in splendid isolation on its spit of land between the River Alde and the sea. This is the most northerly of the great impenetrable fortresses built during the Napoleonic Wars. In this century, buildings put up for similar reasons (though not, of course, against the French) are the concrete pillboxes that can be seen in fields on the side of the road as you approach Aldeburgh.

The **Parish Church of St. Peter and St. Paul** stands on the high ground at the entrance to the old town, and it is a noted landmark for sailors. The original church was Norman, but in 1525 it was altered and enlarged. It has been the setting for many illustrious concerts of the Aldeburgh Festival over the years, and it is fitting that the graveyard is the final resting place for festival founders Britten and Pears. The parents of the poet George Crabbe, who was also the curate of this church in 1781, are buried here too. There is a bust of Crabbe in the Chapel of St. Clement and St. Catherine. Close by is the Benjamin Britten Memorial Window. It is the work of artist John Piper, a close friend of Britten's, and it depicts the composer's church parables "Curlew River," "The Burning Fiery Furnace," and "The Prodigal Son."

STAYING AND DINING IN ALDEBURGH

Opposite the church is a large Georgian house, now the ▶ **Uplands Hotel**. This comfortable, privately run inn has 20 bedrooms, most with private bath. The fact that the rooms are quite small is compensated for by the friendly service. This interesting house was the childhood home of the remarkable Elizabeth Garrett Anderson, the first woman in Britain to qualify as a physician and a surgeon, who in 1908 also became the first woman mayor of Aldeburgh.

At the bottom of the hill, to the left on the seafront, is the ▶ **Wentworth Hotel**, a pleasant place both to eat and to stay. It had been in the hands of one family for nearly 60 years when present owner Michael Pritt took it over in 1978 and carried out extensive and attractive renovations. The public rooms, which are light and airy, face the sea. The bedrooms are nicely decorated and comfortable, and most have en-suite facilities. The hotel is popular with musicians during Festival time.

Thorpeness

Just a mile north along the beach from Aldeburgh is the village of **Thorpeness**, the brainchild of one man, Stuart Ogilvie, who designed it as a holiday village in 1910. He created the Meare, a delightful and shallow lake where children can rent boats and go off adventuring to the Pirates' Lair, Peter Pan's Island, and Wendy's House. It's all slightly shabby now but still enormous fun for children, and it also has good picnicking sites (if the ducks don't get the food first). From the Meare you can see the **House in the Clouds**, an eccentric building that looks like a dollhouse on a column but is actually a water tower set on top of living accommodations. Adjacent to it is a windmill, which is now the information center for the Suffolk Heritage Coast.

The beach at Thorpeness is one of the best in Suffolk. If you are brave enough to venture into the cold North Sea you will find that the water is marginally warmed by the outfall from Sizewell Nuclear Power Station, which is a mile to the north along the coast—perhaps a dubious benefit. A more positive aspect of the coast is that there are two fine golf courses here, at Thorpeness and Aldeburgh.

Dunwich

Another few miles along the coast north of Aldeburgh is the minute cliff-top village of Dunwich. Like Aldeburgh, this village has suffered from the rampaging sea, but to a much greater extent. In the seventh century Dunwich was such a large and prosperous city that Saint Felix, the first bishop of East Anglia, set up the first Cathedral See of East Anglia here, effectively making this the regional capital. In the early Middle Ages the sea, on which the fortunes of this great port depended, started to invade, and since then almost everything that existed here has been washed away, including nine medieval churches and two monasteries. The last of these, All Saints, disappeared at the beginning of this century, leaving one solitary tombstone on the cliff as a memorial. There is a local legend that when a gale is blowing at sea, the bells of the churches can be heard ringing beneath the waves. The little local museum is an easy way to learn about this lost city. There is a good pub here, the **Ship Inn**, which serves food and where, if you engage a local in conversation, you may be told many more legends of this extraordinary part of the coast.

Adjacent to the village is Dunwich Heath and Minsmere Reserve. Here there are hides (blinds), run by the Royal Society for the Protection of Birds, from which you can watch the ever-fascinating bird life of the Suffolk coast. (For permission to use the hides write to: Royal Society for the Protection of Birds, The Lodge, Sandy, Bedfordshire SG19 2DL; Tel: 0767-68-05-51.)

Blythburgh

Blythburgh, northwest of Dunwich, is another small village that was once a large and thriving port. Now all that is left is a huddle of cottages; the White Hart pub, which was the old courthouse; and the magnificent **Church of the Holy Trinity**, also called, with justification, the Cathedral of the Marshes. As you approach from any direction, its 14th-century tower dominates the skyline with breathtaking grace and beauty. Although the church is huge, the combination of its intricate flushwork and enormous clerestory windows give it an effect of almost floating above the landscape. The vast interior, painted white, is quite bare and wonderfully simple; its light and spaciousness will make your spirits soar. During the Aldeburgh Festival the church is the site of many concerts, and as you sit listening to the music, it is a joy to look upward at the angel roof. General Dowsing did his best to destroy this architectural feature by urging his Puritan soldiers to fire their muskets at it; in fact, during recent restoration work, musket balls were found in some of the woodwork.

Southwold

On May 28, 1672, the English and Dutch fleets engaged each other in the Battle of Sole Bay. It was a fight with no real victor but plenty of carnage. The previous day was Whit Monday, a public holiday, which for the English meant a day devoted to drinking. Thus was the fleet caught totally unprepared; hundreds of sailors were too drunk to move, and it took four hours to round up the few capable of getting on board.

The lovely town of Southwold (northeast of Blythburgh) is so demure and delightful that it is hard to imagine anything so horrific happening near its coast—so close, in fact, that the citizens lined the cliff to watch the spectacle. Yet on these same cliffs is another reminder of a particularly bloody battle: six 18-pound Elizabethan cannons, which were last used at the Battle of Culloden in Scotland, when the Scots were decisively beaten by the English. The cannons were presented to the town in 1746 by the victor, the duke of Cumberland. During World War I they were temporarily buried when the Germans, claiming that the cannons were fortifications, bombed the town.

One of the best-known landmarks of Southwold is the white-painted lighthouse on the cliffs. Also on the cliffs is the **Sailors' Reading Room**, which is open to anyone who wishes to look at its collection of artifacts, old photographs, and almost anything else connected with the sea. Close by is Adnams Brewery. Some of the best beer in England is brewed here, and you can sample it at the pub opposite, the **Sole Bay Inn**. The beer is still delivered locally by magnificent gray dray horses, a wonderful sight as they pull carts loaded with barrels through the lanes.

Special features of this delightful watering place are the greens, seven open spaces that were created by the Great Fire of 1659, when much of the town was destroyed. After the fire these spaces were left open as firebreaks. Much of the quaint town you see today was built immediately after the fire, and since this is the closest point in Britain to Holland, there is a strong Dutch influence in many of the houses.

From the greens, the great common leads down to the town marshes on the River Blyth and to the now silted-up Southwold Harbour. At the beginning of the 16th century the harbor was the source of much prosperity for the town. But as the century drew to a close the North Sea—which tends to eat away the cliffs of some towns, depositing them at others in the form of sand and shingle—did its worst by blocking off Southwold's harbor. Despite an attempt by most able-bodied inhabitants of the town on April 12, 1590, to cut through the shingle and clear the entrance to the harbor, only shallow-drafted vessels can use the waterway.

From the sea four landmarks mark the entrance to the channel: Walberswick and Blythburgh churches on the south, and the lighthouse and Southwold Church on the north. **Southwold Church** is huge, evidence of a once-large congregation. It is dedicated to Saint Edmund, the last king of East Anglia, who was martyred by the Danes at Bury St. Edmunds. Built in the 15th century, it is full of such treasures as the pre-Reformation pulpit, unique in that it stands on one slender pillar, and the glorious painted rood screen, which divides the chancel from the nave; it dates from 1500 and is one of the most beautiful in England. In 1930 the people of Southold, Long Island, USA, provided funds for the pulpit's restoration in memory of John Youngs, who in the 17th century set off with the Puritans from Southwold, where his father was the vicar, for the New World. He founded the settlement of Southold and died there in 1672. Another famous son of Southwold is George Orwell.

In the Lady Chapel are two interesting signs of Henry VIII's presence in East Anglia. On the roof are two carved bosses (ornamental plaster plaques). One represents Mary Tudor, his sister, who is buried in Bury St. Edmunds; the other is of Charles Brandon, duke of Suffolk, who was Mary's second husband. Together they looked after Henry's affairs in Suffolk. Other aspects of the church include the 15th-century Jack o' the Clock, or Southwold Jack, as he is known locally. He stands in the north arch of the tower, and when the service is about to start, he strikes the bell with the battle-ax he holds in his right hand.

STAYING AND DINING IN SOUTHWOLD

Southwold has many tea shops, but for either a simple or an elaborate meal the ▶ Crown Hotel is the place to go. It is almost next door to the ▶ Swan Hotel, the old coaching inn of the town; rooms can be had in both establishments. Both these inns are owned by Adnams Brewery, which, in addition to brewing some of the best prize-winning beer in England, delivers locally by horse and cart (the stables for the handsome gray dray horses are behind the Swan). The Swan has a beautifully decorated dining room, with excellent if expensive food. The bedrooms are adequate, but not to the same standard as the public rooms. The Crown is much used by the locals, less elaborately decorated, and less expensive. Both hotels have a pleasant atmosphere and helpful staff.

AT THE NORFOLK BORDER
Bungay

The River Waveney divides the counties of Suffolk and Norfolk, and the prosperous and attractive towns of

Beccles and Bungay are built on it. (Bungay is at the intersection of A 143 and A 144, northwest of Southwold and west of Beccles.) Lovely as the Waveney looks today skirting commons, golf courses, and children's playgrounds, it has been the cause of much death and destruction. From 802 to 1000 the Danes sailed up it in their longboats and sacked and pillaged the area. Part of the inheritance they left can be seen in many of the local place names.

In the center of Bungay, behind the Swan Hotel, are the remains of **Hugh Bigod's Castle**. From this huge Norman keep, which stood 90 feet high when it was built in 1165, Hugh terrorized the local countryside as had the Danes before him. It was not until King Henry II built Orford Castle and established a stronghold in East Anglia that Hugh Bigod was finally tamed. All that remains of Hugh's fortress are some ruins and fragments of stone incorporated in buildings throughout the town.

In 1160 Gundreda, Roger Bigod's wife, founded a Benedictine priory near the castle. As were other monasteries, this one was dissolved in 1536 by Henry VIII, although some ruins remain in the churchyard at the east end of **St. Mary's Priory Church**. In 1577 the church was full for morning service when a terrible storm suddenly shook the town. Lightning hit the tower, twisting the wheels of the clock and hurling down stones. In the midst of this tumult the Devil himself, in the shape of a black dog, ran through the church, leaving two dead men behind. A black dog running on a bolt of lightning can now be seen on the town's coat of arms. Renowned for its fine tower, this handsome church sadly became unable to sustain a congregation large enough for its enormous size. However, the Redundant Churches Fund has since restored it, and the building is now used for flower festivals, concerts, and exhibitions.

The very much smaller **Church of the Holy Trinity** shares the churchyard with St. Mary's. Its round tower is the oldest building in Bungay (predating the castle by about 100 years) and is possibly the oldest round tower in the country. One noteworthy feature of the church is its finely carved Elizabethan pulpit.

Bungay is the only community in Britain that still has a town reeve. The holder of this ancient Saxon office, which was replaced in most towns by the Norman title of mayor, was responsible to the county shire reeve, known to us as sheriff, who in turn was responsible to the king.

Market day in Bungay is Thursday. In the past, farmers and market women displayed their wares at the **Butter Cross**, which stands at the middle of the marketplace. This attractive centerpiece to the town was created in 1689 to replace a much older cross that was destroyed in a terrible fire in 1688. The Butter Cross was also where offenders were detained and displayed. The stocks were kept there, as was a cage for the detention of prisoners. For culprits guilty of more serious offenses, there was a small dungeon beneath the floor, and if you look hard you will see a pair of wrist irons fixed to a pillar. No doubt all this explains why the figure of Justice surmounts the cross, although, unlike most of her counterparts, this Justice does not wear a blindfold.

The **Bungay Museum**, which is situated in the Council Offices on Broad Street, gives a good view of the town. Its contents include a model of the castle as it was in the 13th century that illustrates what it would have been like to live there in those days.

One of the largest employers in the town is the printer Richard Clay and Company. Founded as John and R. Childs in 1795, it has grown over the years to become one of the most renowned printing firms in Britain. This is not the end of Bungay's literary associations: The famous writer Sir Henry Rider Haggard lived just a mile from the printing works, and the Aldeburgh poet George Crabbe spent several years studying at the grammar school in Bungay.

Bungay is also known to cricketers as the source of the best cricket bats. The willows are grown on the marshes and then made into bats in a factory in town.

Three miles (5 km) from Bungay is the village of Flixton. During World War II a U.S. Air Force airfield was located here; the village is now the home of the **Norfolk and Suffolk Aviation Museum**, which has a varied collection of aircraft from all periods. Also just outside the town, at the village of Earsham, is the Otter Trust. The world's largest group of otters is kept here in seminatural surroundings by the River Waveney.

The town has several good inns that serve lunch; highly recommended are **The Three Tuns** for good pub fare and **Brownes Restaurant** for a more leisurely meal.

Beccles

Beccles (east of Bungay on A 143) is an enchanting town with many Georgian buildings; it suffered a terrible fire in 1586 that destroyed most of the earlier structures. Even the 14th-century church of **St. Michael**, which was built of stone, was severely damaged when all of its woodwork, including the roof, went up in flames. Today the church stands in the center of the town, between the Old Market Place and the New Market Place, both very old. One unusual feature of the church is the 97-foot-high campanile, with its peal of ten bells, which stands apart from the main structure. During the construction of the church the builders felt that the cliff overlooking the River Waveney (on which the tower would have stood if it had been built in the normal place) was not strong enough to bear the enormous weight. The peal of ten bells is one of the finest in East Anglia, and the church is a center for bell ringers from all over the country.

Although there are several porches by which to enter the church, the most impressive is the 15th-century South Porch, the Pride of St. Michael. It is two stories—34 feet—high and has elaborately carved stonework that was once highly colored. The priest's chamber above the porch has a squinch window that looks into the church; through it the priest could watch the altar unobserved. This chamber is now used for Sunday school. Close to the staircase that leads to the chamber is the font. Its bowl was carved in the 12th century.

Another old building in the town is the 16th-century **Roos Hall**. This handsome Elizabethan structure, with its battlemented gables (gables designed to look like the top of a castle wall) was once the home of an ancestor of Lord Nelson. The **Beccles and District Museum** is in Newgate; here you can see a printing press dating to 1842, as Beccles, like Bungay, is the home of an old, established printing firm. William Clowes started printing in London at the end of the 18th century. The company moved to Beccles in 1873 and printed, among many other books, the works of Beatrix Potter. The town's Baptist Chapel is called the Martyrs Memorial after three victims of religious persecution who were burned to death in the marketplace in 1556. It is hard to imagine such horrors occurring in this peaceful town, but when Mary I came to the throne such things happened all over England.

From many points around town glimpses can be caught of the delightful River Waveney and the bustling activity upon it. You can get a particularly attractive view by leaning over the old wall on the top of the cliff behind the church. If you descend the steps here and walk beside the red-brick walls to your right, you will eventually come to the town yacht station. This is another good vantage point from which to observe the river life, and it is situated next to some attractive old maltings. One of these has been converted into a restaurant, the **Loaves and Fishes**, an interesting place to stop for lunch; the menu of good, wholesome English food has a strong emphasis on fish (Tel: 0502-71-38-44).

The little fishing village of Kessingland, on the coast between Southwold and Lowestoft east of Beccles, is the site of the popular **Wild Life and Rare Breeds Park**. The park has a collection of exotic wild birds and animals and, of all things, a large Wurlitzer organ, which is a great attraction.

Lowestoft

Lowestoft (east of Beccles on A 146) is the most easterly point in Britain, and the golden weathercock atop St. Margaret's Church is the first object in the country to catch the light of the morning sun. Since the 14th century, when the little fishing village started to grow, it has become both one of the largest fishing ports in the country and a popular vacation resort. Over the last 20 years it has grown even more as a supply town for the North Sea oil rigs and as a food-processing and shipbuilding center. Many of the huge trawlers that put to sea for 12 days at a time were built at the local yards, as was Richard Branson's *Virgin Atlantic Challenger II*. And, of course, when the fish is brought back to Lowestoft it is sold at the town's fish market, either to be processed locally or sent inland to be sold fresh.

The coming of the railway in 1847 provided a big boost to the town. It carried fish out to the great urban centers and vacationers into the town, where they could take advantage of the newly built pier and hotels and, of course, the fresh but rather fishy air.

The docks are in the center of the town, and a swing bridge over the main road allows vessels to sail in and out of the inner harbor. The two-hour guided tours of the 63-acre fish markets and the docks are interesting and sometimes include a tour of a trawler. Tours can be booked at the Tourist Information Centre, which is situated on the Esplanade by the South Beach. It is also possible to buy a box of smoked fish from one of the local shops to be sent as a gift to a friend,

Lowestoft is renowned for its miles of firm, golden-sand beaches. On the **South Beach** there are all the usual pleasures of a large English seaside resort: Punch and Judy shows, trampolines, yacht ponds, a pier, and a lifeguard on duty. Naturists (nudists) are permitted at the northern end of the **North Beach**, at Corton, where the beach merges into the dunes and marram (beach grass) hills. Still farther north is Pleasurewood Hills, an American-style theme park, offering a day's entertainment for one entrance fee. Lowestoft is also the birthplace of the composer Benjamin Britten, who later moved south along the coast to Aldeburgh, where he founded the Aldeburgh Festival.

There are many more recreational facilities in the area, as well as several attractive parks. At **Sparrow's Nest Park**, site of the local theater, is the most easterly public bar in Britain, the **Bar of the Sparrow's Nest Theatre**. The Maritime Museum at Bowling Green Cottage is also in Sparrow's Nest. On the cliff above is beautiful Belle Vue Park, the site of a memorial to the men of the Royal Naval Patrol Service who have no grave but the sea.

On Oulton Broad, one of the finest stretches of inland water in the country and the site of speedboat racing on Thursday evenings in the summer, is **Nicholas Everitt Park**. In the park's Broad House is the Lowestoft Museum, which has a collection of local archaeological finds and a fine assortment of Lowestoft's famous porcelain.

Just 4 miles (6½ km) northwest of Lowestoft is the picturesque village of **Somerleyton**. Sir Samuel Morton Peto, the railway builder and founder of modern Lowestoft, bought the estate here in 1844 and restored it. Today it is the home of Lord and Lady Somerleyton and is open to the public; there are many attractions for children as well as adults here, including a miniature railway and a maze.

NORFOLK

Norfolk, north of Suffolk, is a large county of huge skies, flat landscape, water, and windmills. With the Wash to the northwest and the North Sea to the north and east, Norfolk is half surrounded by water and, in fact, for centuries was inundated by it. In the 17th century Charles II invited engineers from Holland to solve the problem, which they did by digging drainage canals, or fens, at the west of the county, creating that mysterious area called Fenland. Having been reclaimed from the sea, the soil is very fertile— rich, black, and peaty—and the terrain is very flat, making for perfect agricultural conditions. Approaching Norfolk from the west you will be struck by mile after mile of neatly laid out rows of vegetables and small farmsteads. Because many of the roads are causeways, you have a perfect view down into the fields.

In the east of the county are the **Norfolk Broads**, another unique feature of the East Anglian landscape. A network of lakes and canals, the Broads cover a large area of Norfolk bordering Suffolk. Three major rivers flow into this system, creating more than 120 miles of navigable water. The Broads are one of the most popular holiday destinations in northern Europe.

Boats of all sizes, from a small Norfolk sailing boat to a large ten-berth cruiser, can be rented for anything from a weekend to a month (for booking information see the Getting Around section). For the enthusiast, the sailing boat is hard to beat, and it is a magical sight to see the sails of these small craft appearing to float through the fields. The waterways twist and turn and go back on themselves so much that the Broads often remain hidden until you are actually on them.

In the center of this fascinating county is the regional capital of East Anglia, Norwich.

NORWICH

George Borrow said, "A fine old city, Norwich," and so it is. It is also a civilized one, with the Theatre Royal (one of the best provincial theaters in England, recently closed for restoration but due to reopen in 1993), many excellent museums and art galleries, and much in the way of contemporary arts and crafts, both to view and to buy. Norfolk attracts many artists and artisans, writers, poets, and composers, who find the remote location and atmosphere conducive to their work, the locals tolerant, and the rents lower than in many other parts of England. This is naturally reflected in the social and artistic life of the county.

Probably the best view of Norwich is from Mousehold

Heath northeast of the city. Although Norfolk is mostly flat, Norwich is in a valley, and from the Heath you have a marvelous view down into the old walled city. In the foreground is the cathedral with its tall spire, which at 315 feet is the second highest in England (after Salisbury), and like Salisbury Cathedral it sits on a winding and photogenic river, in this case the Wensum. Another ancient building in view is the dominating Norman castle on its mound in the center of the town. Everywhere church towers rise above the fine medieval buildings; legend has it that among the streets and alleys of this ancient city there are 52 churches, one for every week of the year.

The Market Place

Although very little is left of the city walls, the area within them was for many centuries the second-largest city in England, after London. Today Norwich gives the impression of an attractive and bustling country town rather than a city, with the **Market Place** at its heart. The center of this large and colorful open space is filled with the gaily roofed stalls of the market traders, and it is surrounded by buildings from many periods. The largest of these, and one of the most modern, is the City Hall, which is at the top of the square on the west. (Behind it on Upper St. Giles Street is Greens, one of the best fish restaurants in the area). City Hall's predecessor, the **Guildhall**, is on the north side of the square. The latter, a church-like flint building, was started in 1407, and from then until 1938, 529 mayors presided over the impressive Council Chamber, with its 15th-century glass and Tudor carved ceiling. Displayed within is the sword captured from the Spanish Admiral of the Fleet at the Battle of St. Vincent by Admiral Lord Nelson, who presented it to the town. Nelson was a local boy, having been born the son of the parson of Burnham Thorpe and educated at Norwich School before going off to sea. Although built as the Council Chamber, the Guildhall has also been a cloth market and a prison. Today there is a magistrates' court on the second floor and, on the ground floor, the Tourist Information Centre, worth a stop not only to look at the architectural detailing but also to find out what is on in town.

On the south side of the Market Place is the magnificent **Church of St. Peter Mancroft**. It is a great joy to be in the vicinity of this church on Sundays, because it houses

13 bells, making it one of the finest and most historic set of bells in the world. The church is the center of campanology in East Anglia. Sixty feet tall from the floor to the great hammer-beam roof and 212 feet in length, with huge windows on the north and south, the interior of the church gives the impression of vastness and light. Contributing to this effect is the glorious East Window, a treasure that boasts some of the finest Norwich glass of the 15th century, the same era as the church.

All major cities in the 18th century had a place of assembly where the gentry, notables, and dandies would meet during the season, and Norwich is no exception. Behind St. Peter Mancroft on North Theatre Road is the elegant **Assembly House**, built in 1754 by Thomas Ivory. People would gather there for tea or to play cards in the smaller rooms, and balls and assemblies would take place in the lovely Music Room. One of the greatest of these events was the victory ball to celebrate the Battle of Trafalgar—the battle in which Admiral Lord Nelson lost his life. The Assembly House is a good place to meet before attending the Theatre Royal next door, as the Music Room is now a restaurant, with an art gallery in one of the other rooms.

Running along the bottom (east side) of the Market Place is Gentleman's Walk, a higgledy-piggledy collection of shops, restaurants, and pubs. On the right at the end of the walk is London Street, one of the main shopping streets of Norwich and very enjoyable to stroll down, as this was one of the first pedestrian malls in England.

The Castle

Standing on its man-made mound overlooking all of this a few blocks east of the Market Place is the Norman castle. Built originally of wood in 1067 in the first flurry of Norman defensive construction, it was rebuilt in stone about 60 years later. Its present appearance dates from 1834, when it was refaced with Bath stone. Until 1220, a Norman nobleman was appointed constable of the castle as the king's representative in Norwich, but from that date until 1887 the castle served as the county jail and, indeed, was the site of public executions. It is now a museum and well worth visiting. The galleries show the historical and cultural growth of Norfolk, as well as geological and archaeological finds in the area. But perhaps the most popular galleries are the Art Galleries, which have an unrivaled collection of the Norwich school of painting. The group of artists who formed the Norwich Society were all local men who painted their beloved East Anglian landscape. The two most prominent among them were John Crome, who founded it in 1803, and John Sell Cotman; all told, there were about 30 members, most of whom are well represented here.

The views from the castle's ramparts are spectacular, with the spires and towers of the city's 32 surviving churches much in evidence (several of these have been converted to other uses).

Around the Castle

To the north of the castle can be seen a network of little streets and alleys, of which the enchantingly medieval **Elm Hill** is the heart. From here it is a short stroll past the **Briton's Arms**, once a pub, now a café/restaurant and a good place for lunch. This 15th-century house, which, unusually for Norwich, is thatched, is the oldest in the street. Be sure to visit the **Bridewell Museum**, a display of local industries and crafts, in Bedford Street. It is fascinating, as Norwich has always had a wide variety of industries, mustard making, shoemaking, and printing being just three. It is housed in a 14th-century merchant's home, which became a prison in the 16th century and a factory in the 19th century before being turned into a museum.

A few blocks west is another merchant's house that has been turned into a museum: the **Strangers Hall** in Charing Cross. This large medieval house, the oldest part dating from 1320, is now a museum of English domestic life. The merchants who lived here were wealthy, leaving the house much enlarged and the many rooms filled with lovely furnishings. Just to the west on St. Benedict's Street is **Pinocchio's**, which serves very good Italian food.

Enchanting cobbled streets of medieval shops and houses, most of which are color-washed, lead down from the castle area to Tombland and the cathedral. At the top stands the old church of **St. Peter Hungate**, which is now a museum of church art. This little building is beautifully kept, with highly polished tiled floors and a display of medieval illuminated manuscripts and Russian icons, as well as fascinating ironwork signs of the mayors of Norwich.

From medieval times Norwich had a very strong, if

sometimes turbulent, ecclesiastical life. Most of the great preaching orders had priories within the city walls, which were demolished at the Reformation, when Henry VIII dissolved the monasteries. One of the very few in England to survive was the nave and chancel of the Dominican Friars' church. The nave is now St. **Andrew's Hall**, and the chancel **Blackfriars' Hall**. The splendid Perpendicular building, across the street from St. Peter Hungate, was acquired by the Norwich Corporation in the 16th century and has been used since that time for civic occasions. Many members of the royal family have been entertained here, as have other distinguished visitors over the centuries. It has a good collection of portraits of local worthies, as well as the last portrait painted of Lord Nelson. The halls are also used for art exhibitions, flower shows, concerts, and the like. There is a coffee bar/café in the ancient crypt, which is another good place for lunch.

The name **Tombland** is macabre but apt, because it was here in Tombland Alley that many victims of the Great Plague were buried. On a happier note, the annual Saxon fair took place in this large open space facing the cathedral close until it was transferred to the Market Place. Note should be made of the marvelously lopsided Augustine Steward house, built in 1549. (Steward negotiated with the Crown over the acquisition of St. Andrew's Hall for the citizens of Norwich in the 16th century.)

The ▶ **Maid's Head Hotel** in Tombland is a great deal older and more fascinating than it looks from the outside. Queen Elizabeth slept here on her perambulations through East Anglia in 1578. Her mother's family, the Boleyns, came from Norfolk, and her grandfather Sir William Boleyn is buried in the cathedral. Pleasant rooms are available.

Norwich Cathedral

From Tombland there are two gates into the **cathedral close**, one of the largest and most attractive in England. On the green is the 14th-century St. Ethelbert's Gate, which was built by the townspeople some years after they fought with the Benedictine monks and set fire to the cathedral. Not too much damage was done, but as penance they were set the task of building this gate. Opposite the west end of the cathedral is the 15th-century Erpingham Gate. This is built in the Perpendicular style, of which it is a fine example, and a bust of Sir Thomas Erpingham, who was the commander of the English archers at Agincourt, can be seen in a niche over the arch. On the left through the Erpingham Gate is Norwich School, founded in 1316 as Carnary College and refounded by Edward VI in his name in 1553. As can be imagined of an institution of such age, it has had many famous pupils, but probably the most illustrious is Lord Nelson, whose statue stands nearby. In its ancient undercroft, the school chapel once housed the charnel house for the city churches.

The great **Cathedral Church of the Most Holy and Undivided Trinity** is one of the glories of England. The Norman bishop Herbert de Losinga began building it in 1096, and much of that structure is still evident today in the nave and transepts. Great Norman columns march down the church to the apsidal east end, with ambulatory and side chapels. The side stalls are among the best there are, with carved misericords showing scenes from everyday life in medieval times. Behind the high altar sits the Saxon bishop's throne, the only one of its kind in northern Europe. The soaring clerestory and fan vaulting date from 300 years later and are glorious, as are the carved stone bosses, which were recently repainted and relit. The best way to examine the intricate detailing of these beautiful examples of medieval workmanship so that you don't get a crick in your neck is to look into the mirrors provided around the nave.

Although the original Norman **cloisters** were destroyed by the citizens' riot in 1272, they were subsequently rebuilt, and therefore they are a mixture of periods. They are the largest of any cathedral in England, with a vast greensward in the center. The cathedral **library** is housed above the cloister and contains many rare books and manuscripts.

The simple grave of Nurse Edith Cavell is outside the east end of the cathedral in a plot of land called Life's Green. She, like Horatio Nelson, who is also commemorated in the cathedral close, was the child of a Norfolk parson. She worked in Belgium as a nurse, remaining there even when the Germans overran it in 1914. In 1915 Cavell was arrested and shot for helping Allied soldiers to escape. After the war, her remains were brought back to England and given a funeral service in Westminster Abbey before being buried in Norwich. There is a statue of her in Tombland and another on Charing Cross Road in London. She is remembered each year on the Sunday morning nearest to October 12, the date of her death.

A walk east past some of the buildings that made up the medieval complex of the priory, including the granary, brewery, infirmary, and refectory, leads into a lane that goes down to the River Wensum and **Pull's Ferry**. This is one of the city's most beautiful spots, a 15th-century water gate. When the Normans built the cathedral, they brought the stone from Caen in Normandy. The lane to the ferry was once a canal created to transport building materials to the site of the massive cathedral.

From Pull's Ferry there is a pleasant riverside walk through playing fields to the 13th-century Bishop Bridge. On the far side of the bridge was Lollard's Pit, the horrifying place where many martyrs were burned at the stake.

Bishopgate, the road leading west from the bridge back toward the cathedral, is believed to be the Roman road that crossed Norwich; on the right as you walk along is the **Great Hospital**, built in 1249. Originally designed to house poor priests and laymen, it survived the Reformation by being taken over by the corporation, or city council. Today it is a retirement home, but much of it is open to the public and definitely worth a visit. The refectory can be seen, as can the cloister leading to the transept of St. Helen's Church, which acts as both the chapel and the local parish church. In the 16th century the nave and chancel were divided into wards for single men and women, and they are not open to the public.

If you are looking for a pub lunch this is the place to stop, because the ancient **Adam and Eve** is very close by. This attractive pub serves good, inexpensive food down near the waterfront, just off Bishopgate.

Other Sights in Norwich

There has always been a strong Nonconformist element in Norfolk, and this has resulted in several very attractive buildings being built over the centuries. Just west of the cathedral, cross the Fye Bridge to Colegate, once the home of the prosperous cloth merchants of Norwich. Two of the earliest Nonconformist chapels in England can be found here. The attractive **Old Meeting House**, which was built by the Congregationalists in 1693, is situated up an alley so that it could be defended against rioters, if need be. The Congregationalists were subject to persecution and had been forced to flee to Holland and North America (where they founded Norwich, Connecticut) before they returned home after the Act of Toleration. The elegant **Octagon Chapel**, built by the Presbyterians in 1756 and later taken over by the Unitarians, was the work of the local architect Thomas Ivory.

The Quaker influence in Norwich has also been particularly strong. The Gurney family, of whom prison reformer Elizabeth Fry was the best known, attended the meetings at the Quaker Meeting House in Lower Goat Lane, which is just off the Market Place. The building dates from 1679.

Close to the river was the cell of the 14th-century mystic Mother Julian, a Benedictine nun who wrote *Revelations of Divine Love,* possibly the first book ever written by a European woman. At St. Julian's Church off King Street, a chapel has been built on the site of the cell, incorporating stone from the original building. Nearby is **Dragon Hall**, a marvelous medieval hall house that was once owned by a rich merchant. It has just been lovingly restored and is now open to the public. There is a great deal to see.

The River Wensum runs through Norwich, and there are many riverside walks to stroll along. There are also cruises that can be taken for an hour, half a day, or a day—a lovely way to see the town. If you wish to stay beside the river, book a room at the ▶ **Nelson Hotel** on Prince of Wales Road. A large, modern, and characterless hotel, it is situated close to both the railway station and the yacht station, convenient if you wish to take a boat trip through enchanting and historic Norwich.

KING'S LYNN

Situated on the Wash, that great shallow saucer of water on England's eastern coastline, beautiful King's Lynn, 42 miles (65 km) west of Norwich via the A 47, is rich in history. Looking rather like one of the handsome Hanseatic towns on the other side of the North Sea, it echoes them in its reliance on trade and commerce. A self-confident, self-reliant sort of place, it has long had a strong maritime character that continues to this day. Some of the country's best examples of medieval merchants' houses and adjoining warehouses are actively used in this flourishing port.

At the heart of the area stands the **Customs House**, an elegant building adorned with a statue of King Charles II.

Built in 1683 by Henry Bell, mayor of King's Lynn and a renowned architect, it is situated at the end of King Street, which is full of superlative houses, among them 15th-century **St. George's Guildhall**. This interesting building was a theater during Shakespeare's time; it is known that his company played here. The Guildhall is now the heart of the **King's Lynn Festival** held in July, which features classical, jazz, folk, and other types of music.

King's Street becomes Queen Street, and the magnificent merchants' houses and warehouses continue; each doorway is intriguing. Look into the courtyards and you may see a Hanseatic warehouse or an apprentices' quarters or a counting house, all indicating how rich this isolated town was in the past.

King's Lynn has two market places: Tuesday Market Place (see below), at the north end of King Street, and **Saturday Market Place**, at the south end of Queen Street. Two buildings of considerable importance overlook Saturday Market Place: St. Margaret's Church and the Guildhall. **St. Margaret's Church** was built by Norman bishop de Losinga, who also built Norwich Cathedral; little of his work remains here at St. Margaret's. It is an interesting structure, very long at 230 feet, with touches from practically every period. Two of its special treasures are the great 10-foot-long 14th-century brasses, among the most important in England. One, dedicated to Adam de Walsokne, who died in 1349, and his wife, Margaret, has a revealing scene on the base depicting country life at that time. The other, dedicated to Robert Brauche (who died in 1364) and his two wives, holds an even more dramatic scene: As mayor of King's Lynn when King Edward III visited the town in 1349, Brauche was the host at a great banquet that is shown on the base, with table, guests, roast peacock, and all. The organ was installed in 1755 at the request of Dr. Charles Burney, father of novelist Fanny Burney, who was born in King's Lynn. Dr. Burney is the author of memoirs known to us as *Music, Men, and Manners in France and Italy 1770*.

Also on Saturday Market Place is the **Guildhall**, built of flint and freestone for the Guild of the Holy Trinity in 1421 and a fascinating building both architecturally and historically. The entrance is through an Elizabethan addition built on the side. At the back stands the 18th-century Assembly Room, the scene of many elaborate social gatherings, although two of the most famous ones took place in a previous building on the same site. One, described above, was the peacock feast in honor of Edward III. The other was a peacock feast given for King John on October 11, 1215, four months after he was forced by the barons to put his seal to the Magna Carta. The following day John set off across the Fens, which were not drained in those days and were therefore treacherous marshland. The tide engulfed his baggage train, and, although he made it to Newark Castle in Lincolnshire, his possessions didn't. To this day legends persist about King John's Great Treasure, and the area still attracts treasure hunters. Some surviving regalia of the period is arrayed in the Guildhall. The most astonishing, called King John's Cup, is a beautiful gold and enamel vessel that dates from 1340 and therefore can't be the king's (he died in 1216). But the sword on display did belong to him; he gave it to the town when he provided its first charter in 1204. Also on show are interesting records of King's Lynn and its history, which include that royal charter and all subsequent ones. Another place to see some of the local history is in the little museum in Baxter's Plain, near the South Gate, built in the early 16th century and the only town gate that remains.

The other imposing open space in town is **Tuesday Market Place**, on which the ▶ **Duke's Head Hotel** stands. This fine building, designed in 1689 (also by Henry Bell), is now a Forte hotel, and its large, airy public rooms and comfortable bedrooms with en-suite baths have recently been refurbished in elegant fashion. It is partnered in the square by many fine Georgian buildings, including the Corn Exchange and several hotels, and in the adjoining St. Nicholas Street and Market Lane are several interesting medieval houses.

North from the square are the docks on the Great Ouse, an aptly named river at low tide, if you'll accept the pun—it dries out almost completely, leaving steep mudbanks. A narrow muddy creek, the Fisher Fleet, leads into the great **Bentinck Dock**, built in 1880 and still one of the reasons for King's Lynn prosperity. This is a fascinating place to wander, looking at the flags of the ships that come into this small but important port to continue the trade that has been carried on here for centuries.

GETTING AROUND
To reach Suffolk from London by road, take A 12 through the East End. An alternative route, approaching Suffolk

from the west, is to take the M 11 toward Cambridge, again through east London, then transfer to A 45 into Suffolk.

To reach Suffolk by train from London, go to Liverpool Street Station in the City area. The trains run hourly and reach Ipswich in 70 minutes. To go on up the East Coast, you will transfer to the East Suffolk Line, which runs every two hours. Suffolk can also be approached from across the Channel, as it has several major ports. The main passenger terminals are at Felixstowe and Harwich.

Norwich is about 50 miles (80 km) north of Ipswich on A 140. The drive up the Suffolk coast on A 12 is longer (about 70 miles/112 km) but more scenic. Once in Norwich, cruises on the Norfolk Broads are an excellent way to see the county. Two firms headquartered in Norfolk are: **G. Smith and Sons**, Riverside Road NR12 8UD, Tel: (0603) 78-25-27; and **C. J. Lovewell Southern River Steamers**, 43 Ebbisham Drive NR4 6HQ, Tel: (0603) 50-12-20.

ACCOMMODATIONS REFERENCE
Rates are projected 1994 prices for a double room with breakfast, unless otherwise stated. As prices are subject to change, always double-check before booking.

▶ **Angel Hotel**. 3 Angel Hill, **Bury St. Edmunds** IP33 1LT. Tel: (0284) 75-39-26; Fax: (0284) 75-00-92; in U.S., (708) 251-4110. £99.

▶ **Black Lion Hotel and Countrymen Restaurant**. The Green, **Long Melford** CO10 9DN. Tel: (0787) 31-23-56; Fax: (0787) 37-45-57. £65–£85.

▶ **Bull Hotel**. Hall Street, **Long Melford** CO10 9JG. Tel: (0787) 37-84-94; Fax: (0787) 88-03-07; in U.S. and Canada, (800) 225-5843; in Australia, (008) 22-24-46. £80–£85 (breakfast not included).

▶ **Bull Hotel**. Market Hill, **Woodbridge** IP12 4LR. Tel: (0394) 38-56-88; Fax: (0394) 38-49-02. £52–£57.

▶ **Crown Hotel**. Market Hill, **Framlingham** IP13 9AN. Tel: (0728) 72-35-21; Fax: (0728) 72-42-74; in U.S. and Canada, (800) 225-5843; in Australia, (008) 22-24-46. £80–£95 (breakfast not included).

▶ **Crown Hotel**. High Street, **Southwold** IP18 6DP. Tel: (0502) 72-22-75; Fax: (0502) 72-48-05. £57.

▶ **Duke's Head Hotel**. Tuesday Market Place, **King's Lynn**, Norfolk PE30 1JS. Tel: (0553) 77-49-96; Fax: (0553) 76-35-56; in U.S. and Canada, (800) 225-5843; in Australia, (008) 22-24-46. £75.

▶ **Great White Horse Hotel.** Tavern Street, **Ipswich** IP1 3AH. Tel: (0473) 25-65-58; Fax: (0473) 25-33-96. £48.

▶ **Hintlesham Hall.** Hintlesham, near Ipswich IP8 3NS. Tel: (0473) 872-68; Fax: (0473) 874-63; in U.S. and Canada, (800) 525-4800; in Australia (008) 802-582. £100–£168 (breakfast not included).

▶ **Jolly Sailor.** Quay Street, **Orford** IP1 2NU. Tel: (0394) 45-02-43. £30.

▶ **Maid's Head Hotel.** Tombland, **Norwich** NR3 1LB. Tel: (0603) 76-11-11; Fax: (0603) 61-36-88; in U.S. and Canada, (800) 448-8355; in Australia, (008) 22-11-76. £78–£89.

▶ **Maison Talbooth.** Stratford Road, **Dedham**, Colchester CO7 6HN. Tel: (0206) 32-23-67; Fax: (0206) 32-27-52. £107–£144 (includes Continental breakfast).

▶ **Mill Hotel.** Walnut Tree Lane, **Sudbury** CO10 6BD. Tel: (0787) 37-55-44; Fax: (0787) 37-30-27. £78–£98.

▶ **Nelson Hotel.** Prince of Wales Road, **Norwich** NR1 1DX. Tel: (0603) 76-02-60; Fax: (0603) 62-00-08; in U.S., (914) 833-3303. £86–£92.

▶ **Otley House.** Otley, **Woodbridge** IP6 9NR. Tel: (0473) 89-02-53; Fax: (0473) 89-02-53. £46.50.

▶ **Rutland Arms Hotel.** High Street, **Newmarket** CB8 8NB. Tel: (0638) 66-42-51; Fax: (0638) 66-62-98. £65.

▶ **Seckford Hall Hotel.** Woodbridge IP13 6NU. Tel: (0394) 38-56-78; Fax: (0394) 38-06-10. £90–£99.

▶ **Swan Hotel.** High Street, **Lavenham** CO10 9QA. Tel: (0787) 24-74-77; Fax: (0787) 24-82-86; in U.S. and Canada, (800) 225-5843; in Australia, (008) 22-24-46. £110–£135 (breakfast not included).

▶ **Swan Hotel.** Market Place, **Southwold** IP18 6EG. Tel: (0502) 72-21-86; Fax: (0502) 72-48-00. £82–£116.

▶ **Uplands Hotel.** Victoria Road, **Aldeburgh** IP15 5DX. Tel: (0728) 45-24-20. £60.

▶ **Wentworth Hotel.** Wentworth Road, **Aldeburgh** IP15 5BD. Tel: (0728) 45-23-12; Fax: (0728) 45-43-43. £88–£109.

THE SHIRES OF MIDDLE ENGLAND

By Angela Murphy

Angela Murphy, a British free-lance writer and photographer, has contributed to a number of guidebooks, including the Shell Weekend Guide Book *and the* Hachette Guide to Great Britain.

Connected by the great motorway arteries of the M 1 and the A 1 as they stride northward from London, the Shires of Middle England are often neglected by visitors drawn by the obvious pleasures of Britain's better-known destinations. However, those who bypass this region—also called, less poetically, the Midlands—will miss some excellent attractions. Some of Britain's finest stately homes and castles lie within these boundaries, and several cities, such as Leicester, Nottingham, and Lincoln, contain both splendid architecture and fascinating museums.

Thanks to the improvements made in museums in the last two decades, history is not only displayed in buildings and artifacts but also superbly explained and brought to life. Some of the best places for a dynamic view of the past are the new castle exhibition and the Lace Hall in Nottingham; the prison cells and courtroom of Boston's Guildhall; and the displays in Gainsborough's Old Hall.

The landscape of the Shires ranges from the vast flatlands and gentle Wolds of Lincolnshire in the northeast to the dramatic heights of the Derbyshire Peaks in the northwest. In the south of the region, the hunting country-side of Northamptonshire and Leicestershire was the setting for thousands of 19th-century sporting prints—gently undulating farmland broken occasionally by woods and hilly outcrops. The geographic heart of the region, featuring great forested parks, is Nottinghamshire, the land of Robin Hood and his Merry Men. To the east, in Lincolnshire, vast fields of flowers and vegetables, criss-crossed by drainage ditches, stretch endlessly toward the Wash, a giant bite of sea fed by the Rivers Welland, Witham, and Nene. (This is where America's Pilgrims first gathered in worship and then set off for the New World in search of religious freedom.) The Peak District, in northwesterly Derbyshire, is an area of dramatic uplands, famous for its walks, limestone caverns, and impressive stately homes.

Throughout these shires, the cities and their museums hold many interesting relics of the Industrial Revolution and the burgeoning of manufactured goods—lace, boots and shoes, leather goods, and bicycles. The terraced housing and large Victorian factories and warehouses that survived the vast building schemes of the 1950s and 1960s tell the story of the population explosion of the 19th century and the steady migration of people from the countryside to the cities.

MAJOR INTEREST

Northamptonshire
Northampton: medieval history, modern market, parks and gardens
Canal Museum at Stoke Bruerne
Althorp House, home of the Spencers

Leicestershire
Leicester: Corn Exchange covered market, medieval Guildhall, Georgian buildings
Bosworth Field
Rutland Water: water sports center
Burghley House, monument to the Elizabethan age
Rockingham Castle

Nottinghamshire
Nottingham: literary associations, industrial history, Museum of Costume and Textiles
Sherwood Forest Country Park
Newstead Abbey, home of Lord Byron

D. H. Lawrence's birthplace at Eastwood
Southwell Minster

Lincolnshire
Belvoir Castle
Lincoln: castle and cathedral
Tattershall Castle: medieval fortress
Gainsborough Old Hall, Boston Guildhall, and
    other points along the Pilgrims' trail
Boston: St. Botolph's Church, fine architecture

The Peak District
Moorlands, valleys, caverns, and "edges"
Chatsworth House: one of the stateliest of En-
    gland's stately houses
Haddon Hall: medieval family home

NORTHAMPTONSHIRE

In the last century, Northamptonshire, north of Oxfordshire and between Warwickshire on the west and
Cambridgeshire on the east, had a reputation for being a
"county of squires and spires," the quintessential rural
county consisting of the large estates of gentleman farmers and little villages gathered around their churches. It
retains its pleasant rural air and attractive villages, and its
squires have left behind a number of important historic
houses that are well worth visiting. Those who enjoy
water-based activities will also find plenty to do here, as
Northamptonshire is crossed by a fine river, the Nene,
and two canals, the Grand Union and the Oxford.

Northampton

Northamptonshire has a rich and eventful history. Its
county town, **Northampton** (68 miles/109 km northwest
of London), was treasured by the medieval kings of England and once contained a large castle, long favored by
monarchs from Henry I to Richard II. Charles II pulled
down the castle and the town walls as a punishment for
the town's support of Cromwell during the Civil War. The
richly decorated Norman church of **St. Peter** on Mare Fair,
to the west of Northampton, is one of the few reminders
of the time it was a fortified city. Another sign of its
medieval importance is the **Eleanor Cross** at the edge of
the town at Hardingstone on the A 508. This was one of 13

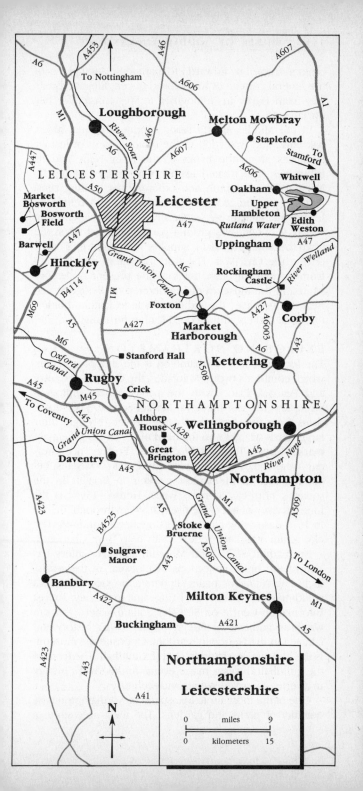

Northamptonshire and Leicestershire

crosses erected by Edward I to mark the resting places of
the funeral cortege of his beloved queen, Eleanor, on its
way from Harby in Nottingham to Westminster for her
burial in 1290.

In the Middle Ages a ready supply of animal hides,
oak bark, and water led to the establishment of leather
tanneries along the banks of the River Nene and its
tributaries. The treated leather was shipped along the
Nene to Northampton and other nearby trading sites,
and this encouraged the city to develop as a center for
leather manufacturing, especially boot and shoemaking
which, it is said, was given a particular boost when the
town became the main supplier to Cromwell's army
during the Civil War. The story of leather and its uses
from ancient Egyptian times to the present is demonstrated in the **Museum of Leathercraft** on Bridge Street.
Besides footwear, the exhibits include leather bottles,
medieval caskets, and modern leather furniture.

EXPLORING NORTHAMPTON

The focal point of Northampton is the shopping center,
which combines two new arcades, the Grosvenor Centre
and Peacock Place, with the pedestrianized Abington
Street and the vast medieval **Market Square**. The square
dates from the days when cattle drovers brought their
large herds straight into the heart of the city. On the main
market days—Tuesday, Wednesday, Friday, and Saturday—the square is filled with more than 200 stalls, becoming one of the largest markets in Britain. In the
square's northeast corner, **Welsh House** (1595) is the
lone survivor of a terrible fire that swept through the city
in 1675 destroying almost all its medieval buildings. The
city center was later rebuilt, with help from Charles II.

Northampton's **Central Museum and Art Gallery** has
one of the finest collections of footwear in the world,
including Nijinsky's ballet slippers and Queen Victoria's
wedding shoes. Follow the bridge link to the new Tourist
Information Centre on St. Giles Square, where you can
watch an audiovisual display on the town's history and
take tea in the Georgian tearoom. Opposite the museum
is the impressive Victorian Gothic **Guildhall**. The front of
the guildhall displays major events in the town's history
in a series of carved statues and sculptures.

One of the most attractive aspects of Northampton is its
quantity of parks and gardens. The most accessible of

these is **Beckett's Park**, just a five minutes' walk southeast from the town center on the banks of the River Nene, a very pleasant spot for riverside walks and picnics. The riverside path here is part of the **Nene Way**, a long-distance path following the route of the river; the Nene Way stretches from Badby in the west (2 miles/3 km south of Daventry) to Wansford in the east (8 miles/13 km west of Peterborough).

Around Northampton

Visitors driving to the city from the north or the south will probably travel on the M 1 motorway, which bisects the southern half of the county and runs close by the city. It also provides easy access to three of the county's most notable houses and to the canal museum at Stoke Bruerne.

CANAL MUSEUM

The Canal Museum is just ten minutes from junction 15 of the M 1, down a pleasant country road (A 508) to the little village of Stoke Bruerne. Here, up a low embankment, visitors will find a cluster of mellow stone houses around a lock on the Grand Union Canal. If you're not a canal enthusiast already, a couple of hours here will make you one. Have a look around the museum first to get an insight into a colorful way of life that lasted for 200 years before vanishing forever. The museum shows the life of the bargees and their families as they travelled the country's canals transporting goods from town to town. Adults, as well as children, will enjoy feeding coins into the working engines and models or watching a demonstration of the traditional canal-boat painting art of "Roses and Castles," developed by working bargees to decorate barge woodwork and their metal buckets, jugs, and similar items (distinctive images of roses and castles are characteristic of this decorative painting style).

The thatched **Boat Inn**, on the other side of the canal, has a restaurant and two traditional canal-side bars that offer excellent food. Here you can sit and watch vacationers and canal enthusiasts manhandle the massive lock gates to move their narrowboats through the lock. Alternatively, enjoy a leisurely cruise along the canal itself or take a canal-side walk. You can go southward where the canal drops through seven locks into the Ouse valley, or northward to the entrance of the 3,056-yard-long Blisworth

Tunnel, the second longest canal tunnel still in use in England. To book boat trips, Tel: (0604) 86-21-07 or (0604) 86-24-28.

STATELY HOUSES

In the southern part of the county, halfway between the M 1 and the M 40, is **Sulgrave Manor,** a fine stone manor house built for Lawrence Washington in the 16th century and located off the B 4525 at Sulgrave village. The three stars and two stripes of the family coat of arms, carved above the front porch, are said to have been the inspiration for the American flag designed when one of Lawrence's descendants, George Washington, was made the first president of the United States. "Living history" events are frequently held here (Tel: 029-576-0205).

One of the most popular stately houses in this area is **Althorp House** (6 miles/10 km northwest of Northampton on the A 428 near Great Brington village; signposted from junction 16 on the M 1). Princess Diana's childhood home, this is now the residence of her brother and his wife, the earl and countess Spencer. The original medieval mansion was extensively remodeled in the 16th, 17th, and 18th centuries, and it has a fine collection of paintings and furniture from those eras.

Just off the M 1, and by the side of the River Avon where it forms the Leicestershire–Northamptonshire border, is **Stanford Hall** (open weekends and bank holidays from Easter through September). This beautiful William and Mary mansion has been the seat of the Cave family for more than 500 years, and its collections reflect their diverse enthusiasms, from Stuart paintings and relics to motorcycles.

LEICESTERSHIRE

The city of Leicester is at the heart of this relatively small county. To the northwest of the city are the gray stone buildings and windswept crags of the Charnwood Forest, while, to the west, brick villages nestle in classically English rolling countryside. The far east side of the county is occupied by the district of Rutland, once England's smallest county, now one of its most attractive regions. Rutland resolutely holds on to its former character as a self-contained area, attaching its name to museums and other attractions. Also to the east are the attractive market towns of Melton Mowbray, Market Harborough, and Oakham, and the traditional hunting country of the Leicestershire hunts.

Leicester

Located 100 miles (160 km) northwest of London and 44 miles (70 km) northeast of Birmingham, Leicester has been a thriving trading center since before the Roman occupation, and there is plenty to do and see here. In spite of this, it does not attract visitors to the same extent as other major cities. Its historic buildings are not gathered together in a coherent and easily visited area, and building schemes of the 1950s and 1960s did nothing to enhance its attractions. Leicester's city planners are now rectifying this matter. Indeed, Leicester was designated Britain's first "Environment City" for its "outstanding achievement and ongoing commitment" to the environment. An attractive shopping center, The Shires, has been built in the heart of the city, and the pedestrianized shopping area around St. Martin's Square has been enhanced by pleasant seating, hanging baskets, tearooms, and even a bandstand.

Just southeast of St. Martin's Square, the **Corn Exchange** area contains one of the largest and busiest covered markets in Europe. It has served the citizens of Leicester for more than seven centuries and still operates six days a week, selling everything from cheap and cheerful knickknacks to foodstuffs from the surrounding farmlands. Principal market days are Wednesday, Friday, and Saturday. Try the bustling **Water Margin** Chinese restaurant nearby (76–78 High Street; Tel: 0533-51-64-22) for dim sum or a meal.

ROMAN LEICESTER

The Romans built a fort at present-day Leicester and laid out the ancient city of Ratae Coritanorum on the banks of the River Soar. The fort was a staging post on the Fosse Way, a formidable Roman road that went all the way from Axminster, in Devon, to Lincoln. The present B 4114 and A 46 largely follow the route of the Fosse Way through Leicester. The Fosse Way was joined in Leicester by a smaller Roman road, Gartree Lane, probably an early Roman supply route from Colchester. Its route is marked today by New Walk (see below), which runs from the university to Belvoir Street in the city center. The largest physical evidence of the Roman settlement is the impressive **Jewry Wall**, just west of the Guildhall (see below) near St. Nicholas Circle. This was originally part of a complex of buildings that included Roman baths. Next to it, the **Jewry Wall Museum**, one of several fine museums dotted around the city, contains a wealth of Roman remains.

MEDIEVAL LEICESTER

Occupying a prime position in the heart of the Midlands, Leicester continued to be an important regional center and thriving market town. Like so many others, Leicester's **castle** was built just after the Norman Conquest. It remained an important seat of power and was occupied in the 13th century by Simon de Montfort, earl of Leicester, who led the revolt against Henry III and became a founder of the first English parliament. Little remains of the castle now except its original motte, or mound, in the Castle Gardens by the river to the west of the city. The gardens contain a fine statue of King Richard III, who lost his life at nearby Bosworth Field. The castle's 12th-century Great Hall, although vastly altered over the centuries, still stands, within 18th-century brickwork that surrounds it, and is used as a magistrate's court. An attractive half-timbered medieval gatehouse also survives. River cruises run from the Waterside Centre in Abbey Meadows, near the castle, on Sunday and bank holiday afternoons from April through October.

Not far from the castle gardens, a few minutes' walk to the east, the **Newarke Houses Museum** has a variety of displays, covering local crafts and history, toys, games, clocks, and mechanical instruments, in a 16th-century chantry house once attached to a medieval foundation. This area was once fortified, and its 15th-century gatehouse (renamed the Magazine) now stands on the traffic island between Newarke Street and Oxford Street, housing the Museum of the Royal Leicestershire Regiment. Another reminder of the Middle Ages is the building once lived in by Leicester's medieval merchant princes, the Wigston family. It now houses the **Museum of Costume** and contains some interesting reconstructed shops. The **Guildhall** opposite is, perhaps, the finest of all the medieval structures remaining in Leicester. Built in 1390, it was used as the town hall until the 1870s. Besides the great hall itself, the building includes some early-19th-century prison cells, a 17th-century library and bedroom, and the paneled Mayor's Parlour.

INDUSTRIAL LEICESTER

As early as the Middle Ages, Leicester was known for leather tanning and textiles and, later, for shoemaking and boot and hosiery making. The enormous success of the hosiery trade depended initially on the stocking frame knitting machine, invented in nearby Hinckley and operated in cottages throughout the county. By the mid-18th century, approximately 1,000 knitting frames were in use throughout Leicestershire, and this number rose to more than 20,000 a century later. The increasing mechanization of the knitting frame also swelled the number of city-based small workshops, trebling Leicester's population in the 18th century. At the onset of the 19th century, more than 40 percent of the city's inhabitants depended on the trade.

Evidence of the town's prosperity at that time can be found in its many fine Georgian buildings. A particularly delightful place to search them out is in the city center on either side of the tree-lined footpath of **New Walk**, first laid out in 1785 and developed over the next 30 years. Although most of the houses here have been converted to offices, the car-free environment makes it easier to picture the city as it was in the last century. **Nikki's**, at the city end of New Walk, is a complex consisting of a nightclub, a wine bar, and the **Blue Elephant** restaurant, which serves Thai food in a light, pleasant atmosphere—ideal for a medium-priced meal (Tel: 0533-54-45-44).

New Walk follows the line of the Roman Gartree Lane for a mile and links the city center with the **Leicestershire Museum and Art Gallery**, built in 1836. Displays of Egyptian mummies and tomb ornaments rub shoulders with natural history exhibitions and a permanent first-floor gallery of paintings and sculptures. You'll find some fine early-20th-century British art here, including Stanley Spencer's *Adoration of Old Men,* Epstein busts, and paintings by Sickert, Wadsworth, and Nash.

The growth of Leicester's traditional industries and subsequently of a third industry, engineering, continued to increase the population of the city in the 19th and 20th centuries. By 1911 about 50,000 workers, nearly a quarter of the population, were employed in the interrelated trades of hosiery and boot and shoemaking, both now carried on in large factories. All three industries are still important here.

STAYING IN LEICESTER

Leicester has several large, modern hotels catering mainly to businesspeople. Three of the best are the Holiday Inn, the Belmont House, and the Hotel Saint James, all centrally located and with well-appointed public rooms and modern bedrooms. The ► **Holiday Inn** is the largest and has the most amenities, including indoor swimming pool, sauna, and gymnasium. The ► **Hotel Saint James** has particularly fine panoramic views of the city from its airy restaurant, and the ► **Belmont House** is located near the railway station.   •

Around Leicester

John Taylor's famous bell foundry in Loughborough (11 miles/18 km northwest of Leicester via the A 6) has been making church bells for centuries. The **Bell Foundry Museum** on Freehold Street demonstrates the foundry's history and techniques of the bell founder's craft. Visitors who phone ahead can join special conducted tours of the foundry, showing the work in progress (Tel: 0509-23-34-14). A carillon of 47 bells, created as a memorial to those who died in World War I, is housed at the top of the 150-foot bell tower in the middle of Queen's Park on Granby Street.

BOSWORTH FIELD

To the southwest of Leicester off the A 447, the **Bosworth Battlefield Visitor Centre and Country Park** marks the site of one of the most important battles in English history, when in 1485 King Richard III of England met Henry Tudor in the final battle of the Wars of the Roses. Afterward, Richard lay dead on the battlefield, and Henry survived to become the first of the Tudor line of monarchs. Using models, replicas, life-size tableaux, and relief maps, exhibitions in the visitor center show what it was like to live and fight battles in the 15th century. Trails across the park trace the course of the battle, and visitors can get light refreshments in the café. On occasional summer weekends there are special events, such as jousts and battle reenactments (open every afternoon, April through October; Tel: 0455-29-22-39).

There is special bus service to the site from Humberstone Gate Bus Station in Leicester city center on Sunday mornings that returns in the afternoon, but for those who are driving there are two unusual forms of transport to and from the battlefield. The **Battlefield Line Steam Railway** operates a limited Sunday and bank holiday service in summer between the battlefield and two stations just to the north of it, Market Bosworth (on B 585) and Shackerstone (3 miles/5 km farther north); Tel: (0827) 88-07-54 for the Battlefield Line. Alternatively, visitors can hire a boat from the **Ashby Narrow Boat Company** in Stoke Golding, 2 miles (3 km) east of Barwell and some 15 miles (24 km) west of Leicester, and cruise to the battlefield or up to the attractive little market town of Market Bosworth (Tel: 0455-21-26-71). Walkers can follow part of the 22-mile canal towpath. Boat trips can also be taken from **Foxton Locks** on the Grand Union Canal south of Leicester, near Market Harborough. Some beautiful countryside surrounds this historic flight of ten locks on the Grand Union Canal.

MELTON MOWBRAY

A thriving country market town east of Loughborough famous for its pork pies and Stilton cheese, Melton Mowbray is the traditional boundary of the celebrated Quorn, Cottesmore, and Belvoir hunts. Hunting has been a popular sport in England for centuries, and nowhere has its survival been more dogged than in Leicestershire, where the great landowning families planted woodland to encourage the survival of foxes. These woodlands now provide a varied landscape ideal for the gentler pursuits of cycling, riding, and walking.

Three miles (5 km) east of Melton is one of the finest country-house hotels in England, ▶ **Stapleford Park**. This superb 16th-century mansion was the home of the Sherard family, later the earls of Harborough, for more than 450 years until it was bought by the American hotelier Bob Payton, who opened it in 1989 as the ultimate luxury hotel. Since then the accolades have kept coming, not just for its grandeur and comfort but also for the welcoming nature of its staff and the excellence of its cuisine. It has few equals in Britain.

Rutland

Tucked into the southeast corner of Leicestershire, just west of Peterborough, is the former county of Rutland. Once the smallest county in England, Rutland was absorbed into Leicestershire by parliamentary decree in 1974. Nearly 20 years later, and although its character has

greatly changed, it retains a strong sense of its own identity, which has given the area a particular charm to be
found nowhere else in England. Two main factors contribute to this: first, the physical preservation of its towns and
villages, most of which survived the building explosion of
the last few decades, and, second, the creation in 1976 of
the largest man-made lake in Britain, Rutland Water. Today, the area is one of the country's best-kept secrets.

RUTLAND WATER

Rutland Water is located just southeast of the village of
Oakham (see below); it is bordered on the north by A 606
and on the west by A 6003. When this enormous reservoir
was first built in the early 1970s, it caused a great deal of
consternation among those who feared its effect on the
environment. However, the sympathetic design, landscap-
ing, and management of the reservoir and its surrounding area have made it a leisure and water sports center of
national importance, especially for fishing, sailing, cycling, and nature watching (for the Tourist Information
Centre at Rutland Water, Tel: 0780-863-21). Fishing is very
popular here. One of the finest trout fisheries in Europe,
the lake is stocked annually with more than 100,000
mature brown and rainbow trout. Visitors can obtain rod
licenses, day permits, and motorboats from the fishing
lodge at Whitwell (Tel: 0780-867-70). Novices may also
attend courses or obtain individual instruction here.

Whitwell, on the lake's northern shore, is the area's
main leisure center, with sailing and windsurfing facilities
(Tel: 0780-864-64), ample parking, and an excellent bicycle rental concession (Tel: 0780-867-05). The *Rutland
Belle* operates hourly cruises around the lake from Whitwell in the summer. Most of the lake's 2,000 acres can be
sailed on, and Rutland Water is one of England's best
inland venues for windsurfing. The Rutland Sailing Club,
on the other side of the lake at Edith Weston, offers instruction (Tel: 0780-72-02-92, except Tuesday and Wednesday).

Cyclists have 25 miles (40 km) of traffic-free waterside
track for touring the perimeter of the five-mile-long lake.
On the way they will pass the elegant Neoclassical **Normanton Church**, which stands on a causeway into the
lake and now houses a fascinating museum about the
history of the reservoir.

The shoreline and western end of the lake are restricted
as part of a nature reserve that provides a glorious haven

for birds over 350 acres. There are two main sections: **Lyndon Hill Reserve** has a visitor center with displays, audiovisual programs, and three bird-watching blinds overlooking the water; **Egleton Reserve** has ten blinds, one designed for wheelchair access (Tel: 0572-72-41-01).

THE MARKET TOWNS

There are three market towns near Rutland Water: Oakham and Uppingham to the west, and Stamford to the east. A natural target of a visit here is **Oakham**, a charming, sleepy hamlet that comes alive on Saturday when everyone comes in to do their weekly shopping and visit the market (Wednesday is also a market day). The old market place is at the town center and still contains the Buttercross (where the farmers' wives used to sit and sell their dairy produce) and the town stocks. The cattle market is held just off South Street on Fridays. Not far away is the incorrectly named **Oakham Castle**, the oldest stone-built aisled hall to have survived more or less intact in Britain. Part of a large 12th-century manor house, the hall contains an extensive collection of horseshoes, testimony to Oakham's ancient right to demand a horseshoe from any peer entering the town. On Mondays the hall doubles as the local magistrate's court.

For a riveting insight into the old county's history, be sure to visit the **Rutland County Museum** at the east end of town. Here a vast collection of agricultural bygones are displayed in a large and airy restored riding school, built around 1800. Nearby, the Rutland Farm Park houses a fascinating menagerie of farm animals, including woolly sheep, long-horned cattle, and spotty pigs. The park has a picnic area and some pleasant walks (open April through September).

Oakham and the town of Uppingham, to the south, are home to two famous public schools of the same names. Although a quiet little town largely dominated by its school, **Uppingham** has a number of interesting antiques shops, bookshops, and galleries, notably the **Goldmark gallery and bookshop** on Orange Street.

Stamford, to the east of Rutland Water via the A 606, is another pleasant country borough with a large number of fine houses, old coaching inns, and medieval churches built during the town's long period of prosperity, when it was an important stop on the main road to the North (now the A 1). Stamford lost its prominence when the railways were built, as it was served only by a branch line. Some fine examples of Georgian architecture can be seen on All Saints Place, Barn Hill, and the High Street. **St. Martin's Church** on the High Street contains a large alabaster monument to Lord Burghley, lord treasurer to Queen Elizabeth I. The town's **museum** is also Stamford's visitor center, with a fine display on local history and archaeology.

BURGHLEY HOUSE

Lord Burghley (William Cecil) built what is now considered to be the largest and most impressive example of Elizabethan architecture to have survived in England. Located a mile (1½ km) south of Stamford, Burghley House is an astonishing monument to the Elizabethan age, containing a fabulous collection of paintings, furniture, and other works of art that reflect its grandeur. Visitors can take an hour-long guided tour of the 18 magnificent rooms open to the public or tour at their own speed on Sunday afternoons (open Easter through October). The house stands in grounds that were landscaped by the 18th-century gardener Capability Brown. The internationally known Burghley Horse Trials take place here every September.

ROCKINGHAM CASTLE

While Burghley House is interesting for its pomp and magnificence, the great attraction of Rockingham Castle (2 miles/3 km north of Corby, which is 16 miles/26 km southwest of Stamford via the A 43) is its intimate relationship with history. The original castle here was built by no less than William the Conqueror on a high bluff overlooking the valley of the River Welland, and it served as a popular royal residence for more than 300 years, after which it fell into semi-ruin. In 1530 Henry VIII gave the castle to Edward Watson, who converted it into a comfortable Tudor residence, and it has been lived in by the Watson family ever since. Of particular interest are the Tudor "street" that contains the castle's domestic buildings—the laundry, brew house, bakery, larder, and dairy; the oak-beamed Great Hall with its Civil War relics; and the Panel Room with its collection of 20th-century paintings.

The Long Gallery became the principal reception room in the 19th century, and Charles Dickens, a frequent visitor, produced and acted in a number of his plays here.

He used Rockingham as the model for Chesney Wold in *Bleak House*. The gardens are set on a series of terraces and include a formal rose garden, a bank of seasonal flowers, and a double yew hedge shaped like a line of elephants. A new exhibition tells the fascinating story of the development of castles, using local examples to illustrate how they functioned and the way people lived in them (open Sundays, Thursdays, and bank holidays, April through September). Good homemade teas are served at the **castle tearoom**. For stronger drink try the ancient **Sondes Arms**, just below the castle among the perfectly preserved buildings of Rockingham village.

STAYING AND DINING IN RUTLAND

Of the pleasant places to stay or have lunch around Rutland Water, undoubtedly the finest is the delightful ▶ **Hambleton Hall**, which stands on a large peninsula jutting out into the lake near the beautiful little village of Upper Hambleton, just a mile (1½ km) east of Oakham (see above). In its superb location, Hambleton Hall is one of those rare luxury hotels that combines absolute comfort and stylish elegance, without the stuffiness that often comes with them. If the room rates are too much of a strain on your pocket, try at least to have lunch at the hotel—it has one of the finest chefs in the country, the talented Aaron Patterson. You can eat in the restaurant or, in fine weather, on the lawn in front overlooking the lake. If you are staying at the hotel, the manager may be able to arrange for you to go lake fishing with the captain of the English Fly Fishing Team or, in autumn, fox hunting with one of the internationally famous packs of hounds in the area—the Belvoir, Quorn, or Fernie. If you like this area but cannot afford the hotel, you may be able to get a room in the village at the delightful ▶ **Finches Arms**, where the rooms are pleasantly and simply furnished, and which is also a good place to have a drink or a pub lunch.

There are a number of pleasant, medium-priced hotels in this area, such as the ▶ **Barnsdale Lodge**, just up the hill from the lake near the Barnsdale Country Park and not far from Whitwell. If you would rather stay in the town of Oakham, the ▶ **Boultons Country House Hotel**, near the County Museum, is a small, friendly place, ever wreathed in a profusion of flowers and run with great enthusiasm and efficiency by a charming young couple.

NOTTINGHAMSHIRE

The county of Nottinghamshire, north of Leicestershire, stretches for about 50 miles from the large industrial city of Nottingham in the south to Worksop and the great parklands of the Dukeries in the north. The M 1 motorway runs almost parallel to Nottinghamshire's western boundary and the River Trent, once central to Nottingham's industry, forms part of its eastern boundary.

The county is probably best known for its association with the outlaw Robin Hood and Nottingham's infamous sheriff. Robin Hood lore is a major attraction, and those interested should visit both the city and the forestland some 30 miles to its north.

Lord Byron lived for some time at romantic Newstead Abbey, to the north of Nottingham. D. H. Lawrence spent his childhood and adolescence in Eastwood, seven miles east of the city center, and, more recently, Alan Sillitoe made the Nottingham back streets famous through his celebrated novel *Saturday Night and Sunday Morning*. All three writers have contributed to Nottinghamshire's popularity with visitors, and those who visit always find that the county and its capital contain a wealth of other interesting places to visit and things to do.

Nottingham

The large, bustling city of Nottingham stands at the heart of the Shires of Middle England and at the southern edge of the county of Nottinghamshire. Dominated by its castle, it developed around a series of sandstone bluffs overlooking the mighty River Trent. Today Nottingham spreads over a wide radius, with a population of more than 230,000 and a thriving industrial base.

From its residents' point of view, Nottingham has other claims to fame. For two centuries the textile industry, particularly lace making and hosiery, has dominated the city and, since Victorian times, a range of other industries have been closely associated with it. These include three world-famous companies: Boots the Chemist, John Player's Cigarettes, and Raleigh Bicycles, all of which started up in the mid-19th century. Recognized as a sporting center, with two first-class football (soccer) teams, a noted county cricket ground at Trent Bridge, and the National Water Sports Centre at nearby Holme

Pierrepoint, Nottingham is also the home of the Olympic ice champions Jayne Torvill and Christopher Dean.

MEDIEVAL NOTTINGHAM

During the Middle Ages Nottingham stood at one of the few crossing points of the River Trent and so developed as a flourishing trading community. In 1155 it became the site of a great Cluniac priory. However, the prior and his monks were hanged by Henry VIII for "treason" and the priory was destroyed in the 16th century. Nevertheless, the town continued to prosper and has remained an important commercial center. The city's importance as a market is celebrated in the annual Goose Fair held at the Forest Recreation Ground on the first Thursday, Friday, and Saturday of October. Once the main hiring fair and autumn market of the Midlands, this is now a giant amusement fair that descends on the city for three days.

Anyone looking for a medieval stone fortress in Nottingham will be disappointed. Almost all traces of the 12th-century castle that existed in the days of Robin Hood and the sheriff of Nottingham were obliterated by the Parliamentarians after a Civil War siege in 1651. A castle built in the late 1670s by the duke of Newcastle was, in turn, destroyed in a fire started during the Reform Bill riots of 1831. The corporation restored the ruins in 1875, and today **Nottingham Castle**, just southwest of the city center on Castle Road, is an elegant Victorian mansion but with a rather institutional atmosphere. The only medieval remnant is the fine **gatehouse** that visitors enter on their way to the main building.

Over the years the sandstone ridge that supports the castle has been riddled with a number of caves and underground passages, some of these possibly used for prisoners or as hiding places. **Mortimer's Hole** is a 321-foot-long tunnel that winds from the Upper Bailey of the castle to the foot of the cliff 134 feet below. It is associated with the dramatic capture of Roger Mortimer, earl of March, in 1330. Visitors can join guided tours of the tunnel by booking in advance (Tel: 0602-48-35-04, ext. 3652).

The castle houses the city's **art gallery and museum**, including a superb new "History of Nottingham" exhibition about the castle, the town, and the surrounding area. The detailed model of the castle in 1500 and the fascinating "Castle of Care" audiovisual show are well worth seeing at the start of any visit to the city, as they provide a context for its other, more specialized attractions. Notable

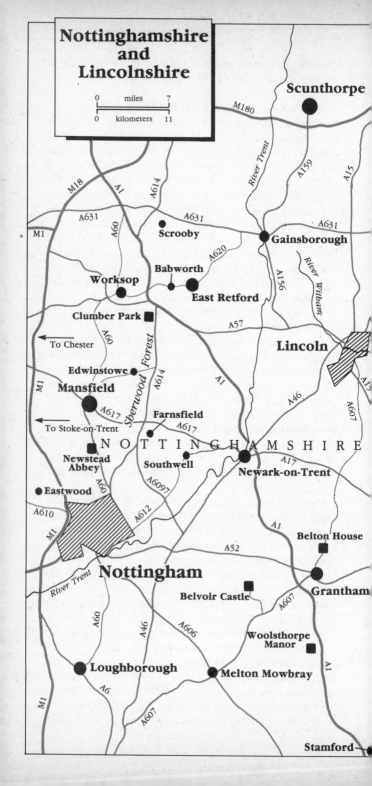

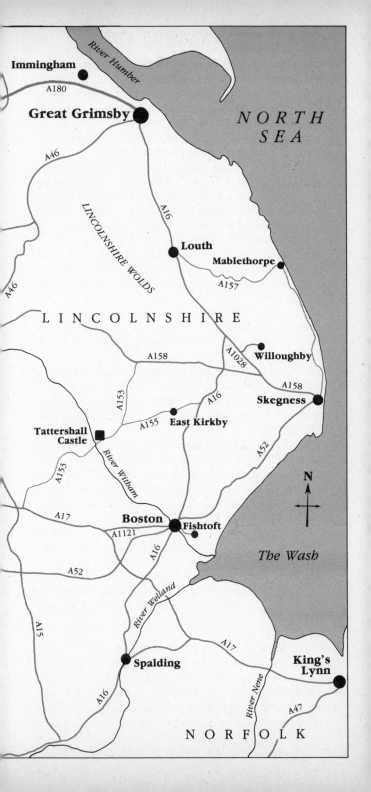

among the museum's collections are the fine glass, medieval alabasters, English domestic silver, and ceramics, including a particularly fine collection of early Wedgwood. The art gallery has a small but varied collection, including watercolors by the Nottingham-born Sandby brothers, Thomas (1723–1798) and Paul (1730–1809), whose father had been a framework knitter.

Another interesting domestic museum is housed in the **Brewhouse Yard,** a cluster of five 17th-century houses that stand below the castle at the foot of the cliff. The buildings contain reconstructed shops, offices, and other rooms displaying a wealth of domestic items from the last two centuries. Visitors can sit at desks in the little schoolroom or pull out drawer after drawer of toys in the 1930s toy shop. Caves carved into the rock behind the houses show their traditional uses as washhouses, stores, and air-raid shelters.

Next door, **Ye Olde Trip to Jerusalem** claims to be the oldest pub in England and the spot from which Nottingham's Crusaders left in 1189. Another old pub worth dropping into is **Ye Olde Salutation,** from the 14th century. Visitors can explore a warren of passages beneath it dating back to the seventh century. The pub serves good, inexpensive bar food and reserves an upstairs room for motorbike enthusiasts—but only those in appropriate dress are admitted.

Visitors keen to discover more about Nottingham's legendary heroes should proceed first to a building on Maid Marian Way, not far from the castle, called **The Tales of Robin Hood** (open daily). Here local entrepreneurs have set up an indoor theme ride based on Robin Hood and his adventures. The building also houses an exhibition, two audiovisual shows, an archery room, and a small restaurant that features a replica of the "greenwood tree." For visitors making a brief visit to the city this may be their only contact with Sherwood Forest. Those who want to see what remains of the real thing will have to make a 30-mile (48-km) journey north via the A 60 and A 614 (see below).

INDUSTRIAL NOTTINGHAM

Nottingham's later history is dominated by the effects of the Industrial Revolution, particularly the history of lace making and hosiery. By the 1850s Nottingham had monopolized the machine-made lace industry, which was concentrated in large factories where vast steam-powered machines performed intricate movements to produce an infinite variety of lace patterns. Today these machines have disappeared, and computers plot lace designs copied from 19th-century pattern books. The story of Nottingham lace is told in a series of audiovisual displays and exhibits at the **Lace Hall**, a converted chapel with some fine Burne-Jones stained glass windows, set in the heart of the old lace-making area on High Pavement, which can be reached by walking northwest from the castle along Castle Gate and Low Pavement.

A working example of the complex machines that dominated the industry in the 19th century can be seen in action in the Lace Hall. Samples of machine and handmade lace can be bought here or at the **Lace Centre**, in the medieval Severns Building opposite the castle. Bobbin lace making is demonstrated at both places (every Thursday afternoon at the Lace Centre). Finally, to see examples of the use of these textiles, visitors should tour the **Museum of Costume and Textile**, near the Severns Building, on Castle Gate. It has one of the largest costume collections in Britain and includes displays of shoes, underwear, hats, and accessories. Further insight into Nottingham's history can be gained from a visit to the **Ruddington Framework Knitter's Workshop**, off the A 60, 5 miles (8 km) south of Nottingham, or the **Industrial Museum** housed in the stables at **Wollaton Hall**, an extravagant Elizabethan mansion with a fine deer park, which also houses Nottingham's Natural History Museum (off A 609, 3 miles/5 km west of Nottingham).

Ease of transport has always been an important factor in Nottingham's prosperity. The construction of a direct railway line to London in 1840 was of vital importance to industry. Before this, however, the city's lifeline was the Trent and its associated canals. These are celebrated in the **Canal Museum** on Canal Street, just a short walk away from Brewhouse Yard near Castle Road. Lodged in a warehouse containing the former canal basin, just off the Nottingham and Beeston Canal, the exhibition includes two narrowboats and a variety of fascinating displays.

DINING AND STAYING IN NOTTINGHAM

A charming spot for lunch or dinner is **Jesse's Restaurant**, on Goosegate (Tel: 0602-50-01-11), the site of Jesse Boot's first chemist shop, now restored and filled with memorabilia of early Boots the Chemist shops. For spacious, central, and modern accommodations, book a room at the ▶ **Royal Moat House International**, on Wollaton Street, with its squash court, shops, and numerous extras like bathrobes, toiletries, and in-house movies. Another modern hotel, for those on a more modest budget, is the ▶ **Holiday Inn Garden Court**, situated near the canal to the southwest of the city, although its location makes it suitable only for those travelling by car.

Visitors who are not driving or would prefer a knowledgeable guide to take them around the sites are advised to call **Blue Badge Guides** (Tel: 0602-87-19-61) or **Sherwood Explorer** (Tel: 0602-62-23-12; Fax: 0602-78-80-12), who will arrange guided tours of any size with a personalized itinerary. Sherwood Explorer also organizes weekends based on a particular interest (e.g., crafts, literature, etc.) in and around Nottingham, for very reasonable prices. Contact Catherine Strauss or Matt Graham (Tel: 0602-62-23-12 or 0623-82-21-90; Fax: 0602-78-80-12).

Around Nottingham

Although small sections of the forest still exist around Nottinghamshire, the largest remaining part of Robin Hood's mighty Sherwood Forest is the 450 acres of the **Sherwood Forest Country Park**, off the B 6034 near Edwinstowe. Crisscrossed by signposted paths and unmarked footpaths, the forest is a delight for walkers. It is also the site of the renowned **Major Oak**, an ancient oak tree whose trunk is more than 30 feet in diameter and propped up by posts. Robin Hood is reputed to have concealed his Merry Men beneath its branches. The park is open year-round and is free. The Sherwood Forest Visitor Centre has a Robin Hood exhibition, films, a shop, and a restaurant. There are some other major forest parks just north of here in an area of former great estates called the Dukeries. **Clumber Park** is particularly worth a visit for its landscape of woodland paths and lakeside picnic spots.

On the way back to Nottingham is the **White Post Modern Farm Centre** at Farnsfield, 12 miles (19 km) north of Nottingham just off the A 614. Part of a working mixed farm, White Post displays a variety of animals at close quarters, and visitors can wander through a fascinating range of exhibits. Try to get a personal tour from farmer Tim Clark if he is around. Also worth a visit is the **Longdale**

Rural Craft Centre, a collection of craft workshops started by sculptor Gordon Brown more than 20 years ago. This is on Longdale Lane in Ravenshead, 8 miles (13 km) north of Nottingham and not far from Newstead Abbey. Visitors can watch silversmiths, masons, wood-carvers, stained glass artists, toy makers, and other craftspeople at work in a re-created early-19th-century village street and then buy their crafts in the attractive shop (Tel: 0623-79-48-58). The excellent **restaurant** serves delicious homemade traditional English food.

LITERARY LANDMARKS
Lovers of the Romantic poets will find plenty to enthrall them at **Newstead Abbey**, also north of Nottingham and west of the A 60. The Abbey once housed a community of Augustinian canons but was abandoned during Henry VIII's dissolution of the monasteries. Converted into a family home by Sir John Byron in 1540, Newstead was eventually inherited by his descendant, the poet Lord Byron, in 1798. The Byron family converted part of the compound's buildings and left the west wall of the Abbey standing alone overlooking the lake. In the garden beyond it is Byron's famous monument to his faithful dog, Boatswain. Part of the house was derelict when Byron came to live here in 1808, so he occupied just a few rooms, which have been restored to their former state. Byron wrote some of his finest poetry here, and the house contains a collection of his manuscripts, letters, and other memorabilia.

In direct contrast to Newstead, the home of D. H. Lawrence, Nottinghamshire's other world-famous writer, was a terraced house in the coal-mining village of Eastwood, on the B 610, 10 miles (16 km) northwest of Nottingham. **Lawrence's Birthplace**, at 8A Victoria Street, is now a museum, furnished in the style of a working-class home of the 1880s. An upstairs exhibition room contains various Lawrence memorabilia as well as a video presentation. The shop sells leaflets describing walks in the surrounding village and countryside so that enthusiasts can find the real-life settings of Lawrence's semiautobiographical novels. Lawrence lived on Victoria Street for only two years, after which his family moved to a house in the valley, just a ten-minute walk away. Number 28 Garden Road (formerly The Breach) was the model for The Bottoms, Paul Morel's house in *Sons and Lovers*. It was privately restored a decade ago; the lower floor is furnished in period style, while the upper floor has been converted into a self-contained flat, which can be rented from Blakes Holidays (Tel: 0603-78-32-21).

SOUTHWELL MINSTER

Also worth a detour is lovely Southwell Minster, 12 miles (19 km) northeast of Nottingham on the A 612, widely regarded as one of the most beautiful churches in England because of its glorious twin Norman towers and pyramidal twin spires. The 13th-century chancel is famous for its intricate carvings of foliage. The town of Southwell contains some delightful old buildings, including the elegant **Burgage Manor**, where Byron lived before he inherited Newstead, and the 17th-century ▶ **Saracen's Head**, where Charles I surrendered to the Scots, ending the Civil War; the Head is now a pleasant, medium-priced hotel. While you are in Southwell, snack on a Bramley apple, a variety discovered in a local orchard in 1805.

Just south of Southwell, at Gunthorpe Marina on the A 6097, **Tamar Belle River Cruises** (Tel: 0602-40-01-81) operates cruises on the beautiful River Trent, once the main trading artery of the region. Contact them directly to see whether they are still running all-day trips to **Newark**, 23 miles (37 km) northeast of Nottingham via the A 612 and A 617. Situated just off the A 1 motorway, Newark has a fine church, impressive ruins of a 12th-century castle (once one of the most important strongholds of the north), and an Air Museum (see below for more on airfield museums). The Lock and Castle Line operates river trips on the Trent from Newark Town Wharf (Tel: 0636-70-79-39).

LINCOLNSHIRE

East of Nottinghamshire and facing Norfolk southward across the Wash, Lincolnshire is by far the largest of the Midland shires, with a wide variety of scenery and places to visit. The county divides into three main regions. In the south is the immense fenland, stretching inland from the Wash and centering on Boston and Spalding (which has a magnificent flower festival every May). Here, crisscrossed by drainage ditches, fenland farms grow vast, flat fields of root vegetables, flowers, and fruit. Two of the county's principal rivers, the Welland and the Witham, cross the fens to reach the sea in the southwest corner of the Wash, near Boston.

In the west are rolling uplands and mixed farmland with a multitude of small villages, dominated by the beautiful town of Lincoln on its high limestone plateau. East of the town are the glorious Lincolnshire Wolds with their pretty wooded slopes and villages. Louth stands guard on the eastern slopes of the Wolds, overlooking the wide coastal plain with its string of seaside towns from Somercotes to Skegness.

Grantham

Situated just off the Great North Road (now the A 1), halfway between Stamford and Newark, the market town of Grantham was an important staging post in the 18th and 19th centuries. Although still an important town, it has suffered from the architectural ravages and uncontrolled development of the 1960s and 1970s. The fine 14th-century church of **St. Wulfram** stands in what is left of the town's Georgian center. In 1483, Richard III signed the death warrant of the duke of Buckingham at the ▶ **Angel and Royal Hotel**, which dates from the 13th century and has a late-15th-century façade. The Angel and Royal is a pleasant hotel with comfortable accommodations and reasonably good food.

Grantham Museum in Peter Street illustrates the local history of the area and contains exhibitions on the lives of Grantham's two most famous personalities: Isaac Newton and Margaret Thatcher. The corner grocery shop where Thatcher grew up has now been converted into a pleasant French restaurant with a few rooms: **The Premier** stands at 2–6 North Parade, where it meets the old A 1 (Tel: 0476-778-55). Newton attended the local grammar school, King's School, and carved his name on a windowsill there.

Three miles (5 km) northeast of Grantham and signposted from the A 607, **Belton House** is a late 17th-century Wren-style house with a richly carved interior, set in a landscaped park. It has a large adventure playground and a miniature railway. Seven miles (11 km) south of Grantham and 1 mile (1½ km) west of the A 1, 17th-century **Woolsthorpe Manor** was Isaac Newton's birthplace, and he came here on extended visits during the plague years. He was sitting in the garden of this small limestone farmhouse when an apple dropped in the orchard and demonstrated the force of gravity to him. Scientific graffiti in the house were probably written by him (open Saturday through Wednesday afternoons, and bank holidays).

Belvoir Castle

Just 7 miles (11 km) southwest of Grantham, off the A 607, is the magnificent ancestral seat of the dukes of Rutland, Belvoir Castle, standing on a ridge overlooking the Vale of Belvoir (pronounced "beaver"). Visitors park at the foot of the hill and walk up a wooded path to the castle (the disabled and elderly can obtain permission to drive up to the castle entrance). The core of this castle is a medieval fortress built by Robert de Todeni, William the Conqueror's standard bearer at the Battle of Hastings. It later fell into ruins but by 1555 had been rebuilt by a de Todeni descendant, the first earl of Rutland. It was rebuilt and destroyed twice more, once after the Civil War and once after a disastrous fire in 1816 that destroyed many of the castle's most famous paintings. The present castle, in every way a grand stately home, was designed in the Gothic style by James Wyatt for the fifth duke, under the direction of his talented duchess. Every room was carefully planned and decorated to convey the power and wealth of its owner.

Visitors can see a succession of impressive rooms, including the ballroom with its splendid family portraits; the Elizabeth Saloon with its ornate ceiling; the Grand Dining Room containing an enormous 17th-century silver punch bowl; and the King's Rooms, elaborately decorated for the visits of George IV. A recent addition to the visitor's tour is the splendid paneled library. Among the many treasures on display at Belvoir are the magnificent paintings in the Picture Gallery. These include Holbein's full-length portrait *Henry VIII*, Poussin's *Seven Sacraments*, and *The Proverbs*, by David Teniers II. Jousting tournaments or other events are held here every Sunday (open April through September; closed Fridays and Mondays).

Lincoln

Visitors who do not have time to see the farther reaches of the county should try to spare at least a day for Lincoln, one of Britain's loveliest small cities. This ancient metropolis is built on a high plateau next to the River Witham that attracted settlers as far back as the Bronze and Iron ages. The Romans built a timber fortress here in A.D. 60, and by the fourth century Lindum Colonia, as it was known, was a large self-governing community and the capital of one of the four Roman provinces of Britain. Lincoln continued to be an important town during Anglo-Saxon and Danish rule, with a population of between 5,000 and 8,000 at the time of the Domesday Survey (1085–1086). Its importance was confirmed when William the Conqueror chose Lincoln as the site of both a new, large castle in 1068 and a cathedral in 1072.

LINCOLN CASTLE

When Lincoln Castle was built, 160 houses had to be destroyed to make way for it. Today its surrounding walls enclose more than six acres, and the large bailey is frequently the site of special events and concerts. The Lincoln Castle Longbowmen display their skill at archery and combat on most summer weekends. Part of the walls of the 12th-century stone keep of the castle still stand on the Conqueror's original great earth mound, now called the Lucy Tower. Visitors can see the gravestones of prisoners who were hanged at the castle in the 1800s. Over the intervening centuries a variety of buildings would have stood within the vast curtain wall of the bailey. The red-brick buildings standing now were built as courts and a prison. Facing the East Gate that most visitors enter is the Shire Hall, or Crown Courts, built between 1822 and 1826 and currently undergoing restoration.

To the left are **Lincoln County Gaol** (built in the 1840s and now the County Archives office and a magistrate's court). A ground-floor room contains a lively audiovisual presentation on the castle, and the main door leads through to two cells and up to the unique **Prison Chapel**, built in the late 18th century according to the Pentonville system that assumed that solitary confinement would cure prisoners of criminal tendencies. Claustrophobic individual pews walled in by wood ensured that prisoners could see only the chaplain, not each other, when attending chapel.

Visitors can walk the castle walls and view the surrounding town and countryside from the top of Observatory Tower, from which Boston Stump (St. Botolph's Church; see Boston, below) and the Lincolnshire Wolds (also see below) can be seen, or from Cobb Hall, where prisoners used to be hanged on the County Gallows (1816–1859). From either vantage point there is a fine view of the cathedral beyond.

From Castle Square, visitors can walk down the aptly named Steep Hill and The Strait, past a collection of fine old buildings dating from the 14th century. These include a former inn, the Harlequin; a 16th-century merchant's house, Harding House; and two unusual Norman houses, the Jew's House and the Jew's Court.

LINCOLN CATHEDRAL

Most of the original cathedral, built by William the Conqueror and his successors between 1072 and 1092, was destroyed in an earthquake in 1185. Its successor, masterminded by the great bishop Hugh of Avalon, was to become one of the finest cathedrals in Europe. The magnificent west front includes the rounded Norman doorways of the original cathedral and a superb sculptured 12th-century frieze that is presently undergoing restoration. The nave (completed in 1250) was built in a then completely new style, now called Early English Gothic. Based on the pointed arch, it incorporates huge windows that give the impression of tremendous light and space. Bishop Hugh was made a saint 20 years after his death, and his tomb became a place of pilgrimage. As a result the cathedral was enlarged (1256–1280) and the glorious Angel Choir, at its east end, was built to house his tomb. The choir is named after the angels that decorate the topmost windows. High up on the pillar next to the tomb (just above a carved head) is the famous Lincoln Imp, who was supposed to have been turned to stone by the angels for misbehaving.

Other notable elements in the cathedral are the two rose windows of the Great Transept (known as the Dean's Eye and the Bishop's Eye), the carved 12th-century Tournai marble font, and the richly carved canons' stalls of St. Hugh's Choir, the center of worship in the cathedral. Among the beautiful buildings attached to the cathedral are the **Cloister**, the **Wren Library**, and the superb **Chapter House**, whose windows contain scenes from the cathedral's history. The area around the castle and cathedral is called the Bailgate, after its central street. Here visitors will find a multitude of delightful old buildings housing charming little shops and restaurants, as well as the Tourist Information Centre opposite Eastgate.

LINCOLN MUSEUMS

Opposite the City and County Museum, over Pelham Bridge, is the City Bus Station, where visitors can take a bus back up Lindum Hill, past Lincoln's famous **Usher Gallery**. The displays here include the world-famous Usher collection of antique watches, miniatures, porcelain, and enamels; a notable collection of English silver and glass; Tennyson memorabilia; and works by the noted 19th-century English watercolorist Peter de Wint, who had close associations with the city. Try not to miss **The Incredibly Fantastic Old Toy Show** (just behind the castle, opposite the Westgate car park), a remarkable collection of children's toys and entertainments from the past (Tel: 0522-52-05-34 for opening times). The **Museum of Lincolnshire Life** on Burton Street, housed in an extensive former barracks, exhibits everything from domestic bygones to steam traction engines.

DINING AND STAYING IN LINCOLN

One of the city's best restaurants is **Harvey's Cathedral Restaurant** in Castle Square. The owner also runs the less expensive brasserie next door, **Troffs**, which specializes in burgers and vegetarian foods. Another satisfying and inexpensive restaurant is **Brown's Pie Shop** at 33 Steep Hill, offering traditional pies with a variety of delicious fillings, as well as other dishes.

There are a number of interesting little streets in the area known as Bailgate, including the street called Bailgate, which contains several pleasant accommodations, such as the ▶ **White Hart Hotel**, where guests pay moderately high prices for the advantage of being in comfortable and elegant lodgings in the heart of old Lincoln. This popular hotel has a good restaurant. Just around the corner on Eastgate, for about half the price visitors can have bed and breakfast in the Georgian ▶ **D'Isney Place Hotel**, which has a garden backing onto the cathedral. There are no public rooms; breakfast is served in the delightful bedrooms. A short walk away, the ▶ **Hillcrest Hotel** is a former Victorian rectory built into the side of a hill. Guests at this reasonably priced little hotel are assured of a warm welcome in relaxing surroundings.

The Lincolnshire Wolds

To the east of Lincoln are the peaceful hills of the Lincolnshire Wolds, a mixture of lovely valleys and intensively farmed chalk uplands. Crops produced for the frozen-food factories around Grimsby (especially peas) are often harvested by night using floodlights. Visitors should either walk or tour the Wolds on tiny back roads to see the best of these quiet rolling hills and deep wooded valleys. The **museum** of the thriving little Georgian town of **Louth** contains a display on the life of the poet Tennyson, who was born in 1809 at the rectory of the lovely village of Somersby, about ten miles to the south.

Another famous native is Captain John Smith, the first governor of Virginia and lover of Pocahontas. He was born in Willoughby (east of the A 1028, southeast of Louth), near the parish church that contains a memorial window to him.

The Lincolnshire Coast

The introduction of bank holidays in 1871, followed by the construction of the railway that connected Skegness and Mablethorpe to the main railway network, led to their development as resorts for the largely working-class populations of the industrial Midland cities. **Skegness** was turned into a model resort by the ninth earl of Scarborough, who laid out wide, tree-lined streets, spacious gardens, and the fourth-longest pier in the country. Although the whole plan was not completed, it can be understood clearly from the air. You can take a pleasure flight from Skegness Aerodrome in nearby Ingoldmells (Tel: 0754-22-40).

Visitors thronged by the trainload to these resorts, which stayed immensely popular right into the 1950s and 1960s, when cheap travel abroad dented their appeal. The two resorts still attract large numbers of visitors, because of their long golden beaches, leisure and amusement parks, live family entertainment, value-for-money lodgings, and, above all, for the chance to be part of a crowd. Funcoast World leisure complex, one of Europe's largest covered water and leisure parks, gets about 200,000 visitors annually. Also popular are the area's two small zoos. **Animal Gardens** at the north end of Mablethorpe is also a sanctuary for sick and injured animals (open Easter through October). **Skegness Natureland Marine Zoo**, on North Parade, specializes in rescuing injured or abandoned seals and returning them to the wild, and has a large collection of tropical birds and animals (open daily).

Although this coastline appears to be completely lined with bungalows and trailer parks, it also has two fine nature reserves. Just over 3 miles (5 km) south of Skegness is the **Gibraltar Point National Nature Reserve**, a 1,000-acre stretch of salt marsh and dunes harboring thousands of birds and other wildlife (open daily May through October; weekends in winter). Guided walks start at the informative visitor center on most summer days. Farther up the coast, off the A 1031, the **Saltfleetby– Theddlethorpe National Nature Reserve** has a rare colony of natterjack toads that can be heard for miles on warm spring or summer evenings. This wildlife haven is also a seal reserve (open daily).

Tattershall Castle

Standing about 20 miles (32 km) southeast of Lincoln on the A 153 between Sleaford and Horncastle, this medieval brick fortress is an impressive reminder of the strategic importance of the area in the Middle Ages, although it was probably built as much for simple domestic security in those turbulent times. Erected in about 1440 by Ralph Cromwell, lord treasurer to Henry VI, the castle rises to a height of 110 feet through a series of enormous central rooms on four floors. Designed for the comfort of the Cromwell family, the castle would have been richly furnished and decorated with tapestries. It was saved from ruin in 1911 by Lord Curzon of Kedelstone, who rescued its two great fireplaces and devoted much time and money to its restoration. Tattershall is remarkably well preserved except for the absence of its outer walls.

Opposite the castle is the 15th-century church of the **Holy Trinity**, reputedly the burial place of Tom Thumb in 1620. The lakes beyond the castle belong to the Tattershall Park Country Club, a family vacation and leisure complex set in 365 acres of park and woodland with a campground and water-sports facilities that day visitors can also use. Those who prefer the indoors might drop into the **Mike Chambers Gallery** in the village to explore an Aladdin's Cave of paintings, watercolors, art supplies, needlework, and tapestries.

Coningsby Airfield, just east of the village, was one of more than 700 World War II fighter and bomber bases in

Britain, of which 49 were in Lincolnshire. Today it is the home of the **Battle of Britain Memorial Flight**, which operates five Spitfires, two Hurricanes, and one of only two Lancasters still flying in the world today. The planes are frequently away, flying at air shows or at displays, but those at the station can be toured any weekday from 10:00 A.M. to 5:00 P.M. (last tour at 3:30 P.M.; Tel: 0526-440-41). Visitors interested in aircraft displays can also visit the **Lincolnshire Aviation Heritage Centre** at East Kirkby (off A 155), a former Lancaster bomber and USAF C-47 base, as well as the **Newark Air Museum** at the former Winthorpe bomber base in Nottinghamshire (33 miles/53 km to the west of Coningsby via the A 153 and A 17; open daily April through October, Sundays in winter). A leaflet describing an Airfield Trail of the area is available from the Tourism Officer, North Kesteven District Council, Kesteven Street, Sleaford, Lincolnshire NG34 7EA (Tel: 0529-41-41-55).

On the Trail of the Pilgrims

When the *Mayflower* set sail for America in 1620 she carried 150 passengers, including a group of families from villages on the Lincolnshire–Nottinghamshire border around the River Trent. They were not the first settlers to set sail for the New World, but their beliefs and determination were to make them some of the most famous, so that 450 years later their leaders are remembered as among the Founding Fathers of the United States of America. **Worksop** (25 miles/40 km northwest of Newark, just west of the A 1) is a good starting point for exploring places related to the Pilgrims, and the exhibition at the **Worksop Museum** provides a good introduction to their history.

The quest for religious freedom that eventually led this small band of folk to the practically uncharted American shores began in the country church of All Saints in the tiny village of **Babworth** (5 miles/8 km east of Worksop). Here, in the late 1500s, a group of earnest Christians led by their rector, Richard Clyfton, had been influenced by the teachings of the Separatist preacher Robert "Troublechurch" Browne, who wanted to worship separately from the "corrupt" religious and political framework of the Protestant Church. Delightful little **All Saints** church sits at the end of a tree-lined lane off the A 620. Stop first at the little group of houses at the top of the lane to collect the church key from the Post Office (the small white house behind the flagpole) or from the manager of the business now occupying Clyfton's old white-painted rectory. Clyfton, a "grave and reverend preacher," attracted to his congregation two men who were to have a major role in the Separatist movement and in the American colonies: William Brewster, the master of the Royal Posts at Scrooby, and William Bradford, a young man from nearby Austerfield.

Shortly after James I came to the throne in 1603, more than 300 Nonconformist preachers, including Richard Clyfton, were removed from their posts. For a couple of years the Babworth Separatists joined the congregation formed by John Smyth, who held regular Nonconformist meetings at a manor house in Gainsborough, the rich grain- and wool-trading port on the River Trent. **Gainsborough Old Hall** (on the A 631, 18 miles/29 km northwest of Lincoln) is a magnificent timber-framed and brick mansion built between 1460 and 1480, and one of the best-preserved medieval manor houses in Britain. Today it is a startling sight, rising up in the middle of an assortment of Edwardian terraces and not far from the decaying warehouses of this once-thriving town. But it is well worth the detour, not only for its link with the Pilgrims but also for its associations with Richard III, who was entertained here by Sir Thomas Burgh in 1483, and with Henry VIII, who met Catherine Parr, his sixth and last wife, here. Displays and reconstructed room sets illustrate all phases of the history of the house. In particular, look at the large kitchen, which displays preparations for a medieval royal feast, and the rooms depicting the life of the remarkable Hickman family, who hosted the Separatist prayer meetings at considerable risk to themselves.

In 1606 the Babworth Separatists moved their prayer meetings to William Brewster's house in **Scrooby**, with Clyfton as pastor, Brewster as the elder, and the newly arrived and charismatic John Robinson as teacher. (Once an important staging post on the Great North Road, Scrooby is just north of Babworth, off the A 638.) Brewster's large manor house here still stands, but it is privately owned. After increasing pressure from the authorities, both the Scrooby and the Gainsborough Separatists decided that they would have to get away from Britain in order to be free to pursue their own beliefs. The Gainsborough group slipped away sometime in the winter of 1607 and joined 300 Separatists already settled in Amsterdam. Just before this, the Scrooby Separatists had tried to leave from Scotia Creek, near Boston, some 60 miles to the south (see below). They were betrayed by the ship's captain, however, robbed of all their money and belongings, and thrown into prison in the Boston Guildhall (see below) for a month.

The Scrooby group's second attempt took place the next spring when a Dutch captain agreed to meet them off the coast at **Killingholme Creek**, just north of Immingham (a few miles inland from Great Grimsby, along the banks of the River Humber). Some 60 men, women, and children arrived there by barge and foot, but as some of the men were being ferried aboard, the captain saw a large armed crowd approaching a waiting party of men, women, and children and sailed immediately. In spite of this setback these last few were eventually freed and sent on to Holland so that all were reunited there by the end of 1608.

John Robinson led about 100 Separatists, including William Brewster and William Bradford, to Leyden in Holland in 1609, and they established a strong Separatist group there until they decided, in about 1616, that they would gain true freedom only if they could set up a colony of their own in the newly explored territories of America. On September 6, 1620, after two false starts and the abandonment of one unseaworthy ship, Robinson's group set off from Plymouth, arriving off Cape Cod on November 10, 1620. During the next few years, with the vital help of the Native Americans Samoset and Squanto, and with William Bradford as their governor, the colony started to pay back their enormous debts. In spite of losing three cargoes of furs and other goods to pirates, they eventually became self-supporting and later joined the larger colony of Massachusetts.

Two monuments celebrate the Pilgrims' attempts to leave Britain. The Pilgrim Fathers Monument at Scotia Creek, Fishtoft, some 4 miles (6½ km) east of Boston, is set in a pleasant picnic area with a fine view of the River Witham. The Immingham Monument stands outside the church of St. Andrew in the town of Immingham.

Boston

ST. BOTOLPH'S CHURCH

Approached from the west, across the endless flat fields of the Fens, the town (27 miles/43 km east of Grantham on the A 52) rises like a mirage under the massive tower of its parish church, St. Botolph's. Called affectionately the Boston Stump, the slim, graceful medieval tower can be seen from miles around and was a useful landmark for travellers and seamen in the past and, more recently, for the airmen of World War II. Visitors can climb to the first stage of the tower (open Monday through Saturday).

The name "Boston" is a shortened version of "St. Botolph's town," after the saint who founded a monastery here in 654. St. Botolph's Day (June 17) is the focal point of the annual Boston Festival, and an annual May Fair is held on May 3. In the Middle Ages, the town was one of Britain's main seaports, and its merchants grew rich from the wine, wool, and cloth trades. Some fine tombs and carvings in St. Botolph's Church date from this period. Look for one carving showing a schoolmaster birching a boy, under a choir stall on the north side of the chancel.

The stained glass windows commemorate events in Boston's past. One shows the historic departure of a group of Boston Puritans for the New World in 1629 and 1630, including the sister of the earl of Lincoln, Lady Arbella Johnson. The *Arbella* led a fleet of seven ships carrying 1,000 emigrants. Three years later, the church's rector, John Cotton, also left for America. He was to spend the next 19 years as the teacher of the First Church in the young American city of Boston, and he was a leading figure in the newly formed colony. The Cotton Chapel in St. Botolph's Church is named after him. Much of the extensive restoration of the church in the 1920s and 1930s was jointly paid for by the citizens of Boston, Massachusetts, and Boston, Lincolnshire. On the south wall under the tower they also put up a memorial to the five English Bostonians who were elected governors of the American state of Massachusetts.

BOSTON ARCHITECTURE

Boston contains some fine architecture, most dating from the 16th, 17th, and early 18th centuries. Look for the Corporation Buildings (1772) and the elegant Assembly Rooms (1822), near the Market Square; the Custom House (1725) and Shodfriars Hall (a 19th-century copy of a 15th-century half-timbered house) on South Street; the Grammar School (14th–16th century) on South End; and the fine Georgian **Fydell House** on South Square. Once home to Boston's most influential family, Fydell House is now a college and has an American Room set aside for the use of visitors from Boston, Massachusetts. If you leave the town by the Horncastle Road, near the Bargate Bridge, you will see the **Maud Foster Windmill** (1819) on Willoughby Road. Standing an impressive seven floors high, this five-sailed windmill is the tallest working one in Britain (open Wednesdays and Sundays). The small health-food shop here sells the mill's stone-ground flour.

BOSTON GUILDHALL

The Guildhall Museum on South Street is a fine brick building dating from 1450 that was first a guildhall and, from 1546, the Town Hall. As such, it was the place to which the hapless Separatists were taken in 1607, and it still contains the 16th-century kitchen and the bare cells they were kept in, which visitors can enter. The court-room where the Separatists were tried is being restored to its former appearance. The Guildhall's small collection of paintings includes one of John Wesley preaching from his father's tombstone at Epworth and a portrait of Sir Joseph Banks, the Lincolnshire gentleman-botanist who accompanied Captain Cook on the *Endeavour*'s voyage of 1768–1771 and who later introduced sheep to Australia.

THE PEAK DISTRICT

Lying between the great conurbations of Manchester and Sheffield and stretching south as far as Ashbourne in Derbyshire west of Nottingham city, the great **Peak District National Park** covers 542 square miles of craggy windswept moorlands and lovely wooded valleys. Dramatic uplands are most typical of the Dark Peak in the north, where coarse dark grit forms the area's distinctive "edges" (low, black lines of crag that occur near the summits of some hills) and where the land rises to 2,088 feet (on Kinder Scout). To the south are the gentler limestone dales of the White Peak, including the lovely wooded ravine called Dovedale, to the northwest of Ashbourne.

THE PENNINE WAY

For a true understanding of the area, start your visit in the north, at the Peak District National Park Information Centre in Edale off A 625, 5 miles (8 km) northwest of Castleton. Displays on the underlying geology, wildlife, and history of the area are combined with an exhibition on the work of the Park Rangers and the Mountain Rescue

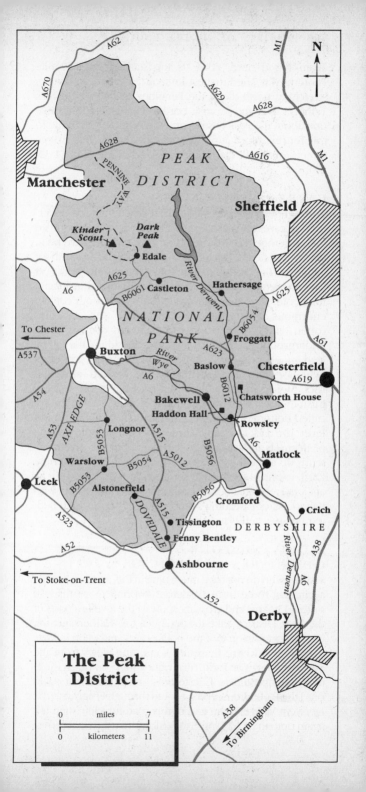

The Peak District

| 0 | miles | 7 |
| 0 | kilometers | 11 |

Team based here. Edale is the start of the 250-mile Pennine Way, the toughest long-distance path in Britain, stretching north along the Pennines all the way to Kirk Yetholm over the Scottish border. For detailed information about the Peak District and the Pennine Way, write to the Tourist Information Centre, Old Market Hall, Bridge Street, Bakewell, Derbyshire DE4 1DS (Tel: 0629-81-32-27).

CAVERNS AND CAVES

Throughout the Peak District there are numerous underground caves and passages, formed as rainwater dissolved the limestone. Four outstanding cave systems have been discovered near Castleton, all sited just off the A 625. About a mile west of Castleton, **Blue John Cavern** and **Treak Cliff Cavern** were opened up to mine the unique translucent, multicolored mineral known as Blue John. Both contain enormous underground caverns, some with stalactites (open daily). Nearby **Speedwell Cavern** consists of an underground canal cut straight into the side of the hill by lead miners in about 1771. Boats formerly were propelled by miners who lay on their backs and "walked" along the roof. Motors are now used, but passengers also help to push the boat with their hands. The canal leads to the so-called Bottomless Pit Cavern some 600 feet below ground level. The dark lake, which lies 70 feet beneath the viewing platform, is in fact only 30 feet deep, but the cavern extends up more than 450 feet (open daily). **Peak Cavern** at Castleton has a spectacular series of caves hollowed out by ancient rivers that occasionally nearly deafen visitors with the sound of cascading water (open Easter through September, weekends in February and March).

A DRIVING TOUR
OF THE PEAK DISTRICT

Visitors who do not have much time in this area can pursue a circular route from Castleton covering more than 70 miles (112 km) and crossing some of the loveliest parts of the Peak District. Take the A 625 east to **Hathersage**, the inspiration for some of the houses and landscape in *Jane Eyre*. Beyond here there are some fine views from the Surprise View Car Park. Turn right when you reach the B 6055 (signposted to Chesterfield) and then right again onto the B 6054, descending south through Froggatt to the Derwent Valley. At the end of this road turn left, then left again onto the A 623 south to Baslow. Take the right turn at the roundabout onto the A 619, then turn onto the B 6012, stopping on the way at Chatsworth House (see below).

Go south to the junction with the A 6 and then, after a detour to Haddon Hall (see below), go south on the A 6 along the Derwent Valley through Matlock and Matlock Bath (see below) to Cromford, site of the **Arkwright Mill**, the world's first (1771) water-powered cotton-spinning mill (open daily). (*Note:* On Sundays and bank holiday evenings in the height of summer, avoid the A 6 on either side of Matlock and Matlock Bath by turning right off the B 6012 at Rowsley onto the A 6 toward Bakewell and Haddon Hall, and then left onto the B 5056, crossing the A 5012 at Grangemill.)

Visitors with young children or with an interest in old modes of transport will be thrilled by a trip to the **Tramway Museum** at Crich; continue on down the A 6 until you reach the left turning to Crich, and then follow the signs. On leaving the museum, retrace your steps to the Arkwright Mill at Cromford and turn left.

Motorists driving south along the A 6 should turn right at the traffic lights by the mill and then take the first right toward Buxton along the A 5012. In Grangemill, turn left down the B 5056 toward Ashbourne. At the end of this very scenic road (you are now at the southern edge of the Peak District) turn right up the A 515 through the village of **Fenny Bentley**, with its fortified manor house. Don't miss the curious tomb in the village church showing Thomas Beresford, his wife, and their 21 children, all dressed in shrouds. Just north of here, a short detour will take you to the beautiful little village of **Tissington**, where the route of a disused railway has been turned into the **Tissington Trail** for walkers and cyclists. Tissington is best known for the Peak District custom of well-dressing, and is traditionally the first place to dress its wells with flowers on Ascension Day, a custom that draws thousands of visitors to the national park throughout the summer.

From here continue north along the A 515 for 1½ miles (2½ km) and then turn left to Alstonefield and down into the beautiful **Valley of the Dove** (there is a walk along Dovedale from nearby Milldale). From Alstonefield take the road north to Hulme End, and then turn left toward Warslow (B 5054) and, after a mile, right toward Buxton (B 5053). Just after Longnor make a left turn to Hollinsclough—and a striking view of some dramatic peaks will open up on your right. About ½ mile (¾ km) past the village turn left just before the sign "Not suitable for motor vehicles." Then turn right at the next junction and right again onto the A 53 toward Buxton. This road runs along **Axe Edge**, which forms an important watershed and the boundary between the eastern White Peak and the Dark Peak to the west.

Buxton, a spa town that once rivaled Bath in popularity, has some fine Georgian houses. You can sample the spa water at St. Ann's Well opposite the Tourist Information Centre. The **Micrarium** situated in the town's lovely crescent is well worth visiting for an extraordinary view of the microscopic world around us (open daily, April through October). Visitors not going into Buxton should take the A 6 bypass (signposted Stockport) and then turn onto the B 6061 toward Castleton. This brings you to the left turn for Edale and Blue John Cavern. Continue straight on over **Winnat's Pass**, one of the Peak District's most impressive gorges, back to Castleton, dominated by the lovely ruined keep of **Peveril Castle**, built by the Normans to protect the Peak Forest and used as the setting in Sir Walter Scott's novel *Peveril of the Peak*.

CHATSWORTH HOUSE
A visit to the home of the duke and duchess of Devonshire should be considered a must for any visitor to the Peak District. One of the most magnificent of England's fine stately homes, Chatsworth is managed superbly and deserves a full day to do it justice. Arrive early to avoid the crowds in summer. (Chatsworth is 11 miles/18 km west of Chesterfield, near the village of Baslow.)

The formidable Bess of Hardwick, widow of Sir William Cavendish, completed the first building here in 1564, but little of it has survived the creation of the present "palace." Chatsworth's appearance today is due to the work of three dukes of Devonshire: the first duke, champion of William of Orange; the fourth duke, a prominent Whig politician; and the sixth, "bachelor" duke. The first duke's building plans at the beginning extended only to changing the south front of the original Elizabethan mansion, but by the time of his death in 1707 he had completely rebuilt Chatsworth to its present design. Capability Brown was the fourth duke's instrument of change; employed to transform the park and gardens, he eventually altered the course of the River Derwent and moved the cottages of the nearby village of Edensor to improve the view. The last major changes were made by the sixth duke, who became a great friend of Joseph Paxton when he was a young gardener at Kew. The duke appointed Paxton head gardener at Chatsworth, and together they made the garden that can be seen today.

The tour of the house, which takes at least an hour, reveals a collection of treasures rarely found under one roof. The Cavendish family maintained and increased their wealth over the centuries through marriage, wise investments, and the ownership of vast tracts of land. They also enjoyed spending their wealth on priceless treasures from all over the world, which are now available for everyone to enjoy.

Visitors enter the house by the north entrance and the vast Painted Hall, with scenes from the life of Julius Caesar. A succession of vast **State Rooms**—superbly painted, carved, and furnished—are not for living but purely for display. Look for the violin hanging on a door in the State Music Room: it is a trompe l'oeil painting. Beyond the State Rooms are a variety of galleries, stairs, and rooms, each with its own identity and each housing yet another galaxy of treasures, from furniture and china to paintings and tapestries. Finally, visitors enter the **Great Dining Room**, with a series of magnificent portraits by Van Dyck and a gallery built to house the sixth duke's outstanding collection of sculpture. The exit is through the orangery, now converted into a large shop.

After touring the house you can walk out into the nearby formal gardens or explore the 1000-acre park. The garden includes a cascade, spectacular fountains and rocks, a tropical greenhouse, herbaceous borders, a rose garden, and various walks through the woods. At the top of the short incline to the north of the house are the 18th-century stables, now glassed in and transformed into a splendid restaurant, the **Carriage House**, which serves delicious lunches and teas.

The elegant ▶ **Cavendish Hotel** at Baslow has excellent views of the Chatsworth estate. Much of the hotel's furniture was made in the workshops of Chatsworth House, and the fine antique pieces and pictures reflect the part played by the present duchess of Devonshire in the recent transformation of the Cavendish from a simple 18th-century inn.

HADDON HALL

While Chatsworth House is a true stately home, built as a display of wealth and power, Haddon Hall, despite its size and elegance, is a medieval family home. This is apparent as soon as you enter this delightful house, located south of Bakewell off the A 6. It has an intimate atmosphere and charm that is impossible in larger houses like Chatsworth and Belvoir Castle. When Haddon was first built on a bluff overlooking the River Wye, it would have been a much smaller fortified manor house consisting of the Peverel Tower, the chapel, and some ancillary buildings. The Vernon family acquired the hall in the 12th century but did not add to it substantially until the 14th century, when Richard de Vernon built the perfectly preserved banqueting hall and the kitchen. From then on until the mid-17th century, nearly every generation added to the hall. Today it is a fine crenellated two-storied stone building that follows an oblong shape. The oblong courtyard within is divided in two by the central chapel.

At the height of its splendor, in about 1563, Haddon was the scene of Dorothy Vernon's romantic elopement with John Manners, the second son of the earl of Rutland. She is said to have fled her father's house, during a ball to celebrate her sister's marriage, by running down the stone steps to the packhorse bridge over the River Wye where her lover was waiting for her. Their great-grandson became the ninth earl of Rutland and in 1703 was created a duke. By this time the family had moved to Belvoir Castle, and for the next 200 years Haddon was largely untouched. It owes its remarkable atmosphere to this fact and to the meticulous restoration carried out by the ninth duke after he moved back into Haddon in 1912.

Visitors will be charmed by the attractive setting, a profusion of roses and other flowers over mellowed stonework, paneled rooms with unusual carvings, and the lovely oak furniture. To experience the intimate atmosphere, arrive early to tour the house. Lunch and tea can be taken in the rooms over the stables (open daily, Easter through September).

MATLOCK AND MATLOCK BATH

Once a quiet and featureless village, Matlock (south of Haddon Hall on the A 6) was transformed in the 18th and early 19th centuries into a massively popular spa attracting fashionable people from miles around to "take the waters." When the railway was built it also drew the middle classes, many of whom came not just for the waters but for a holiday, enticed by the popular hotels and attractions developed by entrepreneur John Smedley.

He also owned the ruined **Riber Castle**, now the site of a large wildlife park (open daily). Every summer visitors still come by the thousands to Matlock and Matlock Bath, drawn by boat trips on the River Derwent, cable-car rides from the wooded Heights of Abraham (a hilltop park above Matlock Bath), a lead-mining museum in The Pavilion at Matlock Bath, and numerous other attractions.

GETTING AROUND

If you have a car, you will be able to get around the Shires of Middle England quite easily. All of them are connected by Britain's two main arteries—the M 1 motorway and the A 1, which go through the region on their way from London to the North of England and Scotland. Visitors often prefer to travel on the A 1 as, while long stretches of it are motorway, it is mercifully free of large trucks. Away from the motorways, driving is generally a pleasure if you avoid the major cities during rush hour. In the big towns and cities, parking is usually fairly easy.

National Express provides good bus service linking the region's major cities with London; for details, Tel: (071) 730-0202. Bus service in rural areas is a different matter; study the timetables carefully so you don't get stranded, particularly on Sundays.

The region is well served by British Rail. Direct high-speed InterCity trains run regularly from London's Euston Station to Northampton; travel to Leicester and Nottingham originates at London's St. Pancras Station. Lincoln is only occasionally served by direct trains; when not, travellers must change at Newark-on-Trent in Nottinghamshire. Visitors who want to use the railways to explore the region should consider a Rail Rover ticket. Ticket holders can travel throughout the Shires of Middle England and as far west as Stoke-on-Trent. Visitors who want to travel almost continuously can buy a 7-day ticket, while others may prefer the cheaper 3-in-7 ticket, which allows unlimited travel within the region for any 3 days out of a 7-day period.

There are several particularly scenic rail routes through the Shires. The route between Leicester and Peterborough goes through Melton Mowbray, Oakham, and Stamford, and is a convenient way to explore these attractive market towns. The Peak District has two scenic rail routes that can be combined with a short bus ride; travellers can start at either Manchester or Derby. The Manchester trains run via Stockport across the White Peaks to Buxton; another line connects Matlock and Derby. Visitors with the time and energy can walk the 20 miles between Buxton and Matlock via the disused railway track or via the High Peak Trail.

ACCOMMODATIONS REFERENCE

Rates are projected 1994 prices for a double room with breakfast, unless otherwise stated. As prices are subject to change, always double-check before booking.

▶ **Angel and Royal Hotel**. High Street, **Grantham**, Lincolnshire NG31 6PN. Tel: (0476) 658-16; Fax: (0476) 671-49; in U.S. and Canada, (800) 225-5843; in Australia, (008) 22-24-46. £80 (does not include breakfast).

▶ **Barnsdale Lodge**. The Avenue, Rutland Water, near Oakham, Leicester LE15 8AH. Tel: (0572) 72-46-78; Fax: (0572) 72-49-61. £73–£84.

▶ **Belmont House Hotel**. De Montfort Street, **Leicester**, Leicestershire LE1 7GR. Tel: (0533) 54-47-73; Fax: (0533) 47-08-04; in U.S. and Canada, (800) 528-1234; in Australia, (008) 222-166. £84–£92.

▶ **Boultons Country House Hotel**. 4 Catmos Street, **Oakham**, Rutland, Leicestershire LE15 6HW. Tel: (0572) 72-28-44; Fax: (0572) 72-44-73. £60–£70.

▶ **Cavendish Hotel**. **Baslow**, Derbyshire DE45 1SP. Tel: (0246) 58-23-11; Fax: (0246) 58-23-12; in U.S., Fax: (800) 235-5845. £94–£105 (does not include breakfast).

▶ **D'Isney Place Hotel**. Eastgate, **Lincoln**, Lincolnshire LN2 4AA. Tel: (0522) 53-88-81; Fax: (0522) 51-13-21. £49–£70.

▶ **Finches Arms**. Hambleton, **Oakham**, Leicestershire LE15 8PO. Tel: (0572) 75-65-75. £35–£45.

▶ **Hambleton Hall**. Hambleton, **Oakham**, Leicestershire LE15 8TH. Tel: (0572) 75-69-91; Fax: (0572) 72-47-21. £120–£262.

▶ **Hillcrest Hotel**. 15 Lindum Terrace, **Lincoln**, Lincolnshire LN2 5RT. Tel: (0522) 51-01-82; Fax: (0522) 51-01-82. £56–£62.50.

▶ **Holiday Inn**. St. Nicholas Circle, **Leicester**, Leicestershire LE1 5LX. Tel: (0533) 53-11-61; Fax: (0533) 51-31-69; in U.S. and Canada, (800) 465-4329; in Australia, (008) 22-10-66. £99–£114.

▶ **Holiday Inn Garden Court**. Castle Marina Park, **Nottingham**, Nottinghamshire NG7 1GX. Tel: (0602) 50-06-00; Fax: (0602) 50-04-33; in U.S. and Canada, (800) 465-4329; in Australia, (008) 22-10-66. £60–£67.

▶ **Hotel Saint James**. Abbey Street, **Leicester**, Leicestershire LE1 3TE. Tel: (0533) 51-06-66; Fax: (0533) 51-51-83. £45 (does not include breakfast).

▶ **Royal Moat House International**. Wollaton Street, **Nottingham** NG1 5RH. Tel: (0602) 41-44-44; Fax: (0602) 47-56-67. £104.

▶ **Saracen's Head**. Market Place, **Southwell**, Nottinghamshire NG25 OHE. Tel: (0636) 81-27-01; Fax: (0636) 81-54-08; in U.S. and Canada, (800) 225-5843; in Australia, (008) 22-24-46. £80–£95.

▶ **Stapleford Park**. **Melton Mowbray**, Leicestershire LE14 2EF. Tel: (057) 28-45-22; Fax: (057) 28-46-51. £125–£195.

▶ **White Hart Hotel**. Bailgate, **Lincoln** LN1 3AR. Tel: (0522) 52-62-22; Fax: (0522) 53-17-98. £90–£135 (does not include breakfast).

THE HEART OF ENGLAND

STRATFORD AND WARWICK TO THE WELSH BORDER

By Angela Murphy

Just a few hours from London is the region loosely known as the "Heart of England." This area, stretching from the ancient towns of Stratford-upon-Avon and Warwick west to the Welsh border, encompasses some of the finest and most historic countryside in England. Shakespeare country, centered around his birthplace, Stratford, and the mighty castle at Warwick, attracts many thousands of visitors every year. But if you explore the areas to the west you'll discover sleepy villages and bustling market towns that have remained largely unspoiled. A network of canals crisscrosses the land. Once essential in transporting goods across the country, they now provide a superb touring resource, and you should not fail to take at least one river or canal trip during your stay. (See Getting Around, at the end of this chapter, for specific booking information.)

MAJOR INTEREST

Shakespearean sites in Stratford
Warwick Castle
Kenilworth Castle
Worcester Cathedral

Malvern Hills
Chained Library in Hereford Cathedral
Forest of Dean
Tintern Abbey
Shrewsbury's fine old buildings
Ironbridge Gorge industrial museum
Ludlow and the Shropshire Hills
Chester's cathedral and Roman amphitheater

STRATFORD-UPON-AVON

A visit to England would be incomplete without at least a brief stop at Shakespeare's birthplace, Stratford. Although it draws crowds of visitors from all over the world, Stratford is still a delightful town, with many less-frequented side roads where ancient houses and unusual crafts and antiques shops are to be found. Regular guided tours of Stratford and some of the nearby sites are available, and Guide Friday runs open-top double-decker buses connecting the Shakespeare properties every 15 minutes in summer and hourly in winter. Tickets can be bought on the bus or from the Guide Friday Stratford Centre of Tourism at 14 Rother Street. Probably the best way to see and understand the town is to use these buses to visit the historic houses first, and later to visit the theater buildings and take a trip along the river.

To start your visit, see the lavish audiovisual production called "The World of Shakespeare," just along the road from the Royal Shakespeare Theatre on Waterside. Superbly designed to present the everyday life of the Elizabethans, it can be a great help to visitors touring the general sites. From here you can walk to the other side of Bridge Foot to catch the open-top Guide Friday bus in front of the Pen & Parchment Inn.

Stratford drew few Shakespearean pilgrims before the early 18th century, when interest in Shakespeare's writings revived. From then on there was a steady stream of literary visitors, encouraged by the first Shakespeare Festival, organized in 1769 by the celebrated actor and impresario David Garrick. Modern-day tourists visit the same places those first tourists did, particularly the Tudor houses associated with Shakespeare. Many of them are now run by the Shakespeare Birthplace Trust, which issues a combined admission ticket to all its buildings. The ticket is available at any of their properties.

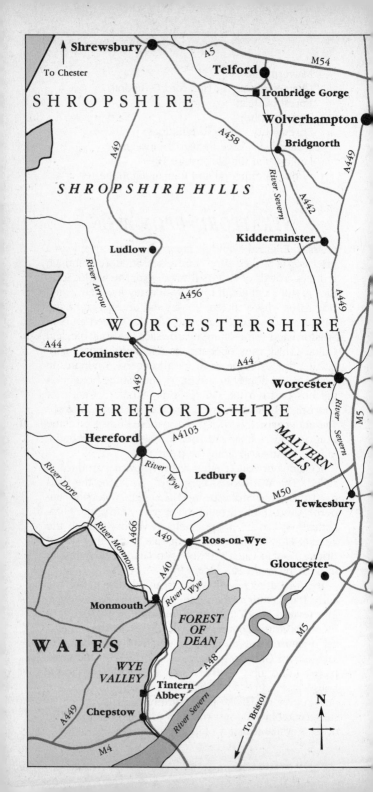

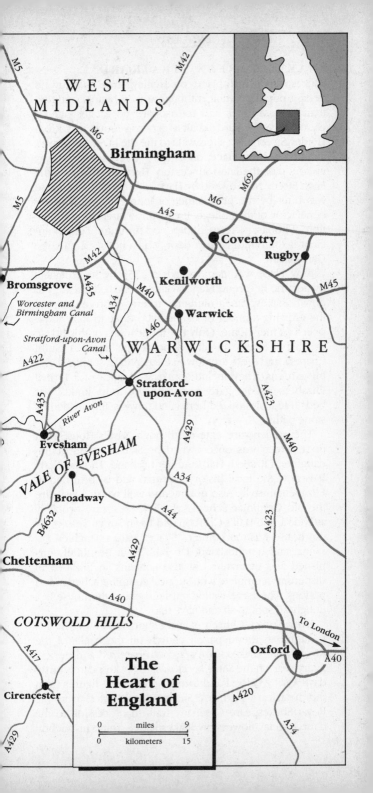

SHAKESPEAREAN STRATFORD

Shakespeare's Birthplace, on Henley Street, has always been a popular venue, although it is in better condition than in past times and tourists are no longer offered chunks from the Bard's chair as expensive souvenirs. From Henley Street it is a short walk to the site of Shakespeare's last home, **New Place,** on Chapel Street. Along the way visitors pass the late-16th-century **Harvard House** on the High Street. Now owned by Harvard University, the house was built by the grandfather of John Harvard, an early benefactor of the college. It contains a fascinating collection of books, pictures, and period furniture. Equally ancient is the building next door, which houses a pub, the **Garrick Inn**.

New Place was demolished in 1759 by its crotchety owner, the Reverend Francis Gastrell. He had already cut down Shakespeare's mulberry tree as a protest against the growing number of visitors who came to look at the poet's former home. Only the foundations of this house in Chapel Street remain (opposite the fine old Guild Chapel), and these are now in the center of some delightful gardens. They include an exact replica of a formal Elizabethan knot garden, comprising four "knotts," or beds filled with mixed herbs and flowers and divided by stone paths.

The gardens are entered through **Nash's House** next door, which was once owned by Shakespeare's granddaughter, Elizabeth Hall, and her husband, Thomas Nash. It is now the local history museum and is furnished in Elizabethan style. Also nearby, and well worth a visit, are the old **Grammar School,** which Shakespeare probably attended, and **Hall's Croft** on Old Town Street. This lovely old house was the home of Shakespeare's daughter, Susanna, and her husband, Dr. John Hall. Beautifully furnished and maintained, it also contains an Elizabethan dispensary, complete with surgical equipment, herbs, and potions. The large walled garden behind the house is a delightful spot to sit and have tea.

Holy Trinity Church is just a short walk away. At this beautiful medieval parish church on the banks of the River Avon, Shakespeare was both baptized and buried. Every year on the Saturday closest to Shakespeare's birthday (April 23) local and foreign dignitaries, figures from the theatrical world, and Shakespearean actors from the Royal Shakespeare Company walk in procession to the church to lay flowers on **Shakespeare's Tomb** in celebra-

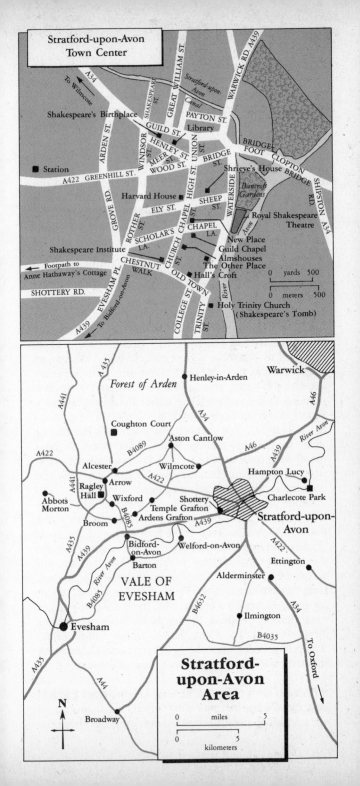

Stratford-upon-Avon Town Center

To Wilmcote
A34
Shakespeare's Birthplace
Station
A422 GREENHILL ST.
Harvard House
Shakespeare Institute
Footpath to
Anne Hathaway's Cottage
SHOTTERY RD.
A439
To Bidford-on-Avon

SHAKESPEARE ST.
GREAT WILLIAM ST.
PAYTON ST.
Stratford-upon-Avon Canal
WARWICK RD. A439
GUILD ST.
HENLEY ST.
Library
ARDEN ST.
WINDSOR ST.
MEER ST.
WOOD ST.
UNION ST.
HIGH ST.
BRIDGE ST.
BRIDGE FOOT
CLOPTON BRIDGE
SHIPSTON RD. A34
Shrieve's House
Bancroft Gardens
GROVE RD.
ROTHER ST.
ELY ST.
CHAPEL ST.
SHEEP ST.
WATERSIDE
Sheep
CHAPEL LA.
SCHOLAR'S LA.
CHURCH ST.
Avon
Royal Shakespeare Theatre
New Place
Guild Chapel
Almshouses
The Other Place
CHESTNUT WALK
EVESHAM PL.
OLD TOWN
Hall's Croft
0 yards 500
0 meters 500
COLLEGE ST.
TRINITY ST.
River
Holy Trinity Church (Shakespeare's Tomb)

Stratford-upon-Avon Area

A435
Forest of Arden
Henley-in-Arden
Warwick
A441
Coughton Court
A34
A46
A422
Aston Cantlow
A46
A439
River Avon
Alcester
Wilmcote
Hampton Lucy
A441
Arrow
A422
Charlecote Park
Ragley Hall
Wixford
Shottery
Stratford-upon-Avon
Abbots Morton
B4085
Temple Grafton
Ardens Grafton
A439
A422
Broom
Welford-on-Avon
Ettington
Bidford-on-Avon
A435
A439
Barton
Alderminster
A34
VALE OF EVESHAM
River Avon
B4085
B4632
Ilmington
To Oxford
Evesham
B4035
A435
A44
N
Broadway
0 miles 5
0 kilometers 5

tion of the Bard's birthday. If your visit to Stratford coincides with this or with the traditional Mop Fair, usually held on or about October 12 (originally an annual hiring fair for servants, it is now an amusement fair), you will miss the summer crush of tourists and see some of the town's true life.

THE THEATERS
Following the river from Holy Trinity back toward the Clopton Bridge, you arrive at the **Royal Shakespeare Theatre**, which contains a small exhibition of paintings, costumes, and mementos. Shakespearean plays are performed here from the end of March to the end of January. A small number of medium-priced tickets are sold on the day of the performance, but advance booking is always highly advisable. The Royal Shakespeare Company will arrange tickets along with food and accommodations. Another fine theater, the Swan, has been built next to it in the shell of the original Victorian Memorial Theatre (destroyed by fire in 1926) and is designed to resemble a Jacobean playhouse. The **Swan Theatre** stages the works of Shakespeare's contemporaries and followers, among other works, and a smaller, modern theater nearby, **The Other Place**, also stages a variety of productions. (Tel: 0789-29-56-23 for bookings or 0789-691-91 for 24-hour recorded information, or write to the Box Office, Royal Shakespeare Theatre, Stratford-upon-Avon CV37 6BB.) Visitors can tour backstage at the Royal Shakespeare Theatre and view the costume exhibition most afternoons.

Other unusual attractions in town include the marvelous **Teddy Bear Museum** in Greenhill Street and the Brass Rubbing Centre in **Avon Bank Park** (between the Swan Theatre and Holy Trinity Church), where visitors can make their own brass rubbings. In Bancroft Gardens and just across the footbridge at the Boathouse pub in Swan's Nest Lane you can take a short cruise or rent boats and canoes for short excursions on the river. There are always a few canal barges moored in the basin here, where the Stratford-upon-Avon Canal begins. In the middle of the riverside gardens opposite is the brasserie **Colette's by the Riverside**, which has a lovely view of the river.

STAYING AND DINING IN STRATFORD
Visitors looking for reasonably priced accommodations are advised to book early and select with care from the

many available choices. Several hotels offer reduced prices for weekend bookings. Two popular, upmarket, and very central hotels with strong historic connections are the luxurious ▶ **Shakespeare Hotel** on Chapel Street, which is housed in an original Tudor building, and the larger and slightly less atmospheric ▶ **White Swan Hotel** opposite Market Place. Part of the Shakespeare Hotel used to be the 15th-century home of Sir Hugh Clopton, a former lord mayor of London who built the town's attractive bridge. The fine 16th-century wall paintings in the White Swan, uncovered in the 1920s, illustrate the story of Tobias and the angel and owe their remarkable state of preservation to Jacobean paneling.

Those looking for a more intimate ambience might try the small but exclusive ▶ **Stratford House Hotel,** just 100 yards from the theater on Sheep Street. It has a charming conservatory-restaurant and the staff will book theater tickets for you. Another pleasant hotel in a peaceful canalside setting is ▶ **Duke's Hotel** on Payton Street. A large family-run hotel, it has a relaxed country-house atmosphere. An excellent and inexpensive bed-and-breakfast accommodation out of town is ▶ **Folly Farm Cottage** at Ilmington, a beautiful village on the northern edge of the Cotswolds. Take a magical walk through this village's back alleys and finish off with an excellent dinner at the restaurant of the **Howard Arms**.

For a really good dinner try **Shepherd's Garden Restaurant** at the Stratford House Hotel (see above) or **Sir Toby's** in Church Street. Theatergoers and others can also dine at the Royal Shakespeare Theatre, either at the elegant **Box Tree Restaurant** overlooking the river (not always good value) or at the more informal **River Terrace Restaurant**. Just across the road is the popular actors' pub, the **Black Swan** (known to regulars as the "Dirty Duck"). In the center of town, the **Slug and Lettuce** pub-cum-bistro on Guild Street offers a lively alternative with an excellent range of dishes, in spite of its unappealing name. For more exotic but inexpensive fare, try **Lord's Bistro** on Union Street or, for first-class Indian food, **Hussain's** on Chapel Street. Also fun to eat at is **Fatty Arbuckle's**, opposite New Place on Chapel Street.

There are also a number of fine hotels around Stratford. Two luxury establishments, housed in large, historic mansions, each with its own first-class restaurant, are the ▶ **Ettington Park Hotel** on the A 34 near Alderminster and the ▶ **Welcombe Hotel** on Warwick Road. Both stand in superb parklands and offer a wide range of amenities, including outstanding accommodation and services.

Opposite the entrance to Ragley Hall, near Wixford a few miles west of Stratford, the ▶ **Arrow Mill** on the River Arrow has been converted into a delightful small hotel. Although situated in a rather featureless area next to the river, the Arrow Mill is an excellent hotel, decorated to the highest standards and with a well laid-out garden. It makes an excellent base for touring the area. The village of Arrow, for which it was named, is nearby.

Attractions near Stratford

A pleasant stroll along the footpaths leading west from the town center will take you to the place where Shakespeare did much of his courting. It can also be reached by open-top bus. **Anne Hathaway's Cottage** at Shottery is a classic thatched farmhouse containing original furniture and surrounded by an old-fashioned English garden. Visitors can get lunchtime snacks or excellent cream teas at the **Cottage Tea Garden** opposite.

To the north and west, little remains of the ancient Forest of Arden, which once covered most of the area. However, much of its timber can be seen in use as the frames and gables of houses in the local villages. Notable among these villages are lovely **Abbots Morton**, with its 14th-century stone church and thatched-roof letter box; **Aston Cantlow**, where Shakespeare's parents married; and charming **Wilmcote**, where his mother was raised.

Shakespeare's parents were a comparatively wealthy couple. His father was a glover and tanner, and his mother, Mary Arden, was the daughter of a prosperous farmer. Their attractive farm in Wilmcote has been combined with the nearby Glebe Farm to form a fascinating museum of farming and rural life. Crafts displays are distributed around the farm buildings. It is also the home of a world-famous falconry center, which puts on daily flying displays and offers falconry courses and hawking parties. The area has a pair of fine traditional English pubs with excellent home-cooked bar food: the **King's Head Inn** at Aston Cantlow (where Shakespeare's parents are reputed to have held their wedding breakfast in 1557), and the **Mason's Arms** in Wilmcote.

Legend has it that the young William Shakespeare poached deer in the grounds of **Charlecote Park** near Stratford to the east, and deer can still be seen grazing there. Whatever the truth of the tale, this magnificent Tudor mansion in its great landscaped park makes for a satisfying visit. Still the home of the Lucy family, the house is now the property of the National Trust, and the ground-floor rooms are open to the public from Easter to October. It has some impressive Victorian rooms, a vast kitchen and brewhouse, and a museum of local and family relics. While there, drive or walk to the village of **Hampton Lucy** to see the family church of St. Peter and a restored 18th-century water mill where traditional stone-ground flour is still made.

VILLAGES TO TOUR
The countryside immediately south of Stratford is fairly flat meadow and farmland sustained by the River Avon. To the west, however, are a number of pleasant villages with Shakespearean associations, which can form the basis of a pleasant drive or bike ride. Take the A 439 west from Stratford for 3½ miles, then turn left through Welford-on-Avon. Much of this village has been built up, but the red, white, and blue maypole still stands, and local children dance around it every May Day. Turn right through Barton and right again onto the B 4085 to Bidford-on-Avon, which has some pleasant riverside meadows. Turn immediately right over the medieval stone bridge (past the church) and cross the A 439 to rejoin the B 4085 toward Wixford.

After about 1½ miles and just before Wixford, one more right turn leads you toward the delightful villages of Exhall, Ardens Grafton, and Temple Grafton. A short detour to the south in Ardens Grafton will take you to the **Golden Cross** pub, which has a fine collection of 300 antique dolls and Victoriana in its restaurant. Otherwise go straight on through Temple Grafton and stop for an excellent light lunch at the **Blue Boar Inn** before continuing across the A 422, past Billesley, to Wilmcote and then back to Stratford.

West of Stratford off the A 435, two important mansions are worth a visit—Coughton Court and Ragley Hall. **Coughton Court**, just north of Alcester, was the home of a powerful Catholic family, the Throckmortons, and is now run by the National Trust. Its ugly frontage conceals a superb brick courtyard and a fascinating interior that includes relics of the infamous Gunpowder Plot. The outstanding Palladian mansion **Ragley Hall**, west of Wixford, is set in a 400-acre park landscaped by

Capability Brown. In addition to a remarkable collection of paintings and furniture, its great hall contains some of the most splendidly ornate plasterwork in Britain. A more recent treasure is *The Temptation* by Graham Rust, a magnificent mural painted (1969–1983) for the present marquess of Hertford.

THE VALE OF EVESHAM

Southwest of Stratford, the River Avon flows through the Vale of Evesham, edged to the south by the Cotswold Hills. This fertile vale gained its fame for the fruit and vegetables grown there when the great abbeys dominated the region, and it is still well known as a major producer of vegetables and for its massed orchards of plums, cherries, and apples. In spring the orchards form part of a signposted "Blossom Trail" from Evesham. Telephone the Tourist Information Centre (Tel: 0386-44-69-44) for up-to-the-minute news of the blossoms from late March.

The two great Benedictine abbeys of the region, Pershore and Evesham, both fell victim to the ravages of the Reformation.

EVESHAM

Evesham's abbey, one of the finest ever built, was completely destroyed after 1540, leaving only its magnificent bell tower (1539) and the 14th-century half-timbered gateway in the marketplace. Among other fascinating displays of local history, a model of the abbey is on view in the **Almonry Museum** on Vine Street near Abbey Park. This lovely old building, which is also the Tourist Information Centre, has a pleasant walled garden. Two fine medieval churches situated side by side in Evesham also survive from this era—the townspeople's church of **All Saints** and the **Church of St. Lawrence**, built for the many pilgrims who flocked to pay homage to Simon de Montfort, a popular hero because of his role in founding the House of Commons. De Montfort was killed by Prince Edward (later Edward I) at the Battle of Evesham in 1265 and is buried beneath the abbey's high altar.

An attractive market town, Evesham has many interesting old buildings, including the beautifully restored Round House, which today contains the National Westminster Bank. At the town hall, the broad High Street splits

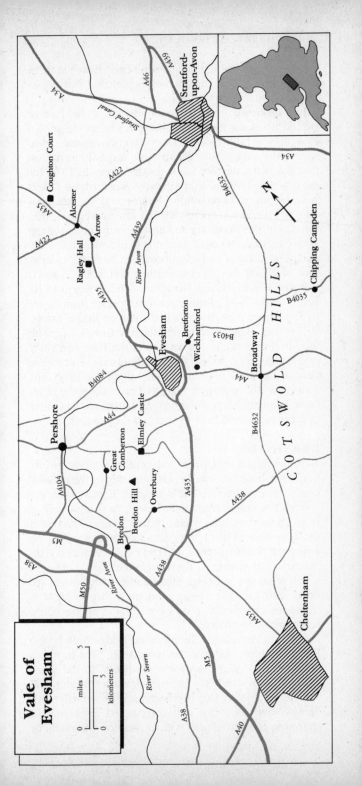

into two roads leading down to the river. Between them lie the abbey ruins, surrounded by parkland that slopes gently down to the riverbank.

Just upstream from Workman Bridge at the foot of Bridge Street, the modern **lockkeeper's house** deserves a look. It was built by the Lower Avon Navigation Trust, which, since the 1940s, has restored the Avon to navigation through voluntary labor contributions. In 1974, for the first time in more than a century, Stratford was linked with the Severn (which flows southwest down past Bristol), and a cruising route—via the River Avon, the Stratford Canal, the Worcester and Birmingham Canal, and the River Severn—was made available to pleasure craft. Fully equipped cruisers and canal boats can be hired in Stratford and Evesham through Blakes (Tel: 0603-78-29-11; Fax: 0603-78-28-71) or Hoseasons (Tel: 0502-50-10-10; Fax: 0502-50-05-32). Daily river trips operate from Easter to September from Boater's Wine Bar on Bridge Street.

Down the lane leading off Merstow Green (opposite the Almonry Museum) is the site of the Hampton Ferry (the oldest rope-pulled ferry in England). From here visitors can walk a circular route along the riverbank, across the Abbey Road bridge, and back along the other bank. Evesham is a popular boating center, and a number of regattas are held here throughout the summer.

PERSHORE

To the west, the important tenth-century Benedictine abbey at Pershore was largely destroyed during the dissolution of the monasteries. The townspeople paid to save the lovely 13th-century choir and transept; these now serve as **Holy Cross**, the town's parish church. Most spectacular is the impressive 14th-century lantern tower, standing on four great Norman arches, and two richly decorated 17th-century monuments to the Hazelwood family are also worth seeking out. Bridge Street and the High Street are lined with attractive Georgian houses, many with bow fronts and ornamental iron balconies. Several now house restaurants or tearooms.

South of Pershore is the medieval bridge built by the Benedictine monks over the River Avon. Next to it is a large riverside picnic area and footpaths. To the south the land rises slowly toward the summit of **Bredon Hill** (961 feet). Bredon Hill is crisscrossed by attractive bridleways and footpaths and surrounded by a ring of charming country villages with clusters of stone-built or half-timbered houses. At its summit are the remains of a large Iron Age fort and, within these, the 18th-century tower **Parson's Folly**.

Walkers can approach the hill from any of the little villages, although the gentlest approach is to drive part of the way up the south side of the hill in Kemerton. Then park and walk northward up the hill past another 18th-century folly, **Bell's Castle**. Other main routes are through nearby Overbury or by walking south from Elmley Castle in the north, first stopping at St. Mary's Church to see its fine 17th-century monuments. The views across the Avon valley are superb from the summit; on a clear day, as many as nine counties can be seen.

VILLAGES IN THE VALE

To the northwest of the hill, the village of **Great Comberton** has one of the largest dovecotes in England, with more than 1,400 nesting holes. Dovecotes were, in reality, pigeon-houses essential in the Middle Ages and later for providing the local gentry with fresh meat in the winter months. Their numbers were restricted to one per lordly household because of the damage pigeons did to local corn crops, but this law was often sidestepped by enormous buildings such as this one. In 1659 there were still more than 26,000 dovecotes in the country.

The village of **Bredon**, southwest of Bredon Hill on the B 4080, has a superb example of an early 14th-century tithe barn, built to hold the crops collected by the church as a tax on the local people. At this time the tax was usually a tithe, or tenth part, of the crop; in this case, it was gathered for the bishops of Worcester to the north.

The country church at **Wickhamford**, 2 miles (3 km) southeast of Evesham, contains the 17th-century tomb of one of George Washington's ancestors, Penelope Washington. Here you can see the Washington family coat of arms—three stars and one stripe—which served as a model for the U.S. flag.

STAYING AND DINING
IN AND AROUND EVESHAM

In Evesham, the comfortable, family-run ▶ **Evesham Hotel** has a friendly and slightly eccentric atmosphere. Worth a detour for a meal, at any time of year, is the **Fleece Inn** at Bretforton, a beautifully preserved 19th-century tavern, part of which dates from the 14th century. It has a superb orchard garden.

On the eastern side of Pershore several hotels and inns back onto gardens by the river, including the friendly 16th-century ▶ **Angel Inn**, which has comfortable rooms and serves good homemade food. An important gardening center, Pershore has a large market on Wednesdays, Fridays, and Saturdays.

WARWICKSHIRE OUTSIDE THE STRATFORD AREA

Stratford attracts hordes of visitors, as does Warwick, but the countryside of surrounding Warwickshire offers delightful exploration too. This has long been a prosperous place: The River Avon provided an early trade route to Bristol, and later the Stratford-upon-Avon Canal linked the area with the industrial center of Birmingham. Mighty castles also gave Warwickshire immense political importance in the Middle Ages. Today the center of this region is Warwick.

Warwick

The historic town of Warwick, just 8 miles (13 km) north of Stratford on A 46, merits at least a daylong visit, not only for its justly famed, monumental Warwick Castle but also for the town itself. Although it is the administrative capital of the county, Warwick is quite small, with a network of crooked streets, many fine old houses, and a special charm and intimacy. It is situated on top of a low hill overlooking the Avon, and its center is largely contained within a triangle of ancient streets grouped around St. Mary's Church in Old Square.

The base of this triangle is the High Street (leading onto Jury Street), which separates the town from the castle and connects the east and west gates of the town's original medieval walls. Although the layout of medieval Warwick has survived, fire destroyed much of the town in 1694, and most of the houses remaining date from the late 17th and 18th centuries. The fire also destroyed the main body of **St. Mary's Church**. (The nave and the superb tower were rebuilt in the early 18th century.) However, the jewel of the church survived: the 15th-century **Beauchamp Chapel**, with its famous tomb of Richard Beauchamp. Other re-

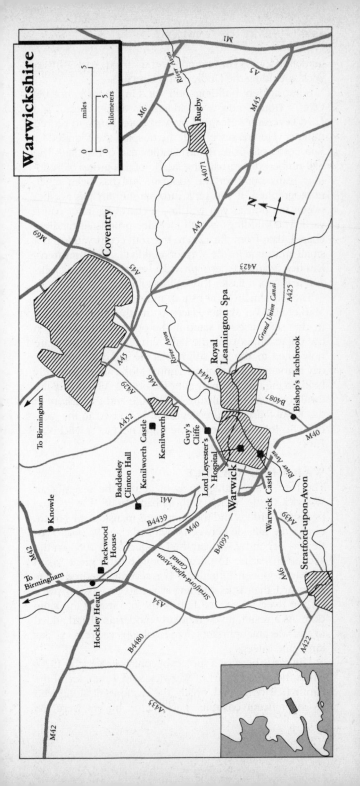

markable tombs commemorate the various earls of Warwick, including the Dudleys and Grevilles.

Some ancient buildings still stand in the town, notably **Oken's House**, now a world-famous doll museum, and **Lord Leycester's Hospital** by West Gate. Home to retired military veterans since 1571, the hospital was founded by Elizabeth I's favorite, Robert Dudley, earl of Leicester. The half-timbered, overhanging façade of this group of buildings leans out over the footpath and has been much photographed. If you walk through the tiny passage between the houses you will find a charming inner courtyard. The buildings, which include an unusual candlelit chapel, date from the 12th to the 16th century; there is a small museum in the former guildhall. The **Brethren's Kitchen** tearoom here provides excellent light snacks and teas (open Easter through October).

The city's main local history museum is housed in the **Market Hall** on Market Place. As in other English towns, market stalls used to stand in the open arcades between the pillars supporting the hall. Although the arcades are now filled in, the hall still marks the site of the present-day marketplace and of the annual Mop Fair, traditionally held on the first Saturday after October 9. A branch of the local museum specializing in folk life and the history of the Royal Warwickshire Regiment is housed in the Jacobean **St. John's House** at Coten End next to St. Nicholas' Park.

WARWICK CASTLE

The town's star attraction is of course the magnificent Warwick Castle, which, with its battlements, towers, and beautiful gardens and the enormous mansion at its heart, covers the hillside between town and river. Warwick Castle was begun by William the Conqueror in 1068 on the site of an earlier fortification built by the great Saxon monarch Queen Ethelfleda. For several hundred years afterward, the castle, standing at a strategic crossing place on the river, was a vital link in the defense of the kingdom. As a result, it was regularly modernized and added to and was an important gift to loyal subjects from various kings and queens.

The castle became a subject of controversy in the 1970s when the present earl of Warwick sold a number of the family heirlooms and, finally, the castle itself along with its magnificent contents. Luckily, the buyers were the owners of Madame Tussaud's, the famous waxworks museum, and they have restored the castle beautifully. They have also added to the collection by buying items associated with the castle's history.

The castle is filled to the brim with visitors in high summer (to be avoided, if possible), and lines to see the state apartments have been known to stretch beyond the castle walls. However, in summer the grounds are at their best; so if you go and want to avoid the worst of the crush, visit in the early morning. Thursdays and Saturdays are the least-crowded days. A winter's afternoon, when visitors are few, can be one of the most rewarding times to visit the castle.

The tour of the private apartments is thrilling. They have been arranged to replicate a weekend house party that occurred here in June 1898, complete with lifelike models of the distinguished guests and appropriate sound effects. It is one of the best-presented exhibits of its kind, and you may feel like an invisible eavesdropper who has travelled back in time. Other fascinating exhibits at the castle include the dungeon, fine armory, and the medieval Great Hall. The main entrance and gift shop are in the stables (through the Castle Lane car park) on a hill above the castle and close to the town center.

A fine view of the castle can be had from the "new" **Banbury Bridge**, built in the 1780s to replace the old bridge at the foot of the castle walls. The delightful ribbon of ancient houses along Bridgend owes its survival to the decision made by George Greville, second earl of Warwick, to move the bridge upstream. Beautiful private gardens at 55 Mill Street are occasionally open for charity, and they too provide a magnificent view of the castle and the remains of the old bridge. However, the finest views of the castle are from the river itself. Boats can be rented riverside at St. Nicholas's Park, which also has recreational facilities, a café, and picnic areas.

Just a mile north of Warwick on the road to Coventry is **Guy's Cliffe**, named after Guy of Warwick, the legendary hero of the Dark Ages who ended his days as a hermit in the caves above the river. Above the cliff are the ruins of an 18th-century house where the great actress Sarah Siddons once worked. Below, on the river, is a pleasant inn and steak house, **Saxon Mill**, where you can watch the mill wheel turning and water rushing underfoot. If you have a car, it is worth visiting for the magnificent setting.

DINING AND STAYING
IN AND AROUND WARWICK

For a light lunch, try **Pizza Piazza** on Jury Street, which serves good homemade pizzas in a 15th-century house near East Gate. Light meals and afternoon tea can also be had at **John Paul's** on the High Street and **Charlotte's Tea Rooms** on Jury Street. You can even take part in a medieval banquet at the castle if you reserve ahead; Tel: (0926) 49-54-21; Fax: (0926) 40-16-92.

Visitors are advised to lodge outside Warwick, in Royal Leamington Spa or Stratford. Alternatively, for inexpensive but very comfortable bed-and-breakfast accommodation try ▶ **Ashleigh House** in Henley-in-Arden, or ▶ **Northleigh House** at Hatton.

Kenilworth

A great castle is also the main attraction at nearby Kenilworth, 5 miles (8 km) north of Warwick on A 46. All that remains of this once formidable royal stronghold are some dramatic ruins left after Cromwell's troops dismantled the castle at the end of the Civil War. The 12th-century keep of **Kenilworth Castle** and its outer curtain wall were once surrounded by a vast man-made lake that was a defensive system in the early Middle Ages. Later the lake became a place of entertainment and leisure, so much so that Elizabeth I and her 400-member retinue made four visits to the castle when it belonged to Robert Dudley. The best documented of these occurred in July 1575 and formed the background for the novel *Kenilworth* by Sir Walter Scott.

Today the lake has been drained and the buildings are decayed and roofless. Their sheer scale, however, is very impressive, especially the walls of John of Gaunt's Great Hall, the massive gatehouse, and the stables erected by the earl of Leicester. Your visit will be enhanced if you first tour "The World of Shakespeare" exhibit in Stratford, part of which illustrates Queen Elizabeth's triumphal procession to Kenilworth in 1575. Make sure, too, that you have a close look at the postcard sold at the castle—it shows a drawing of Kenilworth as it was during Elizabeth's visit.

Between the castle and Kenilworth's center is a large open space named **Abbey Fields**, in which stand the remains of the town's abbey. The main part of the town is modern, but the area near the castle (particularly

Castle Green, Little Virginia on Castle Hill, and the High Street) has retained its original buildings, including many of the charming bow-fronted cottages characteristic of this region.

DINING IN KENILWORTH

Just up Castle Hill is a pleasant, inexpensive restaurant called **George Rafters**, which serves lunch and dinner. For something a little more special, seek out **Restaurant Bosquet** on Warwick Road, which serves superb food and wine at reasonable prices (reservations are essential; Tel: 0926-524-63).

Royal Leamington Spa

A couple of miles east of Warwick, on A 425, is Royal Leamington Spa (generally referred to as simply Leamington Spa), an elegant, early-19th-century Regency town with gracious houses and broad streets. Leamington and other important British spa towns such as Bath and Cheltenham (see The Cotswolds to Winchester chapter) came to prominence in the late 18th century on a wave of enthusiasm for "taking the waters" at mineral springs. By 1814 several baths had been built in Leamington, together with the large, distinguished buildings housing the **Pump Room** and the **Assembly Rooms**. The town continued to prosper in the early 19th century, a fact attested to by its spacious avenues and crescents lined with houses that are handsomely embellished with porticoes and ornate iron balconies. However, the spa's popularity began to decline in the mid-19th century, and the Pump Room is no longer in use.

Just opposite the Pump Room, by the River Leam, are the delightful **Jephson Gardens**. Also worth a visit is the **Leamington Spa Art Gallery and Museum** on Avenue Road, which has a fine collection of Dutch and Flemish masterpieces. The shopping in Royal Leamington Spa is excellent; the High Street has a full range of shops, from Next to Marks and Spencer.

Two stately homes are nearby: Baddesley Clinton Hall, 6 miles (10 km) north of Warwick off A 4177 near Knowle, and Packwood House, near A 3400 at Hockley Heath. Both are owned by the National Trust. **Baddesley Clinton Hall** is a superb moated manor house, much of which dates from the 14th and 15th centuries. It has several priest holes (for concealing Catholic priests during the Reformation) and Elizabethan fireplaces; fine tapestries and some notable paintings hang in paneled rooms. A 17th-century yew topiary garden representing the Sermon on the Mount is probably the most famous feature of **Packwood House**, but the building itself is an outstanding example of domestic Tudor architecture, with some fine tapestries, needlework, and furniture on display.

STAYING AND DINING IN AND AROUND ROYAL LEAMINGTON SPA

Royal Leamington Spa offers a wide variety of hotels, guest houses, and restaurants to choose from. For a pleasant, inexpensive hotel try the ► **Lansdowne Hotel** on Clarendon Street or the ► **Coverdale Private Hotel** on Portland Street. If you prefer more luxurious surroundings, head for ► **Mallory Court**, an outstanding country-house hotel with a superb restaurant, at Bishop's Tachbrook just south of Leamington.

WORCESTERSHIRE
Worcester

Thirty miles (48 km) west from Stratford on A 422 is the ancient cathedral city of Worcester (pronounced w'sster). The city lies on the River Severn, just where the valley broadens into a wide, fertile plain. To the east, gently rolling farmland stretches to the valley of the River Avon and the Vale of Evesham, while to the west are the fertile, hop-producing slopes of the lovely Teme Valley and the sharply defined ridge of the Malvern Hills.

An important settlement as early as Roman times, Worcester later flourished as the marketplace for surrounding agricultural areas and as a staging post between the North and Gloucester and between Wales and London. Worcester has also played a vital role in British history: In 1651, at the Battle of Worcester, the city was the last in England to surrender to Oliver Cromwell. Today much of the old city has disappeared under successive layers of development, but enough fascinating reminders of its varied history remain to make a visit here rewarding. Its many attractions include some well-designed exhibitions, such as the Commandery and Tudor House, that bring these events to life.

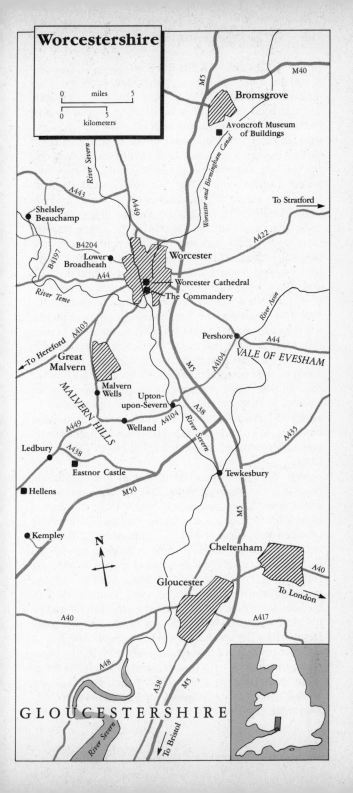

Worcestershire

miles 5
kilometers 5

River Severn

A443

A449

To Stratford

M5

M40

Bromsgrove

Avoncroft Museum
of Buildings

Worcester and Birmingham Canal

A422

Shelsley
Beauchamp

B4204

Lower
Broadheath

B4197

A44

Worcester

Worcester Cathedral
The Commandery

River Teme

A4103

To Hereford

Great
Malvern

Pershore

A44

River Avon

VALE OF EVESHAM

A4104

M5

Malvern
Wells

Upton-
upon-Severn

A4104

A38

MALVERN HILLS

Welland

River Severn

A449

Ledbury

A438

A435

Eastnor Castle

Hellens

M50

Tewkesbury

M5

Kempley

N

Cheltenham

A40

Gloucester

To London

A40

A417

GLOUCESTERSHIRE

A48

A38

M5

To Bristol

River Severn

WORCESTER CATHEDRAL

If you are a first-time visitor, you should make the magnificent Worcester Cathedral your first stop. Originally the cathedral church of a Benedictine monastery that thrived here until 1540, it is built on a low hill overlooking the Severn, just upstream of the town's impressive arched bridge. Its majestic bulk dominates the city skyline and provides a spectacular backdrop to the well-known Worcestershire County Cricket Ground. (You can buy tickets for any of the matches at the grounds.) Parts of the present structure, notably the fine crypt, date back to Norman times; indeed the crypt is the largest Norman crypt in England and the only surviving part of the original cathedral (1084). However, most of the cathedral was constructed under royal favor during the 13th and 14th centuries, when a constant stream of pilgrims visited its tombs and surrounding monastic buildings.

Many of the monastery buildings have survived, including the magnificent round Chapter House and the monks' refectory (now the hall of the King's School and recently renovated). Viewed from across the college green, to the south of the cathedral, these buildings are testaments to the binding link between church and monastery that existed before the dissolution of the monasteries by Henry VIII. From this side it's possible to walk around the **cloisters**, where side doors lead to a tearoom and a shop; you can enter the cathedral itself through the "Prior's Door."

After the intimacy of the cloisters, the magnificent nave is a breathtaking sight. Take special note of the elaborately carved pulpits and tombs, especially that of King John of Magna Carta fame, who was buried here between two saints at his own request in 1216. Other items of interest include some cunningly carved misericords under the choir seats, a carved marble reredos, and Prince Arthur's Chantry, with its delicate tracery. (Prince Arthur, whose tomb is here, died of measles before he could succeed to the throne and so his place was taken by his younger brother, who became Henry VIII.) The cathedral's upkeep is expensive, and its constant program of restoration is funded solely by donations, so you may wish to contribute as you leave. Every three years (next in 1995) the cathedral is host to the annual Three Choirs Festival. (The location is alternately Worcester, Gloucester, and Hereford.) This is the oldest choral festival in Europe, and it features first-class orchestral, choral, and chamber music concerts.

AROUND IN WORCESTER

The **Commandery**, an important 15th-century building, is southeast of the cathedral, next to the Worcester and Birmingham Canal at the foot of the hill. Erected on the site of a medieval hospital, or commandery, this was the Royalist headquarters during the Civil War and the site of some of Charles II's war councils. The restored building, with its superb Great Hall, now houses the Civil War Centre—a mixture of permanent displays and some very imaginative life-size reconstructions of various events throughout the Civil War. These bring the past to life in an exceptional way and should be a first stop for anyone interested in this fascinating period of British history. Allow two hours for a complete tour of the center. In fine weather the tearoom here serves by the side of the canal.

Some of the best-preserved reminders of the city's past are the ancient half-timbered houses on nearby Friar Street, particulary the 15th-century **Greyfriars** and **Tudor House**, now a folk museum with a well-organized display of the social and domestic life of the town over the past two centuries, including reconstruction of many shops and rooms from the past. **King Charles's House** in New Street, now a restaurant of the same name, is where Charles II hid after he lost the disastrous Battle of Worcester in 1651.

Of the three things for which Worcester is most famous—gloves, sauce, and porcelain—glove making is the only industry to have declined significantly. The curious spire off Deansway, once part of a church, was renamed the Glover's Needle by the townspeople in honor of the trade. Worcestershire sauce is still made in quantity here at the Lea & Perrins factory. Its founder, C. W. Dyson Perrins, established the unique **Dyson Perrins Museum** of historic Worcester porcelain at the Royal Worcester Porcelain Company. On display is the first piece ever made here, the Wigornia cream boat.

The **Royal Worcester Porcelain Company**, founded in 1751, conducts fascinating tours of the factory continually every weekday, during which you can watch at close hand the processes used in making porcelain. You can buy the results in the retail showroom and seconds shop. Reservations are essential in the summer and advisable at other times; however, a phone call before 10:00 A.M. will sometimes produce a reservation for the same day (Tel: 0905-232-21, Fax: 0905-236-01; no children under eight). Longer (two hours) and more detailed connoisseur's tours are also available. A restaurant serves afternoon teas and light lunches. If you come to Worcester by car, you can park at the Royal Worcester factory for a small fee and walk up to the cathedral along the cobbled College Precinct. From there, it is a pleasant walk around the center of the town and then back down to the Commandery and the factory. On summer Saturdays visitors can join the regular guided walks from the Guildhall.

Other attractions in Worcester include the narrowboats, or barges, in the Diglis Basin and on Lowesmoor Wharf on the canal; **St. Helen's County Record Office**, housed in a former church at the corner of the High Street and Fish Street, which holds the marriage document of William Shakespeare and Anne Hathaway; the **City Museum and Art Gallery**, near Foregate Street Railway Station; and the picturesque Pitchcroft Racecourse, by the Severn. Riverboats, rowing boats, and canoes can be rented at North and South Quay, and there are regular summer river trips from South Quay, opposite the cricket ground; for details, Tel: 0905-259-73. There is also regular ferry service on summer weekends across the river from the cathedral steps to Slingpool Walk near the cricket ground, which affords one of the finest views of the cathedral. You can rent bicycles and accessories at the **Cadence Café and Cycle Hire**, at the Foregate Street Railway Station; weekend booking advisable (Tel: 0905-61-35-01).

DINING AND STAYING
IN AND AROUND WORCESTER

You can get light snacks at the Cadence Café. For more substantial fare try **Hodsons Coffee House**, at the top of the High Street near the cathedral (closed Sundays), or one of the little restaurants on Friar Street. For a more stylish meal, dine overlooking the river at **Brown's Restaurant**, a converted granary on Quay Street (lunch and dinner).

The newly restored ▶ **Fownes Resort Hotel** on City Walls Road is an elegant modern hotel on the side of the canal. Out of town, you can get excellent home-cooked meals and accommodations at the ▶ **Birche Hotel** (just 7 miles/11 km northeast of Worcester in Shelsley Beauchamp off B 4204).

The Malvern Hills

Composer Sir Edward Elgar was born in the nearby village of Lower Broadheath and lived in Worcester. (A statue of him stands in Worcester at the top of the High Street, across from the cathedral.) His beloved Malvern Hills can be seen from the riverside garden in front of Worcester Cathedral, and the local tourist board has devised a 45-mile/72-km-long signposted **Elgar Trail** for motorists, which leads to the houses where he lived—including the **Elgar Birthplace Museum** in Lower Broadheath—and the places that inspired his music. An accompanying booklet and cassette are available.

These hills that inspired Elgar also provide some lovely walks. From their highest point, the **Worcestershire Beacon** (1,395 feet), just west of Great Malvern, you can walk the entire nine-mile range south to the Herefordshire Beacon. On a clear day you will be able to see into Wales. Nestled below the hills is the old spa town of **Great Malvern**, southwest of Worcester on A 449, built around a splendid priory church containing some stunning medieval stained glass and tiles. This pleasant town holds an annual festival of music at the end of May called the Malvern Festival.

Two other attractive towns just to the south of the Malvern Hills are **Ledbury** (on A 449) and Upton-upon-Severn (on A 4104, just off A 38). Ledbury's Heritage Centre, in the **Old Grammar School** on cobbled Church Lane, offers local history exhibits that trace the development of this thriving market town from its beginnings as an Anglo-Saxon village; the medieval **Church of St. Michael's** has an interesting collection of tombs. There are many fine half-timbered houses in Ledbury; two of the town's most handsome old buildings are the oak-pillared **Market House** (1617) in Market Place and, beyond it, the 16th-century Feathers Hotel (see below).

Eastnor Castle, 1 mile (1½ km) to the east of Ledbury, is a 19th-century building housing an important collection of tapestries, furniture, and ancient armor. Farther south, the historic **Hellens** mansion at Much Marcle is definitely worth a detour. This charming house has changed little since some major alterations made just before the Civil War. Two-hour guided tours leave hourly. The Norman church at nearby **Kempley** is famous for a remarkable series of 12th-century frescoes.

The beautiful old country town of **Upton-upon-Severn**,

southeast of Great Malvern, is a perfect center for boating trips on the river. Information about boating and town and riverside walks can be obtained at the local Heritage Centre, an unusual eight-sided cupola crowning an old church tower by the river; it is the town's oldest surviving building.

About 5 miles (8 km) south of Upton on the A 38 is the lovely town of **Tewkesbury**, on the edge of the Cotswolds, which lie to the south in Gloucestershire (see The Cotswolds to Winchester chapter). It commands a historic and strategic position at the confluence of the Rivers Severn and Avon. The massive **Abbey**, which dominates the town, sits foursquare, seemingly rooted to the earth. Inside, the nave is striking in its simplicity. Its decorative elements are mainly confined to the east end, where there is a magnificent stained-glass window and a series of elaborate chantries. A tour of the town is worthwhile: It is full of interesting old buildings and attractive alleyways. Church Street contains two fascinating local history museums and some fine buildings. Tewkesbury also has two important literary associations. Mrs. Craik wrote the 1856 novel *John Halifax, Gentleman* while staying at the charming ▶ **Bell Hotel** on Church Street, and there is a museum near the abbey commemorating the 20th-century novelist and short-story writer John Moore.

The town of Bromsgrove, 14 miles (22 km) north of Worcester off M 5, is well worth a visit, chiefly for its fascinating **Avoncroft Museum of Buildings** just outside the town at Stoke Prior. The buildings range from a working windmill, which sells its own stone-ground flour, to a cockpit and a fully equipped nail- and chain-making workshop. They have been collected from all over Britain and re-erected in a large 15-acre park.

STAYING AND DINING
IN THE MALVERN HILLS

▶ **Holdfast Cottage** in Welland is a rambling hotel with views of the Malvern Hills. To the south, in Malvern Wells, is the tiny **Croque-en-Bouche**, one of the best restaurants in England. In high season you may have to book well ahead, especially for a Saturday (dinner only Wednesday through Saturday; Tel: 0684-56-56-12).

In Ledbury, the ▶ **Feathers Hotel** has a good restaurant and plenty of character. On the edge of town, the excellent ▶ **Hope End Hotel** provides superb English cooking from home-grown ingredients and luxurious rooms in a delightful setting. Nonresidents can eat dinner here too.

In Tewkesbury, stop for a delicious light dinner at **Oscar's** on the High Street (closed Sunday and Monday) or for cream teas at **Wintor House** on Church Street (closed Mondays). The ▶ **Tewkesbury Park Hotel**, on Lincoln Green Lane, is a large, tourist-oriented hotel. There is also a good small hotel in the area; the ▶ **Corse Lawn House Hotel** (in Corse Lawn, on the B 4211 southwest of Tewkesbury) is a spacious, peaceful country hotel with an excellent restaurant.

HEREFORDSHIRE AND THE WYE VALLEY AREA

From its source in the mountains of Wales, the River Wye runs down to rural Herefordshire and flows, twisting and turning, south from the cathedral city of Hereford, through Ross-on-Wye and Monmouth, and on to Chepstow at the mouth of the Severn. The Wye Valley and the ancient Forest of Dean, to the east, form one of the loveliest areas in Britain. Although not readily accessible by public transport, this is great touring country for motorists and provides many lovely walks, particularly along the river valley itself. From Stratford the best way to reach this region is on A 422 to Worcester, and from there A 4103 to Hereford.

Hereford

Hereford, just 26 miles (42 km) from Worcester and 22 miles (35 km) from the Welsh border, was once a Saxon capital and took its name from the local ford, the only way of crossing the river before bridges were built. For many centuries the city was battered by border conflicts, and its castle was destroyed and rebuilt several times. Finally, it was dismantled after the Civil War, and today all that remains is part of the moat around **Castle Green**. Hereford also became known as a thriving marketplace for the products of the rich agricultural land around it, especially beef cattle. Indeed, it still has a thriving cattle and sheep market every day except Tuesday.

If you are travelling by car, one of the most attractive ways to approach Hereford and appreciate its history is to

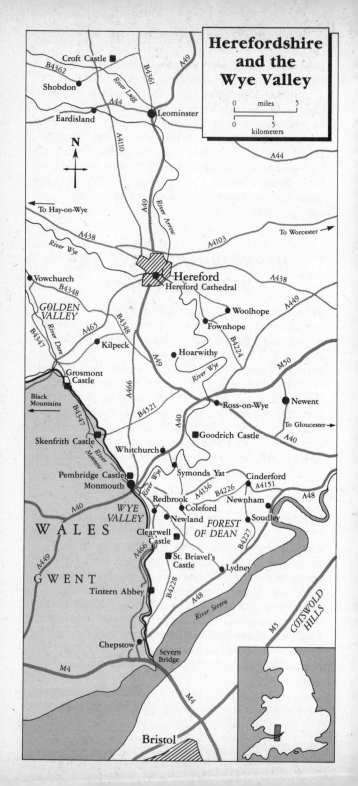

Herefordshire and the Wye Valley

miles 0 — 5
kilometers 0 — 5

Croft Castle
B4362
Shobdon
Eardisland
B4361
A49
River Lugg
Leominster
A44
A44
A4110
N
To Hay-on-Wye
A438
River Wye
River Arrow
A49
A4103
To Worcester
Vowchurch
B4348
Hereford
Hereford Cathedral
A438
A449
GOLDEN VALLEY
River Dore
A465
B4347
B4348
A466
A49
Woolhope
Fownhope
Kilpeck
Hoarwithy
River Wye
B4224
M50
Grosmont Castle
Black Mountains
B4521
A40
Ross-on-Wye
Newent
To Gloucester
Skenfrith Castle
River Monnow
Whitchurch
Goodrich Castle
A40
Pembridge Castle
Monmouth
River Wye
Symonds Yat
Cinderford
A4151
A4136
B4226
Newnham
A48
WALES
A40
Redbrook
Coleford
Newland
FOREST OF DEAN
Soudley
B4227
WYE VALLEY
Clearwell Castle
A466
St. Briavel's Castle
Lydney
GWENT
A449
Tintern Abbey
B4228
A48
River Severn
COTSWOLD HILLS
M5
Chepstow
Severn Bridge
M4
M4
Bristol

leave the car and walk the short distance to the town center. Park in the lot on Wye Street, just to the south of the old town bridge, which stands parallel to the new road bridge carrying traffic from the south. From here visitors can walk across Bishop's Meadow to the **Victoria Footbridge**. There is a stunning view of the city's fine cathedral from here, and the footbridge leads to a pleasant walk through Castle Green and Redcliffe Gardens to the cathedral. It is possible to park closer to the city center, but there are more restrictions there. Hereford is particularly lively in May, when the May Fair, the Regatta, and a raft race down the river are held.

HEREFORD CATHEDRAL

Hereford Cathedral is the jewel of the city today. Although founded in about A.D. 700, the present building dates mainly from the 12th century and later. Inside, the massive bulk of its pillars and the imposing semicircular arches in the nave display its Norman origins, while the great sandstone tower is a 14th-century structure. Also notable are the lovely early English Lady Chapel and some fine sculpted tombs.

The cathedral's two greatest treasures are the famous **Chained Library** and the 13th-century **Mappa Mundi**—a unique five-foot-wide map of a flat world with Jerusalem at its center. This is now the centerpiece of a small, specially built museum. In the historic library, more than 1,400 books are chained to rods attached to the four 17th-century bookcases. The extraordinary collection of books includes a copy of the eighth-century Anglo-Saxon Gospels. Also worth visiting is the 15th-century **College of Vicars' Choral**, a quadrangle surrounded by cottages where the 27 priests who chanted the services lived. Visitors can obtain a light lunch in the restaurant in the 13th-century Bishop's Cloister. This year the cathedral is also host to the annual Three Choirs Festival, held alternately in Worcester, Gloucester, and Hereford.

The profile of the cathedral dominates the skyline, and the cathedral is surrounded by a medieval network of ancient streets. The houses in this part of the city are of many different ages and include some fine Georgian buildings on **Broad Street**, one of which is the ▶ **Green Dragon Hotel**, a well-restored coaching inn open to overnight guests, with comfortable accommodations. From the cathedral, Church Street, lined with attractive old buildings, leads up to the ancient Saxon marketplace of High Town, now a modern pedestrian precinct lined with stores. Only the 17th-century **Old House** in the marketplace is a reminder of an earlier age. This fine black-and-white timbered building houses a museum of 17th-century life and is well worth a visit.

ELSEWHERE IN HEREFORD

Another fascinating building just outside the center of Hereford is Coningsby Hospital on Widemarsh Street. This delightful 13th-century edifice contains the **St. John Medieval Museum**, which has armor and relics from the crusaders' order of Saint John and tells the story of its wars during the 300 years of the Crusades. The city's main museum and art gallery, with its fine collection of 19th-century watercolors, is near the cathedral and next to the library on Broad Street. If you'd like a more detailed look at the city and its surroundings, you should go on one of the guided city walks organized by the local tourist office in St. Owen's Street (daily during the summer; Tel: 0432-26-84-30 for details).

Many visitors come to Hereford to visit H. P. Bulmer's world-famous cider factory, on Plough Lane off Whitecross Road (the A 438 to Brecon); tours are arranged from the **Cider Museum** on Grimmer Road (Tel: 0432-35-42-07). Cider making is closely linked with the history of the region, and the story of this industry is outlined in the museum. Many traditional cider makers still work in the villages around Hereford. Bulmer's also owns the **Railway Centre**, where its own train as well as the King George V, Princess Elizabeth, and Clan Line steam locomotives are kept, with many other examples of steam-railway memorabilia. Both sites can be reached by a walk down Eign Street. Note that the Railway Centre is open only on weekends and bank holidays from Easter to September. For details of special Steam Open Days, Tel: (0432) 35-88-92 or 27-43-78. Another fascinating steam museum is the **Herefordshire Waterworks Museum** on Broomy Hill, near the river to the east of the town. Here, on selected weekends, visitors can operate some of the pumps and see many of them in steam; for details, Tel: (0432) 82-03-82.

Around Hereford

All year round Hereford is a popular center for exploring the immediate area as well as Wales and the Welsh Black Mountains. There is a string of fine Norman castles along the Welsh border, testaments to the long and troubled history of the border region. The finest are Croft, to the north near Leominster; Grosmont, Skenfrith, and Pembridge, along the border itself; and Goodrich, near Ross-on-Wye to the south of Hereford. All have superb settings and are open to the public. There is a particularly fine walk from **Croft Castle** up to the Iron Age hill fort of **Croft Ambrey**, with its magnificent views of the Welsh mountains. Croft Castle, 5 miles (8 km) northwest of Leominster, has been almost continuously inhabited by the same family for more than 800 years. Its fine Gothic interiors and furniture can be viewed on most summer afternoons.

It is an easy trip from Hereford north to the sleepy little town of **Leominster**. In addition to the nearby castle, this delightful old wool town boasts some impressive architecture, including a fine 12th-century **priory church**. On display in the church is a ducking stool last used as a punishment for troublesome women in 1809. About 6 miles (10 km) northwest of Leominster is the church at Shobdon, a 1755 rococo Gothic structure that looks like an elaborate piece of confectionery and, on the River Arrow, the delightful village of Eardisland (4 miles/6½ km west of Leominster off the A 44).

Another popular regional base is the charming town of **Ross-on-Wye**, south of Hereford on A 49. (In summer this normally quiet little market town can get very busy, especially as the M 50/M 5 link here makes it very accessible from the Midlands.) Ross-on-Wye, which stands on a hill overlooking a bend in the Wye and the Welsh hills beyond, has a fine 17th-century market house and, in Brookend Street, the charming **Lost Street Museum** with its Edwardian shops and displays. The town owes much of its charm to the work of its most famous citizen, John Kyrle, the so-called Man of Ross, whose good deeds were immortalized in Alexander Pope's *Moral Essays* in the early 18th century. Just outside the town are the impressive **Hill Court Gardens and Garden Centre**.

The lovely town of **Newent**, a few miles east of Ross, is well worth visiting for the fascinating complex of Victorian shops called **The Shambles**, and for the world-famous **National Birds of Prey Centre** nearby, where visitors can see the largest collection of birds of prey in Western Europe at close quarters and watch some excellent flying demonstrations. If you want to cycle around this area or the Forest of Dean or canoe on the River Wye, you can rent transport from **Pedalaway** in Llangarron, to the southwest of Ross-on-Wye (Tel: 098-98-43-57). They will deliver bicycles to your accommodation and also rent kayaks and canoes. You can rent bicycles in Ross-on-Wye (Little and Hall on Broad Street; Tel: 0989-626-39) or in Hereford (Coombes Cycles on Widemarsh Street; Tel: 0432-35-43-73).

The less energetic may be attracted by the pioneering **Three Choirs Vineyard**, situated just off the B 4215 two miles/3 km northwest of Newent. This is one of the six largest vineyards in Britain and is open to visitors year-round. They also run conducted tours with free tastings on request; Tel: (0531) 89-02-23 or 89-05-55.

DINING AND STAYING AROUND HEREFORD

Between Newent and the Forest of Dean, the **Cider Press** at Drybrook is an excellent little restaurant that bases many of its dishes on locally made cider. Teas are served in the mansion's attractive walled garden; reservations are recommended (Tel: 0594-54-44-72).

Excellent food in a relaxed country-house setting is also available from the admirable ▶ **Glewstone Court**, just south of Ross-on-Wye. Here, William and Christine Reeve-Tucker run a charming hotel with a restaurant that matches up to the highest country-house standards. The hotel is worth visiting for itself, but guests can also participate in many other activities, from hot-air ballooning to art courses. Glewstone is good value for its medium-priced rates. For budget accommodation, visitors should try the charming ▶ **Butcher's Arms** in Woolhope, a traditional 14th-century half-timbered inn with a simple restaurant and some excellent walks nearby.

Another relatively inexpensive lodging is the ▶ **Croft Country Guest House** at Vowchurch, at the heart of the so-called Golden Valley, west of Hereford. The valley runs north to Dorstone along the course of the River Dore, which may have taken its name from *d'or,* the French phrase for "of gold." The **Abbey Dore Court Garden** to the south of the valley has a fine garden next to the river, an unusual plant center, a collection of teddy bears, and a restaurant serving lunches and cream teas.

Hay-on-Wye

A trip that combines some wonderful natural sights with a cultural attraction leads west of Hereford to the town of Hay-on-Wye on the Welsh border. This small, sleepy Welsh market town, reached via A 438, has over the last ten years become a mecca for book lovers and is said to contain the largest number of secondhand books in the world. West from Hereford, the A 438 runs along the River Wye on the river's way down from the Black Mountains, which glower in the distance. If you take the first turn signposted to Hay, you will pass through the tiny hamlet of Bredwardine—famous as the parish of the late-19th-century Anglican curate and diarist Francis Kilvert. A booklet about Kilvert and a map of a walk around the village can be bought in the parish church.

Hay is dominated by its 12th-century castle, whose ruins now enclose the remains of a fine Jacobean mansion that is being restored after a recent fire. Its present owner, Richard Booth, was the first to open a secondhand bookshop in the town, and the growth of this and his own flair for publicity led to Hay's present renown. Hay now has over 20 major bookshops—some general and some specializing in subjects as diverse as the Native American, poetry, cooking, children's books, and Dickensiana. Prices are extremely reasonable, especially when compared to those in London, and most shops are open every day. Call at the tourist and crafts center near the car park at the top of the town for more information. Market day is on Thursday.

Hay has a lively Festival of Literature at the end of May. For information and tickets write to the Festival Office, Hay-on-Wye HR3 5BX; Tel: (0497) 82-12-17.

DINING AND STAYING
IN AND AROUND HAY-ON-WYE

The Granary restaurant near the clock tower on Broad Street is a delightful health-food restaurant, or you can buy excellent picnic provisions at **Hay Wholefoods and Delicatessen** on Lion Street. For a more sophisticated ambience, try **Colin's** restaurant and piano bar on Broad Street.

For inexpensive accommodations, try the ▶ Swan, a very central Georgian hotel with a beautiful garden and an excellent restaurant, or ▶ Bredwardine Hall, 7 miles (11 km) east of Hay via the B 4352, for a more rural and spacious setting.

The Wye Valley

South of Ross-on-Wye are the undulating hills and lovely woods of the Forest of Dean, just east of the magnificent Wye Valley. The River Wye flows in great loops through its beautiful wooded valley and provides some of the finest river views in Britain—and, incidentally, some of the best fishing.

LOWER WYE VALLEY WALK

One of the most desirable ways to see and enjoy this spectacular piece of countryside is to walk alongside the river on part of the 34-mile Lower Wye Valley Walk. Guidebooks and cards describing the walk are available in local bookshops, and the walk, which runs from near Monmouth to Chepstow, is very well signposted. You can start anywhere. An alternative is to join one of the many guided walks organized by the Wye Valley Countryside Service year round. Details can be obtained from local Tourist Information Centres.

Particularly interesting on the first stretch of this walk are the view from Kerne Bridge, the formidable ruins of **Goodrich Castle**, and Symonds Yat, where there is a famous outcrop of rock 1,500 feet high. Hardy walkers can climb 400 feet up the hillside from the river for a marvelous vista; the less energetic can drive to the forest parking lot at the top.

SYMONDS YAT

The east and west halves of the village of Symonds Yat are on either side of the river and are linked by two hand-operated ferries. Half-hour river tours can be taken from points on either side of the water. Symonds Yat East is the more attractive of the two little hamlets. It has a number of small guest houses and a congenial pub, the **Saracen's Head**. However, parking in the village is limited, so arrive in the early morning during the summer. The **Wyedean Canoe and Adventure Centre** here organizes canoeing, caving, and climbing and other trips and rents canoes and equipment (Tel: 0600-89-01-29).

Far less attractive but with lots of space for parking, Symonds Yat West and its garish entertainment complexes lie on the flat plain near the river. The first of these complexes contains a tropical butterfly garden and the rather more interesting **Jubilee Maze**—a traditional hedge labyrinth containing a museum of mazes. Nearer the river there are amusement arcades and, next to one of the river-trip pickup points, a tropical bird garden. Farther downstream, where the river goes into a little gorge, **Ye Olde Ferrie Inn** has some large terraces facing across the river to Symonds Yat East and makes a pleasant stop for a snack or a drink.

If you take the exit off A 40 toward Symonds Yat East but make a right turn before reaching the town, you can follow the signs up Great Doward Hill to the **Rural Heritage Museum**. This collection of domestic and agricultural bygones in the midst of woodland must be one of the largest in England and is the remarkable result of one family's endeavors. Although not very well labeled, the collection is a fascinating mixture of everything from steam threshing machines and domestic mangles to a fully equipped blacksmith's shop.

MONMOUTH

Downstream from here is ancient Monmouth, just over the Welsh border. Situated where the River Monnow joins the Wye, the town was a strategic site from the time of the Romans and figured in the defeat of the Welsh princes in the 13th century. The bridge over the Monnow has a fine fortified gatehouse. **Great Castle House** (now a regimental headquarters and museum) stands on the site of the castle, which was destroyed during the Civil War.

The heart of the town is pretty **Agincourt Square**, with its attractive buildings and Saturday market. Here you can see statues of two of Monmouth's most famous sons—Henry V and Charles Rolls, co-founder of Rolls-Royce and an early aviator. Nearby is a museum in the Victorian Market Hall largely devoted to a collection of memorabilia related to Lord Nelson (who visited here in 1802—see below—but otherwise has no connection to the town), donated by Rolls's mother. You can rent canoes, with or without instruction, at Monmouth Canoe Hire, which also organizes caving and climbing trips locally (Tel: 0600-71-34-61).

OFFA'S DYKE LONG-DISTANCE FOOTPATH

To the east of Monmouth, **Kymin Hill** is topped by the Round House, or Pavilion, built by a local dining club in 1793 so that they could enjoy the magnificent panorama at their weekly dinners. The same dining club (long since disbanded) built the nearby Naval Temple in 1800 in honor of Nelson, "the hero of the Nile." Admiral Nelson made a triumphant visit to the temple on August 19, 1802. You can reach Kymin Hill via an access road off B 4136 or by following part of the Offa's Dyke Long-Distance Footpath up the hill from Monmouth. This footpath runs the entire length of the English-Welsh border. Part of it follows the rampart built by the Saxon king Offa in the eighth century to defend England from the Welsh tribes. If you follow the footpath across the disused railroad bridge at Redbrook (on A 466 south of Monmouth), you can get a good meal at the Boat Inn, which has a lovely setting overlooking the River Wye.

The Forest of Dean

To the east of the Wye Valley in Gloucestershire is the Forest of Dean. Many of its 22,000 acres are covered in mixed woodland—mostly oak and beech—and crisscrossed by hundreds of paths where wildlife of all kinds can be seen in abundance. The tourist board and some individuals have published maps of forest trails, and there is the signposted Forest of Dean Scenic Drive around the area. You can also tour the forest by bicycle or on horseback. For details, contact the local Tourist Information Centres at Coleford (Tel: 0594-363-07) or Ross-on-Wye (Tel: 0989-627-68).

Industry once flourished in the forest, chiefly charcoal burning and coal mining. Over a million tons of coal a year were being mined at the beginning of the 20th century. Today some small mines are still worked by the so-called Free Miners, who have a traditional right to dig coal. They are among the many Foresters who have retained inherited rights to graze their animals, mine for coal, and cut stone in the quarries. Nowadays, however, most of their children are born in the county hospital outside the forest and are therefore losing their inheritance. Fine monuments, including one of a 15th-century Forester showing his traditional dress and tools, can be found in the 13th-century All Saints' Church—the so-called Cathedral of the Forest—in Newland, west of Coleford. Even more unusual is the curious little brass there depicting a local miner. Just opposite the ancient lych-gate the ▶ Ostrich Inn serves excellent bar and restaurant food and provides inexpensive accommodations. The rights of the Foresters were maintained through meetings at the ▶ Speech House, which stands on the B 4226 halfway between Coleford and Cinderford. It is now an attractive hotel and an ideal center for exploring the forest. The old courtroom in the Speech House is preserved and still used for the transaction of business by the verderers, officials in charge of the forest.

Nearby, visitors can follow the remarkable **Sculpture Trail**, a three- to four-hour walk through the forest past more than 15 modern sculptures. For information about guided walks through the forest throughout the year, contact Timewalk (Tel: 0594-83-35-44). A pleasant place for shorter walks is the unique Puzzle Wood near Coleford on B 4228—the site of ancient open iron workings transformed in the 1800s into a maze of beautiful woodland paths.

The **Clearwell Caves** (just south of Coleford off B 4228) are ancient iron mines that were worked for more than 2,500 years, until 1945. Guides from local mining families make a visit to this small mine and museum particularly interesting (open March through October). Nearby ▶ **Clearwell Castle** (1727), the earliest Neo-Gothic building in Britain, is now a charming country hotel and restaurant standing in eight acres of parkland. Most of its rooms have four-poster beds. You can also get snacks or full meals in the ▶ **Wyndham Arms** in Clearwell, a large 14th-century inn with an attractive garden and several rooms; children are welcome.

Some of the best views of the forest can be had from **St. Briavels Castle**, just south of Clearwell to the west of the forest. Royal visitors once stayed in this medieval castle when they came to hunt wild boar and deer; it is now a youth hostel. A congenial and lively place for a home-made snack and a pint is the **George Pub** at the foot of the castle walls; it's worth a detour.

The **Dean Heritage Centre** at Camp Mill in Soudley, south of Cinderford, is on the other side of the forest. It is a fascinating collection of buildings situated in a beautiful wooded valley by a mill pond. The many exhibitions illustrating the life of the area include such displays as "The Living Forest," as well as others on charcoal burning, woodcraft, and the region's industrial history; there is also a Museum of Forest Life and a reconstructed forester's cottage. You can get information on nature trails and guided tours of the forest (open daily all year) here too. It is well worth a visit and serves as an excellent introduction to the whole area.

The widespread improvement of England's road system in the mid-18th century led to a rapid increase in travel for its own sake, and the beauty of the Wye Valley soon attracted many visitors. One of the most famous was William Gilpin, who wrote *Observations on the River Wye* in 1782. The Wye Tourists, as they came to be known, would usually take a boat trip south from Ross or Monmouth to Chepstow, and most stopped at the beautiful ruins of Tintern Abbey, north of Chepstow.

Tintern Abbey

Tintern is known to many people through Wordsworth's poem "Lines Composed a Few Miles Above Tintern Abbey." Its majestic bulk, situated next to the river, is an impressive sight, even though the stone ruins are no longer romantically covered in ivy and moss, which were removed around the turn of the century.

An abbey was first built on this site for Cistercian monks in the early 12th century; however, the present building dates mostly from the 13th century, when it was rebuilt by Roger, earl of Norfolk. For several hundred years it was an important trading center, but it gradually declined and was stripped of its treasures at the dissolution of the monasteries. The roof was dismantled and much of the stone removed, but the mighty shell of the abbey remains, and it's still possible to trace the position of the domestic buildings attached to the church. A little museum and tourist information center stand nearby.

It is hard to believe that sleepy Tintern was also an industrial center for more than 300 years, and that works producing brass, iron, and wire lined the little Angidy valley. Nowadays just a few millponds and ruins remain to commemorate their passage. A mile above the abbey on the A 466 Chepstow–Monmouth road, the old Tintern railway station has been preserved. It has a picnic site and a car park, which makes this a convenient base for walks around the area.

Staying in Tintern
Tintern contains quite a number of hotels. The ▶ **Royal George Hotel**, a long-established coaching inn, and the ▶ **Parva Farmhouse** both provide comfortable accommodations.

Chepstow

South of Tintern, the River Wye goes around in two giant loops before widening out on its way down to join the mighty Severn. Here, west of the river, is the Welsh town of Chepstow; at its northern edge is the famous Chepstow Racecourse at Piercefield Park, the site of both flat racing and steeplechasing events. The town, to the south, has been a trading settlement since Saxon times, and the first stage of **Chepstow Castle** was built here in 1067, just a year after the Norman Conquest.

The magnificent ruins of this once-mighty castle give a very clear picture of how it must have functioned. It stretches along the giant cliffs overlooking the River Wye on the north side of the town (there is a fine view of the castle from A 48) and is open to the public daily. There is a large car park at the foot of the hill, near the entrance to the castle, and a new building here houses the Tourist Information Centre. Across the road the **Castle View Hotel** serves good bar food. A small local history museum is located next door. Walking up toward the town, you will see the **Stuart Crystal Craft Centre**, where you can watch artisans engrave lead crystal and then, if you wish, buy the end product.

An ancient town wall encloses the maze of steep, narrow streets that cluster above the castle, and the city's fine west gate still stands. Close by, the church of St. Mary contains the tomb of Henry Marten. An unrepentant signatory of Charles I's death warrant, Marten spent 20 years under house arrest in the castle until his death in 1680. Book lovers will enjoy a visit to **Glance Back Books** in Upper Church Street. Its rabbit warren of rooms contains over 60,000 antiquarian and secondhand books as well as rare coins, postcards, medals, stamps, and prints.

The luxurious ▶ **St. Pierre Hotel** in St. Pierre Park, a couple of miles west of Chepstow, provides an impressive array of facilities for its guests, including tennis and an internationally famous golf course.

South of Chepstow is the western end of the mighty Severn Bridge. This is where the M 4 motorway crosses from England to Wales, and it is also a convenient link straight into London or to the southwest of England. Westbound vehicles are now charged a toll for the crossing; eastbound vehicles go for free. The tolls will finance a new road bridge, due for completion in 1996, that is being built 3 miles (5 km) downstream from the existing bridge.

THE UPPER SEVERN VALLEY AND THE SHROPSHIRE HILLS

Between the industrial city of Birmingham and the high, harsh mountains of the Welsh border country is the beautiful winding valley of the River Severn and the rich farming land and bare escarpments of the Shropshire Hills. The **Shropshire Hills** occupy a great triangle of land north of Herefordshire and Worcestershire, bounded by the Severn Valley to the north and east, the Teme Valley to the south, and the Long Mynd escarpment and Clun Forest to the west; they are bisected by A 49. Vivid reminders of the past fill this superb landscape, from fortified manor houses to later remnants of the Industrial Revolution. The effort of travelling off the beaten tourist track to get here will be rewarded.

The area has been settled from the earliest times. Traces of Bronze and Iron Age settlements and hill forts have been found at Caer Caradoc, near Church Stretton, and Croft Ambrey, near Leominster. One of the largest cities of the Roman era, Viroconium, stood near Wroxeter southeast of Shrewsbury, and later the area was heavily fortified by the Normans against the unruly Welsh princes. At the same time, land was cleared and small permanent communities began to develop in the valleys and on the lower slopes of the hills. Timber from the cleared forests provided frames for the area's characteristic black-and-white, half-timbered houses. Local oak was first blackened with pitch, then the frame was erected on a sandstone base, filled in with brick or wattle and daub, plastered, lime-washed, and finally roofed in Welsh slate. Dairy and sheep farming were the dominant industries, and, as local conflicts died out, the area rapidly grew in prosperity, which prompted the growth of several important market towns.

Shrewsbury

The most important market town in this area was Shrewsbury (pronounced SHROZE-bree), which is situated in a superb defensive position on gently rising ground enclosed by a tight loop of the Severn. It is an attractive, sleepy old town, in the center of Shropshire, about 55

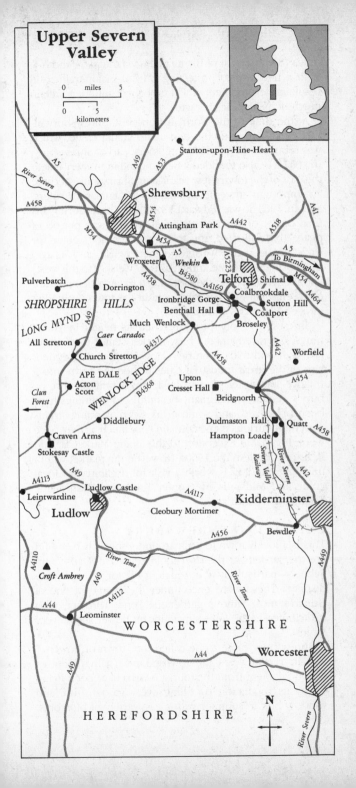

Upper Severn Valley

0 miles 5

0 kilometers 5

Stanton-upon-Hine-Heath

River Severn

A5

A49

A53

A458

Shrewsbury

M54

Attingham Park

A442

A518

A41

A5

To Birmingham

M54

M54

A5

Wroxeter

Wrekin ▲

A5223

Telford

Shifnal

M54

A464

Pulverbatch

Dorrington

B4380

A4169

Coalbrookdale

Sutton Hill

SHROPSHIRE HILLS

Ironbridge Gorge

Benthall Hall

Coalport

LONG MYND

A49

Much Wenlock

Broseley

Caer Caradoc ▲

A442

Worfield

All Stretton

B4371

A458

A454

Church Stretton

APE DALE

WENLOCK EDGE

Upton
Cresset Hall

Acton
Scott

B4368

Bridgnorth

*Clun
Forest*

←

Diddlebury

Dudmaston Hall

Quatt

A458

Hampton Loade

Craven Arms

*Severn
Valley
Railway*

River Severn

A442

Stokesay Castle

A4113

A49

Ludlow Castle

A4117

Kidderminster

Leintwardine

Cleobury Mortimer

Ludlow

A456

Bewdley

A4110

River Teme

A449

Croft Ambrey ▲

A49

A4112

River Teme

A44

Leominster

W O R C E S T E R S H I R E

A49

A44

Worcester

H E R E F O R D S H I R E

N

River Severn

miles (88 km) west of Birmingham via the M 54 and A 5. With a new bypass protecting it from major traffic and resultant development, it will probably continue to retain much of its historic character.

At the time of the Norman Conquest, Shrewsbury already had five churches and a substantial castle, which was rebuilt by Roger de Montgomery, earl of Shrewsbury, in 1067. He also founded a Benedictine monastery just to the east of the town a few years later. Shrewsbury became an important strategic stronghold for England's rulers, and in 1283 it was Edward I's military base during his final defeat of the Welsh princes. During the period of peace that followed, the town was a major center for trade between the Welsh and the English, and its two main bridges became known as the "Welsh" (to the west) and the "English" (to the east). Even today, a rich mixture of accents can be heard throughout the town on market days (Wednesdays and Fridays).

Shrewsbury's prosperity reached its height in Tudor times, but it remained a busy market center throughout the 18th and 19th centuries. However, the subsequent rise of the great industrial cities turned the town into a relative backwater. Today the happy result of Shrewsbury's decline is that many beautiful old buildings have been preserved, and some of its steep, winding streets with their curious names remain very much as they once were. A notable exception to this is the Market Hall in Bellstone, built in the 1960s. However, the market within this ugly building is worth a visit for a glimpse of local color and Midlands life (open Tuesdays, Wednesdays, Fridays, and Saturdays).

EXPLORING SHREWSBURY

This is a lovely town to walk around; especially beautiful are **the gardens** by the river looking toward Shrewsbury School—particularly the Dingle Dell for its elaborate displays. These were once under the charge of one of Britain's most famous gardeners, Percy Thrower, who contributed to the town's magnificent flower show every August.

Shrewsbury came to be called the "town of flowers," and in recent years the townspeople (with plenty of encouragement from the tourist board) have been living up to its reputation by filling every garden, tub, and window box in summer with a vast variety of blossoms.

Shrewsbury's once-great castle was largely dismantled after the town's stand against Cromwell in the Civil War. However, in 1787 the keep was transformed into a private house by Thomas Telford, the great civil engineer, for his patron William Pulteney, the local M.P. The castle now houses the Shropshire regimental museum. All that remains of the great Benedictine monastery of Sts. Peter and Paul is the **Abbey church** and the refectory pulpit, just over the English Bridge. It contains several interesting tombs and is the setting for the popular Brother Cadfael novels by Ellis Peters.

One of the best ways to get to know Shrewsbury is to take an organized town walk. These are offered on weekends in April and daily from May to October at 2:30 P.M.; lasting about two hours, they leave from the Tourist Information Centre in the Square. Failing this, follow one of the walking routes outlined in the information center's leaflets. You can arrange a tour in the off-season through Tourist Information (Tel: 0743-35-07-61).

Some of the town's finest buildings were erected by the great cloth merchants of the 16th and 17th centuries. **Rowley's House,** on Barker Street, is one; Rowley's son built the neighboring Rowley's Mansion, one of the first brick houses in town. Together the two house a fine local history museum, which has a sizable display of important Roman remains from nearby Viroconium (see below).

The oldest part of Shrewsbury is at the highest point of the town between the Square, Dogpole, and the pedestrian shopping area of Pride Hill. Many of Shrewsbury's fine old buildings are here, including the Old Market Hall, Ireland's Mansion on the High Street, the Abbott's House in Butcher Row, and the group of medieval buildings in St. Alkmund's Square known as **Bear Steps,** part of which houses a pleasant tearoom. Just across St. Alkmund's Square from here, **St. Julian's Craft Centre** is good for local crafts shopping, especially on Saturdays (closed Thursdays and Sundays).

Architectural splendors from the Georgian Age are also in abundance in Shrewsbury, especially between St. John's Hill and Belmont. One of these, on College Hill, is now the **Clive House Museum**, with a beautiful garden. The period rooms provide an elegant setting for a specialized collection of Shropshire pottery and porcelain. Another attractive Georgian building is now the Parade Shopping Centre on St. Mary's Place.

STAYING AND DINING
IN AND AROUND SHREWSBURY

Most of Shrewsbury's inns and restaurants are in the center of town around Butcher Row, St. Alkmund's Square, and Wyle Cop (*cop* means "hilltop" in Welsh). The ► **Lion Hotel**, an old coaching inn with leaded windows on Wyle Cop, is large and comfortable and has an elegant Adam-style ballroom. However, the best hotel is the ► **Prince Rupert**, part of which is housed in a 17th-century mansion. Centrally located on Butcher Row, the hotel has recently been refurbished to a very high standard.

For an excellent but not too expensive meal, try the **Cornhouse Restaurant and Wine Bar**, at the bottom of Wyle Cop. Simpler fare is available at the **New Delaney's** restaurant, a vegetarian eatery at St. Julian's Craft Centre on St. Alkmund's Square (closed on Sundays and bank holidays). The **Good Life** is another good-value vegetarian restaurant, in a delightful 14th-century building in Barrack's Passage, off Wyle Cop (closed Sundays). An excellent out-of-town restaurant, **Country Friends**, in Dorrington south of town on the A 49, serves seasonal food in an attractive old building.

The Upper Severn Valley and
Ironbridge Gorge

From Shrewsbury, the Severn continues to wind eastward across a broad, fertile plain broken occasionally by hilly outcrops. The most spectacular of these is the abrupt, conical shape of the **Wrekin**, east of Wroxeter, which, at 1,335 feet, affords some fine views to those hardy enough to climb it. One of Shropshire's greatest houses is nearby at Atcham: **Attingham Park** (4 miles/6½ km southeast of Shrewsbury on A 5), a magnificent Regency mansion built for the first Lord Berwick and now run by the National Trust. Its impressive state rooms are lined with paintings and fine furniture, and it has a superb collection of Regency silverware acquired in Italy by the third Lord Berwick. The great park was elaborately landscaped by the legendary gardener Sir Humphrey Repton.

Just south on B 4380 at Wroxeter is another historic site, but from a much earlier period. The Roman city of **Viroconium**, built between A.D. 50 and 125, was the fourth-largest Roman city in Britain. Although little of the original town remains standing, the Roman baths there are illuminating to see in that they show how much still lies under neighboring fields.

IRONBRIDGE GORGE

The real gem of this part of the Upper Severn Valley is Ironbridge Gorge, an area that is celebrated throughout Britain as the birthplace of the Industrial Revolution. Today nearly six square miles of the gorge, from the town of Coalbrookdale in the north to Coalport in the south, is a museum where the remains of Britain's Industrial Revolution have been restored and rebuilt into a fascinating exhibit.

This area's unique combination of natural assets—coal, timber, ironstone, clay, limestone, and water transport—created ideal conditions for the development of the region's fledgling iron-smelting industry. It expanded even more rapidly after 1708, when Abraham Darby arrived and began to use coke rather than charcoal to fuel his furnaces. Rapid advances in the mass production of iron followed, and in 1779 Abraham Darby III built the massive **Iron Bridge**—the first cast-iron bridge in the world. Today it takes a leap of imagination to understand what a masterpiece of invention and engineering skill it was at the time. At the other end of the gorge, a thriving ceramics industry developed around the Coalport China Works.

After the decline of its industries, the area remained relatively untouched for more than 90 years, until some of its industrial buildings were restored in the 1960s. It is now the country's largest museum, and to do it full justice you'll need at least two days. There are six museum sites: the **Museum of the River Visitor Centre**, which offers an exhibition introducing the area and an audiovisual show on its history; the **Coalbrookdale Furnace and Museum of Iron**; the Iron Bridge; the **Coalport China Works Museum**, which has a fascinating display of some of the finest china produced in Britain; the **Jackfield Works and Tile Museum**; and the **Blists Hill Open Air Museum**, a recreation of a Victorian township where the everyday life of local tradespeople is reenacted around the visitor.

If your time is limited, start your tour at the visitors' center in the Museum of the River, then visit the Coalbrookdale Furnace and Museum of Iron and Blists Hill, including the Hay inclined plane, which moved boats between the two levels of the Shropshire Canal. The bridge and Ironbridge town are nearby; you can get a light meal and other refreshments in the town, which also contains some fascinating antiques shops, or at various tearooms throughout the museum complex. (For more on the subject of the early industry in this area, see the chapter The Industrial Heritage.)

OTHER AREA ATTRACTIONS

Twelfth-century **Buildwas Abbey** (off B 4380, two miles/3 km east of Ironbridge), with its fine vaulted chapter house, stands in a picturesque setting by the river. South of Ironbridge are the 16th-century Benthall Hall, with its delightful church; the charming little village of Broseley; and **Much Wenlock**, a small market town with many old timbered buildings and the extensive ruins of a 12th-century priory (worth a visit for its famous topiary). The **Old Courtyard** and the **Malthouse** on the High Street here both serve an excellent and inexpensive light lunch.

Just to the northeast is **Boscobel House**, where the future King Charles II hid in the "royal oak" while fleeing Cromwell, and **Weston Park**, a beautiful house designed by Lady Wilbraham in the 17th century. Weston has an assortment of Georgian furniture and a particularly fine collection of paintings, including some by Holbein, Gainsborough, and Van Dyck. The Capability Brown–designed park has architectural and nature trails, an aquarium, and the Weston Park miniature railway. The park is crowded in summer with families from the neighboring industrial cities and is also host to various fairs.

STAYING AND DINING IN AND AROUND IRONBRIDGE GORGE

There are three luxurious hotels in the immediate vicinity of Ironbridge. The ▶ **Telford Hotel, Golf and Country Club** at Great Hay in Sutton Hill, just north of Coalport, is a comfortable, welcoming hotel, contained in a series of modernized farm buildings and houses. Nearby at Shifnal is ▶ **Park House Hotel**, in two adjoining Georgian houses. Park House is a luxurious hotel with a grill room and an excellent, though formal, restaurant. The third is ▶ **Madeley Court Hotel**—a beautiful, sympathetically restored and extended Elizabethan house with a restaurant.

For cheaper but central accommodations try the family-run ▶ **Valley Hotel** in Ironbridge Gorge, which is within walking distance of several of the main attractions.

Bridgnorth

Bridgnorth (south of Ironbridge Gorge on A 442) is an ancient market town on the River Severn. The river divides the town in two: The quaint, Italianate High Town is perched on a 200-foot-high sandstone cliff, and Low Town is set on the other side of the river. A steep, winding road, several passageways of steps, and a two-car funicular cliff railway, which climbs a four-in-seven gradient, link the two parts of the town. The remaining wall of a late-Norman castle sits at the top of the cliff and leans 17 degrees off the perpendicular (more than the Leaning Tower of Pisa). The more upright, classical **Church of St. Mary Magdalene** is next to it; designed by Thomas Telford in 1794, the church is surrounded by some pleasant gardens.

Just 4 miles (6½ km) to the west, set in beautiful countryside, is **Upton Cresset Hall**, a lovely Elizabethan manor with a magnificent gatehouse and a 14th-century Great Hall (open Thursday afternoons in summer, or by appointment; Tel: 074-63-13-07). **Dudmaston Hall**, to the southeast at Quatt, is slightly more accessible (open Wednesday and Sunday afternoons in summer). Fine furniture and interesting exhibits fill this 17th-century house.

Anyone interested in steam trains should take the **Severn Valley Railway** for a scenic 16-mile journey along the river valley between Bridgnorth and Kidderminster. It is well worth a detour. You can get on or off the trains at any of the stations in between; Bewdley is a good place to start. Trains run daily from mid-May to the end of September and on most weekends for the rest of the year. There are refreshment facilities at most of the stations, and if you take a picnic basket you can stop at the little station of Hampton Loade or Arley and walk down to a picnic spot by the river before catching a train back later in the day. The Bridgnorth Railway Station is home to the largest collection of standard-gauge steam and diesel locomotives in Britain.

One mile (1½ km) south of Bridgnorth is the family-owned **Daniel's Mill**. This picturesque working water mill has the largest waterwheel powering a cornmill still working in England. Open to individuals; guided tours by arrangement (Tel: 0746-76-27-53.)

Staying and Dining near Bridgnorth
An excellent small hotel to the northeast is the ▶ **Old Vicarage Hotel**, in Worfield, which serves fine food in a pleasant, relaxed setting.

The Shropshire Hills

To the south of Shrewsbury lies the vast area known as the Shropshire Hills. These 300 square miles of land, where the wild Welsh mountains gradually give way to the gentler vales and uplands of the Midlands, have been designated an Area of Outstanding Natural Beauty. It's best to explore the hills by car at first, but whenever possible, get out and walk. From Shrewsbury, A 49 goes directly south to the town of Craven Arms along the path of an ancient Roman road between the two massive escarpments—Long Mynd (west) and Wenlock Edge (east)—that run northeast to southwest.

LONG MYND

Long Mynd dominates the landscape, rising abruptly from the valley to a high (1,700 feet) plateau of heather-covered moorland ten miles long. A series of valleys cuts into its eastern edge, and these provide fine walks for both the serious walker and those who prefer a gentle stroll.

One popular short walk begins in the parking lot at the National Trust Information Centre (which has a shop and café) in Carding Mill Valley and climbs up to New Pool Hollow. (Carding Mill Valley is about 12 miles/19 km south of Shrewsbury off A 49 near All Stretton.) You can also drive up the Long Mynd on minor roads, and on a fine day you may get some good views of hang-glider enthusiasts from the southern end of the ridge. To the west is a strange outcrop of rocks known as the **Stiperstones**. Legend has it that devils gather here to select a leader on midwinter nights.

There is a small, comfortable hotel with an excellent restaurant—the ▶ **Mynd House Hotel**—near the little market town of Church Stretton on the A 49, at the foot of Long Mynd. One of Shropshire's most famous literary figures, the novelist Mary Webb, spent her honeymoon here and named it Shepwardine in her novels. The **Acton Scott Historic Working Farm** nearby provides a fascinating glimpse of life as it was on a 19th-century farm before the advent of mechanization, and it is well worth a detour (open daily, April through October).

WENLOCK EDGE

A narrow, wooded limestone escarpment, Wenlock Edge stretches southwest from Much Wenlock near Ironbridge for 15 miles (24 km). A footpath along its crest is part of the unofficial long-distance footpath called the **Shropshire Way.** B 4371 runs along the top of Wenlock Edge, and, if you drive, it's possible to leave your car at any of the small parking areas along the road and explore the area on foot. (Be careful of the unfenced "edge" itself.) There are excellent views across Ape Dale to the Stretton Hills. Southward, past the town of Craven Arms on A 49, is the massive 13th-century fortified manor house of **Stokesay Castle** (open daily except Tuesdays, April through October; in November, open on weekends). This unusual building has been renovated by English Heritage and, although empty of furnishings, merits viewing.

Ludlow

The major town in this region is the ancient market center of **Ludlow,** south of Craven Arms on A 49. It is famous for its attractive black-and-white half-timbered houses and the great Norman **Ludlow Castle.** The town's wealth was built on the wool trade, which is celebrated in the local museum at Butter Cross. The **Church of St. Laurence** is one of the largest and finest medieval churches in the country; it contains several fine monuments, some notable wood carvings, and lovely stained glass. **Broad Street,** which runs southeast from the church, has claims to being Britain's prettiest street.

Ludlow is an excellent center for exploring the beautiful rolling landscape to the north and west, the "blue remembered hills" that the poet A. E. Housman described in *A Shropshire Lad* (his ashes are scattered in the St. Laurence churchyard). The composer Ralph Vaughan Williams was also inspired by this landscape when he wrote his celebrated and haunting vocal piece "On Wenlock Edge" based on the Housman poem.

A good time to come to Ludlow is during the Ludlow Festival, the last week of June and the first week of July. The castle makes a spectacular backdrop for the Shakespeare play performed on the castle grounds. Reserve ahead, as there are rarely tickets available on the night of performance; also, dress warmly and take blankets, cushions, rainwear, a picnic basket, and a warming drink to the play (Tel: 0584-87-21-50 for information, May through July).

DINING AND STAYING IN LUDLOW
In Ludlow there are two delightful and inexpensive vegetarian restaurants—**Hardwicks**, on Quality Square just off the Market Square, and the **Olive Branch** on Old Street (both open 10:00 A.M. to 5:00 P.M.).

Ludlow has two excellent hotels. The ▶ **Feathers** is an attractive Jacobean half-timbered building in the town center; ▶ **Dinham Hall** near the castle is a superb new hotel in a large Georgian house with an exceptional restaurant. Less expensive is the charming ▶ **Redfern Hotel**, east of Ludlow in Cleobury Mortimer, which has a good restaurant.

Directly south of Ludlow on A 49 is Leominster and, beyond that, Hereford, discussed earlier.

CHESTER

Some 40 miles north of Shrewsbury, near the mouth of the River Dee, lies Chester, a charming, well-preserved city, with historic architecture, beautiful riverside walks, and superb museum and visitor centers.

Chester has been an important locus of English life since Roman times, when it was the fortress Diva, the farthest western outpost of the Roman Empire and the garrison headquarters of the elite Valeria Victrix legion that crushed the uprising led by the warrior queen Boadicea. Viking raiders subsequently landed here, and later still Chester was the capital of the Anglo-Saxon kingdom ruled by Alfred the Great's daughter, Aethelflaeda. Chester was the site of a formidable Norman castle built by William the Conqueror's nephew, Hugh Lupus; from here he carried out attacks on the Welsh, and the castle continued to be an important border stronghold throughout the Middle Ages, when Chester was also the largest port in northwest England, shipping out quantities of cheese, candles, and salt.

In the 17th century Chester was still a thriving city and port but, as a Royalist stronghold during the Civil War, it suffered a two-year siege by Cromwell's troops. This period is vividly recalled by an exhibition at King Charles's Tower on the city walls. Chester's fortunes soon revived, and its prosperity was reflected in an intensive period of rebuilding (1788–1822) that resulted in some glorious Georgian buildings and the Shropshire Union Canal. Throughout the Victorian and Edwardian ages Chester continued to flourish, and today it is a prosperous place largely untouched by the rebuilding that blighted other Midland cities in the mid-20th century.

A regular summertime occurrence is the appearance of the Town Crier at the Cross, where Chester's four main streets converge. At 12:00 noon and 3:00 P.M., every day except Sunday and Monday, visitors gather to hear him give his public proclamations. The town can become very congested in the summer months, so try to visit in spring or autumn or even during the weeks before Christmas, when the ancient streets are filled with gaily colored decorations.

EXPLORING CHESTER

First-time visitors might take one of the daily sightseeing walks around the city led by Blue Badge Guides. Guided walks depart daily from the Tourist Information Centre at the Town Hall (10:45 A.M. all year and 2:30 P.M. April through October; Tel: 0244-31-31-26 or 31-83-56) and from the Chester Visitor Centre, opposite the Roman amphitheater (10:30 A.M. all year and 2:00 P.M. April through October; Tel: 0244-35-16-09). There are also a number of regular guided walks that follow particular themes, such as the Roman Soldier Wall Patrol that takes place frequently during the summer.

If the guided walks do not fit in with your schedule, walk unguided along Chester's fortified **city walls**, which offer a series of delightful views of the city's historic center along their two-mile circuit. This tour will take an hour or two and can be started at any one of the city's six gates. From the city walls you will see the largest **Roman amphitheater** ever uncovered in Britain, with seating for 7,000 spectators; the city's magnificent cathedral; the medieval **Water Tower** built to guard the port; and the **Roodee**, the city's racecourse and once the site of a massive Roman harbor. The country's oldest horseraces are held here; unusually, the races run counterclockwise.

One of Chester's most famous features is the **Rows**, a series of double-tiered shop galleries that date from the

Middle Ages and that line both sides of the city's main thoroughfares, such as Watergate, Eastgate, and Bridge Street. Shoppers can walk along one of these streets past shops at ground level and then walk back past another series of shops along wooden galleries built one story higher. Fine architecture of all periods can be found throughout Chester's city center, where attractive modern buildings blend with older styles.

Chester's superbly conserved buildings are enough reason to visit the city, but there are also a number of other attractions. The Victorian era is commemorated by the splendid **Eastgate Clock**, erected on top of the Georgian gate that in 1769 replaced the original Roman city gate. The clock was built to celebrate Queen Victoria's Jubilee of 1897. Then there is the **Chester Heritage Centre** on Street Row, with fascinating audiovisual shows, and the **Chester Visitor Centre** on Vicars Lane, which contains a life-size street scene showing the Rows in Victorian times, with accompanying sounds—and smells.

Be sure to visit Chester's **cathedral** in the city center near Market Square, noting the superb 13th-century choir and unusual carved choir stalls; the **Grosvenor Museum** on Grosvenor Street near the castle, with its fine collection of paintings and silver and its exhibitions covering local history; and the **Toy Museum** on Lower Bridge Street.

DINING AND STAYING IN CHESTER
Chester has one of Britain's finest vegetarian restaurants, the **Abbey Green**, just off Northgate Street. Here a wide range of international dishes are served in a pleasant, welcoming atmosphere. Hotels and guest houses are plentiful in and around Chester, and several have good restaurants attached. Notable is the ► **Chester Grosvenor Hotel**, well-established and recently refurbished, with an attractive half-timbered façade, spacious, comfortable bedrooms, and two fine restaurants; prices at the elegant **Arkle Restaurant** are high, while the hotel's less expensive **Brasserie** offers quality and good value. Book early for this popular hotel. Around the corner on St. John Street is ► **Blossoms Hotel**, with well-furnished rooms in a historic building that also contains a moderately priced restaurant. The exceptional ► **Castle House** on Castle Street, a centrally located guest house that is also the home of the owners, has five well-equipped bedrooms, most with their own showers.

GETTING AROUND

The Heart of England is accessible through three major cities: London, Birmingham, and Bristol. Travellers by air will come via London's Gatwick or Heathrow, or through the international airports at Birmingham and Manchester. Birmingham has direct flights from major European and North American cities and feeder connections to the London airports and other domestic airports. Luxury-coach services by Flightlink (Tel: 021-554-5232) run from all these airports, and National Express (Tel: 021-622-4373) has bus services between all the major towns and cities in the Heart of England. Overseas visitors can also obtain from National Express a 30-day BritExpress Card, which provides a discount on long-distance travel services.

The area is well served by the railway network, and high-speed trains run frequently to Coventry, Birmingham, Wolverhampton, and Chester from London's Euston Station. The southern part of this region is served by trains running from London's Paddington Station. There are discounted fares for off-peak travel, and overseas visitors can buy Rail Rover tickets, which entitle them to periods of inexpensive, unlimited travel. Visitors to Stratford-upon-Avon can also go via Guide Friday's fast rail/road service from Euston via Coventry to Stratford. Several services operate daily, including a post-theater service. Tickets are available from London's Euston Station or any British Rail Travel Centre. If your visit is solely to go to the theater, you can take the Royal Shakespeare Shuttle, a bus service that travels from London in the afternoon and returns after the evening performance. For details, Tel: (071) 379-1564 or, in the U.S., (800) 223-6108.

For those visitors who want to venture away from the main centers, a car is almost essential. The motorways make the area easily accessible; most points can be reached within two to three hours from London and four or five hours from Dover and Folkestone. The most efficient and attractive point of entry for car drivers travelling from London is across the Severn Bridge to Chepstow via the M 4. You can then explore the Heart of England and return via Shrewsbury and the M 54/M 6/M 1; or via Bromsgrove and the M 42, Stratford and the A 46, or the Cotswolds and the A 40—the latter three all link up with the M 40 into London. You can do this circular trip in the reverse order and avoid the tolls on the Severn Bridge (for cars, £2.80), as they are charged only in the westward direction. It is also possible to travel around by bus along some beautifully scenic routes, but plan your journey carefully and be sure you are armed with the latest timetables or you might get stranded.

If you are going to Stratford first and want to enjoy the surrounding countryside, Guide Friday Ltd., Civic Hall, Market Place, 14 Rother Street (Tel: 0789-29-44-66), can arrange car rentals through the major national and international companies. Taxis can be very expensive.

River and canal trips are an increasingly popular way to explore the area. Two major firms that book these trips, as well as offer cruises along the Thames and other waterways of England, are: **Hoseasons Holidays**, Sunway House, Lowestoft NR32 3LT, Tel: (0502) 50-10-10; Fax: (0502) 51-43-98; and **Blake's Holidays**, Wroxham, Norwich NR12 8DH, Tel: (0603) 78-29-11; Fax: (0603) 78-28-71.

ACCOMMODATIONS REFERENCE
Rates are projected 1994 prices for a double room with breakfast, unless otherwise stated. As prices are subject to change, always double-check before booking.

▶ **Angel Inn.** 9 High Street, **Pershore**, Worcestershire WR10 1AF. Tel: (0386) 55-20-46; Fax: (0386) 55-25-81. £45–£67.

▶ **Arrow Mill. Arrow,** near Alcester, Warwickshire B49 5NL. Tel: (0789) 76-24-19; Fax: (0789) 76-51-70. £65–£85.

▶ **Ashleigh House.** Whitley Hill, **Henley-in-Arden** B95 5DL. Tel: (0564) 79-23-15; Fax: (0564) 79-41-33. £52.

▶ **Bell Hotel.** 52 Church Street, **Tewkesbury** GL20 5SA. Tel: (0684) 29-32-93; Fax: (0684) 29-66-90; in U.S. and Canada, (800) 528-1234. £75–£85.

▶ **Birche Hotel. Shelsley Beauchamp**, Worcestershire WR6 6RD. Tel: (088-65) 251; Fax: (088-65) 731. £57.

▶ **Blossoms Hotel.** St. John Street, **Chester**, Cheshire CH1 1HL. Tel: (0244) 32-31-86; Fax: (0244) 34-64-33; in U.S. and Canada, (800) 225-5843; in Australia, (008) 22-24-46. £80 (does not include breakfast).

▶ **Bredwardine Hall. Bredwardine**, Herefordshire HR3 6DB. Tel: (0981) 50-05-96. £44.

▶ **Butcher's Arms. Woolhope**, Herefordshire HR1 4RF. Tel: (0432) 86-02-81. £43.

▶ **Castle House.** 23 Castle Street, **Chester**, Cheshire CH1 2DS. Tel: (0244) 35-03-54. £42.

▶ **Chester Grosvenor Hotel.** Eastgate Street, **Chester**, Cheshire CH1 1LT. Tel: (0244) 32-40-24; Fax: (0244) 31-

32-46; in U.S. and Canada, (800) 525-4800; in Australia, (008) 80-08-96. £185–£210.

▶ **Clearwell Castle. Clearwell**, Coleford, Gloucestershire GL16 8LG. Tel: (0594) 83-23-20; Fax: (0594) 83-55-23. £80–£120.

▶ **Corse Lawn House Hotel. Corse Lawn**, Gloucestershire GL19 4LZ. Tel: (0452) 78-07-71; Fax: (0452) 78-08-40. £72.50–£100.

▶ **Coverdale Private Hotel**. 8 Portland Street, **Royal Leamington Spa**, Warwickshire CV32 5HE. Tel: (0926) 33-04-00; Fax: (0926) 83-33-88. £39–£42.

▶ **Croft Country Guest House. Vowchurch**, Herefordshire HR2 0QE. Tel: (0981) 55-02-26. £40–£50.

▶ **Dinham Hall Hotel**. Dinham, **Ludlow**, Shropshire SY8 1EJ. Tel: (0584) 87-64-64 or 87-36-69; Fax: (0584) 87-60-19. £89.50–£104.

▶ **Duke's Hotel**. Payton Street, **Stratford-upon-Avon**, Warwickshire CV37 6UA. Tel: (0789) 26-93-00; Fax: (0789) 41-47-00. £68–£89.

▶ **Ettington Park Hotel**. Alderminster, near **Stratford-upon-Avon**, Warwickshire CV37 8BS. Tel: (0789) 45-01-23; Fax: (0789) 45-04-72; in U.S., (212) 247-6200.£145–£160.

▶ **Evesham Hotel**. Cooper's Lane, off Waterside, **Evesham** WR11 6DA. Tel: (0386) 76-55-66; Fax: (0386) 76-54-43. £82–£94.

▶ **Feathers Hotel**. The Bull Ring, **Ludlow**, Shropshire SY8 1AA. Tel: (0584) 87-52-61; Fax: (0584) 87-60-30; in U.S., (800) 323-5463 or (708) 251-4110. £104–£124.

▶ **Feathers Hotel**. High Street, **Ledbury**, Herefordshire HR8 1DS. Tel: (0531) 63-52-66; Fax: (0531) 63-20-01. £85–£99.

▶ **Folly Farm Cottage. Ilmington**, near Shipston-on-Stour, Warwickshire CV36 4LJ. Tel: (0608) 68-24-25. £42–£50.

▶ **Fownes Resort Hotel**. City Walls Road, **Worcester** WR1 2AP. Tel: (0905) 61-31-51; Fax: (0905) 237-42. £75–£100.

▶ **Glewstone Court**. Near **Ross-on-Wye**, Herefordshire HR9 6AW. Tel: (0989) 770-367; Fax: (0989) 770-282. £75–£90.

▶ **Green Dragon Hotel**. Broad Street, **Hereford**, Herefordshire HR4 9BG. Tel: (0432) 27-25-06; Fax: (0432) 35-21-39; in U.S. and Canada, (800) 225-5843; in Australia, (008) 22-24-46. £80.

▶ **Holdfast Cottage Hotel**. Marlbank Road, **Welland**, near Malvern WR13 6NA. Tel: (0684) 31-02-88. £68–£76.

▶ **Hope End Hotel.** Hope End, **Ledbury,** Herefordshire HR8 1JQ. Tel: (0531) 63-36-13; Fax: (0531) 63-63-66. £99–£141 (closed Dec. 15–Feb. 15).

▶ **Lansdowne Hotel.** 87 Clarendon Street, **Royal Leamington Spa,** Warwickshire CV32 4PE. Tel: (0926) 45-05-05; Fax: (0926) 42-06-04. £58.

▶ **Lion Hotel.** Wyle Cop, **Shrewsbury,** Shropshire SY1 1UY. Tel: (0743) 35-31-07; Fax: (0743) 35-27-44; in U.S. and Canada, (800) 225-5843; in Australia, (008) 22-24-46. £80.

▶ **Madeley Court Hotel.** Castlefields Way, **Madeley,** Telford, Shropshire TF7 5DW. Tel: (0952) 68-00-68; Fax: (0952) 68-42-75. £95.

▶ **Mallory Court.** Harbury Lane, **Bishop's Tachbrook,** near Royal Leamington Spa CV33 9QB. Tel: (0926) 33-02-14; Fax: (0926) 45-17-14. £145–£210.

▶ **Mynd House Hotel. Little Stretton,** Church Stretton, Shropshire SY6 6RB. Tel: (0694) 72-22-12; Fax: (0694) 72-41-80. £60.

▶ **Northleigh House.** Five Ways Road, **Hatton,** near Warwick CV35 7HZ. Tel: (0926) 48-42-03. £42–£54.

▶ **Old Vicarage Hotel. Worfield,** Bridgnorth, Worcestershire WV15 5JZ. Tel: (0746) 44-97; Fax: (0746) 45-52. £88–£106. A suite specially designed for the disabled is available.

▶ **Ostrich Inn. Newland,** near Coleford, Gloucestershire GL16 8NP. Tel: (0594) 83-32-60. £40.

▶ **Park House Hotel.** Park Street, **Shifnal,** Shropshire TF11 9BA. Tel: (0952) 46-01-28; Fax: (0952) 46-16-58. £94.50. Some rooms adapted for the partially disabled.

▶ **Parva Farmhouse. Tintern,** Chepstow, Gwent NP6 6SQ. Tel: (0291) 68-94-11; Fax: (0291) 62-56-14. £48–£58.

▶ **Prince Rupert Hotel.** Butcher Row, **Shrewsbury,** Shropshire SY1 1UQ. Tel: (0743) 23-60-00; Fax: (0743) 35-73-06. £85.

▶ **Redfern Hotel. Cleobury Mortimer,** Shropshire DY14 8AA. Tel: (0299) 27-03-95; Fax: (0299) 27-10-11; in U.S., Fax: (800) 654-0494. £66.

▶ **Royal George Hotel. Tintern,** Chepstow, Gwent NP6 6SF. Tel: (0291) 68-92-05; Fax: (0291) 68-94-48. £67.

▶ **St. Pierre Hotel.** St. Pierre Park, **Chepstow,** Gwent NP6 6YA. Tel: (0291) 62-44-44; Fax: (0291) 62-79-77. £80–£100.

▶ **Shakespeare Hotel.** Chapel Street, **Stratford-upon-Avon,** Warwickshire CV37 6ER. Tel: (0789) 29-47-71; Fax: (0789) 41-54-11; in U.S. and Canada, (800) 225-5843; in Australia, (008) 22-24-46. £100–£115.

► **Speech House.** Forest of Dean, **Coleford**, Gloucestershire GL16 7EL. Tel: (0594) 82-26-07; Fax: (0594) 82-36-58; in U.S. and Canada, (800) 225-5843; in Australia, (008) 22-24-46. £95–£110.

► **Stratford House Hotel.** 18 Sheep Street, **Stratford-upon-Avon**, Warwickshire CV37 6EF. Tel: (0789) 26-82-88; Fax: (0789) 29-55-80. £61–£76.

► **Swan.** Church Street, **Hay-on-Wye**, Hereford HR3 5DQ. Tel: (0497) 82-11-77; Fax: (0497) 82-14-24. £60–£80.

► **Telford Hotel, Golf and Country Club.** Great Hay, **Sutton Hill**, Telford, Shropshire TF7 4DT. Tel: (0952) 58-56-42; Fax: (0952) 58-66-02. £88.50–£98.50.

► **Tewkesbury Park Hotel.** Lincoln Green Lane, **Tewkesbury**, Gloucestershire GL20 7DN. Tel: (0684) 29-54-05; Fax: (0684) 29-23-86. £85–£101.

► **Valley Hotel. Ironbridge**, Telford, Shropshire TF8 7DW. Tel: (0952) 43-22-47; Fax: (0952) 43-23-08. £72.

► **Welcombe Hotel.** Warwick Road, **Stratford-upon-Avon**, Warwickshire CV37 0NR. Tel: (0789) 29-52-52; Fax: (0789) 41-46-66; in U.S. and Canada, (800) 237-1236; in Australia, (008) 22-11-76. £126–£152.

► **White Swan Hotel.** Rother Street, **Stratford-upon-Avon**, Warwickshire CV37 6NH. Tel: (0789) 29-70-22; Fax: (0789) 26-87-73; in U.S. and Canada, (800) 225-5843; in Australia, (008) 22-24-46. £85–£100.

► **Wyndham Arms. Clearwell**, near Coleford, Gloucestershire GL16 8JT. Tel: (0594) 3-36-66; Fax: (0594) 3-64-50. £60. Some rooms with wheelchair access.

YORK

By Frank Victor Dawes

In no other English city are the strata of history more visible than in York. Its peat-rich soil has preserved, layer upon layer, the buildings and artifacts of almost two millennia of civilization. Every epoch since the Roman occupation has left its mark on York.

Three miles of stout limestone wall, with just a few gaps here and there, encompass an almost theatrically medieval city dominated by York Minster, the largest Gothic cathedral north of the Alps; its great square towers are visible for miles across the relatively flat countryside. "The antiquity of York," wrote Daniel Defoe in 1724 in *A Tour Thro' the Whole Island of Great Britain,* "showed itself so visibly at a distance that we could not but observe it before we came quite up to the city."

What was remains so today, although York is no museum but a thriving commercial and shopping center, the home of chocolate and candy manufacturers, with new-technology coal mines just a short drive away.

It is historic York, of course, that draws two million visitors each year. The people who live and work here cope easily and cheerfully with the tides of tourists. Although on the whole not given to boastfulness (self-mockery is more their style), the folks of York are quietly proud of their city's attractions. Citizens' inquisitive interest in strangers ("Where are tha from? What does tha do?") may embarrass their southern cousins, but most visitors find it engaging.

If you have only a limited time to spend in York, go immediately to the minster—without a doubt the city's most spectacular treasure. After you have explored the cathedral, take a walk, no matter how brief, on the famed city walls. The views they command are spectacular, and they give you a magical taste of what living in a medieval town was like. For those who can explore York at a more leisurely pace, choose a tour that takes you all the way around the city walls, beginning with Micklegate Bar, York's royal entrance, and ending at York Minster and the old medieval city.

York Tour at 8 Tower Street (Tel: 0904-64-51-51) offers a variety of tours in and around the city, including one operated by Guide Friday. At 9 Tower Street is a first for Britain, the Museum of Automata, incorporating "George," a life-size skeleton demonstrating the tedium of assembly-line work. Anything but robot-like is the lately reintroduced Town Crier, who parades the streets shouting out the news.

MAJOR INTEREST

Jorvik Viking Centre
City walls and gates
York Minster (largest English medieval cathedral, with glorious stained glass)
Medieval streets and buildings
The Shambles

Historic York

EBORACUM

When the invading Roman legions marched north less than 100 years after the death of Christ, they set up a temporary camp at the confluence of the Rivers Ouse and Foss. In time, this became a permanent fort, and Eboracum, as the Romans called it, grew into a city of the first importance. Not only was it the headquarters of the Sixth Legion and capital of the province of Lower (that is to say, Northern) Britain, it also flourished as a port served by galleys that were able to navigate the River Ouse 50 miles inland from the North Sea. At its peak, the garrison reached 6,000 men.

A network of arrow-straight Roman roads converged on Eboracum, where Emperor Hadrian made his base. When Constantius Chlorus died here in A.D. 306, his son was proclaimed emperor from York and became, as Constantine the Great, the first Roman emperor to embrace Christianity.

The Romans ruled Britain for three and a half centuries

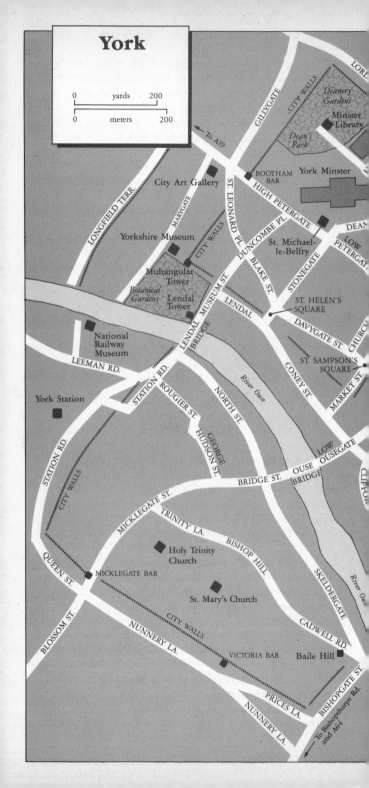

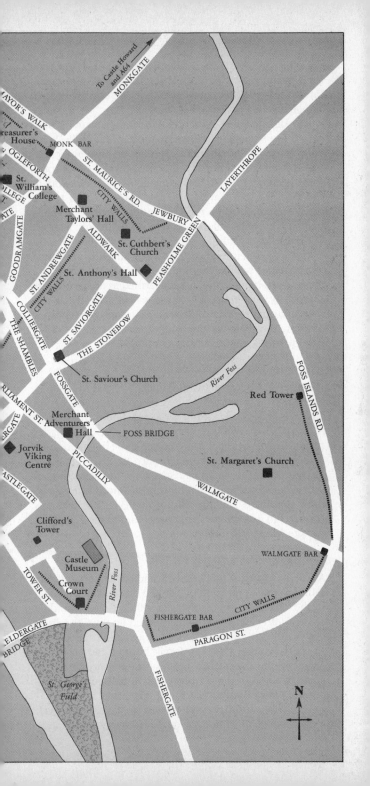

(61–409) until they left to defend their native soil. In York their paved streets lie buried beneath today's thorough-fares—Via Praetoria ran where Stonegate is today and Via Principalis lies under Petergate.

The only tangible evidence of the long Roman occupation is the Multangular Tower in the gardens of the **York-shire Museum and Botanical Gardens** on Museum Street. The tower was originally the west-corner tower of a fourth-century fortress, and from the Roman brickwork at the base the eye travels up some 19 feet or so to the medieval structure on top. The museum, recently refurbished with new galleries, is concerned mainly with archaeology and natural history, with a strong emphasis on Yorkshire. Roman coffins are displayed here, remnants that together with kitchen utensils, mosaics, jewelry, and the like are being constantly unearthed as archaeologists scrape away at the city's substrata. As recently as the 1960s, during repairs to the central foundations of York Minster, the walls of the Sixth Legion's administrative headquarters, the Principia, were uncovered.

EOFORWIC

During what is known as the Anglian period (627–867), Eboracum was known as Eoforwic, the capital of the Saxon kingdom of Northumbria and, under the scholar Alcuin (735–804), the center of learning. (Later, at Charlemagne's court in Aachen, Alcuin was to be the intellectual leader of the Carolingian renaissance.)

The Saxons accepted Christianity in the seventh century when Saint Paulinus converted King Edward, who then appointed Paulinus bishop in 634. The king was baptized in a small wooden chapel said to have been on the site of today's minster.

JORVIK

After the Romans departed, Scandinavian adventurers found it easy to raid and pillage the coasts of Britain, and by the 850s they came in fleets of 300 ships. In the middle of the ninth century the Vikings sailed up the Ouse from the North Sea in their longships and took the city by storm, renaming it Jorvik. Jorvik became the capital of Danelaw, the conquered north and eastern part of England, while Alfred the Great clung to his southern kingdom of Wessex, with its capital at Winchester.

The Vikings brought with them their culture, and even today all over Yorkshire you can find villages with Scandinavian names. Many of York's main thoroughfares are called "gates," from the Norse for "street." (Gates are confusingly called "bars.") The Vikings repaired and extended Jorvik's old walls and laid out the streets as they remain today. It became one of Europe's major ports, thronged by traders from overseas, its warehouses stuffed with merchandise.

Jorvik Viking Centre

Between 1976 and 1981, the York Archaeological Trust carried out a major dig on Coppergate and discovered one part of the old Viking city: four rows of buildings, deep beneath the foundations of their 20th-century successors. Preserved in the damp peat-rich soil, plant and insect remains as well as those of human beings, along with their everyday tools and implements—even boots and shoes—have been found by archaeologists.

At the site of the dig, Heritage Projects, an offshoot of the Trust, built the underground Jorvik Viking Centre. The museum displays two rows of reconstructed buildings as they were 1,000 years ago; another two are preserved as they were when found in the late 1970s, deep beneath a shopping mall. Visitors climb aboard "time cars," which carry them back through the years, past the sights and sounds of 30 generations of York citizens, until the clock stops at Coppergate on a late October day in 948. The scene is re-created vividly for all the senses, even smell: A whiff of appetizing stew mingles with the odors of a pigsty and a latrine. Even the diseases and the rudimentary dentistry of our ancestors have been re-created with merciless authenticity.

The Jorvik Viking Centre was a huge success from the moment it opened in 1984 and almost always has a long line at its doors. If you have the patience to wait, you'll find the experience a rewarding one.

Archaeological Resource Centre

Quieter but hardly less exciting than the Jorvik Viking Centre, the Archaeological Resource Centre is in St. Saviour's, a Norman church only 300 yards away. The memorials include a marble tablet for Mary Morris, who was courted by George Washington.

At St. Saviour's you can "Touch the Past" by handling authentic finds from excavations and speak with archaeologists about their work. There is a computer database for those seeking specific objects. On display is the

Viking-style ship *Tormodson* ("brave son of Thor"), built at the turn of this century in Aafjord, Norway, and saved from destruction by a maritime historian.

MEDIEVAL YORK

The earls of Northumbria took over Jorvik from the departing Danes; 100 years later, in 1066, the Normans invaded England and marched north from the landing beaches of the Channel. They sacked Jorvik, but York rose from this traumatic upheaval to become a powerful medieval city (except for London the greatest in the land), the civil and ecclesiastical capital of the north, and a thriving port from which ships sailed to Europe with cargoes of grain, wool, hides, and lead. To this day, the archbishop of York has the title Primate of England, second only in the Anglican church to its head, the archbishop of Canterbury, who is called Primate of All England.

The City Walls

The old city, no more than a mile across, is encircled by fortified walls, which are open from dawn to dusk. An almost complete walking circuit can be made on top of the wall, but wear sensible shoes, for there are many breaks in the wall, and its grassy slopes are steep. Given the vagaries of the English climate, as always it is a good idea to carry an umbrella. The circuit can be started at any of the "bars" (gates), which resemble the turreted gateways of medieval castles, or at the occasional breaks in the wall, where steps lead to the top. In springtime, Wordsworthian "hosts of golden daffodils" adorn the slopes of the moat that runs outside the walls.

The River Ouse divides the wall into two parts. A good way to cover the walls is to start at Lendal Tower just north of the river on the west side of town and go counterclockwise. From Lendal Tower cross Lendal Bridge, going south past the railway station and the splendidly Victorian ▶ **Royal York Hotel**, where despite modernization, gentility will prevail as you linger over tea and crumpets beneath high, ornate ceilings. The Royal York was built more than 100 years ago and, now carefully restored, is a splendid example of the grand Victorian railway hotel. The food is not outstanding, but the 148 bedrooms offer a high standard of comfort with every modern convenience. The immensely popular **National Railway Museum** is west, beyond the station on Leeman Road. The museum tells the story of railways and railway engineering in Britain with period platform tableaux in a recently opened Great Railway Show reached by a tunnel under the road. The refurbished Great Hall contains *Mallard,* the world's fastest steam locomotive, Queen Victoria's royal carriage of 1869, and a bullion box from the first Great Train Robbery in 1855.

MICKLEGATE BAR

Continuing south, you will come to the most important of the four original gates, Micklegate Bar, which guarded York from the hostile south. In the Middle Ages, heads of vanquished rebels were often displayed here, among them those of Richard, duke of York, and Sir Henry "Hotspur" Percy, who helped put Henry IV on the throne of England but was executed for later rebelling against him.

From Micklegate, the wall runs parallel to Nunnery Lane between St. Mary's Convent, founded in 1686, and two churches, **Holy Trinity** and **St. Mary's.** The latter has a Saxon tower and is partly constructed of Roman masonry. The former was once the church of a Benedictine priory, and stocks remain in the churchyard.

At **Baile Hill** the wall runs northeast to meet the Ouse at Skeldergate Bridge. Baile Hill was the first of two mounds raised by William the Conqueror, but nothing remains of the castle that once stood upon it.

Across the river, the second of William's man-made hills is topped by **Clifford's Tower,** an imposing stone quatrefoil keep with a gatehouse and chapel, built around 1300 and reached by an exhausting flight of steps. It is named after Roger de Clifford, who was executed here in 1596. Clifford's Tower was preceded by an earlier wooden Norman castle that burned to the ground on March 16, 1190, after 150 Jews took refuge inside from an anti-Semitic mob. Rather than surrender they committed mass suicide like those who died at Masada in Israel. The head of each household was responsible for killing his own immediate family. The rabbis then killed the remaining men and set fire to the tower, incinerating themselves.

In the shadow of the present stone tower is the ▶ Holiday Inn. Somehow its light, airy rooms and smart cocktail bars, **Clifford's** and **Turpin's,** don't seem out of place in this historic setting. Many of the 128 bedrooms have a view of the ancient battlements, as well as modern creature comforts, such as minibars and in-house movies.

Three rooms have their own Jacuzzi baths and three are specially fitted for disabled people. An even newer addition to the list of York's hotels is the Grange Hotel, converted from an early-19th-century town house (see the section on hotels below).

Close by Clifford's Tower is the **Assize Court** (now known as the Crown Court), located in a magnificent building designed by John Carr in 1773, and the **Castle Museum**, a former women's prison on Tower Street that today depicts ordinary Yorkshire life from the 18th century onward. It is a leading folk museum, best known for its reconstruction of 18th- and 19th-century city life. For example, Kirkgate, a cobbled street, has an original horse-drawn hansom cab (the invention of a York man, Joseph Hansom, who was born at 114 Micklegate) parked outside the shops of candlemakers and blacksmiths. Half Moon Court is an Edwardian street complete with a gaslit pub. The Castle Museum has the cell in which the infamous highwayman Dick Turpin was held for three months before being hanged in 1739.

Other exhibits in this imaginative museum include policemen's truncheons, old valentines, vintage firearms, musical instruments, and snuffboxes.

South of the Castle Museum is **St. George's Field**; here the citizens of York have ancient rights "to walk, shoot with bows and arrows, and dry linen." Needless to say, the first is the only right that is regularly exercised today. To the northwest of the museum, on Coppergate, is the Jorvik Viking Centre.

FISHERGATE BAR AND WALMGATE BAR

Resume your walk along the city walls at Fishergate Bar, and continue on east to Walmgate Bar, which has its original barbican and portcullis, with inner oak gates and a wicket. Nearby on Walmgate is **St. Margaret's Church**, its Norman porch richly decorated with the signs of the zodiac. This part of the wall turns and ends at the **Red Tower**. Walk north along Foss Islands Road to rejoin the ramparts. En route, you will come to Peasholme Green and the **Black Swan Inn**, built for a merchant in the 16th century. Later, when it became a pub, one of the upstairs rooms was used for illegal cockfighting. Today it is still a pub, but an entirely law-abiding one. **St. Anthony's Hall**, also on Peasholme Green, is a fine, timber-framed guildhall, as is **Merchant Taylors' Hall**, which you will pass as you continue toward the city walls. (The finest and grandest guildhall is the **Merchant Adventurers' Hall**, built in the 14th and 15th centuries by city notables concerned mainly with the export of cloth. It is located to the south, near the Foss Bridge, and it is well worth visiting to see its beautiful medieval timberwork.)

THE CITY WALLS CONCLUDED

At **Monk Bar**, the gate just north of Merchant Taylors' Hall, the most dramatic section of the walls begins, traversing two sides of the Roman city of Eboracum. It is from here that the soaring triple towers of the minster can be seen at their best. Within the enclave are the **Treasurer's House**, the **Minster Library** (with an exhibition hall open to the public), **St. William's College**, and the lawns of the **Deanery Gardens**.

These ancient walls took a terrific battering from Cromwell's cannonballs during the Civil War, when the Royalists were besieged here, having set up a printing press in St. William's College to wage a war of words against Parliament. In 1644 Prince Rupert arrived with reinforcements for the beleaguered city, but to no avail.

The wall ends at **Bootham Bar**, a bit north of Lendal Tower. Its Norman portcullis remains, as if ready to be lowered at any moment against an invading army. **Bootham Tea Room**, located in the old wall at High Petergate, is a good place for a refreshing "cuppa" after all that exercise.

York Minster

It is impossible to approach this, the largest and most glorious medieval cathedral in Britain, without reverence and awe. In 1984 the world was horror-struck when the minster was badly damaged in a fire started by a bolt of lightning, engulfing the 13th-century south transept in flames. After the conflagration, a team of 67 stonemasons, joiners, woodcarvers, scaffolders, and painters rebuilt the roof and the intricately vaulted ceiling using 150 large oak trees, some from the Queen's estates. Carvings illustrate the words of the canticle "Benedicte—all ye works of the Lord, praise ye the Lord." A thousand books of 22-carat gold leaf were used in the new decorations. The restoration, completed a year ahead of schedule, took four years—an infinitesimally small period in the long history of the minster. Twice before the church had been ravaged—in 1829, when a blaze burned out the choir, and in 1840, when a workman accidentally ignited the timber roof of the nave. The noble cathedral has always survived such disasters, just as it has survived wars and sieges throughout the ages.

The present structure took 250 years to build and was completed in 1480. Many of the masons who labored on it were swept away by the plague, but their magnificent work lives on. The south transept, restored by their 20th-century heirs, is an imposing sight by day or by night, when floodlights dramatically illuminate it. High above the door is the famous **Rose Window**, which was cracked and splintered into 40,000 fragments by the 1984 fire but is now almost miraculously restored. Its red and white roses commemorate the end of the bloody 15th-century feud between the "Red Rose" House of Lancaster and the "White Rose" House of York. This window is only one of the minster's 130 stained-glass windows. The church's chief glory, these priceless examples of English Gothic glass were removed in 1939 to secure them from possible bomb damage. After the war, it took 20 years to reinstall them under the painstaking direction of Dean Milner-White.

The west window's heart-shaped traceries, known as the Heart of Yorkshire, are particularly beautiful, yet it is the **"Five Sisters" Window** that attracts the most attention. Each lancet of this odd, early-English grisaille glass is more than 50 feet tall and 5 feet wide.

Among the startlingly lifelike statues inside the minster are many of past archbishops, including the Purbeck marble effigy of Archbishop Walter de Gray, who began the building.

A more recent memorial is the astronomical clock in the north transept, which is dedicated to the 18,000 men of the Royal Air Force stationed at bases in the northeast who died during World War II.

The main entrance to the cathedral is at the west end, where you will find information on tape. The cathedral is open daily. The octagonal **Chapter House** is noted for its 13th-century vaulting, and the **Foundations Museum** exhibits archaeological finds. In 1967 it was discovered that York Minster was in imminent danger of collapse due to structural fatigue, erosion, and changes in the water table under the foundations. Repairs in reinforced concrete were quickly begun and are visible in the museum.

The Streets of Old York

The narrow streets and alleys near York Minster are packed with curiosities and are best explored either on foot or in one of the horse-drawn carriages for hire opposite the minster. You can get information from the **Tourist Information Centre** on Rougier Street, off Station Road; Tel: (0904) 62-05-57 or 62-05-76. If you choose to explore by carriage, you will invariably get a commentary from the driver. He will almost certainly point out the birthplace of Guy Fawkes, the man who hatched the Gunpowder Plot and tried to blow up Parliament in 1605. There is some confusion over the actual place—it may be on Stonegate or on High Petergate—but there is no doubt that Fawkes was born in York.

There are plenty of hostelries where a pint of the local Theakston's Best Bitter, Old Peculiar, or John Smith's Bitter can be taken in old-fashioned ease without the accompaniment of Muzak. The **Roman Bath** on St. Sampson's Square has the remains of one in its basement, and the **King's Arms** on King's Staith has a board recording the flood level as early warning to its customers. Also by the river, at Acaster Malbis 3 miles (5 km) south of the city, the **Ship Inn** has its own moorings and fishing and serves drinks in the garden.

In **Coffee Yard** off Stonegate, the town's oldest print-shop is marked by a carving of a red devil. (Apprentices to what is now the archaic craft of hot-metal printing are still known as "printers' devils.") Boot scrapers can be seen at many doorways, surviving from the days when cobbles were a rarity and mud plentiful—only in 1541, when Henry VIII and Catherine Howard visited York, were the streets "swept, sanded and gravelled" for the first time. The Red House on Duncombe Place has a torch snuffer for the convenience of the linkmen (torchbearers) who used to escort people through the unlit streets, and a former tobacconist's at 76 Petergate displays a gilded horse's head at its door. A gas flame used to spurt from its mouth for anyone wanting a light.

Another curiosity of the old York streets is the "fire-mark," a plaque mounted on houses before a municipal fire service existed. Fire engines were operated by insurance companies and called only at those houses bearing their company mark, no matter how desperate the blaze.

The best-known York street is **The Shambles**, once the butchers' quarter, with its medieval timbered gables overhanging so far that it is possible to shake hands across facing upper stories. The Shambles leads to the city's shortest street, which boasts its longest name: **Whip-Ma-Whop-Ma-Gate**. As guides will delight in telling you, this is where petty criminals were flogged.

Northwest of York Minster on Exhibition Square is the **City Art Gallery**, noted for its British paintings and for the Lycett Green Collection of works by old masters.

SHOPPING IN YORK

Shopping here is not unlike visiting Aladdin's Cave. There is an open-air market on Newgate every day except Sundays, a new pedestrians-only mall on Coppergate, and an array of department stores on Coney Street. **Liberty** and **Laura Ashley** can be found on Davygate. The medieval lanes and alleys are crammed with shops of all varieties. In The Shambles, **Cox of Northampton** sells sheepskin; for leather go to Walmgate and **Ralph Ellerker's**, which started as a saddlery in 1796. On Goodramgate, **Donald Butler** sells fine china and **Trinity** all manner of dolls. **Spelman's** on Micklegate is the place for antiquarian books, while the **Little Gallery** on Low Petergate ships "all gifts to all countries."

For a break, **Taylors Tea Rooms** on Stonegate serve not just tea but toast, Earl Grey fruitcake, and a Yorkshire rarebit made with Theakston's ale and roasted ham as well. Its partner is **Betty's Café** on St. Helen's Square, which can get overcrowded at peak times, with consequent long waits for service. **Grandma Batty's Yorkshire Pudding Emporium** on Jubbergate, off Parliament Street, serves giant versions of the celebrated local dish with various fillings. Bakers such as **Yates** on Low Petergate sell parkin and Pontefract cakes as well as fresh bread, and **Scott's**, the pork butcher on the same street, does excellent black puddings, another northern delight.

STAYING IN AND AROUND YORK

In addition to the Holiday Inn and the Victorian Royal York mentioned in the City Walls section above, the city and its environs abound with hotels and guest houses to suit every taste and budget, although in peak season accommodations are heavily booked. As its name suggests, ▶ **Judge's Lodging**, a Georgian house at 9 Lendal, used to be the residence of Assize Court judges. Every bedroom has a four-poster, and the food and wine are French—and French at its best. ▶ **Middlethorpe Hall**, on

Bishopthorpe Road outside the city by the racecourse, is stately, complete with liveried footman. Game features prominently on the menu, along with roast beef with Yorkshire pudding.

The ▶ **Grange Hotel**'s transformation from period town house to luxurious 29-room hotel filled with antiques was performed by Christophe Golut, Swiss designer of the new restaurant at the House of Lords in London. The Grange has two restaurants, one a brasserie.

▶ **Fairfield Manor**, reopened in 1992 after a major refurbishment, is a short distance from town at Skelton on the northern outskirts, but there is ample parking, and buses for York (10 to 15 minutes away) stop outside. Its 90 rooms retain some 18th-century features, such as carved oak paneling, combined with bright new furnishings and fabrics. Many of the rooms are reserved for nonsmokers, and all rooms have additional security to reassure women guests travelling alone. Two rooms are specially adapted for disabled people.

If you want a view of the minster from your window, the ▶ **Viking Hotel** in North Street can offer it from many of its 187 bedrooms. It is built on the riverside within the city walls in a totally up-to-date style, yet its restaurant prides itself on traditional English country fare such as apple pie and Wensleydale cheese. In an unusual touch, its leisure center incorporates a golf driving range. Much smaller, with 35 bedrooms, the ▶ **Dean Court Hotel** can be found in Duncombe Place beneath the minster's west front. Its atmosphere is reminiscent of Trollope and *Barchester Towers,* yet all bedrooms are equipped with bath, television, and phone. The food is solidly traditional.

Also centrally placed, **St. Williams** in College Street looks more like a monastery refectory than the popular restaurant it is. In summer long trestle tables are set in the courtyard outside a 15th-century building. The food is wholesome and comes in large portions.

SEASONAL EVENTS

Just as the Vikings welcomed the approach of spring with *Jolablot* (winter festivities), so York brightens up the otherwise dreary month of February with its annual **Jorvik Viking Festival**. This includes longships racing on the Ouse, Viking battles in the streets, fireworks, and the recitation of sagas. The **York Races** take place every month from May through October, and the Ebor Handicap is in August. The **York Festival** of drama, dance, music, opera, and art is held in June and early July. Every fourth year it includes the York Cycle of Mystery Plays, a colorful medieval-style reenactment of the story of mankind. The mystery plays are traditionally held in the open air, with a large cast, predominantly amateur. The next performance is due in 1996.

Castle Howard

Fifteen miles (24 km) northeast of York on A 64, toward the Yorkshire Moors, **Castle Howard**, a Baroque, domed 18th-century mansion stands by a lake on an arrow-straight five-mile (8-km) drive. The impressive setting of the television version of Evelyn Waugh's *Brideshead Revisited*, it was designed by Sir John Vanbrugh with the help of Nicholas Hawksmoor for the third earl of Carlisle, Charles Howard, and remains the home of his descendants, although it is open to visitors. The interior, especially the Great Hall under the dome, with its Italianate frescoes and chimneypiece, is richly furnished, and works by Holbein and Van Dyck are displayed in the Long Gallery. York Tour (see above) includes Castle Howard in its Yorkshire Countryside Tour.

GETTING AROUND
The drive from London to York is north on A 1 or M 1, turning onto A 64 through Tadcaster, and totals 193 miles (309 km). By train the journey is two hours from London's King's Cross Station, a considerable improvement on the stagecoach travel of Defoe's day, which took four days. The bus trip, via National Express from Victoria Coach Station, takes four to five hours.

ACCOMMODATIONS REFERENCE
Rates are projected 1994 prices for a double room with breakfast, unless otherwise stated. As prices are subject to change, always double-check before booking.

▶ **Dean Court Hotel.** Duncombe Place, **York** YO1 2EF. Tel: (0904) 62-50-82; Fax: (0904) 62-03-05; in U.S. and Canada, (800) 528-1234; in Australia, (02) 212-6444. £100–£120.
▶ **Fairfield Manor.** Shipton Road, Skelton, **York** YO3 6XW. Tel: (0904) 67-02-22; Fax: (0904) 67-03-11. £90.
▶ **Grange Hotel.** Clifton, **York** YO3 6AA. Tel: (0904) 64-47-44; Fax: (0904) 61-24-53; in U.S., (800) 323-5463. £107.

► **Holiday Inn**. 1 Tower Street, **York** YO1 1SB. Tel: (0904) 64-81-11; Fax: (0904) 61-03-17; in U.S. and Canada, (800) 465-4329. £110–£143 (breakfast not included).

► **Judge's Lodging**. 9 Lendal, **York** YO1 2AQ. Tel: (0904) 63-87-33; Fax: (0904) 67-99-47. £73–£115.

► **Middlethorpe Hall**. Bishopthorpe Road, **York** YO2 1QB. Tel: (0904) 64-12-41; Fax: (0904) 62-01-76; in U.S. and Canada, (800) 525-4800; in Australia, (008) 802-582. £121–£173 (breakfast not included).

► **Royal York Hotel**. Station Road, **York** YO2 2AA. Tel: (0904) 65-36-81; Fax: (0904) 62-35-03; in U.S. and Canada, (800) 448-8355). £94–£126.

► **Viking Hotel**. North Street, **York** YO1 1JF. Tel: (0904) 65-98-22; Fax: (0904) 64-17-93; in U.S. and Canada, (800) 448-8355. £90–£145.

THE NORTH COUNTRY

LAKE DISTRICT, NORTH YORKSHIRE MOORS, DURHAM, HADRIAN'S WALL

By Frank Victor Dawes

The North—"Up North" to those who live in the southern parts of Great Britain—is not as it was. If J. B. Priestley were to revisit Bradford, where he was born, he might well imagine himself to be in the Punjab; a whole area here has been colonized by various ethnic groups who came to work in the mills in the 1960s and have adhered strictly to their own traditions, customs, and language. Indeed, the traditional idea of the North as a place of flat caps, clogs, and shawls, warm beer, fish and chips, black pudding, whippets, backyard pigeon lofts, and mill chimneys, as portrayed by L. S. Lowry in his paintings and Walter Greenwood in *Love on the Dole,* is now mere nostalgia.

What has *not* changed is the scenery that captured the hearts and imaginations of poets and writers from Wordsworth to the Brontës to Priestley. Within an area defined by what used to be called simply the Great North Road (A 1, up the east side of the North), the Road to the Lakes (M 6, up the west side of the North), and the Scottish border (the area of Hadrian's Wall) lies a beguiling combination of superb scenery—rich in historical and literary associations—and ample opportunities for outdoor exercise.

MAJOR INTEREST

The Great North Road
North Yorkshire Moors and Dales
Durham City (cathedral and castle)
Castles: Warkworth, Alnwick, Dunstanburgh, and
     Bamburgh
The Farne Islands for bird-watching
Holy Island (Lindisfarne) castle and ecclesiastical
     ruins

The Road to the Lakes
Spectacular views from the Trough of Bowland
Lake District's Wordsworth sites and atmosphere

Border Country
Carlisle
Border Forest Park
Berwick-upon-Tweed
Hadrian's Wall

Exploring the North of England can take a few weeks or a
few days. It is even possible to sample Yorkshire, Cumbria,
and Northumberland in a single day from London, leaving
King's Cross at 7:45 A.M. on one of the special excursions
(including Nostalgic Steam Days Out) arranged by British
Rail InterCity.

Breakfast is served in the Pullman car as the **Hadrian**
speeds through Peterborough, and a couple of hours
later the great cathedrals of York and then Durham are
gliding past (there's a particularly fine view of the latter
from the railway viaduct spanning the valley). The train
skirts the metropolis of Newcastle-upon-Tyne, then deposits passengers at Hexham for a journey by bus along an
arrow-straight Roman military road, followed by a walk
along the wall Hadrian built at the northernmost frontier
of the Roman Empire nearly 2,000 years ago.

Passengers rejoin the train, which has travelled empty
across the narrowest part of England from the Tyne to the
Solway, at a station on the 72-mile "Long Drag" between
Carlisle and Settle, a masterpiece of Victorian railway engineering. The viaducts, tunnels, cuttings, and embankments
were accomplished with dynamite, pick and shovel, and
the sweat—and sometimes the blood—of vast armies of
"navvies." More than a hundred of them lie buried in the
little churchyard at Chapel-le-Dale.

While dinner is served aboard the train, the incompara-

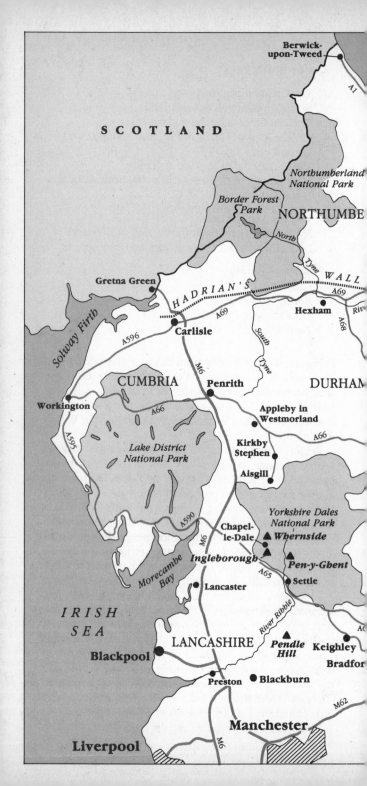

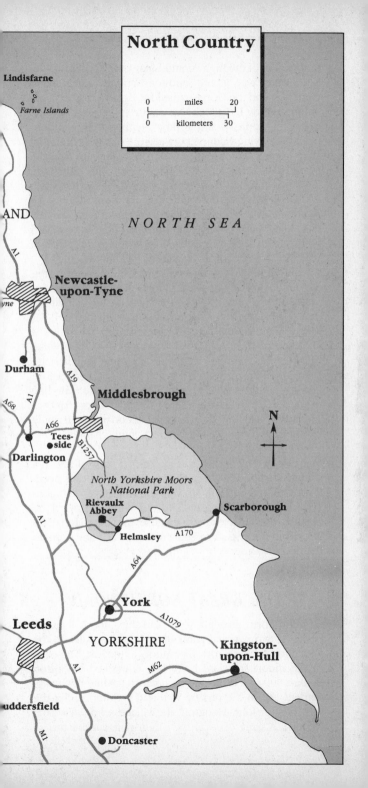

ble scenery of the high Pennines passes the windows: the Eden Valley with its red sandstone bridges, villages, and churches, and the Gorge, famed for its salmon; the Druid temple beside Long Meg Viaduct; Cross Fell; and the hill towns of Appleby and Kirkby Stephen—all glimpsed from high-flying viaducts between the darkness of tunnel after tunnel, carrying the track to its summit at Aisgill, more than 1,000 feet above sea level. The train then descends through the upland sheep farms of Garsdale and Dentdale, crossing the head of the River Ribble on a viaduct with 24 arches, a quarter of a mile long and 105 feet high, and passing through the limestone-walled fields of the Yorkshire Dales beneath the three peaks of Whernside, Ingleborough, and Pen-y-ghent to Settle.

From Hellifield you can see Pendle Hill, home of the ten so-called witches who were publicly hanged at Lancaster in 1612 for a host of alleged crimes, including murder, desecration of graves, and "communing with the Devil." At Keighley, the Worth Valley line, the setting for the films *The Railway Children* and *The Adventures of Sherlock Holmes,* branches into Brontë country. By the time the charlotte russe is served, the train is pausing briefly at Leeds before heading south through Doncaster to rejoin the main line to London, arriving back at King's Cross just after 10:00 P.M. This admittedly long day trip from London traces a triangle explored in more detail in the rest of this chapter.

Our closer look at the most interesting parts of the area roughly covered by this train excursion first heads north through North Yorkshire to Durham and Newcastle-upon-Tyne, then follows England's eastern coast up toward the Scottish border. Next, we explore the Cumbrian Lake District in northwestern England before heading north to the border country above and along Hadrian's Wall.

THE GREAT NORTH ROAD

Heading north through North Yorkshire, the A 1 passes between two national parks: the Yorkshire Dales to the west and the North Yorkshire Moors to the east. The edge of the moors, reached by A 170, is marked by **Sutton Bank**, a 700-foot escarpment on which a white horse was marked out in the turf by Victorian children under the direction of John Hodgson, the village schoolmaster at Kilburn. A gang of local men then dug out the turf to create a lasting monument 314 feet long and 228 feet high. Kilburn's other claim to fame is the cottage of the "Mouseman," the furniture maker Robert Thompson, who left his unusual trademark on every item he crafted and whose tradition is carried on today by his grandsons. At nearby Coxwold is Shandy Hall, where Laurence Sterne, the author of *Tristram Shandy,* lived as vicar, preaching at the church of St. Michael.

The Yorkshire Moors

HELMSLEY

The poet William Wordsworth and his sister Dorothy, on their way from Grasmere to Hackness to visit Wordsworth's future wife, abandoned their carriage in the old market town of Thirsk and decided to negotiate Sutton Bank on foot. They reached Helmsley on the south fringe of the moor (20 miles/32 km east of the A 1 on A 170, and due north of York) and stayed the night at the ▶ **Black Swan**, on the north side of the town's market square. They stayed there again on their way home, and Dorothy wrote in her diary: "My heart danced at the sight of its cleanly outside, bright yellow walls, casements overshadowed with jasmine and its low, double gavel-ended front."

The Black Swan, which until the railway arrived in the 1870s was a coaching inn from which the "Helmsley Highflyer" ran to Leeds and York, is as welcoming today as it was to the Wordsworths. In the 1960s the train suffered a fate similar to the stagecoach, so the way to get there now is by car or bus — or, like the Wordsworths, on foot. The inn is four distinct buildings (Tudor, Elizabethan, Georgian, and modern) that stand amid apple trees in a walled garden next to the parish church. Its 44 rooms, some reserved for nonsmokers, are furnished in a pretty, homey style. The dining room, where local and traditional dishes, such as steak in strong ale and mustard in Yorkshire pudding, are served, is presided over by motherly women in white caps and aprons.

Helmsley, with its market cross (where stalls are set out every Friday) and ruined 12th-century Norman castle, is a delightful town and a convenient base for exploring the wild moors. A mile out of town, **Duncombe Park**, opened to visitors for the first time in 1990, is a fine early-18th-century mansion with a landscaped garden occupying

300 acres on the banks of the River Rye. Its soaring ash and lime trees, classical temples, and vast lawns were laid out in 1713 by the forebears of the present owners, Lord and Lady Feversham.

RIEVAULX ABBEY

Two miles (3 km) northwest on B 1257 is Rievaulx Abbey (pronounced REE-vo), built by the Cistercians in 1131 on the banks of the River Rye. It fell into disuse 400 years later during Henry VIII's dissolution of the monasteries, and now, after another four centuries, it is in ruins. Even so, the abbey is majestic and moving in its quiet and beautiful setting amid trees and next to the river. A shrine to Saint William, the first abbot, who made Rievaulx the leading Cistercian abbey in Britain, is set in the west wall of the chapter house. The empty coffin here is said to have been that of his successor, Saint Aelred, renowned for his gentleness and patience. In his book, *Christian Friendship,* he wrote: "Wonderful must be he who can afford to do without friends and without love—more wonderful assuredly than God himself."

Beyond, to the north and northeast, are the moors, mile upon mile of heather-covered hills where sheep roam free and grouse and pheasant start up as you approach. Out on the lonely moor, where tracks are still marked with stone crosses, the few roads can be treacherous in bad weather. Ghostly bells have been heard ringing out from the ruins of Rievaulx Abbey, and low bridges crossing the streams can become fords when the rain lashes down. It is hard to believe, once out among the heather away from the few main roads, that this lonely country is part of a small, overcrowded island. Osmotherley, just off the A 19 north of Thirsk, is typical of little Yorkshire moor towns of stone buildings clustered around a square. The **Three Tuns** inn makes a cheerful stopping place for a drink or a hearty lunch. Fresh country cheese can be bought from the local woman who makes it from the output of just two or three cows (inquire at the inn).

Farmhouses, let alone villages, are few and far between and even in peak season it's possible to walk for hours without seeing any living creature other than sheep. The now unused "golf ball" structures of the NATO early-warning station looming out of the mist at **Fylingdales Moor** merely emphasize the feeling of nature in isolation. Masses of daffodils blossom in the green valleys such as **Farndale** in spring, and in August when the heather blooms on the hills the landscape glows deep purple. Trails are well marked, but it's a good idea to carry a compass and an Ordnance Survey map in case you stray.

On August 12, the "Glorious Twelfth," the deep valleys and sharply rising hills echo to the cracks of shotguns as the grouse-shooting season opens. Scotland may boast the finest grouse shooting, but when it comes to pheasant the moors of Helmsley and Ryedale are preeminent; the Black Swan has a gun room and a drying room next to the garden lounge.

The Cleveland Way

The 100-mile Cleveland Way, a walking route (see Getting Around, below, for information on North Country walks), describes a horseshoe from Helmsley up through the moors and back down along the coast to Filey south of Scarborough. At its northernmost edge is Roseberry Topping, a peak-shaped outcrop that looks down grassy slopes toward the chimneys and iron bridges of industrial Tees-side and Middlesbrough some 10 miles (16 km) to the northwest. Perched high on nearby Easby Moor is a 51-foot monument to Captain James Cook, who attended school in the village of Great Ayton below, a couple of miles to the west of the Cleveland Way. The school is now a museum, and there are details of Cook's life and voyages around Australia, New Zealand, and North America near his birthplace at Stewart Park in Marton, just outside Middlesbrough. This town on the northern edge of the moors did not exist in Cook's day, but the steel that came later from its blast furnaces went into railways and bridges around the world, notably, by a nice coincidence, the Sydney Harbour Bridge.

Leaving the moors behind, the Cleveland Way follows the coast south along some of the highest cliffs in England. At Staithes, where James Cook was apprenticed to a grocer before running away to sea, a steep road winds down to a tiny harbor where fishing cobles anchor. Whitby, with its wheeling seagulls, steep streets, and ruined abbey, was where Cook first went to sea in colliers and where his ships were later built. In his day whalers plied out of Whitby; today only token fishing fleets put out to sea here, but otherwise the moors and coast of North Yorkshire are much as Cook knew them.

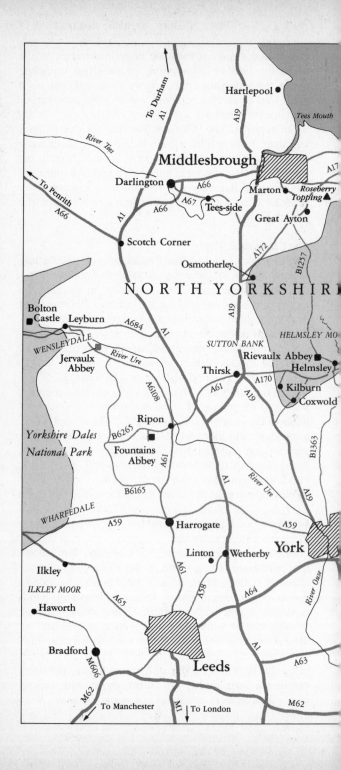

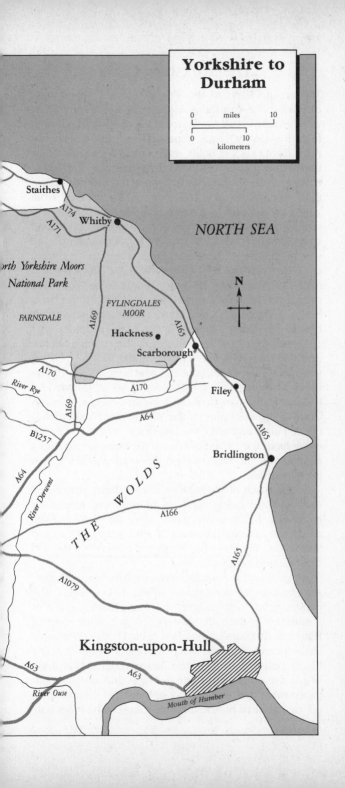

Yorkshire to Durham

0 — miles — 10

0 — 10 — kilometers

Staithes

A174

A171

Whitby

NORTH SEA

North Yorkshire Moors
National Park

FARNSDALE

FYLINGDALES
MOOR

A169

Hackness

A165

Scarborough

N

A170

River Rye

A170

A169

Filey

A64

B1257

A64

River Derwent

T H E   W O L D S

A165

Bridlington

A166

A1079

A165

Kingston-upon-Hull

A63

A63

River Ouse

Mouth of Humber

The Yorkshire Dales

The green valleys to the west of the A 1 are in stark contrast to the vast industrial conurbation of the former woollen textile mill towns stretching east, west, and south from the city of Leeds. Patterned with dry stone walls marking out ancient fields, these valleys were sculpted by the melting glaciers of the Ice Age, which also created the rushing rivers and waterfalls that give the Yorkshire Dales their dramatic beauty. Limestone is the material from which the scenery is created, fashioned by centuries of water flowing into the cliffs, gorges, tunnels, caves, and shafts, where "potholers" explore for new underground streams and lakes. Those who prefer to stay above ground can follow way-marked heather tracks: the **Dales Way** and the **Ribble Way**, as well as the tougher **Pennine Way**, which runs from the Peak District in Derbyshire up the back-bone of England to the Cheviot Hills on the Scottish border (see Getting Around, at end of this chapter).

Some of the loveliest villages in the country are just north of **Ilkley Moor** (celebrated in the Yorkshire dialect song "On Ilkley Moor baht 'at," which means, simply, on Ilkley Moor without a hat) along A 65 in Wharfedale. ▶ **Wood Hall**, a part Jacobean and part Georgian mansion overlooking the valley of the Wharfe near Wetherby on the A 1 and reached by a mile-long drive through the estate from the village of Linton, has been turned into a comfortable and welcoming hotel—with a teddy bear in every bedroom.

To the south of Ilkley Moor lies **Bradford**, where mill chimneys are being replaced by minarets. Ringed by more than half a dozen golf courses and home of the acclaimed **National Museum of Photography, Film, and Television**, Bradford has broken the mold of the old cloth-capped North.

Westward are the somber moors that feature in *Wuthering Heights* and other novels of the Brontë sisters. The **parsonage** where the sisters lived from 1820 to 1861 is now a museum in the little slate-roofed, gray-stone town of **Haworth**. It bears comparison with Hardy's Dorset or Shakespeare's Stratford as a place of literary interest. The highly polished table in the dining room is that upon which the sisters put their thoughts and dreams onto paper while their father slept upstairs and their supposedly more gifted brother Branwell drank at the Black Bull.

The pub is still there, unexceptional were it not for its many mementos of this famous customer. Haworth gets uncomfortably crowded with visitors at holiday times.

Possibly the most attractive of all the ecclesiastical ruins in England lies north of Leeds and 3 miles (5 km) west of Ripon off B 6265 in the wooded valley of the River Skell. **Fountains Abbey**, taken over from the Benedictines by the Cistercians in the 12th century, preserves the spirit of the monastic life with its nave and Chapel of the Nine Altars, its cloister, dormitories, refectories and infirmary, and cellars and workshops, which somehow survived total destruction at the hands of Henry VIII. Its monks played a leading role in developing the Yorkshire wool industry. A short bit east along the banks of the little river are the lovely gardens of **Studley Royal**, part of the same National Trust property as the abbey. The gardens were landscaped in formal Dutch style by John Aislabie, member of Parliament for Ripon and chancellor of the Exchequer until his involvement in the South Sea Bubble forced him from office in 1720.

Just outside Leyburn (north of Ripon and west of the A 1 on A 684), a lane climbs to **Bolton Castle**, which has guarded the green folds of hills beside the River Ure for 600 years. Mary, Queen of Scots, was imprisoned here for six months in 1568. The dining room of this remarkably preserved fortified medieval manor is now a restaurant, efficiently managed by the former butler of Lord Bolton at Bolton Hall. The ruins of the 12th-century **Jervaulx Abbey**, built by Cistercian monks who bred excellent horses and sheep and who created Wensleydale cheese, can be seen on the road south to Ripon (A 6108). **Wensleydale** is perhaps the most beautiful of all the Yorkshire Dales.

Durham County

Going north from Yorkshire, the A 1 and the InterCity rail line cross into the county of Durham, the land of the prince bishops. For centuries the heads of the Christian church ruled here with the power of kings; they commanded their own armies, courts, and coinage. Their bishopric extended from the River Tees to the Scottish border, a kingdom within a kingdom. In more recent times, the countryside was blackened with slag heaps from the coal mines that were a major industry here.

BARNARD CASTLE

At Scotch Corner, the A 66 branches off northwest toward the Pennines, following the route laid down by the Roman legions. Just after it crosses the border with County Durham, an unclassified road splits off from A 66 and meanders its way north across rolling countryside to the River Tees and the town of Barnard Castle, where Charles Dickens came by stagecoach in 1838 to gather background material about the notorious "Yorkshire schools" for his novel *Nicholas Nickleby*. William Shaw and his Bowes Academy, the models for Wackford Squeers and Dotheboys Hall, had been successfully sued by the parents of two children who became blind from untreated infections. The local churchyard contains the graves of 25 boys, as young as seven years, who died in Shaw's care between 1810 and 1834. Dickens, accompanied by the artist "Phiz," travelled under an assumed name and pretended to be in search of a school for the son of a widowed friend. The one-eyed Shaw was suspicious and let them see little; however, they learned everything from a local attorney they met at the **King's Head** pub, which still serves food and drink today. Dickens and "Phiz" also stayed at the George and New Inn at nearby Greta Bridge, where "a rousing fire halfway up the chimney" was more than welcome after a two-day journey from London through raging snowstorms.

One building looks out of place among the Georgian and Victorian stone houses that line the steep streets leading down to the river—a French-style château set in a formal garden reminiscent of the Tuileries in Paris. This is the **Bowes Museum** (which celebrated its centenary in 1992), the jewel in Barnard Castle's crown. Its former owner, John Bowes, illegitimate son of the earl of Strathmore, packed it with lovely things collected from the great houses of Europe with his wife, Josephine, a French actress: furniture and fine paintings by Goya, Tiepolo, and El Greco, plus 5,000 pieces of pottery, the most comprehensive collection in Britain. There are dollhouses and toys, too, and a magnificent silver swan swimming on a lake of spun glass; at appointed hours, to the minute, an attendant ceremoniously winds it up, and the swan's head twists realistically on its graceful neck before darting down to snatch up and swallow a silver fish.

TEESDALE

A winding road (B 6277) between dry stone walls leads northwest up the dale from Barnard Castle and through the former Quaker lead-mining town of Middleton-in-Teesdale to **High Force**, the highest waterfall in England. The water, stained brown from the iron in the rocks, tumbles 70 feet into a wooded gorge filled with wild-flowers and ferns. This is very near Cross Fell, where the Tees rises, fed by countless streams furrowing the slopes. It is wild country, with a few whitewashed farmhouses that have been occupied by the same families for genera-tions, and some ancient stone barns where the hardy sheep are sheltered from winter snowdrifts. Three major rivers rise in these high fells of the Pennines: the Tees, the Wear, and the South Tyne.

Durham City

Back east on the A 1, head north to Durham City. Along with the Grand Canyon, the Great Barrier Reef, the Taj Mahal, the palace of Versailles, and other such places, Durham's magnificent cathedral and castle appear in the list of World Heritage sites. Their towers and battlements dominate a wooded promontory of rock around which the River Wear winds a graceful loop. One of the best views is from a train on the great viaduct that carries the railway line from London to Edinburgh across the deep valley on the western side of the city. Another is from Prebends' Bridge, which bears the verse Sir Walter Scott was inspired to write from it, beginning "Grey towers of Durham . . . ." The Great North Road, transformed at this point into a six-lane motorway, bypasses the city to the east.

Secure in their fortress-church—"Half church of God, half castle 'gainst the Scot," as Sir Walter Scott phrased it—the prince bishops were able to repel not only the repeated and ferocious attacks of the Scots but also rebel-lious Sassenachs (the English).

In addition to its historic castle and cathedral, Dur-ham's university adds a special vitality to the city.

DURHAM CATHEDRAL

Celebrating its 900th anniversary in 1993 and arguably the finest Norman cathedral in Europe, Durham was origi-nally the site of a shrine for the miraculously preserved body of Saint Cuthbert, which monks carried from the island of Lindisfarne in 875 to escape marauding Danes. They paused during their flight to rest on this rocky hilltop and then, according to legend, found the coffin impossible to move. In 1020 the remains of the Venerable Bede, who wrote the earliest surviving ecclesiastical history of England, joined those of Saint Cuthbert in the Saxon church that predated the cathedral.

In 1104 Saint Cuthbert's remains were enshrined behind the high altar in the present cathedral, begun 11 years earlier to replace the Saxon church, of which no trace remains, and after another two centuries the remains of the Venerable Bede were moved to a simple tomb in the Galilee Chapel at the opposite end. Among the list of Prince Bishops appointed to serve at the cathedral is John of Washington (1416), whose family provided the United States with its first president three and a half centuries later.

The interior of the cathedral is celebrated for its soaring nave and stout, incised Norman columns. Dr. Johnson was struck by its "rocky solidity and indeterminate duration." The ribbed vaulting of the roof high above is the earliest of its kind in England, and the pointed arches of the nave are thought to be the first example of their use in Europe. A curiosity to visitors is the sanctuary knocker outside, which throughout the Middle Ages offered the protection of Saint Cuthbert to any hunted criminal who grasped its ring.

DURHAM CASTLE

Generations of Durham undergraduates have made their temporary home in this splendid pile, with its Norman gatehouse, tiny chapel in the crypt, and Bishop Cosin's 17th-century "Black Staircase." The 15th-century kitchens, much modernized, still operate to serve the students at the refectory tables in the Norman great hall. When the students are on vacation their rooms (and the refectory) are open to visitors without advance booking at very inexpensive rates, and there is a restaurant in the Norman undercroft of the Monk's Dormitory that serves fresh food at moderate prices. Surprisingly, there are no outstanding hotels or restaurants in Durham City.

University life is reflected in the bookshops and pubs along the steep streets and alleys, called "vennels," beneath the castle walls. They lead down to the river, where daffodils crowd the banks in spring and rowboats can be rented. At the **Shakespeare Pub** next door to the tall, dusty offices of the *Northern Echo,* pints of Eighty Shillings Ale can be quaffed in small back rooms offering unobtrusive access to the vennel at the side. Durham is a compact city best toured on foot, so leave your automobile at one of the parking lots on the outskirts of the fortified hill.

STAYING IN DURHAM

The largest and most convenient local hotel is the ▶ **Royal County** in the Old Elvet neighborhood west across the river from the cathedral; the hotel has been extensively renovated.

WASHINGTON

North of Durham on the A 1 nearing Newcastle, there are signposts to Washington. This is the place from which George Washington's family took its name, although George himself never came here. Unfortunately, the village green of old Washington, with its sandstone houses and former smithy, has been all but swallowed up by a hideous urban development.

Washington Old Hall was the home of George Washington's direct ancestors for five generations, until they sold it in 1613. George's great-grandfather emigrated to Virginia in 1656, possibly because *his* father, a Loyalist parson, fell foul of the Roundheads during the Civil War. Three centuries later the house that had been built on the foundations of the old hall was due for demolition, but it was saved by a preservation committee with generous donations from both sides of the Atlantic. It now belongs to the National Trust and is lovingly maintained. The 18th-century gates leading to the hall, just below the church on a wooded hill, were the gift of the Colonial Dames of America.

Newcastle-upon-Tyne

The Great North Road, skirting the hinterland of Sunderland and the industrialized estuary of the River Wear, dives northward under the Tyne through a toll tunnel. Apart from the Tyne Bridge, the model for the Sydney Harbour Bridge, there are five others spanning this celebrated river and dominating the Geordie capital of the Northeast.

Like Scousers (from Liverpool in northwest England), Geordies are an unofficial Anglo-Saxon subtribe with a culture and dialect all their own. The latter, with an

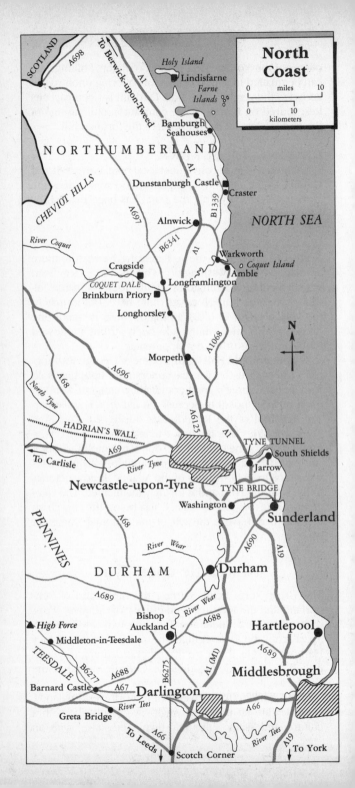

entirely different set of vowels from standard English, includes phrases such as "wor lass," which means "my wife, daughter, or sister," and "Howay, man!" which from a Southerner would sound more like "I say, you over there!" The lethal local brew—Newcastle Brown Ale—is sometimes referred to as "jawney inter spayus," which means "journey into space."

HISTORIC NEWCASTLE

The **New Castle** that gave the city its name was built in 1080, and a 12th-century keep erected on the site of the earlier fortress survives, together with a stretch of the medieval walls. The **cathedral** has a distinctive 15th-century lantern tower. **Blackfriars,** built in the 13th century, is a Dominican friary that survived the dissolution of the monasteries. An excellent series of "Heritage Trails" leaflets and other literature is available from the Tourist Information Centre next to the Central Library in Princess Square and at Central Railway Station. The trails are marked with stainless steel studs set firmly into the sidewalks.

The town of **Jarrow** on the southern side of the Tyne Tunnel was the home of the Venerable Bede and has a church dating back to the year 685. There is also a museum and a reconstructed gate of a Roman fort that once stood there commanding the river. But the name of Jarrow is remembered more for the Hunger Marchers who in 1935 walked almost 350 miles to London to demand work and subsistence; after the cruiser *York* had been launched at Palmers Shipyard in 1931, the gates stayed locked—and Palmers, the town's major employer, *was* Jarrow.

THE MODERN CITY

The prosperity of the Tyneside area was based on coal, ships, and the river. It suffered terribly during the Depression, and the novels of Catherine Cookson, who was raised by her grandparents in the docklands of South Shields (to the east of Newcastle at the south side of the river's mouth) reflect the harshness of that period. The South Tyne is now "Catherine Cookson country," and a section of the **South Shields Museum** is devoted to her life and work. Since World War II many of the shipyards and coal mines have closed for good, but there is a new sense of vitality and enterprise about Newcastle. As for the river, it is now clean enough for thousands of salmon to return, and fishing for them is once again a thriving sport. South Shields is only a few stops from the city center on the Tyneside Metro, which makes the London Underground look antediluvian, with spotless stations and trains and special facilities for the disabled. An inexpensive Day Rover ticket provides unlimited travel on the Shields ferries, most buses, and the Metro.

Monument Mall, opened in 1992, and Eldon Square shopping center in Newcastle, together with the 1980s-vintage Metro shopping mall on the outskirts, contrast with an older generation of buildings such as the Central Exchange and Arcade and the Grainger Market, which was considered by the Victorians to be "the most spacious and magnificent in Europe." Today shoppers descend on Newcastle by plane and ferry from Scandinavia across the North Sea and even from Iceland. But these latter-day Vikings are armed with nothing more lethal than credit cards. Happily, the city hasn't allowed itself to be overwhelmed by glass and concrete towers. Sir John Betjeman rated Grey Street as "one of the best streets in England," and its original grandeur, overseen by a 135-foot statue of Earl Grey (the prime minister who not only saw the Great Reform Bill of 1832 through parliament but also gave his name to a brand of tea), has been restored by the removal of decades of soot deposits. The Theatre Royal and other Classical buildings give Newcastle a sense of style and sophistication sometimes absent in other English provincial cities. Unlike them, Newcastle even provides a nightlife with its discos and clubs.

Other good things about Newcastle are some of the local foods like Singin' Hinny (hot, buttered fruit scones), pease pudding (mashed yellow peas), and prize leeks, as well as workingmen's clubs and pigeon racing.

STAYING AND DINING IN NEWCASTLE-UPON-TYNE

There is a wide choice of hotels here, including, on the historic Quayside, the ▶ Copthorne Newcastle, which opened in 1991. Its 156 rooms look out over the River Tyne, and facilities include a swimming pool and fitness center, two restaurants, and two cocktail bars. It is a ten-minute drive from the airport and two minutes from Central Station. Even nearer to the latter, on Neville Street, are the ▶ Royal Station and the recently renovated ▶ County Thistle, with its elegant Café Mozart. Both of these occupy vast Victorian buildings with wood paneling and ornately decorated plaster ceilings that recall an era when steam was king and everyone travelled by train. Now they have the facilities expected of modern hotels, including parking and easy access to shopping, theaters, and restaurants that offer everything from Madras curry to French nouvelle cuisine. If you want Singin' Hinny or pease pudding, alas, you have to get yourself invited into the homes of real Geordies, unless you can find an old-fashioned workingmen's "café" (diner).

Newcastle is a good base for day trips to the ancient Roman sites along Hadrian's Wall, to the west of the city; if pressed for time you can view the wall from above in a light aircraft (see Hadrian's Wall, below).

Castles on the Coast

Between Newcastle and the Scottish border to the north, and lying more or less parallel to the Great North Road, is one of the finest unspoiled stretches of coastline in Great Britain, the **Northumberland Coast**. Mile upon mile of clean, soft sand, fringed by dunes and golf courses, is watched over, as it has been for centuries, by medieval castles. A few miles north of Morpeth, the A 1 crosses the River Coquet (pronounced cocket), a lovely stream rich in trout and salmon. Upstream in Coquet Dale, reached by B 6341 or B 6344, is **Cragside**, the mansion estate of the Tyneside magnate who invented the rifled cannon and became the first Lord Armstrong. It was the first house in the world to be lit by hydroelectricity, with a system Armstrong designed using artificial lakes and subterranean pipes. In the 900-acre park, he planted literally millions of trees and shrubs, including spectacular rhododendrons, and laid down 40 miles of paths and driveways. The property is owned by the National Trust and is open to visitors.

The Coquet winds its way to the sea, looping around the 12th-century **Brinkburn Priory**, inviting anglers and others to linger in perfect tranquillity on the wooded banks that the Augustinian canons knew. ▶ **Embleton Hall**, on the edge of Longframlington on A 697 to Coldstream, is a country house made into a homey hotel by Trevor Thorne and his wife, Judith. It is an early-18th-century stone house with a late Victorian wing, where the Fenwick family lived for two centuries, leaving their family crest on the pediment above the main entrance. The five-acre garden includes a ha-ha (an ornamental sunken fence), a grass tennis court, and a croquet lawn. Nearby in

Longframlington, the **Besom Barn** uses locally grown provisions to create imaginative dishes, such as Ewesley Fell lamb baked with root vegetables and rosemary and served with a sauce of Port wine and fresh mint. To the south on A 697 in Longhorsley is ▶ **Linden Hall**, a country-house hotel standing in its own park of 450 acres. This is more a stately home than a hotel, with spacious period rooms and a wide range of leisure facilities, all reflected in the price.

WARKWORTH CASTLE

Little more than a mile before it reaches the sea, the Coquet forms a horseshoe around the ancient town of Warkworth (on A 1068), with its narrow, humpbacked cobbled bridge alongside the parvenu 1960s structure that usurped its function after six centuries. The town is dominated by what Shakespeare's Henry IV described as a "worm-eaten hold of ragged stone," and three scenes from the two parts of *Henry IV* are set at Warkworth Castle, which dates to the 12th century. It is distinguished by its cruciform keep, great hall, chapel, and tower carved with the Percy lion. Upstream, and reached only by a rowboat that operates on weekends, is **Warkworth Hermitage**, a tiny chapel in a cave hewn out of the rock. Warkworth was the ancestral home of the Percy family, and it was the third Lord Percy and his son, Harry Hotspur (who rode "as if his spurs were hot"), who placed Henry IV on the throne of England in 1399. Later the Percys conspired against the king, and Hotspur's head ended up on Micklegate Bar in York.

Brightly painted fishing boats called cobles are still made in the Amble boatyard, to the south of Warkworth, in an estuary once busy with colliers but now the domain of yachters (a splendid new marina has been built here) and golfers attracted by the links on the dunes by the sea. One mile offshore is the low-lying Coquet Island, with sandy beaches and a lighthouse, a sanctuary for puffins, terns, eiders, fulmars, and oystercatchers carefully managed by the Royal Society for the Protection of Birds. There are boat trips from Amble Harbour around the island, with commentaries.

ALNWICK CASTLE

North of Warkworth the Great North Road used to squeeze its way through the Hotspur Gate at the heart of the old market town of Alnwick, the seat of the earls of Northumberland. Now A 1 bypasses the town, but the Percy lion still adorns the gate and sits atop the Tenantry Column, erected by grateful tenants after their rents were reduced during a depression in the early 19th century. The Norman Alnwick Castle sits elegantly in its pastoral setting, with stone-carved soldiers staring out from the battlements over the meadows beside the River Aln, where horses and cattle graze. This 12th-century structure is the home of the present duke and duchess of Northumberland; inside are a collection of Meissen china and a superb library with Second Folio editions of Shakespeare. Paintings by Titian, Van Dyck, and Canaletto hang beside modern photographs and greeting cards from various members of the royal family.

The firm of Hardy's, sponsor of the Fishing Tackle Museum in Alnwick, also had its brush with royalty. Soon after King George V came to the throne, the novelist Thomas Hardy attained his 70th birthday, and the king was reminded that it might be a good idea to send a telegram to "old Hardy." The maker of the royal fishing rods at Alnwick was surprised to receive the king's misdirected congratulations on reaching an age he was still far from attaining on a day that was not his birthday.

Staying in Alnwick

Hardy Pie (made from fish, of course) is on the menu at the ▶ **White Swan Hotel** on Bondgate, which is also remarkable for its Olympic Room. In 1911 the *Olympic* and the *Titanic* were the world's biggest steamships. The *Olympic* was broken up at Palmers in Jarrow in 1935, and its first-class lounge was taken out and reassembled at the White Swan. The 43 guest rooms here have all the modern amenities and traditional, comfortable furnishings.

DUNSTANBURGH CASTLE

Around the tiny, almost circular harbor of **Craster**, a few miles northeast of Alnwick on B 1339, the stone jetties are strewn with crab and lobster pots. The village is famed, however, for fish that are no longer caught off its shores. The herring that are smoked in a harborside shed to make Craster kippers are now brought from the west of Scotland. Be that as it may, Craster kippers (not to mention its smoked salmon) are delectable and much sought after.

Beyond the village, on a rock ledge high above the sea, is the commanding bulk of Dunstanburgh Castle. This was the stronghold of John of Gaunt, who as uncle of the boy-king Richard II was the most powerful baron in England. The castle was severely knocked about during the Wars of the Roses, changing hands no fewer than five times. Its impressive ruins can be reached only on foot along a grassy coastal path strewn with boulders and through a wicket gate at the north side of Craster. From there, it is a mile to the great gatehouse, with its two towers and walls several feet thick. The site covers 11 acres, and the path continues beyond the castle around Embleton Bay, skirting golf links and golden sands. At the seaward side of Dunstanburgh, Gull Crag drops sheer to the rocks below. Peer over the edge and you will see innumerable gulls riding the air currents as they come and go from their nests on the cliff ledges, their cries competing with the crash of the waves.

THE FARNE ISLANDS

Gull Crag's population of seabirds is merely the overspill from the Farnes. Terns, comical puffins, clumsy cormorants, kittiwakes, and eiders are to be found in these 30 rocky outcrops a few miles offshore. This is also one of the main breeding grounds of the gray seal. Like the coastal strip, the islands are owned by the National Trust, but landing is allowed on some of them, and boats sail every day, weather permitting, from the harbor at **Seahouses**. In summer the harbor is often crowded with daytrippers. The cruise around the islands, with an hour ashore, provides magical opportunities to see and photograph at close range nesting birds, Manx shearwaters skimming the waves, or gannets crash-diving on shoals of mackerel and herring.

BAMBURGH CASTLE AND
HOLY ISLAND

There is a memorial to Grace Darling in the churchyard at her home village of **Bamburgh** just north of Seahouses (on B 1342), and a small museum devoted to the gallant rescue she made with her father in 1838 of the crew of the stricken ship *Forfarshire* off the coast here. But her heroics are overshadowed by the pink-walled castle perched atop a 150-foot outcrop. Little survives of the early fortifications of the kings of Northumbria except a deep well. Within the stout walls of the 12th-century keep the ambience is Victorian, reflecting its ownership by the first Lord Armstrong, who lavished the money he made out of armaments on rebuilding it.

On a clear day there are stunning views from the battlements up and down the sandy coast. Another dramatic castle can be seen on the nearby Holy Island, or **Lindisfarne**, which is really only a half-time island—when the tide goes out a causeway emerges (reached via a small road that branches west from A 1 at West Mains). There is a hut on stilts, reached from the causeway by a flight of stairs, for those who fail to get the tide timings right, even though they are clearly displayed on a board.

Colonies of wildfowl and waders feed on the sands and flats as they did when Saint Aidan, journeying from that far-off island of the western shore, the holy Iona, crossed the sands at low tide and founded the monastery of Lindisfarne in the year 634. An illuminated manuscript of the Lindisfarne Gospels survives in the British Museum, although the monastery, which first brought Christianity to these northern parts, was sacked successively by the Vikings in the two centuries after the manuscript was written.

As Bishop Lightfoot said, "When Finian [another early missionary] built his first church on lonely Lindisfarne, with its wooden walls and thatched roof, it was destined, nevertheless, to be the precursor of stately, imperial Durham."

The red-stone walls of the priory church built by Benedictine monks from Durham in the latter part of the 11th century are still standing, and the carved pillars and zigzag-ornamented arches mirror those in Durham Cathedral. A new museum at the priory illustrates the horrific raids of the Vikings on these shores in earlier times. Northumberland's historic themes of religion and war are repeated on Holy Island, with the castle perched on its crag near the priory in stark silhouette at sunrise or sunset. Among castles, however, this was a Johnny-come-lately: Built in the mid-16th century to defend Holy Island against the Scots, it was never to loose a single cannonball from its battlements. It was renovated in 1903 in the romantic style of Sir Edwin Lutyens.

THE ROAD TO THE LAKES

The fact that there is superhighway (the M 1 and M 6) for the entire 250 miles (400 km) from London to the Lake District makes for a speedy journey through the Midlands, which used to be known, and not without reason, as "the Black Country." Just north of the industrialized conurbations of Lancashire (Manchester), due west from Preston on the M 55, however, is **Blackpool**, a resort town with six miles of beaches, three piers, a "Golden Mile" of fun fairs, and a 518-foot structure aping the Eiffel Tower. But for a more attractive detour, turn off the M 6 at junction 31 and take the road northeast toward Clitheroe, which accompanies the River Ribble inland from Preston.

At Clitheroe there's the diminutive, 800-year-old **Whalley Abbey**, founded by the Cistercians in the 13th century, and nearby are charming stone-built villages such as Bolton-by-Bowland and Downham, with their greens, brooks, and ancient stocks, where miscreants were pinioned to be pelted with garbage and rotten fruit and vegetables. Toward Lancaster and the Lake District to the northwest lies the **Forest of Bowland**, which now has few trees but stupendous scenery: wave after wave of rocky hills, purple in late summer and autumn when the heather is out. The **Trough of Bowland** is a natural cleft climbing more than 1,500 feet from the Ribble valley to provide views on a clear day of the Isle of Man to the west and the distant mountains of North Wales to the southwest.

STAYING AND DINING
EN ROUTE TO THE LAKES

▶ **Northcote Manor**, a Victorian cotton mill owner's aspiration to gentility, now a country hotel, stands foursquare behind stone walls on the outskirts of Langho, just before Clitheroe. The 14 bedrooms are all spacious, with carpeted bathrooms, Victorian furniture, and cheerful wallpaper. The windows look out on cows and sheep grazing contentedly in the meadows of the Ribble valley; Pendle Hill, the haunt of such Lancashire witches as Mother Demdike, Old Chattox, and Mistress Nutter, looms on the horizon. In its oak-paneled dining room lit by candles and chandeliers, Northcote Manor serves superb terrines and sweets and imaginative main courses such as lobster in Champagne and dill sauce and breast of wood pigeon (from local shoots) on foie gras, garnished with black grapes. The vegetables are fresh from the kitchen garden.

Lancaster

The narrow, winding, unclassified road through the Trough of Bowland drops down to Lancaster, which is also on the M 6. **Hornsea Pottery**, on Wyersdale Road in

Lancaster, set in 42 acres of landscaped parkland, offers guided factory tours and a wide range of china, earthenware, and glass at reduced prices. A maritime museum in the Georgian **Custom House** on St. George's Quay beside the River Lune tells the story of Lancaster's once-thriving "triangular" trade to the Americas, taking slaves out of Africa and returning from America with tobacco and cotton, and of the fishing industry that was based on Morecambe Bay's famous prawns and shrimps. Morecambe, on the coast, offers traditional English seaside attractions, including a rival to the more famous Illuminations at Blackpool, in which the seafront is lit up in August with a dazzling display of colored bulbs that form tableaux. Lancaster remains the administrative center of Lancashire and the home of one of Britain's newer universities. The skyline is still dominated by a medieval castle where in 1612 the Lancashire witches were imprisoned awaiting trial.

STAYING AND DINING NEAR LANCASTER

About 10 miles (16 km) north of Lancaster, a mile to the right off the M 6, 18th-century ▶ **Lupton Tower** near Kirkby Lonsdale in Lupton is a guest house with a vegetarian restaurant. Its seven bedrooms offer views across the River Lune to the fells that John Ruskin described as "the loveliest in England, therefore in the world."

The Southern Lakes

Some of Ruskin's watercolors and Turner's *Passage of the St. Gothard* can be seen at **Abbot Hall** in Kendal (22 miles/35 km north of Lancaster), as can the work of the portraitist George Romney, who grew up in this market town, then as now the gateway to the southern lakes. Alfred Wainwright, whose guidebooks on walking the Lakeland Fells are definitive, was borough treasurer here for many years. Within this tiny area are to be found England's highest mountain and largest lake, but the scale is not grand: Scafell Pike reaches 3,206 feet (beating neighboring Sca Fell by about 100 feet), and Lake Windermere is ten miles long and just over a mile at its widest.

Despite their Lilliputian proportions (by Alpine standards) the crags of volcanic black rock towering above the open moors, or "fells"—boulder-strewn treeless expanses covered with gorse—are unmistakably *moun-*

tains. Shrouded in clouds and mist or battered by rain and strong winds, they can be menacing, but under clear skies magnificent vistas open up. Lower down, shaggy Lakeland sheep graze the precipitous slopes within drystone walls, tended by the occasional shepherd. Waterfalls and thousands of tiny streams, or becks, tumble down from the fells, keeping the pastures lushly green and filling innumerable little lakes (tarns) that in turn feed into the larger lakes (meres). Crooked fingers of water dotted with islands lend enchantment to wooded valleys, golden with daffodils in spring, verdant in summer, and a blaze of rainbow colors in the fall. In contrast to the high fells, the vales are soft and pastoral, their stone buildings mellowed by mosses and lichens. In sunshine the scene has lyrical beauty, but the ever-changing pattern of clouds on water has its charms, too. Lovers of the Lake District—who are legion—take the weather as it comes. Rarely are two days the same.

This is an outdoor area that attracts both serious walkers and climbers and casual ramblers—whichever you are, one of Wainwright's splendid guides should go with you. If walking is too tame, mountain bicycles with fat tires and 15 gears can be rented locally, as can horses. If you prefer a guide, the Mountain Goat Bus and Holiday Company, in the rear of the Outfellows Pub yard, opposite the municipal parking lot in Keswick (Tel: 0768-77-39-62) or at Windermere (Tel: 05394-451-61) organizes day excursions.

In his long life William Wordsworth tramped the fells in all weather and foresaw the need to protect his native countryside by making it a national park, which it is today. In his *Guide through the District of the Lakes,* Wordsworth wrote of the "persons of pure taste throughout the whole island, who, by their visits (often repeated) to the Lakes in the North of England, testify that they deem the district a sort of national property, in which every man has a right and interest who has an eye to perceive and a heart to enjoy." Given that Wordsworth could scarcely have imagined the pressures that 20th-century mass tourism and ease of transportation would place on his beloved lakes, the sentiment is especially prescient.

Despite everything—horrendous motor traffic on the narrow roads, acid rain, fallout scares, nuclear processing plants and power stations on the coast, and the persistent use of the Lake District's contours for games of "chicken" by low-flying combat jets—the natural attractions of the

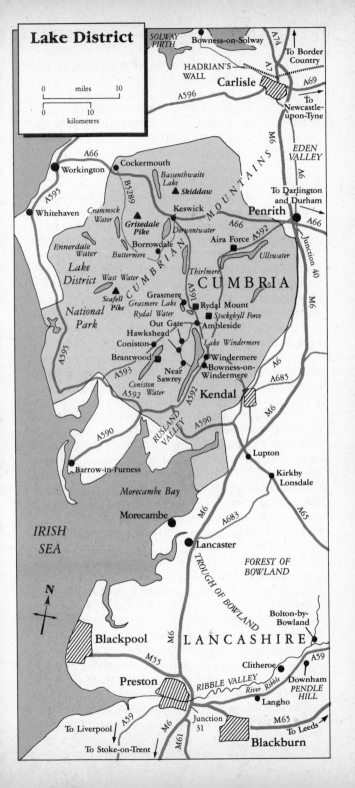

place remain much as they were when they inspired the age of English romanticism. Whatever season you choose, the weather remains a gamble. That being so, it makes sense to avoid, if possible, public and school holiday times and the peak summer season. April–May and September–October are good times for missing excessive crowds and taking advantage of lower hotel rates.

LAKE WINDERMERE

This long and narrow lake, the largest in England and surrounded by gentle wooded hills, is undeniably beautiful. But in summer its waters are overcrowded with craft of all descriptions, everything from powerboats, sailing cruisers, and sightseeing launches down to dinghies and rowboats. Vintage steam yachts such as the *Osprey* (built 1902), which is available for pleasure trips, against the backdrop of Belle Isle with its classical 18th-century round house, maintain Windermere's romantic reputation.

The town of Windermere barely existed before the railway came in the mid-19th century—despite the opposition of the then-aging Wordsworth. He knew Bowness, also on the lake's eastern shore, and mentions the White Lion there.

The young Wordsworth used the ferry that still runs across the lake between Ferry Nab and Ferry House, providing a shortcut to **Hawkshead**, to the west of the lake, where he attended grammar school between 1779 and 1787. (His name is carved into the wood of his old desk there, which can be seen in the schoolroom when it is open to visitors.) The center of Hawkshead is closed to through traffic, which helps greatly toward preserving the character of the poet's "beloved Vale."

Hill Top Farm, 2 miles (3 km) south at Near Sawrey, "as nearly perfect a little place as I ever lived in," was the home of Beatrix Potter, whose children's books featuring Peter Rabbit, Jemima Puddle-Duck, and others were illustrated with sketches and paintings of the hills and lakes hereabouts. Potter bought local farmlands to save them from developers and left these and her 17th-century farmhouse to the National Trust when she died in 1943. The "New Room," where she did much of her work, is open to visitors and displays her furniture and china. Hill Top Farm is, however, very small in relation to the huge crowds it attracts, and should be avoided on weekends and bank holidays. There is a permanent gallery on Main Street in Hawkshead; formerly the office of Potter's husband, a local attorney, it features a rotating selection of 500 watercolor illustrations from her books.

A new year-round exhibition, the **World of Beatrix Potter**, has been opened at the Old Laundry just outside Bowness on the opposite shore of the lake. Audiovisual technology is used to animate the Potter menagerie in a show that is very popular with children.

Staying and Dining at Lake Windermere

One of the oldest established hotels in the Lake District, the White Lion of Wordsworth's day now calls itself the ▶ **Royal Hotel** in memory of past royal patronage, having upgraded its 29 rooms to the highest standards in the budget price range. Many of the rooms have lake views, and guests are given free mooring and launching at the nearby Low Wood Watersports Center and free access to the leisure club at ▶ **Low Wood Hotel**, which has a 50-foot-long swimming pool, gym, squash courts, solarium, and Jacuzzi. The latter hotel, originally built around a 17th-century coaching inn and stable block, has also undergone extensive refurbishment. It has 99 rooms with baths and a highly rated restaurant. Considerably more expensive, the 13-room ▶ **Miller Howe** enjoys an international reputation for the comforts of its 13 rooms and its magical menus.

CONISTON WATER

Coniston Water is half the size of its neighbor lake, Windermere, and much less used. This was one of the reasons why it was chosen for successful attempts on the world water speed records by Malcolm Campbell in 1939 and 20 years later by his son Donald, with their *Bluebird* boats. In 1967 Donald lost his life on Coniston Water while trying to improve on the world record of 276.3 MPH, which he had set in Australia three years earlier. The lake nestles peacefully at the feet of the Old Man of Coniston, a peak rising to 2,631 feet, its gloriously wooded shores mostly undisturbed by the noise of powerboats. One of three enticing islets on its waters was given the fictional name of Wild Cat Island by Arthur Ransome in *Swallows and Amazons,* his classic children's yarn of the 1930s.

John Ruskin lies in the churchyard at Coniston, and a museum in the village is devoted to his life and work as an artist, writer, scientist, critic, and fighter for social justice. He moved here in 1871, long after Wordsworth was dead, yet Ruskin was influenced by the English

Romantics. **Brantwood**, his home on the eastern side of the lake, is open to visitors.

Tennyson spent his honeymoon by Coniston Water. Its haunting beauty wreathed in dawn mists is captured by Turner in a painting now in the Tate Gallery in London. One of the best ways to see the real lake now is from the richly upholstered opulence of the steam yacht *Gondola,* launched in 1859 and now owned and operated by the National Trust; it runs between Coniston and Park-a-Moor.

Ambleside, Rydal, and Grasmere

To the north of Lake Windermere, in the shadow of the high fells, the associations with Wordsworth are stronger than anywhere else in the Lake District. Every wood, mere, beck, tarn, and fell seems to echo evocative lines. His visitors here included Sir Walter Scott, Shelley, Keats, Emerson, Hawthorne, Charlotte Brontë, and Mrs. Gaskell.

At Ambleside, where Stockghyll Force sends its waters cascading from a height of 70 feet, is **Old Stamp House**, now a law office, where Wordsworth was the official distributor of stamps for Westmorland, a county now merged with Cumberland into Cumbria. **Rydal Mount**, on the road (A 591) to Keswick, was Wordsworth's home from 1813 until his death in 1850. Both the house and the garden he lovingly designed are open to visitors year-round. The road to Grasmere (A 549) skirts Rydal Water, one of the smallest of the lakes, and the neighboring lake, Grasmere.

Overlooking Grasmere lake's placid waters is **Dove Cottage**, on the outskirts of Grasmere. Wordsworth and his sister Dorothy lived here in the opening years of the 19th century while he wrote, among other works, *Michael, Resolution and Independence,* and *Ode on Intimations of Immortality* and completed *The Prelude.* The house and museum next door contain the world's foremost collection of his manuscripts and possessions. After Wordsworth married he turned the cottage over to his friend Thomas De Quincey, best known as the author of *Confessions of an English Opium Eater,* and moved briefly to Allan Bank, planting the grounds there, and then to the old rectory before settling finally at Rydal Mount. For a short spell Wordsworth taught at the Lych Gate school by St. Oswald's Church, and his son John was a pupil there. It is now Sarah Nelson's Original Gingerbread Shop. The yew trees in the churchyard at Grasmere were planted by Wordsworth, and he and his wife, Mary, are buried here beneath a simple headstone.

Considered by many to be the heart of the Lake District, Grasmere is sheltered at the foot of the fells, radiating rustic charm. Its buildings of blue-green local slate cluster around the narrow winding road above the pretty lake, which, no more than a mile across at its widest, is hardly more than a pond. There is a lovely view of the lake from the Wishing Gate just south of Dove Cottage and an easy walk around its wooded shores—take the old road to Rydal and cross the footbridge over the River Rothay. With a single green islet set into it like an emerald, Grasmere is an enchanting place, especially in May and early June when vast clumps of rhododendrons are in fiery bloom of purple, red, and pink.

On the Thursday nearest August 20 every year Grasmere holds the Lakeland's largest festival of sports—a rare opportunity to see fell running, hound trailing, and Cumberland and Westmorland wrestling.

STAYING AND DINING AT GRASMERE
Overlooking Grasmere among the rhododendrons in a three-acre garden is ▶ **Michaels Nook Country House Hotel**, built in 1859 as the summer home of a Lancashire mill owner who named it after the shepherd in Wordsworth's lines,

> Upon the forest-side at Grasmere Vale
> There dwelt a shepherd, Michael was his name.

In 1969 the house was opened as an 11-room hotel; filled with antiques, it is patrolled by Jake, a harmless Great Dane. A tempting menu is served by candlelight. Michaels has an arrangement with the nearby ▶ **Wordsworth Hotel**, which has 37 rooms, whereby the latter's swimming pool, saunas, and solarium are available to the guests of both establishments.

The Northern Lakes

The unofficial frontier between the southern and northern lakes is the broad pass of Dunmail Raise, and within a ten-mile radius of Keswick there is a wide variety of lakes. Thirlmere, dammed in 1876, supplies Manchester with water. **Buttermere** and **Crummock Water** are quiet places, rarely disturbed by anything more than an occasional rowboat. **Bassenthwaite Lake**, skirted by a main road, A 66, is the base of a sailing club but is nonetheless uncrowded.

DERWENTWATER

Just south of Keswick (see below), Derwentwater is surrounded by perfect picnic spots and is busy with boats of all kinds from a club, a marina, and rental shops as well as canoeists, water-skiers, and wind-surfers. There are jetties at intervals, where pleasure boats from Keswick embark and disembark passengers. Derwentwater, three miles long by a mile wide, is dotted with small islands such as Derwent, Lord's, and St. Herbert's, the last where this disciple of St. Cuthbert is said to have lived as a hermit in the seventh century. The shores are more wild and dramatic than those of the southern lakes, with wooded slopes erupting into rock crags, waterfalls, and gorges.

Staying and Dining at Derwentwater

The ▶ **Stakis Lodore Swiss Hotel**, large by Lakeland standards and impressively sited with views of the lake and the Lodore Falls, offers international cuisine and indoor and outdoor pools, as well as saunas. The rooms are furnished in solid English oak. The ▶ **Derwentwater Hotel**, at Portinscale just outside Keswick, is a rambling building on 16 acres of lawn and shrubbery at the water's edge. It has grown over the years to include the Tower, originally the home of John Grave, thrice lord mayor of Manchester. No two of the 86 rooms of the hotel are the same size or shape.

KESWICK

The town of Keswick lies on the River Greta in a natural amphitheater, surrounded by the peaks of Skiddaw, Blencathra, Catbells, and Grisedale Pike. Walking the fells here calls for stout shoes and raincoats, and Keswick is a good place to buy them, together with rucksacks, sheepskins, and all kinds of woollens. (The **Sheepskin Warehouse Shop** at the Royal Oak Hotel on Station Road has a wide selection at good prices.) Wordsworth used to walk the 13 miles from Grasmere and back to visit his friends, the other "Lake Poets" Coleridge and Southey, who both lived at Keswick. He fought against the coming of the railway; now the railway station has been closed and transformed into a year-round leisure center where an indoor pool has a wave-making machine and a simulated tropical climate.

The old **Moot Hall** in the market square, which as recently as 20 years ago was filled with market stalls selling eggs, butter, and flowers, is now a visitors' information center. However, the Saturday market outside continues a six-century tradition, and the clerks in the old-fashioned shops off the marketplace are unfailingly courteous. One of the local traders, **Myers of Keswick**, has opened a shop in New York City's Greenwich Village to purvey Cumberland sausage, pork pies, and black pudding to expatriates. Keswick is as famous for its pencils as Kendal is for its "mint cake" confection. The Pencil Museum at the Cumberland Pencil Company traces the history of plumbago (graphite) mining in Borrowdale—the town 6 miles (10 km) south of Keswick on B 5289 that penetrates the high fells and offers a stunning view over Derwentwater from Friar's Crag.

ULLSWATER

The largest of the northern lakes, east of Lake Thirlmere and Derwentwater, is Ullswater, seven and a half miles long, with a main road (A 592) now winding along the shore where Wordsworth once "wandered lonely as a cloud." In April and May the bank is still covered with golden *Narcissus pseudo-narcissus,* but the large pleasure boats, motor cruisers, powerboats, and yachts make the surface of Ullswater almost as busy in the summer as the road along its northwest side. It is more peaceful to walk the southern shore, where there are no major roads. Below Howtown, a calling place for the passenger launch linking Pooley Bridge and Glenridding at opposite ends of the lake, the scenery is at its most impressive, with 3,114-foot Helvellyn towering over it.

A climb up the slopes of the fell is rewarded with a sweeping view of the region's second-largest lake after Windermere, made more interesting by its three distinct parts. According to Wordsworth it has "the happiest combination of beauty and grandeur which any of the Lakes afford." **Aira Force**, the waterfall that inspired his poem *The Somnambulist,* can be reached on foot through the woods on either side of Aira Beck from the National Trust parking lot.

Staying and Dining at Ullswater

The ▶ **Sharrow Bay Hotel** stands at the water's edge with steep, wooded slopes rising behind it to the high fells. The early Victorian house, stuffed with antiques and set in a classic garden, offers its guests superb food, including sticky puddings and real English breakfasts. After more than 40 years, Sharrow Bay is justifiably in the top bracket of country-house hotels, with prices to match. A marginally cheaper (and in its own way no less attractive) alternative may be found not far away along the lakeside near Watermillock. The ▶ **Old Church Hotel**, approached by a lane across a meadow, has the same homey feel, if not the same snob appeal, as Sharrow Bay. Afternoon tea includes cucumber-and-egg sandwiches, scones and cream, and a mountain of freshly baked cakes. The house, from the 18th century, is on the site of a 12th-century church, hence its name. Delectable fabrics and furnishings render the rooms—each named rather than numbered—delightful to stay in.

Penrith

It is only a short drive north on A 592 from the head of Ullswater (or east on A 66 from Keswick) to Penrith, the hometown of Wordsworth's parents. Although born near the coast in Cockermouth, the poet, his sister, and his future wife all attended nursery school here in the 1770s. His excursion to Penrith Beacon as a five-year-old is remembered in *The Prelude*. Main roads from all directions, including the A 66 across the Pennines from Durham, meet the M 6 here.

STAYING AND DINING NEAR PENRITH
The ▶ **North Lakes Hotel** is next to junction 40 on M 6 just outside the old town. Surrounded by a new housing development, it offers access to a leisure center with two squash courts, a gym and solarium, indoor pools, and a whirlpool. Although ancient barn timbers are incorporated in the restaurant to give it an "Olde World" character, this is plainly a hotel of the 1980s, comfortable, functional, and conveniently situated for motorists.

Located northeast of Penrith and within a half hour's drive of the best of the Lake District are four skillfully converted self-catering cottages that formerly were barns but would now satisfy the most discriminating vacationer. Called ▶ **Howscales**, they are just uphill from the red-sandstone village of Kirkoswald in the Eden Valley.

THE BORDER COUNTRY

Emperor Hadrian built his wall across the neck of North Britain from Bowness on the Solway Firth, north of Penrith and Carlisle, to Wallsend-on-Tyne in order to forestall the northern barbarians. The present-day frontier separating Scots and Sassenachs (the English) runs instead diagonally from Gretna Green, where eloping couples from England used to be married "over the anvil" by the village blacksmith, who exercised an ancient right to officiate at weddings. The present border meets the sea just north of Berwick-upon-Tweed. There is no wall now or custom post to mark it, merely signs by lonely roadsides announcing to travellers that they have just entered Scotland.

Carlisle

It is Carlisle's not too serious boast that it is Britain's largest city, with boundaries stretching along the Scottish border, down the North Pennines, and across the Eden Valley to the Solway Firth—a staggering 347 miles. For all that, it remains a border outpost so far as the rest of England is concerned.

The cannons of the Citadel, a round, red-stone, crenellated tower outside the railway station, were last fired in anger by the Scots against the duke of Cumberland's forces in 1745. Parts of the city wall survive and can be walked. Mary, Queen of Scots, was a prisoner in the castle, which displays the improvements and modifications of monarchs over eight centuries. **Mary's Tower** now houses the museum of the Border Regiment, whose regimental march "D'ye ken John Peel?" commemorates the foxhunter in "his coat so gay" who is buried at Caldbeck, 16 miles (26 km) southwest of the city. It happens also to be the unofficial anthem of Cumbrians everywhere.

Carlisle Cathedral is one of the smallest in Britain and has been in its time both a priory and a prison. Its interior is graced by an exquisite 14th-century east window with tracery lights showing the Last Judgment. The canopied choir stalls have misericords carved with beasts, birds, and monsters; paintings of the Apostles and scenes from the lives of Saint Anthony, Saint Cuthbert, and Saint Augustine decorate the backs. It was in this cathedral that Robert

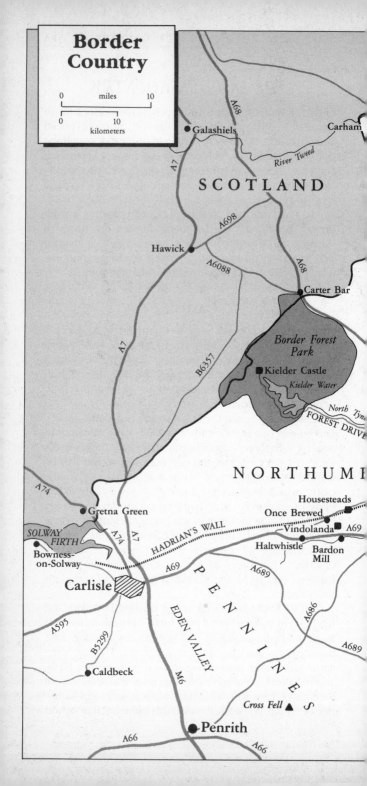

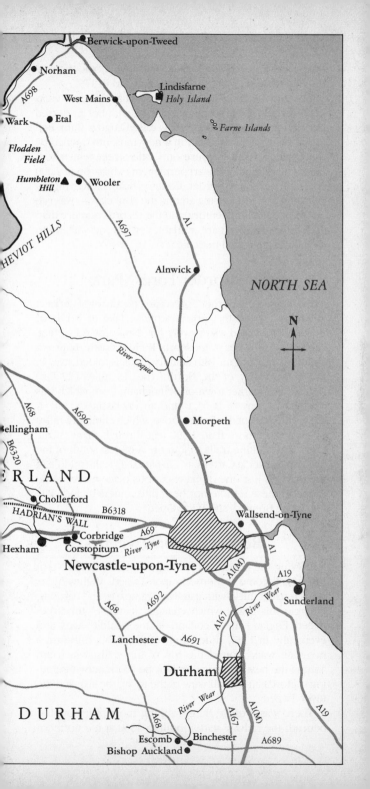

the Bruce was excommunicated with "bell, book, and candle" and that Sir Walter Scott was married in 1797.

The Roman city of fountains and statuary here, its villas kept warm in the inhospitable climate with hot air ducted beneath mosaic-tiled floors, was called Luguvallium. Relics of this lost city are kept in a new museum opened by the Queen in **Tullie House** on Castle Street, which contains a huge state-of-the-art permanent exhibition of 2,000 years of turbulent Border Country history. "Reiving"—pillaging and plundering among the rival clans—was rife up to the mid-17th century, and the records of more than 70 families involved are available for anyone wishing to delve into a colorful heritage.

The Border Forest Park

At the heart of the Border Forest Park, northeast of Carlisle, is Kielder Water, the largest artificial lake in Northern Europe. It is used extensively for fishing, wind-surfing, canoeing, and other water sports. **Kielder Castle**, built as a shooting lodge by an 18th-century duke, is folded away in the green valley of the North Tyne, 18 miles (29 km) beyond the market town of Bellingham, from which it is reached by way of B 6320 and an unclassified road. It marks the start of the Forest Drive, which climbs 12 miles (19 km) and more than 1,500 feet through many picnic areas and walking trails to join the A 68 just south of the Scottish border at Carter Bar. Oh Me Edge, at the middle of the drive, is just one of many curious place names to be found in these remote northern hills; others include Pity Me, Once Brewed, and Wide Open.

Berwick-upon-Tweed

Following the border all the way northeast to the North Sea, you'll come to Berwick-upon-Tweed. Mighty Tudor walls ten feet thick, with gateways, ramparts, and bastions, encircle this town, which changed hands 13 times between England and Scotland in the Middle Ages and eventually, in 1482, ended up in England, but only just. A two-mile walk around the top of the walls, which are among the best preserved in Europe (York notwithstanding), affords an overall view of the town, the sea, and the River Tweed.

There was a castle here, too, but most of it now lies beneath the railway station built in 1850 at the northern end of Robert Stephenson's Royal Border Bridge. The bridge spans the Tweed Valley on 28 of the most graceful arches to be seen anywhere.

From the 1,333-foot summit of **Halidon Hill** on the outskirts of Berwick a panorama of the Borders unfolds. To the south Holy Island and the Farnes are visible on a clear day. Landward are the Cheviot Hills and the Scottish Lowlands, between which the castles at Norham, Etal, and Wark are impassive survivors of historic battles on Flodden Field (where the English vanquished the Scots in the 16th century) and at Carham (where in 1018 the victorious Scots claimed all the land between the Tweed and Edinburgh as their spoil). In the distance, above the sleepy town of Wooler, is Humbleton Hill, where Hotspur and his father obliterated the Scots army led by Lord Douglas. Part I of Shakespeare's *Henry IV* opens with the news of that battle. Halidon Hill itself was the site of another conflict in which the Scots were defeated.

Hadrian's Wall

The ancient wall stretched 73 miles — or 80 Roman miles—from Bowness (Ituna) on the Solway Firth in the west to Wallsend-on-Tyne (Segedunum) in the east. It was originally composed of stone 10 feet thick and 15 feet high, and, in the middle reaches where limestone and mortar were in short supply, of turf 12 feet high on a 20-foot-wide base. The turf construction did not stand up too well to the rigors of the Pennine winters; its builders may have rushed the job and, in any case, were unused to working in such wet and windy conditions. After a mere 60 or 70 years the wall had to be rebuilt and was then executed in stone eight feet wide. It was an enormous construction job, but the Roman Empire, with eight centuries of conquest and colonization behind it when it invaded Britain, was equal to the task.

Every Roman mile (1,620 yards) along the wall a fort, or mile castle, was placed. The auxiliary troops who manned these forts during a 250-year period came from all over the Roman Empire, of which this was the northernmost bastion. As Parnesius, a centurion of the seventh cohort of the 13th Legion, says in *Puck of Pook's Hill* by Rudyard Kipling: "Just when you think you are at the world's end, you see a smoke from East to West as far as the eye can turn, and then, under it, also as far as the eye can stretch, houses and temples, shops and theatres, barracks and granaries, trickling along like dice behind—always behind—one long, low, rising and falling, and hiding and showing line of towers. And that is the Wall!"

A more recent feat of civil engineering, the Tyne Valley railway, built in the 1830s, runs between Carlisle and Newcastle alongside Hadrian's Wall. Haltwhistle, Bardon Mill, and Hexham are convenient stops for visiting three of the best-preserved and most interesting Roman sites, which are also easily reached off the main A 69 road. Yet another way of seeing the wall (and Kielder Water or Durham Cathedral as well) is in a Cessna Skylane from Newcastle airport; Tel: (0325) 33-27-52 for details.

Vindolanda (in present-day Chesterholm) was a fort on the Stanegate, or "Stone Way," the road running east to west behind the wall, and it has been excavated and restored to give a vivid impression of garrison life 17 to 19 centuries ago. In the museum, a wood tablet sent to a Roman soldier from a loving relative, perhaps his mother, reads in translation: "I have sent you pairs of socks and from Sattia two pairs of sandals and two pairs of underpants." The poet W. H. Auden put himself into the sandals of a legionnaire on guard when he wrote,

> Over the heather the wet wind blows,
> I've lice in my tunic
> and a cold in my nose.
> The rain comes pattering out of the sky,
> I'm a Wall soldier, I don't know why.

There are full-scale reconstructions of the turf wall, a turret from the stone wall, and a timber gate tower as well as the *vicus,* the civilian settlement near Vindolanda.

Housesteads (Vercovicium), about 2 miles (3 km) east, is the best preserved of the forts actually on the wall, which snakes over the green hills and can be walked for a considerable stretch. The fort extended over five acres and housed 1,000 soldiers. Its ruins, dating from 122 to the end of the fourth century, include walls, gateways, granaries, barracks, and a latrine with a flushing tank.

In a wooded valley half a mile west of Chollerford, between Housesteads and Newcastle, **Chesters Fort** (Cilurnum) contains the best surviving example of a Roman military bathhouse, used by the 500-strong cavalry unit, the Second Ala of Asturians, that was based here. Stones from the bridge that carried Hadrian's Wall across the North Tyne can be seen on the riverbank opposite the bathhouse.

Dere Street

At Corbridge (junction of A 68 and A 69), Dere Street, the Roman road linking York and the far north, met Stanegate running east to west. This was the site of **Corstopitum**, a supply town for the cohorts guarding the Wall. The ruins of their military compounds, temples, storehouses, and granaries survive, and the museum contains an intricately sculpted fountainhead known as the Corbridge Lion.

Dere Street can still be traced north of Scotch Corner (southwest of Middlesbrough and Darlington) on the B 6275, which joins A 68 near Bishop Auckland. The Roman fort of Vinovium stood at Binchester on the River Wear, downriver from the 800-acre park surrounding Auckland Castle, seat of the bishops of Durham since Norman times and open to visitors on Tuesday mornings and Sunday, Wednesday, and Thursday afternoons during the summer; Tel: (0388) 60-16-27 for details. Stones were carried from the fort to build the **Saxon church** at nearby Escomb that is thought to be the earliest complete example of its kind anywhere in Britain. The splendid Roman chancel arch and a stone, upside down with LEG VI (Sixth Legion) carved in it, in the north wall, as well as diamond broaching in many other stones, display the antiquity of the church.

At Lanchester, north of Bishop Auckland, a Norman church was again built from stones from the fort of Longovicium, and there is a Roman altar in the porch. North of Corbridge, long, straight stretches of the A 68 retrace the route of Dere Street, which was wide enough to take two lanes of chariots. Stretches were built on embankments raised above the surrounding moor, making it, literally, the High Road to Scotland, which it remains to this day.

GETTING AROUND

Most visitors to Britain from overseas arrive in the southeast, but the distance involved in travelling to the North is not great: 300 miles at the outside. The InterCity 225 trains on the London–Edinburgh East Coast main line travel at up to 140 MPH, taking less than 3 hours to Durham, and National Express "Rapide" buses, using the motorways, get there in 5 to 6 hours. There are numerous interconnecting bus and rail services between towns. If time is at a premium, it is possible to fly from Gatwick or

Heathrow to regional airports such as Newcastle or Tees-side. They also handle some international flights, but the majority go to either Manchester or Prestwick (Glasgow), both of which are more convenient starting points for touring the North Country than London; car rental can be arranged easily at these airports. There are sea-ferry routes between North Shields on the Tyne and Scandinavia, between Liverpool and Ireland, and between Heysham (Lancaster) and the Isle of Man.

An excellent source of information on North Country walks (the various "ways" referred to in the chapter above) is the Ramblers Association, 1–5 Wandsworth Road, London SW8 2XX; Tel: (071) 582-6878.

ACCOMMODATIONS REFERENCE
Rates are projected 1994 prices for a double room with breakfast, unless otherwise stated. As prices are subject to change, always double-check before booking.

▶ **Black Swan Hotel.** Market Place, **Helmsley** YO6 5BJ. Tel: (0439) 704-66; Fax: (0439) 701-74; in U.S. and Canada, (800) 225-5843; in Australia, (008) 22-24-46. £130–£160 (includes breakfast and dinner).

▶ **Copthorne Newcastle.** The Close, Quayside, **Newcastle-upon-Tyne** NE1 3RT. Tel: (091) 222-0333; Fax: (091) 230-1111; in U.S., (800) 44-UTELL; in Canada, (800) 668-1513. £110 (breakfast not included).

▶ **County Thistle Hotel.** Neville Street, **Newcastle-upon-Tyne** NE99 1AH. Tel: (0912) 32-24-71; Fax: (0912) 32-12-85; in U.S., (800) 847-4358. £85 (breakfast not included).

▶ **Derwentwater Hotel.** Portinscale, **Keswick** CA12 5RE. Tel: (0768) 77-25-38; Fax: (0768) 77-10-02; in U.S., (800) 223-6764. £96.

▶ **Embleton Hall. Longframlington**, near Morpeth NE65 8DT. Tel: (0665) 57-02-49. £69.

▶ **Howscales.** Kirkoswald, near **Penrith** CA10 IJG. Tel: (0768) 89-86-66; Fax: (0768) 89-87-10. £150–£375 per week.

▶ **Linden Hall Hotel.** Longhorsley, **Morpeth** NE65 8XF. Tel: (0670) 51-66-11; Fax: (0670) 885-44. £115–£185.

▶ **Low Wood Hotel. Windermere** LA23 1LP. Tel: (053-94) 333-38; Fax: (053-94) 340-72. £129–£159.

▶ **Lupton Tower. Lupton**, near Kirkby Lonsdale LA6 2PR. Tel: (053-95) 674-00. £48.

▶ **Michaels Nook Country House Hotel. Grasmere**

LA22 9RP. Tel: (053-94) 354-96; Fax: (053-94) 357-65. £179–£336 (includes breakfast and dinner).

▶ **Miller Howe.** Reyrigg Road, **Windermere** LA23 1EY. Tel: (0539) 44-25-36; Fax: (0539) 44-56-64. £150–£260 (includes breakfast and dinner).

▶ **Northcote Manor.** Northcote Road, Langho, **Black-burn** BB6 8BE. Tel: (0254) 24-05-55; Fax: (0254) 24-65-68. £70.

▶ **North Lakes Hotel.** Ullswater Road, **Penrith** CA11 8QT. Tel: (0768) 681-11; Fax: (0768) 682-91. £108–£128.

▶ **Old Church Hotel.** Waterwillock, **Penrith,** Cumbria CA11 0JN. Tel: (0768) 48-62-04; Fax: (0768) 48-63-68. £90–£150.

▶ **Royal County Hotel.** Old Elvet, **Durham** DH1 3JN. Tel: (0913) 86-68-21; Fax: (0913) 86-07-04; in U.S. and Canada, (800) 444- 1454. £115.

▶ **Royal Hotel.** Queens Square, **Bowness-on-Winder-mere** LA23 3DB. Tel: (053-94) 430-45; Fax: (053-94) 449-90. £39.

▶ **Royal Station Hotel.** Neville Street, **Newcastle-upon-Tyne** NE1 5DH. Tel: (0912) 32-07-81; Fax: (0912) 22-07-86. £55.

▶ **Sharrow Bay Hotel.** Pooley Bridge, **Ullswater** CA10 2LZ. Tel: (0768) 48-63-01; Fax: (0768) 48-63-49; in U.S., (713) 783-8033. £168–£300 (includes breakfast and dinner).

▶ **Stakis Lodore Swiss Hotel.** Borrowdale, **Keswick** CA12 5UX. Tel: (0768) 77-72-85; Fax: (0768) 77-73-43; in U.S., (800) 448-8355; in Canada, (800) 668-8355. £110 (breakfast not included).

▶ **White Swan Hotel.** Bondgate Within, **Alnwick** NE66 1TD. Tel: (0665) 60-21-09; Fax: (0665) 51-04-00. £40–£75.

▶ **Wood Hall. Linton,** near Wetherby LS22 4JA. Tel: (0937) 58-72-71; Fax: (0937) 58-43-53. £89–£125.

▶ **Wordsworth Hotel.** Grasmere LA22 9SW. Tel: (053-94) 355-92; Fax: (053-94) 357-65. £110–£140.

WALES

By Charlotte Atkins

Formerly deputy editor of the UK Holiday Guide *and* Family Holidays in Britain *magazines, Charlotte Atkins is a freelance travel writer and travel editor of* Woman's Own *magazine. She is also coauthor of* The French Channel Ports.

While the Principality of Wales, that pouch bulging on England's left hip into the Irish Sea, shares the English monarchy and government, it has its own distinct culture. Indeed, Wales is the nearest "foreign" country to England. Yet British subjects don't need a passport to visit, and there's no language barrier—although Wales has one of the oldest languages and literatures in Europe.

Wales is Celtic from the moment you pass the *Croeso i Gymru* (Welcome to Wales) signs on the border. In fact, some people argue that place names like Llanrhaeadr (pronounced th-lan-rah-ED-uhr and meaning the Village of the Waterfall), Betws-y-Coed (pronounced bet-oos-uh-KOeed and meaning the Sanctuary in the Wood), and Llangollen (pronounced lan-GOTH-lan) were invented to trip the foreign tongue.

The visitor, however, will encounter no problems. Everyone speaks English—although for many it's a second language. In Gwynedd, the most northwesterly county, for example, around 75 percent of the children are monoglot Welsh until they go to school, and in the morning the village streets echo to hails of *"bore da!"* ("good morning"). The most obvious remnants of the Celtic heritage are people's names: At today's christening ceremonies, first names like Angharad, Gareth, Bet, Rhiannon, Thomas, and Megan are coupled with centuries-old surnames like

Jones, Roberts, Evans, Lloyd, and Davies. These are all unmistakably Welsh. And besides its own patron saint, David, honored on March 1, a national flag and emblem (a red dragon on a green-and-white background), and its own postage stamps, Wales can boast more than 50 national cheeses and mineral water that stands proud on restaurant tables in Italy and France. The country also lays claim to the *eisteddfod* (pronounced eye-STETH-vod), a festival of music, poetry, and dancing that is a significant part of Welsh tradition.

There are several such jamborees held throughout Wales every year, but the two most famous are the National Eisteddfod (the first week in August) and the International Musical Eisteddfod (held every July in a field just outside Llangollen).

MAJOR INTEREST

Snowdonia National Park and Snowdon Mountain
  Railway
Portmeirion Italianate village
International Musical Eisteddfod in Llangollen
Ffestiniog Railway
Castles, especially Harlech, Conwy, and Caernarfon
  in North Wales
Isle of Anglesey
Pembrokeshire Coast National Park
Brecon Beacons National Park
Cardiff

Although there is no geographical north/south divide in Wales, the two areas are different. It's even said that a northerner finds it difficult to understand a southerner—and vice versa—when conversing in Welsh. Rock-solid community spirit runs high in North and West Wales. When a villager dies, for example, it's not unusual for several hundred people to turn out for the funeral. The north also has the edge on rural solitude—apart from a pocket of heavy industry on the banks of the River Dee, most of the area is devoted to mountains, lakes, hill farms, rivers, and sheep-farming pastures (Wales grazes a total of six million sheep).

Slate has been a part of everyday life in North Wales for centuries. In the 19th century the industry boomed, and an escalating demand for the product throughout the world led to the development of ports (such as Porthma-

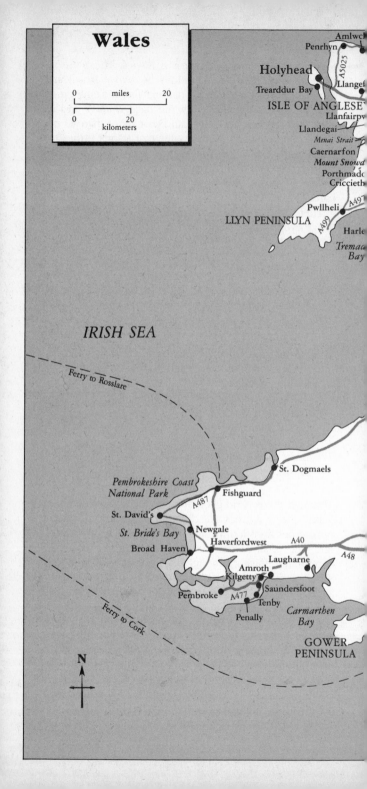

dog and Portdinorwig) and the building of slate-heaving railways (for example, the narrow-gauge Ffestiniog Railway, which runs from Porthmadog to Blaenau Ffestiniog). With the decline in demand, most of the quarries ceased production, but several, especially those at Blaenau Ffestiniog and Bethesda, have responded to a new demand from visitors who come to pay their respects to the area's industrial archaeology and see demonstrations of the skills that earlier generations had mastered. Architects, environmentalists, and conservationists are also helping to create a period of quarry resurgence.

The majority of the Welsh population lives in the more heavily industrialized south, particularly along the seaboard between Swansea and Newport, and the South Wales valleys. Here steel making and manufacturing have provided most of the employment for as long as anyone can remember. In its mid-19th-century heyday, the thriving Welsh coal industry, booming in green and peaceful valleys, attracted workers from England, Ireland, Italy, Greece, and Spain, but as competition grew the Welsh mines went into steady decline; by the end of World War I many coal-mining villages were silent and deserted. Now government rulings on closures are speeding up the process of decline: By January 1992 there was only one working deep mine left in the South Wales coalfield; thus there are no longer any mines operating in the Rhondda Valley, once synonymous with coal.

At just over 8,000 square miles, Wales is so small that the sea is always within easy reach. Seaside towns have obvious appeal to families. To the north, there are the brash and breezy Rhyl, the dignified Victorian resort of Criccieth, dandy Colwyn Bay, and elegant Llandudno. In mid-Wales, there's Aberystwyth, and to the south, Tenby, where massive low-tide sands and gaily painted houses lend an almost Caribbean flavor. Much of the seashore between Barmouth and Harlech is peppered with recreational vehicles, campsites, and chalets. The rock pools and woody river valleys of the **Gower Peninsula** in the south, the first area in Britain to be designated an Area of Outstanding Natural Beauty, are also popular with vacationers.

Despite its humble proportions, Wales manages to squeeze three of the United Kingdom's 11 national parks into its borders, each one an ideal retreat for the touring motorist: Snowdonia, at the top of the map, Brecon Beacons, in the southeast (nudging the border with England at Ross-on-Wye), and Pembrokeshire in the southwest. The 1945 National Parks and Access to Countryside Act defined these areas of wonderful countryside as national parks, although they were owned by private landowners. In agreement with the landowners, the act opened up the areas for the enjoyment of all, with plenty of public footpaths, but the public does not have the right of access to every inch of the parks.

NORTH WALES

Although all of Wales could be tackled in a two-week whip around, it is more sensible to concentrate on one particular part. For first-timers, the north, and particularly Gwynedd in the scenic northwest corner, makes a perfect introduction. In high summer this is the area most popular with British vacationers. The best time to tour is in the spring, when the slopes and fields are covered in wild rhododendrons and gorse, the verges dancing with daffodils and blossoms, or in autumn, under a crisp blue sky, when the leaves are turning orange brown, sharp frosts turn the bare landscape white, and early-morning mists lend the mountain peaks and river valleys a ghostly air. From October through March most tourist attractions are closed, but the uncluttered landscape more than compensates.

The coast from Prestatyn around to Barmouth is strung with popular holiday towns, and on hot summer days the broad, shallow, sandy-pebbly beaches are crowded with the bucket-and-spade brigade. Each resort can be relied upon to display at least one of the traditional characteristics of the British seaside: pinball machines along the pier, donkey rides, Formica-topped café tables, and the occasional brass-band stand.

Colwyn Bay has one of the best beaches along the north coast, a sweeping arc of golden sand fringed by a wide promenade built for deck-chair lounging. It's the haunt of yachters, as the clattering of halyards around the jetties testifies, but its most loyal clientele are older folk, attracted by the resort's sedateness, although the giant flumes at Rhyl's Sun Centre, one of the largest amusement parks in Britain, echo to the sounds of frenzied screams.

Llandudno

Llandudno is undoubtedly the grande dame of North Wales resorts. Her claims to fame are her size (the largest seaside resort in the country) and her literary association with the Reverend Charles Lutwidge Dodgson, a.k.a. Lewis Carroll, the author of *Alice's Adventures in Wonderland,* who lived and wrote here. Don't miss the White Rabbit memorial opposite the Gogarth Abbey Hotel, unveiled in 1933 by David Lloyd George as part of the celebration of Carroll's centenary. Llandudno's other attractions are less cerebral; the wide bay revives childhood beach memories beside the Victorian pier, one of the best such examples in Britain, now lined by postcard, souvenir, and candy stalls. A stroll along the **West Shore** beach affords staggering views of the Conwy Estuary, Puffin Island, and the Menai Strait. Or you can take a walk or a drive, or ride the cable car or tram up to the visitor center at the top of Great Orme Country Park and Nature Reserve. Little Orme, the headland at the opposite end of town, is smaller but significant to naturalists and bird watchers.

Out of season the only sounds here are the gentle crashing of waves and the screeching of scavenging sea gulls as the towns sink into hibernation, building up energy for the next summer's onslaught.

STAYING AND DINING IN LLANDUDNO

Although the seafront is lined with moderately priced Victorian establishments, the best place to stay in Llandudno is ► **Bodysgallen Hall**, hidden in the woods just south of town. The building's dark oak paneling, chunky drapes and carpets, antiques, stone-mullioned windows, massive fireplaces, and glorious gardens, backed by moody views of Snowdonia, define it as a world apart from the seaside hostelry. Martin James works wonders in the kitchen.

Snowdonia National Park

A few miles southwest of Colwyn Bay on A 470 lies Parc Cenedlaethol Eryri (Land of the Eagles), the Welsh name for the 840 square miles that lie within the boundary of the Snowdonia National Park, tucked into the northwest corner of Wales. It includes **Snowdon** itself, the "monstrous peak," as Daniel Defoe described it, at 3,560 feet the highest mountain south of the Scottish border, as well as 13 other summits that are more than 2,900 feet high.

The park roughly covers the medieval kingdom of Gwynedd, a military stronghold ruled by Owain Glyndwr, one of Wales's greatest heroes, and historically the seat of the dynasty of Welsh princes. It is a fascinating geographical site, studded with glaciated U-shaped valleys, lakes, razor-sharp mountain edges, and other legacies of its Ice Age torment. It is a mecca for lovers of the outdoors—walkers, backpackers, climbers, pony trekkers, and white-water canoeists—but even the most sedate tourists will find the peaks, forests, lakes, raging streams, and undulating lowland scenery spectacular.

A quick-thinking entrepreneur has established a restaurant, bar, and shop on Snowdon's summit. The Snowdon Mountain Railway, one of the remaining steam-driven, narrow-gauge "Great Little Trains of Wales" (some regrettably now run on diesel), will take you on a four-and-a-half-mile run from Llanberis almost to the top of the mountain at half-hour intervals throughout the summer. But it is arguably more pleasant to climb. The easiest route is the Llanberis Path from **Llanberis** itself—it parallels the railroad tracks for five miles and climbs to 3,200 feet. Dolgellau and Betws-y-Coed are excellent starting points for more challenging, spectacular walks through the park itself.

It's no coincidence that it was here that Sir John Hunt's victorious Everest team of 1953 did their training; or that 88 years earlier Edward Whymper chose the same region to prepare for his conquest of the Matterhorn. The best views of Snowdon are from the Llanberis Pass, where it's easy to pull off the road (if you don't mind appearing sedentary as teams of climbers scale the rocks). On the descent to the wooded valley of Nant Gwynant, another site gives views westward over the shimmering lakes of Gwynant and Dinas. But the finest views of Snowdon are from the parking lot in the tiny village of Rhyd-Ddu, where you feel on top of the mountain, rather than overshadowed by it.

Mull over Snowdon's presence from **Y Bistro** restaurant in Llanberis, a longtime favorite as much with locals as visitors. The menu is set price, but there is a choice of five or six dishes per course, including roast rack of lamb in almond and cream sauce, and salmon or prawns, both smoked locally. There's even a Welsh wine on the list.

BALA AND ENVIRONS

On the eastern edge of the park, the one-street town of Bala, especially popular with ramblers, is easily outshone by its five-mile-long lake, Llyn Tegid, also known as **Bala Lake**. Access is easy, and it's possible to completely circumnavigate it by road. One of the few hotels in town to raise its head above mediocre modesty is ▶ **Fron Feuno Hall**. Built as a hostel for monks in the 16th century, it was later enlarged to become a family house. There are three large bedrooms, each with its own bathroom and views over the gardens, woods, and lake.

If you don't mind driving in and out a few miles from Bala, there are two commendable hotels on the outskirts. ▶ **Tyddyn Llan Country House**, a member of the Welsh Rarebits group of prestigious hotels, is a gray-stone Georgian property in the Vale of Edeyrnion, on the road to Llangollen. It bulges with antiques and paintings, passions of its owners, Peter and Bridget Kindred, and the superb quality extends to the evening menu, which features lamb, salmon, and other local specialties. It's also very quiet here—birdsong is the only sound outside most bedrooms. ▶ **Palé Hall**, the second, is a stately Victorian mansion of golden stone, grand and expensive but nonetheless made homey by Tim and Jain Ovens, right down to the blazing fire in the great hall and the sporting activities they will arrange for you around and about.

BETWS-Y-COED

To the north, Betws-y-Coed, at the confluence of the rivers Conwy, Llugwy, and Lledr, is a major gateway to the national park and, as such, is crowded in summer, particularly on weekends. Among its gray-stone buildings are a handful of Welsh woollen and craft shops, such as **Pennant Crafts**, which sells local pottery, with its characteristic white flower pattern on a dark-blue background. As a major tourist spot, the town is well served by hotels and guest houses. It even has its own Fairy Glen, a waterfall 1 mile (1½ km) from the village on the A 470 road to Dolgellau and reached by a footpath up from the whitewashed ▶ **Fairy Glen Hotel**, a cozy 17th-century house overlooking the River Conwy.

PORTMEIRION

The village of Portmeirion, situated about 10 miles (16 km) south of Snowdon on a wooded headland near Porthmadog (access from the A 487), is best known as the setting for the cult television series "The Prisoner," although it also inspired Noël Coward to write *Blithe Spirit*. The village itself, at the end of a private road, was the fantasy creation of an eccentric architect, Sir Clough Williams-Ellis, who bought the site in 1925; it resembles a stage set more than a popular holiday village. The community's center point is the 14-room ► **Portmeirion Hotel**; still in the Williams-Ellis family, it was closed by fire in 1981 but reopened in 1988. The hotel's interior is almost as fantastical as the village. Many rooms are decorated thematically: The mirror room, for example, not for the self-conscious, is lined from floor to ceiling with gilt-framed glass. Another relies solely on Indian imports, while others contain antiques shipped from around the globe. Portmeirion itself exhibits Oriental, Indian, and Italian influences. Twenty of the pastel pink, yellow, and blue houses in the village are self-catering units belonging to the hotel, interspersed with the occasional shop, restaurant, and even a town hall, and leading down to a beautiful sweep of beach and a residents' swimming pool.

LLANGOLLEN

Buried at the heart of the Dee Valley to the east of the national park on A 5, Llangollen makes an important appearance on the international map every July with its **International Musical Eisteddfod**. Hotels are booked up months in advance, hardly surprising when festival participants include the likes of Luciano Pavarotti (who made his debut at the Eisteddfod in 1955) and the Vienna Boys Choir. One favorite hotel is the ► **Bryn Howel**, a 19th-century family-run country house. The town also stirs when orange-and-yellow-coated canoeists hold slalom races on the River Dee. But most of the time Llangollen is the quintessential quiet Welsh town, enough of a backwater for the local laundromat to double as the video store. It attracts a small but steady flow of visitors exploring the valley, calling in at the woollen mill or the pottery works, riding to the Horseshoe falls on board the nostalgic Llangollen Railway Society steam train and returning on a horse-drawn canal boat, climbing up to the ruins of the 12th-century fortress—Castell Dinas Bran, which towers over the town—or taking a ride on a horse-drawn barge from the wharf along the canal that parallels the river. The Dee flows through town, and the gardens behind several hotels and restaurants end abruptly at its banks. One such is **Gales,** a restaurant and wine bar that also has eight daintily decorated bedrooms on Bridge Street; another is **Caesar's Restaurant**, right beside the bridge.

BLAENAU FFESTINIOG

The 153-year-old **Ffestiniog Railway** follows a route alongside which heaps of slate were once piled from the massive quarries at Blaenau Ffestiniog. Vacationers now trundle the 27-mile round trip that departs every hour or so from Porthmadog's High Street to Blaenau Ffestiniog, one of the most famous slate towns in Wales. A small railway museum in the station supplies history and details. The round trip takes approximately two hours.

Blaenau Ffestiniog is popular for the underground floodlit tours (helmets provided) of the **Llechwedd Slate Caverns** and **Gloddfa Ganol Slate Mine**, once the world's largest slate mine and now an open-air museum. Tours take in the machinery in the mill, plus a ride by Land Rover through part of the tunnel system and a Narrow-Gauge Railway Centre, with both locomotives and rolling stock.

One of the largest studio pottery works in rural Wales is down the road, housed in a converted mill that used to grind flour for ships' biscuits. Pottery is for sale, but you can also tour the workshop and watch craftsmen molding, baking, and painting the earthenware—they'll encourage you to make your own with the help (or hindrance) of a potter's wheel. The building can't be missed; its entire outer wall has been painted by Ed Povey with a mural called *Pots,* which includes the figures of Lloyd George and other less famous local personages. Tourist Information Centres are located in many towns and villages, including Llanberis, Blaenau Ffestiniog, Harlech, Bala, Conwy, Porthmadog, Betws-y-Coed, and Dolgellau.

Welsh Castles

Some 700 years ago, King Edward I of England built 17 massive castles to dissuade the fiery Celts from challenging his authority. This enormous campaign to Anglicize Wales cost the king dearly, yet the money was well spent: Apart from one major revolt, his castles succeeded in keeping the peace for the next 100 years.

Built by a small army of workers under a French master mason, the castles marked the end of Welsh independence. But Edward's fortresses (Caernarfon, Conwy, Harlech, and Beaumaris, all in North Wales, are the four most noteworthy) are not the only castles Wales has to offer the visitor. There are plenty of truly Welsh-built examples, like Dolbadarn and Castell-y-Bere. And even earlier, after William the Conqueror had sailed from Normandy in 1066 and seized the English throne, the Normans looked westward from their newly acquired position of strength along the English–Welsh border and spotted a country torn apart by civil war and ripe for conquest. They stormed the land, building castles as symbols of their power. At first, these were simple wooden affairs on top of grassy mounds (or *mottes*); later came massive multiwalled buildings that were the last word in military technique.

Today Wales is stocked with an abundance of Norman and Gothic castles, their aged battlements illustrating more than anything else the country's turbulent history. Politics aside, castles are a vital part of both the heritage of Wales and its glorious landscapes. When they were built they became obvious focal points for civilian settlements, giving the rural Welsh their first taste of urban life. In North Wales they are particularly varied and magnificent and constitute the most concentrated group of medieval castles in Europe. A large proportion of them are now maintained and managed by Cadw, the Welsh equivalent of English Heritage.

"Put yourself in the mind of an attacking force," advises the Welsh Office, the government body that administers the country. "It's the only way to understand just what castles are all about." The hefty, seemingly impenetrable gateways are nowadays the easiest of entrances. In medieval days there would usually have been a long ramp followed by a drawbridge. You can probably see just where the drawbridge would have hinged into its original pivot holes. The next line of defense was the portcullis (iron grating), its sliding grooves clearly visible in the castle walls, followed by the stout doorways of the gate passage. All along the journey attackers would have been picked off by archers and would have had boiling water poured on them from aptly named murder holes.

HARLECH CASTLE
Whether you approach the little town of Harlech (off A 496 in Snowdonia) from the north or the south, the view of its castle as you round the last corner is breathtaking. One of Edward's coastal fortresses, Harlech was built in the late 13th century. It commands the most impressive

location of all Welsh castles, perched 200 feet above sea level at the foot of a cliff, overlooking the grand sand-duned sweep of Tremadog Bay and the Royal St. David's Golf Course. It was the last Royalist castle to capitulate to the Parliamentarians in 1647 and in Elizabethan times had been a debtors' prison. Its gates are now open to visitors throughout the year.

A walk around the castle's breezy ramparts on a fine day offers a constant change of scenery: the neck of the Llŷn Peninsula, the gray rooftops of Harlech's white houses, a fleet of sand dunes, and the bulk of Mount Snowdon. The castle sits on a promontory once lapped by waves; although the immediately surrounding land is now reclaimed, a stairway still plunges down the rock face to a water gate at the bottom.

The walls of Harlech Castle stand sturdy, but the central core, the Inner Ward, is open to the elements. It is a grassy quadrangle strewn with foundations of walls now only knee high. Apart from a 143-step climb to the top of the gatehouse, there's a freestanding exhibition about the Edwardian conquest in one of the few rooms still intact.

One of Wales' grandest country-house hotels lies at the end of a long driveway in Talsarnau, 3 miles (5 km) to the north of Harlech. The ▶ Hotel Maes-y-Neuadd (pronounced mice-er-NAY-aath) is the kind of place that, once you discover it, you will want to keep secret— especially if you have been lucky enough to get a front bedroom overlooking Snowdon and the Traeth Bach estuary. It's run by two families; one family member, Olive Horsfall, heads the kitchen team, preparing a daily menu of such Welsh specialties as lamb in honey, cider, and rosemary; herrings with apple and sage; and Welsh Amber Pudding (apple tart with orange curd and marmalade). Lunch reservations are essential at the popular restaurant (Tel: 0766-78-02-00).

CONWY CASTLE

The most important room inside all medieval castles is the Great Hall, and the one at Conwy is a grand example. Although it is now roofless and floorless, it's easy to imagine the three gaping fireplaces in full flame and the fine tracery windows in their prime in the Middle Ages. From the farthest tower, built high on a buttress of rock, the view is spectacular, looking down on streets still laid out on their original medieval lines and across to the estuary of the foaming River Conwy.

The old town of Conwy itself, on the coast north of

Snowdon on A 55, sits wrapped in three-quarters of a mile of medieval stone walls. On a stroll along the crest, no place for acute vertigo sufferers, you will encounter only sea gulls on their battlement perches. In Conwy's High Street an Elizabethan town house, Plas Mawr, is currently being restored to its former glory by the National Trust; the Visitor Centre, in Rose Hill Street, has exhibitions, film shows, and a crafts store. Down on the quay, Conwy possesses what is reputed to be the smallest house in Britain, furnished as a mid-Victorian Welsh cottage.

CAERNARFON CASTLE

This "camp on the land opposite Anglesey," as the name translates, shot to modern-day fame with the investiture of the present Prince of Wales in July 1969. On the day of the ceremony 500 million television viewers worldwide tuned in to the castle.

Caernarfon Castle, which is just across the Menai Strait from the Isle of Anglesey in North Wales, looks the part—after all, it was Edward I's royal seat of government for North Wales. Shaped like an hourglass, its interior once housed a 100-foot Great Hall where all of the castle's residents could eat, drink, and be merry—though perhaps their mirth waned when the food arrived stone cold after being carried from the kitchen on the far side of the courtyard (a deliberate segregation because of fire hazards). In the Eagle Tower you can see a Prince of Wales exhibition and trace the royal family tree. And you can see how the crafty Edward made his own son, born in Caernarfon, Prince of Wales after subduing the Welsh princes.

The mammoth Caernarfon Castle and its towering cliff walls are best encompassed from the opposite bank of the River Seiont. Its pretty bands of red sandstone were inspired by the spectacular fifth-century walls at Constantinople, which King Edward had admired on his travels.
▶ **Seiont Manor Hotel** in Llanrug east of Caernarfon has taken its name from the salmon-filled waters that flow through its estate. The gardens also contain a traditional millpond, an herb garden, and a lake; the building is the original farmstead of a Georgian manor house.

The town of **Caernarfon**, on the Menai Strait, is small and quiet, little more than a square, a modest handful of stores, the Black Boy Inn, and a castle. Drive directly south on route A 487 and you cross the neck of the Llŷn Peninsula. Although on the map it looks as if its landscapes will be flat, on the ground you are in for surprisingly bumpy scenery. This neglected limb of land, the "Land's End of Wales," basks in accolades as an Area of Outstanding Natural Beauty, as well as boasting David Lloyd George's boyhood home at Llanystumdwy. His simple grave on the banks of the River Dwyfor is much visited, as are the stone cottage opposite the Feathers public house that was his home until 1890 and the town museum, which contains many mementos of his political career.

The Llŷn Peninsula also boasts one of the best "restaurants with rooms" in Wales, Chris Chown's ▶ **Plas Bodegroes** (pronounced bod-E-groyce and meaning the Place of the Cross) near Pwllheli. It is small, with only eight bedrooms, but very beautiful, surrounded by beech woods and six acres of garden yet only a pebble's throw from the Atlantic. Food, supplied by a network of locals, includes Welsh black beef, free-range veal, chickens and ducks, and salmon and sea trout fished by the Bangor boats, all served with organically grown vegetables and local wild mushrooms. Five-course menus cost around £30. If you stay the night you'll find that bedrooms are given equally tender loving care—the rooms with four-posters have particularly worthy views.

OTHER CASTLES

Criccieth Castle

Standing above its tiny, timeless seaside town on the Llŷn Peninsula's southern flank, Criccieth Castle is backed by the mountains of Snowdonia and fronted by the broad sweep of Tremadog Bay. On a clear day you can see Harlech Castle in the distance. Although there's some disagreement about who actually built it, majority opinion seems to support the view that it is a native Welsh castle to which Edward added a few strengthening touches. Its main feature is a twin-towered gatehouse, a rare type of structure, built by Llywelyn the Great (1173–1240), a man whose "nickname" fitted him well, as'he was probably the greatest of the rulers of medieval Wales. In 1205 he married the English King John's daughter Joan, and in 1209 accompanied his father-in-law on an expedition against King William of Scotland. The relationship came to an abrupt end, however, in 1211, when John invaded Gwynedd, Llywelyn's stronghold in northwest Wales. Llywelyn later recovered the lands he had lost, and in 1216 he presided over what was virtually a Welsh parliament at Aberdovey. Criccieth is certainly a much simpler, more irregularly shaped, and altogether far less sophisticated affair than any of the pure Edwardian castles.

Dolwyddelan Castle

If Dracula had owned a Welsh pied-à-terre it could well have been Dolwyddelan Castle, about 5 miles (8 im) southwest of Betws-y-Coed on A 470. Not that there's anything remotely Gothic about this native Welsh structure, but if you see it wrapped in patches of mist and bathed with eerie shafts of light, its simple solitary square tower is quite awesome. The castle is barely penetrable, even today. Its first line of defense is a five-bar gate, followed by a farmyard full of barking dogs. Next there is a trudge up a steep track, through a siege of chomping Friesian cattle (and a final slosh through mud if there's been any rain), and then a perilous climb up inside the tower to its battlements, from which the view over the Lledr valley is, literally, breathtaking. It clearly wasn't weaponry that kept the enemy at bay here—physical exhaustion sufficed.

Rumor has it that Llewelyn was born here, but he wasn't. (It is likely that he was born in a castle built earlier somewhere down in the valley.) It is almost certain, however, that he built Dolwyddelan. The reason may be difficult to fathom, since the castle's isolated position seems to bestow no defensive role whatsoever. But it did, in fact, guard an old road, the medieval pass from Meirionnydd to the Vale of Conwy. From the battlements, restored by the Victorians, its location makes much more sense.

Rhuddlan Castle

All of Edward's castles had the sea in common—or at least a river leading to it. Since the English communities were so isolated in the midst of hostile terrain, it was clearly impractical to bring supplies overland across miles of Wales and utterly impossible to reach the castles in times of siege. At Rhuddlan Castle, a mile or two inland from Rhyl, an army of diggers worked six days a week for three years to divert the canal, which is still the main artery of the River Clwyd as you see it today.

Penrhyn Castle

North Wales contains a number of weird and wonderful 19th-century shams. From the outside, Penrhyn Castle, on the A 55 Conwy road 2 miles (3 km) east of Bangor, looks like an ancient monument, with its insurmountable walls, toothy battlements, turrets, and the castellated like. But its roots date no further back than the 19th century, when the architect Thomas Hopper built the Neo-Gothic structure for an army of servants rather than soldiers. It is an utter fake, an extravagance designed to reflect the enormous wealth accumulated by the Douglas Pennants from their sugar interests in the West Indies and later from the nearby slate mines.

Outside, the grassy banks are awash with nodding daffodils throughout the spring, while inside there is hardly an undecorated surface in the entire place. The furniture, wall panelings, and mighty doors were all made specially for the house, mostly from oaks grown on the estate, and carved with motifs that echo those found on the exterior walls. There are highly polished slate fireplaces and even a slate bed, weighing nearly a ton, on which Queen Victoria refused to sleep. The castle also houses a huge collection of dolls. Whether or not the style of Penrhyn is to your taste, one thing is certain: You can't possibly ignore it.

The Island of Anglesey and Beaumaris Castle

It can be snowing in Snowdonia, they say, while daffodils are blooming in Anglesey. Separated from the Llŷn Peninsula by the Menai Strait but easily reached on the Menai Suspension Bridge or the neighboring Britannia Bridge, the island of Anglesey has 125 miles of coastline, a large proportion of which are classified as Areas of Outstanding Natural Beauty; three sizable sections are listed among Britain's Heritage Coasts. The clear blue waters at Trearddur Bay in the west are ideal for swimming, sailing, and water-skiing, while the cruising center at Holyhead, the chunk of northwest Anglesey that "drifted" away, bursts at the seams every August for the Menai Strait Regatta Fortnight boat races. Away from the water there are five golf courses, sports centers at Amlwch and Llangefni, and a bird-watching reservoir three miles long. And if you thought Snowdonia had the monopoly on heights, you'll think differently after a bracing walk up the main street of Moelfre village.

Anglesey's **Beaumaris Castle**, in the town of Beaumaris, sits right at the end of a street of Georgian houses, making the town one of the prettiest in Wales. It used to be one of the busiest, too, in the days when its ferry was Anglesey's only link to the mainland. Since the construction of bridges, however, Beaumaris has become a peaceful backwater.

The immediately obvious difference between Beaumaris and the rest of Edward's castles is that it doesn't perch on a haughty rock. It stands on a flat, seemingly vulnerable stretch of marshland, so all its barriers had to be constructed. The best example of concentric castle design in Britain, Beaumaris is a highly compact unit—thus defenders on the higher inner walls could fire their missiles over the heads of their fellows on the outer wall. Today the fields are full of passive bowls players and a few gardeners.

Beaumaris, built in the 1290s, was Edward's last Welsh bastion, and it remains unfinished. Edward had competing demands on his resources, and since peace was established in this part of the world at about this time, Beaumaris was no longer a priority.

▶ **Ye Olde Bull's Head** inn on Castle Street is almost as old as the castle. Details reveal its age (over 500 years): back-breakingly low ceilings, timber beams, and a courtyard where stagecoach horses were once watered. The place is run by Keith Rothwell, David Robertson, and their wives, who will be happy to fill you in on the latest catch; fish is the inn's culinary specialty.

As you leave Anglesey, pick up a platform ticket from the railway station in the village of Llanfairpwll. No ordinary ticket this, it contains all 58 letters of the town's proper name: Llanfairpwllgwyngyllgogerychwyrndrobwll-llantysyliogogogoch, which roughly translates as "St. Mary's (church) by the White Aspen over the Whirlpool and St. Tysilio's (church) by the Red Cave." (The extension of the original name, Llanfair Pwllgwyngyll, was a 19th-century hoax to impress tourists!)

SOUTH WALES
Pembrokeshire Coast National Park

The smallest of the three national parks in Wales, Pembrokeshire's 225 square miles mainly hug the southwest coast in the form of the **Pembrokeshire Coast Path**. The path follows the ups, downs, ins, and outs of the shoreline of Britain's only coastal national park for 167 miles, from St. Dogmaels in the north to Amroth in the south, taking in the enormous sweep of St. Bride's Bay. The ragged outline and craggy cliffs of Pembrokeshire resemble the coastline of Cornwall, but this beautiful corner of Wales remains far less known and visited. Even during the peak holiday season it feels remote, a wild seascape where you can wander for hours on end without meeting a soul. Come here in the depths of winter and you could be at the very edge of the world.

Apart from the beauty of its landscape, the Pembrokeshire coastline enjoys the year-round presence of beautiful wildflowers and hordes of seabirds, including cormorants, shags, choughs, guillemots, and razorbills. The area is also a favorite haunt of geologists, who come to examine rocks that date back 2,000 million years; even the untrained eye will appreciate the elemental forces that have twisted and folded the land masses and the erosive power of the sea that has created caves, arches, stacks, and other geological features. Although this is now rather a remote, thinly populated region, the coast path abounds in evidence of earlier inhabitants in the flint chippings left by Stone Age people some 10,000 years ago, and in the Iron Age forts built on several promontories.

There is a halfway point on the Pembrokeshire Coast Path—in culture as well as in miles. The so-called **Landsker Line**, drawn inland at Newgale, marks the northern limits of Norman influence in Wales. To the south are bold, castellated church towers, English and even some Scandinavian village names, and a relatively dense pattern of settlement. To the north the villages are more scattered, the chapels more modest, and the village names Welsh.

The path can be overgrown in places, especially in the winter, when it is little used. Wear long pants to protect yourself from the gorse and brambles. Because many of the villages are little more than a clutch of cottages, chapel, and pub, accommodation has to be planned carefully, although hot, filling lunches (often based on seafood) can almost always be bought in pubs. Four miles off the path as it passes near Fishguard (a town rather lacking in good looks whose sole raison d'être is as a departure point for ferries to southern Ireland, though its more photogenic Lower Town was the setting for the movie of Dylan Thomas's *Under Milk Wood*) is the ▶ **Penlan Oleu**, a renovated Welsh farmhouse. It scores high on location, with views over Fishguard Bay, and has everything the weary walker could want—simple rooms, fine cuisine (often fish from the bay), and hearty breakfasts in the morning.

TENBY
Another nice place to break the wearying journey is the resort of Tenby, built on a peninsula and surrounded by sea on three sides. Its pastel pink, yellow, blue, and green houses and seafront hotels have drawn holiday visitors for two centuries with the promise of health-giving sea breezes. Described as one of the most romantic spots in Europe, it has a network of casbahlike alleyways of shops and cafés that echo to the screeches of gulls. **Mangle's Pantry**, serving thick vegetable soups, ploughman's platters, and homemade apple crumble, is a good lunch stop. Overnighters are a three-minute drive away from a wonderful hotel in the village of Penally, Steven and Elleen Warren's ▶ **Penally Abbey**. It has been their home for almost ten years, and the personal touch is what makes it so special—there is no reception desk, for example—but the informality disguises a keen, low-key professionalism. The bedrooms are large and very beautiful, with original arched doors and four-posters. There's a small, heated indoor pool for weary feet and the kind of candlelit dinners that would carry anyone through another week's trekking.

ST. DAVID'S
The coastal path next passes through St. David's, the smallest city in Britain. The modestly sized cathedral (which defines it as a city) and the remains of the Bishop's Palace sit incongruously down in a dip, strategically built there to be hidden from invading Vikings. Although the cathedral now ranks low on Britain's ecclesiastical scale, it was once a vital center of pilgrimage—two visits to St. David's equaled one to Rome or Canterbury. The

town's modern-day claim to fame is as home to the Oceanarium, the largest purpose-built sea aquarium in Wales. It is also the departure point (at nearby Whitesands Bay Beach) for two-hour voyages around Pembroke-shire's offshore islands, sailing under 500-foot sea cliffs, past gray seals and nesting seabirds, and into the longest sea caves in Wales. Those prepared to wade out to the rigid-inflatable boats should contact Thousand Islands Expeditions; Tel: (0437) 72-16-86. The whitewashed ▶ **St. Non's Hotel,** yards from the cathedral, takes its name from the mother of St. David, the country's patron saint. It's not fancy but perfectly comfortable, and the food, though publike, is filling.

▶ **St. Bride's Hotel** in Saundersfoot, on the edge of the park, is an excellent place to start or finish a trip along the path. Worn-out walkers will find a night of moderately priced luxury—perhaps a two-hour soak in a bath. You need to wear something smart for dinner, but it's worth the effort just for the views over Carmarthen Bay.

The Boat House, Dylan Thomas's blue, sea-shaken home from 1949 until his death in 1953, is 10 miles (16 km) east of Saundersfoot in Laugharne (pronounced larn). Built on a rocky breakwater, the house, particularly the wooden hut where Thomas penned his most famous works, has stunning views of the estuary. It's now a "house of information," with relics and memoirs of the poet's life. Nearby, fans can down a pint at Thomas's favorite watering hole, Brown's Hotel; you can also buy copies of his works in the tiny bookshop across the street and visit the church-yard of St. Martin's, where he is buried.

Pembrokeshire Coast National Park Information Cen-tres are at St. David's, Haverfordwest, Pembroke, Tenby, Fishguard, Broad Haven, and Kilgetty.

Brecon Beacons National Park

Wales's third national park is in South Wales north of Cardiff and west of Pembrokeshire. Brecon Beacons's 519 square miles of high hills, crags, and bleak moorland is effectively three distinct areas, namely, the western flank, an empty upland wilderness dominated by the Black Mountain; the shapely Brecon region; and the flat-topped Black Mountains in the east (not to be confused with the singular and solitary Black Mountain in the northwestern part of the park). Apart from the park's geographical high points, topped by the 2,907 feet of Pen-y-Fan, the area contains wooded patches, farmlands, lakes, and the gentle valley of the River Usk. In common with its two sisters, it attracts a vast number of outdoor enthusiasts (particularly pony trekkers) as well as people who tour by car.

The park's natural focal point is the ancient town of **Brecon**, whose narrow streets and tiny shops are dominated by the massive, 13th-century **Priory Church of St. John the Evangelist**, towering high above the River Honddu. ▶ **Llangoed Hall**, just outside town near Llyswen village on the road to Builth Wells, is one of Wales's newest country-house hotels and the brainchild of Sir Bernard Ashley, husband of the late Laura Ashley. Since its opening in 1990, everything possible has been done to ensure that this Edwardian mansion overlooking the River Wye feels more like a grand house than a hotel—there is no reception desk, for example—and its designer has arranged for superb furnishings and fabrics in the 23 rooms. **Brecon Castle**, built by William the Conqueror's half-brother, is best viewed from the gardens of the ▶ **Castle of Brecon Hotel**, suitably high up on Castle Square, with views across the Usk valley and the imposing Brecon Beacons. Or descend into the river valley to the market town of Crickhowell, where the kitchen at the ▶ **Bear Hotel**, a family-run 15th-century coaching inn in the center, serves young salmon caught by fishermen, as well as local lamb, wild duck, and *sewin* (Welsh sea trout). Brecon also has one of Wales's most welcoming working farms, ▶ **Trehenry Farm**, where the owners treat guests to simple, home-cooked food in falling-off-the-plate portions, spotless rooms, and a real fire burning in the sitting-room hearth.

Cardiff

Wales is not a country of big cities, as the modest proportions of its capital city (population 275,000) testify. Even the most expensive hotels and restaurants, concentrated around the triangle of roads formed by Westgate Street, Castle Street, and High Street/St. Mary Street, charge prices comparable to those in a provincial English city.

Cardiff, down on the southeastern coast of Wales, is an attractive, green city facing England across the mouth of the Severn, its pleasant aesthetics helped along by the fact that its more prestigious monuments are built in local white Portland stone and are floodlit during civic functions. **Cardiff Castle**, bang in the center of town, is really a three-in-one affair, a stylistic hodgepodge with thick Roman outer walls, a Norman keep, and a 19th-century wing full of richly decorated rooms. But the castle constitutes only one-seventh of the Civic Centre—its neighbors, all worthy of attention, are the Law Courts, the City Hall, the Welsh Office, the University College, the Institute of Science and Technology, the Temple of Peace, and the National Museum of Wales. This latter is essential viewing for enthusiasts of all things Welsh, as well as for fans of French Impressionist painting.

Cardiff's covered "arcades" add a dimension of interest to the modern, could-be-anywhere shopping arteries. Their Art Nouveau entrances are heralded by such names as Morgan, Royal, Castle, Dominion, and Duke Street. Down these narrow alleyways lurk specialist, antiquary, eccentric, and crafts stores, among them **Lear's Bookshop** (the largest in town) in the Royal Arcade and **Things Welsh** in the Duke Street Arcade.

STAYING AND DINING IN CARDIFF

The ▶ **Park Hotel**, with 125 bedrooms and just off the main shopping precinct, has everything you might expect from a city center hotel with all the modern conveniences, yet it is still quite traditional in style. But if you prefer to stay in green-belt country and make occasional forays to the city, a good choice would be the ▶ **Celtic Manor**, a 19th-century house with huge bedrooms in Coldra Woods, 12 miles (19 km) out of town along the M 4 to Newport. Although essentially a businessman's hotel, with traffic roaring below the windows on the M 4, the place has a lot of charm, woodland views, good sports facilities, and an impressive restaurant.

Anyone in Cardiff during the fall is only 40 miles (64 km) from the **Swansea Festival**, which runs for seven weeks every year from mid-September to the beginning of November. This is an arts festival extraordinaire, with performances by the English Shakespeare Company and national ballet and opera troupes, full programs of orchestral, choral, and chamber music, as well as films, jazz, and other events. For performance details and tickets, Tel: (0792) 30-24-32.

GETTING AROUND

Some corners of Britain demand a car; Wales is one of them. The M 4 motorway runs from London to Newport, Cardiff, and Swansea (it takes roughly two and a half hours to Cardiff). Visitors to North Wales can take the M 1 and M 6, and then join the A 5. Apart from the stretch of M 4, which runs well into South Wales just north of the Gower Peninsula, there are no motorways in Wales, although the "A" roads are fast and wide, and the A 55 Expressway along the North Wales coast is designated a Euroroute, meeting motorway standards.

Regular InterCity trains run from London to Cardiff (two hours) and Chester, just across the border from North Wales (three hours). Cars can be rented at both stations.

ACCOMMODATIONS REFERENCE

Rates are projected 1994 prices for a double room with breakfast, unless otherwise stated. As prices are subject to change, always double-check before booking.

▶ **Bear Hotel.** High Street, **Crickhowell**, Powys NP8 1BW. Tel: (0873) 81-04-08; Fax: (0873) 81-16-96. £52–£70.

▶ **Bodysgallen Hall.** **Llandudno**, Gwynedd LL30 1RS. Tel: (0492) 58-44-66; Fax: (0492) 58-25-19; in U.S. and Canada, Tel: (800) 525-4800; in Australia, (008) 802-582. £108–£155 (breakfast not included).

▶ **Bryn Howel Hotel.** **Llangollen**, Clwyd LL20 7UW. Tel: (0978) 86-03-31; Fax: (0978) 86-01-19. £80–£119.

▶ **Castle of Brecon Hotel.** Castle Square, **Brecon**, Powys LD3 9DB. Tel: (0874) 62-46-11; Fax: (0874) 62-37-37. £53–£68.

▶ **Celtic Manor.** Coldra Woods, **Newport**, Gwent NP6 2YA. Tel: (0633) 41-30-00; Fax: (0633) 41-29-10. £99 (breakfast not included).

▶ **Fairy Glen Hotel.** **Betws-y-Coed**, Gwynedd LL24 0SH. Tel: (0690) 71-02-69. £42.

▶ **Fron Feuno Hall.** **Bala**, Gwynedd LL23 7YF. Tel: (0678) 52-11-15. £50–£55.

▶ **Gales.** 18 Bridge Street, **Llangollen**, Clwyd LL20 8PF. Tel: (0978) 86-00-89; Fax: (0978) 86-13-13. £51.

▶ **Hotel Maes-y-Neuadd.** **Talsarnau**, Gwynedd LL47 6YA. Tel: (0766) 78-02-00; Fax: (0766) 78-02-11; in U.S., Tel. and Fax: (800) 635-3602. £100–£138.

▶ **Llangoed Hall.** **Llyswen**, **Brecon**, Powys LD3 0YP. Tel:

(0874) 75-45-25; Fax: (0874) 75-45-45; in U.S. and Canada, (800) 525-4800; in Australia, (008) 802-582. £135–£185.

▶ **Ye Olde Bull's Head.** Castle Street, **Beaumaris**, Isle of Anglesey, Gwynedd LL58 8AP. Tel: (0248) 81-03-29; Fax: (0248) 81-12-94. £72.

▶ **Palé Hall.** Llandderfel, near **Bala**, Gwynedd LL23 7PS. Tel: (06783) 285; Fax: (06783) 220. £132–£149 (including dinner).

▶ **Park Hotel.** Park Place, **Cardiff** CF1 3UD. Tel: (0222) 38-34-71; Fax: (0222) 39-93-09; in U.S., (800) 847-4358; in Canada, (800) 448-8355; in Australia, (008) 22-11-76. £90–£106 (breakfast not included).

▶ **Penally Abbey. Penally**, near Tenby, Pembrokeshire, Dyfed SA70 7PY. Tel: (0834) 84-30-33; Fax: (0834) 84-47-14. £84–£128.

▶ **Penlan Oleu.** Llanychaer, **Fishguard**, Dyfed SA65 9TL. Tel: (0348) 88-13-14. £40.

▶ **Plas Bodegroes Hotel and Restaurant.** Plas Bodegroes, Nefyn Road, **Pwllheli**, Gwynedd LL53 5TH. Tel: (0758) 61-23-63; Fax: (0758) 70-12-47. £70–£110.

▶ **Portmeirion Hotel. Portmeirion**, Gwynedd LL48 6ET. Tel: (0766) 77-02-28; Fax: (0766) 77-13-31. £59–£129 (breakfast not included).

▶ **St. Bride's Hotel.** St. Bride's Hill, **Saundersfoot**, Dyfed SA69 9NH. Tel: (0834) 81-23-04; Fax: (0834) 81-33-03; in U.S., (813) 957-3200. £88–£98

▶ **St. Non's Hotel.** St. David's, Haverfordwest, Dyfed SA62 6RJ. Tel: (0437) 72-02-39; Fax: (0437) 72-18-39. £73.

▶ **Seiont Manor Hotel. Llanrug**, Caernarfon, Gwynedd LL55 2AQ. Tel: (0286) 67-33-66; Fax: (0286) 67-28-40. £96.50–£105.

▶ **Trehenry Farm.** Felin-fach, **Brecon**, Powys LD3 0UN. Tel: (0874) 75-43-12. £34.

▶ **Tyddyn Llan Country House. Llandrillo**, near Corwen, Clwyd LL21 0ST. Tel. and Fax: (049084) 264. £88–£96.

THE INDUSTRIAL HERITAGE

By Anthony Burton

After leaving a career in publishing, Anthony Burton has been writing full-time for the past 25 years. Concentrating on the industrial and transport history of his native Britain, he has written several books and television and radio series on those subjects.

The Industrial Revolution, which began in Britain in the middle of the 18th century, was one of the turning points of history. It also brought in the filth and noise of the first industrial towns, the squalor of slums, and the hard, monotonous, grinding toil of the first factories. But that pain has become a distant memory, and what is left is a story of endeavor, ingenuity, and pioneering spirit. The physical remains of that revolution, most of which are located from the Midlands to the north and in Wales, are as important and fascinating as the Roman ruins or the country estates that have been standard fare on the British tourist menu for generations.

In this chapter we depart from our format of focusing on a defined region because the important sites of the Industrial Revolution are widely dispersed.

It sometimes seems from historical accounts that industry appeared, full-fledged, somewhere around 1760. But recognizable industrial activity dates back far beyond that year, and those who want a truly romantic start to the

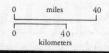

Industrial Heritage

0	miles	40
0	40	
kilometers		

Great Ormes Head

Live

● Llanberis

▲ *Mt. Snowdon*

Porthmadog ●   ● Blaenau
             Ffestiniog

GWYNEDD

IRISH SEA

● Tywyn

A487

W A L E

■ Dolaucothi
Pumpsaint

A40   *River Cothi*

DYFED

GW

Cardi●

DEVON

● Sticklepath   *A30*

River Tamar   **DARTMOOR**

CORNWALL   ● Tavistock

Cotehele ●   ■ Morwellham
         Quay

A30   ● Plymouth

A38

N

history of industry cannot do better than to head for two sites in Wales: Great Ormes Head, Gwynedd, and Pumpsaint in Dyfed. The **Great Orme mines** were first worked for copper in the Bronze Age almost 4,000 years ago. Modern visitors can observe the underground workings and the archaeologists at work on this very important site, opened to the public for the first time in 1991. The Romans came to Wales in search of wealth and found it in what is now the **Dolaucothi gold mine**, near modern Pumpsaint. It is a vast site where the Roman engineers diverted water from the nearby Rivers Cothi and Annell and used it to wash away the topsoil to expose the rock with its veins of rich ore. Later, the Romans quarried out the stone and dug tunnels deep into the hillside. Centuries after that, Victorian engineers came back to reopen the mines, creating a labyrinth of tunnels and shafts. Mining engineers now take groups into this underground world.

Coal

SOUTH WALES: BLAENAVON
Coal mines are more commonplace than gold mines, and it was coal that literally fueled the Industrial Revolution. At their peak, British mines were turning out nearly 300 million tons of coal a year, and mining dominated many of the industrial areas. The world of the miner was, however, a mystery to most people—until recently, when the decline in demand for coal closed many pits while some found new life as museums, among them the **Big Pit** at Blaenavon in South Wales. This was a working colliery until 1980, and the aim today is to introduce visitors to the everyday life of the pit. On the surface you will see the changing rooms and pit-head baths, the railway, and a reconstructed miner's cottage, but the principal attraction is underground. Fitted out with helmets and cap lamps, you enter the cage and are lowered to the galleries and the coal face, where former miners explain what went on down there.

COUNTY DURHAM: BEAMISH
Miners must go where the coal is, and villages with a strong sense of community grow up around the pit. Both mine and village are fully represented in the large open-air museum of Beamish, in the heart of the northeastern

coalfield some 10 miles (16 km) northwest of the city of Durham in the North Country. One of the main features is the pit head with its original steam winding engine, which first began work in 1855. A railway leads from the mine to a row of 19th-century pit cottages, restored to show life at different periods. The Beamish Railway carries a working replica of George Stephenson's early-19th-century steam engine Locomotion, built in 1975 for the 150th anniversary of the Stockton and Darlington Railway. The railway also passes by a re-creation of a typical small-town street of the 1920s. Here are the station, a row of houses, the Cooperative store, and the pub. Everything, from shop fittings to the trams that run down the street, is of the period. Add a farm with animals, a transport collection, and a vintage fairground, and you have a museum that reflects every aspect of life in the region.

Iron

SHROPSHIRE: COALBROOKDALE AND IRONBRIDGE

The area of Coalbrookdale and Ironbridge in Shropshire has been called the birthplace of the Industrial Revolution. The story began in the early 18th century, when Abraham Darby established his ironworks here using a revolutionary technique of smelting iron ore using coke. The whole area can now be thought of as one giant museum, split up into different sections, some consisting of conventional displays in buildings, others based on existing features in the industrial landscape, but it is at the Coalbrookdale works that any tour of the area should start. Darby's original furnace is preserved as part of the **Coalbrookdale Furnace and Museum of Iron**. It was from this furnace that iron flowed to be cast into the parts of the first iron bridge, which still spans the River Severn and which gives Ironbridge its name. Between Coalbrookdale and the bridge is another museum in an old warehouse by the Severn, but the major site in the area is **Blists Hill**, higher up the hill above Ironbridge. Blists Hill is still a working industrial complex. There are remains of its giant blast furnaces, and wrought iron is still made in a puddling furnace, a genuine industrial rarity. But there is also a wealth of other exhibits—a miniature town with shops and a pub, a colliery with a steam winding engine, a foundry, a candle factory, print works, and a curious canal where the boats, resting on cradles, were lowered down a steep incline to a lower level of the canal beside the River Severn. Down here, too, is the **Coalport China Works Museum**. There is more than enough of interest in the area to fill a whole day's touring.

DARTMOOR: MUSEUM OF WATERPOWER

Not all the museums of the iron industry are on such a large scale. The little village of Sticklepath, on the edge of Dartmoor, is home to the Museum of Waterpower where edged tools such as scythes were once made. Here a succession of waterwheels provides the power for the various processes. One wheel moves the bellows that blast air into the furnace where the iron is heated, another powers the mighty hammers used to shape the metal on the anvil, and a third turns the grindstones on which the blades are sharpened. The latter gives literal significance to "keep your nose to the grindstone," for the grinder lies on a platform with his head just above the turning wheel.

SOUTH YORKSHIRE: ABBEYDALE INDUSTRIAL HAMLET

The same system can be seen at work, on a grander scale, at the Abbeydale Industrial Hamlet on the edge of the Yorkshire city of Sheffield. Steel was manufactured on the site, and you can also see the whole range of machinery needed to turn an iron bar into a razor-sharp scythe blade. Elsewhere in the city the story of Sheffield steel is told in more detail—from the overview presented at the Kelham Island **Industrial Museum** to the specialized work to be seen at **Shepherd Wheel**, a cutlery-grinding establishment.

Wool and Cotton

WEST YORKSHIRE: COLNE VALLEY MUSEUM

Historically, Britain's industrial wealth derived from the wool trade: the complex business of taking wool from the sheep, spinning it into yarn, and weaving that yarn into cloth. At first, this depended on individual spinners and weavers working in their own homes. Memories of those days are preserved in the Colne Valley Museum at Golcar in West Yorkshire, housed in a restored group of weavers' cottages. Here the women and children worked on the lower floors turning the wool into yarn, which then went to the men working at the hand looms on the upper floors. Spinning and weaving are still practiced here as they have been for centuries. Originally, the cloth would have been taken by the weavers or their masters to sell at one of the major trading centers. A magnificent example, the **Piece Hall**, built in 1775, has survived in nearby Halifax. Two floors of offices, joined by a colonnaded walkway, surround a central courtyard. The old offices now contain shops; a new industrial museum is also part of the complex.

GREATER MANCHESTER: HELMSHORE

Before being used, the cloth from the loom needed to be "fulled"—pounded in water by giant hammers—so that the fibers shrank and matted together. A water-powered fulling mill has survived at Helmshore in Lancashire. A cotton spinning mill was added to the complex in the middle of the 19th century, and this has now become home to the **Helmshore Textile Museums**. Displays tell the story of cotton, but the real attraction here is the old mill itself and its machinery, notably its spinning mules. The mules each spin 714 strands of yarn by means of whirring spindles on a moving carriage, which trundles back and forth across the mill floor. The mule, first devised at the end of the 18th century and for many decades the mainstay of the cotton industry, is fascinating to watch.

DERBYSHIRE: CROMFORD

The first successful cotton mill, using the power of the waterwheel to turn many spindles, was built by Richard Arkwright at Cromford in Derbyshire in 1771. It was here that the factory age was born, and the village that Arkwright built to house the new work force was, in effect, the first mill town. The old mill still stands, though it is now little more than an empty shell. But the village retains much of its old atmosphere. North Street, in particular, shows the quality of Arkwright's houses. The long windows on the upper floors mark the workshops where the men wove while the women and children went off to the mill. A better-preserved example of an early Arkwright mill can be seen nearby at Matlock Bath. Cromford established a pattern—a water-powered spinning mill was built, then a village housing the work force grew up around it.

CHESHIRE: STYAL

A fine example of the system is to be seen in the perfectly preserved complex at Styal in Cheshire. The mill at Styal was begun in 1784, was gradually expanded over the years, and remained at work for nearly two centuries. At first it relied entirely on waterwheels, but later steam power was added and power looms joined the spinning machinery. The atmosphere of this country mill in a delightful setting is very different from that of the crowded textile towns farther to the north. The mill is now in the care of the National Trust, and its original character has been preserved. Styal's importance, however, lies largely in the story it tells of the mill workers. Like the mill itself, the little village has remained virtually unchanged. The most poignant reminder of the old days is the apprentice house, which was home to more than 100 poor and orphaned children who worked 12 hours and more each day in the mill.

LANCASHIRE: WIGAN

By the beginning of the 20th century, steam engines in mills had reached a monstrous size. Trencherfield Mill at Wigan, west of Manchester, had one of the biggest. Four huge cylinders were fed by steam to turn the enormous flywheel, around which ropes were wrapped to transfer the drive to all parts of the mill and set more than 80,000 spindles turning. The mill is now part of a new museum complex at **Wigan Pier**—there really was a Wigan Pier—a stop on the Leeds and Liverpool Canal marked by old warehouses that now contain industrial exhibits. Local citizens have even forgiven George Orwell for his less-than-flattering portrayal of the town in his book *The Road to Wigan Pier* and have named the new pub after him. The museum is designed to tell the story of the area, and the past is brought to life by actors. Children can sit in the schoolroom furnished with slates and chalk and be shouted at by a suitably stern disciplinarian. The canal, which runs through the center of the site, can be explored on foot along a towpath or by boat (there is a regular water-bus service).

Canals

Canals fed the industries of Britain from the 1760s through the 1820s, when the railway first became established. A complex network of more than 1,000 miles of waterway was constructed across Britain, and most of it is still in use—no longer to carry cargo but for the pleasure of boaters. Even a short trip on a canal is a good introduction to industrial Britain. But most canals also contain long, quiet rural stretches: The Leeds and Liverpool Canal, for example, once clear of the mill towns, runs through a landscape of moorland and rough fells. For those who are interested in history, there are excellent museums along the canals.

CHESHIRE: ELLESMERE PORT

The **Boat Museum** at Ellesmere Port in Cheshire occupies what was once a major inland port complex that grew up where the Shropshire Union Canal met the River Mersey. The port and warehouses, designed by the engineer Thomas Telford, gained new importance with the construction of the Manchester Ship Canal at the end of the 19th century. Some of the original structures remain, including the steam engine used for the hydraulic system of the docks. But the principal interest lies in a collection of boats that once plied the inland waterways. Pride of place here belongs to the narrowboats, crafts approximately 70 feet long and 7 feet wide that were once in use on many of England's canals. One of the museum's prize exhibits is *Friendship,* the last privately owned horse-drawn narrowboat to work on the system. The tiny back cabin, where the family who operated the boat once lived, is perfectly preserved. Not all canals and rivers had the same size locks, so other boats were also in use, and the museum also has a collection of wide boats and short boats. Preserved cottages, a working forge, and the boat horses in their stable block complete the busy scene here.

GLOUCESTERSHIRE

A new **National Waterways Museum** opened in 1988 at The Docks in Gloucester, at the end of the Gloucester and Sharpness Canal. It is sited in a magnificent Victorian warehouse and has three floors of displays and exhibits telling the story of Britain's canals. Outside on the water are historic craft of all kinds, including a massive steam dredger. This is a splendid museum in a beautiful setting in the heart of the city.

WEST MIDLANDS: DUDLEY

The **Black Country Museum** at Dudley (some 10 miles/16 km west of Birmingham) is a large open-air museum similar to those of Beamish and Ironbridge but firmly based on its canal location. The name "Black Country" was given to this region in the days when the smoking chimneys of industry darkened the skies. The museum reflects those days but, happily, without the dirt. The old canal basin, with its limekilns and workshops, has been preserved. The principal attraction here, though, is the narrow Dudley Tunnel, which links vast caverns where limestone was once quarried. The Dudley Canal Trust runs trips by electric narrowboat into the tunnel. In one of the narrowest sections, passengers are encouraged to try "legging." There was never a towpath in Dudley Tunnel, so the boatmen lay on their backs, put their feet against the tunnel wall, and walked the boat along. Thomas Newcomen constructed one of the first steam engines in Dudley in 1712, and a working replica is on display in the museum. Other Black Country industries, from chain making to coal mining, are also represented here, and there is a full range of buildings, from a Methodist chapel to a town pub.

Ports

The canal system joined the industries to the ports, and so to the rest of the world. Some of the early ports were a good way inland on navigable rivers and were often built to serve particular local needs.

RIVER TAMAR PORTS

The River Tamar, which divides Cornwall from Devon, runs through the heart of a countryside rich in copper mines and tin mines. Small ports line the riverbanks, among them the one at **Cotehele**, where a typical Tamar sailing barge is preserved. Although the vessel looks romantic, it spent its trading days carrying manure. Farther upstream is a much greater port, **Morwellham**, whose wharves were connected to the local canal system and the mines by a complex railway that carried trucks high above the quays on wooden trestles. The workshops and houses that grew up around the quays form the basis of the open-air museum, and you can combine a visit there with a train ride into the heart of a hill to enter one of the old mines. Even in its heyday Morwellham could hardly claim to be a major port—though it could, with some justice, claim to have a beautiful setting.

LIVERPOOL

If you want to see a port that is a true child of the Industrial Revolution, the place to go is Liverpool. Manchester was the commercial heartland of the Lancashire cotton industry, but it was through the port of Liverpool that the raw cotton came in from America and the finished products went out to the world. A new cargo was added in the 19th century—emigrants, many from Ireland, heading for a new life across the Atlantic. The **Merseyside Maritime Museum**, on the docks near the heart of the city, includes a superb example of Victorian industrial design, the Albert Dock. This is a closed dock ringed by warehouses, some now converted into housing, others to shops, and one block to the museum. There is an air of nobility about these buildings on giant iron pillars that lift them above the cobbled quay. Iron is the keynote here; even the classical façade on the office building at the entrance to the dock is iron. The museum has two aspects: the docks themselves, where ships such as the Mersey pilot cutter are displayed and dockside machinery is demonstrated; and the displays inside the various buildings. The most ambitious, and one of the most popular, is "Emigrants to a New World," where role-players help re-create the story of European emigration from 1830 to 1930. Other exhibits vary in scale from full-size ships to miniature ones, and an expert shows just how to put a ship in a bottle. In 1988 Albert Dock also became home to the **Tate Gallery Liverpool**, which, like the original gallery in London, specializes in the best of modern art.

Shipbuilding

PORTSMOUTH

The story of British shipping is seen with greatest clarity in Portsmouth, on the south coast, where you can trace warships from the 16th to the 20th century. The story begins with the raising of Henry VIII's warship **Mary Rose** from the waters of the Solent in 1982. The vessel is by no means complete, but enough remains to give a clear picture of how she was built and how she would have looked. Experts are now at work in Portsmouth conserving the ancient timbers and replacing others. The remarkable salvage operation on the *Mary Rose* did more than reveal the remnants of the old structure—it also brought to life the different artifacts carried on board, from the bows and arrows of the military to the more mundane articles of everyday use. All these are displayed in a special museum alongside the old ship in the naval dockyard at Portsmouth, under the shadow of Admiral Nelson's flagship. The *Victory* is now restored, so what is seen today is the vessel very much as she was when she achieved her finest hour at the Battle of Trafalgar in 1805. She was a first-rate ship—which is not to say that she was excellent, but merely to define her as a ship bearing at least 100 guns. By the time of Nelson's great battle she was already old-fashioned, work having started on her in 1759—something like fighting a World War II engagement with a Victorian battleship. The *Victory* represents the end of a long tradition of wooden ships moved by sails and engaging the enemy by firing broadsides from cannon set in lines all down the sides of the boat. The end it might have been, but it was a glorious end for *Victory*.

A new generation of warships appeared in the 19th century as the cannonball was replaced by the explosive shell and sails gradually gave way to steam. In 1861 the frigate *Warrior* was launched and the new age arrived. Everything about her was new: The old muzzle-loaded cannon had given way to breech-loaded guns with rifled bores, the steam engine supplemented the sail, and, most important, she was armor-plated. Her hull consists of a sandwich, with iron as the filling and wood on the outsides. She was faster, more maneuverable, better protected, and better armed than any ship of Nelson's navy. Now that she is restored, it is possible to see just what a very fine ship she is. The *Warrior* is berthed at the quay just inside the dockyard gates.

The story of warships at Portsmouth does not end here, for at neighboring Gosport is the **Royal Navy Submarine Museum**, based on the World War II submarine H.M.S. *Alliance*. This sleekly functional craft seems very far removed from the ancient timbers of the *Mary Rose*.

Railways

DURHAM: SHILDON

By far the most important change in transport took place not at sea but on land, with the arrival of the steam locomotive running on iron rails. Academics debate over which railway first began the modern age, but the designation generally goes to George Stephenson's Stockton and Darlington line, opened in 1825. The locomotive works were established at Shildon in Durham under the supervision of Timothy Hackworth. Here you can see something of the original line, parts of the works, and the Hackworth museum, based in the house where he lived and telling the story of his life and achievements. Here, too, is a working replica of Hackworth's most famous engine, Sans Pareil, which he built to compete in the Rainhill Trials of 1829, tests devised so that a locomotive could be chosen for the new Liverpool and Manchester Railway. The winner was Stephenson's Rocket, but Sans Pareil put up a brave fight.

YORK: NATIONAL RAILWAY MUSEUM

Those who want a view of Britain's railway heritage from the earliest days to the most modern innovations should make their way to the National Railway Museum in York. Here is a vast range of locomotives covering the whole story of steam. The world record holder for steam locomotives, Mallard, is here, as is the last to be built for British Rail, Evening Star. The story is then continued into the age of diesel and electric trains. Locomotives represent only a part of train history, for rolling stock, too, has changed over the years: Compare the Bodmin and Wadebridge coach of the 1830s, little better than a cattle truck, with the splendor of Queen Victoria's coach of 1869. Around these main features are displayed railway paraphernalia, from signals to posters.

WALES: TALYLLYN RAILWAY

For many enthusiasts, however, the railways come to life only when the old engines have fire in their bellies. There is no shortage of preserved railways in Britain, though the movement began only in 1950 when a group of enthusiasts got together to try to save the little seven-and-a-quarter-mile-long Talyllyn Railway, which starts by the coast at Tywyn in Wales. It is little only in the sense of being narrow gauge, with the rails a mere two feet, three inches apart, but it makes a giant effort, climbing from sea level high into the hills using engines up to a century old. The magnificent scenery is accompanied by the sound of the locomotives struggling to take you there.

SEVERN VALLEY RAILWAY

The steam railway is perhaps better typified by the main lines and their innumerable lesser branches, and no railway has ever won more hearts than the G.W.R., prosaically the Great Western Railway, but to its thousands of enthusiasts, God's Wonderful Railway. The Severn Valley Railway, once a part of that great railway empire, runs for 16 miles between Kidderminster and Bridgnorth and is dedicated to keeping the G.W.R. tradition alive. Stations have been restored to look just as they did half a century ago and carriages are vintage stock, but the chief attractions are the old steam engines, everything from main-line locomotives to diminutive tank engines.

WALES: FFESTINIOG RAILWAY

It is easy to lose sight of the importance of railways when indulging in nostalgia, so a useful corrective is to visit a line originally built for the process of hauling goods, not passengers. The 13½-mile-long Ffestiniog Railway was originally intended to take slate from Blaenau Ffestiniog to the port of Porthmadog. It just happened to pass through some of the most beautiful mountain scenery in Wales along the way, and scenery is part of the lure that draws the crowds today. But it also has a special place in the affections of railway enthusiasts. This was the first narrow-gauge railway to carry steam locomotives, and it still runs double-ended Fairlies, extraordinary contraptions that look like two conventional engines that have backed into each other and become permanently stuck together. It is a railway in which all the best elements of railroading come together, and to add to its appeal, it takes visitors to the heart of the most Welsh of Welsh industrial centers.

Slate

WALES: BLAENAU FFESTINIOG

Blaenau Ffestiniog is the slate capital of Wales. Here people have quarried and mined to dig out the stones that would roof millions of houses. The town seems overwhelmed by slate, mountains of it all over the valley, great mounds that after rain gleam like jewels in the sun. The **Gloddfa Ganol Slate Mine** is more than just a mine, certainly more than just a museum: It is a mountain of slate into which miners have burrowed to create tunnels and caverns. The scale is spectacular. There are 30 different levels to the mine—the lowest some 500 feet below the town and the highest 1,600 feet above sea level. Visitors see deep into the workings of a slate mine and also catch a glimpse of the life and craft of the slate workers. Those who find themselves fascinated by this industry can find out more by visiting the **Welsh Slate Museum** at Llanberis, under the shadow of Snowdon and the Snowdon Mountain Railway.

Other Industries

The preceding, of course, is just a brief glimpse of Britain's industrial heritage. Nearly 100 railway museums and preserved railways go unmentioned here, and entire industries have been left untouched. One or two, however, are so well served by museums that you should add them to your itinerary.

GLADSTONE POTTERY MUSEUM

At Longton, near Stoke-on-Trent in the Midlands, the Gladstone Pottery Museum is one such place. Like many of the best industrial museums, it is based on an old working site. Gladstone was never one of the great names like Wedgwood or Spode, and that is perhaps part of its appeal. It is plain, honest, no-nonsense pottery, proving that true beauty exists in the commonplace. There are the wonderful sinuous shapes of the tall bottle ovens where the pots were fired, matched by the beauty of the pots on display. Here visitors can see every step of pottery making, from the shaping of the clay to the addition of the final decorative touches.

BASS MUSEUM

All this dashing about from steam engine to furnace is warm work, so what could be a more appropriate way to finish than with a cooling draught? Brewing must surely rank among the great British trades, and the story of beer is told in loving detail with opportunities for sampling at the brewing capital of England, Burton-upon-Trent, northeast of Birmingham in Staffordshire. The Bass Museum occupies only one section of what is still a major working brewery—which is very much a part of the Industrial Revolution. It has its own steam engine (on display), it was built near a canal, and it has its own railway system. The brewery differs from most factories in that few industrial processes can boast such a palatable end product.

CHRONOLOGY
OF THE HISTORY OF
ENGLAND & WALES

The aim of this chronology is to give a quick guide to the historic context of the towns, buildings, and monuments that visitors will see on their travels through England and Wales. Although the human race first came to Britain around half a million years ago, and there is ample evidence of the life of cave dwellers, there is little to see beyond stone axes preserved in museums. So, this chronology begins at the period when people first began to leave significant monuments on the landscape.

The Neolithic Age

The Neolithic Age, or New Stone Age (c. 4000 B.C. to 2000 B.C.), was the age of forest clearance and settlement, crop growing, and stock raising. Tools were manufactured from the hard stones, especially flints, the latter sometimes coming from deep mines, such as those of Grimes Graves, Norfolk. The dead were buried in communal burial places, either long barrows, great mounds surrounded by ditches, or stone chambers. The most striking memorials of the age are the henge monuments, the rings of bank and ditch of which Avebury and Stonehenge are the finest examples.

The Bronze Age

The Bronze Age (c. 2000 B.C. to 500 B.C.) saw the arrival of metal tools and weapons, and, as with the Neolithic Age, we know it now from its burial mounds and strange, mysterious monuments. The round barrows are familiar marks in the landscape, hemispherical humps that dot the tops of ridges. But the most impressive features are the stone rings and standing stones, such as the Rollright Stones in Oxfordshire.

The Iron Age

The end of prehistory is marked by a sophisticated Celtic culture in Britain (c. 500 B.C. to 50 B.C.). There is ample evidence of a settled way of life in such villages as Chysauster in Cornwall. Defense was a prime concern, however, resulting in the typical hill forts of the period. Maiden Castle near Dorchester in Dorset—an area of 45 acres surrounded by earth ramparts and ditches—is a fine example, while nearby South Cadbury hill fort is said to be the site of King Arthur's Camelot.

The Romans

The Romans (55 B.C. to A.D. 409) founded many of Britain's cities, among them London, York, and Lincoln, and joined them together by a network of roads, many of which survive in the routes that modern roads follow. Surviving villas with decorated pavements, central heating, and elaborate baths point to a rich, highly civilized lifestyle. Forts, fortifications, and military roads serve as reminders that the Romans came as military conquerors.

- **55–54 B.C.:** Caesar's expedition.
- **A.D. 43–47:** Claudian invasion and conquest of southern England. Foundation of Londinium (London).
- **60–61:** Revolt of Queen Boadicea.
- **122:** Hadrian's Wall begun.
- **c. 340–369:** Barbarian raids in Britain.
- **410–446:** Roman withdrawal from Britain.

The Anglo-Saxons and the Vikings

With the end of the Roman Empire came invading armies of Saxons, Angles, and Jutes. They brought with them Norse religion and culture, still remembered in our days of the week: "Tiw's day," "Woden's day," and "Thor's day." In time, the country became divided between the Anglo-Saxon kingdoms of what is now England and the Celtic realms of Wales. It was not a peaceful time, and the kingdoms were soon to be invaded by the Vikings from

Scandinavia, who eventually established the Danelaw of North and East England. Christian missionaries arrived in the country, and their success can be seen in the early churches and crosses.

This period saw the establishment of many of the towns that are still important in Britain today. Some were simply developments of Roman centers, but others, such as Southampton, were essentially new Saxon towns. The Saxons also established "burhs," fortified towns, such as Oxford. The Norse established their own capital at York. The arts were represented by rich ornamental work such as that found in the Sutton Hoo burial ship, discovered in East Anglia and now in the British Museum, and by epic poems such as *Beowulf.* The period's finest accomplishment is to be seen in the beautiful illuminated manuscripts of the Christian church.

- **429:** Saint Germanus comes to Britain.
- **c. 450:** Saxon settlements in Kent.
- **477–495:** Saxon settlement of Sussex and Wessex.
- **c. 500:** British princes, said to include Arthur, establish peace at the Battle of Mons Badonicus.
- **597:** The mission of Saint Augustine of Canterbury arrives in Kent.
- **663–664:** Synod of Whitby establishes a unified church in England.
- **731:** Bede's ecclesiastical history completed.
- **757:** Offa becomes king of Mercia and begins fortifying the Welsh border by building the so-called Offa's Dyke.
- **793:** First Danish raids.
- **865:** The "Great Army" of Danes invades England.
- **871:** Alfred the Great becomes king.
- **878:** Alfred defeats the Danes.
- **919:** Foundation of Norse kingdom at York.
- **c. 940:** Monasteries founded at Glastonbury and Abingdon.
- **978:** Ethelred the Unready crowned.
- **1003:** Danes invade.
- **1014:** Danes elect Canute as king.
- **1016:** Ethelred dies and Canute becomes king of all England.
- **1037:** Harold I becomes king.
- **1066:** Harold II defeats Danes at Battle of Stamford Bridge; a month later the English are defeated by William of Normandy at the Battle of Hastings.

Normans and Plantagenets

The conquering Normans had one overriding priority: to establish their own rule. Consequently, the first and most important contribution they made to the English landscape was the castle. In its simplest form, the castle consisted of the motte and bailey—a motte, or mound, with a wooden tower on top, surrounded by a bailey, or courtyard, protected by a moat. Soon, the wooden tower was replaced by the stone keep, a daunting fortress of which the great White Tower of London is a particularly impressive example. The medieval castle reached its ultimate expression with Edward I's conquest of Wales, when he promptly set about defending his newly won land with a string of border fortresses.

The Normans also brought with them elaborate religious rituals that required large churches, cathedrals, abbeys, and monasteries. The local churches remained comparatively simple in form but were often richly decorated with wall paintings explaining the scriptures to a largely illiterate populace. Architectural change came with the building of Durham Cathedral, begun in 1093, where the introduction of ribbed vaulting led to the full flowering of the Gothic style. The period also saw the establishment of the great religious houses, the monasteries and abbeys with their fine churches and extensive lands. The medieval Church had a power to match that of the monarchy itself, a power that can still readily be seen in ruins such as those of Tintern and Fountains abbeys. Learning, too, was advanced with the establishment of universities at Oxford (1249) and Cambridge (1281).

The feudal system of the Normans was based on the lord of the manor, who gathered his wealth from the work of the villagers who plowed the fields and tended the stock. It was a society of contrasts and seldom a land at peace. Discontent between peasant and lord, between church and state, and between lord and lord, and the wider issues of international wars, including the Crusades in the Holy Land, combined to make this a period of seemingly endless turmoil.

- **1086**: The Domesday survey.
- **1087**: Accession of William II.
- **1100**: Accession of Henry I.
- **1135**: Accession of Stephen.

- **1139–1153**: Civil War as Stephen is challenged by Geoffrey and Matilda of Anjou.
- **1154**: Accession of Henry II, the first Plantagenet king.
- **1162**: Thomas à Becket appointed archbishop of Canterbury.
- **1170**: Becket murdered in Canterbury Cathedral.
- **1189**: Accession of Richard I.
- **1190**: Start of Richard I's crusades, which end in his imprisonment in Germany.
- **1199**: Accession of John.
- **1215**: Signing of Magna Carta.
- **1264**: Simon de Montfort's rebellion begins.
- **1272**: Accession of Edward I.
- **1276–1283**: Wars with Wales, culminating in the conquest of the principality.
- **1296**: Edward I invades Scotland.
- **1306**: Rebellion of Robert the Bruce.
- **1314**: Scots defeat the English at the Battle of Bannockburn.
- **1327**: Deposition of Edward II in favor of his son Edward III.

The Late Middle Ages

This period—which received its most notable, if not always its most accurate, chronicling in the plays of William Shakespeare—was dominated by war: the Hundred Years War between England and France and the seemingly endless civil wars between the houses of York and Lancaster (Wars of the Roses). Wars abroad cost a great deal of money, and taxation was resisted, most violently in the Peasants' Revolt. To this bloodshed that washed over the country was added the horror of the Black Death, which reduced Britain's population by a third. Yet this period showed a fine, exuberant flowering of many arts. In architecture, the Gothic achieved its greatest expression in majestic cathedrals with tall spires, complex tracery windows, pointed arches, and elaborate decoration. Even today, the strong, sweeping curves of, say, Wells Cathedral seem almost incredibly bold. Perhaps the principal feature of the age was the birth of a truly English literature, based in part on the high romance and chivalry of courtly life and in part on the experience of the rougher world of ordinary men and women. Its first masterpiece was Langland's *Piers Plowman,* but that was soon surpassed by Geoffrey Chaucer's *Canterbury Tales.* Another great work of the time is Malory's *Morte d'Arthur.* Literature was given a further boost at the end of the period with the arrival of William Caxton's printing press.

- **1337**: Start of the Hundred Years War.
- **1346**: Battle of Crécy.
- **1348**: Beginning of the Black Death.
- **1356**: Battle of Poitiers.
- **1362**: First version of *Piers Plowman.*
- **1377**: Accession of Richard II.
- **c. 1386**: *The Canterbury Tales.*
- **1399**: Accession of Henry IV.
- **1400–1410**: Rebellion of Owen Glendower of Wales.
- **1413**: Accession of Henry V.
- **1415**: Battle of Agincourt.
- **1422**: Accession of Henry VI.
- **1450**: Jack Cade's rebellion.
- **1470**: *Le Morte d'Arthur* completed.
- **1475**: Edward IV invades France.
- **1477**: Caxton's first book printed in England.
- **1483**: Death of Edward IV and Edward V and accession of Richard III.
- **1485**: The Battle of Bosworth and the death of Richard III marks the end of the Wars of the Roses.
- **1492**: Columbus in the New World.

The Tudors

The accession of Henry Tudor brought an end to the apparently endless struggle of the Wars of the Roses. Peace at home was also marked by a new prosperity founded, in good measure, on the wool trade, while at the same time the country was looking increasingly to its overseas connections with the Americas and the Far East. This was an age of discoveries and innovations. Britain built up a navy under Henry VIII that was to prove its worth with the defeat of the Spanish Armada. The arts flourished, particularly architecture. The wealthy no longer needed to concentrate on grim castles for defense but could turn to exuberantly decorated homes instead—houses such as Burghley House and Hardwick Hall. The Gothic style also reached its climax, typified by the extraordinary fan-vaulted ceiling of King's College Chapel, Cambridge. The old religious houses were less fortunate, reduced to ruin by Henry VIII's dissolution of the monasteries and the break with Roman Catholicism. Other arts, however, thrived. Painters such as Holbein depicted the famous, while the English miniaturist Nicholas Hilliard provided the most telling images of the age. British music found a distinctive voice in the works of William Byrd. But it was in literature that the period reached its peak of achievement—first with the poems of Edmund Spenser, then with the plays of Christopher Marlowe, and finally with the genius of William Shakespeare.

- **1509**: Accession of Henry VIII.
- **1515**: Cardinal Wolsey appointed lord chancellor.
- **1517**: Martin Luther's 95 theses posted at Wittenberg.
- **1533**: Henry VIII marries Anne Boleyn.
- **1536**: The union of England and Wales and dissolution of the monasteries; publication of the first English-language Bible.
- **1545**: Sinking of Henry VIII's ship *Mary Rose*.
- **1552**: Birth of Edmund Spenser.
- **1553**: Accession of Mary.
- **1558**: Accession of Elizabeth I.
- **1562**: Sir John Hawkins's first voyage transporting slaves from Africa to America.
- **1564**: Births of Christopher Marlowe and William Shakespeare.
- **1587**: Execution of Mary Stuart.
- **1588**: Defeat of the Spanish Armada.
- **1603**: Death of Elizabeth I.

The 17th Century

This century of contrasts saw the Stuart dynasty take the throne, lose it in the Civil War, and regain it at the Restoration. It ended with the firm establishment of Protestant domination with the accession of William of Orange in the English Revolution. The period saw the flamboyance of the Restoration and the austerity of Puritanism. It was above all a century of religious conflict, which appeared in such diverse forms as the Catholic Gunpowder Plot to blow up Parliament and the departure of many Puritans to look for a new and better life in America. These differences spilled over into other areas, notably literature and the world of ideas. On one side there was the metaphysics of the poet John Donne and on the other the austere majesty of Milton and the plainer allegory of Bunyan. The world was viewed in different lights, colored by the philosophical thoughts of Thomas Hobbes and the scientific discoveries of Isaac Newton. In architecture, there were new themes to explore in the styles of the Baroque and the Classical. Christopher Wren, the master of the Baroque, set his mark on London following the Great Fire, while Inigo Jones produced such formal masterpieces as Somerset House in London. The outstanding composer of the age was Henry Purcell.

- **1603**: James VI of Scotland becomes James I of England and Wales.
- **1605**: The Gunpowder Plot.
- **1611**: Authorized Version of the Bible published.
- **1616**: Death of Shakespeare.
- **1620**: Pilgrims set sail from Plymouth.
- **1625**: Accession of Charles I.
- **1642**: Civil War begins.
- **1649**: Execution of Charles I.
- **1651**: Thomas Hobbes, in *Leviathan,* develops a pessimistic rationalism.
- **1653**: Oliver Cromwell becomes lord protector.
- **1660**: Charles II restored.
- **1666**: Great Fire of London.
- **1667**: Publication of *Paradise Lost*.
- **1685**: Accession of James II; Edict of Nantes revoked; thousands of French Protestants arrive in England.
- **1687**: Publication of Newton's *Principia Mathematica*.
- **1688**: Accession of William of Orange and Mary.
- **1690**: John Locke completes his *Essay Concerning Human Understanding*.

The 18th Century

The period tends to be associated with the term "Georgian," for George I came to the throne in 1714 and George III was still alive when the century ended. Britain did not experience the political revolutions that convulsed Continental Europe, yet there were profound changes. Britain lost one colony in the American Revolution, but at the same time a new empire was being built in India. This age presented two faces to the world. One showed an urbane, cleanly classical aspect, epitomized in the architecture of Bath; the other was a dirtier, rougher visage, representing the new and exciting age of industrial development. These divisions were fundamental. On the one hand were the arts, notably architecture, in which a severe Classicism ruled, where a dining room by Robert Adam would be furnished by Sheraton or Chippendale and the food would be eaten off plates by Wedgwood, possibly to the accompaniment of music by the fashionable composer of the day, Handel. The other side appeared in the rush toward industrialization—canal building, the construction of the first factories, and the appearance of the steam engine. Literature showed an equally lively sense of innovation: The novel was born with the work of Richardson, Fielding, and Sterne, while others, led by the poets Blake and Wordsworth, turned away from the aggressive industrial world. This was also a period when changes in agriculture produced the pattern of neat fields and farms that now seem typical of the attractive British landscape.

- **1702**: Accession of Queen Anne.
- **1712**: Thomas Newcomen builds a steam engine at Dudley.
- **1714**: Accession of George I.
- **1726**: *Gulliver's Travels* published.
- **1727**: Accession of George II.
- **1735**: William Hogarth's *The Rake's Progress.*
- **1738**: John Wesley founds Methodism.
- **1740**: David Hume finishes *A Treatise of Human Nature.*
- **1745**: Bonnie Prince Charlie leads unsuccessful Jacobite Rebellion.
- **1760**: Accession of George III; construction of Britain's first true canal.
- **1771**: First powered cotton mill opens.
- **1773**: The Boston Tea Party.
- **1776**: American Declaration of Independence.
- **1776**: Adam Smith's *An Inquiry into the Nature and Causes of the Wealth of Nations* published.
- **1779**: Completion of the world's first iron bridge.
- **1789**: Start of the French Revolution.
- **1791**: Thomas Paine's *Rights of Man.*

The 19th Century

The 19th century can be split into two periods: the Georgian age shading off into the Regency, and the Victorian age. In terms of the arts the distinction has some validity, but as regards the development of society as a whole, there is no such division. The new world of industry and trade went on expanding: Factories continued developing, the steam engine appeared on rails as a steam locomotive, and a new generation of industrial cities grew up. But while engineers such as Isambard Brunel looked for new forms for their bridges, ships, and railway stations, architects increasingly turned back to the older styles of the Gothic for churches, town halls, and mansions. In the arts, the Romantic movement that had begun with Wordsworth and his contemporaries was extended by artists such as Turner, the poets Keats and Shelley, and such novelists as the Brontë sisters. Increasingly, however, there was a growing concern with social questions, and changes can be seen most clearly in the novel. At the beginning of the century, Jane Austen conducted her minute dissections of an enclosed society, and at the end Charles Dickens created his loud, teeming world.

- **1804**: The first steam locomotive runs on rails.
- **1805**: Battle of Trafalgar.
- **1815**: Battle of Waterloo.
- **1820**: Accession of George IV.
- **1832**: The Great Reform Bill extends the franchise.
- **1836**: Dickens's *Pickwick Papers*.
- **1837**: Accession of Queen Victoria.
- **1838**: First steamship crosses the Atlantic.
- **1851**: The Great Exhibition.
- **1854**: Start of the Crimean War.
- **1859**: Charles Darwin's *Origin of Species*.
- **1869**: Opening of the Suez Canal.
- **1876**: Victoria declared empress of India.
- **1880**: Start of the Boer Wars.

The 20th Century

In the 19th century Britain was one of the great powers of the world, with a huge empire and a manufacturing industry that earned it the title "workshop of the world." That structure has slipped and crumbled in the 20th century. One by one, the old colonies have achieved independence, and industrial innovation has largely become the provenance of other countries. Britain has been a participant, rather than an innovator, in the major developments of the age—the motor car, the airplane, and the computer. The process has been accelerated by two world wars, and the bombings of the second necessitated major rebuilding in many towns and cities. The confidence that produced the Gothic extravaganzas of the Victorian age has evaporated, however, so that there has been little new architectural development to warrant more than modest praise. In the arts, literature has continued to be the most innovative and successful medium, though music, not historically one of Britain's stronger arts, has thrived, covering a wide range from Benjamin Britten to the most successful of popular musicians, the Beatles. Much of the character of modern Britain derives from a long history; it remains to be seen whether that character will be preserved, adapted, or simply lost.

- **1901**: Death of Victoria, accession of Edward VII.
- **1910**: Accession of George V.
- **1914–1918**: World War I.
- **1918**: Women win the vote.
- **1922**: Formation of the BBC.
- **1924**: First Labour government.
- **1936**: Death of George V, abdication of Edward VIII, and accession of George VI.
- **1939–1945**: World War II.
- **1947**: India given independence.
- **1952**: Accession of Elizabeth II.
- **1973**: Britain enters the European Economic Community.
- **1979**: Margaret Thatcher is the first woman to become prime minister.
- **1982**: War in the Falklands.
- **1990**: John Major replaces Margaret Thatcher as prime minister.

—Anthony Burton

INDEX

Abbey Church (Shrewsbury), 519

Abbey Church Yard (Bath), 287

Abbey Court, 138

Abbeydale Industrial Hamlet, 624

Abbey Dore Court Garden, 508

Abbey Fields, 494

Abbey Green, 528

Abbot Hall, 575

Abbotsbury, 268

Abbots Morton, 484

Abinger Hammer, 245

Ackermann & Johnson, 177

Acton Scott Historic Working Farm, 524

Adam and Eve, 424

Admiral Benbow Coffee Tavern, 359

Agglestone, 266

Agincourt Square, 511

Aira Force, 583

Airey & Wheeler, 176

Ajimura, 53

Alandale Hotel, 298, 321

Alastair Little's, 152

Albion Hotel, 260, 272

Aldeburgh, 407

Aldeburgh Festival, 407

Alexander House, 239, 249

Alexandra Hotel, 271, 272

Al Hamra, 149

All England Club, 89

All Saints' Church: Babworth, 462; Evesham, 486; Newland, 512

Al Maroush, 149

Al Maroush II, 149

Al Maroush III, 149

Almonry Museum, 486

Alnwick Castle, 570

Alresford, 318

Al-Shami, 197

Althorp House, 436

Alverton Manor Hotel, 362, 370

Amberley Castle, 249

Ambleside, 580

American Bar, 128

Anchor Inn: Hartfield, 240; London, 169

Ancient Gate House Hotel, 301, 321

Anemos, 150

The Angel, 119

Angel Arcade, 107

Angel Hotel, 397, 428

Angel Inn, 490, 530

Angel and Royal Hotel, 455, 474

Anglesey, 610

Animal Gardens, Lincolnshire, 460

Annabel's, 166

Anne Hathaway's Cottage, 484

Ann's—The Lizard Pasty Shop, 359

Antiquarius Antique Market, 83, 182

Antique and General Trading Centre, 311

Anything Lefthanded, 179

Apsley House Hotel, 292, 321

Aquarium, 216

Aquascutum, 174

Archaeological Resource Centre, 539

Arkle Restaurant, 528

Arkwright Mill, 469

Arlington Court, 330

Arlington Row, 283
Arrow Mill, 484, 530
Arundel, 218, 248
Arundel Castle, 248
Arundell Arms Hotel, 339, 370
Ashby Narrow Boat Company, 441
Ashdown Forest, 239
Ashford, 231
Ashford Post House, 231, 249
Ashleigh House, 494, 530
Ashmolean Museum, 195
Aspinall's, 168
Asprey, 177
Assembly House, 420
Assembly Rooms, 495
Assize Court, 542
Aston Cantlow, 484
Astor House Hotel, 134
Astoria Theatre, 167
Attingham Park, 520
Auberge de Provence, 145
Austin Reed, 174
Avebury Stone Circle, 319
Avis, 125
Avon Bank Park, 482
Avoncroft Museum of Buildings, 502
Axe Edge, 470

Babworth, 462
The Backs, 200
Baddesley Clinton Hall, 495
Badgers Holt Café, 340
Bahn Thai, 148
Baile Hill, 541
Baker Street, 95
Bala, 602
Bala Lake, 602
Bamburgh, 572
Bamburgh Castle, 572
Banbury Bridge, 493
Banqueting House, 74
Barbara Hepworth Museum and Sculpture Garden, 355
Barbarella 2, 168
Barbican, 346
Barbican Arts Centre, 43, 165
Barnard Castle, 562
Barnsdale Lodge, 445, 474

Barnstaple, 332
Baron of Beef, 202
Bar of the Sparrow's Nest Theatre, 417
Basil Street Hotel, 134
Bass Clef, 165
Bassenthwaite Lake, 582
Bass Museum, 633
Batemans, 242
Bath, 286, 288 (map)
Bath Spa Hotel, 291, 321
Batsford Arboretum, 283
Battle of Britain Memorial Flight, 462
Battlefield Line Steam Railway, 441
Bayswater, 94 (map)
Bay Tree Hotel, 281, 321
Beach's Bookshop, 311
Beales, 265
Beamish, 622
Bear Hotel: Crickhowell, 615, 617; Woodstock, 285, 321
Bear Steps, 519
Beauchamp Chapel, 490
Beauchamp Place, 80, 181
Beaufort, 134
Beaulieu Abbey, 261
Beaumaris Castle, 610
Beccles, 414
Beccles and District Museum, 415
Beckett's Park, 435
Bedford Square, 57
Bedruthan Steps, 354
Beefeaters, 39
Bekynton House, 301, 321
Belgravia, 80
Bell Foundry Museum, 440
Bell Hotel, 502, 530
Bell Inn, 243, 250
Bell's Castle, 489
Belmont House Hotel, 440, 474
Belton House, 455
Belvoir Castle, 456
Bennett's Cashmere House, 179
Bentinck Dock, 427
Bentleys, 347
Beotys, 150
Berkeley, 135

Berners Park Plaza Hotel, 128
Berwick-upon-Tweed, 588
Besom Barn, 570
Bethnal Green Museum of Childhood, 116
Betty's Café, 546
Betws-y-Coed, 602
Bibendum, 152, 181
Bideford, 333
Big Pit, 622
Binns, 229
Birche Hotel, 500, 530
Bishop's Palace, 300
Bistro Carapace, 145
Black Country Museum, 628
Blackfriars' Hall, 422
Blackfriars Monastery, 567
Black Lion Hotel and Countrymen Restaurant, 388, 428
Blackpool, 574
Black Swan Hotel (Helmsley), 555, 592
Black Swan Inn (York), 542
Black Swan Pub (Stratford), 483
Blaenau Ffestiniog, 604, 632
Blaenavon, 622
Blanchards, 317
Bleak House, 237
Blenheim Palace, 285
Blists Hill Open Air Museum, 521, 623
Bloom's, 116, 149
Bloomsbury, 53
Bloomsbury Rare Books, 178
Blossoms Hotel, 528, 530
Blue Anchor, 89
Blue Boar Inn, 485
Blue Elephant: Leicester, 439; London, 148
Blue John Cavern, 468
Blueprint Café, 118
Blunderbuss, 95, 173
Blythburgh, 410
The Boat House, 614
Boat Inn: Redbrook, 512; Stoke Bruerne, 435
Boat Museum, 627
Bodleian Library, 193
Bodmin Moor, 348
Bodysgallen Hall, 600, 617

Bolebroke Mill, 240, 250
Bolton Castle, 561
Bombay Brasserie, 147
Bond Street, 64
Bonham's, 177
Bookbinders Arms, 196
Boot and Flogger, 160
Bootham Bar, 543
Bootham Tea Room, 543
Border Country, 585, 586 (map)
Border Forest Park, 588
Borovicks, 178
Boscastle, 352
Boscobel House, 522
Bosham, 255
Boston, 464
Boston Guildhall, 466
Bosworth Battlefield Visitor Centre and Country Park, 440
Bottlescrue, 159
Boulestin, 53
Boulevard Restaurant, 344
Boultons Country House Hotel, 445, 474
Bournemouth, 263
Bourton-on-the-Water, 281
Bowes Museum, 562
Boxford, 391
Box House, 293
Box Tree Restaurant, 483
Bradford, 560
Bradford-on-Avon, 303
Brahms and Liszt, 160
Brantwood, 580
Brasserie: Chester, 528; London, 101
Brass Rubbing Center, 330
Brecon, 615
Brecon Beacons National Park, 614
Brecon Castle, 615
Bredon, 489
Bredon Hill, 488
Bredwardine Hall, 509, 530
Brentor, 340
Brethren's Kitchen, 492
Brewhouse Yard, 450
Bridewell Museum, 421
Bridge of Sighs, 200
Bridgnorth, 523

Bridport, 270

Brighton, 213

Brighton International Festival, 217

Brighton Metropole, 217, 219

Brighton Square, 215

Brinkburn Priory, 569

Bristol, 293

Bristol Cathedral, 297

Bristol Hilton Hotel, 298, 321

Bristol Holiday Inn Crown Plaza, 298, 321

British Casino Association, 168

British Home Stores, 173

British Museum, 53

British Travel Centre, 122, 123

Briton's Arms, 421

Broadlands, 258

Broadstairs, 236

Broad Street: Bristol, 296; Hereford, 505; Ludlow, 525; Oxford, 194

Broadway, 282

Broadway Hill, 283

Brownes Restaurant (Bungay), 414

Browns Boutique, 172

Brown's Brasserie, 258

Brownsea Island, 265

Brown's Hotel, 66, 129, 161

Brown's Pie Shop, 459

Brown's Restaurant: Cambridge, 206; Oxford, 197; Worcester, 500

Brunel's Tunnel House Hotel, 298, 321

Bryher Island, 366

Bryn Howel Hotel, 603, 617

Buckerell Lodge Hotel and Restaurant, 337, 370

Buckfast Abbey, 340

Buckingham Palace, 67

Buckland Abbey, 345

Buckland Manor, 282, 321

Buckland-in-the-Moor, 340

Bucklers Hard, 261

Budget, 125

Budleigh Salterton, 342

Budock Vean Golf and Country House Hotel, 361, 370

Buildwas Abbey, 522

Bull and Bush Tavern, 100

Bull Hotel: Burford, 281, 321; Long Melford, 388, 428; Woodbridge, 401, 428

Bull's Head, 89, 165

Bungay, 412

Bungay Museum, 414

Burberry's, 174

Burford, 281

Burgage Manor, 454

Burgh Island Hotel, 345, 370

Burghley House, 444

The Burlington, 347

Burlington Arcade, 64, 176

Burwash, 242

Bury St. Edmunds, 395

The Bush, 163

Butcher's Arms, 508, 530

Butler's Wharf, 117

Butler & Wilson, 173

Butley Orford Oysterage, 402

Butter Cross, 414

Buttermere, 581

Buxton, 470

Cabinet War Rooms, 74

Cabot Place, 119

Cabot Tower, 295

Cadence Café and Cycle Hire, 500

Cadogan Arms, 159

Cadwallader's Coffee Shop, 296

Caernarfon, 607

Caernarfon Castle, 607

Caesar's Restaurant, 604

Café Delancey, 101

Café du Jardin, 153

Café du Marché, 111

Café Pacifico, 53

Café de París, 166

Calabash, 53

Calverley Park, 229

Cambridge, 197, 198 (map)

Camden Lock, 184

Camden Lock's Weekend Market, 101

Camden Palace, 101

Camden Passage, 107, 184

Camden Town, 98 (map), 100

Camilla Hotel, 358, 371
Canal Museum: Nottingham, 451; Stoke Bruerne, 435
Canary Wharf, 119
Canterbury, 231
Canterbury Exhibitions, 232
Canterbury Heritage, 233
Capital Hotel, 135
Le Caprice, 144, 154
Cardiff, 615
Cardiff Castle, 616
Carfax Tower, 188
Carisbrooke Castle, 259
Carlisle, 585
Carlisle Cathedral, 585
Carlton Hotel, 264, 272
Carlyon Bay Hotel, 365, 371
Carn Euny, 349
Carriage House, 471
Carved Angel, 344
Casper's Restaurant, 144
Casterbridge Hotel, 270, 272
Castle of Brecon Hotel, 615, 617
Castle Drogo, 338
Castle Green, 503
Castle Hall, 315
Castle House, 528, 530
Castle Howard, 548
Castle Inn, 263
Castle Museum (York), 542
The Castle Restaurant, 212
Castle View Hotel, 515
Catamaran Cruises, 169
Cathedral Church of the Most Holy and Undivided Trinity, 423
Cathedral Church of St. James, 396
The Causerie, 151, 154
Cavendish Hotel, 471, 474
Celtic Manor, 616, 617
Central London, 41, 54 (map)
Central Museum and Art Gallery, 434
Chained Library, 505
Chalk Farm, 102
Chambercombe Manor, 331
Chandos, 155
Changing of the Guard, 70

Chapel of the Charnel, 396
Chapel of the Order of the Garter, 209
Chappells, 177
Chapter House: Lincoln, 458; York, 544
Charing Cross Road, 58
Charingworth Manor, 282, 321
Charlecote Park, 484
Charleston, 240
Charlotte's Tea Rooms, 494
Charterhouse, 107
Chart Room, 355
Chartwell Manor, 225
Chatham Historic Dockyard, 234
Chatsworth House, 470
Chawton, 247
Cheddar Gorge, 302
Chedworth Roman Villa, 280
Chelsea, 81
Chelsea Bun Diner, 83
Chelsea Harbour, 91
Chelsea Physic Garden, 83
Chelsea Potter, 159
Chelsea Room, 146
Cheltenham, 280
Chepstow, 514
Chepstow Castle, 515
Cherrybrook Hotel, 341, 371
Chesil Beach, 268
Chester, 526
Chester Cathedral, 528
Chesterfield, 130
Chester Grosvenor Hotel, 528, 530
Chester Heritage Centre, 528
Chesters Fort, 590
Chester Visitor Centre, 528
Chewton Glen, 261, 272
Chez Fred, 265
Chez Nico, 145
Chiang Mai, 148
Chichester, 255
Chichester Cathedral, 255
Chichester Harbour, 255
Chilham, 231
Chiltern Street, 96, 173
Chinatown, 60
Chinehead, 264, 272

Chipping Camden, 281

Christchurch, 263

Christ Church, 115

Christ Church College, 189

Christchurch Mansion, 394

Christie's, 177

Christopher, 212

Christopher's—The American Grill, 150

Christopher Wray's, 82, 182

Chuen Cheng Ku, 148

Church of the Holy Trinity: Blythburgh, 410; Bungay, 413

Churchill's, 167

Church of St. Laurence (Ludlow), 525

Church of St. Lawrence (Evesham), 486

Church of St. Margaret, 232

Church of St. Mary Magdalene, 523

Church of St. Mary-the-Virgin, 193

Church of St. Michael the Archangel, 406

Church of St. Michael's, 501

Church of St. Peter Mancroft, 419

Church of Sts. Peter and Paul, 389

Church's Shoes, 176

Chysauster, 349

Cibo, 151

Cider Museum, 506

Cider Press, 508

Circus, 287

The City, 42, 44 (map)

City Art Gallery (York), 546

City Museum and Art Gallery: Bristol, 297; Worcester, 500

Clare House, 362, 371

Claridge's, 130

Clarke's, 152

Claverton Manor, 291

Clearwell Castle, 513, 531

Clearwell Caves, 513

Cleeve Hill, 283

Clerkenwell, 107

Cleveland Way, 557

Clifford's, 541

Clifford's Tower, 541

Clifton, 295

Clifton Restaurant, 116

Clifton Suspension Bridge, 295

Clink Museum, 41

Clive House Museum, 519

Cloisters Restaurant, 337

Clovelly, 333

Clubman's Club, 168

Clumber Park, 452

Coalbrookdale Furnace and Museum of Iron, 521, 623

Coalport China Works Museum, 521, 624

Cobham, 235

Cobham Hall, 235

Le Cochonnet, 161

Cock Tavern, 158

Coffee Yard, 545

Colette's by the Riverside, 482

Colin's, 509

College of Matrons, 309

College of Vicars' Choral, 505

Colne Valley Museum, 624

Colwyn Bay, 599

Commandery, 499

Commodore Hotel, 332, 371

Compton Acres, 266

Coningsby Airfield, 461

Coniston Water, 579

Connaught Grill, 131

Connaught Hotel, 131, 143, 161

Conran, 181

Conwy Castle, 606

Cooling, 236

Copthorne Hotel, 347, 371

Copthorne Newcastle, 568, 592

Corfe Castle, 266

Cork and Bottle, 160

Corner Cupboard Dining Room, 283

Corn Exchange, 437

Cornhouse Restaurant and Wine Bar, 520

Cornwall, 347, 350 (map)

Corpus Christi College, 192

Corse Lawn House Hotel, 503, 531

Corstopitum, 591

Costa Dorada, 168
Cotehele, 628
Cotswold House Hotel and Restaurant, 281, 321
Cotswolds, 275, 278 (map)
Cotswold Way, 283
Cottage Tea Garden, 484
Cott Inn, 343, 371
Coughton Court, 485
Country Friends, 520
County Hotel, 233, 250
County Thistle Hotel, 568, 592
Courtauld Institute Galleries, 47
Courtfield Private Hotel, 197, 219
Covent Garden, 51
Coverdale Private Hotel, 496, 531
Cowes, 260
Cox of Northampton, 546
Crabtree & Evelyn, 175
Cragside, 569
Cranley Gardens Hotel, 135
Craster, 571
Criccieth Castle, 608
Crockford's, 168
Croft Ambrey, 507
Croft Castle, 507
Croft Country Guest House, 508, 531
La Croisette, 146
Cromford, 625
Croque-en-Bouche, 502
Cross Guns, 303
Cross Keys, 407
Cross Keys Chequer, 308
Crown Hotel: Framlingham, 405, 428; Lyndhurst, 262, 272; Southwold, 412, 428; Wells, 301, 321
Crown Inn: London, 158; Long Melford, 389
Crown Jewels, 39
Croyde, 332
Crummock Water, 581
Crust, 265
Crystal Palace, 292
Custom House (Lancaster), 575
Customs House (King's Lynn), 425

Dales Way, 560
Daniel's Mill, 523
D'Arcy's, 217
Dartmoor National Park, 339
Dartmoor Prison, 340
Dartmouth, 344
Dart Valley Steam Railway, 341
David Leach, 342
Dawlish, 343
D-Day Museum, 256
Deals, 91
Dean Court Hotel, 547, 548
Deanery Gardens, 543
Dean Heritage Centre, 513
Delmere Hotel, 131
Dere Street, 591
Derwentwater, 582
Derwentwater Hotel, 582, 592
Design Center, 171
Designers Sale Studio, 182
Design Museum, 118
Devil's Punch Bowl, 245
Devon, 325, 328 (map)
Devon Motel, 338, 371
Devonshire Craft Center, 334
Dickens Centre, 235
Dickens House Museum, 56
The Dickens Inn by the Tower, 117, 169
Dillons, 58, 178
Dinham Hall Hotel, 526, 531
Director's Lodge, 167
Dirty Dick's, 115
D'Isney Place Hotel, 459, 474
Disney Store, 174
Dobwalls Family Adventure Park, 364
Docklands, 112 (map), 116
The Docklands Light Railway Route, 118
Dr. Johnson's House, 47
Dog & Duck, 156
Dolaucothi Gold Mine, 622
Doll's House Toys Ltd., 180
Dolphin & Anchor, 256, 273
Dolphin Hotel, 259, 272
Dolphin Square, 140
Dolphin's Restaurant, 258
Dolphin Tavern, 359
Dolwyddelan Castle, 609

Dome Café, 96
Dome Theater, 215
The Dôme Wine Bar, 110
Donald Butler, 546
Dorchester, 269
Dormy House Hotel, 282, 321
Dorset, 252, 263
Dorset Coast Path, 267
Dorset Square Hotel, 128
The Dove, 89
Dove Cottage, 580
Dove Inn, 169
Dover, 238
Dover Castle, 157
Dover Street Wine Bar, 165
Dragon Hall, 425
Draycott House, 140
Drewsteignton, 340
Drill Hall, 164
Drury Lane Theatre, 162
Dublin Castle, 101
Duchy Restaurant, 361
Dudley, 628
Dudmaston Hall, 523
Duke of Edinburgh's Royal Regiment Museum, 309
Duke's Head Hotel, 427, 428
Dukes Hotel: London, 131; Stratford-upon-Avon, 483, 531
Duncombe Park, 555
Dunhill, 176
Dunstanburgh Castle, 571
Dunster, 327
Dunwich, 409
Durham Castle, 564
Durham Cathedral, 563
Durham City, 563
Durham County, 561
Durley House, 140
Durrant's, 161
Dyson Perrins Museum, 499

The Eagle, 206
East Anglia, 16, 375, 376 (map)
East Bergholt, 383
East End, 111, 112 (map)
Eastgate Clock, 528
Eastnor Castle, 501
Eastwell Manor, 230, 250
Eaton Garden Restaurant, 217

Ebford House Hotel, 338, 371
Eboracum, 535
Ebury Wine Bar, 81
Eccleston Hotel, 132
Eclipse, 317
Ed's Easy Diner, 150
Edward's Café, 280
Efes II, 162
Effingham Park Hotel, 239, 250
Egleton Reserve, 443
Eight Bells Inn, 393
Eleanor Cross, 432
Electric Ballroom, 101
Eleven Cadogan Gardens, 135
Elgar Birthplace Museum, 501
Elgar Trail, 501
Elgin Marbles, 56
Elizabeth Hotel, 132
Ellesmere Port, 627
Elm Hill, 421
Embleton Hall, 569, 592
Empire Ballroom, 166
Emporio Armani Express, 144
English Garden, 142
English House, 142
English National Opera, 165
English's, 217
Eoforwic, 538
Episode, 181
L'Escargot, 143
Eton, 211
Ettington Park Hotel, 483, 531
Europ Car InterRent, 125
Euston Plaza Hotel, 128
Evan Evans, 126
Evesham, 486
Evesham Hotel, 489, 531
Exeter, 335
Exeter Cathedral, 335
Exeter Maritime Museum, 336
Exhibition Road, 83
Exmoor Bird Gardens, 330
Exmoor National Park, 330
Exmouth, 342

Fairfield Manor, 547, 548
Fairy Glen Hotel, 602, 617
Falmouth, 360
Falmouth Beach Hotel, 361, 371
Falstaff Hotel, 233, 250

Farndale, 557
Farne Islands, 572
Farnham, 247
Farringford, 260, 273
Fatty Arbuckle's, 483
Faversham, 236
Feathers Hotel: Ledbury, 502, 531; Ludlow, 526, 531; Woodstock, 285, 322
Fenny Bentley, 469
Fenton House, 100
Fenwicks, 177
Ffestiniog Railway, 604, 632
Fields, 154
Finches Arms, 445, 474
Fishergate Bar, 542
Fitzbillies, 205
Fitzroy Square, 57
Fitzwilliam Museum, 205
"Five Sisters" Window, 544
The Flask, 97
Flatford Mill, 384
Fleece Inn, 489
Fleet Street, 46
Floating Harbour, 293
Floris, 176
Folkestone, 238
Folly Farm Cottage, 483, 531
Ford Farm House, 344, 371
Forest of Bowland, 574
Forest of Dean, 512
Forte Crest Hotel, 318, 322
Forte Posthouse Hotel, 347, 371
Fortnum & Mason, 64, 175
47 Park Street, 140
Foundations Museum, 544
Fountain House, 383
Fountains Abbey, 561
Four Seasons, 147
Fownes Resort Hotel, 500, 531
Fox & Anchor, 158
Foxton Locks, 441
Foyles, 178
Frames Rickards, 126
Framlingham, 405
Francis Hotel, 292, 322
French House, 60, 156
Frensham Pond Hotel, 245, 250
Freud's, 162
Friars Restaurant, 387

Fron Feuno Hall, 602, 617
Fung Shing, 148
Fydell House, 465
Fylingdales Moor, 556

Gad's Hill Place, 235
Gainsborough Old Hall, 463
Gainsborough's House, 386
Gales, 604, 617
Garden Court Hotel, 138
Garden House Hotel, 205, 219
Garlands, 292
Garrard, 174
Garrick Inn, 480
Garter Inn, 208
Gaslight Club, 167
Gate Diner, 91
Gate Theater, 164
Gatwick, 122
Le Gavroche, 140, 145
Gee's Brasserie, 197
Geffrye Museum, 116
Geological Museum, 84
George Hotel, 244, 250
George Inn, 169
George and Pilgrims Hotel, 302, 322
George Pub: Clearwell, 513; London, 46
George Rafters, 495
George Tavern (Portsmouth), 257
Georgian House, 297
Gerrard Street, 60
Gibraltar Point National Nature Reserve, 461
Gilberts, 317
Gino's Spaghetti House, 359
Gladstone Pottery Museum, 633
Glance Back Books, 515
Glastonbury, 301
Glastonbury Tor, 302
Glendurgan, 361
Glewstone Court, 508, 531
Globe Theatre, 42
Gloddfa Ganol Slate Mine, 604, 633
Gloucester Hotel, 267
Glyndebourne Manor, 241
Golden Cross, 485

Golden Valley Thistle Hotel, 284, 322

Goldmark Gallery and Bookshop, 443

Gonville and Caius College, 203

Good Life, 520

Goodrich Castle, 510

Goonhilly Downs, 360

Goonhilly Earth Station, 360

Gore Hotel, 135

Goring Hotel, 133

Gossips, 166

Gower Peninsula, 598

Graham and Jo Webb, 215

Grammar School, 480

The Granary, 509

Le Grandgousier, 217

Grand Hotel: Brighton, 218, 219; Bristol, 298, 322; Plymouth, 347, 371

Grandma Batty's Yorkshire Pudding Emporium, 546

The Grange, 242

Grange Hotel, 547, 548

Grantham, 455

Grantham Museum, 455

The Grapes, 119

Grapevine Hotel, 281, 322

Grasmere, 580

Gravetye Manor, 239, 250

Gray's Antique Market, 173

Gray's Inn, 49

Great Castle House, 511

Great Comberton, 489

Great Court, 203

Great Dining Room, 471

Great Hall, 229

Great Hospital, 424

Great Malvern, 501

Great Orme Mines, 622

Great St. Mary's Church, 204

Great Tew, 277

Great Torrington, 334

Great White Horse Hotel, 395, 429

Grecian Taverna & Grill, 168

Greenbank Hotel, 361, 371

Green Dragon Hotel, 505, 531

Green Lawns Hotel, 361, 371

Green Line, 126

Green Man & French Horn, 156

Green Park, 71

Green's, 154

Greenwich, 120, 184

Greyfriars, 499

Greyhound Inn, 390

Grill St. Quentin, 146

Grosvenor Museum, 528

Groton, 391

Gugh Island, 366

The Guildhall: Bury St. Edmonds, 398; Hadleigh, 392; King's Lynn, 426; Lavenham, 389; Leicester, 438; Northampton, 434; Norwich, 419; Windsor, 208

Guy's Cliffe, 493

Habitat, 178

Hackett, 180

Haddon Hall, 471

Hadleigh, 392

The Hadrian, 551

Hadrian's Wall, 589

Hailes Abbey, 283

Halcyon Hotel, 138

Half Moon Inn, 333, 371

Halidon Hill, 589

Halkin Arcade, 80

Hall's Croft, 480

Hambleton Hall, 445, 474

Hamleys, 174

Hammersmith Palais, 166

Hammersmith Terrace, 89

Hampshire, 245, 246 (map), 252

Hampstead, 96, 98 (map)

Hampstead Heath, 96

Hampton Court, 89

Hampton Lucy, 485

Hannington's, 215

Hard Rock Café, 150

Hardwicks, 526

Hare and Hounds, 383

Harlech Castle, 605

Harper's, 311

Harrietsham, 230

Harrods, 77, 180

The Harrow, 230, 250

Harvard House, 480

Harvey Nichols, 77, 180

Harvey's, 152

Harvey's Cathedral Restaurant, 459

Harvey's Wine Museum, 297

Hatchard's, 176

Hathersage, 468

Hatton Court Hotel, 284, 322

Haunch of Venison, 310

Hawkshead, 578

Haworth, 560

Hay's Galleria, 41

Hay Wholefoods and Delicatessen, 509

Hay-on-Wye, 509

Headland Hotel, 354, 371

Heart of England, 476, 478 (map)

Heathrow, 122

Helen Hotel, 206, 219

Hellens, 501

Helmingham, 404

Helmingham Hall, 405

Helmshore Textile Museums, 625

Helmsley, 555

Helston, 359

Henderson's, 335

Henry J. Bean's, 159

Hereford, 503

Hereford Cathedral, 505

Herefordshire, 503, 504 (map)

Herefordshire Waterworks Museum, 506

Heritage Museum (Charlestown), 364

Her Majesty's Dockyard, 256

Hertz, 125

Hever Castle, 226

Hidcote Manor Garden, 283

High Force, 563

Highgate, 100

Highgate Cemetery, 100

Hill Court Gardens and Garden Centre, 507

Hillcrest Hotel, 459, 474

Hill Top Farm, 578

Hilton National: Bath, 291, 322; Southampton, 258, 273

Hintlesham Hall, 393, 429

Hippodrome, 166

HMV, 172

Hobbs Pavilion, 206

Hodsons Coffee House, 500

Hog's Back, 245

Holburne of Menstrie Museum of Art, 291

Holdfast Cottage Hotel, 502, 531

Holiday Inn: Leicester, 440, 474; York, 541, 549

Holiday Inn Garden Court (Nottingham), 452, 474

Holland Park, 91, 92 (map)

Holland Park Hotel, 138

Holne Chase Hotel and Restaurant, 341, 371

Holy Cross, 488

Holy Island, 572

Holy Trinity Church: Stratford-upon-Avon, 480; Tattershall, 461; York, 541

Holywell Music Room, 195

Hope End Hotel, 502, 532

Horn of Plenty, 340

Hornsea Pottery, 574

Horse Guards Parade, 74

Horsted Place, 241, 250

Hospitality Inn Brighton, 217, 219

Hospital of St. Cross, 316

L'Hotel, 136

Hotel Crichton, 128

Hotel George, 136

Hotel Maes-y-Neuadd, 606, 617

Hotel Saint James, 440, 474

House in the Clouds, 409

House of Commons, 75

Houses of Parliament, 74

Housesteads, 590

Howard Arms, 483

Howscales, 584, 592

Hugh Bigod's Castle, 413

Hugh Town Museum, 368

Hungerford, 318

Hungry Monk, 245

Huntsham Court Country House, 335, 371

Hussain's, 483

Hyde Park, 81

Hyde Park Hotel, 136
Hyper-Hyper, 183

Ian Hastie, 311
Ickworth, 398
Idle Rocks Hotel, 363, 372
Ikkyu, 149
Ilchester Arms, 268, 273
Ilfracombe, 331
Ilkley Moor, 560
L'Incontro, 151
The Incredibly Fantastic Old
    Toy Show, 459
Industrial Heritage, 619, 620
    (map)
Industrial Museum: Notting-
    ham, 451; Sheffield, 624
In the English Manner, 141
Inner Temple, 48
Inns of Court, 48
Institute of Contemporary Arts,
    71
International Musical
    Eisteddfod, 603
Ipswich, 393
Irish Linen Company, 176
Ironbridge Gorge, 521, 623
Island History Trust, 119
Island Hotel, 368, 372
Island House, 346
Isle of Dogs, 119
Isles of Scilly, 325, 365
Isle of Wight, 259
Islington, 106, 108 (map)

Jackfield Works and Tile Mu-
    seum, 521
Jack Straw's Castle, 100
Jamaica Inn, 352
James Lock & Company, 175
Jarrow, 567
Jason's Trip, 125
Jazz Café, 101
Jeake's House, 244, 250
Jephson Gardens, 495
Jermyn Street, 64
Jervaulx Abbey, 561
Jesse's Restaurant, 451
Jewish Museum, 56
Jewry Wall, 438

Jewry Wall Museum, 438
J. Floris, 175
Joe Allen's, 53, 150
Joe's Café, 144
John Lewis, 173
John Paul's, 494
Jolly Sailor, 402, 429
Jorvik, 538
Jorvik Viking Centre, 539
Jorvik Viking Festival, 547
Joseph Tricot, 181
Jubilee Maze, 510
Judge's Lodging, 546, 549
Julie's Wine Bar and Restaurant,
    91

Kalamaras, 150
Katharine Hamnett's, 181
Keats House, 100
Keep of Rochester Castle, 234
Kempley, 501
Kenilworth, 494
Kenilworth Castle, 494
Kensington, 78 (map)
Kensington Gardens, 81
Kensington High Street, 182
Kensington Place, 143
Kent, 220
Kent Battle of Britain Museum,
    238
Kentwell Hall, 387
Kenwood House, 97, 165
Kersey, 390
Keswick, 582
Kettle's Yard, 202
Kettners, 151
Kew Gardens, 88
Khan's, 91
Kielder Castle, 588
Killerton, 338
Killingholme Creek, 464
King Alfred's Kitchen, 270
King Charles's House, 499
Kings Arms Hotel (Dorchester),
    270, 273
Kings Arms Pub: Oxford, 194;
    Salisbury, 310; York, 545
King's College, 200, 204
King's College Chapel, 204
Kingsgate Street, 316

King's Head Hotel
  (Cirencester), 284, 322
King's Head Inn (Aston
  Cantlow), 484
King's Head Pub: Barnard Cas-
  tle, 562; London, 166
King's Head Restaurant (Or-
  ford), 403
King's Head Theater, 110, 163
King's Lynn, 425
King's Lynn Festival, 426
King's Parade, 204
King's Road, 82, 182
Kittiwell House Hotel and Res-
  taurant, 332, 372
Knightsbridge, 77, 78 (map)
Knightsbridge Hotel, 136
Knole, 227
Kutchinsky, 181
Kuti's, 258
Kyber, 91
Kymin Hill, 511

Lace Centre, 451
Lace Hall, 451
Lainston House Hotel, 318,
  322
Lake District, 550, 577 (map)
Lake Windermere, 578
Lal Qila, 147
Lambeth Palace, 76
Lamb & Flag, 157
Lamb House, 243
Lamb Pub (London), 157
The Lamb Restaurant (Burford),
  281
Lancaster, 574
Land's End, 356
Landsker Line, 612
The Lanes, 215
Lanesborough Hotel, 137
Langan's Brasserie, 143
Langford House Cottages, 277,
  322
Langtry Manor, 264, 273
Lanhydrock, 353
Lansdowne Hotel, 496, 532
Lanyon Quoit, 358
The Last Days of the Raj, 147
Launceston Place, 142

Laura Ashley: London, 174;
  York, 546
Lavenham, 389
Lawrence's Birthplace, 453
Leamington Spa Art Gallery and
  Museum, 495
Lear's Bookshop, 616
Leather Bottle Inn, 235
Ledbury, 501
Leeds Castle, 230
Leicester, 437
Leicester Castle, 438
Leicestershire, 433 (map), 436
Leicestershire Museum and Art
  Gallery, 439
Leicester Square, 58
Leith's, 91, 142
Lemonia, 102
Lensfield Hotel, 205, 219
Leominster, 507
Lewes, 240
Lewtrenchard Manor, 339, 372
Liberties Bar, 101
Liberty: London, 174; York, 546
Lillywhites, 175
Limelight, 166
Lincoln, 456
Lincoln Castle, 457
Lincoln Cathedral, 458
Lincoln County Gaol, 457
Lincolnshire, 448 (map), 454
Lincolnshire Aviation Heritage
  Centre, 462
Lincolnshire Wolds, 459
Lincoln's Inn, 49
Linden Hall Hotel, 570, 592
Lindisfarne, 573
Lindsay House, 142
Lion Hotel, 520, 532
Literary Southeast, 220, 222
  (map)
Little Angel Marionette Theatre,
  164
Little Chart, 231
Little Gallery, 546
Little Venice, 106
Lively Lady, 257
Liverpool, 629
Livingston's, 362
Lizard Peninsula, 359

Llanberis, 601
Llandudno, 600
Llangoed Hall, 615, 617
Llangollen, 603
Llechwedd Slate Caverns, 604
Loaves and Fishes, 416
London, 7, 29, 30 (map), 36 (map)
London Environs, 187 (map)
London–London Hotel, 131
London Palladium, 162
London Park Tower Casino, 168
London Pavilion, 65, 176
London and Provincial Antique Dealers Association, 182
London School of Economics, 48
London Tourist Board and Convention Bureau, 123
London Tourist Information Centre, 123
London Transport, 123, 124
London Transport Museum, 53
London Visitor Travelcard, 124
London Zoo, 102
Long Barn, 227
Longdale Rural Craft Centre, 452
Long Island Iced Tea Shop, 162
Longleat House, 306
Long Melford, 387
Long Melford Church, 387
Long Mynd, 524
Longstone Heritage Center, 368
Looe, 364
Loon Fung Supermarket, 179
Lord Leycester's Hospital, 492
Lord's Bistro, 483
Lord's Cricket Ground, 103
Lords of the Manor, 284, 322
Lost Street Museum, 507
Louis Pâtisserie, 96
Louth, 460
Louth Museum, 460
Lower Slaughter Manor, 284, 323
Lower Wye Valley Walk, 510
Lowestoft, 416
Low Wood Hotel, 579, 592
Ludlow, 525

Ludlow Castle, 525
Lugger Hotel, 363, 372
Lupton Tower, 575, 592
Lydford, 338
Lydford House Hotel, 339, 372
Lygon Arms, 282, 323
Lyme Regis, 271
Lymington, 261
Lyndhurst, 262
Lyndon Hill Reserve, 443
Lynmouth, 330
Lynton, 330
Lyric Studio, 163

Madame Jo Jo's, 168
Madame Tussaud's Waxworks Museum, 95
Madeley Court Hotel, 522, 532
Mad Meg's, 337
Magdalen College (Oxford), 193
Magdalene College (Cambridge), 201
Maggs, 67
Magna Carta, 56
Magno's, 153
Magpie & Stump, 158
Maid's Head Hotel, 422, 429
Maids of Honour Row, 86
Maids of Honour Tearoom, 86
Maison Bertaux, 60
Maison Sagne, 95, 173
Maison Talbooth, 382, 429
Major Oak, 452
The Mall, 107
Mallory Court, 496, 532
Malthouse, 522
Malvern Hills, 501
Mandeville Hotel, 129
Mangle's Pantry, 613
Man in the Moon, 83, 159, 163
Map House, 181
Maples and Heals, 177
Mappa Mundi, 505
Mappin & Webb, 181
Marble Arch, 63
La Marinade, 217
Los Marinos, 258
Maritime Heritage Centre, 294
Market Hall, 492

Market House, 501
Market Place: Norwich, 419; Wells, 299
Market Porter, 158
Market Square (Northampton), 434
Markham Arms, 83
Marks and Spencer, 172
Marlborough, 318
Marsham Court, 264, 273
Marylebone High Street, 95, 173
Marylebone Road, 95
Mary Rose, 256, 630
Mary's Tower, 585
Mason's Arms: Bury St. Edmonds, 397; Wilmcote, 484
Master Builder's House, 262, 273
Matlock, 472
Matlock Bath, 472
Maud Foster Windmill, 466
Mayfair, 66
Mayflower Steps, 346
Melford Hall, 387
Melton Mowbray, 441
Memories of China, 148
Memories of China Chelsea, 148
Merchant Adventurers' Hall, 543
Merchant Taylors' Hall, 543
Mermaid Inn, 244, 250
Merseyside Maritime Museum, 629
Merton Chapel, 192
Merton College, 192
Methuselah's, 160
Le Metro Bistro, 136
The Metro Pub, 161
Mevagissey, 364
Michaels Nook Country House Hotel, 581, 592
Micklegate Bar, 541
Micrarium, 470
Middle House Hotel, 243, 250
Middlesex Street, 184
Middle Temple, 48
Middlethorpe Hall, 546, 549
Midsummer House, 206

Mike Chambers Gallery, 461
Miller Howe, 579, 593
Mill Hotel, 387, 429
Mimmo d'Ischia, 80
Minogues, 110
Minster Library, 543
Mitre House, 311
Miyama, 148, 149
Mock Turtle Restaurant, 217
Mompesson House, 309
Monk Bar, 543
Monk's House, 241
Monmouth, 511
Mon Plaisir, 53
Mon Plaisir du Nord, 110
Montagu Arms, 261, 273
Monument, 46
Moonfleet Manor, 268, 273
The Moon & Sixpence, 292
Moot Hall: Aldeburgh, 407; Keswick, 583
Morgan's, 161
Mortimer's Fish Restaurant, 394
Mortimer's Hole, 447
Morwellham, 628
Mo's, 311
Mostyn Hotel, 129
Mottisfont Abbey, 314
Mousehole, 356
Moyses Hall, 398
Much Wenlock, 522
Munchy Munchy, 197
Museum of Costume: Bath, 290; Leicester, 438
Museum of Costume and Textile (Nottingham), 451
Museum of the History of Science, 195
Museum of the Household Cavalry, 209
Museum of Leathercraft, 434
Museum of Lincolnshire Life, 459
Museum of London, 42
Museum of Mankind, 64
Museum of Modern Art, 196
Museum of the Moving Image, 40
Museum of the River Visitor Centre, 521

Museum Store, 180
Museum Tavern, 157
Museum of Waterpower, 624
Myers of Keswick, 583
Mynd House Hotel, 524, 532
Mysteries, 180

Nash's House, 480
National Army Museum, 83
National Birds of Prey Centre, 507
National Car Parks, 125
National Gallery, 72
National Horseracing Museum, 399
National Maritime Museum, 121
National Motor Museum, 261
National Museum of Photography, Film, and Television, 560
National Portrait Gallery, 73
National Railway Museum, 540, 631
National Waterways Museum, 627
Natural History Museum, 84
Naturally British, 179
Nazrul, 116
Neal Street, 179
Neal's Yard, 179
The Needles, 259
Nelson Hotel, 425, 429
Nene Way, 435
Neptune's Statue, 293
Newark, 454
Newark Air Museum, 462
Newarke Houses Museum, 438
New Castle, 567
Newcastle Cathedral, 567
Newcastle-upon-Tyne, 565
New Delaney's, 520
New End, 164
Newent, 507
New Forest, 261
New Forest Pony Sales, 262
New Inn, 260
Newmarket, 398
New Place, 480
Newport, 260
Newquay, 354
New Row, 179

New Serpentine Restaurant, 143
Newstead Abbey, 453
New Walk, 439
New World, 148
Nicholas Everitt Park, 417
Nikki's, 439
Nine, The Square, 318
Noel Arms, 281, 323
Norfolk, 417
Norfolk Broads, 418
Norfolk Royale, 264, 273
Norfolk and Suffolk Aviation Museum, 414
Normanton Church, 442
Northampton, 432
Northamptonshire, 432, 433 (map)
North Beach, 417
North Coast, 566
Northcote Manor, 574, 593
North Country, 14, 550, 552 (map)
North Downs Way, 237
North Lakes Hotel, 584, 593
Northleigh House, 494, 532
Northumberland Coast, 569
Norwich, 418
Norwich Castle, 420
Norwich Cathedral, 422
Nottingham, 446
Nottingham Castle, 447
Nottinghamshire, 446, 448 (map)
Notting Hill, 90, 92 (map)
Novotel, 347, 372
Number 1 Royal Crescent, 290
Number Sixteen, 137
No. 3 Hotel and Restaurant, 302, 323
Nutshell, 397

Oakham, 443
Oakham Castle, 443
Oak Room, 147
Oare Church, 330
Observatory Restaurant, 357
Octagon Chapel, 425
Odette's, 102
Offa's Dyke Long-Distance Footpath, 511

Okehampton, 340
Oken's House, 492
Old Albion Inn, 354
Old Bailey, 50
Old Church Hotel, 584, 593
Old Coffee House, 156
Old Compton Street, 60
Old Courtyard, 522
Old Custom House Inn, 353, 372
Olde Cheshire Cheese, 160
Olde Wine Shades, 158, 160
Old Grammar School, 501
Old House, 506
Old Meeting House, 424
Old Parsonage Hotel, 197, 219
Old Red Lion, 163
Old Royal Observatory, 121
Old Sarum, 307
Old Ship Hotel, 217, 219
Old Stamp House, 580
Old Station Museum, 120
Old Success Inn, 357, 372
Old Vic, 162
Old Vicarage Hotel, 524, 532
Oldway Mansion, 343
Olive Branch, 526
100 Club, 165
One Ninety Queen's Gate, 136
192, 91
Open-Air Theatre, 162
Opera Terrace, 53
Orestone Manor House, 344, 372
Orford, 402
Orford Castle, 402
Oriel College, 192
Orso, 53, 151
Os Aquanos, 168
Osborne House, 259
Oscar's, 503
Ostrich Inn, 512, 532
The Other Place, 482
Otley, 403
Otley Hall, 404
Otley House, 404, 429
Ovations, 153
Overlord Embroidery, 257
Owlpen Manor, 277, 323
Oxenham Arms, 339, 372
Oxford, 186, 190 (map)

Oxford and Cambridge Boat Race, 87
Oxford Cathedral, 189
The Oxford Story, 196
Oxford Street, 62

Pack o' Cards, 330
Packwood House, 496
Padstow, 353
Palace House, 261
Palace Pier, 216
Palace of Westminster, 74
Palé Hall, 602, 618
Pall Mall, 72
Palm Court, 132
Pamela Teignmouth, 183
The Pandora, 362
Pantiles, 228
Paperchase, 178
Paradise House, 292, 323
Parish Church of St. Peter and St. Paul, 408
Park Hotel: Barnstaple, 333, 372; Cardiff, 616, 618
Park House Hotel, 522, 532
Park Street, 296
Parson's Folly, 489
Parva Farmhouse, 514, 532
Pâtisserie Valerie, 60, 179
Paulise de Bush Costume Collection, 338
Pavilion Hotel, 139
Paxton & Whitfield, 176
Peak Cavern, 468
Peak District, 466, 467 (map)
Peak District National Park, 466
Pearl Harbor, 258
Peckwater Quad, 192
Pedalaway, 508
Pelham Hotel, 137
Pembroke Lodge, 88
Pembrokeshire Coast National Park, 612
Pembrokeshire Coast Path, 612
Penally Abbey, 613, 618
Pencarrow, 353
Pendennis Castle, 361
Penhaligons, 176
Peninsula Barracks, 316
Penlan Oleu, 613, 618

Pennant Crafts, 602
Pennine Way, 466, 560
Penrhyn Castle, 610
Penrith, 584
Penshurst Place, 226
Penzance, 357
Pepys Library, 202
Percival David Foundation of Chinese Art, 56
Periquito, 229, 250
Pershore, 488
Peterhouse, 205
Petticoat Lane, 114
Petticoat Lane Designer Fashion Market, 184
Peveril Castle, 470
The Pheasantry, 83
Phillip's, 177
Piccadilly Circus, 65
Piece Hall, 625
The Pilgrims Way, 230
Pinocchio's, 421
Pinstripe, 167
Piper's Bench, 345, 372
Pizza Express, 165
Pizza Piazza, 494
Planetarium, 95
Plas Bodegroes Hotel and Restaurant, 608, 618
Playhouse Theatre, 195
The Plough, 196
Plough at Clanfield, 284, 323
Plymouth, 345
Plymouth Dome, 346
Plymouth Hoe, 345
Plymouth Moat House, 347, 372
Pogey's, 248
Polka, 164
Pollock's Toy Museum, 56
Pollock's Toy Theatres, 180
Polperro, 364
Poltimore, 339, 372
Le Pont de la Tour, 118
Pooh Corner, 240
Poole, 265
Poon's, 53, 148
Popjoy's, 287
Port Gaverne Hotel, 353, 372
Porthminster Hotel, 356, 372

Portland Heights Hotel, 268, 273
Portloe, 363
Portmeirion, 602
Portmeirion Hotel, 603, 618
Portobello Hotel, 139
Portobello Road, 184
Portobello Road Market, 91
Portsmouth, 256, 629
Portsmouth Marriott, 257, 273
Postbridge, 340
Posthouse Hotel, 257, 273
The Premier, 455
Primrose Hill, 101
Prince Henry's Room, 47
Prince of Orange, 165
Prince Regent, 157
Prince Rupert Hotel, 520, 532
The Print Room, 178
Priory (Lavenham), 390
Priory Church of St. John the Evangelist, 615
Priory Hotel, 292, 323
Prison Chapel, 457
Prospect of Whitby, 119
Puffin, 180
Pull's Ferry, 424
Pulpit Pub, 160
Pulteney Bridge, 287
Pump Room: Bath, 290; Royal Leamington Spa, 495
Puppet Theatre Barge, 164
Purbeck Pottery, 265
Pyramid, 215

Le Quai St. Pierre, 146
Queen's College: Cambridge, 204; Oxford, 193
Queen's Gallery, 70
Queen's Head, 157
Queen's Hotel: Cheltenham, 284, 323; Penzance, 358, 372
Queen's House, 121
Queen's Larder, 157
Quince Honey Farm, 334

Radcliffe Camera, 193
Radcliffe Square, 193
Radio Taxis, 125
Radisson Kenilworth Hotel, 128

Rafferty, 183
Ragam, 147
Ragley Hall, 485
Railway Centre, 506
Ralph Ellerker's, 546
Ramsgate, 237
Randolph Hotel, 197, 219
Rebecca's, 334
Redfern Hotel, 526, 532
Red Lion Hotel: Salisbury, 310, 323; Wells, 301, 323
Red Lodge, 297
Red Tower, 542
Regency Square, 214
Regent's Canal, 106
Regent's Park, 102, 104 (map)
Regent Street, 63
Restaurant Bosquet, 495
Restormel Castle, 364
Revuebar, 168
Rhuddlan Castle, 609
Ribble Way, 560
Riber Castle, 473
Rib Room, 147
Richborough, 238
Richmond, 85
Richmond Park, 87
Rievaulx Abbey, 556
Ringlestone, 230
Rising Sun Hotel, 331, 373
Ritz, 131
Riverbus, 126
River Café, 151
River Room, 47
Riverside Walk, 41, 87
River Terrace Restaurant, 483
R. M. Williams, 181
Robert Hales, 183
Rochester, 234
Rockingham Castle, 444
Rock Island Diner, 150
Roger Bigod's Castle, 405
Rollright Stones, 283
Roman Amphitheater (Chester), 527
Roman Bath Pub, 545
Romance of London, 169
Roman Palace (Chichester), 255
Ronnie Scott's, 61, 165
Roodee, 527

Roos Hall, 415
Rose & Crown Hotel, 311, 323
Roseland Peninsula, 362
Rosemundy House Hotel, 354, 373
Rosetta Stone, 56
Rose-in-Vale Country House Hotel, 355, 373
Ross-on-Wye, 507
Rottingdean, 242
Rougemont House Museum of Costume and Lace, 336
Round Church, 202
Rowley's House, 519
The Rows, 527
Royal Academy, 64
Royal Albert Hall, 85, 165
Royal Albert Memorial Museum, 336
Royal Albion, 217, 219
Royal Bath Hotel, 264, 273
Royal Citadel, 346
Royal Clarence Hotel, 337, 373
Royal County Hotel, 565, 593
Royal Court Hotel, 133
Royal Courts of Justice, 50
Royal Court Theatre, 162
Royal Crescent, 287
Royal Crescent Hotel, 292, 323
Royal Duchy Hotel, 362, 373
Royal Festival Hall, 40
Royal & Fortescue Hotel, 333, 373
Royal George Hotel, 514, 532
Royal Horseguards Thistle Hotel, 127
Royal Hospital, 83
Royal Hotel: Bideford, 333, 373; Bowness-on-Windermere, 579, 593
Royal Leamington Spa, 495
Royal Mews, 70
Royal Moat House International, 452, 475
Royal National Theatre, 162
Royal Naval Museum, 256
Royal Navy Submarine Museum, 630
Royal Oak, 317
Royal Opera House, 52, 164

The Royal Pavilion, 214
Royal Shakespeare Company, 162
Royal Shakespeare Theatre, 482
Royal Station Hotel, 568, 593
Royal Tunbridge Wells, 228
Royalty and Empire Exhibit, 208
Royal Victoria and Bull Hotel, 234, 250
Royal Windsor Horse Show, 212
Royal Worcester Porcelain Company, 499
Royal York Hotel, 540, 549
RSJ, 154
Rubens Hotel, 133
Ruddington Framework Knitter's Workshop, 451
Rugantino's, 301
Rules, 153
Runnymede, 212
Rural Heritage Museum, 511
Rutland, 441
Rutland Arms Hotel, 399, 429
Rutland Arms Pub, 89
Rutland County Museum, 443
Rutland Water, 442
Rydal Mount, 580
Rye, 243

Sadler's Wells Theatre, 110, 165
Sailors' Reading Room, 411
St. Agnes, 354
St. Agnes Island, 366
St. Andrew's Hall, 422
St. Anne Church, 119
St. Ann's Gate, 308
St. Ann's Street, 308
St. Anthony's Hall, 542
St. Bartholomew-the-Great Church, 111
St. Bartholomew's Church, 403
St. Botolph's Church, 464
St. Briavels Castle, 513
St. Bride Church, 47
St. Bride's Hotel, 614, 618
St. Christopher's Place, 63, 173
St. Clement Danes, 47
St. David's, 613
St. Enodoc Churchyard, 353

St. George in the East, 118
St. George's Field, 542
St. George's Guildhall, 426
St. Gregory's Church, 386
St. Helen's County Record Office, 500
St. Ives, 355
St. James's Court Hotel, 133
St. James's Palace, 67
St. James's Park, 71
St. John Medieval Museum, 506
St. John's College, 203
St. John's House, 492
St. Julian's Craft Centre, 519
St. Just-in-Roseland, 363
St. Katharine's Dock, 117
St. Margaret's Church: King's Lynn, 426; York, 542
St. Martin-in-the-Fields, 73
St. Martin's Church, 444
St. Martin's Island, 366
St. Mary Magdalene, 235
St. Mary Redcliffe, 296
St. Mary's Church: Boxford, 391; Bury St. Edmonds, 397; Hadleigh, 392; Stratford St. Mary, 382; Warwick, 490; York, 541
St. Mary's Island, 365
St. Mary's Priory Church (Bungay), 413
St. Mary the Virgin, 384
St. Mawes, 363
St. Mawes Castle, 361
St. Michael's Church, 415
St. Michael's Mount, 358
St. Nicholas Priory, 336
St. Non's Hotel, 614, 618
St. Olaves Court Hotel, 337, 373
St. Paul's Cathedral, 41
St. Paul's Church, 51
St. Peter Hungate, 421
St. Peter's Church, 432
St. Pierre Hotel, 515, 532
St. Quentin, 146
St. Thomas's Church, 309
St. William's College, 543
St. Williams Restaurant, 547
St. Wulfram, 455
Salisbury, 306

Salisbury Arts Festival, 307
Salisbury Cathedral, 307
Salisbury Plain, 302, 304 (map)
Salisbury Pub, 156
Salisbury and South Wiltshire
  Museum, 309
Sally Lunn's, 292
Saltfleetby–Theddlethorpe National Nature Reserve, 461
Saltram, 346
San Lorenzo, 151
Santini, 151
Saracen's Head Hotel, 454, 475
Saracen's Head Pub, 510
Saturday Market Place, 426
Saunton Sands Hotel, 332, 373
Savernake Forest, 319
Savoy Bar, 161
Savoy Court Hotel, 129
Savoy Grill, 128, 153
Savoy Hotel, 47, 127
Saxon Mill, 493
Science Museum, 85
Scotch House, 181
Scottish Merchant, 179
Scott's, 546
Scrooby, 463
Sculpture Trail, 513
Seafood Restaurant, 354
The Seagull, 257
Seahouses, 572
Seckford Hall Hotel, 401, 429
Seiont Manor Hotel, 607, 618
Selborne, 248
Selfridges', 172
Sevenoaks, 227
Severn Valley Railway, 523, 632
Shakespeare Hotel, 483, 532
Shakespeare Pub, 564
Shakespeare's Birthplace, 480
Shakespeare's Head, 156
Shakespeare's Tomb, 480
Shaldon, 343
The Shambles: Newent, 507;
  York, 545
Shampers, 160
Sharrow Bay Hotel, 583, 593
Sheepskin Warehouse Shop,
  582
Sheldonian Theatre, 195

Shelley Park, 264
Shelleys Hotel, 240, 250
Shepherd Market, 66
Shepherd's Garden Restaurant,
  483
Shepherd Wheel, 624
Sherwood Forest Country Park,
  452
Shiki Restaurant, 149
Shildon, 631
The Ship Hotel (Chichester),
  255, 274
Ship Inn: Dunwich, 409; Exeter,
  337; Mousehole, 356; York,
  545
The Ship Pub, 89
Ship and Star, 387
Shipwreck Centre, 364
Shire Hall, 400
Shrewsbury, 516
Shropshire Hills, 516, 524
Shropshire Way, 525
Sidmouth, 342
Silbury Hill, 319
Simply Nico, 145
Simpson's, 175
Sir John Soane's Museum, 51
Sir Toby's, 483
Sissinghurst Castle, 227
Sittingbourne, 236
Skegness, 460
Skegness Natureland Marine
  Zoo, 460
Sloane Street, 77
Sloop Inn, 355
Slug and Lettuce, 483
Smeaton's Tower, 346
Smithfield Central Market, 110
Smythson, 177
Snell's, 309
Snowdon, 600
Snowdonia National Park, 600
Snowshill Manor, 283
Soar Mill Cove Hotel, 344, 373
Soho, 58
Soho Brasserie, 143
Soho Square, 59
Sole Bay Inn, 411
Somerleyton, 417
Somerset House, 47

Sondes Arms, 445
Sophisticates, 265
Sotheby's, 177
Le Soufflé, 147
Southampton, 257
Southampton Moat House, 259, 274
South Bank Arts Centre, 40, 165
South Beach, 417
South Downs Way, 244
South Hams, 344
South Kensington, 83
South Molton Street, 63, 172
Southover Grange, 240
South Shields Museum, 567
Southwell Minster, 454
Southwold, 410
Southwold Church, 411
The Spa, 229, 251
Spanish Garden Club, 167
Sparrow's Nest Park, 417
Speech House, 512, 533
Speedwell Cavern, 468
Spelman's, 546
The Spotted Dog, 227
Stafford Hotel, 132, 161
Stakis Lodore Swiss Hotel, 582, 593
Stamford, 443
Stamford Museum, 444
The Standard, 91
Stanford Hall, 436
Stanford's Map Shop, 179
Stapleford Park, 441, 475
Star Castle, 367, 373
Star Hotel, 301, 323
State Apartments, 210
State House Hotel, 357, 373
Stiperstones, 524
Stoby's, 311
Stokesay Castle, 525
Stonehenge, 312
Stourhead, 306
Stourhead House, 306
Stow-on-the-Wold, 280
Strait of Dover, 237
The Strand, 47
Strangers Hall, 421
Stratford House Hotel, 483, 533
Stratford St. Mary, 382

Stratford-upon-Avon, 477, 481 (map)
Stringfellow's, 166
Stuart Crystal Craft Centre, 515
Studley Priory Hotel, 284, 323
Studley Royal, 561
Styal, 626
Sudbury, 384
Sudbury Quay, 385
Sudeley Castle, 282
Sudeley Castle Cottages, 282, 324
Suffolk, 375, 379
Sulgrave Manor, 436
Sullys, 233
The Sun, 155
Suntory, 148
Le Suquet, 146
Surrey, 245, 246 (map)
Sussex, 13, 220, 252
Sutherlands, 152
Sutton Bank, 554
Sutton Hoo Burial Site, 400
Swallow Royal Hotel, 297, 324
Swanage, 266
Swan Hotel: Hay-on-Wye, 509, 533; Lavenham, 390, 429; Southwold, 412, 429; Wells, 301, 324
Swan Inn (Stratford St. Mary), 382
Swan Pub: Ipswich, 394; London, 166
Swan Theatre, 482
Swan Upping, 87
Swiss House, 138
Symonds Yat, 510
Syon House, 89

The Tales of Robin Hood, 450
Tall Orders, 144
Tall Trees, 285, 324
Talyllyn Railway, 631
Tamar Belle River Cruises, 454
Tamar Road Bridge, 347
La Tante Claire, 145
Tarka Country, 332
Tarka Trail, 332
Tate Gallery (London), 76
Tate Gallery Liverpool, 629

Tate Gallery of St. Ives, 355
Tattershall Castle, 461
Tavistock, 340
Taylors Tea Rooms, 546
Tea Shoppe, 327
Teddy Bear Museum, 482
Teesdale, 563
Teignmouth, 343
Telford Hotel, Golf and Country Club, 522, 533
Temple, 48
Temple Church, 48
Temple Meads Station, 295
Tenby, 613
10 Downing Street, 74
Terrace Garden, 154
Tewkesbury, 502
Tewkesbury Park Hotel, 503, 533
Thackeray's House, 228
Thames Barrier, 120
Thayer Street, 173
Theater District, 65
Theatre Line, 164
Theatre Museum, 53
Theatre Royal, 397
Theatre Tonight, 163
Theatre Upstairs, 163
Things Welsh, 616
Thomas Luny House, 342, 373
Thorpeness, 409
Three Choirs Vineyard, 508
The Three Tuns: Bungay, 414; Osmotherley, 556
Thurlestone Hotel, 345, 373
Tidal Cruises, 169
Tide's Reach Hotel, 344, 373
Tintagel, 352
Tintern Abbey, 514
Tissington, 469
Tissington Trail, 469
Tobacco Dock, 183
Tolsey Museum, 281
Tombland, 422
Tom Tower, 189
Topkapi, 149
Toppesfield Bridge, 393
Torbay, 341, 343
Torquay, 343
Torridge, 333

Totnes, 341
Tottenham Court Road, 177
Tourist Information Centre (York), 545
Tower Bridge, 39
Tower of London, 38
Tower Thistle Hotel, 127
Town of Ramsgate Pub, 118
Toy Museum, 528
Trafalgar Square, 72
Tramway Museum, 469
Travel Information Centres (London), 124
Treak Cliff Cavern, 468
Treasurer's House, 543
Treglos Hotel, 353, 373
Trehenry Farm, 615, 618
Trerice, 354
Tresco Abbey Gardens, 366, 368
Tresco Island, 366
Tricycle, 164
Trinity, 546
Trinity College, 203
Trocadero Centre, 65, 176
Troffs, 459
Trough of Bowland, 574
Truro, 362
Tubby Isaacs', 116
Tudor House Museum, 499
Tudor House Restaurant, 337
Tuesday Market Place, 427
Tullie House, 588
Turf Tavern, 194
Turk's Head, 359
Turnbull & Asser, 176
Turpin's, 541
Twenty Two, 206
Tyddyn Llan Country House, 602, 618

Uley, 277
Ullswater, 583
Unicorn Hotel: Bristol, 298, 324; Stow-on-the-Wold, 280, 324
Unicorn Theatre, 164
Unitarian Chapel, 394
University Arms, 205, 219
University of London, 57
University Museum (Oxford), 196

Uplands Hotel, 408, 429
Upper Severn Valley, 516, 517 (map), 520
Upper Street, 107
Upper Street Fish Shop, 110
Upper Thames, 207 (map)
Uppingham, 443
Upstairs at the Savoy, 153
Upton Cresset Hall, 523
Upton-upon-Severn, 501
Usher Gallery, 459

Vale of Evesham, 486, 487 (map)
Valhalla Maritime Museum, 366
Valley of the Dove, 469
Valley Hotel, 522, 533
Valley Walk, 385
Vic's Tour, 367
Victoria and Albert Museum, 84
Victoria Arms, 193
Victoria Footbridge, 505
Victoria Hotel, 342, 374
Viking Hotel, 547, 549
Village Pâtisserie, 258
Vindolanda, 590
El Vino, 46, 160
Virgin Megastore, 172
Viroconium, 520
Volkers, 161

Wag Club, 166
The Wakes, 248
Wales, 14, 594, 596 (map)
Wallace Collection, 63
Walmgate Bar, 542
Warehouse, 163
Warkworth Castle, 570
Warkworth Hermitage, 570
Warwick, 476, 490.
Warwick Castle, 492
Warwickshire, 490, 491 (map)
Washington, 565
Washington Old Hall, 565
Waterfront Museum, 266
Waterloo Arms Pub, 262
Waterman's Arms, 342, 374
Water Margin, 437
Watershed, 295
Waterside Inn, 212

Waterstones, 178
Water Tower, 527
Watson's, 310
Wedgwood Gift Center, 174
Welcombe Hotel, 483, 533
The Well House, 365
Wells, 298
Wells Bookshop, 317
Wells Cathedral, 300
Wells Museum, 299
Welsh House, 434
Welsh Slate Museum, 633
Wenlock Edge, 525
Wensleydale, 561
Wentworth Hotel, 408, 429
Wesley's Chapel, 46
Wessex, 13, 252
Wessex Shore, 253 (map)
Westaway and Westaway, 178
West End, 62
West End Cares, 163
Westerham, 224
Westford House, 368, 374
Westgate Hotel, 197, 219
Westminster, 67, 68 (map)
Westminster Abbey, 75
Westminster Hotel, 139
Westminster Pier, 38
Weston Park, 522
West Pier, 216
West Shore Beach, 600
Weymouth, 267
Whalley Abbey, 574
Wheeler's (Brighton), 217
Wheeler's Oyster Bar (Whitstable), 236
Whip-Ma-Whop-Ma-Gate, 546
Whistles, 173
Whitechapel Art Gallery, 116
Whitechapel Manor, 334, 374
Whitehall, 73
White Hart Hotel: Lewes, 240, 251; Lincoln, 459, 475; Salisbury, 311, 324; Wells, 301, 324
White Hart Pub, 158
White Horse Hill, 319
White Horse Pub, 166
Whiteley's, 91, 183
White Post Modern Farm Centre, 452

Whites Hotel, 139
White Swan Hotel: Alnwick, 571, 593; Stratford-upon-Avon, 483, 533
White Tower, 150
Whitstable, 236
Whitwell, 442
Wickhamford, 489
Widecombe-in-the-Moor, 340
Wife of Bath Restaurant, 233
Wigan, 626
Wigan Pier, 626
Wigham, 335, 374
Wigmore Hall, 165
Wildensteins, 177
Wild Life and Rare Breeds Park, 416
William Cobbett Inn, 247
Willmead Farm, 342, 374
Willy Lott's Cottage, 384
Wilmcote, 484
Wimbledon Common, 89
Winchester, 315
Winchester Cathedral, 316
Winchester College, 315
Windsor, 206
Windsor Castle, 208
Windsor Great Park, 211
Winnat's Pass, 470
Wintor House, 503
Withington, 277
Wollaton Hall, 451
Wong Kei, 148
Woodbridge, 399
Woodbridge Museum, 401
Woodford Bridge Hotel, 333, 374
Wood Hall, 560, 593
Woodlands Hotel, 331, 374
Woodlands Park Hotel, 245, 251
Woods, 293
Wookey Hole, 302
Woolley Grange Hotel, 306, 324
Woolpack Inn, 231, 251

Woolsthorpe Manor, 455
Worcester, 496
Worcester Cathedral, 498
Worcestershire, 496, 497 (map)
Worcestershire Beacon, 501
Wordsworth Hotel, 581, 593
Worksop, 462
Worksop Museum, 462
World of Beatrix Potter, 579
Worth Matravers, 266
Wrekin, 520
Wren Library, 458
Wyck Hill House, 281, 324
Wyedean Canoe and Adventure Centre, 510
Wye Valley, 504 (map), 510
Wykeham Arms, 318
Wyndham Arms, 513, 533
Wyn Gillett, 215

Yates, 546
Y Bistro, 601
Ye Olde Bell and Steelyard, 401
Ye Olde Bull's Head, 611, 618
Ye Olde Cheshire Cheese, 46
Ye Olde Ferrie Inn, 511
Ye Olde Mitre, 158
Ye Olde Salutation, 450
Ye Olde Trip to Jerusalem, 450
York, 534, 536 (map)
York Festival, 547
York Minster, 543
York Races, 547
Yorkshire, 558 (map)
Yorkshire Dales, 560
Yorkshire Moors, 555
Yorkshire Museum and Botanical Gardens, 538
Young's, 110
Yung's, 148

Zen, 148
Zen Central, 148
Zwemmer, 178